ARAMAIC PESHITTA NEW TESTAMENT

Vertical Interlinear

Volume 1

Matthew - Luke

Janet M. Magiera
Light of the Word Ministry

Copyright © 2005, 2009, Janet M. Magiera

Published by LWM Publications
A Division of Light of the Word Ministry

ISBN 978-0-9679613-8-5

Introduction

Traditionally, an interlinear is composed of the original language with a translation underneath the word and perhaps a numbering system above the word. When reading Semitic languages such as Hebrew and Aramaic, it becomes difficult to determine the word order. First of all, one is reading right to left and secondly, needs to then deal with the grammatical differences with English.

This edition of an interlinear for the Aramaic Peshitta New Testament is composed in a vertical layout. The English translation of the verse is first written out directly above the list of individual words. This makes it easy for the Bible student to follow the change in the order of the words when it is translated into English. The list is to be read from top to bottom.

There are several markings in the interlinear of note. Words that have brackets like these < > mean that they are in the Peshitta text, but are not translated. Brackets like these [ ] are words added in the text to make the English translation complete. <?> is used to denote the word *lema* which introduces a question and is not always translated. Words that have an asterisk * mean that the phrase goes with the word before it and form a phrase or idiom. Please see the idiom list in the *Aramaic Peshitta New Testament Translation* or on our website at www.lightofword.org. Words that are in all capital letters indicate that this part of the verse is a quotation from the Old Testament.

To the left of each individual word is the Dictionary Number used by all the Light of the Word Ministry publications. Further study can be made by searching the *Word Study Concordance* and looking up the number in the *Dictionary Number Lexicon*.

The following chart is a list of the Aramaic alphabet and the English code equivalents. The font used in this publication was designed by www.peshitta.org and is freely available on their website.

English	Syriac	Name	Sound
A	ܐ	Aleph	a, ah
B	ܒ	Beth	b, bh
G	ܓ	Gamel	g, gh
D	ܕ	Daleth	d, dh
H	ܗ	He	h
O	ܘ	Wau	w, o, u
Z	ܙ	Zain	z
X	ܚ	Kheth	kh
Y	ܛ	Teth	t
I	ܝ	Yudh	y, i, e
K	ܟ	Kaph	k
L	ܠ	Lamed	l
M	ܡ	Mem	m
N	ܢ	Nun	n
S	ܣ	Semketh	s
E	ܥ	Ai	ai
P	ܦ	Pe	p
/	ܨ	Tzaddi	ts, tz
Q	ܩ	Qoph	q
R	ܪ	Resh	r
W	ܫ	Shin	sh
T	ܬ	tau	t, th

Vertical Interlinear

MATTHEW

CHAPTER	1	
VERSE	**1**	The book of the genealogy of Jesus Christ, the son of David, the son of Abraham;
1248	ܟܬܒܐ	The book
1050	ܕܝܠܝܕܘܬܗ	of the genealogy
3257	ܕܝܫܘܥ	of Jesus
1446	ܡܫܝܚܐ	Christ
0323	ܒܪܗ	the son
3159	ܕܕܘܝܕ	of David
0323	ܒܪܗ	the son
3005	ܕܐܒܪܗܡ	of Abraham
VERSE	**2**	Abraham fathered Isaac, Isaac fathered Jacob, Jacob fathered Judah and his brothers,
3005	ܐܒܪܗܡ	Abraham
1046	ܐܘܠܕ	fathered
3033	ܠܐܝܣܚܩ	Isaac
3033	ܠܐܝܣܚܩ	Isaac
1046	ܐܘܠܕ	fathered
3255	ܠܝܥܩܘܒ	Jacob
3255	ܠܝܥܩܘܒ	Jacob
1046	ܐܘܠܕ	fathered
3228	ܠܝܗܘܕܐ	Judah
0043	ܘܠܐܚܘܗܝ	and his brothers
VERSE	**3**	Judah fathered Perez and Zerah by Tamar. Perez fathered Hezron, Hezron fathered Aram,
3228	ܝܗܘܕܐ	Judah
1046	ܐܘܠܕ	fathered
3445	ܠܦܪܨ	Perez
3193	ܘܠܙܪܚ	and Zerah
1388	ܡܢ	by
3532	ܬܡܪ	Tamar
3445	ܦܪܨ	Perez
1046	ܐܘܠܕ	fathered
3203	ܠܚܣܪܘܢ	Hezron
3203	ܚܣܪܘܢ	Hezron
1046	ܐܘܠܕ	fathered
3099	ܠܐܪܡ	Aram

VERSE	**4**	Aram fathered Aminadab, Aminadab fathered Nahshon, Nahshon fathered Salmon,
3099	ܐܪܡ	Aram
1046	ܐܘܠܕ	fathered
3399	ܠܥܡܝܢܕܒ	Aminadab
3399	ܠܥܡܝܢܕܒ	Aminadab
1046	ܐܘܠܕ	fathered
3344	ܠܢܚܫܘܢ	Nahshon
3344	ܠܢܚܫܘܢ	Nahshon
1046	ܐܘܠܕ	fathered
3373	ܠܣܠܡܘܢ	Salmon
VERSE	**5**	Salmon fathered Boaz by Rahab, Boaz fathered Obed by Ruth, Obed fathered Jesse, [and]
3373	ܣܠܡܘܢ	Salmon
1046	ܐܘܠܕ	fathered
3125	ܠܒܥܙ	Boaz
1388	ܡܢ	by
3499	ܪܚܒ	Rahab
3125	ܒܥܙ	Boaz
1046	ܐܘܠܕ	fathered
3389	ܠܥܘܒܝܕ	Obed
1388	ܡܢ	by
3504	ܪܥܘܬ	Ruth
3389	ܥܘܒܝܕ	Obed
1046	ܐܘܠܕ	fathered
3040	ܠܐܝܫܝ	Jesse [and]
VERSE	**6**	Jesse fathered David the king. David fathered Solomon by the wife of Uriah,
3040	ܐܝܫܝ	Jesse
1046	ܐܘܠܕ	fathered
3159	ܠܕܘܝܕ	David
1383	ܡܠܟܐ	the king
3159	ܕܘܝܕ	David
1046	ܐܘܠܕ	fathered
3518	ܠܫܠܝܡܘܢ	Solomon
1388	ܡܢ	by
0135	ܐܢܬܬܗ	the wife
3021	ܕܐܘܪܝܐ	of Uriah

MATTHEW CHAPTER 1

VERSE 7 — Solomon fathered Rehoboam, Rehoboam fathered Abijah, Abijah fathered Asa,

3518	ܫܠܝܡܘܢ	Solomon
1046	ܐܘܠܕ	fathered
3500	ܠܪܚܒܥܡ	Rehoboam
3500	ܪܚܒܥܡ	Rehoboam
1046	ܐܘܠܕ	fathered
3000	ܠܐܒܝܐ	Abijah
3000	ܐܒܝܐ	Abijah
1046	ܐܘܠܕ	fathered
3070	ܠܐܣܐ	Asa

VERSE 8 — Asa fathered Jehoshaphat, Jehoshaphat fathered Joram, Joram fathered Uzziah,

3070	ܐܣܐ	Asa
1046	ܐܘܠܕ	fathered
3229	ܠܝܗܘܫܦܛ	Jehoshaphat
3229	ܝܗܘܫܦܛ	Jehoshaphat
1046	ܐܘܠܕ	fathered
3249	ܠܝܘܪܡ	Joram
3249	ܝܘܪܡ	Joram
1046	ܐܘܠܕ	fathered
3390	ܠܥܘܙܝܐ	Uzziah

VERSE 9 — Uzziah fathered Jotham, Jotham fathered Ahaz, Ahaz fathered Hezekiah,

3390	ܥܘܙܝܐ	Uzziah
1046	ܐܘܠܕ	fathered
3251	ܠܝܘܬܡ	Jotham
3251	ܝܘܬܡ	Jotham
1046	ܐܘܠܕ	fathered
3024	ܠܐܚܙ	Ahaz
3024	ܐܚܙ	Ahaz
1046	ܐܘܠܕ	fathered
3195	ܠܚܙܩܝܐ	Hezekiah

VERSE 10 — Hezekiah fathered Manasseh, Manasseh fathered Amon, Amon fathered Josiah,

3195	ܚܙܩܝܐ	Hezekiah
1046	ܐܘܠܕ	fathered
3320	ܠܡܢܫܐ	Manasseh
3320	ܡܢܫܐ	Manasseh
1046	ܐܘܠܕ	fathered
3058	ܠܐܡܘܢ	Amon
3058	ܐܡܘܢ	Amon
1046	ܐܘܠܕ	fathered
3250	ܠܝܘܫܝܐ	Josiah

VERSE 11 — Josiah fathered Jechoniah and his brothers in the captivity of Babylon.

3250	ܝܘܫܝܐ	Josiah
1046	ܐܘܠܕ	fathered
3234	ܠܝܘܟܢܝܐ	Jechoniah
0043	ܘܠܐܚܘܗܝ	and his brothers
0410	ܒܓܠܘܬܐ	in the captivity
3112	ܕܒܒܠ	of Babylon

VERSE 12 — And after the captivity of Babylon, Jechoniah fathered Shealtiel, Shealtiel fathered Zerubbabel,

1388	ܒܬܪ	after
0215	ܕܝܢ	*
0410	ܓܠܘܬܐ	the captivity
0518	ܕ	And
3112	ܕܒܒܠ	of Babylon
3234	ܝܘܟܢܝܐ	Jechoniah
1046	ܐܘܠܕ	fathered
3519	ܠܫܠܬܐܝܠ	Shealtiel
3519	ܫܠܬܐܝܠ	Shealtiel
1046	ܐܘܠܕ	fathered
3189	ܠܙܘܪܒܒܠ	Zerubbabel

VERSE 13 — Zerubbabel fathered Abiud, Abiud fathered Eliakim, Eliakim fathered Azor,

3189	ܙܘܪܒܒܠ	Zerubbabel
1046	ܐܘܠܕ	fathered
3002	ܠܐܒܝܘܕ	Abiud
3002	ܐܒܝܘܕ	Abiud
1046	ܐܘܠܕ	fathered
3050	ܠܐܠܝܩܝܡ	Eliakim
3050	ܐܠܝܩܝܡ	Eliakim
1046	ܐܘܠܕ	fathered
3391	ܠܥܙܘܪ	Azor

VERSE 14 — Azor fathered Sadoc, Sadoc fathered Achim, Achim fathered Eliud,

| 3391 | ܥܙܘܪ | Azor |

Vertical Interlinear

MATTHEW   CHAPTER 1

1046		fathered		1388		from
3187		Sadoc		3005		Abraham
3187		Sadoc		1747		until
1046		fathered		3159		David
3043		Achim		2605		[were] generations
3043		Achim		0182		fourteen
1046		fathered		1388		and from
3048		Eliud		3159		David

VERSE 15   Eliud fathered Eleazer, Eleazer fathered Matthan, Matthan fathered Jacob,

				1747		until
3048		Eliud		0410		the captivity
1046		fathered		3112		of Babylon
3049		Eleazer		2605		generations
3049		Eleazer		0182		fourteen
1046		fathered		1388		and from
3332		Matthan		0410		the captivity
3332		Matthan		3112		of Babylon
1046		fathered		1747		until
3255		Jacob		1446		the Messiah
				2605		generations
				0182		fourteen

VERSE 16   Jacob fathered Joseph, the husband of Mary, from whom Jesus, who was called the Messiah, was born.

VERSE 18   Now the birth of Jesus Christ was like this: when Mary his mother was engaged to Joseph, before they were joined in marriage, she was found [to be] pregnant from the Holy Spirit.

3255		Jacob				
1046		fathered				
3246		Joseph		1047		the birth
0361		the husband		0518		Now
3325		of Mary		3257		of Jesus
1388		from whom		1446		Christ
1046		was born		0597		like this
3257		Jesus		0603		was
2239		who was called		1128		when
1446		the Messiah		1361		engaged
				0603		was

VERSE 17   Therefore, all the generations from Abraham until David [were] fourteen generations, and from David until the captivity of Babylon, fourteen generations, and from the captivity of Babylon until the Messiah, fourteen generations.

				3325		Mary
				0106		his mother
				3246		to Joseph
1168		all <of them>		1746		before
0596		Therefore		2485		they were joined in marriage
2605		the generations		2510		she was found

MATTHEW CHAPTER 1

0260		[to be] pregnant		1532		to take
1388		from		3325		Mary
2323		the Holy Spirit		0135		your wife
2164		*		0593		he
				0403		for
				1046		that is fathered
				0217		in her
				1388		from
				2323		the Spirit
				0592		is
				2164		Holy

VERSE 19 But Joseph her husband was upright and was not willing to disgrace her and he was thinking that he would dismiss her privately.

3246		Joseph
0518		But
0306		her husband
1150		upright
0603		was
1262		and not
2077		was willing
2036		to disgrace her
2381		and he was thinking
0603		*
1011		that privately
2597		he would dismiss her

VERSE 20 But while he was considering these [things], an angel of the LORD appeared to him in a dream and said to him, "Joseph, son of David, do not be afraid to take Mary your wife, for he that is fathered in her [is] from the Holy Spirit.

1128		while
0598		these [things]
0518		But
2381		he was considering
0758		appeared
1261		to him
1375		an angel
1426		of the LORD
0810		in a dream
0116		and said
1261		to him
3246		Joseph
0323		son
3159		of David
1262		not
0509		do be afraid

VERSE 21 And she will give birth to a son and she will call his name Jesus, for he will give life to his people from their sins."

1046		she will give birth to
0518		And
0323		a son
2239		and she will call
2539		his name
3257		Jesus
0592		<he>
0403		for
0780		he will give life to
1818		his people
1388		from
0771		their sins

VERSE 22 Now all this that happened [was] that it would be fulfilled what was spoken from the LORD by way of the prophet:

0598		this
0518		Now
1168		all <of it>
0603		that happened [was]
1366		that it would be fulfilled
1326		what
0116		was spoken
1388		from
1426		the LORD
0057		by way of
1457		the prophet

Vertical Interlinear

MATTHEW CHAPTER 1

VERSE	23		BEHOLD, A VIRGIN WILL CONCEIVE AND WILL GIVE BIRTH TO A SON AND THEY WILL CALL HIS NAME EMMANUEL, WHICH IS INTERPRETED, OUR GOD [IS] WITH US.
0580	ܗܐ		BEHOLD
0347	ܒܬܘܠܬܐ		A VIRGIN
0259	ܬܒܛܢ		WILL CONCEIVE
1046	ܘܬܐܠܕ		AND WILL GIVE BIRTH TO
0323	ܒܪܐ		A SON
2239	ܘܢܩܪܘܢ		AND THEY WILL CALL
2539	ܫܡܗ		HIS NAME
3400	ܥܡܢܘܐܝܠ		EMMANUEL
2707	ܕܡܬܬܪܓܡ		WHICH IS INTERPRETED
1817	ܥܡܢ		WITH US
0093	ܐܠܗܢ		OUR GOD [IS]
VERSE	**24**		And when Joseph rose up from his sleep, he did as the angel of the LORD had commanded him and he took his wife.
1128	ܟܕ		when
2168	ܩܡ		rose up
0518	ܕܝܢ		And
3246	ܝܘܣܦ		Joseph
1388	ܡܢ		from
2568	ܫܢܬܗ		his sleep
1724	ܥܒܕ		he did
0061	ܐܝܟܢܐ		as
2007	ܕܦܩܕ		had commanded
1261	ܠܗ		him
1375	ܡܠܐܟܗ		the angel
1426	ܕܡܪܝܐ		of the LORD
0477	ܘܕܒܪܗ		and he took
0135	ܠܐܢܬܬܗ		his wife
VERSE	**25**		And he did not know her until she had given birth to her firstborn son. And she called his name Jesus.
1262	ܘܠܐ		And not
0789	ܚܟܡܗ		he did not know her
1747	ܥܕܡܐ		until
1046	ܕܝܠܕܬܗ		she had given birth to
0323	ܠܒܪܗ		her son
0271	ܒܘܟܪܐ		firstborn
2239	ܘܩܪܬ		And she called
2539	ܫܡܗ		his name
3257	ܝܫܘܥ		Jesus
CHAPTER	**2**		
VERSE	**1**		Now when Jesus was born in Bethlehem of Judea in the days of Herod the king, Magi came from the east to Jerusalem
1128	ܟܕ		when
0518	ܕܝܢ		Now
1046	ܐܬܝܠܕ		was born
3257	ܝܫܘܥ		Jesus
3114	ܒܒܝܬܠܚܡ		in Bethlehem
3224	ܕܝܗܘܕܐ		of Judea
1036	ܒܝܘܡܝ		in the days of
3179	ܗܪܘܕܣ		Herod
1383	ܡܠܟܐ		the king
0208	ܐܬܘ		came
3299	ܡܓܘܫܐ		Magi
1388	ܡܢ		from
0557	ܡܕܢܚܐ		the east
3022	ܠܐܘܪܫܠܡ		to Jerusalem
VERSE	**2**		and said, "Where is the king of the Judeans who was born? For we have seen his star in the east and we have come to worship him."
0116	ܘܐܡܪܝܢ		and said
1109	ܐܝܟܘ		Where is
1383	ܡܠܟܐ		the king
3226	ܕܝܗܘܕܝܐ		of the Judeans
1046	ܕܐܬܝܠܕ		who was born
0758	ܚܙܝܢ		we have seen
0403	ܓܝܪ		For
1141	ܟܘܟܒܗ		his star
0557	ܒܡܕܢܚܐ		in the east
0208	ܘܐܬܝܢ		and we have come
1599	ܠܡܣܓܕ		to worship
1261	ܠܗ		him

Vertical Interlinear

MATTHEW   CHAPTER 2

VERSE 3 — And Herod the king heard and was troubled and all Jerusalem with him.

#	Syriac	English
2547		heard
0518		And
3179		Herod
1383		the king
0657		and was troubled
1168		and all
3022		Jerusalem
1817		with him

VERSE 4 — And he gathered all of the chief priests and scribes of the people and was asking them where the Messiah was [to be] born.

#	Syriac	English
1198		And he gathered
1168		all of
2271		the chief
1135		priests
1699		and scribes
1818		of the people
2420		and was asking
0603		*
1261		them
1108		where
1046		was [to be] born
1446		the Messiah

VERSE 5 — And they said, "In Bethlehem of Judea," for so it is written in the prophet:

#	Syriac	English
0592		<they>
0518		And
0116		they said
3114		In Bethlehem
3224		of Judea
0597		so
0403		for
1247		it is written
1457		in the prophet

VERSE 6 — YOU ALSO, BETHLEHEM OF JUDEA, YOU WILL NOT BE THE LEAST AMONG THE KINGS OF JUDEA, FOR FROM YOU WILL GO OUT A KING WHO WILL SHEPHERD MY PEOPLE ISRAEL.

#	Syriac	English
0169		ALSO
0133		YOU
3114		BETHLEHEM
3224		OF JUDEA
1262		NOT
0603		YOU WILL BE
0312		THE LEAST
1383		AMONG THE KINGS
3224		OF JUDEA
1388		FROM YOU
0403		FOR
1542		WILL GO OUT
1383		A KING
0592		WHO
2381		WILL SHEPHERD
1818		MY PEOPLE
3035		ISRAEL

VERSE 7 — Then Herod secretly called the Magi and learned from them at what time the star appeared to them.

#	Syriac	English
0594		Then
3179		Herod
1011		secretly
2239		called
3299		the Magi
1053		and learned
1388		from them
0066		at what
0633		time
0758		appeared
1261		to them
1141		the star

MATTHEW CHAPTER 2

VERSE 8 — And he sent them to Bethlehem and said to them, "Go, search for the boy diligently and when you have found him, come, inform me that I may also go [and] worship him."

Code	Aramaic	English
2458		And he sent
0592		them
3114		to Bethlehem
0116		and said
1261		to them
0042		Go
1867		search
1804		for
0976		the boy
0873		diligently
1313		and when
2510		you have found him
0208		come
0739		inform me
0169		that also
0124		I
0042		may go
1599		[and] worship
1261		him

VERSE 9 — And when they had heard from the king, they went away and behold, the star that they had seen in the east went before them, until it came [and] stood over where the boy was.

Code	Aramaic	English
0592		<they>
0518		And
1128		when
2547		they had heard
1388		from
1383		the king
0042		they went away
0580		and behold
1141		the star
0593		that
0758		they had seen
0557		in the east
0042		went
0603		*
2154		before them
1747		until
0208		it came
2168		[and] stood
1803		over
1388		<from>
1108		where
0069		was
0976		the boy

VERSE 10 — And when they saw the star, they rejoiced [with] very great joy.

Code	Aramaic	English
1128		when
0518		And
0758		they saw
1141		the star
0726		they rejoiced
0727		[with] joy
2271		great
0938		very

VERSE 11 — And they entered the house and they saw the boy with Mary his mother and they fell down [and] worshipped him and they opened their treasures and offered him gifts, gold and myrrh and incense.

Code	Aramaic	English
1796		And they entered
0243		the house
0758		and they saw
0976		the boy
1817		with
3325		Mary
0106		his mother
1538		and they fell down
1599		[and] worshipped
1261		him
2070		and they opened
1627		their treasures
2244		and offered
1261		him
2246		gifts
0489		gold

MATTHEW   CHAPTER 2

1331		and myrrh		1747		until
1270		and incense		0116		I tell
				0124		*
				1261		you
				1914		is going
				0592		*
				0403		for
				3179		Herod
				0296		to seek
				0976		for the child
				0060		in order
				0005		to destroy him

VERSE 12 — And it was shown to them in a dream that they should not return to Herod and by another way, they went to their country.

0758		And it was shown
1261		to them
0810		in a dream
1262		that not
0616		they should return
1288		to
3179		Herod
0038		and by way
0053		another
0042		they went
0214		to their country

VERSE 13 — And when they had gone, an angel of the LORD appeared in a dream to Joseph and said to him, "Get up. Lead the child and his mother and flee to Egypt and stay there until I tell you, for Herod is going to seek for the child in order to destroy him."

1128		when
0518		And
0042		they had gone
0758		appeared
1375		an angel
1426		of the LORD
0810		in a dream
3246		to Joseph
0116		and said
1261		to him
2168		Get up
0477		Lead
0976		the child
0106		and his mother
1904		and flee
3321		to Egypt
2682		and there
0603		stay

VERSE 14 — Now Joseph rose up, took up the child and his mother in the night, and fled to Egypt.

3246		Joseph
0518		Now
2168		rose up
2587		took up
0976		the child
0106		and his mother
1299		in the night
1904		and fled
3321		to Egypt

VERSE 15 — And he remained there until the death of Herod, so that it would be fulfilled what was spoken from the LORD by the prophet who said: FROM EGYPT I HAVE CALLED MY SON.

0603		And he remained
2682		there
1747		until
1335		the death
3179		of Herod
1366		so that it would be fulfilled
1326		what
0116		was spoken
1388		from
1426		the LORD
1457		by the prophet
0116		who said

MATTHEW — CHAPTER 2

Vertical Interlinear

#	Syriac	English
1388		FROM
3321		EGYPT
2239		I HAVE CALLED
0323		MY SON

VERSE 16 — Then Herod, when he saw that he was mocked by the Magi, was very angry and sent [and] killed all the boys of Bethlehem and of all its borders from two years old and under, according to the time that he had investigated from the Magi.

#	Syriac	English
0594		Then
3179		Herod
1128		when
0758		he saw
0246		that he was mocked
1388		by
3299		the Magi
0837		was angry
0938		very
2458		and sent
2179		[and] killed
0976		the boys
1168		all
3114		of Bethlehem
1168		and of all
2659		its borders
1388		from
0323		two years old
2709		*
2559		*
2660		and under
0060		according to
0633		the time
1867		that he had investigated
1388		from
3299		the Magi

VERSE 17 — Then was fulfilled what was spoken by way of Jeremiah the prophet, who said:

#	Syriac	English
0594		Then
1366		was fulfilled
1326		what
0116		was spoken
0057		by way of
3102		Jeremiah
1457		the prophet
0116		who said

VERSE 18 — A VOICE WAS HEARD IN RAMA, CRYING AND GREAT MOURNING, RACHEL CRYING FOR HER SONS AND NOT WANTING TO BE COMFORTED, BECAUSE THEY WERE NOT.

#	Syriac	English
2204		A VOICE
2547		WAS HEARD
3502		IN RAMA
0268		CRYING
0092		AND MOURNING
1596		GREAT
3501		RACHEL
0267		CRYING
1804		FOR
0323		HER SONS
1262		AND NOT
2077		WANTING
0262		TO BE COMFORTED
1347		BECAUSE
1262		NOT
0069		THEY WERE

VERSE 19 — Now when Herod the king died, an angel of the LORD appeared in a dream to Joseph in Egypt.

#	Syriac	English
1128		when
1334		died
0518		Now
3179		Herod
1383		the king
0758		appeared
1375		an angel
1426		of the LORD
0810		in a dream
3246		to Joseph

MATTHEW CHAPTER 2

3321		in Egypt
VERSE 20		And he said to him, "Get up. Lead the child and his mother and go to the land of Israel, for those who were seeking the life of the child have died."
0116		And he said
1261		to him
2168		Get up
0477		Lead
0976		the child
0106		and his mother
0042		and go
0199		to the land
3035		of Israel
1334		have died
1261		*
0403		for
0593		those
0296		who seeking
0603		were
1547		the life
0976		of the child
VERSE 21		And Joseph rose up [and] led the child and his mother and came to the land of Israel.
3246		And Joseph
2168		rose up
0477		[and] led
0976		the child
0106		and his mother
0208		and came
0199		to the land
3035		of Israel
VERSE 22		But when he heard that Archelaus was king in Judah in place of Herod his father, he was afraid to go there and it was shown to him in a dream that he should go to the land of Galilee.
1128		when
0518		But
2547		he heard
3098		that Archelaus
0603		was
1383		king
3224		in Judah
0812		in place of
3179		Herod
0002		his father
0509		he was afraid
0042		to go
2682		there
0758		and it was shown
1261		to him
0810		in a dream
0042		that he should go
0214		to the land
3153		of Galilee
VERSE 23		And he came [and] lived in the city that is called Nazareth, so that it would be fulfilled what was spoken by the prophet: "He will be called a Nazarene."
0208		And he came
1833		[and] lived
0499		in the city
2239		that is called
3354		Nazareth
0060		so that
1366		it would be fulfilled
1326		what
0116		was spoken
1457		by the prophet
3355		a Nazarene
2239		He will be called

CHAPTER 3

VERSE 1		Now in those days John the baptizer came and was preaching in the desert of Judea.
0217		<in them>
0518		Now
1036		In days
0593		those
0208		came
3233		John

MATTHEW CHAPTER 3

1820	ܡܥܡܕܢܐ	the baptizer		1273	ܠܒܘܫܗ	his clothes
1230	ܘܡܟܪܙ	and preaching		1687	ܣܥܪܐ	of the hair
0603	ܗܘܐ	was		0420	ܕܓܡܠܐ	of camels
0892	ܒܚܘܪܒܐ	in the desert		0164	ܘܐܣܪܐ	and a girdle
3224	ܕܝܗܘܕ	of Judea		0876	ܕܚܨܘ	*

VERSE 2 — And he said, "Repent. The kingdom of heaven is near."

0116	ܘܐܡܪ	And he said		1449	ܕܡܫܟܐ	of skin
2649	ܬܘܒܘ	Repent		1804	ܥܠ	[was] on
2244	ܩܪܒܬ	is near		0876	ܚܨܘܗܝ	his loins
1261	ܠܗ	<to him>		0079	ܘܡܐܟܘܠܬܗ	and his food
1385	ܡܠܟܘܬܐ	The kingdom		2213	ܩܡܨܐ	[was] locusts
2543	ܕܫܡܝܐ	of heaven		0484	ܘܕܒܫܐ	and honey
				0320	ܕܒܪܐ	of the desert

VERSE 3 — For this is he about whom it was said by way of Isaiah the prophet: THE VOICE OF ONE CRYING IN THE DESERT: PREPARE THE WAY OF THE LORD AND MAKE STRAIGHT HIS PATHS.

VERSE 5 — Then Jerusalem went out to him and all Judea and all the region that was around the Jordan.

0599	ܗܢܘ	this is he		0594	ܗܝܕܝܢ	Then
0403	ܓܝܪ	For		1542	ܢܦܩܐ	went out
0593	ܗܘ	<who>		0603	ܗܘܬ	<was>
0116	ܕܐܡܝܪ	about whom it was said		1288	ܠܘܬܗ	to him
0057	ܒܝܕ	by way of		3022	ܐܘܪܫܠܡ	Jerusalem
3109	ܐܫܥܝܐ	Isaiah		1168	ܘܟܠܗ	and all
1457	ܢܒܝܐ	the prophet		3224	ܝܗܘܕ	Judea
2204	ܩܠܐ	THE VOICE		1168	ܘܟܠܗ	and all
2239	ܕܩܪܐ	OF ONE CRYING		0214	ܐܬܪܐ	the region
0892	ܒܚܘܪܒܐ	IN THE DESERT		0732	ܕܚܕܪܝ	the was around
0950	ܛܝܒܘ	PREPARE		3248	ܝܘܪܕܢܢ	the Jordan
0038	ܐܘܪܚܗ	THE WAY				
1426	ܕܡܪܝܐ	OF THE LORD				
2461	ܘܐܫܘܘ	AND MAKE STRAIGHT				
2434	ܠܫܒܝܠܘܗܝ	HIS PATHS				

VERSE 6 — And they were baptized by him in the Jordan River when they confessed their sins.

VERSE 4 — Now [this] John, his clothes were of the hair of camels and a girdle of skin [was] on his loins and his food [was] locusts and honey of the desert.

0592	ܗܘ	<he>		1819	ܘܥܡܕܝܢ	And they baptized
0518	ܕܝܢ	Now		0603	ܗܘܘ	were
3233	ܝܘܚܢܢ	[this] John		1388	ܡܢܗ	by him
0069	ܐܝܬܘܗܝ	were		3248	ܒܝܘܪܕܢܢ	in the Jordan
0603	ܗܘܐ	*		1478	ܢܗܪܐ	River
				1128	ܟܕ	when
				1020	ܡܘܕܝܢ	they confessed
				0771	ܒܚܛܗܝܗܘܢ	their sins

MATTHEW CHAPTER 3

Vertical Interlinear

VERSE	7		And when he saw many from the Pharisees and from the Sadducees who came to be baptized, he said to them, "Generation of vipers! Who has informed you to flee from the wrath that will come?
1128			when
0758			he saw
0518			And
1596			many
1388			from
3439			the Pharisees
1388			and from
3188			the Sadducees
0208			who came
1819			to be baptized
0116			he said
1261			to them
1047			Generation
0071			of vipers
1390			who
0739			has informed you
1904			to flee
1388			from
2291			the wrath
0208			that will come
VERSE	8		Produce, therefore, the fruits that are proper for repentance.
1724			Produce
0596			therefore
2016			the fruits
2461			that are proper
2651			for repentance
VERSE	9		And do not think or say within yourselves that we have Abraham [as a] father, for I say to you, God is able from these stones to raise up sons to Abraham.
1262			And not
1588			do think
0116			or say
1547			within yourselves
0002			that [as a] father
0069			we have
1261			*
3005			Abraham
0116			say
0124			I
1261			to you
0403			for
2510			is able
0093			God
1388			from
0598			these
1119			stones
2168			to raise up
0323			sons
3005			to Abraham
VERSE	10		Now behold, the ax is placed on the root of the trees. Therefore, every tree that does not bear good fruit will be cut down and thrown into the fire.
0580			behold
0518			Now
1569			the ax
1625			is placed
1804			on
1877			the root
0063			of the trees
1168			every
0063			tree
0596			Therefore
2016			that fruit
0938			good
1262			not
1724			does bear
1992			will be cut down
1538			and thrown
1494			into the fire

MATTHEW CHAPTER 3

VERSE 11 — I baptize you with water for repentance, but he who comes after me is stronger than I [am], whose sandals I am not worthy to carry. He will baptize you with the Holy Spirit and with fire,

Code	Aramaic	English
0124	ܐܢܐ	<I>
1819	ܡܥܡܕ	baptize
0124	ܐܢܐ	I
1261	ܠܟܘܢ	you
1351	ܒܡܝܐ	with water
2651	ܠܬܝܒܘܬܐ	for repentance
0593	ܗܘ	he
0518	ܕܝܢ	but
0215	ܕܒܬܪܝ	who after me
0208	ܐܬܐ	comes
0862	ܚܣܝܢ	is stronger
0592	ܗܘ	*
1388	ܡܢܝ	than I [am]
0593	ܗܘ	<who>
1262	ܠܐ	whose not
2461	ܫܘܐ	am worthy
0124	ܐܢܐ	I
1582	ܡܣܢܘܗܝ	sandals
2587	ܠܡܫܩܠ	to carry
0592	ܗܘ	<he>
1819	ܡܥܡܕ	He will baptize
1261	ܠܟܘܢ	you
2323	ܒܪܘܚܐ	with the Holy Spirit
2164	ܕܩܘܕܫܐ	*
1494	ܘܒܢܘܪܐ	and with fire

VERSE 12 — he whose winnowing fan [is] in his hand and he will cleanse his threshing floors. And he will gather the wheat to his granaries, and he will burn the chaff in a fire that does not go out."

Code	Aramaic	English
0593	ܗܘ	he
2396	ܕܪܦܫܐ	whose winnowing fan
0057	ܒܐܝܕܗ	[is] in his hand
0521	ܘܡܕܟܐ	and he will cleanse
0022	ܐܕܪܘܗܝ	his threshing floors
0779	ܘܚܛܐ	And the wheat
1198	ܟܢܫ	he will gather
0035	ܠܐܘܨܪܘܗܝ	to his granaries
2630	ܘܬܒܢܐ	and the chaff
1073	ܢܘܩܕ	he will burn
1494	ܒܢܘܪܐ	in a fire
1262	ܠܐ	that not
0558	ܕܥܟܐ	does go out

VERSE 13 — Then Jesus came from Galilee to the Jordan to John to be baptized by him.

Code	Aramaic	English
0594	ܗܝܕܝܢ	Then
0208	ܐܬܐ	came
3257	ܝܫܘܥ	Jesus
1388	ܡܢ	from
3153	ܓܠܝܠܐ	Galilee
3248	ܠܝܘܪܕܢܢ	to the Jordan
1288	ܠܘܬ	to
3233	ܝܘܚܢܢ	John
1819	ܕܢܥܡܕ	to be baptized
1388	ܡܢܗ	by him

VERSE 14 — But John restrained him and said, "I need to be baptized by you and are you coming to me?"

Code	Aramaic	English
0592	ܗܘ	<he>
0518	ܕܝܢ	But
3233	ܝܘܚܢܢ	John
1180	ܟܠܐ	restrained
0603	ܗܘܐ	*
1261	ܠܗ	him
0116	ܘܐܡܪ	and said
0124	ܐܢܐ	<I>
1679	ܣܢܝܩ	I need
0124	ܐܢܐ	*
1388	ܡܢܟ	by you
1819	ܕܐܬܥܡܕ	to be baptized
0133	ܘܐܢܬ	and <you>
1288	ܠܘܬܝ	to me
0208	ܐܬܝܬ	are you coming

VERSE 15 — But Jesus answered and said to him, "Allow [it] now, for so it is proper for us to fulfill all uprightness." And then he allowed him [to baptize him].

Code	Aramaic	English
0592	ܗܘ	<he>

MATTHEW CHAPTER 3

0518		But
3257		Jesus
1838		answered
0116		and said
1261		to him
2440		Allow [it]
0602		now
0597		so
0403		for
1012		it is proper
1261		for us
1366		to fulfill
1168		all
1152		uprightness
0594		And then
2440		he allowed him [to baptize him]

VERSE 16 — And when Jesus was baptized, immediately he came out of the water and heaven was opened to him and he saw the Spirit of God that was descending as a dove and it came on him.

1128		when
1819		was baptized
0518		And
3257		Jesus
0725		immediately
1658		he came out
1388		of
1351		the water
2070		and was opened
1261		to him
2543		heaven
0758		and he saw
2323		the Spirit
0093		of God
1499		that was descending
0060		as
1038		a dove
0208		and it came
1804		on him

VERSE 17 — And behold, [there was] a voice from heaven that said, "This is my beloved Son in whom I am pleased."

0580		And behold
2204		[there was] a voice
1388		from
2543		heaven
0116		that said
0599		This is
0323		my Son
0698		beloved
0217		in whom
2077		I am pleased

CHAPTER 4

VERSE 1 — Then Jesus was led by the Holy Spirit to the wilderness to be tempted by the Accuser.

0594		Then
3257		Jesus
0477		was led
1388		by
2323		the Holy Spirit
2164		*
0480		to the wilderness
1527		to be tempted
1388		by
0078		the Accuser

VERSE 2 — And he fasted forty days and forty nights and afterwards he was hungry.

2093		And he fasted
0180		forty
1036		days
0180		and forty
1299		nights
0051		afterwards
0518		and
1212		he was hungry

MATTHEW CHAPTER 4

VERSE 3 — And he who was tempting came near and said to him, "If you are the Son of God, say that these stones should become bread."

2244		And came near
0593		he
1527		who was tempting
0116		and said
1261		to him
0121		If
0323		the Son
0133		you are
0093		of God
0116		say
0598		that these
1119		stones
0603		should become
1293		bread

VERSE 4 — But he answered and said, "It is written: MAN DOES NOT LIVE BY BREAD ALONE, BUT BY EVERY WORD THAT COMES OUT OF THE MOUTH OF GOD."

0592		\<he\>
0518		But
1838		he answered
0116		and said
1247		It is written
1262		NOT
0603		DOES
1293		BY BREAD
1041		ALONE
0780		LIVE
0325		MAN
0090		BUT
1168		BY EVERY
1364		WORD
1542		THAT COMES OUT
1388		OF
1936		THE MOUTH
0093		OF GOD

VERSE 5 — Then the Accuser led him to the holy city and placed him on the outer edge of the temple.

0594		Then
0477		led him
0078		the Accuser
0499		to the city
2164		holy
2168		and placed him
1804		on
1197		the outer edge
0607		of the temple

VERSE 6 — And he said to him, "If you are the Son of God, throw yourself down, for it is written: HE WILL COMMAND HIS ANGELS CONCERNING YOU, and ON THEIR HANDS THEY WILL BEAR YOU UP, SO THAT YOU SHOULD NOT STRIKE YOUR FOOT ON A STONE."

0116		And he said
1261		to him
0121		If
0323		the Son
0133		you are
0093		of God
2455		throw
1547		yourself
2660		down
1247		it is written
0403		for
1375		HIS ANGELS
2007		HE WILL COMMAND
1804		CONCERNING YOU
1804		and ON
0057		THEIR HANDS
2587		THEY WILL BEAR YOU UP
1262		SO THAT
2697		YOU SHOULD NOT STRIKE
1119		ON A STONE
2293		YOUR FOOT

MATTHEW CHAPTER 4

VERSE 7 — Jesus said to him, "Again it is written: YOU SHOULD NOT TEMPT THE LORD YOUR GOD."

0116	said
1261	to him
3257	Jesus
2650	Again
1247	It is written
1262	NOT
1527	YOU SHOULD TEMPT
1426	THE LORD
0093	YOUR GOD

VERSE 8 — Again, the Accuser took him to a mountain that was very high. And he showed him all the kingdoms of the world and their glory.

2650	Again
0477	took him
0078	the Accuser
0958	to a mountain
0938	that was high
2336	very
0739	And he showed him
1168	all
1385	the kingdoms
1813	of the world
2431	and their glory

VERSE 9 — And he said to him, "All these [kingdoms] I will give to you if you will fall down [and] worship me."

0116	And he said
1261	to him
0598	these [kingdoms]
1168	All <of them>
1261	to you
1030	I will give
0121	if
1538	you will fall down
1599	[and] worship
1261	me

VERSE 10 — Then Jesus said to him, "Go, Satan! For it is written: YOU SHOULD WORSHIP THE LORD YOUR GOD AND FOR HIM ALONE YOU SHOULD WORK."

0594	Then
0116	said
1261	to him
3257	Jesus
0042	Go
1261	<you>
1642	Satan
1247	it is written
0403	For
1426	THE LORD
0093	YOUR GOD
1599	YOU SHOULD WORSHIP
1261	AND FOR HIM
1041	ALONE
1974	YOU SHOULD WORK

VERSE 11 — Then the Accuser left him and behold, angels came near and ministered to him.

0594	Then
2440	left him
0078	the Accuser
0580	and behold
1375	angels
2244	came near
2554	and ministered
0603	*
1261	to him

VERSE 12 — Now when Jesus heard that John had been delivered up, he went away to Galilee.

1128	when
2547	heard
0518	Now
3257	Jesus
3233	that John
2530	had been delivered up
2561	he went away
1261	*

MATTHEW — CHAPTER 4

3153	ܠܓܠܝܠܐ	to Galilee	

VERSE 13 — And he left Nazareth and came [and] lived in Capernaum by the shore of the sea in the territory of Zebulun and of Naphtali,

2440	ܘܫܒܩܗ	And he left
3354	ܠܢܨܪܬ	Nazareth
0208	ܘܐܬܐ	and came
1833	ܥܡܪ	[and] lived
3268	ܒܟܦܪܢܚܘܡ	in Capernaum
1804	ܥܠ	by
0057	ܝܕ	the shore
1057	ܝܡܐ	of the sea
2659	ܒܬܚܘܡܐ	in the territory
3186	ܕܙܒܘܠܘܢ	of Zebulun
3353	ܘܕܢܦܬܠܝ	and of Naphtali

VERSE 14 — that it would be fulfilled what was spoken by way of Isaiah the prophet who said:

1366	ܕܢܬܡܠܐ	that it would be fulfilled
1326	ܡܕܡ	what
0116	ܕܐܬܐܡܪ	was spoken
0057	ܒܝܕ	by way of
3109	ܐܫܥܝܐ	Isaiah
1457	ܢܒܝܐ	the prophet
0116	ܕܐܡܪ	who said

VERSE 15 — THE LAND OF ZEBULUN, THE LAND OF NAPHTALI, THE WAY OF THE SEA, THE CROSSINGS OF THE JORDAN, GALILEE OF THE GENTILES,

0199	ܐܪܥܐ	THE LAND
3186	ܕܙܒܘܠܘܢ	OF ZEBULUN
0199	ܐܪܥܐ	THE LAND
3353	ܕܢܦܬܠܝ	OF NAPHTALI
0038	ܐܘܪܚܐ	THE WAY
1057	ܕܝܡܐ	OF THE SEA
1735	ܥܒܪܘܗܝ	THE CROSSINGS
3248	ܕܝܘܪܕܢܢ	OF THE JORDAN
3153	ܓܠܝܠܐ	GALILEE
1818	ܕܥܡܡܐ	OF THE GENTILES

VERSE 16 — THE PEOPLE WHO SIT IN DARKNESS HAVE SEEN A GREAT LIGHT AND A LIGHT HAS DAWNED TO THEM WHO SIT IN THE LAND AND THE SHADOWS OF DEATH.

1818	ܥܡܐ	THE PEOPLE
1093	ܕܝܬܒ	WHO SIT
0923	ܒܚܫܘܟܐ	IN DARKNESS
1477	ܢܘܗܪܐ	A LIGHT
2271	ܪܒܐ	GREAT
0758	ܚܙܐ	HAVE SEEN
0066	ܘܐܝܠܝܢ	AND <THOSE>
1093	ܕܝܬܒܝܢ	WHO SIT
0214	ܒܐܬܪܐ	IN THE LAND
0971	ܘܒܛܠܠܐ	AND THE SHADOWS
1335	ܕܡܘܬܐ	OF DEATH
1477	ܢܘܗܪܐ	A LIGHT
0555	ܕܢܚ	HAS DAWNED
1261	ܠܗܘܢ	TO THEM

VERSE 17 — From then [on], Jesus began to preach and to say, "Repent, for the kingdom of heaven is near."

1388	ܡܢ	From
0594	ܗܝܕܝܢ	then [on]
2597	ܫܪܝ	began
3257	ܝܫܘܥ	Jesus
1230	ܠܡܟܪܙܘ	to preach
0116	ܘܠܡܐܡܪ	and to say
2649	ܬܘܒܘ	Repent
2244	ܩܪܒܬ	is near
1261	ܠܗ	*
0403	ܓܝܪ	for
1385	ܡܠܟܘܬܐ	the kingdom
2543	ܕܫܡܝܐ	of heaven

VERSE 18 — And while he was walking along the shore of the Sea of Galilee, he saw two brothers, Simon who was called Peter and Andrew his brother, who were casting nets into the sea, for they were fishermen.

1128	ܘܟܕ	And while
0608	ܡܗܠܟ	he was walking
1804	ܥܠ	along

Vertical Interlinear

MATTHEW CHAPTER 4

0057	ܝܡܐ	the shore
1057	ܕܝܡܐ	of the Sea
3153	ܕܓܠܝܠܐ	of Galilee
0758	ܚܙܐ	he saw
2709	ܬܪܝܢ	two
0043	ܐܚܝܢ	brothers
3521	ܠܫܡܥܘܢ	Simon
2239	ܕܐܬܩܪܝ	who was called
3258	ܟܐܦܐ	Cephas
3061	ܘܠܐܢܕܪܐܘܣ	and Andrew
0043	ܐܚܘܗܝ	his brother
2372	ܕܪܡܝܢ	who were casting
2090	ܡܨܝܕܬܐ	nets
1057	ܒܝܡܐ	into the sea
0069	ܐܝܬܝܗܘܢ	they were
0603	ܗܘܘ	*
0403	ܓܝܪ	for
2091	ܨܝܕܐ	fishermen

VERSE 19 And Jesus said to them, "Follow me and I will make you to be fishermen of men."

0116	ܘܐܡܪ	And said
1261	ܠܗܘܢ	to them
3257	ܝܫܘܥ	Jesus
0208	ܬܘ	Follow me
0215	ܒܬܪܝ	*
1724	ܘܐܥܒܕܟܘܢ	and I will make you
0603	ܕܬܗܘܘܢ	to be
2091	ܨܝܕܐ	fishermen
0323	ܕܒܢܝ	of men
0131	ܐܢܫܐ	*

VERSE 20 And they immediately left their nets and went after him.

0592	ܗܢܘܢ	<they>
0518	ܕܝܢ	And
0725	ܡܚܕܐ	immediately
2440	ܫܒܩܘ	they left
2090	ܡܨܝܕܬܗܘܢ	their nets
0042	ܘܐܙܠܘ	and went after him
0215	ܒܬܪܗ	*

VERSE 21 And when he crossed over from there he saw two other brothers, James, the son of Zebedee, and John, his brother, in a ship with Zebedee, their father, who were mending their nets and he called them.

1128	ܘܟܕ	And when
1733	ܥܒܪ	he crossed over
1388	ܡܢ	from
2682	ܬܡܢ	there
0758	ܚܙܐ	he saw
0053	ܐܚܪܢܐ	other
0043	ܐܚܐ	brothers
2709	ܬܪܝܢ	two
3255	ܠܝܥܩܘܒ	James
0323	ܒܪ	the son
3185	ܕܙܒܕܝ	of Zebedee
3233	ܘܠܝܘܚܢܢ	and John
0043	ܐܚܘܗܝ	his brother
0100	ܒܐܠܦܐ	in a ship
1817	ܥܡ	with
3185	ܕܙܒܕܝ	Zebedee
0002	ܐܒܘܗܘܢ	their father
2699	ܕܡܬܩܢܝܢ	who were mending
2090	ܡܨܝܕܬܗܘܢ	their nets
2239	ܘܩܪܐ	and he called
0592	ܐܢܘܢ	them

VERSE 22 And immediately they left the ship and their father and they went after him.

0592	ܗܢܘܢ	<they>
0518	ܕܝܢ	And
0725	ܡܚܕܐ	immediately
2440	ܫܒܩܘ	they left
0100	ܠܐܠܦܐ	the ship
0002	ܘܠܐܒܘܗܘܢ	and their father
0042	ܘܐܙܠܘ	and went after him
0215	ܒܬܪܗ	*

VERSE 23 And Jesus traveled around in all Galilee and taught in their synagogues and preached the gospel of the kingdom and cured every disease and sickness among the people.

1236	ܘܡܬܟܪܟ	And traveled around

MATTHEW CHAPTER 4

0603	ܗܘܐ	*
3257	ܝܫܘܥ	Jesus
1168	ܒܟܠܗ	in all
3153	ܓܠܝܠܐ	Galilee
1053	ܘܡܠܦ	and taught
0603	ܗܘܐ	*
1200	ܒܟܢܘܫܬܗܘܢ	in their synagogues
1230	ܘܡܟܪܙ	and preached
1593	ܣܒܪܬܐ	the gospel
1385	ܕܡܠܟܘܬܐ	of the kingdom
0136	ܘܡܐܣܐ	and cured
1168	ܟܠ	every
1116	ܟܐܒ	disease
1227	ܘܟܘܪܗܢ	and sickness
1818	ܒܥܡܐ	among the people

VERSE 24 And his fame was heard in all Syria and they brought to him all those who were very sick with various diseases and those who were oppressed with severe pains and possessed [ones] and [those] who were insane and paralyzed [ones] and he healed them.

2547	ܘܐܫܬܡܥ	And was heard
0944	ܛܒܗ	his fame
1168	ܒܟܠܗ	in all
3367	ܣܘܪܝܐ	Syria
2244	ܘܩܪܒܘ	and they brought
1261	ܠܗ	to him
1168	ܟܠܗܘܢ	all <of them>
0066	ܐܝܠܝܢ	those
0220	ܕܒܝܫ	who were very
0220	ܒܝܫ	sick
1724	ܥܒܝܕܝܢ	*
1227	ܒܟܘܪܗܢܐ	with diseases
0813	ܡܫܚܠܦܐ	various
0066	ܘܐܝܠܝܢ	and those
0104	ܐܠܝܨܝܢ	who were oppressed
2567	ܒܐܘܠܨܢܐ	with severe pains
0515	ܘܕܝܘܢܐ	and possessed [ones]
0323	ܘܕܒܪܐ	and [those] who were insane
0019	ܐܢܫܐ	*

2598	ܘܡܫܪܝܐ	and paralyzed [ones]
0136	ܘܐܣܝ	and he healed
0592	ܐܢܘܢ	them

VERSE 25 And large crowds followed him from Galilee and from the Decapolis and from Jerusalem and from Judea and from beyond the Jordan.

0042	ܘܐܙܠܘ	And followed him
0215	ܒܬܪܗ	*
1201	ܟܢܫܐ	crowds
1596	ܣܓܝܐܐ	large
1388	ܡܢ	from
3153	ܓܠܝܠܐ	Galilee
1388	ܘܡܢ	and from
3402	ܥܣܪܬ ܡܕܝܢܬܐ	the Decapolis
1388	ܘܡܢ	and from
3022	ܐܘܪܫܠܡ	Jerusalem
1388	ܘܡܢ	and from
3224	ܝܗܘܕ	Judea
1388	ܘܡܢ	and from
1735	ܥܒܪܐ	beyond
3248	ܕܝܘܪܕܢܢ	Jordan

CHAPTER 5

VERSE 1 And when Jesus saw the crowd, he climbed a mountain and when he sat down, his disciples came near to him.

1128	ܟܕ	when
0758	ܚܙܐ	saw
0518	ܕܝܢ	And
3257	ܝܫܘܥ	Jesus
1201	ܠܟܢܫܐ	the crowd
1658	ܣܠܩ	he climbed
0958	ܠܛܘܪܐ	a mountain
1128	ܘܟܕ	and when
1093	ܝܬܒ	he sat down
2244	ܩܪܒܘ	came near
1288	ܠܘܬܗ	to him
1304	ܬܠܡܝܕܘܗܝ	his disciples

VERSE 2 And he opened his mouth and was teaching them and said,

2070	ܘܦܬܚ	And he opened

21

Vertical Interlinear

MATTHEW CHAPTER 5

1936	ܦܘܡܗ	his mouth
1053	ܘܡܠܦ	and teaching
0603	ܗܘܐ	was
1261	ܠܗܘܢ	them
0116	ܘܐܡܪ	and said

VERSE 3 "Blessed [are] the poor in spirit, because theirs is the kingdom of heaven.

0940	ܛܘܒܝܗܘܢ	Blessed [are]
1406	ܠܡܣܟܢܐ	the poor
2323	ܒܪܘܚ	in spirit
0517	ܕܕܝܠܗܘܢ	because theirs
0592	ܗܝ	is
1385	ܡܠܟܘܬܐ	the kingdom
2543	ܕܫܡܝܐ	of heaven

VERSE 4 Blessed [are] the mourners, because they will be comforted.

0940	ܛܘܒܝܗܘܢ	Blessed [are]
0010	ܠܐܒܝܠܐ	the mourners
0592	ܕܗܢܘܢ	because they
0262	ܢܬܒܝܐܘܢ	will be comforted

VERSE 5 Blessed [are] the meek, because they will inherit the earth.

0940	ܛܘܒܝܗܘܢ	Blessed [are]
1355	ܠܡܟܝܟܐ	the meek
0592	ܕܗܢܘܢ	because they
1087	ܢܐܪܬܘܢ	will inherit
0199	ܐܪܥܐ	the earth

VERSE 6 Blessed [are] those who hunger and thirst for uprightness, because they will be satisfied.

0940	ܛܘܒܝܗܘܢ	Blessed [are]
0066	ܠܐܝܠܝܢ	those
1214	ܕܟܦܢܝܢ	who hunger
2087	ܘܨܗܝܢ	and thirst
1152	ܠܟܐܢܘܬܐ	for uprightness
0592	ܕܗܢܘܢ	because they
1585	ܢܣܒܥܘܢ	will be satisfied

VERSE 7 Blessed [are] the merciful, because on them will be mercies.

0940	ܛܘܒܝܗܘܢ	Blessed [are]
2343	ܠܡܪܚܡܢܐ	the merciful
1804	ܕܥܠܝܗܘܢ	because on them
0603	ܢܗܘܘܢ	will be
2346	ܪܚܡܐ	mercies

VERSE 8 Blessed [are] those who are pure in their heart[s], because they will see God.

0940	ܛܘܒܝܗܘܢ	Blessed [are]
0066	ܠܐܝܠܝܢ	those
0521	ܕܕܟܝܢ	who are pure
1268	ܒܠܒܗܘܢ	in their heart[s]
0592	ܕܗܢܘܢ	because they
0758	ܢܚܙܘܢ	will see
0093	ܠܐܠܗܐ	God

VERSE 9 Blessed [are] the peacemakers, because they will be called the sons of God.

0940	ܛܘܒܝܗܘܢ	Blessed [are]
1724	ܠܥܒܕܝ	the peacemakers
2535	ܫܠܡܐ	*
0323	ܕܒܢܘܗܝ	because the sons
0093	ܕܐܠܗܐ	of God
2239	ܢܬܩܪܘܢ	they will be called

VERSE 10 Blessed [are] those who are persecuted because of uprightness, because theirs is the kingdom of heaven.

0940	ܛܘܒܝܗܘܢ	Blessed [are]
0066	ܠܐܝܠܝܢ	those
2304	ܕܐܬܪܕܦܘ	who are persecuted
1347	ܡܛܠ	because of
1152	ܟܐܢܘܬܐ	uprightness
0517	ܕܕܝܠܗܘܢ	because theirs
0592	ܗܝ	is
1385	ܡܠܟܘܬܐ	the kingdom
2543	ܕܫܡܝܐ	of heaven

VERSE 11 You are blessed when they curse you and persecute you and say every evil word against you falsely because of me.

0940	ܛܘܒܝܟܘܢ	You are blessed
0120	ܐܡܬܝ	when
0855	ܕܡܚܣܕܝܢ	they curse
1261	ܠܟܘܢ	you
2304	ܘܪܕܦܝܢ	and persecute
1261	ܠܟܘܢ	you

22

MATTHEW   CHAPTER 5

0116		and say
1804		against you
1168		every
1364		word
0220		evil
1347		because of me
0487		falsely

VERSE 12 — Then rejoice and be glad, because your reward is great in heaven, for so they persecuted the prophets who [were] before you.

0594		Then
0726		rejoice
2320		and be glad
0018		because your reward
1595		is great
2543		in heaven
0597		so
0403		for
2304		they persecuted
1457		the prophets
1388		who [were]
2154		before you

VERSE 13 — You are the salt of the earth, but if the salt should go flat, with what will it be salted? It is not fit for anything, but to be thrown outside and to be trampled on by man.

0133		You
0592		are
1378		the salt
0199		of the earth
0123		if
0518		but
1378		the salt
1962		should go flat
1393		with what
1377		will it be salted
1326		for anything
1262		not
0042		It is fit
0090		but
2455		to be thrown
0322		outside
0507		and to be trampled on
1388		by
0131		man

VERSE 14 — You are the light of the world. It is not possible to hide a city that is built on a mountain.

0133		You
0592		are
1477		the light
1813		of the world
1262		not
2510		It is possible
1009		to hide
0499		a city
1804		that on
0958		a mountain
0281		is built

VERSE 15 — And they do not light a lamp and place it under a basket, but on a lampstand and it lights all those who are in the house.

1262		And not
1474		they do light
2607		a lamp
1625		and place
1261		it
2660		under
1583		a basket
0090		but
1804		on
1402		a lampstand
1474		and it lights
1168		all
0066		those
0243		who in the house
0592		are

Vertical Interlinear

MATTHEW CHAPTER 5

VERSE 16 — Likewise, your light should shine before men, so that they will see your good works and will glorify your Father who is in heaven.

Num	Aramaic	English
0597		Likewise
1474		should shine
1477		your light
2154		before
0325		men
0758		so that they will see
1728		your works
0938		good
2428		and will glorify
0002		your Father
2543		who is in heaven

VERSE 17 — Do not think that I have come to change the law or the prophets. I have not come to change, but to fulfill [them].

Num	Aramaic	English
1262		not
1588		Do think
0208		that I have come
2597		to change
1524		the law
0024		or
1457		the prophets
1262		not
0208		I have come
2597		to change
0090		but
1366		to fulfill [them]

VERSE 18 — For truly I say to you, until heaven and earth pass away, not one jot or one stroke will pass from the law until everything happens.

Num	Aramaic	English
0110		truly
0403		For
0116		say
0124		I
1261		to you
1747		until
1733		pass away
2543		heaven
0199		and earth
1034		jot
0721		one
0024		or
0721		one
1712		stroke
1262		not
1733		will pass
1388		from
1524		the law
1747		until
1168		everything
0603		happens

VERSE 19 — Therefore, whoever changes one [jot] of these small commandments (and will teach so to men) will be called little in the kingdom of heaven. But all who will do and teach this [law] will be called great in the kingdom of heaven.

Num	Aramaic	English
1168		whoever
1389		*
0596		Therefore
2597		changes
0721		one [jot]
1388		of
2009		commandments
0598		these
0686		small
1053		and will teach
0597		so
0325		to men
0312		little
2239		will be called
1385		in the kingdom
2543		of heaven
1168		all
0518		but
1724		who will do
1053		and teach
0598		this [law]
2271		great

MATTHEW CHAPTER 5

#	Syriac	English
2239		will be called
1385		in the kingdom
2543		of heaven

VERSE 20 — For I say to you, unless your uprightness exceeds [that] of the scribes and Pharisees, you will not enter the kingdom of heaven.

#	Syriac	English
0116		say
0124		I
1261		to you
0403		For
0090		unless
1098		exceeds
1152		your uprightness
1100		<more>
1388		<than>
1699		[that] of the scribes
3439		and Pharisees
1262		not
1796		you will enter
1385		the kingdom
2543		of heaven

VERSE 21 — You have heard that it was said to the ancient [ones]: YOU SHOULD NOT KILL. And ANYONE WHO KILLS IS CONDEMNED TO JUDGMENT.

#	Syriac	English
2547		You have heard
0116		that it was said
2157		to the ancient [ones]
1262		NOT
2179		YOU SHOULD KILL
1168		And ANYONE
2179		WHO KILLS
0742		IS CONDEMNED
0592		*
0497		TO JUDGMENT

VERSE 22 — But I say to you, whoever provokes his brother to anger without cause is condemned to judgment. And anyone who says to his brother, '[I] spit [on you]!' is condemned to the assembly. And he, who says, 'Fool,' is condemned to the Gehenna of fire.

#	Syriac	English
0124		<I>
0518		But
0116		say
0124		I
1261		to you
1168		whoever
1389		*
2290		provokes to anger
1804		<on>
0043		his brother
0068		without cause
0742		is condemned
0592		*
0497		to judgment
1168		And anyone
0116		who says
0043		to his brother
2402		[I] spit [on you]
0742		is condemned
0592		*
1200		to the assembly
1389		And he
0116		who says
1297		Fool
0742		is condemned
0592		*
3148		to the Gehenna
1494		of fire

VERSE 23 — If, therefore, you offer your offering on the altar and there you remember that your brother holds a certain grudge against you,

#	Syriac	English
0121		If
0592		<it is>
0596		therefore

MATTHEW   CHAPTER 5

2244	ܩܪܒ	offer	1744	ܥܕ	while
0133	ܐܢܬ	you	1817	ܥܡܗ	with him
2246	ܩܘܪܒܢܟ	your offering	0133	ܐܢܬ	you [are]
1804	ܥܠ	on	0038	ܒܐܘܪܚܐ	on the journey
0475	ܡܕܒܚܐ	the altar	1314	ܕܠܡܐ	so that not
2682	ܘܬܡܢ	and there	0306	ܒܥܠ	your opponent at law
0527	ܬܬܕܟܪ	you remember	0497	ܕܝܢܟ	*
0047	ܐܚܝܕ	that holds	2530	ܢܫܠܡܟ	will deliver you
1804	ܥܠܝܟ	against you	0498	ܠܕܝܢܐ	to the judge
0043	ܐܚܘܟ	your brother	0498	ܘܕܝܢܐ	and the judge
0089	ܐܟܬܐ	a grudge	2530	ܢܫܠܡܟ	deliver you
1326	ܡܕܡ	certain	0352	ܠܓܒܝܐ	to the officer

VERSE 24   leave your offering there before the altar and first go, be reconciled with your brother and then come, offer your offering.

			1538	ܘܬܦܠ	and you fall [into]
			0243	ܒܝܬ	prison
			0163	ܐܣܝܪܐ	*

VERSE 26   And truly I say to you, you will not come out from there until you give back the last coin.

2440	ܫܒܘܩ	leave	0110	ܘܐܡܝܢ	And truly
2682	ܬܡܢ	there	0116	ܐܡܪ	say
2246	ܩܘܪܒܢܟ	your offering	0124	ܐܢܐ	I
2154	ܩܕܡ	before	1261	ܠܟ	to you
0475	ܡܕܒܚܐ	the altar	1262	ܕܠܐ	not
0042	ܘܙܠ	and go	1542	ܬܦܘܩ	you will come out
2151	ܠܘܩܕܡ	first	1388	ܡܢ	of from
2381	ܐܬܪܥܐ	be reconciled	2682	ܬܡܢ	there
1817	ܥܡ	with	1747	ܥܕܡܐ	until
0043	ܐܚܘܟ	your brother	1030	ܬܬܠ	you give back
0594	ܘܗܝܕܝܢ	and then	2541	ܫܡܘܢܐ	the coin
0208	ܬܐ	come	0051	ܐܚܪܝܐ	last
2244	ܩܪܒ	offer			
2246	ܩܘܪܒܢܟ	your offering			

VERSE 27   You have heard that it was said: YOU SHOULD NOT COMMIT ADULTERY.

VERSE 25   Reconcile with your opponent at law quickly while you [are] with him on the journey, so that your opponent at law will not deliver you to the judge and the judge deliver you to the officer and you fall [into] prison.

			2547	ܫܡܥܬܘܢ	You have heard
			0116	ܕܐܬܐܡܪ	that it was said
0603	ܗܘܝܬ	<be>	1262	ܠܐ	NOT
0026	ܡܬܪܥܐ	Reconcile	0385	ܬܓܘܪ	YOU SHOULD COMMIT ADULTERY
1817	ܥܡ	with			
0306	ܒܥܠ	your opponent at law			
0497	ܕܝܢܟ	*			
1738	ܒܥܓܠ	quickly			

VERSE 28   But I say to you, anyone who looks at a woman as desiring her immediately commits adultery with her in his heart.

0124	ܐܢܐ	<I>

MATTHEW CHAPTER 5

Vertical Interlinear

0518	ܕܝܢ	But
0116	ܐܡܪ	say
0124	ܐܢܐ	I
1261	ܠܟܘܢ	to you
1168	ܕܟܠ	anyone
1389	ܡܢ	*
0758	ܕܚܙܐ	who looks at
0135	ܐܢܬܬܐ	a woman
0060	ܐܝܟ	as
2287	ܕܢܪܓܝܗ	desiring her
0725	ܡܚܕܐ	immediately
0385	ܓܪܗ	commits adultery with her
1268	ܒܠܒܗ	in his heart

VERSE 29 Now if your right eye causes you to offend, tear it out and throw it from you. For it is better for you that one of your members should be lost and not [that] your whole body should fall into Gehenna.

0121	ܐܢ	if
0518	ܕܝܢ	Now
1794	ܥܝܢܟ	your eye
1061	ܕܝܡܝܢܐ	right
1242	ܡܟܫܠܐ	causes to offend
1261	ܠܟ	you
0877	ܚܨܝܗ	tear it out
2455	ܘܫܕܝܗ	and throw it
1388	ܡܢܟ	from you
2010	ܦܩܚ	it is better
1261	ܠܟ	for you
0403	ܓܝܪ	For
0005	ܕܢܐܒܕ	that should be lost
0721	ܚܕ	one
0589	ܡܢ ܗܕܡܝܟ	of your members
1262	ܘܠܐ	and not
1168	ܟܠܗ	[that] whole
1929	ܦܓܪܟ	your body
1538	ܢܦܠ	should fall
3148	ܒܓܗܢܐ	into Gehenna

VERSE 30 And if your right hand causes you to offend, cut [it] off [and] throw it from you. For it is better for you that one of your members should be lost and not [that] your whole body should fall into Gehenna.

0121	ܘܐܢ	And if
0057	ܐܝܕܟ	your hand
1061	ܕܝܡܝܢܐ	right
1242	ܡܟܫܠܐ	causes to offend
1261	ܠܟ	you
1992	ܦܣܘܩܝܗ	cut [it] off
2455	ܘܫܕܝܗ	[and] throw it
1388	ܡܢܟ	from you
2010	ܦܩܚ	it is better
1261	ܠܟ	for you
0403	ܓܝܪ	For
0005	ܕܢܐܒܕ	that should be lost
0721	ܚܕ	one
1388	ܡܢ	of
0589	ܗܕܡܝܟ	your members
1262	ܘܠܐ	and not
1168	ܟܠܗ	[that] whole
1929	ܦܓܪܟ	your body
1538	ܢܦܠ	should fall
3148	ܒܓܗܢܐ	into Gehenna

VERSE 31 It was said: HE WHO DISMISSES HIS WIFE MUST GIVE HER A WRITING OF DIVORCE.

0116	ܐܬܐܡܪ	It was said
1389	ܕܡܢ	HE
2597	ܕܫܪܐ	WHO DISMISSES
0135	ܐܢܬܬܗ	HIS WIFE
1030	ܢܬܠ	MUST GIVE
1261	ܠܗ	HER
1248	ܟܬܒܐ	A WRITING
0531	ܕܕܘܠܠܐ	OF DIVORCE

VERSE 32 But I say to you, anyone who dismisses his wife outside of the case of fornication makes her commit adultery and he who marries a dismissed woman commits adultery.

0124	ܐܢܐ	<I>

MATTHEW   CHAPTER 5

0518	ܕܝܢ	But
0116	ܐܡܪ	say
0124	ܐܢܐ	I
1261	ܠܟܘܢ	to you
1168	ܕܟܠ	anyone
1389	ܡܢ	*
2597	ܕܫܪܐ	who dismisses
0135	ܐܢܬܬܗ	his wife
0322	ܠܒܪ	outside
1388	ܡܢ	of
1364	ܡܠܬܐ	the case
0681	ܕܙܢܝܘܬܐ	of fornication
1724	ܥܒܕ	makes
1261	ܠܗ	her
0385	ܕܬܓܘܪ	commit adultery
1389	ܘܡܢ	and he
2587	ܕܢܣܒ	who marries
2440	ܫܒܝܩܬܐ	a dismissed woman
0385	ܓܐܪ	commits adultery

VERSE 33   Again, you have heard that it was said of the ancient [ones]: DO NOT BE FALSE IN YOUR OATH, BUT COMPLETE YOUR OATH TO THE LORD.

2650	ܬܘܒ	Again
2547	ܫܡܥܬܘܢ	you have heard
0116	ܕܐܬܐܡܪ	that it was said
2157	ܠܩܕܡܝܐ	of the ancient [ones]
1262	ܠܐ	NOT
0485	ܬܕܓܠ	DO BE FALSE
1060	ܒܡܘܡܬܟ	IN YOUR OATH
2530	ܬܫܠܡ	COMPLETE
0518	ܕܝܢ	BUT
1426	ܠܡܪܝܐ	TO THE LORD
1060	ܡܘܡܬܟ	YOUR OATH

VERSE 34   But I say to you, you should not swear at all, neither by heaven, which is the throne of God,

0124	ܐܢܐ	<I>
0518	ܕܝܢ	But
0116	ܐܡܪ	say
0124	ܐܢܐ	I
1261	ܠܟܘܢ	to you
1262	ܠܐ	not
1059	ܬܐܡܘܢ	you should swear
1622	ܣܟ	at all
1262	ܠܐ	neither
2543	ܒܫܡܝܐ	by heaven
1159	ܕܟܘܪܣܝܐ	which the throne
0592	ܗܘ	is
0093	ܕܐܠܗܐ	of God

VERSE 35   nor by earth, which is the footstool that is under his feet, not even by Jerusalem, which is the city of the great king.

1262	ܘܠܐ	nor
0199	ܒܐܪܥܐ	by earth
1127	ܕܟܘܒܫܐ	which the footstool
0592	ܗܝ	is
2660	ܕܬܚܝܬ	that is under
2293	ܪܓܠܘܗܝ	his feet
0170	ܐܦܠܐ	not even
3022	ܒܐܘܪܫܠܡ	by Jerusalem
0499	ܕܡܕܝܢܬܗ	which the city
0592	ܗܝ	is
1383	ܕܡܠܟܐ	of the king
2271	ܪܒܐ	great

VERSE 36   You should not even swear by your head, because you are not able to make one separate hair [either] black or white.

0170	ܐܦܠܐ	not even
2362	ܒܪܫܟ	by your head
1059	ܬܐܡܐ	You should swear
1262	ܕܠܐ	because not
2510	ܡܫܟܚ	are able
0133	ܐܢܬ	you
1724	ܠܡܥܒܕ	to make
0217	ܒܗ	<in it>
1403	ܡܢܬܐ	separate hair
0721	ܚܕܐ	one
1687	ܕܣܥܪܐ	<of the hair>
0084	ܐܘܟܡܬܐ	[either] black

MATTHEW CHAPTER 5

0024		or		0220		an evil [one]
0755		white		0090		but
VERSE 37		But your word should be yes, yes, and no, no. Anything that is apart from these [things] abounds from evil.		1389		he
				1341		who strikes
				1261		you
0090		But		1804		on
0603		should be		1961		your cheek
1364		your word		1061		right
0065		yes		1984		turn
0065		yes		1261		to him
1262		and no		0169		also
1262		no		0053		the other
1326		Anything		**VERSE 40**		And he who wants to go to court with you and to take your coat, give him your cloak also.
1388		that is apart from				
0598		these [things]				
1100		abounds		1389		And he
1388		from		2077		who wants
0220		evil		0496		to go to court
0592		<is>		1817		with you
VERSE 38		You have heard that it was said: EYE FOR EYE AND TOOTH FOR TOOTH.		2587		and to take
				1256		your coat
2547		You have heard		2440		give
0116		that it was said		1261		him
1794		EYE		0169		also
0812		FOR		1439		your cloak
1794		EYE		**VERSE 41**		He who compels you [to go] one mile, go with him two.
2558		AND TOOTH				
0812		FOR		1389		He
2558		TOOTH		2496		who compels
VERSE 39		But I say to you, you should not oppose an evil [one], but he who strikes you on your right cheek, turn to him the other also.		1261		you
				1352		[to go] mile
				0721		one
0124		<I>		0042		go
0518		But		1817		with him
0116		say		2709		two
0124		I		**VERSE 42**		Whoever asks you, give to him. And he who wants to borrow from you, you should not refuse him.
1261		to you				
1262		not		1389		Whoever
2168		you should oppose		2420		asks
2135		*		1261		you

MATTHEW CHAPTER 5

1030		give		0477		who take
1261		to him		1261		you
1389		And he		2188		by force
2077		who wants		2304		and persecute
1039		to borrow		1261		you
1388		from you				
1262		not				
1180		you should refuse him				

VERSE 45 so that you may be the sons of your Father who is in heaven, who causes his sun to rise on the good and on the bad and causes his rain to come down on the upright and on the wicked.

VERSE 43 You have heard that it was said: LOVE YOUR NEIGHBOR AND HATE YOUR ENEMY.

2547		You have heard		0061		so that
0116		that it was said		0603		you may be
2342		LOVE		0323		the sons
2248		YOUR NEIGHBOR		0002		of your Father
1673		AND HATE		2543		who is in heaven
0307		YOUR ENEMY		0593		<he>

VERSE 44 But I say to you, love your enemies and bless those who curse you and do that which is pleasing to him who hates you and pray for those who take you by force and persecute you,

0124		<I>		0555		who causes to rise
0518		But		2557		his sun
0116		say		1804		on
0124		I		0938		the good
1261		to you		1804		and on
0696		love		0220		the bad
0307		your enemies		1499		and causes to come down
0335		and bless		1350		his rain
1389		those		1804		on
1284		who curse		1150		the upright
1261		you		1804		and on
1724		and do		1767		the wicked
2583		that which is pleasing				
1389		to him				
1674		who hates				
1261		you				
2106		and pray				
1804		for				
0066		those				

VERSE 46 For if you love those who love you, what is the reward for you? Behold, [do] not even the tax collectors do the same?

0121		if
0403		For
0696		love
0133		you
0066		those
0696		who love
1261		you
1393		what
0018		the reward
0069		is

MATTHEW CHAPTER 5

1261		for you
1262		[do] not
0580		Behold
0169		even
1358		the tax collectors
0592		the same
0598		*
1724		do

VERSE 47 And if you greet only your brothers, what extraordinary [thing] are you doing? Behold, [do] not even the tax collectors do this?

0121		And if
2420		greet you
0133		*
2535		*
0043		your brothers
1041		only
1393		what
1100		extraordinary [thing]
1724		are doing
0133		you
1262		[do] not
0580		Behold
0169		even
1358		the tax collectors
0592		<they>
0598		this
1724		do

VERSE 48 Therefore, be made perfect, as your Father who is in heaven is perfect.'

0603		be
0596		Therefore
0133		<you>
0426		be made perfect
0061		as
0002		your Father
2543		who is in heaven
0426		perfect
0592		is

CHAPTER 6

VERSE 1 And take heed with regard to your almsgiving that you should not do it before men, so that you may be seen by them, otherwise you [will] not have a reward from your Father who is in heaven.

0756		take heed
0518		And
0642		with regard to your almsgiving
1262		that not
1724		you should do it
2154		before
0323		men
0131		*
0060		so
0758		that you may be seen
1261		by them
0090		otherwise
0018		a reward
1264		you [will] not have
1261		*
1288		from
0002		your Father
2543		who is in heaven

VERSE 2 Therefore, whenever you do almsgiving, do not sound a trumpet before you as the hypocrites do in the synagogues and in the marketplaces, so that they may be praised by men. And truly I say to you, they have received their reward.

0120		whenever
0596		Therefore
1724		do
0133		you
0642		almsgiving
1262		not
2239		do sound
2255		a trumpet
2154		before you
0060		as
1724		do
1532		the hypocrites

MATTHEW CHAPTER 6

0173	ܐܢܫܐ	*
1200	ܒܟܢܘܫܬܐ	in the synagogues
2481	ܘܒܫܘܩܐ	and in the marketplaces
0060	ܐܝܟ	so
2428	ܕܢܫܬܒܚܘܢ	that they may be praised
1388	ܡܢ	by
0323	ܒܢܝ	men
0131	ܐܢܫܐ	*
0110	ܘܐܡܝܢ	And truly
0116	ܐܡܪ	say
0124	ܐܢܐ	I
1261	ܠܟܘܢ	to you
2134	ܕܩܒܠܘ	they have received
0018	ܐܓܪܗܘܢ	their reward

VERSE 3 But when you do almsgiving, you should not let your left hand know what your right hand does,

0133	ܐܢܬ	<you>
0518	ܕܝܢ	But
1313	ܡܐ	when
1724	ܕܥܒܕ	do
0133	ܐܢܬ	you
0642	ܙܕܩܬܐ	almsgiving
1262	ܠܐ	not
1023	ܬܕܥ	you should let know
1668	ܣܡܠܟ	your left hand
1393	ܡܢܐ	what
1724	ܥܒܕܐ	does
1061	ܝܡܝܢܟ	your right hand

VERSE 4 so that your almsgiving may be in secret and your Father, who sees in secret, shall repay you openly.

0060	ܐܝܟ	so
0603	ܕܬܗܘܐ	that may be
0642	ܙܕܩܬܟ	your almsgiving
1206	ܒܟܣܝܐ	in secret
0002	ܘܐܒܘܟ	and your Father
0758	ܕܚܙܐ	who sees
1206	ܒܟܣܝܐ	in secret
0592	ܗܘ	<he>

2037	ܢܦܪܥܟ	will repay you
0411	ܒܓܠܝܐ	openly

VERSE 5 And when you pray, you should not be as the hypocrites, who love to stand in the synagogues and on the corners of the marketplaces to pray, to be seen by men. And truly I say to you, they have received their reward.

1313	ܘܡܐ	And when
2106	ܕܡܨܠܐ	pray
0133	ܐܢܬ	you
1262	ܠܐ	not
0603	ܬܗܘܐ	you should be
0060	ܐܝܟ	as
1532	ܢܣܒܝ	the hypocrites
0173	ܐܢܫܐ	*
2342	ܕܪܚܡܝܢ	who love
2168	ܠܡܩܡ	to stand
1200	ܒܟܢܘܫܬܐ	in the synagogues
0654	ܘܒܙܘܝܬܐ	and on the corners
2481	ܕܫܘܩܐ	of the marketplaces
2106	ܠܡܨܠܝܘ	to pray
0758	ܕܢܬܚܙܘܢ	to be seen
0323	ܠܒܢܝ	by men
0131	ܐܢܫܐ	*
0110	ܘܐܡܝܢ	And truly
0116	ܐܡܪ	say
0124	ܐܢܐ	I
1261	ܠܟܘܢ	to you
2134	ܕܩܒܠܘ	they have received
0018	ܐܓܪܗܘܢ	their reward

VERSE 6 But when you pray, enter your room and close your door and pray to your Father, who is in secret, and your Father, who sees in secret, will repay you openly.

0133	ܐܢܬ	<you>
0518	ܕܝܢ	But
0120	ܐܡܬܝ	when
2106	ܕܡܨܠܐ	pray
0133	ܐܢܬ	you
1796	ܥܘܠ	enter
0029	ܠܬܘܢܟ	your room

MATTHEW CHAPTER 6

#	Aramaic	English
0047		and close
2718		your door
2106		and pray
0002		to your Father
1206		who is in secret
0002		and your Father
0758		who sees
1206		in secret
2037		will repay you
0411		openly

VERSE 7 — And when you are praying, you should not talk idly as the heathens [do], for they think that they are heard by much speaking.

#	Aramaic	English
1313		And when
2106		are praying
0133		you
1262		not
0603		you should
2005		talk idly
0060		as
0847		the heathens
1588		they think
0403		for
1365		that by speaking
1596		much
2547		they are heard

VERSE 8 — Therefore, do not imitate them, for your Father knows what is needed by you before you ask him.

#	Aramaic	English
1262		not
0596		Therefore
0540		do imitate
1261		them
0002		your Father
0403		for
1023		knows
1393		what
0296		is needed
1261		by you
1746		before
2420		you ask him

VERSE 9 — Therefore pray like this: 'Our Father, who is in heaven, may your name be holy.

#	Aramaic	English
0597		like this
0596		Therefore
2106		pray
0133		<you>
0002		Our Father
2543		who is in heaven
2160		may be holy
2539		your name

VERSE 10 — May your kingdom come. May your will occur, as in heaven, also on earth.

#	Aramaic	English
0208		May come
1385		your kingdom
0603		May occur
2079		your will
0061		as
2543		in heaven
0169		also
0199		on earth

VERSE 11 — Give us the bread of our need today

#	Aramaic	English
1030		Give
1261		us
1293		the bread
1680		of our need
1037		today

VERSE 12 — and forgive us our debts, as also we have forgiven our debtors.

#	Aramaic	English
2440		and forgive
1261		us
0743		our debts
0061		as
0169		also
0124		we
2440		have forgiven
0745		our debtors

MATTHEW   CHAPTER 6

VERSE 13 And do not let us enter into trial, but deliver us from the Evil [one], because the kingdom and the power and the glory are yours, forever and ever.'

1262	ܘܠܐ	And not
1796	ܬܥܠܢ	do let us enter
1528	ܠܢܣܝܘܢܐ	into trial
0090	ܐܠܐ	but
2002	ܦܨܢ	deliver us
1388	ܡܢ	from
0220	ܒܝܫܐ	the Evil [one]
1347	ܡܛܠ	because
0517	ܕܕܝܠܟ	yours
0592	ܗܝ	are
1385	ܡܠܟܘܬܐ	the kingdom
0786	ܘܚܝܠܐ	and the power
2432	ܘܬܫܒܘܚܬܐ	and the glory
1813	ܠܥܠܡ	forever and ever
1813	ܥܠܡܝܢ	*

VERSE 14 For if you forgive men their offenses, your Father who is in heaven will also forgive you,

0121	ܐܢ	if
0403	ܓܝܪ	For
2440	ܬܫܒܩܘܢ	you forgive
0325	ܠܒܢܝܢܫܐ	men
1652	ܣܟܠܘܬܗܘܢ	their offenses
2440	ܢܫܒܘܩ	will forgive
0169	ܐܦ	also
1261	ܠܟܘܢ	you
0002	ܐܒܘܟܘܢ	your Father
2543	ܕܒܫܡܝܐ	who is in heaven

VERSE 15 but if you do not forgive men, your Father will also not forgive you your offenses.

0121	ܐܢ	if
0518	ܕܝܢ	but
1262	ܠܐ	not
2440	ܬܫܒܩܘܢ	do you forgive
0325	ܠܒܢܝܢܫܐ	men
0170	ܐܦܠܐ	also not
0002	ܐܒܘܟܘܢ	your Father
2440	ܢܫܒܘܩ	will forgive
1261	ܠܟܘܢ	you
1652	ܣܟܠܘܬܟܘܢ	your offenses

VERSE 16 Now when you fast, you should not be sad as the hypocrites, for they distort their faces so that they may be seen by men that they are fasting. And truly I say to you, they have received their reward.

0120	ܐܡܬܝ	when
0518	ܕܝܢ	Now
2093	ܕܨܝܡܝܢ	fast
0133	ܐܢܬܘܢ	you
1262	ܠܐ	not
0603	ܬܗܘܘܢ	you should be
1193	ܟܡܝܪܐ	sad
0060	ܐܝܟ	as
1532	ܢܣܒܝ	the hypocrites
0173	ܐܦܐ	*
0702	ܡܚܒܠܝܢ	they distort
0403	ܓܝܪ	for
2041	ܦܪܨܘܦܝܗܘܢ	their faces
0060	ܐܝܟ	so
0758	ܕܢܬܚܙܘܢ	that they may be seen
0325	ܠܒܢܝܢܫܐ	by men
2093	ܕܨܝܡܝܢ	that they are fasting
0110	ܘܐܡܝܢ	And truly
0116	ܐܡܪ	say
0124	ܐܢܐ	I
1261	ܠܟܘܢ	to you
2134	ܕܩܒܠܘ	they have received
0018	ܐܓܪܗܘܢ	their reward

VERSE 17 But when you fast, wash your face and anoint your head,

0133	ܐܢܬ	<you>
0518	ܕܝܢ	But
1313	ܡܐ	when
2093	ܕܨܐܡ	fast
0133	ܐܢܬ	you
2466	ܐܫܝܓ	wash
0173	ܐܦܝܟ	your face

MATTHEW CHAPTER 6

Vertical Interlinear

1443		and anoint
2362		your head

VERSE 18 — so that [the fact that] you are fasting may not be seen by men, but by your Father who is in secret. And your Father, who sees in secret, will reward you.

0060		so that
1262		that [the fact that] not
0758		may be seen
0325		by men
2093		you are fasting
0133		you
0090		but
0002		by your Father
1206		who is in secret
0002		And your father
0758		who sees
1206		in secret
0592		\<he\>
2037		will reward you

VERSE 19 — You should not place for yourself treasures on earth, where moth and rust corrupt and where thieves break in and steal.

1262		not
1625		You should place
1261		for yourself
1627		treasures
0199		on earth
0214		where
1682		moth
0077		and rust
0702		corrupt
1108		and where
0437		thieves
1983		break in
0436		and steal

VERSE 20 — But place for yourself treasures in heaven, where neither moth nor rust corrupt and where thieves do not break in and do not steal.

0090		But
1625		place
1261		for yourself
1627		treasures
2543		in heaven
1108		where
1262		neither
1682		moth
1262		nor
0077		rust
0702		corrupt
1108		and where
0437		thieves
1262		not
1983		do break in
1262		and not
0436		do steal

VERSE 21 — For where your treasure is, there is also your heart.

1108		where
0403		For
0069		is
1627		your treasure
2682		there
0592		is
0169		also
1268		your heart

VERSE 22 — The lamp of the body is the eye. Therefore, if your eye will be simple, your whole body also is enlightened.

2607		The lamp
1929		of the body
0069		is
1794		the eye
0121		if
1794		your eye
0596		Therefore
0603		will be
2055		simple
0169		also
1168		whole

MATTHEW CHAPTER 6

1929		your body		2342		will love
1474		enlightened		0024		or
0592		is		0721		the one
VERSE 23		But if your eye will be evil, your whole body will be dark. If then the light that is in you is darkness, how great will be your darkness.		1076		he will honor
				0053		and the other
				2474		will treat with contempt
				1262		not
0121		if		2510		are able
0518		But		0133		You
1794		your eye		0093		God
0603		will be		1974		to serve
0220		evil		1387		and wealth
1168		whole		**VERSE 25**		Because of this, I say to you, you should not be worried about your life, what you will eat and what you will drink and not about your body, what you will wear. Behold, is not life more than food and the body [more] than clothing?
1929		your body				
0923		dark				
0603		will be				
0121		If				
0596		then		1347		Because of
1477		the light		0598		this
0217		that is in you		0116		say
0923		darkness		0124		I
0592		is		1261		to you
0923		your darkness		1262		not
1188		how great		1069		you should be worried
0603		will be		1547		about your life
VERSE 24		No man is able to serve two lords. For either he will hate the one and will love the other or he will honor the one and will treat the other with contempt. You are not able to serve God and wealth.		1393		what
				0075		you will eat
				1393		and what
				2620		you will drink
1262		No		1262		and not
0131		man		1929		about your body
2510		is able		1393		what
2709		two		1272		you will wear
1426		lords		1262		not
1974		to serve		0580		Behold
0024		either		1547		life
0403		For		1100		is more
0721		the one		1388		than
1673		he will hate		1594		food
0053		and the other		1929		and the body

MATTHEW   CHAPTER 6

1388		[more] than
1273		clothing

VERSE 26 — Look at the birds in the sky that do not sow nor reap nor gather into storehouses, yet your Father who is in heaven feeds them. Behold, are not you more important than they?

0756		Look at
2026		the birds
2543		in the sky
1262		that not
0691		do sow
1262		nor
0878		reap
1262		nor
0824		gather
0035		into storehouses
0002		yet your Father
2543		who is in heaven
2715		feeds
1261		them
1262		not
0580		Behold
0133		<you>
1104		are more important
0133		you
1388		than they

VERSE 27 — And who among you, while worrying, is able to add one cubit to his height?

1390		who
0518		And
1388		among you
1128		while
1069		worrying
2510		is able
1064		to add
1804		to
2171		his height
0119		cubit
0721		one

VERSE 28 — And why are you worried about clothes? Consider the lilies of the field, how they grow without toil and without spinning.

1804		And about
1273		clothes
1393		why
1069		are worried
0133		you
0316		Consider
2484		the lilies
0478		of the field
0061		how
2280		they grow
1262		without
1265		toil
1262		and without
1782		spinning

VERSE 29 — But I say to you, not even Solomon in all his glory was clothed like one of these.

0116		say
0124		I
1261		to you
0518		But
0170		not even
3518		Solomon
1168		in all
2431		his glory
1206		was clothed
0060		like
0721		one
1388		of these

VERSE 30 — Now if God so clothes the grass of the field that today is and tomorrow falls into the oven, [will he] not much more [clothe] you, oh little of faith?

0121		if
0518		Now
1826		the grass
0884		of the field
1037		that today
0069		is

MATTHEW CHAPTER 6

1345		and tomorrow		2543		who is in heaven
1538		falls		1023		knows
2692		into the oven		0169		that even
0093		God		1261		by you
0597		so		0296		are needed
1272		clothes		0598		these [things]
1262		[will he] not		1168		all <of them>

VERSE 33 — But seek first the kingdom of God and his justification and all these [things] will be added to you.

1596		more
1100		much
1261		[clothe] you
0686		oh little of
0113		faith

0296		seek
0518		But
2151		first
1385		the kingdom
0093		of God
0639		and his justification
1168		and all <of them>
0598		these [things]
1064		will be added
1261		to you

VERSE 31 — Therefore, do not be worried or say, 'What will we eat?' or, 'What will we drink?' or, 'What will we wear?'

1262		not
0596		Therefore
1069		do be worried
0024		or
0116		say
1393		What
0075		will we eat
0024		or
1393		What
2620		will we drink
0024		or
1393		What
1206		will we wear

VERSE 34 — Therefore, do not be worried about tomorrow, for tomorrow will care for itself. Sufficient for the day is its [own] evil.

1262		not
0596		Therefore
1069		do be worried
1345		about tomorrow
0592		<it>
0403		for
1345		tomorrow
1069		will care for
0517		itself
1694		Sufficient is
1261		<for it>
1036		for the day
0220		its [own] evil

VERSE 32 — For the nations of the world seek all these [things]. And your Father who is in heaven knows that even all these [things] are needed by you.

1168		all <of them>
0403		For
0598		these [things]
1818		the nations
0592		<it>
0296		seek
1261		<them>
0002		your Father
0518		And

CHAPTER 7

VERSE 1 — You should not judge, so that you will not be judged.

1262		not

MATTHEW CHAPTER 7

Code	Aramaic	English
0496		You should judge
1262		so that not
0496		you will be judged

VERSE 2 For with the judgment that you judge, you will be judged and by the measure that you measure, it will be measured to you.

Code	Aramaic	English
0497		with the judgment
0403		For
0496		that judge
0133		you
0496		you will be judged
1144		and by the measure
1142		that measure
0133		you
1142		it will be measured
1261		to you

VERSE 3 And why do you see the straw that is in the eye of your brother and you do not observe the beam that is in your eye?

Code	Aramaic	English
1393		why
0518		And
0758		do see
0133		you
0406		the straw
1794		that is in the eye
0043		of your brother
2252		and the beam
1794		that is in your eye
1262		not
0251		do observe
0133		you

VERSE 4 Or how do you say to your brother, 'Allow [me] to take out the straw from your eye,' and behold, a beam [is] in your eye?

Code	Aramaic	English
0024		Or
0061		how
0116		do say
0133		you
0043		to your brother
2440		Allow [me]
1542		to take out
0406		the straw
1388		from
1794		your eye
0580		and behold
2252		a beam
1794		[is] in your eye

VERSE 5 Hypocrite! First take out the beam from your eye and then you will be proved capable to take out the straw from the eye of your brother.

Code	Aramaic	English
1532		Hypocrite
0173		*
1542		take out
2151		First
2252		the beam
1388		from
1794		your eye
0594		and then
0251		will be proved capable
1261		<to> you
1542		to take out
0406		the straw
1388		from
1794		the eye
0043		of your brother

VERSE 6 You should not give a holy [thing] to dogs and you should not throw your pearls before pigs, so that they will not trample them with their feet and turn [and] attack you.

Code	Aramaic	English
1262		not
1030		You should give
2164		a holy [thing]
1183		to dogs
1262		and not
2372		you should throw
1430		your pearls
2154		before
0766		pigs
1314		so that not

MATTHEW CHAPTER 7

0507		they will trample
0592		them
2293		with their feet
0616		and turn
0249		[and] attack you

VERSE 7 — Ask and it will be given to you. Seek and you will find. Knock and it will be opened to you.

2420		Ask
1030		and it will be given
1261		to you
0296		Seek
2510		and you will find
1568		Knock
2070		and it will be opened
1261		to you

VERSE 8 — For everyone who asks will receive and he who seeks will find and to him who knocks, it will be opened to him.

1168		everyone
0403		For
2420		who asks
1532		will receive
0296		and he who seeks
2510		will find
0066		and to him
1568		who knocks
2070		it will be opened
1261		to him

VERSE 9 — Or what man among you, whose son asks him for bread, will hold out a stone to him?

0024		Or
1390		what
1388		among you
0361		man
2420		asks him
0323		whose son
1293		for bread
1316		<?>
1119		a stone
1091		will hold out
1261		to him

VERSE 10 — And if he asks for a fish, will he hold out a snake to him?

0121		And if
1490		a fish
2420		he asks for
1316		<?>
0740		a snake
1091		will he hold out
1261		to him

VERSE 11 — And if therefore you who are evil know to give good gifts to your sons, how much more will your Father who is in heaven give good [gifts] to those who ask him?

0121		And if
0596		therefore
0133		you
0220		who are evil
0133		<you>
1023		know
0133		you
1032		gifts
0938		good
1030		to give
0323		to your sons
1188		how much
1101		more
0002		your Father
2543		who is in heaven
1030		will give
0938		good [gifts]
0066		to those
2420		who ask
1261		him

VERSE 12 — All that you desire that men should do to you, so also do to them, for this is the law and the prophets.

1168		All
1313		that

MATTHEW CHAPTER 7

2077		desire
0133		you
1724		that should do
1261		to you
0323		men
0131		*
0597		so
0169		also
0133		<you>
1724		do
1261		to them
0599		this is
0403		for
1524		the law
1457		and the prophets

VERSE 13 Enter by the straight door because wide is the door and broad [is] the road that leads to loss and many are those who go in it.

1796		Enter
2718		by the door
0104		straight
2066		because wide
0592		is
2718		the door
2330		and broad [is]
0038		the road
0066		that
1015		leads
0006		to loss
1596		and many
0592		are
0066		those
0042		who go
0217		in it

VERSE 14 How narrow the door and straight the road that leads to life and few are those who find it.

1313		How
2183		narrow
2718		the door
0104		and straight
0038		the road
1015		that leads
0782		to life
0686		and few
0592		are
0066		those
2510		who find
1261		it

VERSE 15 Beware of false prophets, who come to you in the clothing of lambs, but within are savage wolves.

0645		Beware
1388		of
1457		prophets
0486		false
0208		who come
1288		to you
1273		in the clothing
0117		of lambs
1388		<from>
0379		within
0518		but
0069		are
0469		wolves
0775		savage

VERSE 16 Now by their fruit you will know them. Do they pick grapes from thorns or figs from thistles?

1388		by
2016		their fruit
0518		Now
1023		you will know
0592		them
1316		<?>
1309		do they pick
1388		from
1139		thorns
1840		grapes
0024		or

MATTHEW   CHAPTER 7

1388		from
2177		thistles
2628		figs
VERSE 17		So every healthy tree bears beautiful fruit, but a diseased tree bears diseased fruit.
0597		So
1168		every
0063		tree
0938		healthy
2016		fruit
2583		beautiful
1724		bears
0063		tree
0518		but
0220		a diseased
2016		fruit
0220		diseased
1724		bears
VERSE 18		A healthy tree is not able to bear diseased fruit and a diseased tree [is not able] to bear healthy fruit.
1262		not
2510		is able
0063		tree
0938		A healthy
2016		fruit
0220		diseased
1724		to bear
1262		and [is] not [able]
0063		tree
0220		a diseased
2016		fruit
0938		healthy
1724		to bear
VERSE 19		Every tree that does not bear healthy fruit is cut down and thrown into the fire.
1168		Every
0063		tree
1262		that not
1724		does bear

2016		fruit
0938		healthy
1992		is cut down
1494		and into the fire
1538		thrown
VERSE 20		So then, by their fruit you will know them.
1324		So then
1388		by
2016		their fruit
1023		you will know
0592		them
VERSE 21		Not all who say to me, 'My Lord, my Lord,' will enter the kingdom of heaven, but he who does the will of my Father who is in heaven.
1262		Not
0603		<it will be>
1168		all
0116		who say
1261		to me
1426		My Lord
1426		my Lord
1796		will enter
1385		the kingdom
2543		of heaven
0090		but
1389		he
1724		who does
2079		the will
0002		of my Father
2543		who is in heaven
VERSE 22		Many will say to me in that day, 'My Lord, my Lord, in your name have we not prophesied and in your name cast out demons and in your name done many miracles?'
1596		Many
0116		will say
1261		to me
0593		in that
1036		day

MATTHEW   CHAPTER 7

1426		My Lord
1426		my Lord
1262		not
2539		in your name
1456		have we prophesied
2539		and in your name
2469		demons
1542		cast out
2539		and in your name
0786		miracles
1596		many
1724		done

VERSE 23 And then I will confess to them, 'I have never known you. Go away from me, workers of wickedness.'

0594		And then
1020		I will confess
1261		to them
1388		never
1450		*
1262		*
1023		I have known you
2353		Go away
1261		<to you>
1388		from me
1976		workers of
1766		wickedness

VERSE 24 Therefore, everyone, who hears these words of mine and does them, will be compared to a wise man who built his house on a rock.

1168		everyone
0596		Therefore
2547		who hears
1364		words of mine
0598		these
1724		and does
1261		them
0540		will be compared
0361		to a man
0790		wise

0593		<he>
0281		who built
0243		his house
1804		on
2477		a rock

VERSE 25 And the rain fell and the floods came and the winds blew and they beat against the house but it did not fail, for its foundations were set on a rock.

1499		And fell
1350		the rain
0208		and came
1478		the floods
1571		and blew
2323		the winds
1004		and they beat
0217		<on it>
0243		against the house
0593		<that>
1262		yet
1538		it did fail
0203		its foundations
0403		for
1804		on
2477		a rock
1626		set
0603		were

VERSE 26 And everyone, who hears these words of mine and does not do them, will be compared to a foolish man who built his house on the sand.

1168		And everyone
1389		who
2547		hears
1364		words of mine
0598		these
1262		and not
1724		does do
1261		them
0540		will be compared
0361		to a man

MATTHEW CHAPTER 7

1651		foolish
0281		who built
0243		his house
1804		on
0796		the sand

VERSE 27 And the rain fell and the floods came and the winds blew and they beat against the house and it fell and its fall was great."

1499		And fell
1350		the rain
0208		and came
1478		the floods
1571		and blew
2323		the winds
1004		and they beat
0243		against the house
0593		<that>
1538		and it fell
0603		and was
1539		its fall
2271		great

VERSE 28 And it happened that when Jesus finished these words, the crowds were amazed at his teaching.

0603		And it happened
1128		that when
2530		finished
3257		Jesus
1364		words
0598		these
2644		amazed
0603		were
1201		the crowds
1804		at
1054		his teaching

VERSE 29 For he was teaching them as [one having] authority and not as their scribes and the Pharisees.

1053		teaching
0603		he was
1261		them
0403		For
0060		as [one having]
2526		authority
1262		and not
0060		as
1699		their scribes
3439		and the Pharisees

CHAPTER 8

VERSE 1 Now when he came down from the mountain, large crowds followed him.

1128		when
1499		he came down
0518		Now
1388		from
0958		the mountain
1565		followed him
1201		crowds
1596		large

VERSE 2 And behold, a certain leper came [and] worshipped him and said, "My Lord, if you desire, you are able to cleanse me."

0580		And behold
0456		a leper
0721		certain
0208		came
1599		[and] worshipped
1261		him
0116		and said
1426		My Lord
0121		if
2077		desire
0133		you
2510		are able
0133		you
0521		to cleanse me

VERSE 3 And Jesus stretched out his hand [and] touched him, and said, "I desire. Be cleansed." And immediately his leprosy was cleansed.

2054		And stretched out

MATTHEW CHAPTER 8

0057		his hand		3257		Jesus
3257		Jesus		3268		Capernaum
2244		[and] touched		2244		approached
1261		him		1261		him
0116		and said		2223		centurion
2077		desire		0721		a certain
0124		I		0296		and entreating
0521		Be cleansed		0603		was
0217		And immediately		1388		<from> him

VERSE 6 — And he said, "My Lord, my child is lying at home and is paralyzed and seriously tortured with pain."

2573		*
0521		was cleansed
0457		his leprosy

VERSE 4 — And Jesus said to him, "See [that] you tell no one, but go, show yourself to the priests and offer an offering, as Moses commanded for their witness."

				0116		And he said
				1426		My Lord
				0976		my child
				2372		is lying
0116		And said		0243		at home
1261		to him		2597		and is paralyzed
3257		Jesus		0221		and seriously
0758		See [that]		2565		tortured with pain

VERSE 7 — Jesus said to him, "I will come and heal him."

1316		<?>				
0131		[no] one				
0116		you tell		0116		said
0133		*		1261		to him
0090		but		3257		Jesus
0042		go		0124		I
0739		show		0208		will come
1547		yourself		0136		and heal him

VERSE 8 — The centurion answered and he said, "My Lord, I am not worthy that you should enter under my roof, but only speak a word and my child will be healed."

1135		to the priests				
2244		and offer				
2246		an offering		1838		answered
0060		as		2223		The centurion
2007		commanded		0593		<that>
3305		Moses		0116		and said
1610		for their witness		1426		My Lord

VERSE 5 — Now when Jesus entered Capernaum, a certain centurion approached him and was entreating him.

				1262		not
1128		when		2461		am worthy
1796		entered		0124		I
0518		Now				

MATTHEW   CHAPTER 8

1796	ܕܬܥܘܠ	that you should enter
2660	ܬܚܝܬ	under
0973	ܡܛܠܠܝ	my roof
0090	ܐܠܐ	but
1041	ܒܠܚܘܕ	only
0116	ܐܡܪ	speak
1364	ܒܡܠܬܐ	\<with\> a word
0136	ܘܢܬܐܣܐ	and will be healed
0976	ܛܠܝܝ	my child

VERSE 9   For I also am a man who is under authority and there are soldiers under my hand. And I say to this one, 'Go,' and he goes, and to another, 'Come,' and he comes and to my servant, 'Do this,' and he does [it]."

0169	ܐܦ	also
0124	ܐܢܐ	\<I\>
0403	ܓܝܪ	For
0361	ܓܒܪܐ	a man
0124	ܐܢܐ	I am
2660	ܕܬܚܝܬ	who is under
2527	ܫܘܠܛܢܐ	authority
0069	ܘܐܝܬ	and there are
2660	ܬܚܝܬ	under
0057	ܐܝܕܝ	my hand
0150	ܐܣܛܪܛܝܘܛܐ	soldiers
0116	ܘܐܡܪ	And say
0124	ܐܢܐ	I
0598	ܠܗܢܐ	to this one
0042	ܙܠ	Go
0042	ܘܐܙܠ	and he goes
0053	ܘܠܐܚܪܢܐ	and to another
0208	ܬܐ	Come
0208	ܘܐܬܐ	and he comes
1727	ܘܠܥܒܕܝ	and to my servant
1724	ܥܒܕ	Do
0598	ܗܢܐ	this
1724	ܘܥܒܕ	and he does [it]

VERSE 10   And when Jesus heard [this], he marveled and said to those who had come with him, "Truly I say to you, not even in Israel have I found faith like this.

1128	ܟܕ	when
2547	ܫܡܥ	heard [this]
0518	ܕܝܢ	And
3257	ܝܫܘܥ	Jesus
0549	ܐܬܕܡܪ	he marveled
0116	ܘܐܡܪ	and said
0208	ܠܕܐܬܝܢ	to those who had come
1817	ܥܡܗ	with him
0110	ܐܡܝܢ	Truly
0116	ܐܡܪ	say
0124	ܐܢܐ	I
1261	ܠܟܘܢ	to you
0169	ܐܦ	even
1262	ܠܐ	not
3035	ܒܝܣܪܐܝܠ	in Israel
2510	ܐܫܟܚܬ	have I found
0060	ܐܝܟ	like
0598	ܗܕܐ	this
0113	ܗܝܡܢܘܬܐ	faith

VERSE 11   And I say to you, many will come from the east and from the west and will lie down to eat with Abraham and Isaac and Jacob in the kingdom of heaven,

0116	ܐܡܪ	say
0124	ܐܢܐ	I
1261	ܠܟܘܢ	to you
0518	ܕܝܢ	And
1596	ܣܓܝܐܐ	many
0208	ܢܐܬܘܢ	will come
1388	ܡܢ	from
0557	ܡܕܢܚܐ	the east
1388	ܘܡܢ	and from
1884	ܡܥܪܒܐ	the west
1664	ܘܢܣܬܡܟܘܢ	and will lie down to eat
1817	ܥܡ	with
3005	ܐܒܪܗܡ	Abraham
3033	ܘܐܝܣܚܩ	and Isaac

MATTHEW CHAPTER 8

3255	ܘܠܝܥܩܘܒ	and Jacob	0758	ܘܚܙܐ	and saw
1385	ܒܡܠܟܘܬܐ	in the kingdom	0823	ܠܚܡܬܗ	his mother-in-law
2543	ܕܫܡܝܐ	of heaven	2372	ܕܪܡܝܐ	who was lying down
VERSE 12		but the sons of the kingdom will go out to outer darkness. There will be crying and gnashing of teeth."	0047	ܘܐܚܝܕܐ	and had taken hold
			1261	ܠܗ	on her
0323	ܒܢܝ	the sons	0204	ܐܫܬܐ	a fever
0518	ܕܝܢ	but	VERSE 15		And he touched her hand and the fever left her and she got up and was serving him.
1385	ܡܠܟܘܬܐ	of the kingdom			
1542	ܢܦܩܘܢ	will go out	2244	ܘܩܪܒ	And he touched
0923	ܠܚܫܘܟܐ	to darkness	0057	ܒܐܝܕܗ	her hand
0321	ܒܪܝܐ	outer	2440	ܘܫܒܩܬܗ	and left her
2682	ܬܡܢ	There	0204	ܐܫܬܐ	the fever
0603	ܢܗܘܐ	will be	2168	ܘܩܡܬ	and she got up
0268	ܒܟܝܐ	crying	2554	ܘܡܫܡܫܐ	and serving
0905	ܘܚܘܪܩ	and gnashing of	0603	ܗܘܬ	was
2558	ܫܢܐ	teeth	1261	ܠܗ	him
VERSE 13		And Jesus said to the centurion, "Go! As you have believed, it will be to you." And his child was healed immediately.	VERSE 16		And when it became evening, they brought to him many possessed of devils and he cast out their devils by a word and he healed all those who were very diseased,
0116	ܘܐܡܪ	And said			
3257	ܝܫܘܥ	Jesus	1128	ܟܕ	when
2223	ܠܩܢܛܪܘܢܐ	to the centurion	0603	ܗܘܐ	it became
0593	ܕܙܠ	<that>	0518	ܕܝܢ	And
0042	ܙܠ	Go	2375	ܪܡܫܐ	evening
0061	ܐܝܟܢܐ	As	2244	ܩܪܒܘ	they brought
0109	ܕܗܝܡܢܬ	you have believed	2154	ܩܕܡܘܗܝ	to him
0603	ܢܗܘܐ	it will be	0515	ܕܝܘܢܐ	possessed of devils
1261	ܠܟ	to you	1596	ܣܓܝܐܐ	many
0136	ܘܐܬܐܣܝ	And was healed	1542	ܘܐܦܩ	and he cast out
0976	ܛܠܝܗ	his child	0514	ܕܝܘܝܗܘܢ	their devils
0217	ܒܗ	immediately	1364	ܒܡܠܬܐ	by a word
2573	ܒܫܥܬܐ	*	1168	ܘܠܟܠܗܘܢ	and all <of them>
VERSE 14		And Jesus came to the house of Simon and saw his mother-in-law who was lying down, and a fever had taken hold on her.	0066	ܐܝܠܝܢ	those
			0221	ܕܒܝܫܐܝܬ	who very
			1724	ܥܒܝܕܝܢ	diseased
0208	ܘܐܬܐ	And came	0603	ܗܘܘ	were
3257	ܝܫܘܥ	Jesus	0136	ܐܣܝ	he healed
0243	ܠܒܝܬܗ	to the house	0592	ܐܢܘܢ	<them>
3521	ܕܫܡܥܘܢ	of Simon			

MATTHEW CHAPTER 8

VERSE 17 — so that it would be fulfilled what was spoken by way of Isaiah the prophet who said: HE WILL TAKE OUR SORROWS AND HE WILL BEAR OUR SICKNESSES.

0060	ܐܝܟ	so that
1366	ܕܢܬܡܠܐ	it would be fulfilled
1326	ܡܕܡ	what
0116	ܕܐܬܐܡܪ	was spoken
0057	ܒܝܕ	by way of
3109	ܐܫܥܝܐ	Isaiah
1457	ܢܒܝܐ	the prophet
0116	ܕܐܡܪ	who said
0592	ܕܗܘ	HE
1532	ܢܣܒ	WILL TAKE
1116	ܟܐܒܝܢ	OUR SORROWS
1227	ܘܟܘܪܗܢܝܢ	AND OUR SICKNESSES
0999	ܢܛܥܢ	HE WILL BEAR

VERSE 18 — And when Jesus saw the many crowds that were surrounding him, he commanded that they should go to the opposite shore.

1128	ܟܕ	when
0758	ܚܙܐ	saw
0518	ܕܝܢ	And
3257	ܝܫܘܥ	Jesus
1201	ܟܢܫܐ	the crowds
1596	ܣܓܝܐܐ	many
0730	ܕܚܕܪܘܗܝ	that were surrounding
1261	ܠܗ	him
2007	ܦܩܕ	he commanded
0042	ܕܢܐܙܠܘܢ	that they should go
1735	ܠܥܒܪܐ	to the opposite shore

VERSE 19 — And a certain scribe approached and said to him, "My Master, I will follow you to the place where you are going."

2244	ܘܩܪܒ	And approached
1699	ܣܦܪܐ	a scribe
0721	ܚܕ	certain
0116	ܘܐܡܪ	and said
1261	ܠܗ	to him
2275	ܪܒܝ	My Master
0208		I will follow you
0215		*
0214		to the place
0042		where are going
0133		you

VERSE 20 — Jesus said to him, "Foxes have holes and the bird of heaven [has] a nest, but the Son of Man has no [home] where he may lay his head."

0116	ܐܡܪ	said
1261	ܠܗ	to him
3257	ܝܫܘܥ	Jesus
2695	ܬܥܠܐ	Foxes
1564	ܢܩܥܐ	holes
0069	ܐܝܬ	have
1261	ܠܗܘܢ	*
2026	ܘܠܦܪܚܬܐ	and the bird
2543	ܕܫܡܝܐ	of heaven [has]
0973	ܡܛܠܠܐ	a nest
0323	ܒܪܗ	the Son
0518	ܕܝܢ	but
0131	ܕܐܢܫܐ	of Man
1264	ܠܝܬ	has no [home]
1261	ܠܗ	*
1108	ܐܝܟܐ	where
1664	ܕܢܣܡܘܟ	he may lay
2362	ܪܫܗ	his head

VERSE 21 — And another of his disciples said to him, "My Lord, allow me first to go [and] bury my father."

0053	ܐܚܪܢܐ	another
0518	ܕܝܢ	And
1388	ܡܢ	of
1304	ܬܠܡܝܕܘܗܝ	his disciples
0116	ܐܡܪ	said
1261	ܠܗ	to him
1426	ܡܪܝ	My Lord
1989	ܐܦܣ	allow
1261	ܠܝ	me
2151	ܠܘܩܕܡ	first
0042	ܐܙܠ	to go

Vertical Interlinear

MATTHEW CHAPTER 8

2142		[and] bury
0002		my father
VERSE 22		But Jesus said to him, "Follow me and leave the dead to bury their dead."
3257		Jesus
0518		But
0116		said
1261		to him
0208		Follow me
0215		*
2440		and leave
1338		the dead
2142		to bury
1338		their dead
VERSE 23		And when Jesus boarded a boat, his disciples boarded with him.
1128		And when
1658		boarded
3257		Jesus
1692		a boat
1658		boarded
1817		with him
1304		his disciples
VERSE 24		And behold, a great earthquake occurred in the sea, so that the boat was covered by the waves. Now Jesus was asleep.
0580		And behold
0658		a earthquake
2271		great
0603		occurred
1057		in the sea
0061		so
0100		that the boat
1206		was covered
1388		by
0407		the waves
0592		<he>
0518		Now
3257		Jesus
0544		asleep
0603		was
VERSE 25		And his disciples came near [and] they woke him and said to him, "Our Lord, save us. We are being destroyed."
2244		And came near
1304		his disciples
1880		[and] they woke him
0116		and said
1261		to him
1426		Our Lord
2002		save us
0005		are being destroyed
0124		We
VERSE 26		Jesus said to them, "Why are you afraid, oh little of faith?" Then he stood and rebuked the wind and the sea and there was a great calm.
0116		said
1261		to them
3257		Jesus
1394		Why
0510		are afraid
0133		you
0686		oh little of
0113		faith
0594		Then
2168		he stood
1113		and rebuked
2323		the wind
1057		and the sea
0603		and there was
2519		a calm
2271		great
VERSE 27		And the men were amazed and said, "Who is this whom the winds and the sea obey?"
0131		the men
0518		And
0549		were amazed
0116		and said
1390		Who is

49

MATTHEW   CHAPTER 8

0598	ܗܢܐ	this		3257	ܝܫܘܥ	Jesus
2323	ܕܪܘܚܐ	whom the winds		0323	ܒܪܗ	Son
1057	ܘܝܡܐ	and the sea		0093	ܐܠܗܐ	of God
2547	ܡܫܬܡܥܝܢ	obey		0208	ܐܬܝܬ	Have you come
1261	ܠܗ	<him>		1111	ܠܟܐ	here

VERSE 28 And when Jesus had come to the opposite shore to the place of the Gadarenes, two [men] possessed of devils met him, who were coming out from the tombs, very evil, so that no one was able to pass by that road.

				2154	ܩܕܡ	before
				0633	ܙܒܢܐ	the time
				2565	ܕܬܫܢܩܢ	to torment us

VERSE 30 Now there was a herd of many pigs a distance from them that was feeding.

1128	ܘܟܕ	And when		0069	ܐܝܬ	there was
0208	ܐܬܐ	had come		0603	ܗܘܐ	*
3257	ܝܫܘܥ	Jesus		0518	ܕܝܢ	Now
1735	ܠܥܒܪܐ	to the opposite shore		1280	ܪܚܝܩ	a distance
0214	ܠܐܬܪܐ	to the place		1388	ܡܢܗܘܢ	from them
3147	ܕܓܕܪܝܐ	of the Gadarenes		0319	ܒܩܪܐ	a herd
0197	ܐܪܥܘܗܝ	met him		0766	ܕܚܙܝܪܐ	of pigs
2709	ܬܪܝܢ	two [men]		1596	ܣܓܝܐܐ	many
0515	ܕܝܘܢܐ	possessed of devils		2381	ܕܪܥܝܐ	that was feeding
1542	ܕܢܦܩܝܢ	who were coming				
1388	ܡܢ	from				
0243	ܒܝܬ	the tombs				
2143	ܩܒܘܪܐ	*				

VERSE 31 And those demons were begging him and said, "If you cast us out, allow us to go to the herd of pigs."

0220	ܒܝܫܐ	evil		0593	ܗܢܘܢ	those
0938	ܕܛܒ	very		0518	ܕܝܢ	And
0060	ܐܝܟ	so that		2469	ܫܐܕܐ	demons
1262	ܕܠܐ	no		0296	ܒܥܝܢ	begging
0131	ܐܢܫ	one		0603	ܗܘܘ	were
2510	ܢܫܟܚ	was able		1388	ܡܢܗ	<from> him
1733	ܠܡܥܒܪ	to pass		0116	ܘܐܡܪܝܢ	and said
0593	ܗܘܐ	by that		0121	ܐܢ	If
0038	ܒܐܘܪܚܐ	road		1542	ܡܦܩ	cast out
				0133	ܐܢܬ	you
				1261	ܠܢ	us
				1989	ܐܦܣ	allow
				1261	ܠܢ	us
				0042	ܕܢܐܙܠ	to go
				0319	ܠܒܩܪܐ	to the herd
				0766	ܕܚܙܝܪܐ	of pigs

VERSE 29 And they cried out and said, "What have we to do with you, Jesus, Son of God? Have you come here before the time to torment us?"

2227	ܘܩܥܘ	And they cried out
0116	ܘܐܡܪܝܢ	and said
1313	ܡܐ	What have we to do with you
1261	ܠܢ	*
1261	ܘܠܟ	*

MATTHEW CHAPTER 8

VERSE 32 — Jesus said to them, "Go!" And immediately they went out and attacked the pigs and that whole herd went straight over a steep rock and they fell into the sea and died in the water.

Number	Aramaic	English
0116		said
1261		to them
3257		Jesus
0042		Go
0725		And immediately
1542		they went out
1796		and attacked
0766		the pigs
1168		and whole
0319		herd
0593		that
2720		went straight
1803		over
2586		a steep rock
1538		and they fell
1057		into the sea
1334		and died
1351		in the water

VERSE 33 — Now those who were tending [the herd] fled and went to the city and made known everything that had occurred and about those possessed of devils.

Number	Aramaic	English
0593		those
0518		Now
2381		who tending [the herd]
0603		were
1904		fled
0042		and went
0499		to the city
0739		and made known
1173		everything
0603		that had occurred
0593		and about those
0515		possessed of devils

VERSE 34 — And the whole city went out for a meeting with Jesus. And when they saw him, they begged him to leave their borders.

Number	Aramaic	English
1542		And went out
1168		whole
0499		the city
0198		for a meeting
3257		with Jesus
1128		And when
0758		they saw him
0296		they begged
1388		<from> him
2561		to leave
1388		<from>
2659		their borders

CHAPTER 9

VERSE 1 — And he boarded the ship and crossed [and] came to his city.

Number	Aramaic	English
1658		And he boarded
0100		the ship
1733		and crossed
0208		[and] came
0499		to his city

VERSE 2 — And they brought to him a paralytic lying on a pallet. And Jesus saw their faith and said to the paralytic, "Take courage, my son, your sins are forgiven."

Number	Aramaic	English
2244		And they brought
1261		to him
2598		a paralytic
1128		lying
2372		*
1897		on a pallet
0758		And saw
3257		Jesus
0113		their faith
0116		and said
0593		to <that>
2598		the paralytic
1267		Take courage

MATTHEW CHAPTER 9

0323		my son
2440		are forgiven
1261		<you>
0771		your sins

VERSE 3 But some of the scribes said among themselves, "This one blasphemes."

0131		some
0518		But
1388		of
1699		the scribes
0116		said
1547		among themselves
0598		This one
0370		blasphemes

VERSE 4 But Jesus knew their thoughts and said to them, "Why do you think evil in your heart[s]?

3257		Jesus
0518		But
1023		knew
0917		their thoughts
0116		and said
1261		to them
1393		Why
0914		do think
0133		you
0220		evil
1268		in your heart[s]

VERSE 5 For what is easier to say, 'Your sins are forgiven,' or to say, 'Get up [and] walk?'

1393		what
0403		For
2061		is easier
0116		to say
2440		are forgiven
1261		<you>
0771		Your sins
0024		or
0116		to say
2168		Get up
0608		[and] walk

VERSE 6 But that you will know that the Son of Man has authority to forgive sins on earth," he said to that paralytic, "Get up, take up your pallet and go to your house."

1023		that you will know
0518		But
2527		that authority
0069		has
0323		the Son
0131		of Man
0199		on earth
2440		to forgive
0771		sins
0116		he said
0593		to that
2598		paralytic
2168		Get up
2587		take up
1897		your pallet
0042		and go
0243		to your house

VERSE 7 And he got up [and] went to his house.

2168		And he got up
0042		[and] went
0243		to his house

VERSE 8 Now when the crowds saw [this], they were frightened and glorified God, who gave authority such as this to men.

1128		when
0758		saw [this]
0518		Now
1201		the crowds
0593		<those>
0509		they were frightened
2428		and glorified
0093		God
1030		who gave
2527		authority
0060		such as

MATTHEW CHAPTER 9

0598		this		1304		his disciples
0325		to men		**VERSE 11**		And when the Pharisees saw, they said to his disciples, "Why does your master eat with tax collectors and sinners?"
VERSE 9		And when Jesus passed over from there, he saw a man who was sitting [at] the customs-house, whose name [was] Matthew. And he said to him, "Follow me." And he rose up [and] went after him.		1128		And when
				0758		saw
				3439		the Pharisees
				0116		they said
1128		And when		1304		to his disciples
1733		passed over		1394		Why
3257		Jesus		1817		with
1388		from		1358		tax collectors
2682		there		0772		and sinners
0758		he saw		1308		does eat
0361		a man		2271		your master
1093		who was sitting		**VERSE 12**		But Jesus when he heard said to them, "The healthy have no need for a doctor, but those who are very diseased.
0243		[at] the customs-house				
1358		*		3257		Jesus
2539		whose name [was]		0518		But
3329		Matthew		1128		when
0116		And he said		2547		he heard
1261		to him		0116		said
0208		Follow me		1261		to them
0215		*		1262		no
2168		And he rose up		1679		have need
0042		[and] went after him		0808		The healthy
0215		*		1804		for
VERSE 10		And as they were sitting to eat in the house, many tax collectors and sinners came and sat to eat with Jesus and with his disciples.		0137		a doctor
				0090		but
				0066		those
1128		And as		0221		who are very diseased
1664		they were sitting to eat		1724		*
0243		in the house		**VERSE 13**		Go, learn what this is: I REQUIRE COMPASSION AND NOT SACRIFICE, for I did not come to call the just [ones], but sinners."
0208		came				
1358		tax collectors				
0772		and sinners		0042		Go
1596		many		1053		learn
1664		[and] sat to eat		1395		what this is
1817		with		0841		COMPASSION
3257		Jesus				
1817		and with				

MATTHEW CHAPTER 9

0296		REQUIRE
0124		I
1262		AND NOT
0474		SACRIFICE
1262		not
0403		for
0208		I did come
2239		to call
0637		the just [ones]
0090		but
0772		sinners

VERSE 14 Then the disciples of John approached him and said, "Why do we and the Pharisees fast much and your disciples do not fast?"

0594		Then
2244		approached
1261		him
1304		the disciples
3233		of John
0116		and said
1394		Why
0124		<we>
3439		and the Pharisees
2093		do fast
0124		we
1596		much
1304		and your disciples
1262		not
2093		do fast

VERSE 15 Jesus said to them, "Are the guests of the wedding feast able to fast as long as the bridegroom [is] with them? But the days are coming when the bridegroom will be taken from them and then they will fast.

0116		said
1261		to them
3257		Jesus
1314		<?>
2510		Are able
0323		the guests of the wedding feast
0431		*
2093		to fast
1188		as long as
0933		the bridegroom
1817		[is] with them
0208		are coming
0518		But
1036		the days
1128		when
2587		will be taken
1388		from them
0933		the bridegroom
0594		and then
2093		they will fast

VERSE 16 No one places a new patch on a worn-out garment, lest the patch should tear away from the garment and the hole become greater.

1262		No
0131		one
2372		places
2405		a patch
0735		new
1804		on
1501		a garment
0275		worn-out
1262		lest
1576		should tear away
1371		the patch
1388		from
0593		<that>
1501		the garment
0603		and become
0250		the hole
1100		greater

MATTHEW CHAPTER 9

Vertical Interlinear

VERSE 17 — And they do not place new wine in worn-out wineskins, lest the wineskins should rip and the wine would be poured out and the wineskins be ruined. But they place new wine in new wineskins and both of them are preserved."

Code	Syriac	English
1262		And not
2372		they do place
0831		wine
0735		new
0687		in wineskins
0275		worn-out
1262		lest
2129		should rip
0687		the wineskins
0831		and the wine
0201		would be poured out
0687		and the wineskins
0005		be ruined
0090		But
2372		they place
0831		wine
0735		new
0687		in wineskins
0735		new
2709		and both of them
1502		are preserved

VERSE 18 — Now while he was speaking these [things] to them, a certain ruler came near [and] worshipped him and said, "My daughter is now dead. But come, place your hand on her and she will live."

Code	Syriac	English
1128		while
0518		Now
0598		these [things]
1362		speaking
0603		he was
1817		to them
0208		came
0194		a ruler
0721		certain
2244		near
1599		[and] worshipped
1261		him
0116		and said
0327		My daughter
0602		now
1334		is dead
0090		But
0208		come
1625		place
0057		your hand
1804		on her
0780		and she will live

VERSE 19 — And Jesus got up and his disciples followed him.

Code	Syriac	English
2168		And got up
3257		Jesus
1304		and his disciples
0042		and followed him
0215		*

VERSE 20 — And behold, a woman, whose blood had flowed [for] twelve years, came from behind him and touched the edge of his clothes,

Code	Syriac	English
0580		And behold
0135		a woman
2299		flowed
0603		had
0539		whose blood
2559		[for] years
2710		twelve
0208		came
1388		from
0295		behind him
2244		and touched
2255		the edge
1273		of his clothes

VERSE 21 — for she was saying within herself, 'If I only touch his clothing, I will be healed.'

Code	Syriac	English
0116		saying
0603		she was
0403		for

MATTHEW CHAPTER 9

Vertical Interlinear

1547		within herself
0172		If
1041		only
1320		his clothing
2244		I touch
0124		*
0136		I will be healed
0124		*

VERSE 22 Now Jesus turned [and] saw her and said to her, "Be comforted, my daughter, your faith has given you life." And that woman was healed immediately.

3257		Jesus
0518		Now
1984		turned
0758		[and] saw her
0116		and said
1261		to her
1267		Be comforted
0327		my daughter
0113		your faith
0780		has given you life
0136		And was healed
0135		woman
0593		that
1388		immediately
0593		*
2573		*

VERSE 23 And Jesus came to the house of the ruler and saw the musicians and the crowds, who were troubled.

0208		And came
3257		Jesus
0243		to the house
0194		of the ruler
0758		and saw
0675		the musicians
1201		and the crowds
2452		who were troubled

VERSE 24 And he said to them, "Go away, for the girl is not dead, but is asleep." And they were laughing at him.

0116		And he said
1261		to them
2042		Go away
1261		<you>
0978		the girl
0403		for
1262		not
1334		is dead
0090		but
0544		is asleep
0592		*
0400		And laughing
0603		they were
1804		at him

VERSE 25 And when he dismissed the crowds, he entered in, took her by the hand and the girl got up.

1128		And when
1542		he dismissed
1201		the crowds
1796		he entered in
0047		took her
0057		by the hand
2168		and got up
0978		the girl

VERSE 26 And this news went out into all this land.

1542		And went out
0944		news
0598		this
1168		into all
0199		land
0593		that

VERSE 27 And when Jesus passed over from there, two blind men followed him, who were crying out and saying, "Have compassion on us, Son of David."

1128		And when
1733		passed over

Vertical Interlinear

MATTHEW   **CHAPTER 9**

3257		Jesus
1388		from
2682		there
0476		followed him
1662		blind men
2709		two
2227		who were crying out
0116		and saying
2342		Have compassion
1804		on us
0323		Son
3159		of David

VERSE 28 — And when he came to the house, those blind men approached him. Jesus said to them, "Do you believe that I am able to do this?" They said to him, "Yes, our Lord."

1128		And when
0208		he came
0243		to the house
2244		approached
1261		him
0593		those
1662		blind men
0116		said
1261		to them
3257		Jesus
0109		Do believe
0133		you
2510		that able
0124		I am
0598		this
1724		to do
0116		They said
1261		to him
0065		Yes
1426		our Lord

VERSE 29 — Then he touched their eyes and said, "As you have believed will it be to you."

0594		Then
2244		he touched
1794		their eyes
0116		and said
0061		As
0109		you have believed
0603		it will be
1261		to you

VERSE 30 — And immediately their eyes were opened and Jesus rebuked them and said, "See [that] no man should know [about this]."

0725		And immediately
2070		were opened
1794		their eyes
1113		and rebuked
0217		them
3257		Jesus
0116		and said
0758		See [that]
1262		no
0131		man
1023		should know [about this]

VERSE 31 — But they went out [and] spread his fame in all that land.

0592		<they>
0518		But
1542		they went out
0943		[and] spread his fame
1168		in all
0199		land
0593		that

VERSE 32 — And when Jesus went out, they brought to him a mute in whom was a devil.

1128		And when
1542		went out
3257		Jesus
2244		they brought
1261		to him
0907		a mute
0069		in whom was
1804		*
0514		a devil

MATTHEW CHAPTER 9

Vertical Interlinear

VERSE 33 — And after the devil went out, that mute spoke and the crowds were amazed and said, "Never was it seen so in Israel."

1388	ܘܡܢ	And after
1542	ܐܦܩ	went out
0514	ܫܐܕܐ	the devil
1362	ܡܠܠ	spoke
0593	ܗܘ	that
0907	ܚܪܫܐ	mute
0549	ܘܐܬܕܡܪܘ	and were amazed
1201	ܟܢܫܐ	the crowds
0116	ܘܐܡܪܝܢ	and said
1262	ܠܐ	Never
1450	ܡܬܘܡ	*
0758	ܐܬܚܙܝ	was it seen
0597	ܗܟܢܐ	so
3035	ܒܐܝܣܪܐܝܠ	in Israel

VERSE 34 — But the Pharisees were saying, "By the chief of devils, he casts out devils."

3439	ܦܪܝܫܐ	the Pharisees
0518	ܕܝܢ	But
0116	ܐܡܪܝܢ	saying
0603	ܗܘܘ	were
2362	ܒܪܫܐ	By the chief
0514	ܕܫܐܕܐ	of devils
1542	ܡܦܩ	he casts out
0514	ܫܐܕܐ	devils

VERSE 35 — And Jesus journeyed into all the cities and into the villages and was teaching in their synagogues and preaching the gospel of the kingdom and healing all their diseases and all their pains.

1236	ܘܡܬܟܪܟ	And journeyed
0603	ܗܘܐ	*
3257	ܝܫܘܥ	Jesus
0499	ܒܡܕܝܢܬܐ	into the cities
1168	ܟܠܗܝܢ	all <of them>
2251	ܘܒܩܘܪܝܐ	and into the villages
1053	ܘܡܠܦ	and teaching
0603	ܗܘܐ	was
1200	ܒܟܢܘܫܬܗܘܢ	in their synagogues
1230	ܘܡܟܪܙ	and preaching
1593	ܣܒܪܬܐ	the gospel
1385	ܕܡܠܟܘܬܐ	of the kingdom
0136	ܘܡܐܣܐ	and healing
1168	ܟܠ	all
1227	ܟܘܪܗܢܝܢ	their diseases
1168	ܘܟܠ	and all
1116	ܟܐܒܝܢ	their pains

VERSE 36 — And when Jesus saw the crowds, he had compassion on them, because they were weary and scattered as sheep that do not have a shepherd.

1128	ܟܕ	when
0758	ܚܙܐ	saw
0518	ܕܝܢ	And
3257	ܝܫܘܥ	Jesus
1201	ܠܟܢܫܐ	the crowds
2342	ܐܬܪܚܡ	he had compassion
1804	ܥܠܝܗܘܢ	on them
1265	ܕܠܐܝܢ	because weary
0603	ܗܘܘ	they were
2597	ܘܫܪܝܢ	and scattered
0060	ܐܝܟ	as
1887	ܥܪܒܐ	sheep
1264	ܕܠܝܬ	that do not have
1261	ܠܗܘܢ	*
2383	ܪܥܝܐ	a shepherd

VERSE 37 — And he said to his disciples, "The harvest is great, and the workers, few."

0116	ܘܐܡܪ	And he said
1304	ܠܬܠܡܝܕܘܗܝ	to his disciples
0879	ܚܨܕܐ	The harvest
1596	ܣܓܝ	is great
1999	ܘܦܥܠܐ	and the workers
0686	ܙܥܘܪܝܢ	few

VERSE 38 — Entreat, therefore, the Lord of the harvest that he would send workers for his harvest."

0296	ܒܥܘ	Entreat
0596	ܗܟܝܠ	therefore
1388	ܡܢ	<from>

Vertical Interlinear

MATTHEW   CHAPTER 9

1426	ܡܪܐ	the Lord		0043	ܐܚܘܗܝ	his brother
0879	ܚܨܕܐ	of the harvest		3255	ܘܝܥܩܘܒ	and James
1542	ܕܢܦܩ	that he would send		0323	ܒܪ	the son of
1999	ܦܥܠܐ	workers		3185	ܘܙܒܕܝ	Zebedee
0879	ܠܚܨܕܗ	for his harvest		3233	ܘܝܘܚܢܢ	and John

CHAPTER 10

				0043	ܐܚܘܗܝ	his brother

VERSE 1 — And he called his twelve disciples and gave them authority over unclean spirits to cast [them] out and to heal every pain and disease.

VERSE 3 — and Philip and Bartholomew and Thomas and Matthew, the tax collector, and James, the son of Alphaeus, and Lebbaeus, who was called Thaddaeus,

2239	ܘܩܪܐ	And he called		3420	ܘܦܝܠܝܦܘܣ	and Philip
2710	ܠܬܪܥܣܪ	twelve		3133	ܘܒܪܬܘܠܡܝ	and Bartholomew
1304	ܬܠܡܝܕܘܗܝ	his disciples		3528	ܘܬܐܘܡܐ	and Thomas
1030	ܘܝܗܒ	and gave		3329	ܘܡܬܝ	and Matthew
1261	ܠܗܘܢ	them		1358	ܡܟܣܐ	the tax collector
2527	ܫܘܠܛܢܐ	authority		3255	ܘܝܥܩܘܒ	and James
1804	ܥܠ	over		0323	ܒܪ	the son of
2323	ܪܘܚܐ	spirits		3196	ܚܠܦܝ	Alphaeus
0991	ܛܢܦܬܐ	unclean		3272	ܘܠܒܝ	and Lebbaeus
1542	ܕܢܦܩܘܢ	to cast [them] out		1196	ܕܐܬܟܢܝ	who was called
0136	ܘܠܡܐܣܝܘ	and to heal		3530	ܬܕܝ	Thaddaeus
1168	ܟܠ	every				
1116	ܟܐܒ	pain				
1227	ܘܟܘܪܗܢ	and disease				

VERSE 4 — and Simon, the Canaanite, and Judas Iscariot, who betrayed him.

3521	ܘܫܡܥܘܢ	and Simon
3482	ܩܢܢܝܐ	the Canaanite
3228	ܘܝܗܘܕܐ	and Judas
3370	ܣܟܪܝܘܛܐ	Iscariot
0593	ܗܘ	<he>
2530	ܕܐܫܠܡܗ	who betrayed him

VERSE 2 — Now the names of the twelve apostles are these: first, Simon, who was called Peter, and Andrew, his brother, and James, the son of Zebedee, and John, his brother,

VERSE 5 — Jesus sent these twelve and commanded them and said, "Do not go on the road of the heathens and do not enter the city of the Samaritans.

0517	ܕܗܠܝܢ	<their>				
0518	ܕܝܢ	Now				
2710	ܕܬܪܥܣܪ	of the twelve				
2522	ܫܠܝܚܐ	apostles				
2539	ܫܡܗܐ	the names		0598	ܗܠܝܢ	these
0069	ܐܝܬܝܗܘܢ	are		2710	ܬܪܥܣܪ	twelve
0598	ܗܠܝܢ	these		2458	ܫܕܪ	sent
2157	ܩܕܡܝܗܘܢ	first		3257	ܝܫܘܥ	Jesus
3521	ܫܡܥܘܢ	Simon		2007	ܘܦܩܕ	and commanded
2239	ܕܡܬܩܪܐ	who was called		0592	ܐܢܘܢ	them
3258	ܟܐܦܐ	Peter		0116	ܘܐܡܪ	and said
3061	ܘܐܢܕܪܐܘܣ	and Andrew		0038	ܒܐܘܪܚܐ	on the road

MATTHEW CHAPTER 10

0847	ܕܚܢܦܐ	of the heathens		1322	ܡܓܢ	freely
1262	ܠܐ	not		1030	ܗܒܘ	give
0042	ܬܐܙܠܘܢ	Do go		**VERSE**	**9**	Do not have gold or silver or brass in your purses
0499	ܘܠܡܕܝܢܬܐ	and the city				
3524	ܕܫܡܪܝܐ	of the Samaritans		1262	ܠܐ	not
1262	ܠܐ	not		2216	ܬܩܢܘܢ	Do have
1796	ܬܥܠܘܢ	do enter		0489	ܕܗܒܐ	gold
VERSE	**6**	But go rather to the sheep that are lost from the house of Israel.		1262	ܘܠܐ	or
				1580	ܣܐܡܐ	silver
0042	ܙܠܘ	go		1262	ܘܠܐ	or
1261	ܠܟܘܢ	<you>		1498	ܢܚܫܐ	brass
0518	ܕܝܢ	But		1165	ܒܟܝܣܝܟܘܢ	in your purses
1101	ܐܝܬܝܪܐܝܬ	rather		**VERSE**	**10**	or a wallet for the journey or two coats or shoes or staff, for a worker is worthy of his food.
1288	ܠܘܬ	to				
1887	ܥܪܒܐ	the sheep		1262	ܘܠܐ	or
0005	ܕܐܒܕܘ	that are lost		2712	ܬܪܡܠܐ	a wallet
1388	ܡܢ	from		0038	ܠܐܘܪܚܐ	for the journey
0243	ܒܝܬ	the house of		1262	ܘܠܐ	or
3035	ܐܝܣܪܝܠ	Israel		2709	ܬܪܬܝܢ	two
VERSE	**7**	And as you are going, preach and say, 'The kingdom of heaven is near.'		1256	ܟܘܬܝܢܝܢ	coats
				1262	ܘܠܐ	or
1128	ܘܟܕ	And as		1582	ܡܣܢܐ	shoes
0042	ܐܙܠܝܢ	going		1262	ܘܠܐ	or
0133	ܐܢܬܘܢ	you are		2433	ܫܒܛܐ	staff
1230	ܐܟܪܙܘ	preach		2461	ܫܘܐ	is worthy of
0116	ܘܐܡܪܘ	and say		0592	ܗܘ	<he>
2244	ܕܩܪܒܬ	is near		0403	ܓܝܪ	for
1385	ܡܠܟܘܬܐ	The kingdom		1999	ܦܥܠܐ	a worker
2543	ܕܫܡܝܐ	of heaven		1594	ܣܝܒܪܬܗ	his food
VERSE	**8**	Heal the sick and cleanse the lepers and cast out devils. Freely you have received, freely give.		**VERSE**	**11**	And into whatever city or village you enter, ask who in it is worthy and there stay until you leave.
1228	ܟܪܝܗܐ	the sick		0066	ܠܐܝܕܐ	into whatever
0136	ܐܣܘ	Heal		0518	ܕܝܢ	And
0456	ܘܓܪܒܐ	and the lepers		0499	ܡܕܝܢܬܐ	city
0521	ܕܟܘ	cleanse		0024	ܐܘ	or
0514	ܘܕܝܘܐ	and devils		2251	ܩܪܝܬܐ	village
1542	ܐܦܩܘ	cast out		1796	ܬܥܠܘܢ	enter
1322	ܡܓܢ	Freely		0133	ܐܢܬܘܢ	you
1532	ܢܣܒܬܘܢ	you have received		1261	ܠܗ	<it>

MATTHEW — CHAPTER 10

Vertical Interlinear

Code	Aramaic	English
2420		ask
1390		who
2461		is worthy
0217		in it
2682		and there
0603		stay
1747		until
1542		leave
0133		you

VERSE 12 — And when you enter a house, greet the household

Code	Aramaic	English
1313		And when
1796		enter
0133		you
0243		a house
2420		greet
2535		*
0243		the household

VERSE 13 — and if the house is worthy, your peace will come on it. But if it is not worthy, your peace will return on you.

Code	Aramaic	English
0121		And if
0592		<it>
2461		is worthy
0243		the house
2535		your peace
0208		will come
1804		on it
0121		if
0518		But
1262		not
2461		it is worthy
2535		your peace
1804		on you
1984		will return

VERSE 14 — And whoever does not receive you and does not hear your words, when you leave the house or that village, shake off the dust from your feet.

Code	Aramaic	English
1389		whoever
1262		not
0518		And
2134		does receive
1261		you
1262		and not
2547		does hear
1364		your words
1128		when
1542		leave
0133		you
1388		<from>
0243		the house
0024		or
1388		<from>
2251		village
0593		that
1541		shake off
0795		the dust
1388		from
2293		your feet

VERSE 15 — And truly I say to you, it will be [more] pleasant for the land of Sodom and Gomorrah in the day of judgment than for that city.

Code	Aramaic	English
0110		And truly
0116		say
0124		I
1261		to you
0199		for the land
3362		of Sodom
3398		and Gomorrah
0603		it will be
1483		[more] pleasant
1036		in the day
0497		of judgment
0024		than
0499		for city
0593		that

VERSE 16 — Behold, I send you as a lamb into the middle of wolves. Be therefore wise as snakes and harmless as doves.

Code	Aramaic	English
0580		Behold

MATTHEW CHAPTER 10

0124	ܐܢܐ	<I>
2458	ܡܫܕܪ	send
0124	ܐܢܐ	I
1261	ܠܟܘܢ	you
0060	ܐܝܟ	as
0117	ܐܡܪܐ	a lamb
0266	ܒܝܢܬ	in the middle of
0469	ܕܐܒܐ	wolves
0603	ܗܘܘ	Be
0596	ܗܟܝܠ	therefore
0790	ܚܟܝܡܐ	wise
0060	ܐܝܟ	as
0740	ܚܘܘܬܐ	snakes
2678	ܘܬܡܝܡܝܢ	and harmless
0060	ܐܝܟ	as
1038	ܝܘܢܐ	doves

VERSE 17 And beware of men, for they will deliver you to the courts and they will beat you in their synagogues.

0645	ܐܙܕܗܪܘ	beware
0518	ܕܝܢ	And
1388	ܡܢ	of
0325	ܒܢܝܢܫܐ	men
2530	ܡܫܠܡܝܢ	they will deliver
1261	ܠܟܘܢ	you
0403	ܓܝܪ	for
0243	ܠܒܝܬ	to the courts
0498	ܕܝܢܐ	*
1200	ܘܒܟܢܘܫܬܗܘܢ	and in their synagogues
1461	ܢܢܓܕܘܢܟܘܢ	they will beat you

VERSE 18 And they will bring you before governors and kings for my sake, for a witness to them and to the Gentiles.

2154	ܘܩܕܡ	And before
0586	ܗܓܡܘܢܐ	governors
1383	ܘܡܠܟܐ	and kings
2244	ܡܩܪܒܝܢ	they will bring
1261	ܠܟܘܢ	you
1347	ܡܛܠܬܝ	for my sake
1610	ܠܣܗܕܘܬܐ	for a witness
0517	ܕܠܗܘܢ	to them
1818	ܘܠܥܡܡܐ	and to the Gentiles

VERSE 19 Now when they deliver you up, do not be concerned how or what you should speak, for it will be given to you immediately what you should speak.

0120	ܐܡܬܝ	when
0518	ܕܝܢ	Now
2530	ܕܡܫܠܡܝܢܠܟܘܢ	they deliver you up
1262	ܠܐ	not
1069	ܬܐܨܦܘܢ	do be concerned
0061	ܐܝܟܢܐ	how
0024	ܐܘ	or
1393	ܡܢܐ	what
1362	ܬܡܠܠܘܢ	you should speak
1030	ܡܬܝܗܒ	it will be given
1261	ܠܟܘܢ	to you
0403	ܓܝܪ	for
0593	ܒܗܝ	immediately
2573	ܫܥܬܐ	*
1313	ܡܐ	what
1362	ܕܬܡܠܠܘܢ	you should speak

VERSE 20 For it will not be you speaking, but the Spirit of your Father speaking in you.

1262	ܠܐ	not
0603	ܗܘܐ	it will be
0403	ܓܝܪ	For
0133	ܐܢܬܘܢ	you
1362	ܡܡܠܠܝܢ	speaking
0090	ܐܠܐ	but
2323	ܪܘܚܐ	the Spirit
0002	ܕܐܒܘܟܘܢ	of your Father
1362	ܡܡܠܠܐ	speaking
0217	ܒܟܘܢ	in you

VERSE 21 But brother will deliver his brother to death and father his son. And children will rise up against their parents and they will kill them.

2530	ܢܫܠܡ	will deliver
0518	ܕܝܢ	But
0043	ܐܚܐ	brother

MATTHEW CHAPTER 10

Vertical Interlinear

#	Syriac	English
0043		his brother
1335		to death
0002		and father
0323		his son
2168		And will rise up
0323		children
1804		against
0002		their parents
1334		and they will kill
0592		them

VERSE 22 — And you will be hated by all men, because of my name. But he who endures until the end will live.

#	Syriac	English
0603		And you will be
1675		hated
1388		by
1175		all men
1347		because of
2539		my name
0066		he
0518		But
1588		who endures
1747		until
0054		the end
0592		<he>
0780		will live

VERSE 23 — Now when they persecute you in this city, flee to another, for truly I say to you, you will not complete all the cities of the house of Israel before the Son of Man will come.

#	Syriac	English
1313		when
2304		they persecute
1261		you
0518		Now
0499		in city
0598		this
1904		flee
1261		<you>
0053		to another
0110		truly
0403		for
0116		say
0124		I
1261		to you
1262		not
2530		you will complete
0592		<them>
1168		all
0499		the cities
0243		of the house
3035		of Israel
1747		before
0208		will come
0323		the Son
0131		of Man

VERSE 24 — There is no disciple who is greater than his master, nor a servant [who is greater] than his lord.

#	Syriac	English
1264		There is no
1304		disciple
1100		who is greater
1388		than
2271		his master
1262		nor
1727		a servant [who is greater]
1388		than
1426		his lord

VERSE 25 — It is sufficient for a disciple to be as his master and for a servant [to be] as his lord. If they call the lord of the house Beelzebub, how much more the sons of his house?

#	Syriac	English
1694		It is sufficient
1261		*
1304		for a disciple
0603		to be
0060		as
2271		his master
1727		and for a servant [to be]
0060		as
1426		his lord

MATTHEW CHAPTER 10

0121		If
1426		the lord
0243		of the house
2239		they call
3127		Beelzebub
0721		how much more
1188		*
0323		the sons
0243		of his house

VERSE 26 Therefore do not be afraid of them, for there is not anything that is covered that will not be revealed, or that is hidden that will not be made known.

1262		not
0596		Therefore
0509		do be afraid
1388		of them
1264		there is not
0403		for
1326		anything
1206		that is covered
1262		that not
0409		will be revealed
1009		or that is hidden
1262		that not
1023		will be made known

VERSE 27 What I say to you in darkness, you speak in the light. And what you hear in your ears, preach on the roofs.

1326		What
0116		say
0124		I
1261		to you
0923		in darkness
0116		speak <it>
0133		you
1475		in the light
1326		And what
0021		in your ears
2547		hear
0133		you

1230		preach
1804		on
0019		the roofs

VERSE 28 And do not be afraid of those who kill the body, but are not able to kill the soul. But be afraid rather of him who is able to destroy the soul and body in Gehenna.

1262		And not
0509		do be afraid
1388		of
0066		those
2179		who kill
1929		the body
1547		the soul
0518		but
1262		not
2510		are able
2179		to kill
0509		be afraid
0518		But
1101		rather
1388		of
1389		him
2510		who is able
1547		the soul
1929		and body
0005		to destroy
3148		in Gehenna

VERSE 29 Are not two sparrows sold for a copper coin? And one of them does not fall on the earth without your Father.

1262		not
2709		two
2125		sparrows
0632		Are sold
0166		for a copper coin
0721		And one
1388		of them
0279		without
1388		*
0002		your Father

Vertical Interlinear

MATTHEW   CHAPTER 10

1262		not
1538		does fall
1804		on
0199		the earth

VERSE 30 — Now yours, even all the hairs of your head are numbered.

0517		yours
0518		Now
0169		even
1403		the hairs
2362		of your head
1168		all
1396		are numbered
0592		*

VERSE 31 — Therefore do not be afraid. You are more important than many sparrows.

1262		not
0596		Therefore
0509		do be afraid
1388		than
2125		sparrows
1596		many
1104		more important
0133		you are

VERSE 32 — Everyone therefore who confesses me before men, I will confess him also before my Father who is in heaven.

1175		Everyone
0596		therefore
1020		who confesses
0217		me
2154		before
0325		men
1020		will confess
0217		him
0169		also
0124		I
2154		before
0002		my Father
2543		who is in heaven

VERSE 33 — But he who denies me before men, I will deny him also before my Father who is in heaven.

1389		he
0518		but
1215		who denies
0217		me
2154		before
0325		men
1215		will deny
0217		him
0169		also
0124		I
2154		before
0002		my Father
2543		who is in heaven

VERSE 34 — Do not think that I have come to bring harmony on earth. I have not come to bring harmony, but a sword.

1262		not
1588		Do think
0208		that I have come
2372		to bring
2505		harmony
0199		on earth
1262		not
0208		I have not come
2372		to bring
2505		harmony
0090		but
0893		a sword

VERSE 35 — For I have come to separate a man from his father and a daughter from her mother and a daughter-in-law from her mother-in-law.

0208		I have come
0403		For
1968		to separate
0361		a man
1804		from
0002		his father

Vertical Interlinear

MATTHEW CHAPTER 10

#	Aramaic	English
0327		and a daughter
1804		from
0106		her mother
1179		and a daughter-in-law
1804		from
0823		her mother-in-law

VERSE 36 — And the enemies of a man [will be] his household.

#	Aramaic	English
0307		And the enemies
0361		of a man
0323		[will be] his household
0243		*

VERSE 37 — He who loves father or mother more than me is not worthy of me and he who loves son or daughter more than me is not worthy of me.

#	Aramaic	English
1389		He
2342		who loves
0002		father
0024		or
0106		mother
1100		more
1388		than
1261		me
1262		not
2461		is worthy
1261		of me
1389		and he
2342		who loves
0323		son
0024		or
0327		daughter
1100		more
1388		than
1261		me
1262		not
2461		is worthy
1261		of me

VERSE 38 — And everyone who does not take up his cross and follow me is not worthy of me.

#	Aramaic	English
1168		And everyone
1262		who not
2587		does take up
0689		his cross
0208		and follow me
0215		*
1262		not
2461		is worthy
1261		of me

VERSE 39 — He who finds his life will lose it, and he who will lose his life because of me will find it.

#	Aramaic	English
1389		He
2510		who finds
1547		his life
0005		will lose it
1389		and he
0005		who will lose
1547		his life
1347		because of me
2510		will find it

VERSE 40 — He who receives you receives me, and he who receives me receives him who sent me.

#	Aramaic	English
1389		He
2134		who receives
1261		you
1261		me
2134		receives
1389		and he
1261		who me
2134		receives
1389		him
2521		who sent me
2134		receives

VERSE 41 — He who receives a prophet in the name of a prophet will receive the reward of a prophet, and he who receives a just [man] in the name of a just [man] will receive the reward of a just [man].

#	Aramaic	English
1389		He
2134		who receives
1457		a prophet

MATTHEW   CHAPTER 10

2539		in the name of		1128		that when
1457		a prophet		2530		completed
0018		the reward		3257		Jesus
1457		of a prophet		2007		directing
1532		will receive		2710		his twelve
1389		and he		1304		disciples
2134		who receives		2561		he went away
0637		a just [man]		1388		from
2539		in the name of		2682		there
0637		a just [man]		1053		to teach
0018		the reward		1230		and to preach
0637		of a just [man]		0499		in their cities
1532		will receive				

VERSE 2   Now when John, [being in] prison, heard of the deeds of the Messiah, he sent [word] by way of his disciples

VERSE 42   And everyone who gives one of these little ones only a cup of cold [water] to drink in the name of a disciple, "Truly I say to you, he will not lose his reward."

				3233		John
1168		And everyone		0518		Now
2585		who gives to drink		1128		when
0721		one		2547		heard of
1388		of		0243		[being in] prison
0598		these		0163		*
0686		little ones		1728		the deeds
1205		a cup		1446		of the Messiah
2238		of cold [water]		2458		he sent [word]
1041		only		0057		by way of
2539		in the name		1304		his disciples
1304		of a disciple				

VERSE 3   and said to him, "Are you he who will come or should we expect another?"

0110		Truly		0116		and said
0116		say		1261		to him
0124		I		0133		you
1261		to you		0592		Are
1262		not		0593		he
0005		he will lose		0208		who will come
0018		his reward		0024		or

CHAPTER 11

				0053		another

VERSE 1   And it happened that when Jesus completed directing the twelve disciples, he went away from there to teach and to preach in their cities.

				0592		<he>
				1646		should expect
0603		And it happened		0124		we

MATTHEW CHAPTER 11

VERSE	**4**	Jesus answered and said to them, "Go. Relate to John those [things] that you have heard and seen.
1838		answered
3257		Jesus
0116		and said
1261		to them
0042		Go
2569		Relate
3233		to John
0066		those [things]
2547		that have heard
0133		you
0758		and seen
VERSE	**5**	The blind see and the lame walk and the lepers are cleansed and the deaf hear and the dead are raised and the poor are given good news.
1662		The blind
0758		see
0719		and the lame
0608		walk
0456		and the lepers
0521		are cleansed
0907		and the deaf
2547		hear
1338		and the dead
2168		are raised
1406		and the poor
1588		are given good news
VERSE	**6**	And he who is not offended by me is blessed."
0940		And is blessed
0066		he
1262		who not
1242		is offended
0217		by me
VERSE	**7**	Now when they had gone, Jesus began to speak to the crowds about John, "What did you go out to the wilderness to see? A reed that is shaken by the wind?
1128		when

0518		Now
0042		they had gone
2597		began
3257		Jesus
0116		to speak
1201		to the crowds
1804		about
3233		John
1393		What
1542		did you go out
0892		to the wilderness
0758		to see
2224		A reed
1388		that by
2323		the wind
0657		is shaken
VERSE	**8**	And if not, what did you go out to see? A man who is clothed in soft robes? Behold, those who are clothed in soft [robes] are [in] the house of kings.
0090		And if not
1393		what
1542		did you go out
0758		to see
0361		A man
1501		who robes
2366		soft
1272		is clothed in
0580		Behold
0066		those
2366		who soft [robes]
1272		are clothed in
0243		[in] the house of
1383		kings
0592		are
VERSE	**9**	And if not, what did you go out to see? A prophet? Yes, I say to you, even [one] greater than the prophets.
0090		And if not
1393		what
1542		did you go out

MATTHEW CHAPTER 11

0758		to see		1388		than
1457		A prophet		3233		John
0065		Yes		1820		the baptizer
0116		say		0686		the least
0124		I		0518		but
1261		to you		1385		in the kingdom of
1100		even [one] greater		2543		heaven
1388		than		2271		greater
1457		the prophets		0592		is
				1388		than him

VERSE 10 For this is he about whom it was written: BEHOLD, I WILL SEND MY MESSENGER BEFORE YOUR FACE THAT HE WOULD ESTABLISH THE WAY BEFORE YOU.

VERSE 12 Now from the days of John the baptizer and until now, the kingdom of heaven was being guided with restraint and the restrainers were robbing it.

0599		this is he		1388		from
0403		For		1036		the days of
1804		about whom		3233		John
1247		it was written		0518		Now
0580		BEHOLD		1820		the baptizer
0124		<I>		1747		and until
2458		WILL SEND		0602		now
0124		I		1385		the kingdom
1375		MY MESSENGER		2543		of heaven
2154		BEFORE		2188		with restraint
2041		YOUR FACE		0477		was being guided
2699		THAT HE WOULD ESTABLISH		2189		and the restrainers
0038		THE WAY		0774		were robbing
2154		BEFORE YOU		1261		it

VERSE 11 Truly I say to you, among those born of women has not stood one who is greater than John the baptizer, but the least in the kingdom of heaven is greater than him.

VERSE 13 For all the prophets and the law have prophesied until John.

0110		Truly		1168		all
0116		I say		0403		For
1261		to you		1457		the prophets
1262		not		0040		and the law
2168		has stood		1747		until
1046		among those born of		3233		John
0135		women		1456		have prophesied
2271		one who is greater				

VERSE 14 And if you desire, accept that this is Elijah who was to come.

0121		And if
2077		desire

69

MATTHEW CHAPTER 11

0133		you
2134		accept
0592		that this is
3047		Elijah
1914		who was
0208		to come

VERSE 15 He who has ears to hear should hear.

1389		He
0069		who has
1261		*
0021		ears
2547		to hear
2547		should hear

VERSE 16 But to what should I liken this generation? It is like children who sit in the marketplace and call out to their friends

1389		to what
0518		But
0540		should I liken
2605		generation
0598		this
0540		It is like
0976		children
1093		who sit
2481		in the marketplace
2227		and call out
0714		to their friends

VERSE 17 and say, 'We sang for you and you did not dance, and we mourned for you and you did not lament.'

0116		and say
0672		We sang
1261		for you
1262		and not
2403		you did dance
0091		and we mourned
1261		for you
1262		and not
2403		you did lament

VERSE 18 For John came not eating and not drinking, and they said, 'There is a devil in him.'

0208		came
0403		For
3233		John
1262		not
0075		eating
1262		and not
2620		drinking
0116		and they said
0514		a devil
0069		There is
0217		in him

VERSE 19 The Son of Man came eating and drinking and they said, 'Behold, a gluttonous man and [one who] drinks wine and a friend of tax collectors and of sinners.' Yet wisdom is justified by its works."

0208		came
0323		The Son
0131		of Man
0075		eating
2620		and drinking
0116		and they said
0580		Behold
0361		a man
0076		gluttonous
2620		and [one who] drinks
0831		wine
2345		and a friend
1358		of tax collectors
0772		and of sinners
0636		Yet is justified
0792		wisdom
1388		by
1728		its works

VERSE 20 Then Jesus began to berate the cities, those in which his many miracles occurred and yet they did not repent.

0594		Then

Vertical Interlinear

MATTHEW   CHAPTER 11

2597	ܫܪܝ	began		**VERSE**	**22**	But I say to you, it will be [more] pleasant for Tyre and Sidon in the day of judgment than for you.
3257	ܝܫܘܥ	Jesus				
0855	ܠܡܚܣܕܘ	to berate		0342	ܕܝܢ	But
0499	ܡܕܝܢܬܐ	the cities		0116	ܐܡܪ	say
0066	ܐܝܠܝܢ	those		0124	ܐܢܐ	I
0603	ܕܗܘܘ	occurred		1261	ܠܟܘܢ	to you
0217	ܒܗܝܢ	in which		3450	ܕܠܨܘܪ	for Tyre
0786	ܚܝܠܘܗܝ	his miracles		3452	ܘܠܨܝܕܢ	and <for> Sidon
1596	ܣܓܝܐܐ	many		0603	ܢܗܘܐ	it will be
1262	ܘܠܐ	and yet not		1483	ܢܝܚ	[more] pleasant
2649	ܬܒܘ	they did repent		1036	ܒܝܘܡܐ	in the day
VERSE	**21**	And he was saying, "Woe to you, Chorazin! Woe to you, Bethsaida! Because if the miracles that were done in you had been done in Tyre and Sidon, doubtless they [would have] repented in sackclothes and in ashes.		0497	ܕܕܝܢܐ	of judgment
				0024	ܐܘ	than
				1261	ܠܟܘܢ	for you
				VERSE	**23**	And you Capernaum, who has been raised up to heaven, will be brought down to Sheol. Because if the miracles had been done in Sodom that were done in you, she would stand to [this] day.
0116	ܘܐܡܪ	And saying				
0603	ܗܘܐ	he was				
0625	ܘܝ	Woe				
1261	ܠܟܝ	to you		0133	ܘܐܢܬܝ	And you
3260	ܟܘܪܙܝܢ	Chorazin		3268	ܟܦܪܢܚܘܡ	Capernaum
0625	ܘܝ	Woe		0593	ܗܝ	who
1261	ܠܟܝ	to you		1747	ܕܥܕܡܐ	up
3118	ܒܝܬܨܝܕܐ	Bethsaida		2543	ܠܫܡܝܐ	to heaven
0097	ܕܐܠܘ	Because if		2331	ܐܬܬܪܝܡܬܝ	has been raised
3450	ܒܨܘܪ	in Tyre		1747	ܥܕܡܐ	to
3452	ܘܒܨܝܕܢ	and <in> Sidon		2422	ܠܫܝܘܠ	Sheol
0603	ܗܘܘ	had been done		2661	ܬܬܚܬܝܢ	will be brought down
0786	ܚܝܠܐ	the miracles		0097	ܕܐܠܘ	Because if
0066	ܐܝܠܝܢ	<those>		3362	ܒܣܕܘܡ	in Sodom
0603	ܕܗܘܘ	that were done		0603	ܗܘܘ	had been done
0217	ܒܟܝ	in you		0786	ܚܝܠܐ	the miracles
1124	ܟܒܪ	doubtless		0066	ܐܝܠܝܢ	<those>
0518	ܕܝܢ	<now>		0603	ܕܗܘܘ	that were done
1702	ܒܣܩܐ	in sackclothes		0217	ܒܟܝ	in you
2182	ܘܒܩܛܡܐ	and in ashes		2174	ܩܝܡܐ	stand
2649	ܬܒܘ	they [would have] repented		0603	ܗܘܬ	she would
				1747	ܥܕܡܐ	to
				1037	ܠܝܘܡܢܐ	[this] day

MATTHEW CHAPTER 11

VERSE 24 — But I say to you, it will be [more] pleasant for the land of Sodom in the day of judgment than for you."

Code	Syriac	Gloss
0342		But
0116		I say
1261		to you
0199		for the land
3362		of Sodom
0603		it will be
1483		[more] pleasant
1036		in the day
0497		of judgment
0024		than
1261		for you

VERSE 25 — At that time, Jesus answered and said, "I give thanks to you my Father, Lord of heaven and of earth, that you have hidden these [things] from the wise and intelligent and you have revealed them to babies.

Code	Syriac	Gloss
0593		At that
0633		time
1838		answered
3257		Jesus
0116		and said
1020		give thanks
0124		I
1261		to you
0002		my Father
1426		Lord
2543		of heaven
0199		and of earth
1206		that you have hidden
0598		these [things]
1388		from
0790		the wise
1650		and intelligent
0409		and you have revealed
0592		them
1048		to babies

VERSE 26 — Yes, my Father, because such was the desire before you.

Code	Syriac	Gloss
0065		Yes
0002		my Father
0597		because such
0603		was
2079		the desire
2154		before you

VERSE 27 — Everything has been delivered to me from my Father and no man knows the Son, except the Father. Also, no man knows the Father, except the Son and he whom the Son desires to reveal [him].

Code	Syriac	Gloss
1168		Everything
1326		*
2530		has been delivered
1261		to me
1388		from
0002		my Father
1262		and no
0131		man
1023		knows
0323		the Son
0090		except
0121		*
0002		the Father
0169		Also
1262		no
0002		the Father
0131		man
1023		knows
0090		except
0121		*
0323		the Son
1389		and he to whom
2077		wants
0323		the Son
0409		to reveal [him]

VERSE 28 — Come to me, all of you [who] labor and bear burdens and I will refresh you.

Code	Syriac	Gloss
0208		Come

Vertical Interlinear

MATTHEW CHAPTER 11

1288		to me		0608		walking
1168		all of you		0603		was
1265		[who] labor		3257		Jesus
2587		and bear		2445		on the Sabbath
1017		burdens		0243		[in] the sown fields
0124		and <I>		0693		*
1483		I will refresh you		1304		and his disciples

VERSE 29 Bear my yoke on you and learn from me that I am restful and I am meek in my heart, and you will find rest for your souls.

				1212		were hungry
				2597		and began
				1376		picking
2587		Bear		2436		grain
1506		my yoke		0075		and eating [it]
1804		on you				

VERSE 2 Now the Pharisees, when they saw them, said to him, "Behold, your disciples are doing what is unlawful to do on the Sabbath."

1053		and learn				
1388		from me				
1483		that restful		3439		the Pharisees
0124		I am		0518		Now
1355		and meek		1128		when
0124		I am		0758		they saw
1268		in my heart		0592		them
2510		and will find		0116		said
0133		you		1261		to him
1485		rest		0580		Behold
1547		for your souls		1304		your disciples

VERSE 30 For my yoke is pleasant and my burden is light."

				1724		are doing
				1326		what
1506		my yoke		1262		is unlawful
0403		For		2528		*
0288		pleasant		1724		to do
0592		is		2445		on the Sabbath
1017		and my burden				
2203		light				
0592		is				

VERSE 3 But he said to them, "Have you not read what David did when he was hungry and those who were with him,

CHAPTER 12

VERSE 1 At that time Jesus was walking on the Sabbath [in] the sown fields and his disciples were hungry and began picking grain and eating [it].

				0592		<he>
				0518		But
				0116		he said
0593		At that		1261		to them
0633		time		1262		not
				2239		Have you read
				1393		what

73

MATTHEW CHAPTER 12

1724		did		0793		break
3159		David		1261		<it>
1128		when		2445		the Sabbath
1212		he was hungry		1262		and without
0066		and those		1749		blame
1817		who were with him		0592		are

VERSE 4 — how he entered the house of God and ate the bread of the table of the LORD, that which was not lawful for him, nor for those who were with him to eat, but only for the priests?

0061		how
1796		he entered
0243		the house
0093		of God
1293		and the bread
2069		of the table
1426		of the LORD
0075		ate
0593		that
1262		which not
2528		lawful
0603		was
1261		for him
0075		to eat
1262		nor
0066		for those
1817		who were with him
0090		but
0121		*
1135		for the priests
1041		only

VERSE 5 — Or have you not read in the law that the priests in the temple break the Sabbath and are without blame?

0024		Or
1262		not
2239		have you read
0040		in the law
1135		that the priests
0607		in the temple

VERSE 6 — But I say to you, a greater [one] than [a priest of] the temple is here.

0116		say
0124		I
1261		to you
0518		But
2271		a greater [one]
1388		than
0607		[a priest of] the temple
0069		is
0600		here

VERSE 7 — Now if you would have known what [was meant by], I DESIRE MERCY AND NOT SACRIFICE, you would not have condemned those who are without blame,

0097		if
0518		Now
1023		known
0603		you would have
1395		what [was meant by]
0841		MERCY
2077		DESIRE
0124		I
1262		AND NOT
0474		SACRIFICE
1262		NOT
0742		condemned
0603		you would not have
0066		those
1262		who without
1749		blame
0592		are

MATTHEW CHAPTER 12

Vertical Interlinear

VERSE 8 — for the Lord of the Sabbath is the Son of Man."

1426		the Lord
0403		for
2445		of the Sabbath
0069		is
0323		the Son
0131		of Man

VERSE 9 — And Jesus went away from there and came to their synagogue.

2561		And went away
1388		from
2682		there
3257		Jesus
0208		and came
1200		to their synagogue

VERSE 10 — And a certain man was there whose hand was withered, and they were asking him and said, "Is it lawful to heal on the Sabbath?" so that they could accuse him.

0361		And a man
0721		certain
0069		was
0603		*
2682		there
1018		was withered
0057		whose hand
2420		and asking
0603		they were
1261		him
0116		and said
0121		Is it
2528		lawful
2445		on the Sabbath
0136		to heal
0060		so that
0075		they could accuse him
2257		*

VERSE 11 — Now he said to them, "What man among you who has a certain sheep, and if it falls into a pit on the Sabbath day, would not grab [it] and lift it out?

0592		<he>
0518		Now
0116		said
1261		to them
1390		What
1388		among you
0361		man
0069		who has
1261		*
1887		a sheep
0721		certain
0121		and if
1538		it falls
0715		into a pit
1036		on the day
2445		<of the> Sabbath
1262		not
0047		would grab [it]
2168		and lift out
1261		it

VERSE 12 — Now how much more important [is] a man than a sheep? So then is it lawful on the Sabbath to do that which is good?"

1188		how much
0518		Now
1100		more important [is]
0325		a man
1388		than
1887		a sheep
1324		So then
2528		lawful
0592		is it
2445		on the Sabbath
1724		to do
2583		that which is good

MATTHEW CHAPTER 12

VERSE 13 Then he said to that man, "Stretch out your hand." And he stretched out his hand and it was restored like the other.

0594	ܗܝܕܝܢ	Then
0116	ܐܡܪ	he said
0593	ܠܗܘ	to that
0361	ܓܒܪܐ	man
2054	ܦܫܘܛ	Stretch out
0057	ܐܝܕܟ	your hand
2054	ܘܦܫܛ	And he stretched out
0057	ܐܝܕܗ	his hand
2699	ܘܬܩܢܬ	and it was restored
0060	ܐܝܟ	like
0714	ܚܒܪܬܗ	the other

VERSE 14 And the Pharisees left and took counsel about him, so that they could destroy him.

1542	ܘܢܦܩܘ	And left
3439	ܦܪܝܫܐ	the Pharisees
1384	ܘܡܠܟܐ	and counsel
1532	ܢܣܒܘ	took
1804	ܥܠܘܗܝ	about him
0060	ܐܝܟ	so that
0005	ܢܘܒܕܘܢܝܗܝ	they could destroy him

VERSE 15 But Jesus knew [of it] and he went away from there. And large crowds followed him and he healed all of them.

3257	ܝܫܘܥ	Jesus
0518	ܕܝܢ	But
1023	ܝܕܥ	knew [of it]
2561	ܘܫܢܝ	and he went away
1261	ܠܗ	<him>
1388	ܡܢ	from
2682	ܬܡܢ	there
0042	ܘܐܙܠܘ	And followed him
0215	ܒܬܪܗ	*
1201	ܟܢܫܐ	crowds
1596	ܣܓܝܐܐ	large
0136	ܘܐܣܝ	and he healed
1168	ܠܟܠܗܘܢ	all of them

VERSE 16 And he charged them that they should not reveal him,

1113	ܘܟܐܐ	And he charged
0217	ܒܗܘܢ	them
1262	ܕܠܐ	that not
0409	ܢܓܠܘܢܝܗܝ	they should reveal him

VERSE 17 that it would be fulfilled what was spoken by way of Isaiah the prophet, who said:

1366	ܕܢܬܡܠܐ	that it would be fulfilled
1326	ܡܕܡ	what
0116	ܕܐܬܐܡܪ	was spoken
0057	ܒܝܕ	by way of
3109	ܐܫܥܝܐ	Isaiah
1457	ܢܒܝܐ	the prophet
0116	ܕܐܡܪ	who said

VERSE 18 BEHOLD, MY SERVANT WITH WHOM I AM WELL PLEASED, MY BELOVED, FOR WHOM MY SOUL LONGS. I WILL PLACE MY SPIRIT ON HIM AND HE WILL DECLARE JUDGMENT TO THE NATIONS.

0580	ܗܐ	BEHOLD
1727	ܥܒܕܝ	MY SERVANT
2077	ܐܨܛܒܝܬ	I AM WELL PLEASED
0217	ܒܗ	WITH WHOM
0698	ܚܒܝܒܝ	MY BELOVED
1619	ܕܣܘܚܬ	LONGS
0217	ܒܗ	FOR WHOM
1547	ܢܦܫܝ	MY SOUL
2323	ܪܘܚܝ	MY SPIRIT
1625	ܐܣܝܡ	I WILL PLACE
1804	ܥܠܘܗܝ	ON HIM
0497	ܘܕܝܢܐ	AND JUDGMENT
1818	ܠܥܡܡܐ	TO THE NATIONS
1230	ܢܟܪܙ	HE WILL DECLARE

VERSE 19 HE WILL NOT DISPUTE AND HE WILL NOT CRY OUT AND NO MAN WILL HEAR HIS VOICE IN THE MARKETPLACE.

1262	ܠܐ	NOT
0889	ܢܬܚܪܐ	HE WILL DISPUTE
1262	ܘܠܐ	AND NOT

Vertical Interlinear

MATTHEW   **CHAPTER 12**

2227		HE WILL CRY OUT
1262		AND NO
0131		MAN
2547		WILL HEAR
2204		HIS VOICE
2481		IN THE MARKETPLACE

VERSE 20 THE BROKEN REED, HE WILL NOT BREAK DOWN, AND THE LAMP THAT IS DYING OUT, HE WILL NOT EXTINGUISH, UNTIL JUDGMENT COMES TO PASS FOR VICTORY

2224		THE REED
2380		BROKEN
1262		NOT
2634		HE WILL BREAK DOWN
2607		AND THE LAMP
1002		THAT IS DYING OUT
1262		NOT
0558		HE WILL EXTINGUISH
1747		UNTIL
1542		COMES TO PASS
0497		JUDGMENT
0665		FOR VICTORY

VERSE 21 AND THE NATIONS WILL TRUST IN HIS NAME.

2539		AND IN HIS NAME
1818		THE NATIONS
1588		WILL TRUST

VERSE 22 Then they brought to him a certain [one] possessed of a devil that was mute and blind and he healed him so that the mute and blind man could talk and could see.

0594		Then
2244		they brought
1261		to him
0515		possessed of a devil
0721		a certain [one]
0906		that was mute
1776		and blind
0136		and he healed him
0061		so that
0907		mute
1662		and the blind man
1362		could talk
0758		and could see

VERSE 23 And all the crowds were marveling and said, "Is this not the Son of David?"

0549		And marveling
0603		were
1168		all <of them>
1201		the crowds
0116		and said
1314		Is not
0599		this
0323		the Son
3159		of David

VERSE 24 But the Pharisees, when they heard [this], were saying, "This [man] does not cast out demons, but by Beelzebub, the chief of devils."

3439		the Pharisees
0518		But
1128		when
2547		they heard [this]
0116		were saying
0598		This [man]
1262		not
1542		does cast out
2469		demons
0090		but
3127		by Beelzebub
2362		the chief
0514		of devils

VERSE 25 Now Jesus knew their thoughts and said to them, "Every kingdom that is divided against itself will be destroyed. And every house and city that is divided against itself will not stand.

3257		Jesus
0518		Now
1023		knew
0917		their thoughts
0116		and said

MATTHEW   CHAPTER 12

1261	ܠܗܘܢ	to them
1168	ܟܠ	Every
1385	ܡܠܟܘ	kingdom
1968	ܕܬܬܦܠܓ	that is divided
1804	ܥܠ	against
1547	ܢܦܫܗ	itself
0891	ܬܚܪܒ	will be destroyed
1168	ܘܟܠ	And every
0243	ܒܝ	house
0499	ܘܡܕܝܢܐ	and city
1968	ܕܢܬܦܠܓ	that is divided
1804	ܥܠ	against
1547	ܢܦܫܗ	itself
1262	ܠܐ	not
2168	ܢܩܘܡ	will stand

VERSE 26 And if Satan casts out Satan, he is divided against himself. How then does his kingdom stand?

0121	ܘܐܢ	And if
1642	ܣܛܢܐ	Satan
1642	ܠܣܛܢܐ	Satan
1542	ܡܦܩ	casts out
1804	ܥܠ	against
1547	ܢܦܫܗ	himself
1968	ܐܬܦܠܓ	he is divided
0061	ܐܝܟܢܐ	How
0596	ܗܟܝܠ	then
2168	ܩܝܡܐ	does stand
1385	ܡܠܟܘܬܗ	his kingdom

VERSE 27 And if by Beelzebub I cast out devils, in what way do your sons cast them out? Because of this, they will be judges of you.

0121	ܘܐܢ	And if
0124	ܐܢܐ	*
3127	ܒܒܥܠܙܒܘܒ	by Beelzebub
1542	ܡܦܩ	cast out
0124	ܐܢܐ	I
0514	ܕܝܘܐ	devils
0323	ܒܢܝܟܘܢ	your sons
1393	ܒܡܢܐ	in what way
1542	ܡܦܩܝܢ	do cast out
1261	ܠܗܘܢ	them
1347	ܡܛܠ	Because of
0598	ܗܢܐ	this
0592	ܗܢܘܢ	<they>
0603	ܢܗܘܘܢ	they will be
1261	ܠܟܘܢ	of you
0498	ܕܝܢܐ	judges

VERSE 28 And if by the Spirit of God I cast out devils, the kingdom of God has come near to you.

0121	ܘܐܢ	And if
2323	ܒܪܘܚܐ	by the Spirit
0093	ܕܐܠܗܐ	of God
0124	ܐܢܐ	<I>
1542	ܡܦܩ	cast out
0124	ܐܢܐ	I
0514	ܕܝܘܐ	devils
2244	ܩܪܒܬ	has come near
1261	ܠܗ	<it>
1804	ܥܠܝܟܘܢ	to you
1385	ܡܠܟܘܬܐ	the kingdom
0093	ܕܐܠܗܐ	of God

VERSE 29 Or how is a man able to enter into the house of a strong man and to rob his possessions, except first he will bind the strong man and then rob his house?

0024	ܐܘ	Or
0061	ܐܝܟܢܐ	how
0131	ܐܢܫ	a man
2510	ܡܫܟܚ	is able
1796	ܕܢܥܘܠ	to enter
0243	ܠܒܝܬ	into the house of
0862	ܚܣܝܢܐ	a strong man
1320	ܘܡܐܢܘܗܝ	and his possessions
0244	ܢܒܘܙ	to rob
0090	ܐܠܐ	except
0121	ܐܢ	*
2151	ܠܘܩܕܡ	first
0160	ܢܐܣܪܝܘܗܝ	he will bind
0862	ܠܚܣܝܢܐ	the strong man

Vertical Interlinear

MATTHEW CHAPTER 12

0594	ܘܗܝܕܝܢ	and then
0243	ܒܝܬܗ	his house
0244	ܢܒܘܙ	rob

VERSE 30 — He who is not with me is against me. And he who does not gather with me indeed scatters.

1389	ܡܢ	He who
1262	ܠܐ	not
0603	ܗܘܐ	is
1817	ܥܡܝ	with me
2135	ܠܘܩܒܠܝ	against me
0592	ܗܘ	is
1389	ܘܡܢ	And he who
1262	ܠܐ	not
1198	ܟܢܫ	does gather
1817	ܥܡܝ	with me
0229	ܡܒܕܪܘ	indeed scatters
0229	ܡܒܕܪ	*

VERSE 31 — Because of this, I say to you, all sins and blasphemies will be forgiven to men, but blasphemy that is against the Spirit will not be forgiven to men.

1347	ܡܛܠ	Because of
0598	ܗܢܐ	this
0116	ܐܡܪ	say
0124	ܐܢܐ	I
1261	ܠܟܘܢ	to you
1168	ܕܟܠ	all
0771	ܚܛܗܝܢ	sins
0371	ܘܓܘܕܦܝܢ	and blasphemies
2440	ܢܫܬܒܩܘܢ	will be forgiven
0325	ܠܒܢܝܢܫܐ	to men
0371	ܓܘܕܦܐ	blasphemy
0518	ܕܝܢ	but
1804	ܕܥܠ	that is against
2323	ܪܘܚܐ	the Spirit
1262	ܠܐ	not
2440	ܢܫܬܒܩ	will be forgiven
0325	ܠܒܢܝܢܫܐ	to men

VERSE 32 — And anyone who will say a word against the Son of Man will be forgiven. But anyone who will speak against the Holy Spirit will not be forgiven, neither in this age nor in the age that is to come.

1168	ܘܟܠ	And anyone
1389	ܡܢ	who
0116	ܕܢܐܡܪ	will say
1364	ܡܠܬܐ	a word
1804	ܥܠ	against
0323	ܒܪܗ	the Son
0131	ܕܐܢܫܐ	of Man
2440	ܢܫܬܒܩ	will be forgiven
1261	ܠܗ	<him>
1168	ܟܠ	anyone
0518	ܕܝܢ	But
1804	ܕܥܠ	who against
2323	ܪܘܚܐ	the Holy Spirit
2164	ܕܩܘܕܫܐ	*
0116	ܢܐܡܪ	will speak
1262	ܠܐ	not
2440	ܢܫܬܒܩ	will be forgiven
1261	ܠܗ	<him>
1262	ܠܐ	neither
1813	ܒܥܠܡܐ	in age
0598	ܗܢܐ	this
1262	ܘܠܐ	nor
1813	ܒܥܠܡܐ	in the age
1914	ܕܥܬܝܕ	that is to come

VERSE 33 — Either make the tree fine and its fruit fine or make the tree bad and its fruit bad, for a tree is known by its fruit.

0024	ܐܘ	Either
1724	ܥܒܕܘ	make
0063	ܐܝܠܢܐ	the tree
2583	ܫܦܝܪܐ	fine
2016	ܘܦܐܪܘܗܝ	and its fruit
2583	ܫܦܝܪܐ	fine
0024	ܐܘ	or
1724	ܥܒܕܘ	make
0063	ܐܝܠܢܐ	the tree

MATTHEW CHAPTER 12

0220	ܒܝܫܐ	bad
2016	ܘܦܐܪܘܗܝ	and its fruit
0220	ܒܝܫܐ	bad
1388	ܡܢ	by
2016	ܦܐܪܘܗܝ	its fruit
0592	ܗܘ	<is>
0403	ܓܝܪ	for
1023	ܡܬܝܕܥ	is known
0063	ܐܝܠܢܐ	a tree

VERSE 34 Generation of vipers! How are you who are bad able to speak good [things]? For from the fullness of the heart the mouth speaks.

1047	ܝܠܕܐ	Generation
0071	ܕܐܟܕܢܐ	of vipers
0061	ܐܝܟܢܐ	How
2510	ܡܫܟܚܝܢ	are able
0133	ܐܢܬܘܢ	you
0938	ܛܒܬܐ	good [things]
1362	ܠܡܡܠܠܘ	to speak
0220	ܕܒܝܫܐ	who are bad
0133	ܐܢܬܘܢ	<you>
1388	ܡܢ	from
1106	ܡܘܬܪܬ	the fullness of
1268	ܠܒܐ	the heart
0403	ܓܝܪ	For
1362	ܡܡܠܠ	speaks
1936	ܦܘܡܐ	the mouth

VERSE 35 A good man from good treasures produces good [things] and a bad man from bad treasures produces bad [things].

0361	ܓܒܪܐ	A man
0938	ܛܒܐ	good
1388	ܡܢ	from
1627	ܣܝܡܬܐ	treasures
0938	ܛܒܬܐ	good
1542	ܡܦܩ	produces
0938	ܛܒܬܐ	good [things]
0361	ܘܓܒܪܐ	and a man
0220	ܒܝܫܐ	bad
1388	ܡܢ	from
1627	ܣܝܡܬܐ	treasures
0220	ܒܝܫܬܐ	bad
1542	ܡܦܩ	produces
0220	ܒܝܫܬܐ	bad [things]

VERSE 36 For I say to you, [for] every idle word that men speak, they will give an account of it in the day of judgment.

0116	ܐܡܪ	say
0124	ܐܢܐ	I
1261	ܠܟܘܢ	to you
0403	ܓܝܪ	For
1168	ܕܟܠ	[for] every
1364	ܡܠܐ	word
0257	ܒܛܠܐ	idle
0116	ܕܢܐܡܪܘܢ	that speak
0323	ܒܢܝ	men
0131	ܐܢܫܐ	*
1030	ܢܬܠܘܢ	they will give
2068	ܦܬܓܡܗ	an account of it
1036	ܒܝܘܡܐ	in the day
0497	ܕܕܝܢܐ	of judgment

VERSE 37 For by your words you will be justified and by your words you will be condemned."

1388	ܡܢ	by
1364	ܡܠܝܟ	your words
0403	ܓܝܪ	For
0636	ܬܙܕܕܩ	you will be justified
1388	ܘܡܢ	and by
1364	ܡܠܝܟ	your words
0742	ܬܬܚܝܒ	you will be condemned

VERSE 38 Then answered some of the scribes and of the Pharisees and said to him, "Teacher, we desire to see a sign from you."

0594	ܗܝܕܝܢ	Then
1838	ܥܢܘ	answered
0131	ܐܢܫܐ	some
1388	ܡܢ	of
1699	ܣܦܪܐ	the scribes

MATTHEW CHAPTER 12

1388		and of		1490		of the fish
3439		the Pharisees		2674		three
0116		and said		1036		days
1261		to him		2674		and three
1055		Teacher		1299		nights
2077		desire		0597		so
0124		we		0603		will be
0758		to see		0323		the Son
1388		from you		0131		of Man
0206		a sign		1268		in the heart
				0199		of the earth
				2674		three
				0064		days
				2674		and three
				1299		nights

VERSE 39 But he answered and said to them, "An evil and adulterous generation seeks a sign, yet a sign will not be given to it, except the sign of Jonah the prophet.

0592		\<he\>
0518		But
1838		he answered
0116		and said
1261		to them
2605		generation
0220		An evil
0388		and adulterous
0206		a sign
0296		seeks
0206		yet a sign
1262		not
1030		will be given
1261		to it
0090		except
0206		the sign
3242		of Jonah
1457		the prophet

VERSE 41 The Ninevite men will stand in judgment with this generation and will condemn it, because they repented at the preaching of Jonah. And behold, one who is greater than Jonah is present.

0361		The men
3346		Ninevite
2168		will stand
0497		in judgment
1817		with
2605		generation
0598		this
0742		and will condemn it
0592		because \<they\>
2649		they repented
1232		at the preaching
3242		of Jonah
0580		And behold
2271		one who is greater
1388		than
3242		Jonah
2694		is present

VERSE 40 For as Jonah was in the belly of the fish three days and three nights, so will the Son of Man be in the heart of the earth three days and three nights.

0061		as
0403		For
0603		was
3242		Jonah
1241		in the belly

MATTHEW CHAPTER 12

VERSE 42 — The queen of the south will stand in judgment with this generation and she will condemn it, because she came from the ends of the earth to hear the wisdom of Solomon. And behold, one who is more than Solomon is here.

#	Aramaic	English
1386		The queen
1062		of the south
2168		will stand
0497		in judgment
1817		with
2605		generation
0598		this
0742		and she will condemn it
0208		because she came
1388		from
1735		the ends
0199		of the earth
2547		to hear
0792		the wisdom
3518		of Solomon
0580		And behold
1100		one who is more
1388		than
3518		Solomon
0600		is here

VERSE 43 — Now when an unclean spirit goes out from a man, it wanders in places in which there is no water and it seeks rest, yet does not find [it].

#	Aramaic	English
0120		when
0518		Now
2323		an spirit
0991		unclean
1542		goes out
1388		from
0325		a man
1236		it wanders
0214		in places
1351		water
1264		there is no
0217		in which
0296		and it seeks
1485		rest
1262		yet not
2510		does find [it]

VERSE 44 — Then it says, 'I will return to my house from where I came out.' And it comes [and] finds that it is empty and swept and set in order.

#	Aramaic	English
0594		Then
0116		it says
0616		I will return
0243		to my house
1388		from
1108		where
1542		I came out
0208		And it comes
2510		[and] finds
1714		that it is empty
0818		and swept
2083		and set in order

VERSE 45 — Then it will go [and] lead with it seven other spirits who are more evil than it and they will enter and dwell in it. And the end of that man will be more evil than his beginning. So it will be to this evil generation."

#	Aramaic	English
0594		Then
0042		it will go
0477		[and] lead
1817		with it
2437		seven
2323		spirits
0053		other
1388		who are more than it
0220		evil
1796		and they will enter
1833		and dwell
0217		in it
0603		And will be
0054		the end
0361		of man
0593		that

MATTHEW CHAPTER 12

0220		more evil
1388		than
2157		his beginning
0597		So
0603		it will be
1261		<to him>
2605		to generation
0598		this
0220		evil

VERSE 46 Now while he was speaking to the crowds, his mother and his brothers came [and] they were standing outside and requesting to speak with him.

1128		while
0592		he
0518		Now
1362		was speaking
1201		to the crowds
0208		came
0106		his mother
0043		and his brothers
2168		[and] they were standing
0322		outside
0296		and requesting
1362		to speak
1817		with him

VERSE 47 Now someone said to him, "Behold, your mother and your brothers are standing outside and requesting to speak with you."

0116		said
1261		to him
0518		Now
0131		someone
0580		Behold
0106		your mother
0043		and your brothers
2168		are standing
0322		outside
0296		and requesting
1362		to speak

1817		with you

VERSE 48 But he answered and said to the one who had spoken to him, "Who is my mother and who are my brothers?"

0592		<he>
0518		But
1838		he answered
0116		and said
1389		to the one
0116		who had spoken
1261		to him
1389		Who
0592		is
0106		my mother
1389		and who
0592		are
0043		my brothers

VERSE 49 And he stretched out his hand toward his disciples and said, "Behold, my mother and behold, my brothers.

2054		And he stretched out
0057		his hand
1288		toward
1304		his disciples
0116		and said
0580		Behold
0106		my mother
0580		and behold
0043		my brothers

VERSE 50 For everyone who does the will of my Father who is in heaven is my brother and my sister and my mother."

1175		everyone
0403		For
1724		who does
2079		the will
0002		of my Father
2543		who is in heaven
0592		is
0043		my brother
0046		and my sister

MATTHEW CHAPTER 12

0106	ܘܐܡܝ	and my mother	0603	ܗܘܐ	he was	
CHAPTER 13			1817	ܥܡܗܘܢ	with them	
VERSE 1		Now on that day, Jesus went out from the house and sat by the shore of the sea.	1967	ܒܦܠܐܬܐ	in parables	
			0116	ܘܐܡܪ	and said	
0593	ܗܘ	on that	0580	ܗܐ	Behold	
0518	ܕܝܢ	Now	1542	ܢܦܩ	went out	
1036	ܒܝܘܡܐ	day	0692	ܙܪܘܥܐ	a sower	
1542	ܢܦܩ	went out	0691	ܕܢܙܪܘܥ	to sow	
3257	ܝܫܘܥ	Jesus	**VERSE 4**		And while he was sowing, it happened that [some seed] fell by the side of the road. And a bird came and ate it.	
1388	ܡܢ	from				
0243	ܒܝܬܐ	the house	1128	ܘܟܕ	And while	
1093	ܘܝܬܒ	and sat	0691	ܙܪܥ	he was sowing	
1804	ܥܠ	by	0069	ܐܝܬ	it happened	
0057	ܝܕ	the shore of	1538	ܕܢܦܠ	that [some seed] fell	
1057	ܝܡܐ	the sea	1804	ܥܠ	by	
VERSE 2		And large crowds were gathered around him so that he boarded a ship to sit down and the whole crowd was standing on the shore of the sea.	0057	ܝܕ	the side of	
			0038	ܐܘܪܚܐ	the road	
			0208	ܘܐܬܬ	And came	
1198	ܘܐܬܟܢܫܘ	And were gathered	2026	ܦܪܚܬܐ	a bird	
1288	ܠܘܬܗ	around him	0075	ܘܐܟܠܬܗ	and ate it	
1201	ܟܢܫܐ	crowds	**VERSE 5**		And other [seed] fell on rocky ground where there was not much soil and immediately it sprouted, because there was no depth of earth.	
1596	ܣܓܝܐܐ	large				
0060	ܐܝܟ	so that				
1658	ܕܢܣܩ	he boarded	0053	ܘܐܚܪܢܐ	And other [seed]	
1093	ܘܢܬܒ	to sit down	1538	ܢܦܠ	fell	
1261	ܠܗ	<him>	1804	ܥܠ	on	
0100	ܠܐܠܦܐ	a ship	2477	ܫܘܥܐ	rocky ground	
1168	ܘܟܠܗ	and the whole	1108	ܐܝܟܐ	where	
1201	ܟܢܫܐ	crowd	1264	ܕܠܝܬ	there was not	
2168	ܩܐܡ	standing	0603	ܗܘܐ	*	
0603	ܗܘܐ	was	1327	ܐܪܥܐ	soil	
1804	ܥܠ	on	1596	ܣܓܝܐܐ	much	
1700	ܣܦܪ	the shore of	0323	ܘܒܪ	and immediately	
1057	ܝܡܐ	the sea	2573	ܫܘܚ	*	
VERSE 3		And he was speaking many [things] with them in parables and said, "Behold, a sower went out to sow.	2472	ܫܘܚ	it sprouted	
			1347	ܡܛܠ	because	
			1264	ܕܠܝܬ	there was no	
1596	ܘܣܓܝ	And many [things]	0603	ܗܘܐ	*	
1362	ܡܡܠܠ	speaking	1831	ܥܘܡܩܐ	depth	

84

MATTHEW CHAPTER 13

0199		of earth

VERSE 6 But when the sun came up, it became hot and because it had no root, it dried up.

1128		when
0555		came up
0518		But
2557		the sun
0818		it became hot
1347		and because
1264		it had no
0603		*
1261		*
1877		root
1018		it dried up

VERSE 7 And other [seed] fell among thorns and the thorns grew up and choked it.

0053		And other [seed]
1538		fell
0266		among
1139		thorns
1658		and grew up
1139		the thorns
0848		and choked it

VERSE 8 And other [seed] fell on good earth and bore fruit, some a hundred and some sixty and some thirty[fold].

0053		And other [seed]
1538		fell
0199		on earth
0938		good
1030		and bore
2016		fruit
0069		some
1317		a hundred
0069		and some
2616		sixty
0069		and some
2676		thirty[fold]

VERSE 9 He who has ears to hear should hear."

1389		He who
0069		has
1261		*
0021		ears
2547		to hear
2547		should hear

VERSE 10 And his disciples came near and said to him, "Why do you speak in parables with them?"

2244		And came near
1304		his disciples
0116		and said
1261		to him
1394		Why
1967		in parables
1362		do speak
0133		you
1817		with them

VERSE 11 Now he answered and said to them, "To you it is given to know the mystery of the kingdom of heaven, but it is not given to them.

0592		\<he\>
0518		Now
1838		he answered
0116		and said
1261		to them
1261		To you
0592		it
1030		is given
1023		to know
0188		the mystery
1385		of the kingdom
2543		of heaven
0593		to them
0518		but
1262		not
1030		it is given

MATTHEW CHAPTER 13

VERSE 12 — For to him who has, it will be given to him and he will have abundance,

Code	Aramaic	English
1389		to him
0403		For
0069		who has
1261		*
1030		it will be given
1261		to him
1098		and he will have abundance
1261		<to him>

VERSE 13 — and to him who has not, even that which he has will be taken from him. Because of this, I speak with them in parables, because they see and do not see, and they hear and do not hear and they do not understand.

Code	Aramaic	English
1389		and to him
1264		who has not
1261		*
0593		even that
0069		which he has
1261		*
2587		will be taken
1388		from him
1347		Because of
0598		this
1967		in parables
1362		speak
0124		I
1817		with them
1347		because
0758		they see
1262		and not
0758		do see
2547		and they hear
1262		and not
2547		do hear
1262		and not do
1647		they understand

VERSE 14 — And the prophecy of Isaiah is fulfilled in them, who said: HEARING YOU WILL HEAR AND YOU WILL NOT UNDERSTAND AND SEEING YOU WILL SEE AND YOU WILL NOT KNOW.

Code	Aramaic	English
2530		And is fulfilled
0217		in them
1458		the prophecy
3109		of Isaiah
0116		who said
2553		HEARING
2547		YOU WILL HEAR
1262		AND NOT
1647		YOU WILL UNDERSTAND
0758		AND SEEING
0758		YOU WILL SEE
1262		AND NOT
1023		YOU WILL KNOW

VERSE 15 — FOR THE HEART OF THIS PEOPLE IS HARDENED AND WITH THEIR EARS THEY ARE HARD OF HEARING AND THEIR EYES ARE CLOSED, LEST THEY WOULD SEE WITH THEIR EYES AND WOULD HEAR WITH THEIR EARS AND WOULD UNDERSTAND WITH THEIR HEART. AND WOULD REPENT AND I [WOULD] HEAL THEM.

Code	Aramaic	English
1722		IS HARDENED
1261		<TO HIM>
0403		FOR
1268		THE HEART
1818		OF PEOPLE
0598		THIS
0021		AND WITH THEIR EARS
1080		THEY ARE HARD OF
2547		HEARING
1794		AND THEIR EYES
1829		ARE CLOSED
1262		LEST
0758		THEY WOULD SEE
1794		WITH THEIR EYES
2547		AND WOULD HEAR
0021		WITH THEIR EARS

MATTHEW CHAPTER 13

1647	ܘܢܣܬܟܠܘܢ	AND WOULD UNDERSTAND
1268	ܒܠܒܗܘܢ	WITH THEIR HEART
1984	ܘܢܬܦܢܘܢ	AND WOULD REPENT
0136	ܘܐܣܐ	AND I [WOULD] HEAL
0592	ܐܢܘܢ	THEM

VERSE 16 But blessed are your eyes, because they see and your ears, because they hear.

0517	ܕܝܠܟܘܢ	<yours>
0518	ܕܝܢ	But
0940	ܛܘܒܝܗܘܢ	blessed are
1794	ܠܥܝܢܝܟܘܢ	your eyes
0758	ܕܚܙܝܢ	because they see
0021	ܘܠܐܕܢܝܟܘܢ	and your ears
2547	ܕܫܡܥܢ	because they hear

VERSE 17 For truly I say to you, many prophets and just [men] have longed to see what you see and they did not see [them], and to hear what you hear and they did not hear [them].

0110	ܐܡܝܢ	truly
0403	ܓܝܪ	For
0116	ܐܡܪ ܐܢܐ	I say
1261	ܠܟܘܢ	to you
1596	ܕܣܓܝܐܐ	many
1457	ܢܒܝܐ	prophets
0637	ܘܙܕܝܩܐ	and just [men]
2287	ܐܬܪܓܪܓܘ	have longed
0758	ܕܢܚܙܘܢ	to see
1326	ܡܕܡ	what
0758	ܕܚܙܝܢ	you see
0133	ܐܢܬܘܢ	*
1262	ܘܠܐ	and not
0758	ܚܙܘ	they did see [them]
2547	ܘܠܡܫܡܥ	and to hear
1326	ܡܕܡ	what
2547	ܕܫܡܥܝܢ	you hear
0133	ܐܢܬܘܢ	*
1262	ܘܠܐ	and not
2547	ܫܡܥܘ	they did hear [them]

VERSE 18 But hear the parable of the seed.

0133	ܐܢܬܘܢ	<you>
0518	ܕܝܢ	But
2547	ܫܡܥܘ	hear
1454	ܡܬܠܐ	the parable
0693	ܕܙܪܥܐ	of the seed

VERSE 19 [From] everyone who hears the message of the kingdom and does not understand, the Evil [one] comes and grabs the word that was sown in his heart. This is that which was sown by the side of the road.

1168	ܟܠ	[From] everyone
2547	ܕܫܡܥ	who hears
1364	ܡܠܬܐ	the message
1385	ܕܡܠܟܘܬܐ	of the kingdom
1262	ܘܠܐ	and not
1647	ܡܣܬܟܠ	does understand
0217	ܒܗ	<it>
0208	ܐܬܐ	comes
0220	ܒܝܫܐ	the Evil [one]
0774	ܘܚܛܦ	and grabs
1364	ܡܠܬܐ	the word
0691	ܕܙܪܝܥܐ	that was sown
1268	ܒܠܒܗ	in his heart
0599	ܗܢܐ	This is
0593	ܗܘ	that
1804	ܕܥܠ	which by
0057	ܝܕ	the side of
0038	ܐܘܪܚܐ	the road
0691	ܐܙܕܪܥ	was sown

VERSE 20 And that which was sown on rocky ground is he who hears the message and immediately receives it with joy.

0593	ܗܘ	that
0518	ܕܝܢ	And
1804	ܕܥܠ	which on
2477	ܫܘܥܐ	rocky ground
0691	ܐܙܕܪܥ	was sown
0593	ܗܘ	<that>
0592	ܗܘ	is he

MATTHEW CHAPTER 13

Vertical Interlinear

2547	ܕܫܡܥ	who hears
1364	ܡܠܬܐ	the message
0323	ܘܒܪ	and immediately
2573	ܫܩܠ	*
0727	ܒܚܕܘܬܐ	with joy
2134	ܡܩܒܠ	receives
1261	ܠܗ	it

VERSE 21 Yet he has no root in him, but is transient. And when trouble or persecution comes because of the word, he is offended quickly.

1264	ܠܝܬ	he has no
1261	ܠܗ	*
0518	ܕܝܢ	Yet
1877	ܥܩܪܐ	root
0217	ܒܗ	in him
0090	ܐܠܐ	but
0633	ܕܙܒܢܐ	transient
0592	ܗܘ	is
1313	ܘܡܐ	And when
0603	ܕܗܘܐ	comes
0103	ܐܘܠܨܢܐ	trouble
0024	ܐܘ	or
2306	ܪܕܘܦܝܐ	persecution
1347	ܡܛܠ	because of
1364	ܡܠܬܐ	the word
1738	ܒܥܓܠ	quickly
1242	ܡܬܟܫܠ	he is offended

VERSE 22 Now that which was sown among thorns is he who hears the word and the care of this world and the deception of riches choke the word and it becomes without fruit.

0593	ܗܘ	that
0518	ܕܝܢ	Now
0266	ܕܒܝܬ	which among
1139	ܟܘܒܐ	thorns
0691	ܐܙܕܪܥ	was sown
0593	ܗܘ	<that>
0592	ܗܘ	is he
2547	ܕܫܡܥ	who hears
1364	ܡܠܬܐ	the word
2377	ܘܨܦܬܐ	and the care
1813	ܕܥܠܡܐ	of world
0598	ܗܢܐ	this
0994	ܘܛܘܥܝܝ	and the deception
1920	ܕܥܘܬܪܐ	of riches
0848	ܚܢܩܝܢ	choke
1261	ܠܗ	<it>
1364	ܠܡܠܬܐ	the word
1262	ܘܕܠܐ	and without
2016	ܦܐܪܐ	fruit
0603	ܗܘܝܐ	it becomes

VERSE 23 But that which was sown on good earth is he who hears my word and understands [it] and produces fruit and yields some a hundred and some sixty and some thirty[fold]."

0593	ܗܘ	that
0518	ܕܝܢ	But
1804	ܕܥܠ	which on
0199	ܐܪܥܐ	earth
0938	ܛܒܬܐ	good
0691	ܐܙܕܪܥ	was sown
0593	ܗܘ	<that>
0592	ܗܘ	is he
2547	ܕܫܡܥ	who hears
1364	ܡܠܬܝ	my word
1647	ܘܡܣܬܟܠ	and understands [it]
1030	ܘܝܗܒ	and produces
2016	ܦܐܪܐ	fruit
1724	ܘܥܒܕ	and yields
0069	ܐܝܬ	some
1317	ܕܡܐܐ	a hundred
0069	ܘܐܝܬ	and some
2616	ܕܫܬܝܢ	sixty
0069	ܘܐܝܬ	and some
2676	ܕܬܠܬܝܢ	thirty[fold]

Vertical Interlinear

MATTHEW   CHAPTER 13

VERSE 24 — He spoke another parable to them and he said, "The kingdom of heaven is compared to a man who sowed good seed in his field.

0053	ܐ̱ܚܪܢܐ	another
1454	ܡܬܠܐ	parable
1453	ܐܡܪ	He spoke <a parable>
1261	ܠܗܘܢ	to them
0116	ܘܐܡܪ	and said
0540	ܕܡܝܐ	is compared
1385	ܡܠܟܘܬܐ	The kingdom
2543	ܕܫܡܝܐ	of heaven
0361	ܠܓܒܪܐ	to a man
0691	ܕܙܪܥ	who sowed
0693	ܙܪܥܐ	seed
0938	ܛܒܐ	good
2251	ܒܩܪܝܬܗ	in his field

VERSE 25 — And when the people were asleep, his enemy came and sowed weeds in the middle of the wheat and [then] left.

1128	ܟܕ	And when
0544	ܕܡܟܘ	were asleep
0131	ܐ̱ܢܫܐ	the people
0208	ܐܬܐ	came
0307	ܒܥܠܕܒܒܗ	his enemy
0691	ܘܙܪܥ	and sowed
0662	ܙܝܙܢܐ	weeds
0266	ܒܝܢܬ	in the middle of
0779	ܚܛܐ	the wheat
0042	ܘܐܙܠ	and [then] left

VERSE 26 — And when the plant sprouted and bore fruit, then the weeds also were seen.

1128	ܟܕ	when
0518	ܕܝܢ	And
1065	ܝܥܐ	sprouted
1845	ܥܣܒܐ	the plant
1724	ܘܥܒܕ	and bore
2016	ܦܐܪܐ	fruit
0594	ܗܝܕܝܢ	then
0758	ܐܬܚܙܝܘ	were seen
0169	ܐܦ	also

0662	ܙܝܙܢܐ	the weeds

VERSE 27 — And the servants of the master [of] the house came near and said to him, 'Our lord, behold, did you not sow good seed in your field? From where are the weeds in it?'

2244	ܘܩܪܒܘ	And came near
1727	ܥܒܕܘܗܝ	the servants
1426	ܕܡܪܐ	of the master
0243	ܒܝܬܐ	[of] the house
0116	ܘܐܡܪܘ	and said
1261	ܠܗ	to him
1426	ܡܪܢ	our lord
1262	ܠܐ	not
0580	ܗܐ	behold
0693	ܙܪܥܐ	seed
0938	ܛܒܐ	good
0691	ܙܪܥܬ	did you sow
2251	ܒܩܪܝܬܟ	in your field
1388	ܡܢ	From
1110	ܐܝܡܟܐ	where
0069	ܐܝܬ	are
0217	ܒܗ	in it
0662	ܙܝܙܢܐ	the weeds

VERSE 28 — But he said to them, 'A man [who is] an enemy did this.' His servants said to him, 'Do you want us to go to pick them out?'

0592	ܗܘ	<he>
0518	ܕܝܢ	But
0116	ܐܡܪ	he said
1261	ܠܗܘܢ	to them
0361	ܓܒܪܐ	A man
0307	ܒܥܠܕܒܒܐ	[who is] an enemy
1724	ܥܒܕ	did
0598	ܗܕܐ	this
0116	ܐܡܪܝܢ	said
1261	ܠܗ	to him
1727	ܥܒܕܘܗܝ	His servants
2077	ܨܒܐ	Do want
0133	ܐܢ̱ܬ	you

MATTHEW CHAPTER 13

0042	ܠܡܐܙܠ	us to go
0351	ܢܒܠܫ	to pick out
0592	ܐܢܘܢ	them
VERSE 29		But he said to them, '[No], lest while you are picking out the weeds, you will uproot the wheat with them also.'
0592	ܗܘ	\<he\>
0518	ܕܝܢ	But
0116	ܐܡܪ	he said
1261	ܠܗܘܢ	to them
1314	ܕܠܡܐ	[No] lest
1128	ܟܕ	while
0351	ܡܠܩܛܝܢ	are picking out
0133	ܐܢܬܘܢ	you
0662	ܙܝܙܢܐ	the weeds
1876	ܬܥܩܪܘܢ	you will uproot
1817	ܥܡܗܘܢ	with them
0169	ܐܦ	also
0779	ܚܛܐ	the wheat
VERSE 30		Allow both to grow together until the harvest. And in the time of harvest, I will say to the reapers, 'Pick out the weeds first and bind them [into] bundles to be burned.' But gather the wheat into my granaries.'"
2440	ܫܒܘܩܘ	Allow
2280	ܪܒܝܢ	to grow
2709	ܬܪܝܗܘܢ	both
0074	ܐܟܚܕܐ	together
1747	ܥܕܡܐ	until
0879	ܠܚܨܕܐ	the harvest
0633	ܘܒܙܒܢܐ	And in the time
0879	ܕܚܨܕܐ	of harvest
0116	ܐܡܪ	will say
0124	ܐܢܐ	I
0880	ܠܚܨܘܕܐ	to the reapers
0351	ܠܩܛܘ	Pick out
2151	ܠܘܩܕܡ	first
0662	ܙܝܙܢܐ	the weeds
0160	ܘܐܣܘܪܘ	and bind
0592	ܐܢܘܢ	them

0165	ܡܐܣܘܪܝܬܐ	[into] bundles
1073	ܠܡܐܩܕ	to be burned
0779	ܚܛܐ	the wheat
0518	ܕܝܢ	But
1198	ܟܢܫܘ	gather
0592	ܐܢܘܢ	\<them\>
0035	ܠܐܘܨܪܝ	into my granaries
VERSE 31		He spoke another parable to them. And he said, "The kingdom of heaven is compared to a grain of mustard seed that a man took [and] sowed in his field.
0053	ܐܚܪܢܐ	another
1454	ܡܬܠܐ	parable
1453	ܐܡܬܠ	He spoke \<a parable\>
1261	ܠܗܘܢ	to them
0116	ܘܐܡܪ	And he said
0540	ܕܡܝܐ	is compared
1385	ܡܠܟܘܬܐ	The kingdom
2543	ܕܫܡܝܐ	of heaven
2019	ܠܦܪܕܬܐ	to a grain
0895	ܕܚܪܕܠܐ	of mustard seed
1532	ܕܢܣܒ	that took
0361	ܓܒܪܐ	a man
0691	ܘܙܪܥ	[and] sowed
2251	ܒܩܪܝܬܗ	in his field
VERSE 32		And this [seed] is smaller than all the small seeds, but when it grows, it is greater than all the small herbs and it becomes a tree, so that a bird of heaven will come [and] nest in its branches."
0592	ܘܗܝ	And this [seed]
0686	ܙܥܘܪܝܐ	smaller
0592	ܗܝ	is
1388	ܡܢ	than
1168	ܟܠܗܘܢ	all \<of them\>
0694	ܙܪܥܘܢܐ	the small seeds
1313	ܡܐ	when
0518	ܕܝܢ	but
2280	ܕܪܒܬ	it grows
2271	ܪܒܐ	greater
0592	ܗܝ	it is

MATTHEW CHAPTER 13

Vertical Interlinear

#		Translation
1388		than
1168		all
1085		the small herbs
0603		and it becomes
0063		a tree
0060		so that
0208		will come
2026		a bird
2543		of heaven
2215		[and] nest
1623		in its branches

VERSE 33 — He spoke another parable to them. "The kingdom of heaven is compared to leaven that a woman took [and] hid in three measures of flour, until all of it was leavened."

#		Translation
0053		another
1454		parable
0116		He spoke
1261		to them
0540		is compared
1385		The kingdom
2543		of heaven
0832		to leaven
0593		that
2587		took
0135		a woman
0986		[and] hid
2674		in three
1583		measures
2210		of flour
1747		until
1168		all of it
0827		was leavened

VERSE 34 — All these [things] Jesus spoke in illustrations to the crowds. And without illustrations he did not speak with them,

#		Translation
0598		these [things]
1168		All
1362		spoke
3257		Jesus
1967		in illustrations
1201		to the crowds
1262		and without
1967		illustrations
1262		not
1362		speak
0603		he did
1817		with them

VERSE 35 — so that it would be fulfilled what was spoken by way of the prophet, who said: I WILL OPEN MY MOUTH WITH PARABLES AND I WILL BRING FORTH HIDDEN [THINGS] THAT WERE FROM BEFORE THE FOUNDATIONS OF THE WORLD.

#		Translation
0060		so that
1366		it would be fulfilled
1326		what
0116		was spoken
0057		by way of
1457		the prophet
0116		who said
2070		I WILL OPEN
1936		MY MOUTH
1454		WITH PARABLES
1459		AND I WILL BRING FORTH
1206		HIDDEN [THINGS]
1388		THAT WERE FROM
2154		BEFORE
2373		THE FOUNDATIONS
1813		OF THE WORLD

VERSE 36 — Then Jesus left the crowds and came to the house and his disciples came near to him and said to him, "Explain to us that parable of the weeds and of the field."

#		Translation
0594		Then
3257		Jesus
2440		left
1201		the crowds
0208		and came
0243		to the house
2244		and came near

MATTHEW CHAPTER 13

Vertical Interlinear

1288		to him
1304		his disciples
0116		and said
1261		to him
2061		Explain
1261		to us
1454		the parable
0593		<that>
0662		of the weeds
2251		and of the field

VERSE 37 — And he answered and said to them, "He who sowed the good seed is the Son of Man.

0592		<he>
0518		And
1838		he answered
0116		and said
1261		to them
0593		He
0691		who sowed
0693		the seed
0938		good
0069		is
0323		the Son
0131		of Man

VERSE 38 — And the field is the age and the good seed are the sons of the kingdom. And the weeds are the sons of the Evil [one].

2251		And the field
0069		is
1813		the age
0693		the seed
0518		and
0938		good
0323		the sons
0592		are
1385		of the kingdom
0662		the weeds
0518		And
0069		are
0323		the sons
0220		of the Evil [one]

VERSE 39 — And the enemy who sowed them is Satan. And the harvest is the culmination of the age and the reapers [are] the angels.

0307		the enemy
0518		And
0691		who sowed
0592		them
0069		is
1642		Satan
0879		the harvest
0518		And
0069		is
2534		the culmination
1813		of the age
0880		the reapers
0518		and
1375		[are] the angels

VERSE 40 — As therefore the weeds are picked out and burned in the fire, so it will be in the culmination of this age.

0061		As
0596		therefore
0351		are picked out
0662		the weeds
1073		and burned
1494		in the fire
0597		so
0603		it will be
2534		in the culmination
1813		of age
0598		this

VERSE 41 — The Son of Man will send his angels and they will pick out from his kingdom all the stumbling blocks and all the servants of wickedness

2458		will send
0323		The Son
0131		of Man
1375		his angels

MATTHEW CHAPTER 13

Vertical Interlinear

0351		and they will pick out		0540		is compared
1388		from		1385		the kingdom
1385		his kingdom		2543		of heaven
1168		all		1627		to a treasure
1244		the stumbling blocks		1009		that is hidden
1168		and all		2251		in a field
1724		the servants of		0593		that
1766		wickedness		2510		found

VERSE 42 and they will throw them into the furnace of fire. In that place will be crying and gnashing of teeth.

				0361		a man
				1009		and hid
2372		and they will throw		1388		And from
0592		them		0727		his joy
0211		into the furnace		0042		he went
1494		of fire		0632		[and] sold
2682		In that place		1168		everything
0603		will be		0069		that he had
0268		crying		1261		*
0905		and gnashing of		0632		and bought
2558		teeth		2251		field
				0593		that

VERSE 43 Then the just [ones] will shine as the sun in the kingdom of their Father. He who has ears to hear should hear.

VERSE 45 Again, the kingdom of heaven is compared to a merchant who was seeking expensive pearls.

0594		Then		2650		Again
0637		the just [ones]		0540		is compared
1474		will shine		1385		the kingdom
0060		as		2543		of heaven
2557		the sun		0361		to a merchant
1385		in the kingdom		2639		*
0002		of their Father		0296		who seeking
1389		He who		0603		was
0069		has		1430		pearls
1261		*		0938		expensive
0021		ears				
2547		to hear				
2547		should hear				

VERSE 46 And when he found a certain precious pearl, he went [and] sold everything that he had and bought it.

VERSE 44 Again, the kingdom of heaven is compared to a treasure that is hidden in a field that a man found and hid. And from his joy, he went [and] sold everything he had and bought that field.

				1128		when
				0518		And
				2510		he found
2650		Again		1430		a pearl

MATTHEW   CHAPTER 13

Vertical Interlinear

Code	Aramaic	English
0721		certain
1079		precious
0543		*
0042		he went
0632		[and] sold
1168		everything
1313		that
0069		he had
1261		*
0632		and bought it

VERSE 47 Again, the kingdom of heaven is compared to a net that was thrown into the sea and gathered together [fish] of every kind.

Code	Aramaic	English
2650		Again
0540		is compared
1385		the kingdom
2543		of heaven
2090		to a net
1538		that was thrown
1057		into the sea
1388		and [fish] of
1168		every
0444		kind
1198		gathered together

VERSE 48 And when it was full, they pulled it out to the shore of the sea and sat down [and] sorted [it]. And the good [fish] they placed in containers and the bad they threw away.

Code	Aramaic	English
1128		And when
1366		it was full
1658		they pulled it out
1700		to the shore of
1057		the sea
1093		and sat down
0351		[and] sorted [it]
0938		And the good [fish]
2372		they placed
1320		in containers
0220		and the bad
2455		they threw
0322		away

VERSE 49 So it will be in the culmination of the age. The angels will go out and separate the evil [ones] from among the just [ones]

Code	Aramaic	English
0597		So
0603		it will be
2534		in the culmination
1813		of the age
1542		will go out
1375		The angels
2046		and separate
0220		the evil [ones]
1388		from
0266		among
0637		the just [ones]

VERSE 50 and they will throw them into the furnace of fire. In that place will be crying and gnashing of teeth.

Code	Aramaic	English
2372		and they will throw
0592		them
0211		into the furnace
1494		of fire
2682		In that place
0603		will be
0268		crying
0905		and gnashing of
2558		teeth

VERSE 51 Jesus said to them, "Do you understand all these [things]?" They said to him, "Yes, our Lord."

Code	Aramaic	English
0116		said
1261		to them
3257		Jesus
1647		Do you understand
1168		all
0598		these [things]
0116		They said
1261		to him
0065		Yes

MATTHEW   CHAPTER 13

1426		our Lord

VERSE 52 — He said to them, "Because of this, every scribe who is instructed for the kingdom of heaven is compared to a man [who is] a master [of] a house, who brings out from his treasures the new and old."

0116		He said
1261		to them
1347		Because of
0598		this
1168		every
1699		scribe
1302		who is instructed
1385		for the kingdom of
2543		heaven
0540		is compared
0361		to a man
1426		[who is] a master [of]
0243		a house
1542		who brings out
1388		from
1627		his treasures
0735		the new
1917		and old

VERSE 53 — And it happened that when Jesus completed these parables, he went away from there.

0603		And it happened
1128		that when
2530		completed
3257		Jesus
1454		parables
0598		these [things]
2561		he went away
1388		from
2682		there

VERSE 54 — And he came to his [own] city and was teaching them in their synagogues, so that they marveled and were saying, "From where [does] this wisdom and [these] miracles [come] to this [man]?

0208		And he came
0499		to his [own] city
1053		and teaching
0603		was
1261		them
1200		in their synagogues
0061		so that
2644		they marveled
0116		and were saying
1110		From where
1261		<to him>
0598		to this [man]
0792		[does] wisdom [come]
0598		this
0786		and [these] miracles

VERSE 55 — Is not this the son of the carpenter? Is not his mother called Mary and his brothers, James and Joses and Simon and Judas?

1262		not
0603		Is
0598		this
0323		the son
1469		of the carpenter
1262		not
0106		his mother
2239		Is called
3325		Mary
0043		and his brothers
3255		James
3244		and Joses
3521		and Simon
3228		and Judas

VERSE 56 — And all his sisters, behold, are they not with us? So from where [do] all these [things] [come] to this [man]?"

0046		And his sisters
1168		all
1262		not
0580		behold
1288		with us
0592		are they
1110		from where [come]

MATTHEW CHAPTER 13

#	Syriac	English
1261		<to him>
0596		So
0598		to this [man]
0598		[do] these [things]
1168		all

VERSE 57 — And they were offended by him. And Jesus said to them, "There is no prophet who is despised, except in his [own] city and in his [own] house."

#	Syriac	English
1242		And offended
0603		they were
0217		by him
0592		<he>
0518		And
3257		Jesus
0116		said
1261		to them
1264		There is no
1457		prophet
2119		who is despised
0090		except
0499		in his [own] city
0243		and in his [own] house

VERSE 58 — And he did not do many miracles there because of their unbelief.

#	Syriac	English
1262		And not
1724		he did do
2682		there
0786		miracles
1596		many
1347		because of
1262		their unbelief
0113		*

CHAPTER 14

VERSE 1 — Now in that time, Herod the Tetrarch heard a report about Jesus.

#	Syriac	English
0593		in that
0518		Now
0633		time
2547		heard
3179		Herod
0961		the Tetrarch
2553		a report
3257		about Jesus

VERSE 2 — And he said to his servants, "This is John the baptizer. He has risen from the dead. Because of this, miracles are done by him."

#	Syriac	English
0116		And he said
1727		to his servants
0599		This is
3233		John
1820		the baptizer
0592		<is>
2168		He has risen
1388		from
0243		the dead
1338		*
1347		Because of
0598		this
0786		miracles
1684		are done
0217		by him

VERSE 3 — For Herod had arrested John and bound him and threw him into prison because of Herodias, the wife of his brother Philip.

#	Syriac	English
0593		<he>
0403		For
3179		Herod
0047		had arrested
0603		*
3233		John
0160		and bound him
2372		and threw him into
0243		prison
0163		*
1347		because of
3178		Herodias
0135		the wife of
3420		Philip
0043		his brother

MATTHEW CHAPTER 14

Vertical Interlinear

VERSE	**4**		For John was saying to him, "It is unlawful that she be a wife to you."
0116	ܐܡܪ	saying	
0603	ܗܘܐ	was	
1261	ܠܗ	to him	
0403	ܓܝܪ	For	
3233	ܝܘܚܢܢ	John	
1262	ܠܐ	It is unlawful	
2528	ܫܠܝܛ	*	
0603	ܕܬܗܘܐ	that she be	
1261	ܠܟ	to you	
0135	ܐܢܬܬܐ	a wife	
VERSE	**5**		And he was desiring to kill him, but he was afraid of the people, who were regarding him as a prophet.
2077	ܘܨܒܐ	And desiring	
0603	ܗܘܐ	he was	
2179	ܠܡܩܛܠܗ	to kill him	
0509	ܘܕܚܠ	but afraid	
0603	ܗܘܐ	he was	
1388	ܡܢ	of	
1818	ܥܡܐ	the people	
0060	ܕܐܝܟ	who as	
1457	ܕܠܢܒܝܐ	a prophet	
0047	ܐܚܝܕܝܢ	regarding	
0603	ܗܘܘ	were	
1261	ܠܗ	him	
VERSE	**6**		Now when the birthday of Herod occurred, the daughter of Herodias danced before the guests and she pleased Herod.
1128	ܟܕ	when	
0603	ܗܘܐ	occurred	
0518	ܕܝܢ	Now	
0243	ܒܝܬ	the birthday	
1047	ܝܠܕܗ	*	
3179	ܕܗܪܘܕܣ	of Herod	
2403	ܪܩܕܬ	danced	
0327	ܒܪܬܗ	the daughter	
3178	ܕܗܪܘܕܝܐ	of Herodias	
2154	ܩܕܡ	before	
1665	ܣܡܝܟܐ	the guests	
2580	ܘܫܦܪܬ	and she pleased	
1261	ܠܗ	<him>	
3179	ܠܗܪܘܕܣ	Herod	
VERSE	**7**		Because of this, with an oath he swore to her that he would give her anything that she asked.
1347	ܡܛܠ	Because of	
0598	ܗܕܐ	this	
1060	ܒܡܘܡܬܐ	with an oath	
1059	ܝܡܐ	he swore	
1261	ܠܗ	to her	
1030	ܕܢܬܠ	that he would give	
1261	ܠܗ	her	
1173	ܟܠܡܕܡ	anything	
2420	ܕܬܫܐܠ	that she asked	
VERSE	**8**		And because she was instructed by her mother, she said, "Give me here on a plate the head of John the baptizer."
0592	ܗܝ	<she>	
0518	ܕܝܢ	And	
1347	ܡܛܠ	because	
1053	ܕܡܠܦܐ	she was instructed	
0603	ܗܘܬ	*	
0106	ܠܐܡܗ	by her mother	
0116	ܐܡܪܐ	she said	
1030	ܗܒ	Give	
1261	ܠܝ	me	
0600	ܗܪܟܐ	here	
1954	ܒܦܝܢܟܐ	on a plate	
2362	ܪܫܗ	the head	
3233	ܕܝܘܚܢܢ	of John	
1820	ܡܥܡܕܢܐ	the baptizer	
VERSE	**9**		And it saddened the king, but because of the oath and the guests, he commanded that it be given to her.
1221	ܘܟܪܝܬ	And it saddened	
1261	ܠܗ	<him>	
1383	ܠܡܠܟܐ	the king	
1347	ܡܛܠ	because of	
0518	ܕܝܢ	but	

MATTHEW CHAPTER 14

1060		the oath		2547		heard [this]
1665		and the guests		2561		he went away
2007		he commanded		1388		from
1030		that it be given		2682		there
1261		to her		0100		in a ship

VERSE 10 — And he sent [and] cut off the head of John [in] the prison.

2458		And he sent
1992		[and] cut off
2362		the head
3233		of John
0243		[in] the prison
0163		*

0214		to a place
0892		desert
1041		alone
1128		And when
2547		heard [this]
1201		the crowds
0042		they followed him
0215		*
1019		by dry land
1388		from
0499		the cities

VERSE 11 — And he brought his head on a plate and it was given to the girl and she brought it to her mother.

0208		And he brought
2362		his head
1954		on a plate
1030		and it was given
0978		to the girl
0208		and she brought it
0106		to her mother

VERSE 14 — And Jesus went out [and] saw the large crowds. And he had compassion on them and he healed their diseases.

1542		And went out
3257		Jesus
0758		[and] saw
1201		the crowds
1596		large
2342		And he had compassion
1804		on them
0136		and he healed
1228		their diseases

VERSE 12 — And his disciples came near, took up his corpse, buried [it] and came [and] made [his death] known to Jesus.

2244		And came near
1304		his disciples
2587		took up
2520		his corpse
2142		buried [it]
0208		and came
0739		[and] made [his death] known
3257		to Jesus

VERSE 15 — Now when it was evening, his disciples came near to him and said to him, "[This] is a desert place and the time has passed. Dismiss the crowds of people that they may go on to the villages and buy food for themselves."

1128		when
0603		it was
0518		Now
2375		evening
2244		came near
1288		to him
1304		his disciples

VERSE 13 — Now when Jesus heard [this], he went away from there in a ship to a desert place alone. And when the crowds heard [this], they followed him by dry land from the cities.

3257		Jesus
0518		Now
1128		when

MATTHEW CHAPTER 14

0116	ܘܐܡܪܘ	and said
1261	ܠܗ	to him
0214	ܐܬܪܐ	a place
0892	ܚܘܪܒܐ	desert
0592	ܗܘ	[This] is
1750	ܘܙܒܢܐ	and the time
1733	ܥܒܪ	has passed
1261	ܠܗ	<to it>
2597	ܫܪܝ	Dismiss
1201	ܠܟܢܫܐ	the crowds
0131	ܕܐܢܫܐ	of people
0042	ܕܢܐܙܠܘܢ	that they may go
2251	ܠܩܘܪܝܐ	to the villages
0632	ܘܢܙܒܢܘܢ	and buy
1261	ܠܗܘܢ	for themselves
1594	ܣܝܒܪܬܐ	food

VERSE 16 But he said to them, "It is not necessary for them to leave. Give them [food] to eat."

0592	ܗܘ	<he>
0518	ܕܝܢ	But
0116	ܐܡܪ	he said
1261	ܠܗܘܢ	to them
1262	ܠܐ	not
0296	ܡܬܒܥܐ	It is necessary
1261	ܠܗܘܢ	for them
0042	ܠܡܐܙܠ	to leave
1030	ܗܒܘ	Give
1261	ܠܗܘܢ	them
0133	ܐܢܬܘܢ	<you>
0075	ܠܡܐܟܠ	[food] to eat

VERSE 17 But they said to him, "We have nothing here, except five [loaves of] bread and two fish."

0592	ܗܢܘܢ	<they>
0518	ܕܝܢ	But
0116	ܐܡܪܘ	they said
1261	ܠܗ	to him
1264	ܠܝܬ	We have nothing
1261	ܠ	*

2694	ܠܢ	here
0090	ܐܠܐ	except
0833	ܚܡܫ	five
0462	ܓܪܨܝܢ	[loaves of] bread
2709	ܘܬܪܝܢ	and two
1490	ܢܘܢܝܢ	fish

VERSE 18 Jesus said to them, "Bring them here to me."

0116	ܐܡܪ	said
1261	ܠܗܘܢ	to them
3257	ܝܫܘܥ	Jesus
0208	ܐܝܬܘ	Bring
0592	ܐܢܘܢ	them
1261	ܠܝ	to me
0600	ܠܗܪܟܐ	here

VERSE 19 And he commanded the crowds to recline on the ground and he lifted up those five [loaves of] bread and two fish and looked into heaven and blessed and broke [them] and gave [them] to his disciples and the disciples set [the food] before the crowds.

2007	ܘܦܩܕ	And he commanded
1201	ܠܟܢܫܐ	the crowds
1664	ܠܡܣܬܡܟܘ	to recline
1804	ܥܠ	on
0199	ܐܪܥܐ	the ground
2587	ܘܫܩܠ	and he lifted up
0593	ܗܢܘܢ	those
0833	ܚܡܫܐ	five
1293	ܠܚܡܝܢ	[loaves of] bread
2709	ܘܬܪܝܢ	and two
1490	ܢܘܢܝܢ	fish
0756	ܘܚܪ	and looked
2543	ܒܫܡܝܐ	into heaven
0335	ܘܒܪܟ	and blessed
2234	ܘܩܨܐ	and broke [them]
1030	ܘܝܗܒ	and gave [them]
1304	ܠܬܠܡܝܕܘܗܝ	to this disciples
0592	ܘܗܢܘܢ	and <they>
1304	ܬܠܡܝܕܐ	the disciples

MATTHEW CHAPTER 14

1625		set [the food]
1201		before the crowds

VERSE 20 — And all of them ate and were satisfied. And they took up the rest of the fragments, twelve baskets full.

0075		And ate
1168		all of them
1585		and were satisfied
2587		And they took up
1106		the rest of
2235		the fragments
2710		twelve
2176		baskets
1128		<being>
1366		full

VERSE 21 — Now those men who ate were five thousand, besides women and children.

0593		those
0518		Now
0131		men
0075		who ate
0603		were
0603		*
0099		thousand
0833		five
1643		besides
1388		*
0135		women
0976		and children

VERSE 22 — And immediately he urged his disciples to board the ship and to go before him to the opposite side, while he dismissed the crowds.

0725		And immediately
0102		he urged
1304		his disciples
1658		to board
1692		the ship
0042		and to go
2154		before him
1735		to the opposite side
1744		while
2597		dismissed
0592		he
1201		the crowds

VERSE 23 — And when he dismissed the crowds, he went up to a mountain alone to pray. And when it became dark, he was alone there.

1128		And when
2597		he dismissed
1201		the crowds
1658		he went up
0958		to a mountain
1041		alone
2106		to pray
1128		And when
0922		it became dark
1041		alone
0603		he was
2682		there

VERSE 24 — And the ship was many furlongs away from land, being tossed greatly by the waves, for the wind was against it.

0100		And the ship
2355		away
0603		was
1388		from
0199		land
0141		furlongs
1596		many
1128		being
2452		tossed
1596		greatly
1388		by
0407		the waves
2323		the wind
0403		for
2135		against it
0603		was

Vertical Interlinear

MATTHEW CHAPTER 14

VERSE 25 — Now in the fourth watch of the night, Jesus came toward them, walking on the water.

1503		in the watch
0518		Now
0184		fourth
1299		of the night
0208		came
1288		toward them
3257		Jesus
1128		walking
0608		*
1804		on
1351		the water

VERSE 26 — And his disciples saw him that he was walking on the water. And they were troubled and were saying, "It is a false vision." And they cried out because of their fear.

0758		And saw him
1304		his disciples
0608		that he was walking
1804		on
1351		the water
0657		And they were troubled
0116		and saying
0603		were
0759		a vision
0592		It is
0486		false
1388		And because
0511		of their fear
2227		they cried out

VERSE 27 — But Jesus immediately spoke with them and said, "Be encouraged, it is I. Do not be afraid."

0592		\<he\>
0518		But
3257		Jesus
0326		immediately
1362		spoke
1817		with them
0116		and said
1267		Be encouraged
0124		it is
0124		I
1262		not
0509		Do be afraid

VERSE 28 — And Peter answered and said to him, "My Lord, if it is you, command me to come to you on the water."

1838		And answered
3258		Peter
0116		and said
1261		to him
1426		My Lord
0121		if
0133		you
0592		it is
2007		command
1261		me
0208		to come
1288		to you
1804		on
1351		the water

VERSE 29 — And Jesus said to him, "Come." And Peter got down from the ship and walked on the water to go to Jesus.

3257		Jesus
0518		And
0116		said
1261		to him
0208		Come
1499		And got down
3258		Peter
1388		from
0100		the ship
0608		and walked
1804		on
1351		the water
0208		to go
1288		to

MATTHEW CHAPTER 14

3257	ܝܫܘܥ	Jesus

VERSE 30 — And when he saw the wind was rough, he feared and began to sink. And he raised his voice and said, "My Lord, save me."

1128	ܘܟܕ	And when
0758	ܚܙܐ	he saw
2323	ܪܘܚܐ	the wind
2265	ܕܩܫܝܐ	was rough
0509	ܕܚܠ	he feared
2597	ܘܫܪܝ	and began
0945	ܠܡܛܒܥ	to sink
2331	ܘܐܪܝܡ	And he raised
2204	ܩܠܗ	his voice
0116	ܘܐܡܪ	and said
1426	ܡܪܝ	My Lord
2042	ܦܪܘܩܝܢܝ	save me

VERSE 31 — And immediately our Lord reached out his hand and grasped him and said to him, "Little of faith, why did you doubt?"

0323	ܒܪ	And immediately
2573	ܫܥܬܗ	*
2054	ܦܫܛ	reached out
0057	ܐܝܕܗ	his hand
1426	ܡܪܢ	our Lord
0047	ܘܐܚܕܗ	and grasped him
0116	ܘܐܡܪ	and said
1261	ܠܗ	to him
0686	ܙܥܘܪ	Little of
0113	ܗܝܡܢܘܬܐ	faith
1394	ܠܡܢܐ	why
1968	ܐܬܦܠܓܬ	did you doubt

VERSE 32 — And when they boarded the ship, the wind quieted.

1128	ܘܟܕ	And when
1658	ܣܠܩܘ	they boarded
0100	ܠܐܠܦܐ	the ship
2516	ܫܠܝܬ	quieted
2323	ܪܘܚܐ	the wind

VERSE 33 — And those who were in the ship came [and] worshipped him and said, "Truly you [are] the Son of God."

0208	ܘܐܬܘ	And came
0593	ܗܢܘܢ	those
0100	ܕܒܐܠܦܐ	who were in the ship
1599	ܣܓܕܘ	[and] worshipped
1261	ܠܗ	him
0116	ܘܐܡܪܘ	and said
2594	ܫܪܝܪܐܝܬ	Truly
0323	ܒܪܗ	the Son
0133	ܐܢܬ	you [are]
0093	ܕܐܠܗܐ	of God

VERSE 34 — And they traveled on and came to the land of Gennesaret.

2299	ܘܪܕܘ	And they traveled on
0208	ܘܐܬܘ	and came
0199	ܠܐܪܥܐ	to the land
3156	ܕܓܢܣܪ	of Gennesaret

VERSE 35 — And the men of that place knew him and they sent [word] to all the villages of the surrounding area. And all those who were very sick came near to him.

1023	ܘܐܫܬܘܕܥܘܗܝ	And knew him
0131	ܐܢܫܐ	the men
0214	ܕܐܬܪܐ	of place
0593	ܗܘ	that
2458	ܘܫܕܪܘ	and they sent [word]
1168	ܠܟܠܗܘܢ	to all
2251	ܩܘܪܝܐ	the villages
0732	ܕܚܕܪܝܗܘܢ	of the surrounding area
2244	ܘܩܪܒܘ	And came near
1261	ܠܗ	to him
1168	ܟܠܗܘܢ	all
0066	ܐܝܠܝܢ	those
0220	ܕܒܝܫ	who were very sick
0220	ܒܝܫ	*
1724	ܥܒܝܕܝܢ	*

MATTHEW CHAPTER 14

VERSE 36 — And they were begging him that they might touch [him], even if only the outer edge of his clothing. And those who touched were healed.

0296		And begging
0603		they were
1388		him
2244		that they might touch [him]
0172		even if
1197		the outer edge
1041		only
1273		of his clothing
0066		And those
2244		who touched
0136		were healed

CHAPTER 15

VERSE 1 — Then the Pharisees and scribes, who were from Jerusalem, came near to Jesus and said,

0594		Then
2244		came near
1288		to
3257		Jesus
3439		the Pharisees
1699		and scribes
1388		who were from
3022		Jerusalem
0116		and said

VERSE 2 — "Why do your disciples cross against the tradition of the elders and do not wash their hands when they eat bread?

1394		Why
1304		your disciples
1733		do cross
1804		against
2533		the tradition
2263		of the elders
1262		and not
2466		do wash
0057		their hands
1313		when
0075		they eat
1293		bread

VERSE 3 — Jesus answered and said to them, "Why do you also cross against the commandment of God because of your tradition?

1838		answered
3257		Jesus
0116		and said
1261		to them
1394		Why
0169		also
0133		<you>
1733		do cross
0133		you
1804		against
2009		the commandment
0093		of God
1347		because of
2533		your tradition

VERSE 4 — For God said: HONOR YOUR FATHER AND YOUR MOTHER and HE WHO REVILES HIS FATHER AND HIS MOTHER SHOULD INDEED BE PUT TO DEATH.

0093		God
0403		For
0116		said
1076		HONOR
0002		YOUR FATHER
0106		AND YOUR MOTHER
1389		and HE WHO
2101		REVILES
0002		HIS FATHER
0106		AND HIS MOTHER
1334		SHOULD INDEED BE PUT TO DEATH
1334		*

Vertical Interlinear

MATTHEW — CHAPTER 15

VERSE 5 — But you say, 'Anyone who will say to a father or to a mother, [Let] whatever you have gained by me [be] my offering, and [then] he does not [need to] honor his father or his mother.'

Number	Aramaic	English
0133		<you>
0518		But
0116		say
0133		you
1168		Anyone
1389		who
0116		will say
0002		to a father
0024		or
0106		to a mother
2246		[Let] my offering [be]
1326		whatever
0613		you have gained
1388		by me
1262		and [then] not
1076		he does [need to] honor
0002		his father
0024		or
0106		his mother

VERSE 6 — And you nullify the word of God because of your tradition.

Number	Aramaic	English
0253		And you nullify
1364		the word
0093		of God
1347		because of
2533		tradition
0517		your

VERSE 7 — Hypocrites! Well did Isaiah prophesy concerning you and say:

Number	Aramaic	English
1532		Hypocrites
0173		*
2583		Well
1456		did prophesy
1804		concerning you
3109		Isaiah
0116		and say

VERSE 8 — THIS PEOPLE HONORS ME WITH THEIR LIPS, BUT THEIR HEART IS VERY FAR FROM ME.

Number	Aramaic	English
1818		PEOPLE
0598		THIS
1701		WITH THEIR LIPS
0592		<IT>
1076		HONORS
1261		ME
1268		THEIR HEART
0518		BUT
1596		VERY
2355		IS FAR
1388		FROM ME

VERSE 9 — AND VAINLY THEY REVERENCE ME, WHILE TEACHING THE DOCTRINES OF THE COMMANDMENTS OF MEN."

Number	Aramaic	English
1715		AND VAINLY
0509		THEY REVERENCE
1261		ME
1128		WHILE
1053		TEACHING
1054		THE DOCTRINES
2009		OF THE COMMANDMENTS
0325		OF MEN

VERSE 10 — And he cried out to the crowds and said to them, "Hear and understand.

Number	Aramaic	English
2239		And he cried out
1201		to the crowds
0116		and said
1261		to them
2547		Hear
1647		and understand

VERSE 11 — It is not what enters the mouth [that] corrupts a man, but what comes out of the mouth, that corrupts a man."

Number	Aramaic	English
1262		not
0603		It is
1326		what
1796		enters
1936		the mouth
1613		[that] corrupts

MATTHEW — CHAPTER 15

#	Syriac	English
0325		a man
0090		but
1326		what
1542		comes out
1388		of
1936		the mouth
0593		that
0592		<is>
1613		corrupts
0325		a man

VERSE 12 — Then his disciples came near and said to him, "Do you know that the Pharisees who heard this saying were offended?"

#	Syriac	English
0594		Then
2244		came near
1304		his disciples
0116		and said
1261		to him
1023		Do know
0133		you
3439		that the Pharisees
2547		who heard
1364		saying
0598		this
1242		were offended

VERSE 13 — Now he answered and said to them, "Every plant that my Father who is in heaven has not planted will be uprooted.

#	Syriac	English
0592		<he>
0518		Now
1838		he answered
0116		and said
1261		to them
1168		Every
1555		plant
0066		that
1262		not
1554		has planted
0002		my Father
2543		who is in heaven
1876		will be uprooted

VERSE 14 — Leave them alone. They are blind leaders of the blind. And if the blind lead the blind, both will fall into a pit."

#	Syriac	English
2440		Leave alone
1261		them
1662		blind
0592		They are
1464		leaders
1662		of the blind
1662		the blind
0518		And
1662		the blind
0121		if
0477		lead
2709		both
0422		into a pit
1538		will fall

VERSE 15 — And Simon Peter answered and said to him, "My Lord, explain to us this parable."

#	Syriac	English
1838		And answered
3521		Simon
3258		Peter
0116		and said
1261		to him
1426		My Lord
2061		explain
1261		to us
1454		parable
0598		this

VERSE 16 — And he said to them, "Until now do you also not understand?

#	Syriac	English
0592		<he>
0518		And
0116		he said
1261		to them
1747		Until
0602		now
0169		also
0133		<you>

MATTHEW CHAPTER 15

1262		not
1647		do understand
0133		you

VERSE 17 — Do you not know that whatever enters the mouth goes to the stomach and from there is cast out [of the body] by a bowel movement?

1262		not
1023		Do know
0133		you
1326		that whatever
1796		enters
1936		the mouth
1241		to the stomach
0592		<it>
0042		goes
1388		and from
2682		there
0526		by a bowel movement
2455		is cast
0322		out [of the body]

VERSE 18 — But what goes out of the mouth goes out of the heart and becomes corrupting to the man.

1326		what
0518		But
1388		of
1936		the mouth
1542		goes out
1388		of
1268		the heart
1542		goes out
0592		and becomes
1613		corrupting
1261		<to him>
0325		to the man

VERSE 19 — For from the heart go out evil thoughts: adultery, murder, fornication, theft, false witness, [and] blasphemy.

1388		from
1268		the heart
0592		<is>
0403		For
1542		go out
0917		thoughts
0220		evil
0386		adultery
2181		murder
0681		fornication
0438		theft
1610		witness
2482		false
0371		[and] blasphemy

VERSE 20 — These are [the things] that corrupt a man. But if a man eats while his hands are not washed, he is not corrupted."

0598		These
0592		are
1613		[the things] that corrupt
0325		a man
0121		if
0131		a man
0518		But
1308		eats
1128		while
1262		not
2466		are washed
0057		his hands
1262		not
1613		he is corrupted

VERSE 21 — And Jesus went out from there and came to the border of Tyre and Sidon.

1542		And went out
1388		from
2682		there
3257		Jesus
0208		and came
2659		to the border
3450		of Tyre
3452		and Sidon

Vertical Interlinear

MATTHEW   CHAPTER 15

VERSE 22 — And behold, a woman of Canaan from those borders came out crying and saying, "Have compassion on me, my Lord, Son of David. My daughter is seriously oppressed by a demon."

Code	Syriac	Gloss
0580	ܘܗܐ	And behold
0135	ܐܢܬܬܐ	a woman
3267	ܟܢܥܢܝܬܐ	of Canaan
1388	ܡܢ	from
2659	ܬܚܘܡܐ	borders
0593	ܗܢܘܢ	those
1542	ܢܦܩܬ	came out
1128	ܟܕ	crying
2227	ܩܥܝܐ	*
0116	ܘܐܡܪܐ	and saying
2342	ܐܬܪܚܡ	Have compassion
1804	ܥܠܝ	on me
1426	ܡܪܝ	my Lord
0323	ܒܪܗ	Son
3159	ܕܕܘܝܕ	of David
0327	ܒܪܬܝ	My daughter
0221	ܒܝܫܐܝܬ	is seriously
0477	ܡܬܕܒܪܐ	oppressed
1388	ܡܢ	by
2469	ܕܝܘܐ	a demon

VERSE 23 — But he did not answer her a word. And his disciples came near [and] begged him and said, "Send her away, because she cries after us."

Code	Syriac	Gloss
0592	ܗܘ	<he>
0518	ܕܝܢ	But
1262	ܠܐ	not
1984	ܦܢܝܗ	he did answer her
2068	ܦܬܓܡܐ	a word
2244	ܘܩܪܒܘ	And came near
1304	ܬܠܡܝܕܘܗܝ	his disciples
0296	ܒܥܘ	[and] begged
1388	ܡܢܗ	him
0116	ܘܐܡܪܝܢ	and said
2597	ܫܪܝܗ	Send her away
2227	ܕܩܥܝܐ	because she cries
0215	ܒܬܪܢ	after us

VERSE 24 — But he answered and said to them, "I have not been sent, except to the sheep that have strayed from the house of Israel."

Code	Syriac	Gloss
0592	ܗܘ	<he>
0518	ܕܝܢ	But
1838	ܥܢܐ	he answered
0116	ܘܐܡܪ	and said
1261	ܠܗܘܢ	to them
1262	ܠܐ	not
2458	ܐܫܬܕܪܬ	I have been sent
0090	ܐܠܐ	except
1288	ܠܘܬ	to
1887	ܥܪܒܐ	the sheep
0993	ܕܛܥܘ	that have strayed
1388	ܡܢ	from
0243	ܒܝܬ	the house of
3035	ܐܝܣܪܝܠ	Israel

VERSE 25 — And she came [and] worshipped him. And she said, "My Lord, help me."

Code	Syriac	Gloss
0592	ܗܝ	<she>
0518	ܕܝܢ	And
0208	ܐܬܬ	she came
1599	ܣܓܕܬ	[and] worshipped
1261	ܠܗ	him
0116	ܘܐܡܪܐ	And she said
1426	ܡܪܝ	My Lord
1751	ܥܕܪܝܢܝ	help me

VERSE 26 — He said to her, "It is not proper to take the bread of the children and to throw [it] to the dogs."

Code	Syriac	Gloss
0116	ܐܡܪ	He said
1261	ܠܗ	to her
1262	ܠܐ	not
2583	ܫܦܝܪ	It is proper
1532	ܠܡܣܒ	to take
1293	ܠܚܡܐ	the bread
0323	ܕܒܢܝܐ	of the children
2372	ܘܠܡܪܡܝܘ	and to throw [it]
1183	ܠܟܠܒܐ	to the dogs

Vertical Interlinear

MATTHEW CHAPTER 15

VERSE 27 — Now she said, "Yes, my Lord, [but] even the dogs eat from the crumbs that fall from the tables of their lords and live."

Code	Syriac	English
0592		<she>
0518		Now
0116		she said
0065		Yes
1426		my Lord
0169		[but] even
1183		the dogs
0075		eat
1388		from
2052		the crumbs
1538		that fall
1388		from
2069		the tables
1426		of their lords
0780		and live

VERSE 28 — Then Jesus said to her, "Oh woman, great is your faith. Let it be to you as you desire." And her daughter was healed at that moment.

Code	Syriac	English
0594		Then
0116		said
1261		to her
3257		Jesus
0025		Oh
0135		woman
2271		great
0592		is
0113		your faith
0603		Let it be
1261		to you
0060		as
2077		desire
0133		you
0136		And was healed
0327		her daughter
1388		at
0593		that moment
2573		*

VERSE 29 — And Jesus went away from there and came to the shore of the Sea of Galilee. And he climbed a mountain and sat there.

Code	Syriac	English
2561		And went away
1388		from
2682		there
3257		Jesus
0208		and came
1804		to
0439		the shore [of]
1057		the Sea
3153		of Galilee
1658		And he climbed
0958		a mountain
1093		and sat
2682		there

VERSE 30 — And large crowds came near to him in which there were the lame and blind and dumb and the maimed and many others. And they laid them at the feet of Jesus and he healed them,

Code	Syriac	English
2244		And came near
1288		to him
1201		crowds
1596		large
0069		there were
0603		*
1817		in which
0719		the lame
1662		and blind
0907		and dumb
2058		and the maimed
0053		and others
1596		many
2372		And they laid
0592		them
1288		at
2293		the feet
3257		of Jesus
0136		and he healed

MATTHEW — CHAPTER 15

0592		them
VERSE 31		so that those crowds were amazed who saw the dumb who spoke and the maimed who were made whole and the lame who walked and the blind who saw. And they praised the God of Israel.
0060		so that
0549		were amazed
1201		crowds
0593		those
0758		who saw
0907		the dumb
1362		who spoke
2058		and the maimed
0807		who were made whole
0719		and the lame
0608		who walked
1662		and the blind
0758		who saw
2428		And they praised
0093		the God
3035		of Israel
VERSE 32		But Jesus called to his disciples and said to them, "I have compassion for this crowd, because, behold, three days they have stayed with me and they do not have anything to eat. And I do not want to send them away fasting, so that they will not lose strength during the journey."
0592		<he>
0518		But
3257		Jesus
2239		called
1304		to his disciples
0116		and said
1261		to them
2342		have compassion
0124		I
1804		for
1201		crowd
0598		this
0580		because behold
2674		three
1036		days
2165		they have stayed
1288		with me
1264		and they do not have
1261		*
1313		anything
0075		to eat
2597		And to send away
0592		them
1128		fasting
2093		*
1262		not
2077		do want
0124		I
1314		so that not
1770		they will lose strength
0038		during the journey
VERSE 33		His disciples were saying to him, "Where is there bread for us in the desert to satisfy this whole crowd?"
0116		were saying
1261		to him
1304		His disciples
1110		Where is there
1261		for us
0892		in the desert
1293		bread
1585		to satisfy
1201		crowd
0598		this
1168		whole
VERSE 34		Jesus said to them, "How many [loaves of] bread do you have?" They said to him, "Seven and a few small fish."
0116		said
1261		to them
3257		Jesus
1188		How many
1293		[loaves of] bread

MATTHEW CHAPTER 15

0069	ܐܝܬ	do you have		1366	ܡܠܝܢ	full
1261	ܠܟܘܢ	*		2437	ܫܒܥܐ	seven
0116	ܐܡܪܝܢ	They said		0159	ܐܣܦܪܝܕܝܢ	baskets
1261	ܠܗ	to him		**VERSE**	**38**	Now those who ate were four thousand men, besides women and children.
2437	ܫܒܥܐ	Seven		0593	ܗܢܘܢ	those
2203	ܘܩܠܝܠ	and a few		0518	ܕܝܢ	Now
1490	ܢܘܢܐ	fish		0075	ܕܐܟܠܘ	who ate
0566	ܕܩܕܩܐ	small		0603	ܗܘܘ	were
VERSE	**35**	And he commanded the crowds to recline on the ground.		0603	ܗܘܘ	*
2007	ܘܦܩܕ	And he commanded		0179	ܐܪܒܥܐ	four
1201	ܠܟܢܫܐ	the crowds		0099	ܐܠܦܝܢ	thousand
1664	ܕܢܣܬܡܟܘܢ	to recline		0361	ܓܒܪܝܢ	men
1804	ܥܠ	on		1643	ܣܛܪ	besides
0199	ܐܪܥܐ	the ground		1388	ܡܢ	<from>
VERSE	**36**	And he took those seven [loaves of] bread and the fish and gave thanks and broke [them] into pieces and gave [them] to his disciples and the disciples gave [them] to the crowds.		0135	ܢܫܐ	women
				0976	ܘܛܠܝܐ	and children
				VERSE	**39**	And when he sent away the crowds, he boarded a ship and came to the border of Magdala.
2587	ܘܢܣܒ	And he took		1128	ܘܟܕ	And when
0598	ܠܗܠܝܢ	those		2597	ܫܪܐ	he sent away
2437	ܫܒܥܐ	seven		1201	ܠܟܢܫܐ	the crowds
1293	ܠܚܡܝܢ	[loaves of] bread		1658	ܣܠܩ	he boarded
1490	ܘܢܘܢܐ	and the fish		0100	ܐܠܦܐ	a ship
2428	ܘܐܘܕܝ	and gave thanks		0208	ܘܐܬܐ	and came
2234	ܘܩܨܐ	and broke [them] into pieces		2659	ܠܬܚܘܡܐ	to the border
1030	ܘܝܗܒ	and gave [them]		3296	ܕܡܓܕܠܐ	of Magdala
1304	ܠܬܠܡܝܕܘܗܝ	to his disciples		**CHAPTER**	**16**	
1304	ܘܬܠܡܝܕܐ	and the disciples		**VERSE**	**1**	And the Pharisees and Sadducees came near, tempting him and asking him to show them a sign from heaven.
1030	ܝܗܒܘ	gave [them]				
1201	ܠܟܢܫܐ	to the crowds		2244	ܘܩܪܒܘ	And came near
VERSE	**37**	And all of them ate and were satisfied. And they took up the rest of the fragments, seven baskets full.		3439	ܦܪܝܫܐ	the Pharisees
				3188	ܘܙܕܘܩܝܐ	and Saducees
0075	ܘܐܟܠܘ	And ate		1527	ܡܢܣܝܢ	tempting
1168	ܟܠܗܘܢ	all of them		1261	ܠܗ	him
1585	ܘܣܒܥܘ	and were satisfied		2420	ܘܫܐܠܝܢ	and asking
2587	ܘܫܩܠܘ	And they took up		1261	ܠܗ	him
1106	ܬܘܬܪܐ	the rest		0206	ܐܬܐ	a sign
2235	ܕܩܨܝܐ	of the fragments		1388	ܡܢ	from

Vertical Interlinear

MATTHEW   CHAPTER 16

2543		heaven
0739		to show
0592		them
VERSE 2		But he answered and said to them, "When it becomes evening, you say, 'It [will be] fair, for the sky is red.'
0592		\<he\>
0518		But
1838		he answered
0116		and said
1261		to them
1313		When
0603		it becomes
2375		evening
0116		say
0133		you
2100		[It will be] fair
0592		\<it\>
1669		is red
0403		for
2543		the sky
VERSE 3		And in the morning you say, 'Today it [will be] stormy for the sky is a gloomy red.' Hypocrites! You know [how] to investigate the appearance of the sky, [but] you do not know [how] to discern the signs of this time.
2124		And in the morning
0116		say
0133		you
1037		today
1718		[it will be] stormy
0592		\<it\>
1669		is red
0403		for
2543		the sky
1194		gloomy
1532		Hypocrites
0173		*
2041		the appearance
2543		of the sky
1023		know
0133		You
0316		[how] to investigate
0206		[but] the signs
0633		of time
0598		this
1262		not
1023		do know
0133		you
2046		[how] to discern
VERSE 4		An evil and adulterous generation seeks for a sign and a sign is not given to it, except the sign of Jonah the prophet." And he left them and went away.
2605		generation
0220		An evil
0388		and adulterous
0206		a sign
0296		seeks for
0206		and a sign
1262		not
1030		is given
1261		to it
0090		except
0206		the sign
3242		of Jonah
1457		the prophet
2440		And he left
0592		them
0042		and went away
VERSE 5		And when his disciples came to the other side, they had forgotten to take bread with them.
1128		And when
0208		came
1304		his disciples
1735		to the other side
0993		they had forgotten
1532		to take
1817		with them
1293		bread

MATTHEW CHAPTER 16

VERSE 6
Now he said to them, "Watch. Beware of the leaven of the Pharisees and the Sadducees."

Code	Syriac	Translation
0592		<he>
0518		Now
0116		he said
1261		to them
0758		Watch
0645		Beware
1388		of
0832		the leaven
3439		of the Pharisees
3188		and the Sadducees

VERSE 7
And they were reasoning among themselves and said that they had not taken bread.

Code	Syriac	Translation
0592		<they>
0518		And
2381		reasoning
0603		they were
1547		among themselves
0116		and said
1293		that bread
1262		not
1532		they had taken

VERSE 8
But Jesus knew and said to them, "What are you thinking to yourselves, little of faith, that [it is because] you did not bring bread?

Code	Syriac	Translation
3257		Jesus
0518		But
1023		knew
0116		and said
1261		to them
1393		What
0914		are thinking
0133		you
1547		to yourselves
0686		little of
0113		faith
1293		that [it is because] bread
1262		not
2587		you did bring

VERSE 9
Do you not yet understand? Do you not remember those five [loaves of] bread for the five thousand and how many baskets you took up?

Code	Syriac	Translation
1262		not
1747		yet
0602		*
1647		Do you understand
1262		not
1756		Do remember
0133		you
0593		those
0833		five
1293		[loaves of] bread
0833		for the five
0099		thousand
1188		and how many
2176		baskets
2587		you took up

VERSE 10
Nor those seven [loaves of] bread for the four thousand and how many baskets you took up?

Code	Syriac	Translation
1262		Nor
0593		those
2437		seven
1293		[loaves of] bread
0179		for the four
0099		thousand
1188		and how many
0159		baskets
2587		you took up

VERSE 11
How do you not understand that it was not about bread [that] I spoke to you, but that you should beware of the leaven of the Pharisees and of the Sadducees?"

Code	Syriac	Translation
0061		How
1262		not
1647		do you understand
1262		that not
0603		it was

Vertical Interlinear

MATTHEW CHAPTER 16

#	Syriac	English
1804		about
1293		bread
0116		[that] I spoke
1261		to you
0090		but
0645		that you should beware
1388		of
0832		the leaven
3439		of the Pharisees
3188		and of the Sadducees

VERSE 12 Then they understood that he did not say that they should beware of the leaven of bread, but of the doctrine of the Pharisees and of the Sadducees.

#	Syriac	English
0594		Then
1647		they understood
1262		that not
0116		he did say
0645		that they should beware
1388		of
0832		the leaven
1293		of bread
0090		but
1388		of
1054		the doctrine
3439		of the Pharisees
3188		and of the Sadducees

VERSE 13 And when Jesus came to the region of Caesarea Philippi, he was asking his disciples and said, "What are men saying about me, who is the Son of Man?"

#	Syriac	English
1128		when
0518		And
0208		came
3257		Jesus
0214		to the region
3485		of Caesarea Philippi
2420		asking
0603		he was
1304		his disciples

#	Syriac	English
0116		and said
1390		What
0116		are saying
1804		about me
0131		men
0069		who is
0323		the Son
0131		of Man

VERSE 14 And they said, "Some say [that you are] John the baptizer, but others [that you are] Elijah and others Jeremiah or one of the prophets."

#	Syriac	English
0592		<they>
0518		And
0116		they said
0069		Some
0116		say
3233		[that you are] John
1820		the baptizer
0053		others
0518		but
3047		[that you are] Elijah
0053		and others
3102		Jeremiah
0024		or
0721		one
1388		of
1457		the prophets

VERSE 15 He said to them, "But who do you say that I am?"

#	Syriac	English
0116		He said
1261		to them
0133		<you>
0518		But
1390		who
0116		say
0133		do you
0069		that I am

113

MATTHEW CHAPTER 16

VERSE 16		Simon Peter answered and said, "You are the Messiah, the Son of the living God."
1838		answered
3521		Simon
3258		Peter
0116		and said
0133		You
0592		are
1446		the Messiah
0323		the Son
0093		of God
0781		the living
VERSE 17		Jesus answered and said to him, "You are blessed, Simon, son of Jonah, because flesh and blood did not reveal [this] to you, but my Father who is in heaven.
1838		answered
3257		Jesus
0116		and said
1261		to him
0940		You are blessed
3521		Simon
3130		son of Jonah
0294		because flesh
0539		and blood
1262		not
0409		did reveal [this]
1261		to you
0090		but
0002		my Father
2543		who is in heaven
VERSE 18		Also I say to you, you are a rock and on this rock I will build my church and the gates of Sheol will not subdue it.
0169		Also
0124		<I>
0116		say
0124		I
1261		to you
0133		you
0592		are
1119		a rock
1804		and on
0598		this
1119		rock
0281		I will build
1755		my church
2718		and the gates
2422		of Sheol
1262		not
0861		will subdue it
VERSE 19		To you I will give the keys of the kingdom of heaven and anything that you bind on earth will be bound in heaven. And that which you loose on earth will be loosed in heaven."
1261		To you
1030		I will give
2205		the keys
1385		of the kingdom
2543		of heaven
1168		and anything
1326		*
0160		that you bind
0199		on earth
0603		will be
0160		bound
2543		in heaven
1326		And that
2597		which you loose
0199		on earth
0603		will be
2597		loosed
2543		in heaven
VERSE 20		Then he commanded his disciples that they should not tell anyone that he was the Messiah.
0594		Then
2007		he commanded
1304		his disciples
0131		that anyone

Vertical Interlinear

MATTHEW CHAPTER 16

#	Syriac	English
1262		not
0116		they should tell
0592		that he was
1446		the Messiah

VERSE 21 — And from then [on], Jesus began to show his disciples that he would go to Jerusalem and suffer much from the elders and from the chief priests and scribes and [that] he would be killed and on the third day would rise up.

#	Syriac	English
1388		And from
0594		then [on]
2597		began
3257		Jesus
0739		to show
1304		his disciples
1914		that <would>
0592		<he>
0042		he would go
3022		to Jerusalem
1596		and much
0911		he would suffer
1388		from
2263		the elders
1388		and from
2271		the chief priests
1135		*
1699		and scribes
2179		and [that] he would be killed
1036		and on the day
2674		third
2168		would rise up

VERSE 22 — Yet Peter took him and began to berate him. And he said, "Forbid it to you, my Lord, that this [thing] should happen to you."

#	Syriac	English
0477		Yet took him
3258		Peter
2597		and began
1113		to berate
0217		him
0116		And he said
0850		Forbid it
1261		to you
1426		my Lord
0603		that should happen
1261		to you
0598		this [thing]

VERSE 23 — But he turned and said to Peter, "Go behind me, Satan! You are a stumbling block to me, because you do not think [the things] of God, but of men."

#	Syriac	English
0592		<he>
0518		But
1984		he turned
0116		and said
3258		to Peter
0042		Go
1261		<to you>
0295		behind me
1642		Satan
2698		a stumbling block
0133		You are
1261		to me
1262		because not
2381		do think
0133		you
0093		[the things] of God
0090		but
0323		of men
0131		*

VERSE 24 — Then Jesus said to his disciples, "He who wants to follow me should deny himself and take up his cross and follow me.

#	Syriac	English
0594		Then
0116		said
3257		Jesus
1304		to his disciples
1389		He who
2077		wants
0208		to follow me
0215		*

115

MATTHEW CHAPTER 16

Code	Syriac	English
1215		should deny
1547		himself
2587		and take up
0689		his cross
0208		and follow me
0215		*

VERSE 25 — For he who wants to save his life will lose it. And he who will lose his life because of me will find it.

Code	Syriac	English
1389		he who
2077		wants
0403		For
0780		to save
1547		his life
0005		will lose it
1389		And he who
0005		will lose
1547		his life
1347		because of me
2510		will find it

VERSE 26 — For what does a man profit if he gains the whole world and loses his life? Or what [thing of] exchange will a man give for his life?

Code	Syriac	English
1393		what
0403		For
0613		does profit
0325		a man
0121		if
1168		whole
1813		the world
2216		he gains
1547		and his life
0865		loses
0024		Or
1393		what
1030		will give
0325		a man
0815		[thing of] exchange
1547		for his life

VERSE 27 — For THE SON OF MAN IS ABOUT TO COME IN THE GLORY OF HIS FATHER WITH HIS HOLY ANGELS. And then he will reward each man according to his works.

Code	Syriac	English
1914		ABOUT
0592		IS
0403		For
0323		THE SON
0131		OF MAN
0208		TO COME
2432		IN THE GLORY
0002		OF HIS FATHER
1817		WITH
1375		HIS ANGELS
2162		HOLY
0594		And then
2037		he will reward
0131		man
0131		each
0060		according to
1728		his works

VERSE 28 — Truly I say to you, there are men who are standing here who will not taste death until they will see the Son of Man come in his kingdom."

Code	Syriac	English
0110		Truly
0116		say
0124		I
1261		to you
0069		there are
0131		men
2168		who are standing
2694		here
1262		who not
0998		will taste
1335		death
1747		until
0758		they will see
0323		the Son
0131		of Man

MATTHEW CHAPTER 16

0208		come
1385		in his kingdom

CHAPTER 17

VERSE 1 — And after six days, Jesus led Peter and James and John his brother and took them up to a high mountain alone.

0215		And after
2615		six
1036		days
0477		led
3257		Jesus
3258		Peter
3255		and James
3233		and John
0043		his brother
1658		and took up
0592		them
0958		to a mountain
2336		high
1041		alone

VERSE 2 — And Jesus was transformed before them and his face was bright like the sun. And his clothes became white like light.

0811		And was transformed
3257		Jesus
2154		before them
1474		and was bright
2041		his face
0060		like
2557		the sun
1501		his clothes
0518		And
0754		became white
0060		like
1477		light

VERSE 3 — And [there] appeared to them Moses and Elijah speaking with him.

0758		And [there] appeared
1261		to them
3305		Moses
3047		and Elijah
1128		speaking
1362		*
1817		with him

VERSE 4 — And Peter answered and said to Jesus, "My Lord, it is good for us that we were here. And if you want, we will make here three booths, one for you and one for Moses and one for Elijah."

1838		answered
0518		And
3258		Peter
0116		and said
3257		to Jesus
1426		My Lord
2583		is good
0592		it
1261		for us
2694		that here
0603		we were
0121		And if
2077		want
0133		you
1724		we will make
2694		here
2674		three
0974		booths
0721		one
1261		for you
0721		and one
3305		for Moses
0721		and one
3047		for Elijah

VERSE 5 — And while he was speaking, behold, a bright cloud overshadowed them. And a voice came from the cloud that said, "This is my beloved Son in whom I am pleased. Hear him."

1744		And while
0592		he
1362		was speaking
0580		behold
1844		a cloud

MATTHEW CHAPTER 17

1475	ܢܗܝܪܐ	bright		1794	ܥܝܢܝܗܘܢ	their eyes
0970	ܐܛܠܬ	overshadowed		0131	ܘܠܐܢܫ	and anyone
1804	ܠܗܘܢ	them		1262	ܠܐ	not
2204	ܘܩܠܐ	And a voice		0758	ܚܙܘ	did see
0603	ܗܘܐ	came		0090	ܐܠܐ	except
1388	ܡܢ	from		0121	ܐܢ	*
1844	ܥܢܢܐ	the cloud		3257	ܠܝܫܘܥ	Jesus
0116	ܘܐܡܪ	that said		1041	ܠܒܠܚܘܕܘܗܝ	alone
0599	ܗܢܘ	This is		**VERSE**	**9**	And while they were coming down from the mountain, Jesus commanded them and said to them, "Do not speak [about] this vision in the presence of anyone until the Son of Man rises from the dead."
0323	ܒܪܝ	my Son				
0698	ܚܒܝܒܐ	beloved				
0217	ܕܒܗ	in whom				
2077	ܐܨܛܒܝܬ	I am pleased		1128	ܘܟܕ	And while
1261	ܠܗ	him		1499	ܢܚܬܝܢ	they were coming down
2547	ܫܡܥܘ	Hear		1388	ܡܢ	from
VERSE	**6**	And when the disciples heard [this], they fell on their faces and were very afraid.		0958	ܛܘܪܐ	the mountain
				2007	ܦܩܕ	commanded
1128	ܘܟܕ	And when		0592	ܐܢܘܢ	them
2547	ܫܡܥܘ	heard [this]		3257	ܝܫܘܥ	Jesus
1304	ܬܠܡܝܕܐ	the disciples		0116	ܘܐܡܪ	and said
1538	ܢܦܠܘ	they fell		1261	ܠܗܘܢ	to them
1804	ܥܠ	on		1794	ܠܥܝܢ	in the presence of
0173	ܐܦܝܗܘܢ	their faces		0131	ܐܢܫ	anyone
0509	ܘܕܚܠܘ	and were afraid		1262	ܠܐ	not
0938	ܛܒ	very		0116	ܬܐܡܪܘܢ	Do not speak
VERSE	**7**	And Jesus came near to them and touched them and said, "Stand up. Do not be afraid."		0759	ܚܙܘܐ	[about] vision
				0598	ܗܢܐ	this
				1747	ܥܕܡܐ	until
2244	ܘܐܬܩܪܒ	And came near		2168	ܕܢܩܘܡ	rises
1288	ܠܘܬܗܘܢ	to them		0323	ܒܪܗ	the Son
3257	ܝܫܘܥ	Jesus		0131	ܕܐܢܫܐ	of Man
2244	ܘܩܪܒ	and touched		1388	ܡܢ	from
1261	ܠܗܘܢ	them		1338	ܡܝܬܐ	the dead
0116	ܘܐܡܪ	and said		**VERSE**	**10**	And his disciples asked him and said to him, "Why then do the scribes say that Elijah ought to come first?"
2168	ܩܘܡܘ	Stand up				
1262	ܠܐ	not				
0509	ܬܕܚܠܘܢ	Do be afraid		2420	ܘܫܐܠܘܗܝ	And asked him
VERSE	**8**	And they raised their eyes and did not see anyone, except Jesus alone.		1304	ܬܠܡܝܕܘܗܝ	his disciples
				0116	ܘܐܡܪܝܢ	and said
2331	ܘܐܪܝܡܘ	And they raised				

MATTHEW CHAPTER 17

1261		to him		0323		the Son
1393		Why		0131		of Man
0596		then		1914		is about
1699		the scribes		0911		to suffer
0116		do say		1388		from them

VERSE 13 Then the disciples understood that he spoke to them about John the baptizer.

3047		that Elijah
0626		ought
0208		to come
2151		first

0594		Then
1647		understood
1304		the disciples
1804		that about
3233		John
1820		the baptizer
0116		he spoke
1261		to them

VERSE 11 Jesus answered and said, "Elijah comes first to fulfill everything.

1838		answered
3257		Jesus
0116		and said
3047		Elijah
0208		comes
2151		first
1168		everything
1326		*
2530		to fulfill

VERSE 14 And when they came to the crowd, a man came near to him and bowed down on his knees

1128		And when
0208		they came
1288		to
1201		the crowd
2244		came near
1261		to him
0361		a man
0335		and bowed down
1804		on
0336		his knees

VERSE 12 But I say to you, behold, Elijah has come and they did not know him and they did with him whatever they desired. So also the Son of Man is about to suffer from them."

0116		say
0124		I
1261		to you
0518		But
0580		behold
3047		Elijah
0208		has come
1262		and not
1023		they did know him
1724		and they did
0217		with him
1168		whatever
1313		*
2077		they desired
0597		So
0169		also

VERSE 15 and said to him, "My Lord, have compassion on me. My son is one who is insane and he is seriously afflicted, for many times he has fallen into the fire and many times in the water.

0116		and said
1261		to him
1426		My Lord
2342		have compassion
1804		on me
0323		My son
0069		is
1261		<to him>

119

MATTHEW CHAPTER 17

#			#		
0323		one who is insane	1111		here
0019		*	VERSE	18	And Jesus rebuked it and the demon went out of him and the child was healed at that moment.
0221		and seriously			
1724		he is afflicted	1113		And rebuked
1188		many	0217		it
0403		for	3257		Jesus
0633		times	1542		and went out
1494		into the fire	1388		of him
1538		he has fallen	2469		the demon
1188		and many	0136		and was healed
0633		times	0976		the child
1351		in the water	1388		at
VERSE	16	And I brought him to your disciples and they were not able to heal him."	0593		that moment
			2573		*
2244		And I brought him	VERSE	19	Then the disciples came near to Jesus alone and said to him, "Why were we not able to heal him?"
1304		to your disciples			
1262		and not			
2510		they were able	0594		Then
0136		to heal him	2244		came near
VERSE	17	Jesus answered and said, "Oh faithless and perverted generation! How long must I be with you and how long must I endure you? Bring him here to me."	1304		the disciples
			1288		to
			3257		Jesus
			1041		alone
1838		answered	0116		and said
3257		Jesus	1261		to him
0116		and said	1394		Why
0033		Oh	0124		<we>
2605		generation	1262		not
1262		faithless	2510		were we able
0114		*	0136		to heal him
1871		and perverted	VERSE	20	Jesus said to them, "Because of your unbelief. For truly I say to you, if you have faith like a grain of mustard seed, you can say to this mountain, 'Move from here,' and it will move and nothing will overcome you.
1747		How long			
0120		*			
0603		must I be			
1817		with you			
1747		and how long	0116		said
0120		*	1261		to them
1588		must I endure you	3257		Jesus
0208		Bring him	1347		Because of
1261		to me	1262		your unbelief

MATTHEW — CHAPTER 17

0113	ܘܐܡܪܝܢ	*		0116	ܐܡܪ	said
0110	ܐܡܝܢ	truly		1261	ܠܗܘܢ	to them
0403	ܓܝܪ	For		3257	ܝܫܘܥ	Jesus
0116	ܐܡܪ	say		1914	ܥܬܝܕ	about to be
0124	ܐܢܐ	I		0592	ܗܘ	is
1261	ܠܟܘܢ	to you		0323	ܒܪܗ	The Son
0121	ܕܐܢ	if		0131	ܕܐܢܫܐ	of Man
0603	ܬܗܘܐ	you have		2530	ܕܢܫܬܠܡ	betrayed
0217	ܒܟܘܢ	<in you>		0057	ܠܐܝܕܝ	into the hands
0113	ܗܝܡܢܘܬܐ	faith		0323	ܒܢܝ	of men
0060	ܐܝܟ	like		0131	ܐܢܫܐ	*
2019	ܦܪܕܬܐ	a grain		**VERSE 23**		And they will kill him and on the third day, he will rise up." And [the saying] saddened them very much.
0895	ܕܚܪܕܠܐ	of mustard seed				
0116	ܬܐܡܪܘܢ	you can say		2179	ܘܢܩܛܠܘܢܝܗܝ	And they will kill him
0958	ܠܛܘܪܐ	to mountain		1036	ܘܠܝܘܡܐ	and on the day
0598	ܗܢܐ	this		2674	ܕܬܠܬܐ	third
2561	ܕܫܢܐ	Move from		2168	ܢܩܘܡ	he will rise up
1112	ܡܟܐ	here		1221	ܘܟܪܝܬ	And [the saying] saddened
2561	ܘܢܫܢܐ	and it will move		1261	ܠܗܘܢ	them
1326	ܘܡܕܡ	and nothing		0938	ܛܒ	very much
1262	ܠܐ	*		**VERSE 24**		And when they came to Capernaum, those who were receiving the two drachmas for the poll tax came near to Peter. And they said to him, "Does not your master give his two drachmas?"
0861	ܢܚܣܢܟܘܢ	will overcome you				
VERSE 21		But this kind does not go out, except by fasting and by prayer."				
0598	ܗܢܐ	this		1128	ܘܟܕ	And when
0518	ܕܝܢ	But		0208	ܐܬܘ	they came
0444	ܓܢܣܐ	kind		3268	ܠܟܦܪܢܚܘܡ	to Capernaum
1262	ܠܐ	not		2244	ܩܪܒܘ	came near
1542	ܢܦܩ	does go out		0593	ܗܢܘܢ	those
0090	ܐܠܐ	except		1532	ܕܢܣܒܝܢ	who were receiving
2094	ܒܨܘܡܐ	by fasting		2709	ܬܪܝܢ	the two
2107	ܘܒܨܠܘܬܐ	and by prayer		2709	ܬܪܝܢ	*
VERSE 22		Now while they were traveling in Galilee, Jesus said to them, "The Son of Man is about to be betrayed into the hands of men."		0651	ܙܘܙܝܢ	drachmas
				1209	ܕܟܣܦ	for the poll tax
				2362	ܪܫܐ	*
1128	ܟܕ	while		1288	ܠܘܬ	to
0616	ܡܬܗܦܟܝܢ	they were traveling		3258	ܟܐܦܐ	Peter
0518	ܕܝܢ	Now		0116	ܘܐܡܪܝܢ	And they said
3153	ܒܓܠܝܠܐ	in Galilee		1261	ܠܗ	to him

121

MATTHEW CHAPTER 17

2271		your master	
1262		not	
1030		Does give	
2709		two	
0651		his drachmas	

VERSE 25 He said to them, "Yes." And when Peter entered the house, Jesus anticipated him and said to him, "What does it appear to you, Simon? The kings of the earth, from whom do they receive tribute and the poll tax, from their children or from strangers?"

0116		He said
1261		to them
0065		Yes
1128		And when
1796		entered
3258		Peter
0243		the house
2150		anticipated him
3257		Jesus
0116		and said
1261		to him
1393		What
0758		does it appear
1261		to you
3521		Simon
1383		The kings
0199		of the earth
1388		from
1389		whom
1532		do they receive
1359		tribute
1209		and the poll tax
2362		*
1389		from
0323		their children
0024		or
1388		from
1522		strangers

VERSE 26 Simon said to him, "From strangers." Jesus said to him, "Then the children are free.

0116		said
1261		to him
3521		Simon
1388		From
1522		strangers
0116		said
1261		to him
3257		Jesus
1324		Then
0323		free
0886		*
0592		are
0323		the children

VERSE 27 But so that [this] should not offend them, go to the sea and cast a fishhook. And the first fish that comes up, open its mouth and you will find a stater. Take that and give [it] for me and for you."

1262		so that not
0518		But
1242		[this] should offend
0592		them
0042		go
1057		to the sea
2372		and cast
0278		a fishhook
1490		And the fish
2157		first
1658		that comes up
2070		open
1936		its mouth
2510		and you will find
0168		a stater
0593		that
1532		Take
1030		and give [it]
0812		for me
0812		and for you

Vertical Interlinear

MATTHEW — CHAPTER 18

CHAPTER 18

VERSE 1 — At that time, the disciples came near to Jesus and said, "Who is indeed great in the kingdom of heaven?"

Code	Aramaic	English
0593		At that
2573		time
2244		came near
1304		the disciples
1288		to
3257		Jesus
0116		and said
1390		Who is
1163		indeed
2271		great
1385		in the kingdom
2543		of heaven

VERSE 2 — And Jesus called a child and set him among them

Code	Aramaic	English
2239		And called
3257		Jesus
0976		a child
2168		and set him
0266		among them

VERSE 3 — and said, "Truly I say to you, if you do not change and become like children, you will not enter into the kingdom of heaven.

Code	Aramaic	English
0116		and said
0110		Truly
0116		I say
1261		to you
0090		if
0616		you do not change
0603		and become
0060		like
0976		children
1262		not
1796		you will enter
1385		into the kingdom
2543		of heaven

VERSE 4 — Therefore, he who humbles himself like this child will be great in the kingdom of heaven.

Code	Aramaic	English
1389		he who
0596		Therefore
1353		humbles
1547		himself
0060		like
0598		this
0976		child
0592		<he>
0603		will be
2271		great
1385		in the kingdom
2543		of heaven

VERSE 5 — And he who receives [one] like this child in my name receives me.

Code	Aramaic	English
1389		And he who
2134		receives
0060		[one] like
0976		child
0598		this
2539		in my name
1261		me
2134		receives

VERSE 6 — And anyone who causes one of these little ones who believe in me to stumble, it would be better for him that the millstone of a donkey would be hung on his neck and he be sunk in the depths of the sea.

Code	Aramaic	English
1168		And anyone
1242		who causes to stumble
0721		one
1388		of
0598		these
0686		little ones
0109		who believe
0217		in me
2010		it would be better
0603		*
1261		for him

Vertical Interlinear

MATTHEW — CHAPTER 18

0603	ܕܗܘܐ	that would be		1388	ܠܟ	from you
2672	ܬܠܐ	hung		0938	ܛܒ	better
2341	ܪܚܝܐ	the millstone		0592	ܗܘ	It is
0830	ܕܚܡܪܐ	of a donkey		1261	ܠ	for you
2097	ܒܨܘܪܗ	on his neck		1796	ܕܬܥܘܠ	to enter
0945	ܘܡܛܒܥ	and he be sunk		0782	ܠܚܝܐ	life
1831	ܒܥܘܡܩܘܗܝ	in the depths		1128	ܟܕ	while
1057	ܕܝܡܐ	of the sea		0718	ܚܓܝܣ	are lame

VERSE 7 — Woe to the world because of offenses! For it is necessary that offenses should come. But woe to the man by whose hand the offenses come!

				0133	ܐܢܬ	you
				0024	ܐܘ	or
				1128	ܟܕ	while
0625	ܘܝ	Woe		2058	ܦܫܝܓ	maimed
1813	ܠܥܠܡܐ	to the world		1262	ܘܠܐ	and not
1388	ܡܢ	because of		1128	ܟܕ	while
1244	ܡܟܫܘܠܐ	offenses		0069	ܐܝܬ	you have
0128	ܐܢܢܩܐ	it is necessary		1261	ܠܟ	*
0403	ܓܝܪ	For		2709	ܬܪܬܝܢ	two
0208	ܕܢܐܬܘܢ	that should come		0057	ܐܝܕܝܢ	hands
1244	ܡܟܫܘܠܐ	offenses		0024	ܐܘ	or
0625	ܘܝ	woe		2709	ܬܪܬܝܢ	two
0518	ܕܝܢ	But		2293	ܪܓܠܝܢ	feet
0361	ܠܒܪܢܫܐ	to the man		1538	ܬܦܠ	to fall
0057	ܕܒܐܝܕܗ	by whose hand		1494	ܒܢܘܪܐ	into fire
0208	ܢܐܬܘܢ	come		1813	ܕܠܥܠܡ	everlasting
1244	ܡܟܫܘܠܐ	the offenses				

VERSE 9 — And if your eye causes you to stumble, tear it out and throw it away from you. It is better for you that you enter life with one eye and not, while you have two eyes, to fall into the Gehenna of fire.

VERSE 8 — Now if your hand or your foot causes you to stumble, cut it off and throw it away from you. It is better for you to enter life while you are lame or while maimed, and not, while you have two hands or two feet, to fall into everlasting fire.

				0121	ܘܐܢ	And if
				0592	ܗܘ	<it>
0121	ܐܢ	if		1794	ܥܝܢܟ	your eye
0518	ܕܝܢ	Now		1242	ܡܟܫܠܐ	causes to stumble
0057	ܐܝܕܟ	your hand		1261	ܠܟ	you
0024	ܐܘ	or		0877	ܚܨܝܗ	tear it out
2293	ܪܓܠܟ	your foot		2455	ܘܫܕܝܗ	and throw it away
1242	ܡܟܫܠܐ	causes to stumble		1388	ܡܢܟ	from you
1261	ܠܟ	you		0938	ܛܒ	better
1992	ܦܣܘܩܝܗ	cut it off		0592	ܗܘ	It is
2455	ܘܫܕܝܗ	and throw it away		1261	ܠܟ	for you

MATTHEW CHAPTER 18

0721		that with one
1794		eye
1796		you enter
0782		life
1262		and not
1128		while
0069		you have
1261		*
2709		two
1794		eyes
1538		to fall
3148		into the Gehenna
1494		of fire

VERSE 10 — See, you should not despise one of these little ones, for I say to you, their angels that are in heaven always see the face of my Father who is in heaven.

0758		See
1262		not
0284		you should despise
1804		<on>
0721		one
1388		of
0598		these
0686		little ones
0116		say
0124		I
1261		to you
0403		for
1375		their angels
2543		in heaven
1170		always
0758		see
2041		the face
0002		of my Father
2543		who is in heaven

VERSE 11 — For the Son of Man has come to make alive that which was perishing.

0208		has come
0403		For
0323		the Son
0131		of Man
0780		to make alive
1326		that
0007		which perishing
0603		was

VERSE 12 — What does it appear to you? If a man had one hundred sheep and one of them strayed, does he not leave the ninety-nine on the mountain and go [and] seek that which has strayed?

1393		What
0758		does it appear
1261		to you
0121		If
0603		had
0131		a man
1317		one hundred
1887		sheep
0993		and strayed
0721		one
1388		of them
1262		not
2440		does he leave
2724		the ninety-
2723		<and> nine
0958		on the mountain
0042		and go
0296		[and] seek
0593		that
0993		which has strayed

VERSE 13 — And if he finds it, truly I say to you, he rejoices at it more than the ninety-nine that did not stray.

0121		And if
2510		he finds it
0110		truly
0116		I say
1261		to you
0726		he rejoices
0217		at it

Vertical Interlinear

MATTHEW   CHAPTER 18

1100		more
1388		than
2724		the ninety-
2723		<and> nine
1262		that not
0993		did stray

VERSE 14   Likewise, it is not the will before your Father who is in heaven that one of these little ones should perish.

0597		Likewise
1264		it is not
2079		the will
2154		before
0002		your Father
2543		who is in heaven
0005		that should perish
0721		one
1388		of
0686		little ones
0598		these

VERSE 15   Now if your brother offends you, go [and] reprove him between you and him alone. If he hears you, you have gained your brother.

0121		if
0518		Now
1647		offends
0217		you
0043		your brother
0042		go
1203		[and] reprove him
0266		between you
1261		and him
1041		alone
0121		If
2547		he hears you
1098		you have gained
0043		your brother

VERSE 16   And if he does not hear you, take with you one or two [others] that, AT THE MOUTH OF TWO OR THREE WITNESSES EVERY WORD WILL BE ESTABLISHED.

0090		And if not
2547		he does hear you
0477		take
1817		with you
0721		one
0024		or
2709		two [others]
1804		that AT
1936		THE MOUTH OF
2709		TWO
0024		OR
2674		THREE
1608		WITNESSES
2168		WILL BE ESTABLISHED
1168		EVERY
1364		WORD

VERSE 17   Now if he will not hear them also, tell the church. And if he will not hear the church also, he will be to you like a tax collector and like a heathen.

0121		if
0518		Now
0169		also
1262		not
0593		them
2547		he will hear
0116		tell
1755		the church
0121		if
0518		And
0169		also
1262		not
1755		the church
2547		he will hear
0603		he will be
1261		to you

MATTHEW   CHAPTER 18

#	Syriac	English
0060		like
1358		a tax collector
0060		and like
0847		a heathen

VERSE 18 — And truly I say to you, anything that you bind on earth will be bound in heaven. And that which you loose on earth will be loosed in heaven.

#	Syriac	English
0110		And truly
0116		say
0124		I
1261		to you
1168		anything
1313		*
0160		that you bind
0199		on earth
0603		will be
0160		bound
2543		in heaven
1326		And that
2597		which you loose
0199		on earth
0603		will be
2597		loosed
2543		in heaven

VERSE 19 — Again I say to you, if two of you agree on earth concerning every matter that they will ask, they will have [an answer] from the presence of my Father who is in heaven.

#	Syriac	English
2650		Again
0116		I say
1261		to you
0121		if
2709		two
1388		of you
2461		agree
0199		on earth
1804		concerning
1168		every
2078		matter
2420		that they will ask
0603		they will have
1261		*
1388		[an answer] from
1288		the presence of
0002		my Father
2543		who is in heaven

VERSE 20 — For where two or three are gathered in my name, there I am among them."

#	Syriac	English
1108		where
0403		For
2709		two
0024		or
2674		three
1198		are gathered
2539		in my name
2682		there
0124		I am
0266		among them

VERSE 21 — Then Peter came near to him and said, "My Lord, if my brother offends me, how many times should I forgive him? Up to seven times?"

#	Syriac	English
0594		Then
2244		came near
1288		to him
3258		Peter
0116		and said
1426		My Lord
1188		how many
0633		times
0121		if
1647		offends
0217		me
0043		my brother
2440		should I forgive
1261		him
1747		Up to
2437		seven
0633		times

MATTHEW   CHAPTER 18

VERSE	**22**	Jesus said to him, "I do not say to you up to seven [times], but up to seventy times, by sevens.
0116		said
1261		to him
3257		Jesus
1262		not
0116		do say
0124		I
1261		to you
1747		up to
2437		seven [times]
0090		but
1747		Up to
2439		seventy
0633		times
2437		by sevens
2437		*
VERSE	**23**	Because of this, the kingdom of heaven is compared to a certain king, who wanted to take an accounting of his servants.
1347		Because of
0598		this
0540		is compared
1385		the kingdom
2543		of heaven
0361		to a certain
1383		king
2077		who wanted
1532		to take
0916		an accounting
1388		of
1727		his servants
VERSE	**24**	And when he began to take [the accounting], they brought to him one who owed ten thousand talents.
1128		And when
2597		he began
1532		to take [the accounting]
2244		they brought

1261		to him
0721		one
0745		who owed
2274		ten thousand
1166		talents
VERSE	**25**	And when he had no [way] to repay, his lord commanded that he should be sold and his wife and his children and everything that was his and [that] he should repay [the debt].
1128		And when
1264		he had no [way]
1261		*
2037		to repay
2007		commanded
1426		his lord
0632		that he should be sold
0592		<he>
0135		and his wife
0323		and his children
1168		and everything
1326		*
0069		that was his
1261		*
2037		and [that] he should repay [the debt]
VERSE	**26**	And the servant fell down [and] worshipped him and said, 'My lord, be patient with me and I will repay everything to you.'
1538		And fell down
0593		<that>
1727		the servant
1599		[and] worshipped
1261		him
0116		and said
1426		My lord
1466		be patient
1804		with me
2323		<spirit>
1168		and everything
1326		*

MATTHEW CHAPTER 18

2037		I will repay
0124		is compared
1261		to you

VERSE 27 — And the lord of that servant had compassion and sent him away and forgave him his debt.

2342		And had compassion
1426		the lord
1727		of servant
0593		that
2597		and sent him away
0743		and his debt
2440		forgave
1261		him

VERSE 28 — Now that servant went out and found one of his fellow-servants, who owed him one hundred denarii, and he grabbed him and was choking him, and said to him, 'Give me that which you owe me.'

1542		went out
0518		Now
1727		servant
0593		that
2510		and found
0721		one
1388		of
1202		his fellow-servants
0745		who owed
0603		*
1261		him
0519		denarii
1317		one hundred
0047		and he grabbed him
0848		and choking
0603		was
1261		him
0116		and said
1261		to him
1030		Give
1261		me

1326		that which
0745		owe
0133		you
1261		me

VERSE 29 — And that [man], his fellow-servant, fell at his feet, begged him and said to him, 'Be patient with me and I will repay you.'

1538		And fell
0593		that [man]
1202		his fellow-servant
1804		at
2293		his feet
0296		begged
1388		him
0116		and said
1261		to him
1466		Be patient
1804		with me
2323		<spirit>
2037		and will repay
0124		I
1261		you

VERSE 30 — And he did not want [to], but went [and] threw him into prison, until he would pay him what he owed him.

0592		<he>
0518		And
1262		not
2077		he did want [to]
0090		but
0042		went
2372		[and] threw him
0243		into prison
0163		*
1747		until
1030		he would pay
1261		him
1313		what
0745		he owed
1261		him

MATTHEW CHAPTER 18

VERSE 31 — Now when their fellow-servants saw what had happened, it saddened them very much. And they came [and] made known to their lord all that happened.

Code	Syriac	English
1128		when
0758		saw
0518		Now
1202		their fellow-servants
1326		what
0603		had happened
1221		it saddened
1261		them
0938		very much
0208		And they came
1023		[and] made known
1426		to their lord
1168		all
0603		that happened

VERSE 32 — Then his lord called him and said to that evil servant, "I forgave you all of the debt because you begged me.

Code	Syriac	English
0594		Then
2239		called him
1426		his lord
0116		and said
1261		to <him>
1727		servant
0220		evil
0593		that
1168		all of
0743		the debt
2440		I forgave
1261		you
0296		because you begged
1388		me

VERSE 33 — Was it not proper for you also to have mercy toward your fellow-servant, as I had mercy on you?"

Code	Syriac	English
1262		not
0626		Was proper
0603		it
1261		for you
0169		also
0133		<you>
0840		to have mercy
1202		toward your fellow-servant
0061		as
0124		I had
0840		mercy on you

VERSE 34 — And his lord was angry and delivered him to the torturers, until he would repay everything that he owed him.

Code	Syriac	English
2290		And was angry
1426		his lord
2530		and delivered him
1462		to the torturers
1747		until
2037		he would repay
1168		everything
1326		*
0745		that he owed
1261		him

VERSE 35 — Likewise my Father who is in heaven will do to you, unless you each forgive his brother his offense from your heart."

Code	Syriac	English
0597		Likewise
1724		will do
1261		to you
0002		my Father
2543		who is in heaven
0090		unless
2440		you forgive
0131		each
0043		his brother
1388		from
1268		your heart
1652		his offense

Vertical Interlinear

MATTHEW

CHAPTER	19	
VERSE	1	And it happened that when Jesus finished these words, he started from Galilee and came to the border of Judea on the other side of Jordan.
0603	ܘܗܘܐ	And it happened
1128	ܕܟܕ	that when
2530	ܫܠܡ	finished
3257	ܝܫܘܥ	Jesus
1364	ܡܠܐ	words
0598	ܗܠܝܢ	these
2587	ܫܩܠ	he started
1388	ܡܢ	from
3153	ܓܠܝܠܐ	Galilee
0208	ܘܐܬܐ	and came
2659	ܠܬܚܘܡܐ	to the border
3224	ܕܝܗܘܕ	of Judea
1735	ܒܥܒܪܐ	on the other side
3248	ܕܝܘܪܕܢܢ	of the Jordan
VERSE	2	And large crowds followed him and he healed them there.
0208	ܘܐܙܠܘ	And followed him
0215	ܒܬܪܗ	*
1201	ܟܢܫܐ	crowds
1596	ܣܓܝܐܐ	large
0136	ܘܐܣܝ	and he healed
0592	ܐܢܘܢ	them
2682	ܬܡܢ	there
VERSE	3	And the Pharisees came near to him and were tempting him and saying, "Is it lawful for a man to put away his wife on any occasion?"
2244	ܘܩܪܒܘ	And came near
1288	ܠܘܬܗ	to him
3439	ܦܪܝܫܐ	the Pharisees
1527	ܘܡܢܣܝܢ	and tempting
0603	ܗܘܘ	were
1261	ܠܗ	him
0116	ܘܐܡܪܝܢ	and saying
0121	ܐܢ	<if>
2528	ܫܠܝܛ	Is it lawful
0131	ܠܓܒܪܐ	for a man
2597	ܠܡܫܪܐ	to put away
0135	ܐܢܬܬܗ	his wife
1168	ܒܟܠ	on any
1801	ܥܠܐ	occasion
VERSE	4	Now he answered and said to them, "Have you not read that he who made [them] from the beginning made them male and female?"
0592	ܗܘ	<he>
0518	ܕܝܢ	Now
1838	ܥܢܐ	he answered
0116	ܘܐܡܪ	and said
1261	ܠܗܘܢ	to them
1262	ܠܐ	not
2239	ܩܪܝܬܘܢ	Have you read
0593	ܕܗܘ	that he
1724	ܕܥܒܕ	who made [them]
1388	ܡܢ	from
2363	ܒܪܫܝܬ	the beginning
0529	ܕܟܪܐ	male
1561	ܘܢܩܒܬܐ	and female
1724	ܥܒܕ	made
0592	ܐܢܘܢ	them
VERSE	5	And he said, "Because of this, A MAN SHOULD LEAVE HIS FATHER AND HIS MOTHER AND SHOULD CLEAVE TO HIS WIFE AND THE TWO OF THEM WILL BECOME ONE FLESH.
0116	ܘܐܡܪ	And he said
1347	ܡܛܠ	Because of
0598	ܗܢܐ	this
2440	ܢܫܒܘܩ	SHOULD LEAVE
0361	ܓܒܪܐ	A MAN
0002	ܠܐܒܘܗܝ	HIS FATHER
0106	ܘܠܐܡܗ	AND HIS MOTHER
1565	ܘܢܩܦ	AND SHOULD CLEAVE
0135	ܠܐܢܬܬܗ	TO HIS WIFE
0603	ܘܢܗܘܘܢ	AND WILL BECOME
2709	ܬܪܝܗܘܢ	THE TWO OF THEM
0721	ܚܕ	ONE

Vertical Interlinear

MATTHEW CHAPTER 19

0294	ܒܣܪ	FLESH

VERSE 6 Therefore, they will not be two, but rather, one flesh. Therefore, that which God has united, man should not separate."

1324	ܡܕܝܢ	Therefore
1262	ܠܐ	not
0603	ܗܘܘ	they will be
2709	ܬܪܝܢ	two
0090	ܐܠܐ	but rather
0721	ܚܕ	one
1929	ܒܣܪ	flesh
1326	ܡܕܡ	that
0596	ܗܟܝܠ	Therefore
0093	ܕܐܠܗܐ	which God
0647	ܙܘܓ	has united
0325	ܒܪܢܫܐ	man
1262	ܠܐ	not
2046	ܢܦܪܫ	should separate

VERSE 7 They said to him, "Why then did Moses command to give a writing of divorce and to dismiss her?"

0116	ܐܡܪܝܢ	They said
1261	ܠܗ	to him
1394	ܠܡܢܐ	Why
0596	ܗܟܝܠ	then
3305	ܡܘܫܐ	Moses
2007	ܦܩܕ	did command
1030	ܕܢܬܠ	to give
1248	ܟܬܒܐ	a writing
2441	ܕܫܘܒܩܢܐ	of divorce
2597	ܘܢܫܪܝܗ	and to dismiss her

VERSE 8 He said to them, "Moses, because of the hardness of your heart, allowed you to dismiss your wives. But previously it was not so.

0116	ܐܡܪ	He said
1261	ܠܗܘܢ	to them
3305	ܡܘܫܐ	Moses
2135	ܠܘܩܒܠ	because of
2267	ܩܫܝܘܬ	the hardness of
1268	ܠܒܟܘܢ	your heart
1989	ܐܦܣ	allowed
1261	ܠܟܘܢ	you
2597	ܕܬܫܪܘܢ	to dismiss
0135	ܢܫܝܟܘܢ	your wives
1388	ܡܢ	previously
2363	ܒܪܫܝܬ	*
0518	ܕܝܢ	But
1262	ܠܐ	not
0603	ܗܘܐ	it was
0597	ܗܟܢܐ	so

VERSE 9 But I say to you, he who forsakes his wife, except [for] adultery, and takes another, commits adultery. And he who takes a forsaken woman commits adultery."

0116	ܐܡܪ	say
0124	ܐܢܐ	I
1261	ܠܟܘܢ	to you
0518	ܕܝܢ	But
1389	ܡܢ	he who
2440	ܕܫܒܩ	forsakes
0135	ܐܢܬܬܗ	his wife
1262	ܐܠܐ	except [for]
0386	ܓܘܪܐ	adultery
1532	ܘܢܣܒ	and takes
0053	ܐܚܪܬܐ	another
0385	ܓܐܪ	commits adultery
1389	ܘܡܢ	And he who
1532	ܕܢܣܒ	takes
2440	ܕܫܒܝܩܬܐ	a forsaken woman
0385	ܓܐܪ	commits adultery

VERSE 10 His disciples said to him, "If such is the case between husband and wife, it is not advantageous to take a wife."

0116	ܐܡܪܝܢ	said
1261	ܠܗ	to him
1304	ܬܠܡܝܕܘܗܝ	His disciples
0121	ܐܢ	If
0597	ܗܟܢܐ	such
0069	ܐܝܬ	is
1749	ܥܕܠܬܐ	the case

MATTHEW — CHAPTER 19

Vertical Interlinear

Code	Aramaic	English
0266		between
0361		husband
0135		and wife
1262		not
2010		it is advantageous
1532		to take
0135		a wife

VERSE 11 But he said to them, "Not every man is fit for this arrangement, except he to whom it is given."

Code	Aramaic	English
0592		<he>
0518		But
0116		he said
1261		to them
1262		Not
1175		every man
1694		is fit
1261		<to him>
1364		for arrangement
0598		this
0090		except
1389		he
1030		it is given
1261		to whom

VERSE 12 For there are believers who were born so from the womb of their mother and there are believers who became believers by men and there are believers who made themselves believers for the sake of the kingdom of heaven. He who is able to understand should understand."

Code	Aramaic	English
0069		there are
0403		For
0115		believers
1388		who from
1241		the womb
0106		of their mother
1046		were born
0597		so
0069		and there are
0115		believers
1388		who by
0325		men
0603		became
0115		believers
0069		and there are
0115		believers
0592		who <they>
1724		made
1547		themselves
0115		believers
1347		for the sake of
1385		the kingdom
2543		of heaven
1389		He who
2510		is able
1694		to understand
1694		should understand

VERSE 13 Then children came near to him that he would lay his hand on them and pray. And his disciples berated them.

Code	Aramaic	English
0594		Then
2244		came near
1261		to him
0976		children
1625		that he would lay
0057		his hand
1804		on them
2106		and pray
1113		And berated
0217		them
1304		His disciples

VERSE 14 But Jesus said to them, "Allow the children [to] come to me and do not hinder them. For of those who are like these is the kingdom of heaven."

Code	Aramaic	English
0592		<he>
0518		But
3257		Jesus
0116		said
1261		to them
2440		Allow

MATTHEW CHAPTER 19

0976	ܛܠܝܐ	the children
0208	ܕܢܐܬܘܢ	[to] come
1288	ܠܘܬܝ	to me
1262	ܘܠܐ	and not
1180	ܬܟܠܘܢ	do hinder
0592	ܐܢܘܢ	them
0066	ܕܕܐܝܠܝܢ	of those
0403	ܓܝܪ	For
0060	ܕܐܝܟ	who are like
0598	ܗܠܝܢ	these
0592	ܐܢܘܢ	<are>
0069	ܐܝܬܝܗ	is
1385	ܡܠܟܘܬܐ	the kingdom
2543	ܕܫܡܝܐ	of heaven

VERSE 15 — And he laid his hand on them and went away from there.

1625	ܘܣܡ	And he laid
0057	ܐܝܕܗ	his hand
1804	ܥܠܝܗܘܢ	on them
0042	ܘܐܙܠ	and went away
1388	ܡܢ	from
2682	ܬܡܢ	there

VERSE 16 — And a certain [man] came [and] approached and said to him, "Good teacher, what good [thing] should I do that I might have eternal life?"

0208	ܘܐܬܐ	And came
0721	ܚܕ	a certain [man]
2244	ܘܩܪܒ	[and] approached
0116	ܘܐܡܪ	and said
1261	ܠܗ	to him
1055	ܡܠܦܢܐ	teacher
0938	ܛܒܐ	Good
1393	ܡܢܐ	what
0938	ܕܛܒ	good [thing]
1724	ܐܥܒܕ	should I do
0603	ܕܢܗܘܘܢ	that I might have
1261	ܠܝ	*
0782	ܚܝܐ	life
1813	ܕܠܥܠܡ	eternal

VERSE 17 — Now he said to him, "Why do you call me good? There is no good [one], except one, God. Now if you want to enter life, keep the commandments."

0592	ܗܘ	<he>
0518	ܕܝܢ	Now
0116	ܐܡܪ	he said
1261	ܠܗ	to him
1393	ܡܢܐ	Why
2239	ܩܪܐ	do call
0133	ܐܢܬ	you
1261	ܠܝ	me
0938	ܛܒܐ	good
1264	ܠܝܬ	There is no
0938	ܛܒܐ	good [one]
0090	ܐܠܐ	except
0121	ܐܢ	*
0721	ܚܕ	one
0093	ܐܠܗܐ	God
0121	ܐܢ	if
0518	ܕܝܢ	Now
2077	ܨܒܐ	want
0133	ܐܢܬ	you
1796	ܕܬܥܘܠ	to enter
0782	ܠܚܝܐ	life
1502	ܛܪ	keep
2009	ܦܘܩܕܢܐ	the commandments

VERSE 18 — He said to him, "Which [ones]?" And Jesus said to him, "DO NOT KILL and DO NOT COMMIT ADULTERY and DO NOT STEAL and DO NOT GIVE FALSE TESTIMONY.

0116	ܐܡܪ	He said
1261	ܠܗ	to him
0066	ܐܝܠܝܢ	Which [ones]
0592	ܗܘ	<he>
0518	ܕܝܢ	And
3257	ܝܫܘܥ	Jesus
0116	ܐܡܪ	said
1261	ܠܗ	to him
1262	ܕܠܐ	NOT

MATTHEW — CHAPTER 19

Vertical Interlinear

#	Aramaic	English
2179		DO KILL
1262		and NOT
0385		DO COMMIT ADULTERY
1262		and NOT
0436		DO STEAL
1262		and NOT
1608		DO GIVE <TESTIMONY>
1610		TESTIMONY
2482		FALSE

VERSE 19 — And HONOR YOUR FATHER AND YOUR MOTHER and LOVE YOUR NEIGHBOR AS YOURSELF."

#	Aramaic	English
1076		And HONOR
0002		YOUR FATHER
0106		AND YOUR MOTHER
0696		and LOVE
2248		YOUR NEIGHBOR
0060		AS
1547		YOURSELF

VERSE 20 — That young man said to him, "All these [things] I have kept from my youth. What do I lack?"

#	Aramaic	English
0116		said
1261		to him
0593		That
1811		young man
0598		these [things]
1168		All
1502		I have kept
0592		<them>
1388		from
0977		my youth
1393		What
0867		do lack
0124		I

VERSE 21 — Jesus said to him, "If you want to be mature, go, sell your possessions and give [them] to the poor and you will have treasure in heaven and follow me."

#	Aramaic	English
0116		said
1261		to him
3257		Jesus
0121		If
2077		want
0133		you
0426		mature
0603		to be
0042		go
0632		sell
2217		your possessions
1030		and give [them]
1406		to the poor
0603		and you will have
1261		*
1627		treasure
2543		in heaven
0208		and follow me
0215		*

VERSE 22 — And that young man heard this word and went away, feeling sorry for himself, for he had many possessions.

#	Aramaic	English
2547		heard
0518		And
0593		that
1811		young man
1364		word
0598		this
0042		and went away
1128		feeling sorry
1221		*
1261		for himself
0069		he had
0603		*
1261		*
0403		for
2217		possessions
1596		many

VERSE 23 — Now Jesus said to his disciples, "Truly I say to you, it is difficult for a rich man to enter into the kingdom of heaven.

#	Aramaic	English
3257		Jesus

MATTHEW CHAPTER 19

0518		Now		0938		very
0116		said		0116		and said
1304		to his disciples		1390		Who is
0110		Truly		1163		indeed
0116		say		2510		able
0124		I		0780		to [gain] life
1261		to you		**VERSE 26**		Jesus looked at them and said to them, "With men, this is not possible, but with God everything is possible."
1788		it is difficult				
0592		*		0756		looked
1921		for a rich man		0217		at them
1796		to enter		3257		Jesus
1385		into the kingdom of		0116		and said
2543		heaven		1261		to them
VERSE 24		And again I say to you, it is easier for a camel to enter into the eye of a needle than [for] a rich man to enter into the kingdom of God."		1288		With
				0325		men
				0598		this
				1262		not
2650		again		2510		is possible
0518		And		1288		with
0116		I say		0093		God
1261		to you		0518		but
0532		it is easier		1173		everything
0592		*		2510		is possible
0420		for a camel		**VERSE 27**		Then answered Peter and said to him, "Behold, we have left everything and have followed you. What indeed will we have?"
1796		to enter				
0888		into the eye				
0748		of a needle				
0024		than		0594		Then
1921		[for] a rich man		1838		answered
1796		to enter		3258		Peter
1385		into the kingdom		0116		and said
0093		of God		1261		to him
VERSE 25		And when the disciples heard [him], they were very amazed and said, "Who is indeed able to [gain] life?"		0580		Behold
				0124		<we>
				2440		we have left
1304		the disciples		1173		everything
0518		And		0208		and have followed you
1128		when		0215		*
2547		heard [him]		1393		What
2644		amazed		1163		indeed
0603		they were				

MATTHEW CHAPTER 19

0603	ܢܗܘܐ	will we have
1261	ܠܢ	*

VERSE 28 — Jesus said to them, "Truly I say you, you who have followed me, when the Son of Man sits on the throne of his glory in the new age, you will also sit on twelve seats of state. And you will judge the twelve tribes of Israel.

0116	ܐܡܪ	said
1261	ܠܗܘܢ	to them
3257	ܝܫܘܥ	Jesus
0110	ܐܡܝܢ	Truly
0116	ܐܡܪ	say
0124	ܐܢܐ	I
1261	ܠܟܘܢ	to you
0133	ܐܢܬܘܢ	you
0208	ܐܬܝܬܘܢ	who have followed me
0215	ܒܬܪܝ	*
1813	ܒܥܠܡܐ	in the age
0735	ܚܕܬܐ	new
1313	ܡܐ	when
1093	ܕܝܬܒ	sits
0323	ܒܪܗ	the Son
0131	ܕܐܢܫܐ	of Man
1804	ܥܠ	on
2711	ܟܘܪܣܝܐ	the throne
2431	ܕܬܫܒܘܚܬܗ	of his glory
1093	ܬܬܒܘܢ	will sit
0169	ܐܦ	also
0133	ܐܢܬܘܢ	you
1804	ܥܠ	on
2710	ܬܪܥܣܪ	twelve
1159	ܟܘܪܣܘܢ	seats of state
0496	ܘܬܕܘܢܘܢ	And you will judge
2710	ܬܪܥܣܪ	twelve
2433	ܫܒܛܐ	the tribes
3035	ܕܐܝܣܪܐܝܠ	of Israel

VERSE 29 — And everyone who has left houses or brothers or sisters or father or mother or wife or children or fields on account of my name will receive one hundred[fold] and will inherit eternal life.

1175	ܘܟܠܢܫ	And everyone
2440	ܕܫܒܩ	who has left
0243	ܒܬܐ	houses
0024	ܐܘ	or
0043	ܐܚܐ	brothers
0024	ܐܘ	or
0046	ܐܚܘܬܐ	sisters
0024	ܐܘ	or
0002	ܐܒܐ	father
0024	ܐܘ	or
0106	ܐܡܐ	mother
0024	ܐܘ	or
0135	ܐܢܬܬܐ	wife
0024	ܐܘ	or
0323	ܒܢܝܐ	children
0024	ܐܘ	or
2251	ܩܘܪܝܐ	fields
1347	ܡܛܠ	on account of
2539	ܫܡܝ	my name
0721	ܚܕ	one
1317	ܒܡܐܐ	hundred[fold]
2134	ܢܩܒܠ	will receive
0782	ܘܚܝܐ	and life
1813	ܕܠܥܠܡ	eternal
1087	ܢܐܪܬ	will inherit

VERSE 30 — But many [are] first, who will be last, and [many are] last, [who will be] first.

1596	ܣܓܝܐܐ	many
0518	ܕܝܢ	But
2157	ܩܕܡܝܐ	[are] first
0603	ܕܢܗܘܘܢ	who will be
0051	ܐܚܪܝܐ	last
0051	ܘܐܚܪܝܐ	and [many are] last
2157	ܩܕܡܝܐ	[who will be] first

MATTHEW

CHAPTER 20

VERSE 1

For the kingdom of heaven is compared to a man, the lord of a house, who went out in the morning to hire laborers for his vineyard.

Code	Aramaic	Translation
0540	ܕܡܐ	is compared
0403	ܓܝܪ	For
1385	ܡܠܟܘܬܐ	the kingdom
2543	ܕܫܡܝܐ	of heaven
0361	ܠܓܒܪܐ	to a man
1426	ܡܪܐ	the lord
0243	ܒܝܬܐ	of a house
1542	ܕܢܦܩ	who went out
2124	ܒܫܦܪܐ	in the morning
0016	ܠܡܐܓܪ	to hire
1999	ܦܥܠܐ	laborers
1240	ܠܟܪܡܗ	for his vineyard

VERSE 2

And he made an agreement with the laborers for a denarius per day. And he sent them to his vineyard.

Code	Aramaic	Translation
2233	ܩܨ	he made an agreement
0518	ܕܝܢ	And
1817	ܥܡ	with
1999	ܦܥܠܐ	the laborers
1388	ܡܢ	for
0519	ܕܝܢܪܐ	a denarius
1036	ܒܝܘܡܐ	per day
2458	ܘܫܕܪ	And he sent
0592	ܐܢܘܢ	them
1240	ܠܟܪܡܗ	to his vineyard

VERSE 3

And he went out in the third hour and saw others who were standing in the marketplace and were idle.

Code	Aramaic	Translation
1542	ܘܢܦܩ	And he went out
2674	ܒܬܠܬ	in the third
2573	ܫܥܝܢ	hour
0758	ܘܚܙܐ	and saw
0053	ܐܚܪܢܐ	others
2168	ܕܩܝܡܝܢ	who were standing
2481	ܒܫܘܩܐ	in the marketplace
0254	ܘܒܛܠܝܢ	and were idle

VERSE 4

And he said to them, 'Go also to the vineyard and I will give to you whatever is right.'

Code	Aramaic	Translation
0116	ܘܐܡܪ	And he said
1261	ܠܗܘܢ	to them
0042	ܙܠܘ	Go
0169	ܐܦ	also
0133	ܐܢܬܘܢ	<you>
1240	ܠܟܪܡܐ	to the vineyard
1326	ܘܡܕܡ	and whatever
0626	ܕܘܠܐ	is right
1030	ܝܗܒ	will give
0124	ܐܢܐ	I
1261	ܠܟܘܢ	to you

VERSE 5

And they went away. And again he came out in the sixth and in the ninth hour and did the same.

Code	Aramaic	Translation
0592	ܗܢܘܢ	<they>
0518	ܕܝܢ	And
0042	ܐܙܠܘ	they went away
1542	ܘܢܦܩ	And he came out
2650	ܬܘܒ	again
2615	ܒܫܬ	in the sixth
2723	ܘܒܬܫܥ	and in the ninth
2573	ܫܥܝܢ	hour
1724	ܘܥܒܕ	and did
0595	ܗܟܘܬ	the same

VERSE 6

And toward the eleventh hour, he went out and found others who were standing and were idle. And he said to them, 'Why are you standing all day and are idle?'

Code	Aramaic	Translation
0173	ܘܠܐܦܝ	And toward
0724	ܚܕܥܣܪܐ	the eleventh
2573	ܫܥܝܢ	hour
1542	ܢܦܩ	he went out
2510	ܘܐܫܟܚ	and found
0053	ܐܚܪܢܐ	others
2168	ܕܩܝܡܝܢ	who were standing
0254	ܘܒܛܠܝܢ	and were idle
0116	ܘܐܡܪ	And he said
1261	ܠܗܘܢ	to them

Vertical Interlinear

MATTHEW CHAPTER 20

1393	ܠܡܢܐ	Why		1261	ܠܗܘܢ	them
2168	ܩܝܡܝܢ	are standing		0018	ܐܓܪܗܘܢ	their wage
0133	ܐܢܬܘܢ	you		2597	ܘܫܪܐ	and begin
1036	ܝܘܡܐ	day		1388	ܡܢ	from
1168	ܟܠܗ	all		0051	ܐܚܪܝܐ	the last
0257	ܘܒܛܠܝܢ	and are idle		1747	ܘܥܕܡܐ	and [proceed] up to

VERSE 7 They said to him, 'No man has hired us.' He said to them, 'Go also to the vineyard and you will receive whatever is right.'

2157 ܠܩܕܡܝܐ the first

VERSE 9 And those of the eleventh hour came [and] each received a denarius.

0116	ܐܡܪܝܢ	They said		0208	ܘܐܬܘ	And came
1261	ܠܗ	to him		0593	ܗܢܘܢ	those
1262	ܠܐ	No		0724	ܕܕܚܕܥܣܪܐ	of the eleventh
0131	ܐܢܫ	man		2573	ܫܥܝܢ	hour
0016	ܐܓܪܢ	has hired us		1532	ܘܢܣܒܘ	[and] received
0116	ܐܡܪ	He said		0519	ܕܝܢܪ	each a denarius
1261	ܠܗܘܢ	to them		0519	ܕܝܢܪ	*
0042	ܙܠܘ	Go				
0169	ܐܦ	also				

VERSE 10 And when the first came, they thought that they would receive more. And they each received a denarius also.

0133	ܐܢܬܘܢ	<you>		1128	ܘܟܕ	And when
1240	ܠܟܪܡܐ	to the vineyard		0208	ܐܬܘ	came
1326	ܘܡܕܡ	and whatever		2157	ܩܕܡܝܐ	the first
0626	ܕܘܠܐ	is right		1588	ܣܒܪܘ	they thought
1532	ܢܣܒܝܢ	will receive		1100	ܕܝܬܝܪ	that more
0133	ܐܢܬܘܢ	you		2587	ܫܩܠܝܢ	they would receive
				2587	ܘܫܩܠܘ	And they received

VERSE 8 Now when it was evening, the lord of the vineyard said to his steward, 'Call the laborers and give them their wage and begin from the last and [proceed] up to the first.'

				0519	ܕܝܢܪ	each a denarius
				0519	ܕܝܢܪ	*
				0169	ܐܦ	also
				0592	ܗܢܘܢ	<they>

VERSE 11 And when they received [it], they murmured against the lord of the house.

1128	ܟܕ	when		1128	ܘܟܕ	And when
0603	ܗܘܐ	it was		2587	ܫܩܠܘ	they received [it]
0518	ܕܝܢ	Now		2360	ܪܛܢܘ	they murmured
2375	ܪܡܫܐ	evening		1804	ܥܠ	against
0116	ܐܡܪ	said		1426	ܡܪܐ	the lord of
1426	ܡܪܐ	the lord of		0243	ܒܝܬܐ	the house
1240	ܟܪܡܐ	the vineyard				
2276	ܠܪܒܝܬܗ	to his steward				
2239	ܩܪܝ	Call				
1999	ܦܥܠܐ	the laborers				
1030	ܘܗܒ	and give				

MATTHEW CHAPTER 20

VERSE 12 — And they said, 'These last [ones] worked one hour and you made them equal with us who bore the burden of the day and its heat.'

0116		And they said
0598		These
0051		last [ones]
0721		one
2573		hour
1724		worked
2461		and you made equal
0592		them
1817		with us
2587		who bore
1078		the burden
1036		of the day
0819		and its heat

VERSE 13 — Now he answered and said to one of them, 'My friend, I did not wrong you. Did you not agree with me for a denarius?

0592		<he>
0518		Now
1838		he answered
0116		and said
0721		to one
1388		of them
0714		My friend
1262		not
1765		did wrong
0124		I
0217		you
1262		not
0603		Did
0519		for a denarius
2233		you agree
1817		with me

VERSE 14 — Take your own and go. But I desire to give to this last [one] as to you.

1532		Take
0517		your own
0042		and go
2077		desire
0124		I
0518		But
0598		to this
0051		last [one]
1030		to give
0060		as
1261		to you

VERSE 15 — Or is it not lawful for me to do with my own what I want? Or is your eye evil because I am good?

0024		Or
1262		not
2528		is it lawful
1261		for me
1326		what
2077		want
0124		I
1724		to do
0517		with my own
0024		Or
1794		your eye
0220		is evil
0124		because <I>
0938		good
0124		I am

VERSE 16 — So the last will be first and the first last. For many are called and few chosen."

0597		So
0603		will be
0051		the last
2157		first
2157		and the first
0051		last
1596		many
0592		<they>
0403		For
2241		are called
0686		and few

MATTHEW CHAPTER 20

0353	ܓܒܝܐ	chosen		0217	ܗܝ	him
VERSE 17		And Jesus was about to go up to Jerusalem. And he took [aside] his twelve disciples privately on the journey and said to them,		1461	ܘܢܢܓܕܘܢܗܝ	and they will beat him
				0688	ܘܢܙܩܦܘܢܗܝ	and they will crucify him
				1036	ܘܠܝܘܡܐ	and on the day
1914	ܥܬܝܕ	about to		2674	ܕܬܠܬܐ	third
0603	ܗܘܐ	was		2168	ܢܩܘܡ	he will rise up
0518	ܕܝܢ	And		**VERSE 20**		Then the mother of the sons of Zebedee came to him, she and her sons. And she worshipped him and was asking him something.
3257	ܝܫܘܥ	Jesus				
1658	ܕܢܣܩ	to go up				
3022	ܠܐܘܪܫܠܡ	to Jerusalem		0594	ܗܝܕܝܢ	Then
0477	ܘܕܒܪ	And he took [aside]		2244	ܩܪܒܬ	came
2710	ܠܬܪܥܣܪ	twelve		1261	ܠܗ	to him
1304	ܬܠܡܝܕܘܗܝ	his disciples		0106	ܐܡܗܘܢ	the mother
0266	ܒܝܢܘܗܝ	privately		0323	ܕܒܢܝ	of the sons of
1261	ܘܠܗܘܢ	*		3185	ܙܒܕܝ	Zebedee
0038	ܒܐܘܪܚܐ	on the journey		0592	ܗܝ	she
0116	ܘܐܡܪ	and said		0323	ܘܒܢܝܗ	and her sons
1261	ܠܗܘܢ	to them		1599	ܘܣܓܕܬ	And she worshipped
VERSE 18		"Behold, we are going up to Jerusalem and the Son of Man will be delivered to the chief priests and to the scribes and they will condemn him to death.		1261	ܠܗ	him
				2420	ܘܫܐܠܐ	and asking
				0603	ܗܘܬ	was
				1261	ܠܗ	him
0580	ܗܐ	Behold		1326	ܡܕܡ	something
1658	ܣܠܩܝܢ	are going up		**VERSE 21**		Now he said to her, "What do you want?" She said to him, "Say that these, my two sons, will sit one on your right and one on your left in your kingdom."
0124	ܚܢܢ	we				
3022	ܠܐܘܪܫܠܡ	to Jerusalem				
0323	ܘܒܪܗ	and the Son		0592	ܗܘ	<he>
0131	ܕܐܢܫܐ	of Man		0518	ܕܝܢ	Now
2530	ܡܫܬܠܡ	will be delivered		0116	ܐܡܪ	he said
2271	ܠܪܒܝ	to the chief priests		1261	ܠܗ	to her
1135	ܟܗܢܐ	*		1393	ܡܢܐ	What
1699	ܘܠܣܦܪܐ	and to the scribes		2077	ܨܒܝܐ	do want
0742	ܘܢܚܝܒܘܢܗܝ	and they will condemn him		0133	ܐܢܬܝ	you
1335	ܠܡܘܬܐ	to death		0116	ܐܡܪܐ	She said
VERSE 19		And they will deliver him to the Gentiles and they will mock him and they will beat him and they will crucify him and on the third day, he will rise up."		1261	ܠܗ	to him
				0116	ܐܡܪ	Say
				1093	ܕܢܬܒܘܢ	that will sit
2530	ܘܢܫܠܡܘܢܗܝ	And they will deliver him		0598	ܗܠܝܢ	these
1818	ܠܥܡܡܐ	to the Gentiles		2709	ܬܪܝܢ	two
0246	ܘܢܒܙܚܘܢ	and they will mock				

141

MATTHEW CHAPTER 20

0323		my sons
0721		one
1388		on
1061		your right
0721		and one
1388		on
1668		your left
1385		in your kingdom

VERSE 22 — Jesus answered and said, "You do not know what you ask. Are you able to drink the cup that I am about to drink or to be baptized [with] the baptism [with] which I [will be] baptized?" They said to him, "We are able."

1838		answered
3257		Jesus
0116		and said
1262		not
1023		do know
0133		You
1393		what
2420		ask
0133		you
2510		Are able
0133		you
2620		to drink
1205		the cup
0124		that I
1914		am about
2620		to drink
0024		or
1821		[with] the baptism
0124		[with] which <I>
1819		[will be] baptized
0124		I
1819		to be baptized
0116		They said
1261		to him
2510		are able
0124		We

VERSE 23 — He said to them, "You will drink my cup and be baptized [with] the baptism [with] which I [will be] baptized. But that you should sit at my right and at my left is not mine to give, except to those [for] whom it is prepared by my Father."

0116		He said
1261		to them
1205		my cup
2620		You will drink
1821		and [with] the baptism
0124		[with] which <I>
1819		[will be] baptized
0124		I
1819		be baptized
1093		that you should sit
0518		But
1388		at
1061		my right
1388		and at
1668		my left
1262		not
0603		is
0517		mine
1030		to give
0090		except
0066		to those
0950		[for] whom it is prepared
1388		by
0002		my Father

VERSE 24 — And when the ten heard [of this], they were angry at those two brothers.

1128		when
0518		And
2547		heard [of this]
1848		the ten
2290		they were angry
1804		at
0593		those
2709		two
0043		brothers

MATTHEW CHAPTER 20

VERSE 25 — And Jesus called them and said to them, "You know that the rulers of the Gentiles are their lords and their nobles are in authority over them.

2239	ܘܩܪܐ	And called
0592	ܐܢܘܢ	them
3257	ܝܫܘܥ	Jesus
0116	ܘܐܡܪ	and said
1261	ܠܗܘܢ	to them
1023	ܝܕܥܝܢ	know
0133	ܐܢܬܘܢ	You
2362	ܕܪܫܢܝܗܘܢ	that the rulers
1818	ܕܥܡܡܐ	of the Gentiles
1426	ܡܪܝܗܘܢ	their lords
0592	ܐܢܘܢ	are
2271	ܘܪܘܪܒܢܝܗܘܢ	and their nobles
2528	ܫܠܝܛܝܢ	are in authority
1804	ܥܠܝܗܘܢ	over them

VERSE 26 — It should not be so among you. But rather, whoever among you wants to be great should be a minister to you.

1262	ܠܐ	not
0597	ܗܟܢܐ	so
0603	ܢܗܘܐ	It should be
0266	ܒܝܢܬܟܘܢ	among you
0090	ܐܠܐ	But rather
1389	ܡܢ	whoever
2077	ܕܨܒܐ	wants
0217	ܒܟܘܢ	among you
0603	ܕܢܗܘܐ	to be
2271	ܪܒܐ	great
0603	ܢܗܘܐ	should be
1261	ܠܟܘܢ	to you
2555	ܡܫܡܫܢܐ	a minister

VERSE 27 — And whoever among you wants to be first should be a servant to you,

1389	ܘܡܢ	And whoever
2077	ܕܨܒܐ	wants
0217	ܒܟܘܢ	among you
0603	ܕܢܗܘܐ	to be
2157	ܩܕܡܝܐ	first

0603	ܢܗܘܐ	should be
1261	ܠܟܘܢ	to you
1727	ܥܒܕܐ	a servant

VERSE 28 — even as the Son of Man did not come to be served, but to serve and to give himself [as] a payment on behalf of many."

0061	ܐܝܟܢܐ	even as
0323	ܕܒܪܗ	the Son
0131	ܕܐܢܫܐ	of Man
1262	ܠܐ	not
0208	ܐܬܐ	did come
2554	ܕܢܫܬܡܫ	to be served
0090	ܐܠܐ	but
2554	ܕܢܫܡܫ	to serve
1030	ܘܕܢܬܠ	and to give
1547	ܢܦܫܗ	himself
2043	ܦܘܪܩܢܐ	[as] a payment
0812	ܚܠܦ	on behalf of
1596	ܣܓܝܐܐ	many

VERSE 29 — And when Jesus went out of Jericho, a large crowd was following him.

1128	ܘܟܕ	And when
1542	ܢܦܩ	went out
3257	ܝܫܘܥ	Jesus
1388	ܡܢ	of
3039	ܐܝܪܝܚܘ	Jericho
0208	ܐܬܐ	following
0603	ܗܘܐ	was
0215	ܒܬܪܗ	<after> him
1201	ܟܢܫܐ	a crowd
1596	ܣܓܝܐܐ	large

VERSE 30 — And behold, two blind men were sitting on the side of the road. And when they heard that Jesus passed by, they gave a cry and said, "Have compassion on us, my Lord, Son of David."

0580	ܘܗܐ	And behold
1662	ܣܡܝܐ	blind men
2709	ܬܪܝܢ	two
1093	ܝܬܒܝܢ	sitting
0603	ܗܘܘ	were

MATTHEW CHAPTER 20

1804		on
0057		the side of
0038		the road
1128		And when
2547		they heard
3257		that Jesus
1733		passed by
1030		they gave
2204		a cry
0116		and said
2342		Have compassion
1804		on us
1426		my Lord
0323		Son
3159		of David

VERSE 31 — But the crowds were admonishing them to be quiet. And they raised their voice more and said, "Our Lord, have compassion on us, Son of David."

1201		the crowds
0518		But
1113		admonishing
0603		were
0217		them
2623		to be quiet
0592		And <they>
1101		more
2331		they raised
2204		their voice
0116		and said
1426		Our Lord
2342		have compassion
1804		on us
0323		Son
3159		of David

VERSE 32 — And Jesus stopped and called them and said, "What do you want me to do for you?"

2168		And stopped
3257		Jesus
2239		and called
0592		them
0116		and said
1393		What
2077		do want
0133		you
1724		me to do
1261		for you

VERSE 33 — They said to him, "Our Lord, that our eyes be opened."

0116		They said
1261		to him
1426		Our Lord
2070		that may be opened
1794		our eyes

VERSE 34 — And Jesus had compassion on them and touched their eyes and immediately their eyes were opened and they followed him.

2342		And had compassion
1804		on them
3257		Jesus
2244		and touched
1794		their eyes
0323		and immediately
2573		*
2070		were opened
1794		their eyes
0042		and they followed him
0215		*

CHAPTER 21

VERSE 1 — And when he came near to Jerusalem and came to Bethphage by the side of the Mount of Olives, Jesus sent two of his disciples.

1128		And when
2244		he came near
3022		to Jerusalem
0208		and came
3117		to Bethphage
1804		by
0439		the side of

MATTHEW — CHAPTER 21

Vertical Interlinear

Code	Aramaic	English
0958		the Mount
0663		of Olives
2458		sent
3257		Jesus
2709		two
1388		of
1304		his disciples

VERSE 2 — and said to them, "Go to this village that is opposite you and immediately you will find a donkey that is tied and a colt with her. Loose [them and] bring [them] to me.

Code	Aramaic	English
0116		and said
1261		to them
0042		Go
2251		to village
0598		this
2135		that is opposite you
0725		and immediately
2510		will find
0133		you
0830		a donkey
0160		that is tied
1793		and a colt
1817		with her
2597		Loose [them and]
0208		bring [them]
1261		to me

VERSE 3 — And if anyone says anything to you, say to him that they are needed for our Lord. And immediately he will send them here."

Code	Aramaic	English
0121		And if
0131		anyone
0116		says
1261		to you
1326		anything
0116		say
1261		to him
1426		that for our Lord
0296		they are needed
0725		And immediately
2458		he will send
1261		them
1111		here

VERSE 4 — Now this which happened [was] so that what was spoken by way of the prophet would be fulfilled, who said:

Code	Aramaic	English
0598		this
0518		Now
0603		which happened
1366		[was] so that would be fulfilled
1326		what
0116		was spoken
0057		by way of
1457		the prophet
0116		who said

VERSE 5 — SAY TO THE DAUGHTER OF ZION, BEHOLD, YOUR KING COMES TO YOU MEEK AND MOUNTED ON A DONKEY AND ON A COLT, THE FOAL OF A DONKEY.

Code	Aramaic	English
0116		SAY
0327		TO THE DAUGHTER
3449		OF ZION
0580		BEHOLD
1383		YOUR KING
0208		COMES
1261		TO YOU
1355		MEEK
2367		AND MOUNTED
1804		ON
0830		A DONKEY
1804		AND ON
1793		A COLT
0323		THE FOAL OF
0213		A <FEMALE> DONKEY

VERSE 6 — And the disciples went and did as Jesus had commanded them.

Code	Aramaic	English
0042		And went
1304		the disciples
1724		and did

145

MATTHEW CHAPTER 21

0061		as
2007		had commanded
1261		them
3257		Jesus

VERSE 7 And they brought the donkey and the colt and placed their garments on the colt and Jesus mounted it.

0208		And they brought
0830		the donkey
1793		and the colt
1625		and placed
1804		on
1793		the colt
1501		their garments
2367		and mounted
1804		<on> it
3257		Jesus

VERSE 8 And a large number of crowds were spreading out their clothes in the road. And others were cutting branches from the trees and throwing [them] on the road.

1598		And a large number
1201		of crowds
2461		spreading out
0603		were
1320		their clothes
0038		in the road
0053		others
0518		And
1992		cutting
0603		were
1623		branches
1388		from
0063		the trees
2372		and throwing [them]
0038		on the road

VERSE 9 And the crowds, who were going before him and were following him, were crying out and saying: HOSANNA TO THE SON OF DAVID. BLESSED IS HE WHO COMES IN THE NAME OF THE LORD. HOSANNA IN THE HIGHEST!

1201		the crowds
0518		And
0066		<those>
0042		who going
0603		were
2154		before him
0208		and were following him
0215		*
2227		crying out
0603		were
0116		and saying
0041		HOSANNA
0323		TO THE SON
3159		OF DAVID
0338		BLESSED
0592		IS
0208		HE WHO COMES
2539		IN THE NAME
1426		OF THE LORD
0041		HOSANNA
2332		IN THE HIGHEST!

VERSE 10 And when he entered Jerusalem, the entire city was in turmoil. And they were saying, "Who is this [man]?"

1128		And when
1796		he entered
3022		Jerusalem
0657		was in turmoil
1168		entire
0499		the city
0116		And saying
0603		they were
1390		Who is
0598		this [man]

MATTHEW CHAPTER 21

Vertical Interlinear

VERSE 11 — And the crowds were saying, "This is Jesus, the prophet, who is from Nazareth of Galilee."

Code	Aramaic	English
1201		the crowds
0518		And
0116		saying
0603		were
0599		This is
3257		Jesus
1457		the prophet
1388		who is from
3354		Nazareth
3153		of Galilee

VERSE 12 — And Jesus entered the temple of God and threw out all who were buying and selling in the temple. And he overturned the tables of the moneychangers and the chairs of those who were selling doves.

Code	Aramaic	English
1796		And entered
3257		Jesus
0607		the temple
0093		of God
1542		and threw out
1168		all
0632		who were buying
0632		and selling
0607		in the temple
1636		And he overturned
2069		the tables
1899		of the moneychangers
1159		and the chairs
0593		of those
0632		who were selling
1038		doves

VERSE 13 — And he said to them, "It is written: MY HOUSE WILL BE CALLED A HOUSE OF PRAYER. But you have made it a den of thieves."

Code	Aramaic	English
0116		And he said
1261		to them
1247		It is written
0592		<it>
0243		MY HOUSE
0243		A HOUSE OF
2107		PRAYER
2239		WILL BE CALLED
0133		<you>
0518		But
1724		you have made it
1775		a den
1306		of thieves

VERSE 14 — And the blind and lame came near to him in the temple and he healed them.

Code	Aramaic	English
2244		And came near
1261		to him
0607		in the temple
1662		the blind
0718		and lame
0136		and he healed
0592		them

VERSE 15 — Now when the chief priests and the Pharisees saw the wonders that he did and the children who were crying out in the temple and saying, "Hosanna to the Son of David," they were displeased.

Code	Aramaic	English
1128		when
0758		saw
0518		Now
2271		the chief priests
1135		*
3439		and the Pharisees
0551		the wonders
1724		that he did
0976		and the children
2227		who were crying out
0607		in the temple
0116		And saying
0041		Hosanna
0323		to the Son
3159		of David
0219		they were displeased
1261		<to them>

Vertical Interlinear

MATTHEW CHAPTER 21

VERSE 16 — And they said to him, "Do you hear what these are saying?" Jesus said to them, "Yes. Have you never read: FROM THE MOUTH OF CHILDREN AND INFANTS YOU HAVE FASHIONED PRAISE?"

Number	Aramaic	English
0116	ܘܐܡܪܝܢ	And they said
1261	ܠܗ	to him
2547	ܫܡܥ	Do hear
0133	ܐܢܬ	you
1393	ܡܢܐ	what
0116	ܐܡܪܝܢ	are saying
0598	ܗܠܝܢ	these
0116	ܐܡܪ	said
1261	ܠܗܘܢ	to them
3257	ܝܫܘܥ	Jesus
0065	ܐܝܢ	Yes
1388	ܠܐ	never
1450	ܡܡܬܘܡ	*
1262	ܠܐ	*
2239	ܩܪܝܬܘܢ	have you read
1388	ܕܡܢ	FROM
1936	ܦܘܡܐ	THE MOUTH
0976	ܕܛܠܝܐ	OF CHILDREN
1048	ܘܕܝܠܘܕܐ	AND INFANTS
2699	ܬܩܢܬ	YOU HAVE FASHIONED
2432	ܬܫܒܘܚܬܐ	PRAISE

VERSE 17 — And he left them and went away outside of the city to Bethany and lodged there.

Number	Aramaic	English
2440	ܘܫܒܩ	And he left
0592	ܐܢܘܢ	them
1542	ܘܢܦܩ	and went away
0322	ܠܒܪ	outside
1388	ܡܢ	of
0499	ܡܕܝܢܬܐ	the city
3116	ܠܒܝܬ ܥܢܝܐ	to Bethany
0242	ܘܒܬ	and lodged
2682	ܬܡܢ	there

VERSE 18 — Now in the morning when he returned to the city, he was hungry.

Number	Aramaic	English
2124	ܒܨܦܪܐ	in the morning
0518	ܕܝܢ	Now
1128	ܟܕ	when
0616	ܗܦܟ	he returned
0499	ܠܡܕܝܢܬܐ	to the city
1212	ܟܦܢ	he was hungry

VERSE 19 — And he saw a certain fig tree by the road and came to it. And he did not find anything on it, except leaves only. And he said to it, "There will not be fruit on you again forever." And immediately that fig tree dried up.

Number	Aramaic	English
0758	ܘܚܙܐ	And he saw
2628	ܬܬܐ	a fig tree
0721	ܚܕܐ	certain
0038	ܒܐܘܪܚܐ	by the road
0208	ܘܐܬܐ	and came
1288	ܠܘܬܗ	to it
1262	ܘܠܐ	And not
2510	ܐܫܟܚ	he did find
0217	ܒܗ	on it
1326	ܡܕܡ	anything
0090	ܐܠܐ	except
0121	ܐܢ	*
1008	ܛܪܦܐ	leaves
1041	ܒܠܚܘܕ	only
0116	ܘܐܡܪ	And he said
1261	ܠܗ	to it
1262	ܠܐ	not
0603	ܢܗܘܘܢ	There will not be
0217	ܒܟܝ	on you
2650	ܬܘܒ	again
2016	ܦܐܪܐ	fruit
1813	ܠܥܠܡ	forever
0725	ܘܡܚܕܐ	And immediately
1018	ܝܒܫܬ	dried up
2628	ܬܬܐ	fig tree
0593	ܗܝ	that

VERSE 20 — And the disciples saw and marveled and said, "How quickly the fig tree dried up!"

Number	Aramaic	English
0758	ܘܚܙܘ	And saw
1304	ܬܠܡܝܕܐ	the disciples
2644	ܘܐܬܕܡܪܘ	and marveled

Vertical Interlinear

MATTHEW CHAPTER 21

0116		and said
0061		How
0323		quickly
2573		*
1018		dried up
2628		the fig tree

VERSE 21 — Jesus answered and said to them, "Truly I say to you, if you have faith and do not doubt, not only will you do this [miracle] of the fig, but even if you say to this mountain, 'Be removed and fall into the sea,' it will happen.

1838		answered
3257		Jesus
0116		and said
1261		to them
0110		Truly
0116		I say*
0124		in the morning
1261		to you
0121		if
0603		you have
0217		*
0113		faith
1262		and not
1968		do doubt
1262		not
1041		only
0598		this [miracle]
2628		of the fig
1724		will you do
0090		but
0172		even if
0958		to mountain
0598		this
0116		you say
2587		Be removed
1538		and fall
1057		into the sea
0603		it will happen

VERSE 22 — And everything that you ask for in prayer and believe, you will receive."

1168		And everything
1326		that
2420		you ask for
2107		in prayer
0109		and believe
1532		you will receive

VERSE 23 — And when Jesus came to the temple, the chief priests and the elders of the people came near to him while he was teaching and said to him, "By what authority do you do these [things]? And who gave you this authority?"

1128		And when
0208		came
3257		Jesus
0607		to the temple
2244		came near
1261		to him
2271		the chief priests
1135		*
2263		and the elders
1818		of the people
1128		while
1053		he was teaching
0116		and said
1261		to him
0066		by what
2527		authority
0598		these [things]
1724		do you do
0133		*
1390		And who
1030		gave
1261		you
2527		authority
0598		this

Vertical Interlinear

MATTHEW CHAPTER 21

VERSE 24 — Jesus answered and said to them, "I will ask you also a certain question and if you answer me, I will also tell you by what authority I do these [things].

#	Syriac	English
1838		answered
3257		Jesus
0116		and said
1261		to them
2420		I will ask you
0169		also
0124		<I>
1364		a question
0721		certain
0121		and if
0116		you answer
1261		me
0169		<and> also
0124		<I>
0116		will tell
0124		I
1261		you
0066		by what
2527		authority
0598		these [things]
1724		do
0124		I

VERSE 25 — The baptism of John, from where is it? Is it from heaven or from men?" Now they were reasoning among themselves and said, "If we say from heaven, he will say to us, 'Why did you not believe him?'

#	Syriac	English
1821		The baptism
3233		of John
1388		from
1110		where
0069		is it
1388		from
2543		heaven
0592		Is it
0024		or
1388		from
0325		men
0592		<they>
0518		Now
2381		reasoning
0603		they were
1547		among themselves
0116		and said
0121		If
0116		we say
1388		from
2543		heaven
0116		he will say
1261		to us
1804		<and> Why
1393		*
1262		not
0109		did you believe him

VERSE 26 — And [if] we say from men, we are afraid of the crowd, for all of them regarded John as a prophet."

#	Syriac	English
0116		And [if] we say
1388		from
0325		men
0509		are afraid
0124		we
1388		of
1201		the crowd
1168		all of them
0403		for
0060		as
1457		a prophet
0047		regarded
0603		*
1261		<him>
3233		John

VERSE 27 — They answered and said to him, "We do not know." Jesus said to them, "Neither will I tell you by what authority I do these [things].

#	Syriac	English
1838		They answered
0116		and said

150

MATTHEW   CHAPTER 21

#		English
1261		to him
1262		not
1023		We do know
0116		said
1261		to them
3257		Jesus
0169		Neither
1262		*
0124		<I>
0116		will tell
0124		I
1261		you
0066		by what
2527		authority
0598		these [things]
1724		do
0124		I

VERSE 28 — But what does it seem to you? A certain man had two sons. And he came near to the first and said to him, 'My son, go today [and] work in the vineyard.'

#		English
1393		what
0518		But
0758		does it seem
1261		to you
0361		A man
0721		certain
0069		had
0603		*
1261		<to him>
0323		sons
2709		two
2244		And he came near
1288		to
2157		the first
0116		and said
1261		to him
0323		My son
0042		go
1037		today
1974		[and] work
1240		in the vineyard

VERSE 29 — Now he answered and said, 'I do not want to.' But later, he regretted [it] and went.

#		English
0592		<he>
0518		Now
1838		he answered
0116		and said
1262		not
2077		do want to
0124		I
0054		later
0518		But
2647		he regretted [it]
0042		and went

VERSE 30 — And he came near to the other and said to him the same. Now he answered and said, 'I am [going], my lord,' and did not go.

#		English
2244		And he came near
1288		to
0053		the other
0116		and said
1261		to him
0595		the same
0592		<he>
0518		Now
1838		he answered
0116		and said
0124		I am [going]
1426		my lord
1262		and not
0042		did go

VERSE 31 — Which of these two did the will of his father?" They said to him, "That first [son]." Jesus said to them, "Truly I say to you, tax collectors and harlots will precede you in the kingdom of God.

#		English
1390		Which
1388		of
0598		these

MATTHEW   CHAPTER 21

2709		two		0169		even
1724		did		1262		not
2079		the will		1128		when
0002		of his father		0758		you saw [him]
0116		They said		2647		did you repent
1261		to him		0054		finally
0593		That		0109		that you might believe
2157		first [son]		0217		in him
0116		said				
1261		to them				
3257		Jesus				
0110		Truly				
0116		say				
0124		I				
1261		to you				
1358		tax collectors				
0680		and harlots				
2150		will precede				
1261		you				
1385		in the kingdom				
0093		of God				

VERSE 33 Hear another parable. A certain man was a lord of a house. And he planted a vineyard. And he set a fence around it and dug a winepress in it. And he built a tower in it and handed it over to laborers and went on a journey.

2547		Hear
0053		another
1454		parable
0361		A man
0721		certain
0069		was
0603		*
1426		a lord of
0243		a house
1554		And he planted
1240		a vineyard
0730		And he set around it
1617		a fence
0875		and he dug
0217		in it
1866		a winepress
0281		And he built
0217		in it
0369		a tower
0047		and handed it over
1977		to laborers
0768		and went on a journey

VERSE 32 For John came to you in the way of uprightness and you did not believe him. But the tax collectors and harlots believed him. But not even when you saw [him], did you finally repent that you might believe in him.

0208		came
0403		For
1288		to you
3233		John
0038		in the way
1152		of uprightness
1262		and not
0109		you did believe him
1358		the tax collectors
0518		But
0680		and harlots
0109		believed him
0133		<you>
0518		But

VERSE 34 Now when the time of harvest arrived, he sent his servants to the laborers that they might send [some] of the fruit of his vineyard to him.

1128		when
0518		Now

152

Vertical Interlinear

MATTHEW   CHAPTER 21

1346	ܡܛܐ	arrived	2458	ܫܕܪ	he sent
0633	ܙܒܢܐ	the time	1288	ܠܘܬܗܘܢ	them
2016	ܕܦܐܪܐ	of harvest	0323	ܠܒܪܗ	his son
2458	ܫܕܪ	he sent	1128	ܟܕ	saying
1727	ܠܥܒܕܘܗܝ	his servants	0116	ܐܡܪ	*
1288	ܠܘܬ	to	1124	ܟܒܪ	Perhaps
1977	ܦܠܚܐ	the laborers	0235	ܢܒܗܬܘܢ	they will respect
2458	ܕܢܫܕܪܘܢ	that they might send	1388	ܡܢ	*
1261	ܠܗ	to him	0323	ܒܪܝ	my son
1388	ܡܢ	[some] of	**VERSE 38**		But the laborers, when they saw the son, said among themselves, 'This is the heir. Come, let us kill him and obtain his inheritance.'
2016	ܦܐܪܐ	the fruit			
1240	ܕܟܪܡܗ	of his vineyard			
VERSE 35		Yet the laborers grabbed his servants and some they beat and some they stoned and some they killed.	1977	ܦܠܚܐ	the laborers
			0518	ܕܝܢ	But
			1128	ܟܕ	when
0047	ܘܐܚܕܘ	Yet grabbed	0758	ܚܙܐܘܗܝ	they saw <him>
1977	ܦܠܚܐ	the laborers	0323	ܠܒܪܐ	the son
1727	ܠܥܒܕܘܗܝ	his servants	0116	ܐܡܪܝܢ	said
0069	ܘܐܝܬ	and some	0266	ܒܢܦܫܗܘܢ	among themselves
1341	ܕܡܚܐܘܗܝ	they beat	0599	ܗܢܘ	This is
0069	ܘܐܝܬ	and some	1089	ܝܪܬܐ	the heir
2296	ܕܪܓܡܘܗܝ	they stoned	0208	ܬܘ	Come
0069	ܘܐܝܬ	and some	2179	ܢܩܛܠܘܗܝ	let us kill him
2179	ܕܩܛܠܘ	they killed	0047	ܘܢܐܚܘܕ	and obtain
VERSE 36		And again he sent other servants, more than the first, and they did the same to them.	1090	ܝܪܬܘܬܗ	his inheritance
			VERSE 39		And they grabbed [him and] took him outside of the vineyard and killed him.
2650	ܘܬܘܒ	And again			
2458	ܫܕܪ	he sent	0047	ܘܐܚܕܘ	And they grabbed [him and]
0053	ܐܚܪܢܐ	other	1542	ܐܦܩܘܗܝ	took him
1727	ܥܒܕܐ	servants	0322	ܠܒܪ	outside
1596	ܕܣܓܝܐܝܢ	more	1388	ܡܢ	of
1388	ܡܢ	than	1240	ܟܪܡܐ	the vineyard
2157	ܩܕܡܝܐ	the first	2179	ܘܩܛܠܘܗܝ	and killed him
0595	ܘܗܟܢܐ	and the same	**VERSE 40**		When, therefore, the lord of the vineyard comes, what should he do to those laborers?"
1724	ܥܒܕܘ	they did			
1261	ܠܗܘܢ	to them			
VERSE 37		And lastly, he sent them his son, saying, 'Perhaps they will respect my son.'	1313	ܡܐ	When
			0208	ܕܐܬܐ	comes
0051	ܐܚܪܝܬ	lastly	0596	ܗܟܝܠ	therefore
0518	ܕܝܢ	And	1426	ܡܪܗ	the lord

Vertical Interlinear

MATTHEW CHAPTER 21

1240		of the vineyard
1393		what
1724		should he do
1977		to laborers
0593		those

VERSE 41 They said to him, "He will utterly destroy them and he will hand over the vineyard to other laborers, those who will give him the fruit in its season."

0116		They said
1261		to him
0220		utterly
0220		*
0005		He will destroy
0592		them
1240		and the vineyard
0047		he will hand over
0053		to other
1977		laborers
0066		those
1030		who will give
1261		him
2016		the fruit
0633		in its season

VERSE 42 Jesus said to them, "Have you never read in the scripture of THE STONE THAT THE BUILDERS REJECTED? IT HAS BECOME THE HEAD OF THE CORNER. THIS [STONE] CAME FROM THE PRESENCE OF THE LORD AND IT IS A WONDER IN OUR EYES.

0116		said
1261		to them
3257		Jesus
1262		never
1451		*
2239		Have you read
1248		in the scripture
1119		of THE STONE
1655		THAT REJECTED
0282		THE BUILDERS
0592		IT
0603		HAS BECOME
2362		THE HEAD
0654		OF THE CORNER
1388		FROM
1288		THE PRESENCE
1426		OF THE LORD
0603		CAME
0598		THIS [STONE]
0069		AND IT IS
0551		A WONDER
1794		IN OUR EYES

VERSE 43 Because of this, I say to you, the kingdom of God will be taken away from you and be given to a people who bear fruit.

1347		Because of
0598		this
0116		say
0124		I
1261		to you
2587		will be taken away
1388		from you
1385		the kingdom
0093		of God
1030		and be given
1818		to a people
1724		who bear
2016		fruit

VERSE 44 And whoever falls on this stone will be bruised, and whomever it falls on, it will blow him away [as chaff]."

1389		And whoever
1538		falls
1804		on
1119		stone
0598		this
2380		will be bruised
1168		and whomever
1389		*
0592		<it>
1538		it falls

MATTHEW CHAPTER 21

#	Aramaic	English
1804		on <him>
0569		it will blow him away [as chaff]

VERSE 45 And when the chief priests and Pharisees heard his parables, they knew that he spoke against them.

#	Aramaic	English
1128		And when
2547		heard
2271		the chief priests
1135		*
3439		and Pharisees
1454		his parables
1023		they knew
1804		that against them
0116		he spoke

VERSE 46 And they sought to arrest him, yet they were afraid of the crowd, because they regarded him as a prophet.

#	Aramaic	English
0296		And they sought
0047		to arrest him
0509		yet they were afraid
1388		of
1201		the crowd
1347		because
0060		as
1457		a prophet
0047		they regarded
0603		*
1261		him

CHAPTER 22

VERSE 1 And Jesus answered again in parables and said,

#	Aramaic	English
1838		And answered
2650		again
3257		Jesus
1454		in parables
0116		and said

VERSE 2 "The kingdom of heaven is compared to a certain king who prepared a wedding feast for his son.

#	Aramaic	English
0540		is compared to
1385		The kingdom
2543		of heaven
0361		to certain
1383		a king
1724		who prepared
2621		a wedding feast
0323		for his son

VERSE 3 And he sent his servants to call the invited [ones] to the wedding feast and they did not want to come.

#	Aramaic	English
2458		And he sent
1727		his servants
2239		to call
0671		the invited [ones]
2621		to the wedding feast
1262		and not
2077		they did want
0208		to come

VERSE 4 Again he sent other servants and told [them] to say to the invited [ones], 'Behold, my feast is prepared and my oxen and my fat [ones] are killed and everything is ready. Come to the wedding feast.'

#	Aramaic	English
2650		Again
2458		he sent
1727		servants
0053		other
0116		and told [them]
0116		to say
0671		to the invited [ones]
0580		Behold
2602		my feast
0950		is prepared
2657		and my oxen
1948		and my fat [ones]
2179		are killed
1168		and everything
1326		*
0950		is ready
0208		Come
2621		to the wedding feast

MATTHEW CHAPTER 22

VERSE 5 — But they scorned [the servants] and went away, one to his field and another to his business.

0592	ܗܢܘܢ	<they>
0518	ܕܝܢ	But
0284	ܒܣܘ	they scorned [the servants]
0042	ܘܐܙܠܘ	and went away
0069	ܚܕ	one
2251	ܠܩܪܝܬܗ	to his field
0069	ܘܚܕ	and another
2638	ܠܬܐܓܘܪܬܗ	to his business

VERSE 6 — Now the rest grabbed his servants and disgraced and killed [them].

2611	ܫܪܟܐ	the rest
0518	ܕܝܢ	Now
0047	ܐܚܕܘ	grabbed
1727	ܠܥܒܕܘܗܝ	his servants
2119	ܘܨܥܪܘ	and disgraced
2179	ܘܩܛܠܘ	and killed [them]

VERSE 7 — Now when the king heard [this], he was angry and sent his armies [and] destroyed those murderers and burned their city.

1128	ܟܕ	when
2547	ܫܡܥ	heard [this]
0518	ܕܝܢ	Now
1383	ܡܠܟܐ	the king
2290	ܪܓܙ	he was angry
2458	ܘܫܕܪ	and sent
0786	ܚܝܠܘܬܗ	his armies
0005	ܐܘܒܕ	[and] destroyed
2180	ܠܩܛܘܠܐ	murderers
0593	ܗܢܘܢ	those
0499	ܘܠܡܕܝܢܬܗܘܢ	and their city
1073	ܐܘܩܕ	burned

VERSE 8 — Then he said to his servants, 'The wedding feast is prepared and those who were invited were not worthy.

0594	ܘܗܝܕܝܢ	Then
0116	ܐܡܪ	he said
1727	ܠܥܒܕܘܗܝ	to his servants
2621	ܡܫܬܘܬܐ	The wedding feast
0950	ܡܛܝܒܐ	is prepared
0593	ܘܗܢܘܢ	and those
0671	ܕܡܙܡܢܝܢ	who invited
0603	ܗܘܘ	were
1262	ܠܐ	not
2461	ܫܘܝܢ	worthy
0603	ܗܘܘ	were

VERSE 9 — Go, therefore, to the limits of the roads and call whomever you find to the wedding feast.'

0042	ܙܠܘ	Go
0596	ܗܟܝܠ	therefore
1544	ܠܡܦܩܢܐ	to the limits
0038	ܕܐܘܪܚܬܐ	of the roads
1168	ܘܟܠ	and whomever
1389	ܡܢ	*
2510	ܕܡܫܟܚܝܢ	find
0133	ܐܢܬܘܢ	you
2239	ܩܪܘ	call
2621	ܠܡܫܬܘܬܐ	to the wedding feast

VERSE 10 — And those servants went out to the roads and gathered all whom they found, bad and good, and the banquet house was filled with guests.

1542	ܘܢܦܩܘ	And went out
1727	ܥܒܕܐ	servants
0593	ܗܢܘܢ	those
0038	ܠܐܘܪܚܬܐ	to the roads
1198	ܘܟܢܫܘ	and gathered
1168	ܟܠ	all
2510	ܕܐܫܟܚܘ	whom they found
0220	ܒܝܫܐ	bad
0938	ܘܛܒܐ	and good
1366	ܘܐܬܡܠܝ	and was filled with
0243	ܒܝܬ	the banquet house
2621	ܡܫܬܘܬܐ	*
1665	ܣܡܝܟܐ	guests

VERSE 11 — And the king entered to see the guests. And he saw there a man who was not wearing wedding clothes.

1796	ܘܥܠ	And entered

MATTHEW — CHAPTER 22

Vertical Interlinear

#	Syriac	English
1383		the king
0758		to see
1665		the guests
0758		And he saw
2682		there
0361		a man
1262		who not
1272		was wearing
1273		wedding clothes
2621		*

VERSE 12 — And he said to him, 'My friend, how did you enter this place, having no wedding garments?' And he was speechless.

#	Syriac	English
0116		And he said
1261		to him
0714		My friend
0061		how
1796		did you enter
1111		this place
1128		<when>
1501		wedding garments
2621		*
1264		having no
1261		*
0592		<he>
0518		And
2623		he was speechless

VERSE 13 — Then said the king to the servers, 'Bind his hands and his feet and throw him into the outer darkness. Crying and gnashing of teeth will be there.

#	Syriac	English
0594		Then
0116		said
1383		the king
2555		to the servers
0160		Bind
0057		his hands
2293		and his feet
1542		and throw him
0923		into the darkness
0321		outer
2682		there
0603		will be
0268		Crying
0905		and gnashing of
2558		teeth

VERSE 14 — For many are called, yet few chosen."

#	Syriac	English
1596		many
0592		are
0403		For
2241		called
0686		yet few
0353		chosen

VERSE 15 — Then the Pharisees went away [and] took counsel how they might trap him with a question.

#	Syriac	English
0594		Then
0042		went away
3439		the Pharisees
1532		[and] took
1384		counsel
0061		how
2089		they might trap him
1364		with a question

VERSE 16 — And they sent him their disciples with the Herodians and said to him, "Teacher, we know that you are true and you teach the way of God with truthfulness and you are not moved by anyone, for you are not a respecter of persons.

#	Syriac	English
2458		And they sent
1288		him
1304		their disciples
1817		with
0243		the Herodians
3179		*
0116		and said
1261		to him
1055		Teacher
1023		we know
2593		that true
0133		you are

MATTHEW CHAPTER 22

0038		and the way
0093		of God
2269		with truthfulness
1053		teach
0133		you
1262		and not
2587		you are moved
0133		*
1072		*
0131		by anyone
1262		not
0403		for
1532		you are a respecter of persons
0133		*
0173		*
0131		<of men>

VERSE 17 Tell us, therefore, how does it seem to you? Is it lawful to give the poll tax to Caesar or not?"

0116		Tell
1261		us
0596		therefore
0061		how
0758		does it seem
1261		to you
2528		Is it lawful
1030		to give
1209		the poll tax
2362		*
3483		to Caesar
0024		or
1262		not

VERSE 18 Now Jesus knew their evil [counsel] and said, "Why do you tempt me? Hypocrites!

3257		Jesus
0518		Now
1023		knew
0222		their evil [counsel]
0116		and said
1393		Why
1527		do tempt
0133		you
1261		me
1532		Hypocrites
0173		*

VERSE 19 Show me the denarius of the poll tax." And they brought to him a denarius.

0739		Show me
0519		the denarius
1209		of the poll tax
2362		*
0592		<they>
0518		And
2244		they brought
1261		to him
0519		a denarius

VERSE 20 And Jesus said to them, "Whose is this image and inscription?"

0116		And said
1261		to them
3257		Jesus
1390		Whose is
2112		image
0598		this
1248		and inscription

VERSE 21 They said, "Caesar's." He said to them, "Give, therefore, Caesar's to Caesar and God's to God."

0116		They said
3483		Caesar's
0116		He said
1261		to them
1030		Give
0596		therefore
3483		Caesar's
3483		to Caesar
0093		and God's
0093		to God

MATTHEW CHAPTER 22

VERSE 22 — And when they heard [this], they were amazed and they left him and went away.

1128	ܕܟܕ	And when
2547	ܫܡܥܘ	they heard [this]
0549	ܐܬܕܡܪܘ	they were amazed
2440	ܘܫܒܩܘܗܝ	and they left him
0042	ܘܐܙܠܘ	and went away

VERSE 23 — On the same day, the Sadducees came near and said to him, "There is no resurrection of the dead." And they asked him

0593	ܒܗܘ	On that
1036	ܝܘܡܐ	day
2244	ܘܩܪܒܘ	came near
3188	ܙܕܘܩܝܐ	the Sadducees
0116	ܘܐܡܪܝܢ	and said
1261	ܠܗ	to him
1264	ܠܝܬ	There is no
0784	ܚܝܬ	resurrection of
1338	ܡܝܬܐ	the dead
2420	ܘܫܐܠܘܗܝ	And they asked him

VERSE 24 — and said to him, "Teacher, Moses said to us, IF A MAN DIES WHILE HE HAS NO SONS, HIS BROTHER SHOULD TAKE HIS WIFE AND RAISE UP SEED FOR HIS BROTHER.

0116	ܘܐܡܪܝܢ	and said
1261	ܠܗ	to him
1055	ܡܠܦܢܐ	Teacher
3305	ܡܘܫܐ	Moses
0116	ܐܡܪ	said
1261	ܠܢ	to us
0121	ܐܢ	IF
0131	ܐܢܫ	A MAN
1334	ܡܐܬ	DIES
1128	ܟܕ	WHILE
1264	ܠܝܬ	HE HAS NO
1261	ܠܗ	*
0323	ܒܢܝܐ	SONS
1532	ܢܣܒ	SHOULD TAKE
0043	ܐܚܘܗܝ	HIS BROTHER
0135	ܐܢܬܬܗ	HIS WIFE
2168	ܘܢܩܝܡ	AND RAISE UP
0693	ܙܪܥܐ	SEED
0043	ܠܐܚܘܗܝ	FOR HIS BROTHER

VERSE 25 — Now there were seven brothers with us. The first took a wife and died and since he had no sons, he left his wife to his brother.

0069	ܐܝܬ	there were
0603	ܗܘܘ	*
0518	ܕܝܢ	Now
1288	ܠܘܬܢ	with us
0043	ܐܚܐ	brothers
2437	ܫܒܥܐ	seven
2157	ܩܕܡܝܐ	The first
2587	ܢܣܒ	took
0135	ܐܢܬܬܐ	a wife
1334	ܘܡܝܬ	and died
1264	ܘܕܠܝܬ	and since he had no
0603	ܗܘܐ	*
1261	ܠܗ	*
0323	ܒܢܝܐ	sons
2440	ܫܒܩܗ	he left
0135	ܐܢܬܬܗ	his wife
0043	ܠܐܚܘܗܝ	to his brother

VERSE 26 — Likewise also, the second and also the third, even up to the seventh.

0595	ܗܟܘܬ	Likewise
0169	ܐܦ	also
0593	ܗܘ	<that>
2709	ܬܪܝܢܐ	the second
0169	ܘܐܦ	and also
0593	ܗܘ	<that>
2674	ܬܠܝܬܝܐ	the third
1747	ܘܥܕܡܐ	even up to
2437	ܠܫܒܥܬܗܘܢ	the seventh

VERSE 27 — Now finally, all of them died [and] the woman also.

0054	ܒܚܪܬܐ	finally
0518	ܕܝܢ	Now
1168	ܕܟܠܗܘܢ	all of them

MATTHEW   CHAPTER 22

1334	died
0169	[and] also
0135	the woman

VERSE 28 — In the resurrection, therefore, to which of those seven [brothers] will she be a wife? For all of them married her."

2173	In the resurrection
0596	therefore
0066	to which
1388	of
0598	those
2437	seven [brothers]
0603	will she be
0135	a wife
1168	all of them
0403	For
1532	married her

VERSE 29 — Jesus answered and said to them, "You err, because you do not know the scriptures nor the power of God.

1838	answered
3257	Jesus
0116	and said
1261	to them
0993	err
0133	You
1262	because not
1023	do know
0133	you
1248	the scriptures
1262	nor
0786	the power
0093	of God

VERSE 30 — For in the resurrection of the dead, [men] do not marry women, nor are women [given] to husbands, but they are as the angels of God in heaven.

2173	In the resurrection
0403	For
1338	of the dead
1262	not
1532	[men] do marry
0135	women
0170	nor
0135	women
0603	are [given]
0361	to husbands
0090	but
0060	as
1375	the angels
0093	of God
2543	in heaven
0069	they are

VERSE 31 — Now concerning the resurrection of the dead, have you not read that which was spoken to you by God, who said:

1804	concerning
2173	the resurrection
0518	Now
1338	of the dead
1262	not
2239	have you read
1326	that
0116	which was spoken
1261	to you
1388	by
0093	God
0116	who said

VERSE 32 — I AM THE GOD OF ABRAHAM, THE GOD OF ISAAC, [AND] THE GOD OF JACOB? And he is not the God of the dead, but of the living."

0124	I AM
0124	*
0093	THE GOD
3005	OF ABRAHAM
0093	THE GOD
3033	OF ISAAC
0093	[AND] THE GOD
3255	OF JACOB
0093	And the God
1262	not

MATTHEW CHAPTER 22

0603	ܗܘܐ	he is
1338	ܕܡܝܬܐ	of the dead
0090	ܐܠܐ	but
0781	ܕܚܝܐ	of the living

VERSE 33 — And when the crowds heard [this], they were amazed by his teaching.

1128	ܘܟܕ	And when
2547	ܫܡܥܘ	heard [this]
1201	ܟܢܫܐ	the crowds
2679	ܡܬܕܡܪܝܢ ܗܘܘ	they were amazed
0603	ܗܘܘ	*
1054	ܒܝܘܠܦܢܗ	by his teaching

VERSE 34 — Now when the Pharisees heard that he had silenced the Sadducees, they assembled together.

3439	ܦܪܝܫܐ	the Pharisees
0518	ܕܝܢ	Now
1128	ܟܕ	when
2547	ܫܡܥܘ	heard [this]
2623	ܕܫܬܩ	that he had silenced
3188	ܠܙܕܘܩܝܐ	the Sadducees
1198	ܐܬܟܢܫܘ	they assembled
0074	ܐܟܚܕܐ	together

VERSE 35 — And one of them who knew the law asked, tempting him,

2420	ܘܫܐܠܗ	And asked
0721	ܚܕ	one
1388	ܡܢܗܘܢ	of them
1023	ܕܝܕܥ	who knew
1524	ܢܡܘܣܐ	the law
1128	ܟܕ	tempting
1527	ܡܢܣܐ	*
1261	ܠܗ	him

VERSE 36 — "Teacher, what commandment is great in the law?"

1055	ܡܠܦܢܐ	Teacher
0066	ܐܝܢܐ	what
2009	ܦܘܩܕܢܐ	commandment
2271	ܪܒ	is great
1524	ܒܢܡܘܣܐ	in the law

VERSE 37 — And Jesus said to him, "YOU SHOULD LOVE THE LORD YOUR GOD WITH ALL YOUR HEART AND WITH ALL YOUR SOUL AND WITH ALL YOUR STRENGTH AND WITH ALL YOUR MIND.

3257	ܝܫܘܥ	Jesus
0518	ܕܝܢ	And
0116	ܐܡܪ	said
1261	ܠܗ	to him
2342	ܕܬܪܚܡ	YOU SHOULD LOVE
1426	ܠܡܪܝܐ	THE LORD
0093	ܐܠܗܟ	YOUR GOD
1388	ܡܢ	WITH
1168	ܟܠܗ	ALL OF
1268	ܠܒܟ	YOUR HEART
1388	ܘܡܢ	AND WITH
1168	ܟܠܗ	ALL OF
1547	ܢܦܫܟ	YOUR SOUL
1388	ܘܡܢ	AND WITH
1168	ܟܠܗ	ALL OF
0786	ܚܝܠܟ	YOUR STRENGTH
1388	ܘܡܢ	AND WITH
1168	ܟܠܗ	ALL OF
2385	ܪܥܝܢܟ	YOUR MIND

VERSE 38 — This is the great and first commandment.

0599	ܗܢܘ	This is
2009	ܦܘܩܕܢܐ	the commandment
2271	ܪܒܐ	great
2157	ܘܩܕܡܝܐ	and first

VERSE 39 — And the second is like it: YOU SHOULD LOVE YOUR NEIGHBOR AS YOURSELF.

2709	ܘܕܬܪܝܢ	And the second
0540	ܕܕܡܐ	is like
1261	ܠܗ	it
2342	ܕܬܪܚܡ	YOU SHOULD LOVE
2248	ܠܩܪܝܒܟ	YOUR NEIGHBOR
0060	ܐܝܟ	AS
1547	ܢܦܫܟ	YOURSELF

MATTHEW CHAPTER 22

VERSE 40 — On these two commandments suspend the law and the prophets."

0598		On these
2709		two
2009		commandments
2672		suspend
0040		the law
1457		and the prophets

VERSE 41 — Now while the Pharisees were assembled, Jesus asked them

1128		while
1198		were assembled
0518		Now
3439		the Pharisees
2420		asked
0592		them
3257		Jesus

VERSE 42 — and said, "What do you say about the Messiah? Whose son is he?" They said to him, "The Son of David."

0116		and said
1393		What
0116		do say
0133		you
1804		about
1446		the Messiah
0323		son
1390		Whose is he
0116		They said
1261		to him
0323		The Son
3159		of David

VERSE 43 — He said to them, "Yet how does David spiritually call him LORD? For he said:

0116		He said
1261		to them
0061		Yet how
3159		David
2323		spiritually
2239		does call
1261		him
1426		LORD
0116		He said
0403		For

VERSE 44 — THE LORD SAID TO MY LORD, SIT AT MY RIGHT UNTIL I PLACE YOUR ENEMIES UNDER YOUR FEET.

0116		SAID
1426		THE LORD
1426		TO MY LORD
1093		SIT
1261		*
1388		AT
1061		MY RIGHT HAND
1747		UNTIL
1625		I PLACE
0307		YOUR ENEMIES
2660		UNDER
2293		YOUR FEET

VERSE 45 — Therefore, if David called him 'LORD,' how is he his son?"

0121		if
0596		Therefore
3159		David
2239		called
1261		him
1426		LORD
0061		how
0323		his son
0592		is he

VERSE 46 — And no man was able to give him an answer. And no man dared to question him again from that day [on].

1262		And no
0131		man
2510		was able
1030		to give
1261		him
2068		an answer
1262		And no
0131		man
1435		dared

MATTHEW CHAPTER 22

Num	Syriac	English
2650		again
1388		from
0593		that
1036		day [on]
2420		to question him

CHAPTER 23

VERSE 1 — Then Jesus talked with the crowds and with his disciples.

Num	Syriac	English
0594		Then
3257		Jesus
1362		talked
1817		with
1201		the crowds
1817		and with
1304		his disciples

VERSE 2 — And he said to them, "The scribes and the Pharisees sit on the seat of Moses.

Num	Syriac	English
0116		And he said
1261		to them
1804		on
1159		the seat
3305		of Moses
1093		sit
1699		The scribes
3439		and Pharisees

VERSE 3 — Everything, therefore, that they say that you should keep, keep and do. But you should not do according to their deeds. For they speak and do not act.

Num	Syriac	English
1168		Everything
1326		*
0596		therefore
0116		that they say
1261		<to you>
1502		that you should keep
1502		keep
1724		and do
0060		according to
1728		their deeds
0518		But
1262		not
1724		you should do
0116		they speak
0403		For
1262		and not
1724		do act

VERSE 4 — And they bind heavy burdens and place [them] on the shoulders of men, but do not want to touch them with their finger[s].

Num	Syriac	English
0160		And they bind
1017		burdens
1079		heavy
1625		and place [them]
1804		on
1257		the shoulders
0323		of men
0131		*
0592		<they>
0518		but
2081		with their finger[s]
1262		not
2077		do want
2244		to touch
1261		them

VERSE 5 — And they do all of their deeds to be seen by men. For they broaden their phylacteries and lengthen the fringes of their mantles.

Num	Syriac	English
1168		And all of
1728		their deeds
1724		they do
0758		to be seen
0323		by men
0131		*
2066		they broaden
0403		For
2696		their phylacteries
0192		and lengthen
2668		the fringes
1439		of their mantles

MATTHEW CHAPTER 23

VERSE 6 — And they love the chief places at festivals and the chief seats in the synagogues

2342		And they love
2362		the chief
1666		places
0928		at festivals
2362		and the chief
1094		seats
1200		in the synagogues

VERSE 7 — and a greeting in the marketplaces and that they are called Rabbi by men.

2535		and a greeting
2481		in the marketplaces
0603		and that they are
2239		called
1388		by
0131		men
2275		Rabbi

VERSE 8 — But you should not be called Rabbi. For one is your Rabbi and all of you are brothers.

0133		<you>
0518		But
1262		not
2239		you should be called
2275		Rabbi
0721		one
0592		is
0403		For
2271		your Rabbi
0133		<you>
0518		and
1168		all of you
0043		brothers
0133		<you> are

VERSE 9 — And do not call yourselves father on earth. For one is your Father, who is in heaven.

0002		And father
1262		not
2239		do call
1261		yourselves
0199		on earth
0721		one
0592		is
0403		For
0002		your Father
2543		who is in heaven

VERSE 10 — And you should not be called leaders, because one is your leader, the Messiah.

1262		And not
2239		you should be called
0482		leaders
1347		because
0721		one
0592		is
0482		your leader
1446		the Messiah

VERSE 11 — But he who is great among you should be a minister to you.

0593		he
0518		But
2271		who is great
0217		among you
0603		should be
1261		to you
2555		a minister

VERSE 12 — For he who elevates himself will be humbled and he who humbles himself will be elevated.

1389		he who
0403		For
2331		elevates
1547		himself
1353		will be humbled
1389		and he who
1353		humbles
1547		himself
2331		will be elevated

MATTHEW CHAPTER 23

VERSE 13 — Woe to you, scribes and Pharisees! Hypocrites! Because you consume the houses of widows with the occasion that you would lengthen your prayers. Because of this, you will receive greater judgment.

0625		Woe
1261		to you
1699		scribes
3439		and Pharisees
1532		Hypocrites
0173		*
0075		Because consume
0133		you
0243		the houses
0195		of widows
1801		with the occasion
0192		that would lengthen
0133		you
2107		your prayers
1347		Because of
0598		this
2134		you will receive
0497		judgment
1100		greater

VERSE 14 — Woe to you, scribes and Pharisees! Hypocrites! Because you have held the kingdom of heaven closed before men. For you are not entering and those who would enter, you do not allow to enter.

0625		Woe
1261		to you
1699		scribes
3439		and Pharisees
1532		Hypocrites
0173		*
0047		Because have held closed
0133		you
1385		the kingdom
2543		of heaven
2154		before
0323		men
0131		*
0133		<you>
0403		For
1262		not
1796		are entering
0133		you
0066		and those
1796		who would enter
1262		not
2440		do allow
0133		you
1796		to enter

VERSE 15 — Woe to you, scribes and Pharisees! Hypocrites! Because you travel over sea and land to make one convert. And when he has become [a convert], you make him the son of Gehenna more than you.

0625		Woe
1261		to you
1699		scribes
3439		and Pharisees
1532		Hypocrites
0173		*
1236		Because travel over
0133		you
1057		sea
1019		and land
1724		to make
0721		one
0387		convert
1313		And when
0603		he has become [a convert]
1724		make
0133		you
1261		him
0323		a son
3148		of Gehenna
1853		even more
1804		than you

Vertical Interlinear

MATTHEW CHAPTER 23

VERSE 16 — Woe to you, blind guides! Because you say that whoever swears by the temple, it is nothing. But he who swears by the gold that is in the temple is guilty.

Code	Aramaic	English
0625		Woe
1261		to you
1464		guides
1662		blind
0116		Because say
0133		you
1389		that whoever
1059		swears
0607		by the temple
1262		nothing
0603		it is
1326		<anything>
1389		he who
0518		But
1059		swears
0489		by the gold
0607		that is in the temple
0742		is guilty

VERSE 17 — [You are] fools and blind! For what is greater, the gold or the temple? Which sanctifies, the gold?

Code	Aramaic	English
1651		[You are] fools
1662		and blind
1393		what
0403		For
2271		is greater
0489		the gold
0024		or
0607		the temple
0592		Which
2160		sanctifies
1261		<it>
0489		the gold

VERSE 18 — And [you say], whoever swears by the altar, it is nothing. But he who swears by the offering that is on it is guilty.

Code	Aramaic	English
1389		And [you say] whoever
1059		swears
0475		by the altar
1262		nothing
0603		it is
1326		<anything>
1389		he who
0518		But
1059		swears
2246		by the offering
1803		that is on
1388		it
0742		is guilty

VERSE 19 — [You are] fools and blind! What is greater, the offering or the altar that is sanctified by the offering?

Code	Aramaic	English
1651		[You are] fools
1776		and blind
1393		What
2271		is greater
2246		the offering
0024		or
0475		the altar
2160		that is sanctified
2246		by the offering

VERSE 20 — Therefore, he who swears by the altar swears by it and by everything that is on it.

Code	Aramaic	English
1389		he who
1059		swears
0596		Therefore
0475		by the altar
1059		swears
0217		by it
1168		and by everything
1313		*
0069		that is
1803		on
1388		it

VERSE 21 — And he who swears by the temple swears by it and by him who dwells in it.

Code	Aramaic	English
1389		and he who

MATTHEW CHAPTER 23

1059		swears
0607		by the temple
1059		swears
0217		by it
1389		and by him
1833		who dwells
0217		in it

VERSE 22 And he who swears by heaven swears by the throne of God and by him who sits on it.

1389		And he who
1059		swears
2543		by heaven
1059		swears
1159		by the throne
0093		of God
1389		and by him
1093		who sits
1803		on
1388		it

VERSE 23 Woe to you, scribes and Pharisees! Hypocrites! Because you tithe mint and dill and cummin and you overlook the more important [things] of the law, judgment and mercy and faith. Now these were necessary for you to have done and you should not have overlooked those.

0625		Woe
1261		to you
1699		scribes
3439		and Pharisees
1532		Hypocrites
0173		*
1850		Because you tithe
0133		*
1526		mint
2447		and dill
1189		and cummin
2440		and you overlook
1079		the more important [things]
1524		of the law
0497		judgment
0841		and mercy
0113		and faith
0598		these
0518		Now
0626		necessary
0603		were
1724		for you to have done
0598		and those
1262		not
2440		you should have overlooked

VERSE 24 [You are] blind guides, who strain gnats and swallow camels!

1464		[You are] guides
1662		blind
2111		who strain
0315		gnats
0277		and swallow
0420		camels

VERSE 25 Woe to you, scribes and Pharisees! Hypocrites! For you cleanse the outside of the cup and of the dish, but inside are full of violence and wickedness.

0625		Woe
1261		to you
1699		scribes
3439		and Pharisees
1532		Hypocrites
0173		*
0521		For cleanse
0133		you
0320		the outside
1205		of the cup
0629		and of the dish
0379		inside
0518		but
1366		are full of
0776		violence
1766		and wickedness

MATTHEW CHAPTER 23

VERSE 26 — Blind Pharisees! Cleanse first the inside of the cup and of the dish, so that their outside may also be clean.

Number	Aramaic	English
3439		Pharisees
1776		Blind
0521		Cleanse
2151		first
0375		the inside
1205		of the cup
0629		and of the dish
0603		so that may be
0169		also
0320		their outside
0521		clean

VERSE 27 — Woe to you, scribes and Pharisees! Hypocrites! Because you are like white graves that on the outside appear beautiful, but on the inside are full of the bones of the dead and all corruption.

Number	Aramaic	English
0625		Woe
1261		to you
1699		scribes
3439		and Pharisees
1532		Hypocrites
0173		*
0540		Because are like
0133		you
2146		graves
1187		white
1388		that on
0322		the outside
0758		appear
2583		beautiful
1388		on
0379		the inside
0518		but
1366		are full of
0464		the bones
1338		of the dead
1168		and all
0992		corruption

VERSE 28 — So also, on the outside you appear to men as just and on the inside you are full of wickedness and hypocrisy.

Number	Aramaic	English
0597		So
0169		also
0133		<you>
1388		on
0322		the outside
0758		appear
0133		you
0323		to men
0131		*
0060		as
0637		just
1388		and on
0379		the inside
1366		are full of
0133		you
1766		wickedness
1533		and hypocrisy
0173		*

VERSE 29 — Woe to you, scribes and Pharisees! Hypocrites! Because you maintain the graves of the prophets and you adorn the tombs of the just [ones]

Number	Aramaic	English
0625		Woe
1261		to you
1699		scribes
3439		and Pharisees
1532		Hypocrites
0173		*
0281		Because maintain
0133		you
2146		the graves
1457		of the prophets
2083		and adorn
0133		you
0243		the tombs
2143		*
0637		of the just [ones]

MATTHEW CHAPTER 23

VERSE 30 — and you say, 'If we had been in the days of our fathers, we would not have been participants with them in the blood of the prophets.'

0116		and say
0133		you
0097		If
0603		we had been
1036		in the days
0002		of our fathers
1262		not
0603		we would have been
0603		*
1261		with them
2486		participants
0539		in the blood
1457		of the prophets

VERSE 31 — Thereby you witness against yourselves that you are the sons of those who killed the prophets.

1324		Thereby
1608		witness
0133		you
1804		against
1547		yourselves
0323		that the sons
0133		you are
0593		of those
2179		who killed
1457		the prophets

VERSE 32 — And you also fill up the measure of your fathers.

0169		And also
0133		you
1366		fill up
1444		the measure
0002		of your fathers

VERSE 33 — [You] snakes! Offspring of vipers! How will you flee from the judgment of Gehenna?

0740		[You] snakes
1047		Offspring
0071		of vipers
0061		How
1904		will you flee
1388		from
0497		the judgment
3148		of Gehenna

VERSE 34 — Because of this, behold, I send to you prophets and wise men and scribes. Some of them you will kill and you will crucify and some of them you will beat in your synagogues and you will pursue them from city to city,

1347		Because of
0598		this
0580		behold
0124		<I>
2458		send
0124		I
1288		to you
1457		prophets
0790		and wise men
1699		and scribes
1388		Some of them
2179		will kill
0133		you
0688		and will crucify
0133		you
1388		and some of them
1461		will beat
0133		you
1200		in your synagogues
2304		and you will pursue
0592		them
1388		from
0499		city
0499		to city

VERSE 35 — so that all the blood of the just [ones] that has been shed on the earth will come on you, from the blood of Abel the just up to the blood of Zechariah, the son of Barachiah, whom you killed between the temple [and] the altar.

0061		so that

MATTHEW CHAPTER 23

0208		will come		3022		Jerusalem
1804		on you		2179		you have killed
1168		all		1457		the prophets
0539		the blood		2296		and you have stoned
0637		of the just [ones]		0066		those
0201		that has been shed		2521		who were sent
1804		on		1288		to her
0199		the earth		1188		How many
1388		from		0633		times
0539		the blood		2077		have I wanted
3171		of Abel		1198		to gather
0637		the just		0323		your sons
1747		up to		0060		like
0539		the blood		1198		gathers
3191		of Zechariah		2714		a hen
0323		the son of		2022		her chicks
3135		Barachiah		2660		under
0593		<he>		0451		her wings
2179		whom you killed		1262		and not
0266		between		2077		you did want [to be gathered]
0607		the temple				
0475		[and] the altar				

VERSE 38 Behold, your house is left to you desolate.

0580		Behold
2440		is left
1261		to you
0243		your house
0894		desolate

VERSE 36 Truly I say to you, all these [things] will come on this generation.

0110		Truly
0116		say
0124		I
1261		to you
0208		will come
0598		these [things]
1168		all
1804		on
2605		generation
0598		this

VERSE 39 For I say to you, you will not see me from now until you say, BLESSED IS HE WHO COMES IN THE NAME OF THE LORD."

0116		I say
1261		to you
0403		For
1262		not
0758		you will see me
1388		from
0602		now
1747		until
0116		you say

VERSE 37 Jerusalem, Jerusalem, you have killed the prophets and you have stoned those who were sent to her. How many times have I wanted to gather your sons like a hen gathers her chicks under her wings and you did not want [to be gathered]?

3022		Jerusalem

Vertical Interlinear

MATTHEW CHAPTER 23

0338	ܒܪܝܟ	BLESSED
0592	ܗܘ	IS HE
0208	ܕܐܬܐ	WHO COMES
2539	ܒܫܡܗ	IN THE NAME
1426	ܕܡܪܝܐ	OF THE LORD

CHAPTER 24

VERSE 1 — And Jesus came out of the temple to go away. And his disciples came near [and] were showing him the construction of the temple.

1542	ܘܢܦܩ	And came out
3257	ܝܫܘܥ	Jesus
1388	ܡܢ	of
0607	ܗܝܟܠܐ	the temple
0042	ܠܡܐܙܠ	to go away
2244	ܘܩܪܒܘ	And came near
1304	ܬܠܡܝܕܘܗܝ	his disciples
0739	ܡܚܘܝܢ	[and] showing
0603	ܗܘܘ	were
1261	ܠܗ	him
0283	ܒܢܝܢܗ	the construction
0607	ܕܗܝܟܠܐ	of the temple

VERSE 2 — And he said to them, "Behold, do you not see all these [things]? Truly I say to you, [one] stone here will not be left on [another] stone that will not be demolished."

0592	ܗܘ	<he>
0518	ܕܝܢ	And
0116	ܐܡܪ	he said
1261	ܠܗܘܢ	to them
1262	ܠܐ	not
0580	ܗܐ	Behold
0758	ܚܙܝܢ	do see
0133	ܐܢܬܘܢ	you
0598	ܗܠܝܢ	these [things]
1168	ܟܠܗܝܢ	all
0110	ܐܡܝܢ	Truly
0116	ܐܡܪ	say
0124	ܐܢܐ	I
1261	ܠܟܘܢ	to you
1262	ܠܐ	not
2440	ܬܫܬܒܩ	will be left
0600	ܗܪܟܐ	here
1119	ܟܐܦ	[one] stone
1804	ܥܠ	on
1119	ܟܐܦ	[another] stone
1262	ܠܐ	that not
1719	ܬܣܬܬܪ	will be demolished

VERSE 3 — And when Jesus sat on the Mount of Olives, his disciples came near and said among themselves and to him, "Tell us when these [things] will be and what is the sign of your coming and of the end of the age."

1128	ܘܟܕ	And when
1093	ܝܬܒ	sat
3257	ܝܫܘܥ	Jesus
1804	ܥܠ	on
0958	ܛܘܪܐ	the Mount
0663	ܕܙܝܬܐ	of Olives
2244	ܩܪܒܘ	came near
1304	ܬܠܡܝܕܘܗܝ	his disciples
0116	ܘܐܡܪܝܢ	and said
0266	ܒܝܢܝܗܘܢ	among themselves
1261	ܘܠܗ	and to him
0116	ܐܡܪ	Tell
1261	ܠܢ	us
0120	ܐܡܬܝ	when
0598	ܗܠܝܢ	these [things]
0603	ܢܗܘܝܢ	will be
1393	ܘܡܢܐ	and what
0592	ܗܘ	is
0206	ܐܬܐ	the sign
0210	ܕܡܐܬܝܬܟ	of your coming
2534	ܘܕܫܘܠܡܗ	and of the end
1813	ܕܥܠܡܐ	of the age

VERSE 4 — Jesus answered and said to them, "Beware, [so that] no one will deceive you.

1838	ܥܢܐ	answered
3257	ܝܫܘܥ	Jesus

MATTHEW   CHAPTER 24

0116		and said
1261		to them
0645		Beware
1262		[so that] no
0131		one
0993		will deceive you

VERSE 5   For many will come in my name and they will say, 'I am the Messiah.' And they will deceive many.

1596		many
0403		For
0208		will come
2539		in my name
0116		and they will say
0124		I am
0124		*
1446		the Messiah
1596		And many
0993		they will deceive

VERSE 6   Now you are about to hear of battles and a report of wars. See [that] you are not disturbed. For it is necessary that all these [things] occur, but the end [is] not yet.

1914		about to
0133		you are
0518		Now
2547		hear
2131		of battles
2553		and a report
2247		of wars
0758		See [that]
1262		not
0493		you are disturbed
0626		it is necessary
0403		For
1168		that all these [things]
0603		occur
0090		but
1262		not
1745		[is] yet

2534		the end

VERSE 7   For people will rise against people and kingdom against kingdom and famines and pestilence and earthquakes will occur in various places.

2168		will rise
0403		For
1818		people
1804		against
1818		people
1385		and kingdom
1804		against
1385		kingdom
0603		and will occur
1213		famines
1336		and pestilence
0658		and earthquakes
0494		in various places
0494		*

VERSE 8   But all these [things] are [only] the beginning of sorrows.

0598		these [things]
0518		But
1168		all
2362		the beginning
0592		are [only]
0704		of sorrows

VERSE 9   Then they will deliver you to trials and they will kill you and you will be hated by all nations because of my name.

0594		Then
2530		they will deliver you
0103		to trials
2179		and they will kill you
0603		and you will be
1675		hated
1388		by
1168		all
1818		nations
1347		because of
2539		my name

MATTHEW CHAPTER 24

Vertical Interlinear

VERSE 10 — Then many will be caused to stumble and will hate one another and will betray one another.

Code	Aramaic	English
0594		Then
1242		will be caused to stumble
1596		many
1673		and will hate
0721		one
0721		another
2530		and will betray
0721		one
0721		another

VERSE 11 — And many false prophets will rise up and deceive many.

Code	Aramaic	English
1596		And many
1457		prophets
0486		false
2168		will rise up
0993		and deceive
1596		many

VERSE 12 — And because of the abundance of wickedness, the love of many will grow cold.

Code	Aramaic	English
1347		And because of
1597		the abundance of
1766		wickedness
1935		will grow cold
0699		the love
1596		of many

VERSE 13 — But he who endures until the last will have life.

Code	Aramaic	English
1389		he who
1588		endures
0518		But
1747		until
0054		the last
0592		<he>
0780		will have life

VERSE 14 — And this gospel of the kingdom will be preached in the entire world for a testimony to all of the nations and then the end will come.

Code	Aramaic	English
1230		And will be preached
0598		this
1593		gospel
1385		of the kingdom
1168		in the entire
1813		world
1610		for a testimony
1168		to all of
1818		the nations
0594		and then
0208		will come
2534		the end

VERSE 15 — Now when you see the abominable sign of desecration that was spoken of by Daniel the prophet that will stand in the holy place (he who reads should understand),

Code	Aramaic	English
1313		when
0518		Now
0758		you see
0206		the sign
0991		abominable
0892		of desecration
0116		that was spoken of
3167		by Daniel
1457		the prophet
2168		that will stand
0494		in the place
2162		holy
0593		he
2239		who reads
1647		should understand

VERSE 16 — then those who are in Judah should flee to the mountain.

Code	Aramaic	English
0594		then
0066		those
3224		who in Judea
0592		are

MATTHEW — CHAPTER 24

1904		should flee
0958		to the mountain
VERSE 17		And he who is on the roof should not come down to take that which is in his house.
0593		And he who
0019		on the roof
0592		is
1262		not
1499		should come down
1532		to take
0243		that which is in his house
VERSE 18		And he who is in the field should not turn back behind himself to take his clothing.
0066		And he who
0884		in the field
0592		is
1262		not
0616		should turn back
0295		behind himself
1532		to take
1274		his clothing
VERSE 19		But woe to the pregnant women and those who are nursing in those days!
0625		woe
0518		But
0260		to the pregnant women
0066		and those
1063		who are nursing
0593		in those
1036		days
VERSE 20		Now pray, so that your flight will not be in the winter, nor on the Sabbath.
2106		pray
0518		Now
1262		so that not
0603		will be
1905		your flight
1718		in the winter
1262		nor
2445		on the Sabbath
VERSE 21		For then a great ordeal will occur, such as has not been from the beginning of the world until now, nor will be.
0603		will occur
0403		For
0594		then
0103		ordeal
2271		a great
0066		such as
1262		not
0603		has been
1388		from
2363		the beginning
1813		of the world
1747		<and> until
0602		now
1262		nor
0603		will be
VERSE 22		And if those days were not cut short, no flesh would live. But because of the chosen [ones], those days will be cut short.
0097		And if
1262		not
1221		were cut short
1036		days
0593		those
1262		no
0780		would live
0603		*
1168		<all>
0294		flesh
1347		because of
0353		the chosen [ones]
0518		But
1221		will be cut short
1036		days
0593		those

MATTHEW CHAPTER 24

Vertical Interlinear

VERSE 23 Then if anyone should say to you, 'Here is the Messiah or [over] here,' do not believe [him].

Code	Aramaic	English
0594		Then
0121		if
0131		anyone
0116		should say
1261		to you
0600		Here
0592		is
1446		the Messiah
0024		or
0600		[over] here
1262		not
0109		do believe [him]

VERSE 24 For false messiahs and lying prophets will rise up and they will produce signs [and] wonders in order to deceive even the chosen [ones], if possible.

Code	Aramaic	English
2168		will rise up
0403		For
1446		messiahs
0486		false
1457		and prophets
1132		lying
1030		and they will produce
0206		signs
2271		[and] wonders
0060		in order
0993		to deceive
0121		if
2510		possible
0169		even
0353		the chosen [ones]

VERSE 25 Behold, I have told you beforehand.

Code	Aramaic	English
0580		Behold
2150		beforehand
0116		I have told
1261		you

VERSE 26 Therefore, if they say to you, 'Behold, he is in the wilderness,' do not go out, or 'Behold, he is in an inner chamber,' do not believe [them].

Code	Aramaic	English
0121		if
0596		Therefore
0116		they say
1261		to you
0580		Behold
0892		in the wilderness
0592		he is
1262		not
1542		do go out
0024		or
0580		Behold
0029		in an inner chamber
0592		he is
1262		not
0109		do believe [them]

VERSE 27 For as the lightning comes out of the east and is visible into the west, so the arrival of the Son of Man will be.

Code	Aramaic	English
0061		as
0403		For
0344		the lightning
1542		comes out
1388		of
0557		the east
0758		and is visible
1747		into
1884		the west
0597		so
0603		will be
0210		the arrival
0323		of the Son
0131		of Man

VERSE 28 Wherever the carcass will be, there the eagles will be gathered.

Code	Aramaic	English
1108		Wherever
0121		*
0603		will be

MATTHEW CHAPTER 24

#	Aramaic	English
1929		the carcass
2682		there
1198		will be gathered
1575		the eagles

VERSE 29 And immediately after the ordeal of those days, THE SUN WILL GROW DARK AND THE MOON WILL NOT SHINE ITS LIGHT AND STARS WILL FALL FROM HEAVEN AND THE POWERS OF HEAVEN WILL BE SHAKEN.

#	Aramaic	English
0725		immediately
0518		And
0215		after
0103		the ordeal
1036		of days
0593		those
2557		THE SUN
0922		WILL GROW DARK
1611		AND THE MOON
1262		NOT
0739		WILL SHINE
1477		ITS LIGHT
1141		AND STARS
1538		WILL FALL
1388		FROM
2543		HEAVEN
0786		AND THE POWERS
2543		OF HEAVEN
0657		WILL BE SHAKEN

VERSE 30 And then the standard of the Son of Man will be seen in heaven. And then all the tribes of the earth will mourn and they will see THE SON OF MAN WHO COMES ON THE CLOUDS OF HEAVEN WITH POWER AND GREAT GLORY.

#	Aramaic	English
0594		And then
0758		will be seen
1507		the standard
0323		of the Son
0131		of Man
2543		in heaven
0594		And then
2403		will mourn
1168		all
2605		the tribes
0199		of the earth
0758		and they will see
0323		THE SON
0131		OF MAN
0208		WHO COMES
1804		ON
1844		THE CLOUDS OF
2543		HEAVEN
1817		WITH
0786		POWER
2431		AND GLORY
1596		GREAT

VERSE 31 And he will send his angels with a great trumpet and they will gather his chosen [ones] from the four winds, from one end of heaven to the other.

#	Aramaic	English
2458		And he will send
1375		his angels
1817		with
2506		a trumpet
2271		great
1198		and they will gather
0353		chosen [ones]
0517		his
1388		from
0179		four
2323		the winds
1388		from
2362		one end
2543		of heaven
1747		to
2362		the other

VERSE 32 Now learn an illustration from the fig tree. Immediately when its branches are tender and its leaves bud, you know that summer has arrived.

#	Aramaic	English
1388		from

MATTHEW — CHAPTER 24

Vertical Interlinear

Code	Syriac	English
2628		the fig tree
0518		Now
1053		learn
1967		an illustration
0725		Immediately
1623		when its branches
2366		are tender
2037		and bud
1008		its leaves
1023		know
0133		you
1346		that has arrived
2194		summer

VERSE 33 — So also you, when you have seen these [things], will all know that I have arrived at the door.

Code	Syriac	English
0597		So
0169		also
0133		you
1313		when
0758		you have seen
0598		these [things]
1168		all
1023		will know
1346		that I have arrived
1261		<to it>
2718		at the door

VERSE 34 — Truly I say to you, this generation will not pass until all these [things] occur.

Code	Syriac	English
0110		Truly
0116		say
0124		I
1261		to you
1262		not
1733		will pass
2605		generation
0598		this
1747		until
0598		these [things]
1168		all
0603		occur

VERSE 35 — Heaven and earth will pass away, yet my words will not pass away.

Code	Syriac	English
2543		Heaven
0199		and earth
1733		will pass away
1364		yet my words
1262		not
1733		will pass away

VERSE 36 — But about that day and about that hour, no man knows, not even the angels of heaven, but the Father only.

Code	Syriac	English
1804		about
1036		day
0518		But
0593		that
1804		and about
2573		hour
0593		that
0131		man
1262		no
1023		knows
0170		not even
1375		the angels
2543		of heaven
0090		but
0002		the Father
1041		only

VERSE 37 — And as the days of Noah, so will be the arrival of the Son of Man.

Code	Syriac	English
0061		as
0518		And
1036		the days of
3339		Noah
0597		so
0603		will be
0210		the arrival
0323		of the Son
0131		of Man

MATTHEW CHAPTER 24

VERSE 38 For as they were before the flood, eating and drinking and marrying women and giving [women in marriage] to men, up to the day [in] which Noah entered the ark,

0061	ܐܝܟ	as
0403	ܓܝܪ	For
0069	ܕܐܝܬܝܗܘܢ	they were
0603	ܗܘܘ	*
2154	ܩܕܡ	before
0954	ܛܘܦܢܐ	the flood
0075	ܐܟܠܝܢ	eating
2620	ܘܫܬܝܢ	and drinking
1532	ܘܢܣܒܝܢ	and marrying
0135	ܢܫܐ	women
1030	ܘܝܗܒܝܢ	and giving [women in marriage]
0361	ܠܓܒܪܐ	to men
1747	ܥܕܡܐ	up to
1036	ܠܝܘܡܐ	the days of
1796	ܕܥܠ	[in] which entered
3339	ܢܘܚ	Noah
1140	ܠܟܘܝܠܐ	the ark

VERSE 39 and they did not know until the flood came and took all of them, so will be the arrival of the Son of Man.

1262	ܘܠܐ	and not
1023	ܝܕܥܘ	they did know
1747	ܥܕܡܐ	until
0208	ܕܐܬܐ	came
0954	ܛܘܦܢܐ	the flood
2587	ܘܫܩܠ	and took
1168	ܠܟܠܗܘܢ	all of them
0597	ܗܟܢܐ	so
0603	ܬܗܘܐ	will be
0210	ܡܐܬܝܬܗ	the arrival
0323	ܕܒܪܗ	of the Son
0131	ܕܐܢܫܐ	of Man

VERSE 40 Then two [men] will be in the field. One will be taken and one will be left.

0594	ܗܝܕܝܢ	Then
2709	ܬܪܝܢ	two [men]
0603	ܢܗܘܘܢ	will be
2251	ܒܩܪܝܬܐ	in the field
0721	ܚܕ	One
0477	ܡܬܕܒܪ	will be taken
0721	ܘܚܕ	and one
2440	ܡܫܬܒܩ	will be left

VERSE 41 And two [women] will be grinding at the mill. One will be taken and one will be left.

2709	ܘܬܪܬܝܢ	And two [women]
0603	ܢܗܘܝܢ	will be
0960	ܛܚܢܢ	grinding
2341	ܒܪܚܝܐ	at the mill
0721	ܚܕܐ	One
0477	ܡܬܕܒܪܐ	will be taken
0721	ܘܚܕܐ	and one
2440	ܡܫܬܒܩܐ	will be left

VERSE 42 Therefore, watch, because you do not know in what hour your Lord will come.

1880	ܐܬܬܥܝܪܘ	watch
0596	ܗܟܝܠ	Therefore
1262	ܕܠܐ	because not
1023	ܝܕܥܝܢ	do know
0133	ܐܢܬܘܢ	you
0066	ܒܐܝܕܐ	in what
2573	ܫܥܬܐ	hour
0208	ܐܬܐ	will come
1426	ܡܪܟܘܢ	your Lord

VERSE 43 But know this, if the master of the house had known in what watch the thief would come, he would have watched and would not have allowed his house to be broken into.

0598	ܗܕܐ	this
0518	ܕܝܢ	But
1023	ܕܥܘ	know
0097	ܕܐܠܘ	if
1023	ܝܕܥ	had known
0603	ܗܘܐ	*
1426	ܡܪܐ	the master of
0243	ܒܝܬܐ	the house

MATTHEW CHAPTER 24

Code	Syriac	English
0066		in what
1503		watch
0208		would come
0437		the thief
1880		he would have watched
0603		*
1262		and not
2440		would have allowed
0603		*
1983		to be broken into
0243		his house

VERSE 44 Because of this, you should be prepared also, because in an hour that you do not expect, the Son of Man will come.

Code	Syriac	English
1347		Because of
0598		this
0169		also
0133		you
0603		should be
0950		prepared
2573		because in an hour
1262		that not
1588		do expect
0133		you
0208		will come
0323		the Son
0131		of Man

VERSE 45 Who truly is the faithful and wise servant whom his lord has set over his household, to give them food in its time?

Code	Syriac	English
1390		Who
1163		truly
0069		is
1727		the servant
0114		faithful
0790		and wise
2168		whom has set
1426		his lord
1804		over
0323		his household

Code	Syriac	English
0243		*
1030		to give
1261		them
1594		food
0633		in its time

VERSE 46 Blessed [is] that servant who, [when] his lord comes, finds him doing so.

Code	Syriac	English
0940		Blessed [is]
1727		servant
0593		that
0208		who [when] comes
1426		his lord
2510		finds him
1724		doing
0597		so

VERSE 47 Truly I say to you, he will set him over all that he has.

Code	Syriac	English
0110		Truly
0116		say
0124		I
1261		to you
2168		he will set him
1804		over
1168		all
0069		that he has
1261		*

VERSE 48 But if a servant, [being] evil in his heart, says, 'My lord is delaying to come,'

Code	Syriac	English
0121		if
0518		But
0116		says
1727		a servant
0593		<who>
0220		[being] evil
1268		in his heart
1426		My lord
0050		is delaying
0208		to come

MATTHEW CHAPTER 24

VERSE 49 and begins to beat his fellow-servants and is eating and drinking with drunkards,

2597	ܘܫܪܐ	and begins
1341	ܠܡܡܚܐ	to beat
1202	ܟܢܘܬܗ	his fellow-servants
0603	ܘܗܘܐ	and is
0075	ܐܟܠ	eating
2620	ܘܫܬܐ	and drinking
1817	ܥܡ	with
2316	ܪܘܝܐ	drunkards

VERSE 50 the lord of that servant will come in a day that he does not expect and in an hour that he does not know.

0208	ܢܐܬܐ	will come
1426	ܡܪܗ	the lord
1727	ܕܥܒܕܐ	of servant
0593	ܗܘ	that
1036	ܒܝܘܡܐ	in a day
1262	ܕܠܐ	that not
1588	ܣܒܪ	he does expect
2573	ܘܒܫܥܬܐ	and in an hour
1262	ܕܠܐ	that not
1023	ܝܕܥ	he does know

VERSE 51 And he will cut him in pieces and assign [him] his portion with the hypocrites. Crying and gnashing of teeth will be there.

1968	ܘܢܦܠܓܝܘܗܝ	And he will cut him in pieces
1625	ܘܢܣܝܡ	and assign [him]
1399	ܡܢܬܗ	his portion
1817	ܥܡ	with
1532	ܢܣܒܝ	the hypocrites
0173	ܐܦܐ	*
2682	ܬܡܢ	there
0603	ܢܗܘܐ	will be
0268	ܒܟܝܐ	Crying
0905	ܘܚܘܪܩ	and gnashing of
2558	ܫܢܐ	teeth

CHAPTER 25

VERSE 1 Then the kingdom of heaven will be compared to ten virgins, those who took their lamps and went out for the arrival of the bridegroom and bride.

0594	ܗܝܕܝܢ	Then
0540	ܬܬܕܡܐ	will be compared
1385	ܡܠܟܘܬܐ	the kingdom
2543	ܕܫܡܝܐ	of heaven
1848	ܠܥܣܪ	to ten
0345	ܒܬܘܠܢ	virgins
0593	ܗܢܝܢ	those
1532	ܕܢܣܒܝ	who took
1305	ܠܡܦܕܝܗܝܢ	their lamps
1542	ܘܢܦܩܝ	and went out
0198	ܠܐܘܪܥܐ	for the arrival of
0933	ܚܬܢܐ	the bridegroom
1179	ܘܟܠܬܐ	and bride

VERSE 2 Now five of them were wise and five were foolish.

0833	ܚܡܫ	five
0518	ܕܝܢ	Now
1388	ܡܢܗܝܢ	of them
0790	ܚܟܝܡܢ	wise
0603	ܗܘܝ	were
0833	ܘܚܡܫ	and five
1651	ܣܟܠܢ	were foolish

VERSE 3 And those foolish [virgins] took their lamps, but did not take oil with them.

0593	ܘܗܢܝܢ	And those
1651	ܣܟܠܬܐ	foolish [virgins]
1532	ܢܣܒܝ	took
1305	ܠܡܦܕܝܗܝܢ	their lamps
1262	ܘܠܐ	yet not
1532	ܢܣܒܝ	did take
1817	ܥܡܗܝܢ	with them
1445	ܡܫܚܐ	oil

VERSE 4 But those wise [virgins] took oil in vessels with their lamps.

0593	ܗܢܝܢ	those
0518	ܕܝܢ	But

MATTHEW CHAPTER 25

#	Syriac	English
0790		wise [virgins]
1532		took
1445		oil
1320		in vessels
1817		with
1305		their lamps

VERSE 5 — Now when the bridegroom was delayed, all of them tired and went to sleep.

#	Syriac	English
1128		when
0050		was delayed
0518		Now
0933		the bridegroom
1488		tired
1168		all of them
0544		and went to sleep

VERSE 6 — And at midnight there was a shout, 'Behold, the bridegroom comes. Go out to meet him.'

#	Syriac	English
1971		And at midnight
1299		*
0603		there was
2228		a shout
0580		Behold
0933		the bridegroom
0208		comes
1542		Go out
0198		to meet him

VERSE 7 — Then all those virgins got up and put their lamps in good order.

#	Syriac	English
0594		Then
2168		got up
1168		all
0347		virgins
0598		those
2699		and put in good order
1305		their lamps

VERSE 8 — And those foolish [virgins] said to the wise, 'Give us [some] of your oil, because, behold, our lamps have gone out.'

#	Syriac	English
0116		said
0518		And
0593		those
1651		foolish [virgins]
0790		to the wise
1030		Give
1261		us
1388		[some] of
1445		your oil
0580		because behold
0558		have gone out
1261		<to them>
1305		our lamps

VERSE 9 — These wise [virgins] answered and said, 'Will there be enough for us and for you? But rather go to those who sell and buy [some] for yourselves.'

#	Syriac	English
1838		answered
0598		These
0790		wise [virgins]
0116		and said
1316		<?>
1262		<not>
1694		Will there be enough
1261		for us
1261		and for you
0090		But rather
0042		go
1288		to
0066		those
0632		who sell
0632		and buy [some]
1261		for yourselves

VERSE 10 — And while they went to buy, the bridegroom came. And those who were prepared entered with him into the banquet hall and the door was shut.

#	Syriac	English
1128		And while
0042		they went
0632		to buy
0208		came
0933		the bridegroom
0066		And those

Vertical Interlinear

MATTHEW CHAPTER 25

0950		who prepared
0603		were
1796		entered
1817		with him
0243		into the banquet hall
0797		*
0047		and was shut
2718		the door

VERSE 11 — Now later, those other virgins also came and said, 'Our Lord, our Lord, open [the door] for us.'

0054		later
0518		Now
0208		came
0169		also
0593		those
0347		virgins
0053		other
0116		and said
1426		Our Lord
1426		our Lord
2070		open [the door]
1261		for us

VERSE 12 — But he answered and said to them, 'Truly I say to you, I do not know you.'

0592		<he>
0518		But
1838		he answered
0116		and said
1261		to them
0110		Truly
0116		say
0124		I
1261		to you
1262		not
1023		do know
0124		I
1261		you

VERSE 13 — Therefore, watch, for you do not know that day or hour.

1880		watch
0596		Therefore
1262		for not
1023		do know
0133		you
1036		day
0593		that
1262		or <not>
2573		hour

VERSE 14 — For [the kingdom of heaven is] as a man who went on a journey. He called his servants and delivered his possessions to them.

0060		as
0361		a man
0403		For [the kingdom of heaven is]
0768		who went on a journey
2239		He called
1727		his servants
2530		and delivered
1261		to them
2217		his possessions

VERSE 15 — There was one to whom he gave five talents and another two and another one, each according to his ability. And immediately he went on a journey.

0069		There was
1030		one he gave
1261		to whom
0833		five
1166		talents
0069		and another
2709		two
0069		and another
0721		one
0131		each
0131		*
0060		according to
0786		his ability

MATTHEW CHAPTER 25

0768	ܘܣܒܪ	And he went on a journey
0725	ܒܪܫܥܬܗ	immediately

VERSE 16 — Now he who received five talents went, engaged in business with them, and gained five others.

0042	ܐܙܠ	he went
0518	ܕܝܢ	Now
0593	ܗܘ	\<he\>
1532	ܕܢܣܒ	who received
0833	ܚܡܫ	five
1166	ܟܟܪܝܢ	talents
2637	ܐܬܬܓܪ	engaged in business
0217	ܒܗܝܢ	with them
1098	ܘܝܬܪ	and gained
0833	ܚܡܫ	five
0053	ܐܚܪܢܝܢ	others

VERSE 17 — And in the same manner also, he who [received] two engaged in business [and gained] two others.

0595	ܘܗܟܘܬ	And in the same manner
0169	ܐܦ	also
0593	ܗܘ	he
2709	ܕܬܪܬܝܢ	who [received] two
2637	ܐܬܬܓܪ	engaged in business [and gained]
2709	ܬܪܬܝܢ	two
0053	ܐܚܪܢܝܢ	others

VERSE 18 — But he who received one [talent] went [and] dug in the ground and hid the money of his lord.

0593	ܗܘ	he
0518	ܕܝܢ	But
1532	ܕܢܣܒ	who received
0721	ܚܕܐ	one [talent]
0042	ܐܙܠ	went
0875	ܚܦܪ	[and] dug
0199	ܒܐܪܥܐ	in the ground
1009	ܘܛܫܝ	and hid
1209	ܟܣܦܐ	the money
1426	ܕܡܪܗ	of his lord

VERSE 19 — Now after a long time the lord of those servants came and received an accounting from them.

0215	ܒܬܪ	after
0518	ܕܝܢ	Now
0633	ܙܒܢܐ	a time
1596	ܣܓܝܐܐ	long
0208	ܐܬܐ	came
1426	ܡܪܗܘܢ	the lord
1727	ܕܥܒܕܐ	of servants
0593	ܗܢܘܢ	those
1532	ܘܢܣܒ	and received
1388	ܡܢܗܘܢ	from them
0916	ܚܘܫܒܢܐ	an accounting

VERSE 20 — And he who received five talents came near and brought five others and said, 'My lord, you gave me five talents. Behold, I have engaged in business [and gained] five others with them.'

2244	ܘܩܪܒ	And came near
0593	ܗܘ	he
1532	ܕܢܣܒ	who received
0603	ܗܘܐ	*
0833	ܚܡܫ	five
1166	ܟܟܪܝܢ	talents
2244	ܘܩܪܒ	and brought
0833	ܚܡܫ	five
0053	ܐܚܪܢܝܢ	others
0116	ܘܐܡܪ	and said
1426	ܡܪܝ	My lord
0833	ܚܡܫ	five
1166	ܟܟܪܝܢ	talents
1030	ܝܗܒܬ	you gave
1261	ܠܝ	me
0580	ܗܐ	Behold
0833	ܚܡܫ	five
0053	ܐܚܪܢܝܢ	others
2637	ܐܬܬܓܪܬ	I have engaged in business [and gained]
1804	ܥܠܝܗܝܢ	with them

MATTHEW CHAPTER 25

VERSE 21
His lord said to him, 'Well done, good and faithful servant. You have been faithful over little. I will place you over much. Enter into the joy of your lord.'

0116		said
1261		to him
1426		His lord
0058		Well done
1727		servant
0938		good
0114		and faithful
1804		over
2203		little
0109		faithful
0603		You have been
1804		over
1596		much
2168		I will place you
1796		Enter
0727		into the joy
1426		of your lord

VERSE 22
And he who [received] two talents came near and said, 'My lord, you gave me two talents. Behold, I have engaged in business [and gained] two others with them.'

2244		And came near
0593		he
2709		who [received] two
1166		talents
0116		and said
1426		My lord
2709		two
1166		talents
1030		you gave
1261		me
0580		Behold
2709		two
0053		others
2637		I have engaged in business [and gained]
1804		with them

VERSE 23
His lord said to him, 'Well done, good and faithful servant. You have been faithful over little. I will place you over much. Enter into the joy of your lord.'

0116		said
1261		to him
1426		His lord
0058		Well done
1727		servant
0938		good
0114		and faithful
1804		over
2203		little
0109		faithful
0603		You have been
1804		over
1596		much
2168		I will place you
1796		Enter
0727		into the joy
1426		of your lord

VERSE 24
Now he who received one talent also came near and said, 'My lord, I know that you are a hard man and [that] you reap where you have not sown and [that] you gather from where you have not scattered.

2244		came near
0518		Now
0169		also
0593		he
1532		who received
0721		one
1166		talent
0116		and said
1426		My lord
1023		I know
0603		*
1261		<to you>
0361		that a man
0133		you are
2265		hard

MATTHEW CHAPTER 25

0878		and [that] reap
0133		you
1108		where
1262		not
0691		you have sown
1198		and [that] gather
0133		you
1388		from
1108		where
1262		not
0229		you have scattered

VERSE 25 — And I was afraid and went [and] hid your talent in the ground. Behold, you have [what is] yours.'

0509		And I was afraid
0042		and went
1009		[and] hid <it>
1166		your talent
0199		in the ground
0580		Behold
0069		you have
1261		*
0517		[what is] yours

VERSE 26 — His lord answered and said to him, 'Wicked and lazy servant, you know that I reap where I have not sown and gather from where I have not scattered.

1838		answered
1426		His lord
0116		and said
1261		to him
1727		servant
0220		Wicked
0709		and lazy
1023		you know
0603		*
0878		that reap
0124		I
1108		where
1262		not
0691		I have sown
1198		and gather
0124		<I>
1388		from
1108		where
1262		not
0229		I have scattered

VERSE 27 — It would have been right for you to have put my money on the exchange table and I would have come and demanded my own with its interest.

0626		It would have been right
0603		*
1261		for you
2372		to have put
1209		my money
1804		on
2069		the exchange table
0208		and I would have come
0603		*
0124		<I>
2631		and demanded
0603		*
0517		my own
1817		with
2282		its interest

VERSE 28 — Take from him, therefore, the talent and give it to him who has ten talents.

1532		Take
0596		therefore
1388		from him
1166		the talent
1030		and give it
0593		to him
0069		who has
1261		*
1848		ten
1166		talents

MATTHEW CHAPTER 25

VERSE 29 For to him who has it will be given and it will be added to him. But he who does not have, even that which he has will be taken from him.

Code	Aramaic	English
1389		to him
0403		For
0069		who has
1261		*
1030		it will be given
1261		<to him>
1064		and it will be added
1261		to him
0593		<and> he
0518		But
1264		who does not have
1261		*
0169		even
0593		that
0069		which he has
1261		*
2587		will be taken
1388		from him

VERSE 30 And throw the useless servant into outer darkness. Crying and gnashing of teeth will be there.'

Code	Aramaic	English
1727		And the servant
0254		useless
1542		throw <him>
0923		into darkness
0321		outer
2682		there
0603		will be
0268		Crying
0905		and gnashing of
2558		teeth

VERSE 31 And when the Son of Man comes in his glory and all of his holy angels with him, then he will sit on the throne of his glory.

Code	Aramaic	English
1313		when
0208		comes
0518		And
0323		the Son
0131		of Man
2431		in his glory
1168		and all of
1375		his angels
2162		holy
1817		with him
0594		then
1093		he will sit
1804		on
2711		the throne
2431		of his glory

VERSE 32 And all the nations will be gathered before him. And he will separate them one from another as a shepherd who separates the sheep from the goats.

Code	Aramaic	English
1198		And will be gathered
2154		before him
1168		all
1818		the nations
2046		And he will separate
0592		them
0721		one
1388		from
0721		another
0060		as
2383		a shepherd
2046		who separates
1887		the sheep
1388		from
0366		the goats

VERSE 33 And he will set the sheep on his right and the goats on his left.

Code	Aramaic	English
2168		And he will set
1887		the sheep
1388		on
1061		his right
0366		and the goats
1388		on
1668		his left

MATTHEW CHAPTER 25

VERSE 34 — Then the king will say to those who are on his right, 'Come, blessed of my Father, inherit the kingdom that has been prepared for you from the foundations of the world.'

0594	ܗܝܕܝܢ	Then
0116	ܢܐܡܪ	will say
1383	ܡܠܟܐ	the king
0593	ܠܗܢܘܢ	to those
1388	ܕܡܢ	who are on
1061	ܝܡܝܢܗ	his right
0208	ܬܘ	Come
0338	ܒܪܝܟܘܗܝ	blessed
0002	ܕܐܒܝ	of my Father
1087	ܝܪܬܘ	inherit
1385	ܡܠܟܘܬܐ	the kingdom
1914	ܕܡܛܝܒܐ	that has been prepared
0603	ܗܘܬ	*
1261	ܠܟܘܢ	for you
1388	ܡܢ	from
2373	ܬܪܡܝܬܗ	the foundations
1813	ܕܥܠܡܐ	of the world

VERSE 35 — For I was hungry and you gave me to eat. And I was thirsty and you gave me to drink. I was a stranger and you took me in.

1212	ܟܦܢܬ	I was hungry
0403	ܓܝܪ	For
1030	ܘܝܗܒܬܘܢ	and you gave
1261	ܠܝ	me
0075	ܠܡܐܟܠ	to eat
2087	ܘܨܗܝܬ	And I was thirsty
2585	ܘܐܫܩܝܬܘܢܢܝ	and you gave me to drink
0085	ܐܟܣܢܝܐ	a stranger
0603	ܗܘܝܬ	I was
1198	ܘܟܢܫܬܘܢܢܝ	and you took me in

VERSE 36 — I was naked and you covered me. I was sick and you visited me. And I was in prison and you came to me.

1890	ܥܪܛܠܝ	naked
0603	ܗܘܝܬ	I was
1206	ܘܟܣܝܬܘܢܢܝ	and you covered me
1226	ܟܪܝܗ	sick
0603	ܗܘܝܬ	I was
1684	ܘܣܥܪܬܘܢܢܝ	and you visited me
0243	ܘܒܝܬ	And in prison
0163	ܐܣܝܪܐ	*
0603	ܗܘܝܬ	I was
0208	ܘܐܬܝܬܘܢ	and you came
1288	ܠܘܬܝ	to me

VERSE 37 — Then those just [ones] will say to him, 'Our Lord, when did we see that you were hungry and feed you, or that you were thirsty and give you drink?

0594	ܗܝܕܝܢ	Then
0116	ܢܐܡܪܘܢ	will say
1261	ܠܗ	to him
0593	ܗܢܘܢ	those
0637	ܙܕܝܩܐ	just [ones]
1426	ܡܪܢ	Our lord
0120	ܐܡܬܝ	when
0758	ܚܙܝܢܟ	did we see
1214	ܕܟܦܢ	that were hungry
0133	ܐܢܬ	you
2715	ܘܬܪܣܝܢܟ	and feed you
0024	ܐܘ	or
2087	ܕܨܗܐ	that were thirsty
0133	ܐܢܬ	you
2585	ܘܐܫܩܝܢܟ	and give you drink

VERSE 38 — And when did we see that you were a stranger and take you in or that you were naked and cover you?

0120	ܘܐܡܬܝ	And when
0758	ܚܙܝܢܟ	did we see
0085	ܕܐܟܣܢܝܐ	that were a stranger
0133	ܐܢܬ	you
1198	ܘܟܢܫܢܟ	and take you in
0024	ܐܘ	or
1890	ܕܥܪܛܠܝ	that were naked
0133	ܐܢܬ	you
1206	ܘܟܣܝܢܟ	and cover you

MATTHEW CHAPTER 25

VERSE 39 And when did we see you sick or in prison and come to you?'

0120	ܘܐܡܬܝ	And when
0758	ܚܙܝܢܟ	did we see you
1228	ܟܪܝܗܐ	sick
0024	ܐܘ	or
0243	ܒܝܬ	in prison
0163	ܐܣܝܪܐ	*
0208	ܘܐܬܝܢ	and come
1288	ܠܘܬܟ	to you

VERSE 40 And the king will answer and say to them, 'Truly I say to you, whatever you did for one of these, my little brothers, you did for me.'

1838	ܘܥܢܐ	And will answer
1383	ܡܠܟܐ	the king
0116	ܘܐܡܪ	and say
1261	ܠܗܘܢ	to them
0110	ܐܡܝܢ	Truly
0116	ܐܡܪ	say
0124	ܐܢܐ	I
1261	ܠܟܘܢ	to you
1188	ܕܟܡܐ	whatever
1724	ܕܥܒܕܬܘܢ	you did
0721	ܠܚܕ	for one
1388	ܡܢ	of
0598	ܗܠܝܢ	these
0043	ܐܚܝ	my brothers
0686	ܙܥܘܪܐ	little
1261	ܠܝ	for me
0592	ܗܘ	<it>
1724	ܥܒܕܬܘܢ	you did

VERSE 41 Then he will say also to those who are on his left, 'Go away from me, cursed [ones], to the eternal fire that is prepared for the Accuser and his angels.

0594	ܗܝܕܝܢ	Then
0116	ܢܐܡܪ	he will say
0169	ܐܦ	also
0593	ܠܗܢܘܢ	to those
1388	ܕܡܢ	who are on
1668	ܣܡܠܗ	his left
0042	ܙܠܘ	Go away
1261	ܠܟܘܢ	<to you>
1388	ܡܢܝ	from me
1284	ܠܝܛܐ	cursed [ones]
1494	ܠܢܘܪܐ	to the fire
1813	ܕܠܥܠܡ	eternal
0593	ܗܝ	<that>
0950	ܕܡܛܝܒܐ	that is prepared
0078	ܠܐܟܠܩܪܨܐ	for the Accuser
1375	ܘܠܡܠܐܟܘܗܝ	and his angels

VERSE 42 For I was hungry and you did not give me to eat and I was thirsty and you did not give me drink.

1212	ܟܦܢܬ	I was hungry
0403	ܓܝܪ	For
1262	ܘܠܐ	and not
1030	ܝܗܒܬܘܢ	you did give
1261	ܠܝ	me
0075	ܠܡܐܟܠ	to eat
2087	ܘܨܗܝܬ	And I was thirsty
1262	ܘܠܐ	and not
2585	ܐܫܩܝܬܘܢܢܝ	you did give me drink

VERSE 43 And I was a stranger and you did not take me in and I was naked and you did not cover me. And I was sick and I was in prison and you did not visit me.'

0085	ܘܐܟܣܢܝܐ	And a stranger
0603	ܗܘܝܬ	I was
1262	ܘܠܐ	and not
1198	ܟܢܫܬܘܢܢܝ	you did take me in
1890	ܘܥܪܛܠܝ	and naked
0603	ܗܘܝܬ	I was
1262	ܘܠܐ	and not
1206	ܟܣܝܬܘܢܢܝ	did cover me
1228	ܘܟܪܝܗܐ	And sick
0603	ܗܘܝܬ	I was
0243	ܘܒܝܬ	and in prison
0163	ܐܣܝܪܐ	*
0603	ܗܘܝܬ	I was
1262	ܘܠܐ	and not

MATTHEW CHAPTER 25

1684		you did visit me		1724		you did do
VERSE 44		Then they will also answer and say, 'Our Lord, when did we see you hungry or thirsty or a stranger or naked or sick or in prison and not minister to you?'		0721		for one
				1388		of
				0598		these
				0686		little ones
0594		Then		0169		also
1838		they will answer		1262		not
0169		also		1261		for me
0592		<they>		1724		you did do
0116		and say		**VERSE 46**		And these will go to eternal torment and the just [ones] to eternal life."
1426		Our Lord				
0120		when		0042		And will go
0758		did we see you		0598		these
1214		hungry		2567		to torment
0024		or		1813		eternal
2087		thirsty		0637		and the just [ones]
0024		or		0782		to life
0085		a stranger		1813		eternal
0024		or		**CHAPTER 26**		
1890		naked		**VERSE 1**		And it happened that when Jesus completed all of these sayings, he said to his disciples,
0024		or				
1228		sick				
0024		or		0603		And it happened
0243		in prison		1128		that when
0163		*		2530		completed
1262		and not		3257		Jesus
2554		minister to you		1168		all of
VERSE 45		Then he will answer and say to them, 'Truly I say to you, whatever you did not do for one of these little ones, you did also not do for me.'		1364		sayings
				0598		these
				0116		he said
				1304		to his disciples
0594		Then		**VERSE 2**		"You know that after two days will be the Passover and the Son of Man will be betrayed to be crucified.
1838		he will answer				
0116		and say				
1261		to them		1023		know
0110		Truly		0133		You
0116		say		0215		that after
0124		I		2709		two
1261		to you		1036		days
1188		whatever		0603		will be
1262		not		3433		the Passover

189

MATTHEW   CHAPTER 26

0323	ܘܒܪܗ	and the Son
0131	ܕܐܢܫܐ	of Man
2530	ܡܫܬܠܡ	will be betrayed
0688	ܠܡܙܩܦܘ	to be crucified

VERSE 3 Then the chief priests and scribes and elders of the people were gathered at the court of the high priest, who was called Caiaphas.

0594	ܗܝܕܝܢ	Then
1198	ܐܬܟܢܫܘ	were gathered
2271	ܪܒܝ	the chief priests
1135	ܟܗܢܐ	*
1699	ܘܣܦܪܐ	and scribes
2263	ܘܩܫܝܫܐ	and elders
1818	ܕܥܡܐ	of the people
0505	ܠܕܪܬܗ	at the court
2271	ܕܪܒ	of the high priest
1135	ܟܗܢܐ	*
2239	ܕܡܬܩܪܐ	who was called
3473	ܩܝܦܐ	Caiaphas

VERSE 4 And they held counsel against Jesus that they might arrest him by deceit and kill him.

1381	ܘܐܬܡܠܟܘ	And they held counsel
1804	ܥܠ	against
3257	ܝܫܘܥ	Jesus
1513	ܕܒܢܟܠܐ	that by deceit
0047	ܐܚܕܘܢܝܗܝ	they might arrest him
2179	ܘܢܩܛܠܘܢܝܗܝ	and kill him

VERSE 5 And they were saying, "Not during the festival, lest a riot should occur among the people."

0116	ܘܐܡܪܝܢ	And saying
0603	ܗܘܘ	they were
1262	ܠܐ	Not
1721	ܒܥܕܥܕܐ	during the festival
1262	ܕܠܐ	lest
0603	ܢܗܘܐ	should occur
2454	ܫܓܘܫܝܐ	a riot
1818	ܒܥܡܐ	among the people

VERSE 6 And while Jesus was in Bethany in the house of Simon the leper,

1128	ܘܟܕ	And while
0603	ܗܘܐ	was
3257	ܝܫܘܥ	Jesus
3116	ܒܒܝܬܥܢܝܐ	in Bethany
0243	ܒܒܝܬܗ	in the house
3521	ܕܫܡܥܘܢ	of Simon
0456	ܓܪܒܐ	the leper

VERSE 7 a woman approached him who had with her an alabaster vase of oil that was very costly perfume. And she poured it on the head of Jesus while he was lying down [to eat].

2244	ܩܪܒܬ	approached
1261	ܠܗ	him
0135	ܐܢܬܬܐ	a woman
0069	ܐܝܬ	who had
1804	ܥܠܝܗ	with her
2502	ܫܛܝܦܬܐ	an alabaster vase
1445	ܕܡܫܚܐ	of oil
0291	ܕܒܣܡܐ	that was perfume
1596	ܣܓܝ	very
0543	ܕܡܝܐ	costly
2577	ܘܐܫܦܥܬܗ	And she poured it
1804	ܥܠ	on
2362	ܪܫܗ	the head
3257	ܕܝܫܘܥ	of Jesus
1128	ܟܕ	while
1664	ܣܡܝܟ	he was lying down [to eat]

VERSE 8 And his disciples saw [it] and it displeased them. And they said, "Why [was there] this waste?

0758	ܚܙܘ	saw [it]
0518	ܕܝܢ	And
1304	ܬܠܡܝܕܘܗܝ	his disciples
0219	ܘܐܬܒܐܫ	and it displeased
1261	ܠܗܘܢ	them
0116	ܘܐܡܪܝܢ	And they said
1394	ܠܡܢܐ	Why [was there]
0006	ܐܒܕܢܐ	waste

Vertical Interlinear

MATTHEW CHAPTER 26

0598	ܗܢܐ	this
VERSE 9		For this [oil] could have been sold for much and [the money] given to the poor."
2510	ܕܢܙܕܒܢ	could have been
0603	ܗܘܐ	*
0403	ܓܝܪ	For
0632	ܗܢܐ ܡܫܚܐ	sold
0598	ܗܢܐ	this [oil]
1596	ܒܣܓܝ	for much
1030	ܘܢܬܝܗܒ	and [the money] given
1406	ܠܡܣܟܢܐ	to the poor
VERSE 10		But Jesus knew [this] and said to them, "Why are you troubling the woman? She has done a good deed for me.
3257	ܝܫܘܥ	Jesus
0518	ܕܝܢ	But
1023	ܝܕܥ	knew [this]
0116	ܘܐܡܪ	and said
1261	ܠܗܘܢ	to them
1393	ܡܢܐ	Why
1265	ܡܠܐܝܢ	are troubling
0133	ܐܢܬܘܢ	you
1261	ܠܗ	<her>
0135	ܠܐܢܬܬܐ	the woman
1728	ܥܒܕܐ	a deed
2583	ܫܦܝܪܐ	good
1724	ܥܒܕܬ	She has done
1288	ܠܘܬܝ	for me
VERSE 11		For you will always have the poor with you, but you will not always have me.
1170	ܒܟܠܙܒܢ	always
0403	ܓܝܪ	For
1406	ܡܣܟܢܐ	the poor
0069	ܐܝܬ	you will have
1261	ܠܟܘܢ	*
1817	ܥܡܟܘܢ	with you
1261	ܠܝ	me
0518	ܕܝܢ	but
1262	ܠܐ	not
1170	ܒܟܠܙܒܢ	always
0069	ܐܝܬ	you will have
1261	ܠܟܘܢ	*
VERSE 12		Now this [act], that she poured this oil on my body, she did as though for my burial.
0598	ܗܕܐ	this [act]
0518	ܕܝܢ	Now
2372	ܕܐܪܡܝܬ	that she poured
0291	ܒܣܡܐ	oil
0598	ܗܢܐ	this
1804	ܥܠ	on
0389	ܓܘܫܡܝ	my body
0060	ܐܝܟ	as though
2142	ܕܠܡܩܒܪܢܝ	for my burial
1724	ܥܒܕܬ	she did
VERSE 13		And truly I say to you, wherever this my gospel is preached in all the world, what she has done will be spoken also for her remembrance."
0110	ܘܐܡܝܢ	And truly
0116	ܐܡܪ	say
0124	ܐܢܐ	I
1261	ܠܟܘܢ	to you
1108	ܕܐܝܟܐ	wherever
1230	ܕܬܬܟܪܙ	is preached
1593	ܣܒܪܬܝ	my gospel
0598	ܗܕܐ	this
1168	ܒܟܠܗ	in all
1813	ܥܠܡܐ	the world
1362	ܬܬܡܠܠ	will be spoken
0169	ܐܦ	also
1326	ܗܕܐ	what
1724	ܕܥܒܕܬ	she has done
0598	ܗܕܐ	<this>
0528	ܠܕܘܟܪܢܗ	for her remembrance
VERSE 14		Then one of the twelve, who was called Judas Iscariot, went to the chief priests.
0594	ܗܝܕܝܢ	Then
0042	ܐܙܠ	went
0721	ܚܕ	one
1388	ܡܢ	of

191

Vertical Interlinear

MATTHEW   CHAPTER 26

2710	ܬܪܥܣܪ	the twelve
2239	ܕܡܬܩܪܐ	who was called
3228	ܝܗܘܕܐ	Judas
3370	ܣܟܪܝܘܛܐ	Iscariot
1288	ܠܘܬ	to
2271	ܪܒܝ	the chief priests
1135	ܟܗܢܐ	*

VERSE 15 And he said to them, "What do you want to give me? And I will deliver him to you." Now they promised him thirty [pieces] of silver.

0116	ܘܐܡܪ	And he said
1261	ܠܗܘܢ	to them
1393	ܡܢܐ	What
2077	ܨܒܝܢ	do want
0133	ܐܢܬܘܢ	you
1030	ܠܡܬܠ	to give
1261	ܠܝ	me
0124	ܘܐܢܐ	And <I>
2530	ܡܫܠܡ	will deliver
0124	ܐܢܐ	I
1261	ܠܗ	him
1261	ܠܟܘܢ	to you
0592	ܗܢܘܢ	<they>
0518	ܕܝܢ	Now
2168	ܐܩܝܡܘ	they promised
1261	ܠܗ	him
2676	ܬܠܬܝܢ	thirty [pieces]
1209	ܕܟܣܦܐ	of silver

VERSE 16 And from that time on, he was seeking an occasion to betray him.

1388	ܘܡܢ	And from
0594	ܗܝܕܝܢ	that time on
0296	ܒܥܐ	seeking
0603	ܗܘܐ	he was
1261	ܠܗ	<him>
1982	ܦܠܥܐ	an occasion
2530	ܕܢܫܠܡܝܘܗܝ	to betray him

VERSE 17 Now on the first day of the Feast of Unleavened Bread, the disciples came near to Jesus and said to him, "Where do you want us to prepare for you to eat the Passover?"

1036	ܒܝܘܡܐ	on the day
0518	ܕܝܢ	Now
2157	ܩܕܡܝܐ	first
1951	ܕܦܛܝܪܐ	of the Feast of Unleavened Bread
2244	ܩܪܒܘ	came near
1304	ܬܠܡܝܕܐ	the disciples
1288	ܠܘܬ	to
3257	ܝܫܘܥ	Jesus
0116	ܘܐܡܪܝܢ	and said
1261	ܠܗ	to him
1108	ܐܝܟܐ	Where
2077	ܨܒܐ	do want
0133	ܐܢܬ	you
0950	ܕܢܛܝܒ	us to prepare
1261	ܠܟ	for you
1308	ܕܬܐܟܘܠ	to eat
3433	ܦܨܚܐ	the Passover

VERSE 18 And he said to them, "Go to the city to a certain [one] and say to him, 'Our Master says, my time comes.' With you I will serve the Passover with my disciples."

0592	ܗܘ	<he>
0518	ܕܝܢ	And
0116	ܐܡܪ	he said
1261	ܠܗܘܢ	to them
0042	ܙܠܘ	Go
0499	ܠܡܕܝܢܬܐ	to the city
1288	ܠܘܬ	to
1980	ܦܠܢ	a certain [one]
0116	ܘܐܡܪܘ	and say
1261	ܠܗ	to him
2271	ܪܒܢ	Our master
0116	ܐܡܪ	says
0633	ܙܒܢܝ	my time
1346	ܡܛܐ	comes

MATTHEW — CHAPTER 26

1261		<to him>
1288		With you
1724		will serve
0124		I
3433		the Passover
1817		with
1304		my disciples

VERSE 19 — And his disciples did as Jesus had commanded them and they prepared the Passover.

1304		And his disciples
1724		did
0061		as
2007		had commanded
1261		them
3257		Jesus
0950		and they prepared
3433		the Passover

VERSE 20 — And when it was evening, he was lying down [to eat] with his twelve disciples.

1128		And when
0603		it was
2375		evening
1664		lying down [to eat]
0603		he was
1817		with
2710		twelve
1304		his disciples

VERSE 21 — And while they were eating, he said, "Truly I say to you, one of you will betray me."

1128		And while
1308		they were eating
0116		he said
0110		Truly
0116		say
0124		I
1261		to you
0721		one
1388		of you
2530		will betray

1261		me

VERSE 22 — And it made them very sad. And each one of them began to say to him, "Is it I, my Lord?"

1221		And it made sad
1261		them
0938		very
2597		And began
0116		to say
1261		to him
0721		each
0721		one
1388		of them
1316		<?>
0124		Is it I
1426		my Lord

VERSE 23 — But he answered and said, "He who dips his hand with me in the dish, he will betray me."

0592		<he>
0518		But
1838		he answered
0116		and said
1389		He who
2080		dips
0057		his hand
1817		with me
1276		in the dish
0592		<he>
2530		he will betray me

VERSE 24 — And the Son of Man will go as it is written about him. But woe to the man by whose hand the Son of Man is betrayed! It would be better for that man if he had not been born."

0323		And the Son
0131		of Man
0042		will go
0061		as
1247		it is written
1804		about him
0625		woe

Vertical Interlinear

MATTHEW CHAPTER 26

Code	Aramaic	English
1261		<to him>
0518		But
0361		to the man
0593		<who>
0057		by whose hand
0323		the Son
0131		of Man
2530		is betrayed
2010		It would be better
0603		*
1261		<for him>
0361		for man
0593		that
0097		if
1262		not
1046		he had been born

VERSE 25 — Judas, the betrayer, answered and said, "Is it I, my Master?" Jesus said to him, "You have said [it]."

Code	Aramaic	English
1838		answered
3228		Judas
2531		the betrayer
0116		and said
1314		<?>
0124		I
0592		Is it
2275		my Master
0116		said
1261		to him
3257		Jesus
0133		<you>
0116		You have said [it]

VERSE 26 — And while they were eating, Jesus took up bread and blessed [it] and broke [it] and gave to his disciples and said, "Take, eat, this is my body."

Code	Aramaic	English
1128		while
0518		And
1308		they were eating
2587		took up
3257		Jesus
1293		bread
0335		and blessed [it]
2234		and broke [it]
1030		and gave
1304		to his disciples
0116		and said
1532		take
0075		eat
0599		this is
1929		my body

VERSE 27 — And he took up a cup and gave thanks and gave [it] to them. And he said, "Take, drink from it, all of you.

Code	Aramaic	English
2587		And he took up
1205		a cup
1020		and gave thanks
1030		and gave [it]
1261		to them
0116		And he said
1532		Take
2620		drink
1388		from it
1168		all of you

VERSE 28 — This is my blood of the new covenant that is poured out for many for the forgiveness of sins.

Code	Aramaic	English
0599		This is
0539		my blood
0520		of the covenant
0735		new
0812		that for
1596		many
0201		is poured out
2441		for the forgiveness
0771		of sins

VERSE 29 — And I say to you, I will not drink from now [on] from this fruit of the vine until the day in which I drink it with you anew in the kingdom of my Father."

Code	Aramaic	English
0116		say
0124		I

MATTHEW CHAPTER 26

1261		to you
0518		And
1262		not
2620		I will drink
1388		from
0602		now [on]
1388		from
0598		this
1047		fruit
0452		of the vine
1747		until
1036		the day
0217		in which
2620		I drink it
1817		with you
0735		anew
1385		in the kingdom
0002		of my Father

VERSE 30 — And they offered praise and went out to the Mount of Olives.

2428		And they offered praise
1542		and went out
0958		to the Mount of
0663		Olives

VERSE 31 — Then Jesus said to them, "All of you will be offended by me in this night, for it is written: I WILL STRIKE THE SHEPHERD AND THE SHEEP OF HIS FLOCK WILL BE SCATTERED.

0594		Then
0116		said
1261		to them
3257		Jesus
0133		<you>
1168		All of you
1242		will be offended
0217		by me
0598		in this
1299		night
1247		it is written
0403		for
1341		I WILL STRIKE
2383		THE SHEPHERD
0229		AND WILL BE SCATTERED
1887		THE SHEEP
1839		OF HIS FLOCK

VERSE 32 — But after I have risen, I [will go] before you into Galilee."

1388		after
0215		*
2168		have risen
0124		I
0518		But
2150		before
0124		I [will go]
1261		you
3153		into Galilee

VERSE 33 — Peter answered and said to him, "Even if everyone be offended by you, I will never be offended by you."

1838		answered
3258		Peter
0116		and said
1261		to him
0172		Even if
1175		everyone
1242		be offended
0217		by you
0124		<I>
1450		never
1262		*
1242		I will be offended
0217		by you

VERSE 34 — Jesus said to him, "Truly I say to you, in this night before the rooster crows three times, you will deny me."

0116		said
1261		to him
3257		Jesus
0110		Truly
0116		say
0124		I

MATTHEW CHAPTER 26

#	Syriac	English
1261		to you
0598		in this
1299		night
2154		before
2239		crows
2713		the rooster
2674		three
0633		times
1215		you will deny
0217		me

VERSE 35 Peter said to him, "If it be [necessary] for me to die with you, I would not deny you." And so also said all the disciples.

#	Syriac	English
0116		said
1261		to him
3258		Peter
0121		If
0603		it be [necessary]
1261		for me
1334		to die
1817		with you
1262		not
1215		I would deny
0217		you
0595		And so
0169		also
1168		all
1304		the disciples
0116		said

VERSE 36 Then Jesus came with them to a place that was called Gethsemane. And he said to his disciples, "Sit here while I go [and] pray."

#	Syriac	English
0594		Then
0208		came
1817		with them
3257		Jesus
0494		to a place
2239		that was called
3145		Gethsemane
0116		And he said
1304		to his disciples
1093		Sit
0600		here
1744		while
0042		I go
2106		[and] pray

VERSE 37 And he took Peter and the two sons of Zebedee. And he began to be sad and wearied.

#	Syriac	English
0477		And he took
3258		Peter
2709		and the two
0323		sons of
3185		Zebedee
2597		And he began
1192		to be sad
1771		and wearied

VERSE 38 And he said to them, "There is sadness to my soul unto death. Remain with me here and watch with me."

#	Syriac	English
0116		And he said
1261		to them
1221		sadness
0592		There is
1261		<to it>
1547		to my soul
1747		unto
1335		death
2165		Remain
1261		with me
0600		here
2459		and watch
1817		with me

VERSE 39 And he went on a little and fell down on his face and was praying and said, "My Father, if it is possible, let this cup pass by me. Nevertheless not as I want, but as you [want]."

#	Syriac	English
2042		And he went on
2203		a little
1538		and fell down
1804		on

MATTHEW CHAPTER 26

Vertical Interlinear

Code	Syriac	English
0173		his face
2106		and praying
0603		was
0116		and said
0002		My Father
0121		if
2510		it is possible
1733		let pass by me
1205		cup
0598		this
0342		Nevertheless
1262		not
0060		as
0124		<I>
2077		want
0124		I
0090		but
0060		as
0133		you [want]

VERSE 40 And he came to his disciples and found them asleep. And he said to Peter, "What, were you not able to watch with me one hour?

Code	Syriac	English
0208		And he came
1288		to
1304		his disciples
2510		and found
0592		them
1128		asleep
0544		*
0116		And he said
3258		to Peter
0597		What
1262		not
2510		were you able
0721		one
2573		hour
2459		to watch
1817		with me

VERSE 41 Watch and pray, so that you will not enter into temptation. The spirit is ready, but the body is weak."

Code	Syriac	English
1880		Watch
2106		and pray
1262		so that not
1796		you will enter
1528		into temptation
2323		The spirit
0950		is ready
1929		the body
0518		but
1226		is weak

VERSE 42 Again he went a second time [and] prayed. And he said, "My Father, if it is not possible for this cup to pass over, except I drink it, your desire will be [done]."

Code	Syriac	English
2650		Again
0042		he went
2709		a second
0633		time
2106		[and] prayed
0116		And he said
0002		My Father
0121		if
1262		not
2510		it is possible for
0598		this
1205		cup
1733		to pass over
0090		except
0121		*
2620		I drink it
0603		will be [done]
2079		your desire

VERSE 43 And he came again [and] found them asleep, for their eyes were heavy.

Code	Syriac	English
0208		And he came
2650		again
2510		[and] found

MATTHEW   CHAPTER 26

0592		them
1128		asleep
0544		*
1794		their eyes
0403		for
1079		heavy
0603		were

VERSE 44 — And he left them and went again [and] prayed a third time and he said the same thing.

2440		And he left
0592		them
0042		and went
2650		again
2106		[and] prayed
2674		third
0633		a time
1261		and the same
1364		thing
0116		he said

VERSE 45 — Then he came to his disciples and said to them, "Sleep now and be rested. Behold, the hour has arrived and the Son of Man will be delivered into the hands of sinners.

0594		Then
0208		he came
1288		to
1304		his disciples
0116		and said
1261		to them
0544		Sleep
1357		now
1483		and be rested
0580		Behold
1346		has arrived
2573		the hour
0323		and the Son
0131		of Man
2530		will be delivered
0057		into the hands
0772		of sinners

VERSE 46 — Rise up, we will go. Behold, he who has betrayed me has arrived."

2168		Rise up
0042		we will go
0580		Behold
1346		has arrived
0593		he
2530		who has betrayed
1261		me

VERSE 47 — And while he was speaking, behold, Judas the betrayer, one of the twelve, came and with him [was] a large crowd with swords and staffs, from before the chief priests and elders of the people.

1744		And while
0592		he
1362		was speaking
0580		behold
3228		Judas
2531		the betrayer
0721		one
1388		of
2710		the twelve
0208		came
1201		and a crowd
1817		with him [was]
1596		large
1817		with
1693		swords
0778		and staffs
1388		from
1288		before
2271		the chief priests
1135		*
2263		and elders
1818		of the people

VERSE 48 — And Judas the betrayer had given them a sign and said, "It is he whom I kiss. Arrest him."

1030		And had given

MATTHEW CHAPTER 26

Vertical Interlinear

0603		*
1261		them
0206		a sign
3228		Judas
2531		the betrayer
0116		and said
0593		<to him>
1573		whom kiss
0124		I
0592		It is he
1261		him
0047		Arrest

VERSE 49 — And immediately he came near to Jesus and said, "Peace, my Master." And he kissed him.

0725		And immediately
2244		he came near
1288		to
3257		Jesus
0116		and said
2535		Peace
2275		my Master
1573		And he kissed him

VERSE 50 — And Jesus said to him, "Did you come for this [purpose], my friend?" Then they came near and placed their hands on Jesus and arrested him.

0592		<he>
0518		And
3257		Jesus
0116		said
1261		to him
1804		for
0593		this [purpose]
0208		Did you come
0714		my friend
0594		Then
2244		they came near
2372		and placed
0057		their hands
1804		on
3257		Jesus
0047		and arrested him

VERSE 51 — And behold, one of those who [were] with Jesus stretched out his hand and drew a sword and struck a servant of the high priest and cut off his ear.

0580		And behold
0721		one
1388		of
0593		those
1817		who [were] with
3257		Jesus
1091		stretched out
0057		his hand
2542		and drew
1693		a sword
1341		and struck <him>
1727		a servant of
2271		the high priest
1135		*
2587		and cut off
0021		his ear

VERSE 52 — Then Jesus said to him, "Return the sword to its place, for all those who take up swords by swords will die.

0594		Then
0116		said
1261		to him
3257		Jesus
0616		Return
1693		the sword
0494		to its place
1168		all
0403		for
0593		those
1532		who take up
1645		swords
1645		by swords
1334		will die

MATTHEW CHAPTER 26

VERSE 53
Or do you think that I am not able to ask of my Father and would he [not] assign to me now more than twelve legions of angels?

Number	Aramaic	English
0024		Or
1588		do think
0133		you
1262		that not
2510		am able
0124		I
0296		to ask
1388		of
0002		my Father
2168		and would he [not] assign
1261		to me
0602		now
1100		more
1388		than
2710		twelve
1275		legions
1375		of angels

VERSE 54
How then would the scriptures be fulfilled that so it must be?"

Number	Aramaic	English
0061		How
0596		then
1366		would be fulfilled
1248		the scriptures
0597		that so
0626		it must be
0603		*

VERSE 55
At that moment Jesus said to the crowds, "Have you come out as against a robber with swords and with staffs to arrest me? I was sitting and teaching every day with you in the temple and you did not arrest me.

Number	Aramaic	English
0593		At that
2573		moment
0116		said
3257		Jesus
1201		to the crowds
0060		as
1804		against
0402		a robber
1542		Have you come out
1693		with swords
0778		and with staffs
0047		to arrest me
1172		every day
1288		with you
0607		in the temple
1093		sitting
0603		I was
1053		and teaching
1262		and not
0047		you did arrest me

VERSE 56
Now this has occurred so that the writings of the prophets would be fulfilled." Then all the disciples deserted him and fled.

Number	Aramaic	English
0598		this
0518		Now
0603		has occurred
1366		so that would be fulfilled
1248		the writings
1457		of the prophets
0594		Then
1304		the disciples
1168		all
2440		deserted him
1904		and fled

VERSE 57
And those who arrested Jesus led him to Caiaphas, the high priest, where the scribes and elders were gathering.

Number	Aramaic	English
0593		And those
0047		who arrested <him>
3257		Jesus
1015		led him
1288		to
3473		Caiaphas
2271		the high priest
1135		*
1108		where

MATTHEW CHAPTER 26

Vertical Interlinear

1699		the scribes
2263		and elders
1198		were gathering
0603		*

VERSE 58 — And Simon Peter was following him from a distance up to the courtyard of the high priest. And he entered [and] sat inside with the guards that he might see the end.

3521		Simon
0518		And
3258		Peter
0042		following
0603		was
0215		<after> him
1388		from
2354		a distance
1747		up to
0505		the courtyard
2271		of the high priest
1135		*
1796		And he entered
1093		[and] sat
0379		inside
1817		with
0513		the guards
0758		that he might see
0054		the end

VERSE 59 — Now the chief priests and elders and all the assembly were seeking witnesses against Jesus so that they might kill him

2271		the chief priests
1135		*
0518		Now
2263		and elders
1200		and the assembly
1168		all
0296		seeking
0603		were
1804		against
3257		Jesus
1609		witnesses
0060		so that
1334		they might kill him

VERSE 60 — and they did not find [them] and many false witnesses came. But finally, two came near

1262		and not
2510		they did find [them]
0208		and came
1596		many
1609		witnesses
2482		false
0051		finally
0518		But
2244		came near
2709		two

VERSE 61 — and said, "This [man] said, 'I am able to destroy the temple of God and to rebuild it in three days.'"

0116		and said
0598		This [man]
0116		said
2510		am able
0124		I
2597		to destroy
0607		the temple
0093		of God
2674		and in three
1036		days
0281		to rebuild it

VERSE 62 — And the high priest stood up and said to him, "Do you not answer anything [to this] matter? Why do these [men] witness against you?"

2168		And stood up
2271		the high priest
1135		*
0116		and said
1261		to him
1262		not
1326		anything

MATTHEW CHAPTER 26

1984		Do answer
0133		you
2068		[to this] matter
1393		Why
1608		do witness
1804		against you
0598		these [men]

VERSE 63 — But Jesus was silent. And the high priest answered and said to him, "I command you by the living God that you tell us if you are the Messiah, the Son of God."

3257		Jesus
0518		But
2623		silent
0603		was
1838		And answered
2271		the high priest
1135		*
0116		and said
1261		to him
1059		command
0124		inside
1261		you
0093		by the God
0781		living
0116		that you tell
1261		us
0121		if
0133		you are
0592		\<him\>
1446		the Messiah
0323		the Son
0093		of God

VERSE 64 — Jesus said to him, "You have said. But I say to you, from now on you will see THE SON OF MAN SITTING AT THE RIGHT HAND OF POWER AND COMING ON THE CLOUDS OF HEAVEN."

0116		said
1261		to him
3257		Jesus
0133		\<you\>
0116		You have said
0116		I say
1261		to you
0518		But
1388		from
0602		now on
0758		you will see
0323		THE SON
0131		OF MAN
1093		SITTING
1388		AT
1061		THE RIGHT HAND
0786		OF POWER
0208		AND COMING
1804		ON
1844		THE CLOUDS OF
2543		HEAVEN

VERSE 65 — Then the high priest tore his clothes and said, "Behold, he has blasphemed. Why, therefore, do we need witnesses? Behold, now you have heard his blasphemy.

0594		Then
2271		the high priest
1135		*
2129		tore
1320		his clothes
0116		and said
0580		Behold
0370		he has blasphemed
1393		Why
1357		therefore
0296		do we need
1261		\<to us\>
1609		witnesses
0580		Behold
0602		now on
2547		you have heard
0371		his blasphemy

MATTHEW CHAPTER 26

VERSE 66 What do you want [to do]?" They answered and were saying, "He is deserving of death."

1393		What
2077		do want [to do]
0133		you
1838		They answered
0116		and were saying
0745		He is deserving of
0592		*
1335		death

VERSE 67 Then they spit in his face and they were striking him. And others were beating him.

0594		Then
2400		they spit
0173		in his face
2230		and striking
0603		they were
1261		him
0053		others
0518		And
1341		beating
0603		were
1261		him

VERSE 68 And they said, "Prophesy to us, Messiah. Who is the one who beat you?"

0116		And they said
1456		Prophesy
1261		to us
1446		Messiah
1390		Who is
0593		the one
1341		who beat you

VERSE 69 Now Peter was sitting outside in the courtyard and a certain maid came near to him. And she said to him, "You also were with Jesus the Nazarene."

3258		Peter
0518		Now
1093		sitting
0603		was
0322		outside
0505		in the courtyard
2244		and came near
1288		to him
0118		a maid
0721		certain
0116		And she said
1261		to him
0169		also
0133		You
1817		with
3257		Jesus
0603		were
3355		the Nazarene

VERSE 70 But he denied [it] before all of them and said, "I do not know what you are saying."

0592		<he>
0518		But
1215		he denied [it]
2154		before
1168		all of them
0116		and said
1262		not
1023		do know
0124		I
1393		what
0116		are saying
0133		you

VERSE 71 And when he went out to the porch, another [maid] saw him and said to them, "This [man] also was there with Jesus the Nazarene."

1128		And when
1542		he went out
1689		to the porch
0758		saw him
0053		another [maid]
0116		and said
1261		to them
2682		there

MATTHEW CHAPTER 26

0603	ܗܘܐ	was
0169	ܐܦ	also
0598	ܗܢܐ	This [man]
1817	ܥܡ	with
3257	ܝܫܘܥ	Jesus
3355	ܢܨܪܝܐ	the Nazarene

VERSE 72 And again he denied [it] with oaths, "I do not know the man."

2650	ܘܬܘܒ	And again
1215	ܟܦܪ	he denied [it]
1060	ܒܡܘܡܬܐ	with oaths
1262	ܕܠܐ	not
1023	ܝܕܥ	do know
0124	ܐܢܐ	I
1261	ܠܗ	<him>
0361	ܠܓܒܪܐ	the man

VERSE 73 And after a little while, those who were standing by came near and said to Peter, "Surely also you are one of them, for your speech also makes you known."

1388	ܡܢ	after
0215	ܒܬܪ	*
2203	ܩܠܝܠ	a little while
0518	ܕܝܢ	And
2244	ܘܩܪܒܘ	came near
0593	ܗܢܘܢ	those
2168	ܕܩܝܡܝܢ	who were standing by
0116	ܘܐܡܪܝܢ	and said
3258	ܠܟܐܦܐ	to Peter
2594	ܫܪܝܪܐܝܬ	Surely
0169	ܐܦ	also
0133	ܐܢܬ	you are
1388	ܡܢܗܘܢ	one of them
0133	ܐܢܬ	<you>
0169	ܐܦ	also
1365	ܡܡܠܠܟ	your speech
0403	ܓܝܪ	for
1023	ܡܘܕܥ	makes known
1261	ܠܟ	you

VERSE 74 Then he began to curse and to say, "I do not know the man." And immediately the rooster crowed.

0594	ܗܝܕܝܢ	Then
2597	ܫܪܝ	he began
0897	ܠܡܚܪܡܘ	to curse
1059	ܘܠܡܐܡܐ	and to say
1262	ܕܠܐ	not
1023	ܝܕܥ	I do know
1261	ܠܗ	<him>
0361	ܠܓܒܪܐ	the man
0217	ܘܒܗ	And immediately
2573	ܒܫܥܬܐ	*
2239	ܩܪܐ	crowed
2713	ܬܪܢܓܠܐ	the rooster

VERSE 75 And Peter remembered the word of Jesus who said to him, "Before the rooster crows three times, you will deny me." And he went outside [and] cried bitterly.

0527	ܘܐܬܕܟܪ	And remembered
3258	ܟܐܦܐ	Peter
1364	ܡܠܬܐ	the word
3257	ܕܝܫܘܥ	of Jesus
0116	ܕܐܡܪ	who said
1261	ܠܗ	to him
2154	ܕܩܕܡ	Before
2239	ܕܢܩܪܐ	crows
2713	ܬܪܢܓܠܐ	the rooster
2674	ܬܠܬ	three
0633	ܙܒܢܝܢ	times
1215	ܬܟܦܘܪ	you will deny
0217	ܒܝ	me
1542	ܘܢܦܩ	And he went
0322	ܠܒܪ	outside
0267	ܒܟܐ	[and] cried
1421	ܡܪܝܪܐܝܬ	bitterly

MATTHEW

CHAPTER	27	
VERSE	1	Now when it was morning, all the chief priests and elders of the people took counsel against Jesus so that they might put him to death.

1128	ܟܕ	when
0518	ܕܝܢ	Now
0603	ܗܘܐ	it was
2124	ܨܦܪܐ	morning
1384	ܡܠܟܐ	counsel
1532	ܢܣܒܘ	took
1804	ܥܠ	against
3257	ܝܫܘܥ	Jesus
1168	ܟܠܗܘܢ	all
2271	ܪܒܝ	the chief priests
1135	ܟܗܢܐ	*
2263	ܘܩܫܝܫܐ	and elders
1818	ܕܥܡܐ	of the people
0060	ܐܝܟ	so that
1334	ܕܢܡܝܬܘܢܝܗܝ	they might put him to death

| VERSE | 2 | And they bound him and took him and delivered him to Pilate the governor. |

0160	ܘܐܣܪܘܗܝ	And they bound him
1015	ܘܐܘܒܠܘܗܝ	and took him
2530	ܘܐܫܠܡܘܗܝ	and delivered him
3417	ܠܦܝܠܛܘܣ	to Pilate
0586	ܗܓܡܘܢܐ	the governor

| VERSE | 3 | Then Judas, the betrayer, when he saw that Jesus was condemned, repented and went [and] returned those thirty [pieces] of silver to the chief priests and to the elders. |

0594	ܗܝܕܝܢ	Then
3228	ܝܗܘܕܐ	Judas
2531	ܡܫܠܡܢܐ	the betrayer
1128	ܟܕ	when
0758	ܚܙܐ	he saw
0742	ܕܐܬܚܝܒ	that was condemned
3257	ܝܫܘܥ	Jesus
2647	ܐܬܬܘܝ	repented
0042	ܘܐܙܠ	and went
0616	ܐܗܦܟ	[and] returned

0598	ܗܠܝܢ	those
2676	ܬܠܬܝܢ	thirty [pieces]
1209	ܕܟܣܦܐ	of silver
2271	ܠܪܒܝ	to the chief priests
1135	ܟܗܢܐ	*
2263	ܘܠܩܫܝܫܐ	and to the elders

| VERSE | 4 | And he said, "I have sinned, because I have betrayed innocent blood." But they said to him, "What [is it] to us? You know [what to do about it]." |

0116	ܘܐܡܪ	And he said
0770	ܚܛܝܬ	I have sinned
2530	ܕܐܫܠܡܬ	because I have betrayed
0539	ܕܡܐ	blood
0666	ܙܟܝܐ	innocent
0592	ܗܢܘܢ	<they>
0518	ܕܝܢ	But
0116	ܐܡܪܘ	they said
1261	ܠܗ	to him
1261	ܠ	<to us>
1313	ܡܐ	What [is it]
1261	ܠ	to us
0133	ܐܢܬ	<you>
1023	ܝܕܥ	know [what to do about it]
0133	ܐܢܬ	You

| VERSE | 5 | And he threw down the silver in the temple and left and went [and] strangled himself. |

2455	ܘܫܕܝܗܝ	And he threw down
1209	ܟܣܦܐ	the silver
0607	ܒܗܝܟܠܐ	in the temple
2561	ܘܫܢܝ	and left
0042	ܘܐܙܠ	and went
0848	ܚܢܩ	[and] strangled
1547	ܢܦܫܗ	himself

| VERSE | 6 | Now the chief priests picked up the silver and said, "It is not lawful to put [this] in the treasury, because it is the price of blood." |

2271	ܪܒܝ	the chief priests
1135	ܟܗܢܐ	*
0518	ܕܝܢ	Now

205

MATTHEW CHAPTER 27

2587		picked up		1366		it was fulfilled
1209		the silver		1326		what
0116		and said		0116		was spoken
1262		not		0057		by way of
2528		It is lawful		1457		the prophet
2372		to put [this] in		0116		who said
0243		the treasury		1532		I TOOK
2246		*		2676		THE THIRTY [PIECES]
1347		because		1209		OF SILVER
0962		the price of		0543		THE PRICE
0539		blood		1079		OF THE PRECIOUS [ONE]
0592		it is		2233		WHICH [THOSE] AGREED ON
				1388		FROM
				0323		THE SONS OF
				3035		ISRAEL

VERSE 7 And they took counsel and bought with it the field of the potter as a cemetery for strangers.

1532		And they took
1384		counsel
0632		and bought
0217		with it
0014		the field
1947		of the potter
0243		as a cemetery
2143		*
0085		for strangers

VERSE 8 Because of this, that field is called "The Field of Blood" until today.

1347		Because of
0598		this
2239		is called
0014		field
0593		that
2251		The Field
0539		of Blood
1747		until
1037		today

VERSE 9 Then it was fulfilled what was spoken by way of the prophet, who said: I TOOK THE THIRTY [PIECES] OF SILVER, THE PRICE OF THE PRECIOUS [ONE] WHICH [THOSE] FROM THE SONS OF ISRAEL AGREED ON,

0594		Then

VERSE 10 AND I GAVE THEM FOR THE FIELD OF THE POTTER AS THE LORD COMMANDED ME.

1030		AND I GAVE
0592		THEM
0014		FOR THE FIELD
1947		OF THE POTTER
0060		AS
2007		COMMANDED
1261		ME
1426		THE LORD

VERSE 11 Now Jesus stood before the governor. And the governor asked him and said to him, "Are you the king of the Judeans?" Jesus said to him, "You have said."

0592		\<he\>
0518		Now
3257		Jesus
2168		stood
2154		before
0586		the governor
2420		And asked him
0586		the governor
0116		and said
1261		to him

MATTHEW CHAPTER 27

Vertical Interlinear

0133		Are you		1261		him
0592		<he>		2068		an answer
1383		the king		1262		not even
3226		of the Judeans		0721		with one
0116		said		1364		word
1261		to him		1804		And at
3257		Jesus		0598		this
0133		<you>		0549		he marveled
0116		You have said		0938		greatly

VERSE 12 — And while the chief priests and elders were accusing him, he did not give any answer.

VERSE 15 — Now at every feast, the governor was accustomed to free one prisoner to the people, whomever they were desiring.

1128		And while		1168		at every
0075		were accusing him		1720		feast
0603		*		0518		Now
2257		*		1761		accustomed
2271		the chief priests		0603		was
1135		*		0586		the governor
2263		and elders		2597		to free
1326		any		0163		prisoner
2068		answer		0721		one
0592		<he>		1818		to the people
1262		not		0066		whomever
1984		he did give		0592		<they>

VERSE 13 — Then Pilate said to him, "Do you not hear how much they testify against you?"

2077		desiring
0603		they were

VERSE 16 — And they had imprisoned a well-known prisoner who was called Barabbas.

0594		Then		0160		imprisoned
0116		said		0603		they had
1261		to him		1261		*
3417		Pilate		0518		And
1262		not		0163		a prisoner
2547		Do hear		1025		well-known
0133		you		2239		who was called
1188		how much		3128		Barabbas
1608		they testify				
1804		against you				

VERSE 14 — And he did not give him an answer, not even with one word. And he greatly marveled at this.

VERSE 17 — And when they were gathered, Pilate said to them, "Whom do you want me to free to you, Barabbas or Jesus, who is called the Messiah?"

1262		And not		1128		And when
1030		he did give				

MATTHEW   CHAPTER 27

1198		they were gathered		1261		with <you>
0116		said		0593		<and> that
1261		to them		0637		just [man]
3417		Pilate		1596		much
1389		Whom		0403		for
2077		do want		0911		I have suffered
0133		you		0810		in my dream
2597		to free		1037		today
1261		to you		1347		because of him
3128		Barabbas				
0024		or				
3257		Jesus				
2239		who is called				
1446		the Messiah				

VERSE 20 But the chief priests and elders persuaded the crowds to ask for Barabbas and to destroy Jesus.

2271		the chief priests
1135		*
0518		But
2263		and elders
1955		persuaded
1201		the crowds
2420		to ask
3128		for Barabbas
3257		Jesus
0518		and
0005		to destroy

VERSE 18 For Pilate was realizing that they had delivered him up because of envy.

1023		realizing
0603		was
0403		For
3417		Pilate
1388		that because of
0860		envy
2530		they had delivered him up

VERSE 19 Now while the governor sat on his judgment seat, his wife sent to him and said to him, "Have nothing to do with that just [man], for I have suffered much today in my dream because of him."

1128		while
1093		sat
0518		Now
0586		the governor
1804		on
0265		his judgment seat
0517		*
2521		sent
1261		to him
0135		his wife
0116		and said
1261		to him
1262		[Have] nothing [to do]

VERSE 21 And the governor answered and said to them, "Whom do you want me to free to you from the two?" And they said, "Barabbas."

1838		And answered
0586		the governor
0116		and said
1261		to them
1389		Whom
2077		do want
0133		you
2597		me to free
1261		to you
1388		from
2709		the two
0592		<they>
0518		And
0116		they said

MATTHEW CHAPTER 27

3128		Barabbas

VERSE 22 — Pilate said to them, "And what should I do to Jesus, who is called the Messiah?" All of them said to him, "He should be crucified!"

0116		said
1261		to them
3417		Pilate
3257		And to Jesus
2239		who is called
1446		the Messiah
1393		what
1724		should I do
1261		to him
0116		said
1168		All of them
0688		He should be crucified

VERSE 23 — The governor said to them, "For what has he done that is evil?" But they cried out all the more and said, "He should be crucified!"

0116		said
1261		to them
0586		The governor
1393		what
0403		For
0220		that is evil
1724		has he done
0592		<they>
0518		But
1101		all the more
2227		they cried out
0116		and said
0688		He should be crucified

VERSE 24 — Now Pilate, when he saw that nothing helped, but [that] the clamor was increased, he took water [and] washed his hands before the crowd and said, "I am absolved of the blood of this just [man]. You should do [what you will]."

3417		Pilate
0518		Now
1128		when
0758		he saw
1326		that nothing
1262		*
1098		helped
0090		but
1101		increased
2319		[that] the clamor
0603		was
2587		he took
1351		water
2466		[and] washed
0057		his hands
1794		before
1201		the crowd
0116		and said
0851		I am absolved
0124		*
1388		of
0539		the blood
0598		of this
0637		just [man]
0133		<you>
1023		You should do [what you will]

VERSE 25 — And all the people answered and said, "His blood [be] on us and on our children."

1838		And answered
1168		all
1818		the people
0116		and said
0539		His blood [be]
1804		on us
1804		and on
0323		our children

VERSE 26 — Then he released Barabbas to them and scourged Jesus with whips and delivered him up to be crucified.

0594		Then
2597		he released
1261		to them

MATTHEW CHAPTER 27

3128		Barabbas		0246		and mocking
1461		and scourged		0603		were
2017		with whips		0217		him
3257		Jesus		0116		and said
2530		and delivered him up		2535		Hail
0688		to be crucified		1383		king

VERSE 27 Then the soldiers of the governor took Jesus to the Praetorium and assembled all the company of soldiers against him.

3226		of the Judeans

VERSE 30 And they spit in his face and they took the reed and were striking him on his head.

0594		Then		2400		And they spit
0150		the soldiers		2041		in his face
0586		of the governor		2587		and they took
0477		took		2224		the reed
3257		Jesus		1341		and striking
2027		to the Praetorium		0603		were
1198		and assembled		1261		him
1804		against him		1804		on
1168		all		2362		his head
0157		the company of soldiers				

VERSE 28 And they stripped him and clothed him with a robe of purple.

VERSE 31 And after they had mocked him, they stripped him of the robe and dressed him in his clothes and led him away to be crucified.

2521		And they stripped him		1128		And after
1272		and clothed him with		0246		they had mocked
1185		a robe		0217		him
0660		of purple		2521		they stripped him of
				1185		the robe
				1272		and dressed him
				1501		in his clothes
				1015		and led him away
				0688		to be crucified

VERSE 29 And they wove a crown of thorns and placed [it] on his head and a reed in his right hand and they bowed down on their knees before him and were mocking him and said, "Hail, king of the Judeans."

VERSE 32 And while they were going out, they found a man, a Cyrenian, whose name [was] Simon. They compelled this [man] to carry his cross.

0367		And they wove		1128		And while
1178		a crown		1542		they were going out
1763		of thorns		2510		they found
1625		and placed [it]		0361		a man
2362		on his head		3465		a Cyrenian
2224		and a reed		2539		whose name [was]
1061		in his right hand				
0335		and they bowed down				
1804		on				
0336		their knees				
2154		before him				

MATTHEW CHAPTER 27

#	Syriac	English
3521		Simon
0598		this [man]
2496		They compelled
2587		to carry
0689		his cross

VERSE 33 — And they came to the place that is called Golgotha, which is interpreted, "The Skull."

#	Syriac	English
0208		And they came
0494		to the place
2239		that is called
3143		Golgotha
0593		<that>
2061		which is interpreted
2259		The Skull

VERSE 34 — And they gave him vinegar that was mixed with gall to drink. And he tasted [it], yet did not want to drink [it].

#	Syriac	English
1030		And they gave
1261		him
2620		to drink
0794		vinegar
0802		that was mixed
1424		with gall
0998		And he tasted [it]
1262		yet not
2077		did want
2620		to drink [it]

VERSE 35 — And when they crucified him, they divided his clothes by lot.

#	Syriac	English
1128		And when
0688		they crucified him
1968		they divided
1501		his clothes
1991		by lot

VERSE 36 — And they were sitting and watching him there.

#	Syriac	English
1093		And sitting
0603		they were
1502		and watching
1261		him
2682		there

VERSE 37 — And they placed over his head the cause of his death in an inscription, "This is Jesus, king of the Judeans."

#	Syriac	English
1625		And they placed
1803		over
1388		*
2362		his head
1801		the cause
1335		of his death
1248		in an inscription
0599		This is
3257		Jesus
1383		king
3226		of the Judeans

VERSE 38 — And two thieves were crucified with him, one on his right and one on his left.

#	Syriac	English
0688		And were crucified
1817		with him
2709		two
1306		thieves
0721		one
1388		on
1061		his right hand
0721		and one
1388		on
1668		his left

VERSE 39 — And those who were passing by were insulting him and were shaking their heads.

#	Syriac	English
0066		those
0518		And
1733		who passing by
0603		were
0370		insulting
0603		were
1804		him
1481		and were shaking
2362		their heads

MATTHEW CHAPTER 27

VERSE 40 — And they said, "[You who would] tear down the temple and rebuild it in three days, save yourself if you [are] the Son of God and come down from the cross."

ID	Syriac	English
0116		And they said
1719		[You who would] tear down
0607		the temple
0281		and rebuild
1261		it
2674		in three
1036		days
2002		save
1547		yourself
0121		if
0323		the Son
0133		you [are]
0093		of God
1499		and come down
1388		from
0689		the cross

VERSE 41 — Likewise, also, the chief priests were mocking [him] with the scribes and elders and Pharisees.

ID	Syriac	English
0595		Likewise
0169		also
2271		the chief priests
1135		*
0246		mocking [him]
0603		were
1817		with
1699		the scribes
2263		and elders
3439		and Pharisees

VERSE 42 — And they said, "He saved others, [but] is not able to save himself. If he is the king of Israel, let him come down now from the cross and we will believe in him."

ID	Syriac	English
0116		And they said
0053		others
0780		He saved
1547		[but] himself
1262		not
2510		is able
0780		to save
0121		If
1383		the king
0592		he is
3035		of Israel
1499		let him come down
0602		now
1388		from
0689		the cross
0109		and we will believe
0217		in him

VERSE 43 — He put his trust in God. Let him save him now if he is pleased with him, for he said, 'I am the Son of God.'"

ID	Syriac	English
2665		He put his trust
1804		in
0093		God
2042		Let him save him
0602		now
0121		if
2077		he is pleased
0217		with him
0116		he said
0403		for
0323		the Son
0124		I am
0093		of God

VERSE 44 — Likewise, also, those robbers who were crucified with him were insulting him.

ID	Syriac	English
0595		Likewise
0169		also
0402		robbers
0593		those
0688		who were crucified
1817		with him
0855		insulting
0603		were
1261		him

MATTHEW CHAPTER 27

VERSE 45 — Now from the sixth hour there was darkness over all the land until the ninth hour.

1388	ܡܢ	from
2615	ܫܬ	sixth
2573	ܫܥܝܢ	the hour
0518	ܕܝܢ	Now
0603	ܗܘܐ	there was
0923	ܚܫܘܟܐ	darkness
1804	ܥܠ	over
1168	ܟܠܗ	all
0199	ܐܪܥܐ	the land
1747	ܥܕܡܐ	until
2573	ܠܫܥܝܢ	the hour
2723	ܬܫܥ	ninth

VERSE 46 — And about the ninth hour, Jesus cried with a loud voice and said, "God, God, why have you left me?"

0173	ܘܠܐܦܝ	And about
2723	ܬܫܥ	ninth
2573	ܫܥܝܢ	the hour
2227	ܩܥܐ	cried
3257	ܝܫܘܥ	Jesus
2204	ܒܩܠܐ	with a voice
2336	ܪܡܐ	loud
0116	ܘܐܡܪ	and said
3031	ܐܝܠ	God
3031	ܐܝܠ	God
1394	ܠܡܢܐ	why
2440	ܫܒܩܬܢܝ	have you left me

VERSE 47 — And some of those who were standing there, when they heard, were saying, "This [man] calls to Elijah."

0131	ܐܢܫܝܢ	some
0518	ܕܝܢ	And
1388	ܡܢ	of
0593	ܗܢܘܢ	those
2168	ܕܩܝܡܝܢ	who standing
0603	ܗܘܘ	were
2682	ܬܡܢ	there
1128	ܟܕ	when
2547	ܫܡܥܘ	they heard
0116	ܐܡܪܝܢ	saying
0603	ܗܘܘ	were
0598	ܗܢܐ	This [man]
3047	ܠܐܠܝܐ	to Elijah
2239	ܩܪܐ	calls

VERSE 48 — And immediately one of them ran and took a sponge and filled it with vinegar and placed it on a reed and offered [a drink] to him.

0217	ܘܒܗ	And immediately
2573	ܒܫܥܬܐ	*
2312	ܪܗܛ	ran
0721	ܚܕ	one
1388	ܡܢܗܘܢ	of them
2587	ܘܫܩܠ	and took
0155	ܐܣܦܘܓܐ	a sponge
1366	ܘܡܠܗ	and filled it with
0794	ܚܠܐ	vinegar
1625	ܘܣܡܗ	and placed it
2224	ܒܩܢܝܐ	on a reed
2585	ܘܡܫܩܐ	and offered [a drink]
0603	ܗܘܐ	*
1261	ܠܗ	to him

VERSE 49 — But the rest were saying, "Leave [him]. We will see if Elijah comes to rescue him."

2611	ܫܪܟܐ	the rest
0518	ܕܝܢ	But
0116	ܐܡܪܝܢ	saying
0603	ܗܘܘ	were
2440	ܫܒܘܩܘ	Leave [him]
0758	ܢܚܙܐ	We will see
0121	ܐܢ	if
0208	ܐܬܐ	comes
3047	ܐܠܝܐ	Elijah
2042	ܠܡܦܪܩܗ	to rescue him

VERSE 50 — Now Jesus again cried out with a loud voice and gave up his spirit.

0592	ܗܘ	<he>
0518	ܕܝܢ	Now

MATTHEW CHAPTER 27

3257	ܝܫܘܥ	Jesus		0215	ܡܢ ܒܬܪ	And after
2650	ܬܘܒ	again		2173	ܩܝܡܬܗ	his resurrection
2227	ܩܥܐ	cried out		1796	ܥܠܘ	they entered
2204	ܒܩܠܐ	with a voice		0499	ܠܡܕܝܢܬܐ	the city
2336	ܪܡܐ	loud		2162	ܩܕܝܫܬܐ	holy
2440	ܘܫܒܩ	and gave up		0758	ܘܐܬܚܙܝܘ	and were seen
2323	ܪܘܚܗ	his spirit		1596	ܠܣܓܝܐܐ	by many

VERSE 51 And immediately the curtains of the temple were torn in two from the top to the bottom and the earth was shaken and the rocks were split.

0725	ܘܡܚܕܐ	And immediately
0173	ܐܦܝ	the curtains
2718	ܬܪܥܐ	*
0607	ܕܗܝܟܠܐ	of the temple
2129	ܐܨܛܪܝ	were torn
2709	ܠܬܪܝܢ	in two
1388	ܡܢ	from
1803	ܠܥܠ	the top
1747	ܥܕܡܐ	to
2660	ܠܬܚܬ	the bottom
0199	ܘܐܪܥܐ	and the earth
0657	ܐܬܬܙܝܥܬ	was shaken
1119	ܘܟܐܦܐ	and the rocks
2129	ܐܨܛܪܝ	were split

VERSE 52 And the tombs were opened and many bodies of the holy [ones] who were asleep rose up

0243	ܘܒܝܬ	And the tombs
2143	ܩܒܘܪܐ	*
2070	ܐܬܦܬܚܘ	were opened
1929	ܘܦܓܪܐ	and bodies
1596	ܣܓܝܐܐ	many
2162	ܕܩܕܝܫܐ	of the holy [ones]
2509	ܕܕܡܟܝܢ	who asleep
0603	ܗܘܘ	were
2168	ܩܡܘ	rose up

VERSE 53 and went out. And after his resurrection they entered the holy city and were seen by many.

1542	ܘܢܦܩܘ	and went out

VERSE 54 And the centurion and those who were watching Jesus with him, when they saw the earthquake and those [things] that had occurred, they were very afraid and said, "Truly this was the Son of God."

2223	ܩܢܛܪܘܢܐ	the centurion
0518	ܕܝܢ	And
1817	ܘܕܥܡܗ	and those with him
1502	ܕܢܛܪܝܢ	who watching
0603	ܗܘܘ	were
3257	ܠܝܫܘܥ	Jesus
1128	ܟܕ	when
0758	ܚܙܘ	they saw
0658	ܙܘܥܐ	the earthquake
0066	ܘܐܝܠܝܢ	and those [things]
0603	ܕܗܘܝ	that had occurred
0509	ܕܚܠܘ	they were afraid
0938	ܛܒ	very
0116	ܘܐܡܪܘ	and said
2594	ܫܪܝܪܐܝܬ	Truly
0598	ܗܢܐ	this
0323	ܒܪܗ	the Son
0603	ܗܘܐ	was
0093	ܕܐܠܗܐ	of God

VERSE 55 Now there were also there many women who were watching from a distance, those who had followed Jesus from Galilee and had ministered to him.

0069	ܐܝܬ	there were
0603	ܗܘܝ	*
0518	ܕܝܢ	Now
0169	ܐܦ	also
2682	ܬܡܢ	there
0135	ܢܫܐ	women

MATTHEW CHAPTER 27

#	Aramaic	English
1596		many
0758		who watching
0603		were
1388		from
2354		a distance
0593		those
0208		who had followed
0603		*
0215		*
3257		Jesus
1388		from
3153		Galilee
2554		and had ministered
0603		*
1261		to him

VERSE 56 One of them [was] Mary Magdalene, and Mary, the mother of James and John, and the mother of the sons of Zebedee.

#	Aramaic	English
0721		One
1388		of them [was]
3325		Mary
3297		Magdalene
3325		and Mary
0106		the mother
3255		of James
3244		and John
0106		and the mother
0323		of the sons of
3185		Zebedee

VERSE 57 Now when it was evening, a rich man from Ramath came, whose name [was] Joseph, who also was taught by Jesus.

#	Aramaic	English
1128		when
0603		it was
0518		Now
2375		evening
0208		came
0361		a man
1921		rich
1388		from

#	Aramaic	English
3502		Ramath
2539		whose name [was]
3246		Joseph
0169		who also
0592		<he>
1302		taught
0603		was
3257		by Jesus

VERSE 58 This [man] came near to Pilate and asked for the body of Jesus. And Pilate commanded that the body be given to him.

#	Aramaic	English
0598		This [man]
2244		came near
1288		to
3417		Pilate
2420		and asked for
1929		the body
3257		of Jesus
2007		And commanded
3417		Pilate
1030		that be given
1261		to him
1929		the body

VERSE 59 And Joseph took the body and wrapped it in a cloth of clean linen.

#	Aramaic	English
2587		And took
3246		Joseph
1929		the body
1236		and wrapped it
0752		in a cloth
1255		of linen
1562		clean

VERSE 60 And he placed it in his new tomb that was hewn in rock. And they rolled a large stone [and] placed [it] over the opening of the tomb and they went away.

#	Aramaic	English
1625		And he placed it
0243		in tomb
2143		*
0735		new

MATTHEW CHAPTER 27

0517	ܕܝܠܗ	his
1567	ܕܢܚܝܬ	that was hewn
1119	ܒܟܐܦܐ	in rock
1737	ܘܥܓܠܘ	And they rolled
1119	ܟܐܦܐ	a stone
2271	ܪܒܬܐ	large
2372	ܘܐܪܡܝܘ	[and] placed [it]
1804	ܥܠ	over
2718	ܬܪܥܗ	the opening
0243	ܕܒܝܬܐ	of the tomb
2143	ܩܒܘܪܐ	*
0042	ܘܐܙܠܘ	and they went away

VERSE 61 Now Mary Magdalene was there and the other Mary, who were sitting opposite the grave.

0069	ܐܝܬ	was
0603	ܗܘܐ	*
0518	ܕܝܢ	Now
2682	ܬܡܢ	there
3325	ܡܪܝܡ	Mary
3297	ܡܓܕܠܝܬܐ	Magdalene
3325	ܘܡܪܝܡ	and Mary
0053	ܐܚܪܬܐ	the other
1093	ܕܝܬܒܢ	who sitting
0603	ܗܘܝ	were
2135	ܠܩܘܒܠܗ	opposite
2146	ܕܩܒܪܐ	the grave

VERSE 62 And on the next day that was after the preparation, the chief priests and the Pharisees were gathered with Pilate

1036	ܠܝܘܡܐ	on the day
0518	ܕܝܢ	And
1345	ܕܚܪܢܐ	next
0069	ܐܝܬܘܗܝ	that was
0215	ܒܬܪ	after
1886	ܥܪܘܒܬܐ	the preparation
1198	ܐܬܟܢܫܘ	were gathered
2271	ܪܒܝ	the chief priests
1135	ܟܗܢܐ	*
3439	ܘܦܪܝܫܐ	and the Pharisees

1288	ܠܘܬ	with
3417	ܦܝܠܛܘܣ	Pilate

VERSE 63 and said to him, "Our lord, we are reminded that that deceiver was saying while he was alive, 'After three days, I will rise up.'

0116	ܘܐܡܪܝܢ	and said
1261	ܠܗ	to him
1426	ܡܪܢ	Our lord
0527	ܐܬܕܟܪܢ	we are reminded
0593	ܕܗܘ	that that
0996	ܡܛܥܝܢܐ	deceiver
0116	ܐܡܪ	saying
0603	ܗܘܐ	was
1128	ܟܕ	while
0781	ܚܝ	he was alive
1388	ܕܡܢ	After
0215	ܒܬܪ	*
2674	ܬܠܬܐ	three
1036	ܝܘܡܝܢ	days
2168	ܩܐܡ	I will rise up
0124	ܐܢܐ	*

VERSE 64 Command therefore to guard the grave until the third day, so that his disciples will not come [and] steal him in the night and say to the people that he has risen from the dead and the last deception should become more evil than the first."

2007	ܦܩܘܕ	Command
0596	ܗܟܝܠ	therefore
0645	ܡܙܕܗܪܝܢ	to guard
2146	ܒܩܒܪܐ	the grave
1747	ܥܕܡܐ	until
2674	ܠܬܠܬܐ	the third
1036	ܝܘܡܝܢ	days
1314	ܕܠܡܐ	so that not
0208	ܢܐܬܘܢ	will come
1304	ܬܠܡܝܕܘܗܝ	his disciples
0436	ܢܓܢܒܘܢܝܗܝ	[and] steal him
1299	ܒܠܠܝܐ	in the night
0116	ܘܢܐܡܪܘܢ	and say
1818	ܠܥܡܐ	to the people

Vertical Interlinear

MATTHEW   CHAPTER 27

1388		that from
0243		the dead
1338		*
2168		he has risen
0603		and should become
0994		the deception
0051		last
0220		more evil
1388		than
2157		the first

VERSE 65 — Pilate said to them, "You have soldiers. Go, watch as you know [how]."

0116		said
1261		to them
3417		Pilate
0069		You have
1261		*
2226		soldiers
0042		Go
0645		watch
0061		as
1023		know [how]
0133		you

VERSE 66 — And they went [and] set a watch on the tomb and sealed that stone, with the soldiers.

0592		<they>
0518		And
0042		they went
0645		[and] set a watch
2146		on the tomb
0931		and sealed
1119		stone
0593		that
1817		with
2226		the soldiers

CHAPTER 28

VERSE 1 — Now in the evening of the Sabbath, as it was twilight [on] the first of the week, Mary Magdalene and the other Mary came to see the grave.

2375		in the evening
0518		Now
2445		of the Sabbath
1465		as it was twilight
0721		[on] the first
2445		of the week
0208		came
3325		Mary
3297		Magdalene
3325		and Mary
0053		the other
0758		to see
2146		the grave

VERSE 2 — And behold, a great earthquake occurred, for an angel of the LORD came down from heaven and came near [and] rolled the stone from the opening and he was sitting on it.

0580		And behold
0658		a earthquake
2271		great
0603		occurred
1375		an angel
0403		for
1426		of the LORD
1499		came down
1388		from
2543		heaven
2244		and came near
1737		[and] rolled
1119		the stone
1388		from
2718		the opening
1093		and he was sitting
0603		was
1804		on it

MATTHEW CHAPTER 28

VERSE 3 — And his appearance was like lightning and his clothes were white like snow.

Code	Syriac	English
0069		was
0603		*
0518		And
0759		his appearance
0060		like
0344		lightning
1273		and his clothes
0755		white
0603		were
0060		like
2673		snow

VERSE 4 — And those who were watching, trembled with fear of him and became like dead [men].

Code	Syriac	English
1388		And with
0511		fear of him
0657		trembled
0066		those
1502		who watching
0603		were
0603		and became
0060		like
1338		dead [men]

VERSE 5 — Now the angel answered and said to the women, "Do not fear, for I know that you seek Jesus who was crucified.

Code	Syriac	English
1838		answered
0518		Now
1375		the angel
0116		and said
0135		to the women
0133		<you>
1262		not
0509		Do fear
1023		I know
0124		*
0403		for
3257		that Jesus
0688		who was crucified
0296		seek
0133		you

VERSE 6 — He is not here, for he has risen, as he said. Come, see the place in which our Lord was laid.

Code	Syriac	English
1262		not
0603		He is
2694		here
2168		he has risen
1261		<to him>
0403		for
0061		as
0116		he said
0208		Come
0758		see
0494		the place
1625		laid
0603		was
0217		in which
1426		our Lord

VERSE 7 — And go quickly [and] tell his disciples that he has risen from the dead, and behold, [he goes] before you to Galilee. There you will see him. Behold, I have told you."

Code	Syriac	English
0042		And go
1738		quickly
0116		[and] tell
1304		his disciples
2168		that he has risen
1388		from
0243		the dead
1338		*
0580		and behold
2150		[he goes] before
1261		you
3153		to Galilee
2682		There
0758		you will see him
0580		Behold
0116		I have told

MATTHEW CHAPTER 28

VERSE 8
And they went away quickly from the grave with fear and with great joy and ran to tell his disciples.

Code	Syriac	English
0042		And they went away
1738		quickly
1388		from
2146		the grave
0511		with fear
0727		and with joy
2271		great
2312		and ran
0116		to tell
1304		his disciples

VERSE 9
And behold, Jesus met up with them and said to them, "Peace to you." And they came near [and] clasped his feet and worshipped him.

Code	Syriac	English
0580		and behold
3257		Jesus
1928		met up
0217		with them
0116		and said
1261		to them
2535		Peace
1261		to you
0592		they
0518		And
2244		came near
0047		[and] clasped
2293		his feet
1599		and worshipped
1261		him

VERSE 10
Then Jesus said to them, "Do not fear! But go [and] tell my brothers that they should go to Galilee and there they will see me."

Code	Syriac	English
0594		Then
0116		said
1261		to them
3257		Jesus
1262		not
1261		you
0509		Do fear
0090		But
0042		go
0116		[and] tell
0043		my brothers
0042		that they should go
3153		to Galilee
2682		and there
0758		they will see me

VERSE 11
Now when they had gone, some of those soldiers came to the city and told the chief priests everything that had occurred.

Code	Syriac	English
1128		when
0042		they had gone
0518		Now
0208		came
0131		some
1388		of
2226		soldiers
0593		those
0499		to the city
0116		and told
2271		the chief priests
1135		*
1168		everything
1326		that
0603		had occurred

VERSE 12
And they were gathered with the elders and took counsel and gave no little money to the soldiers

Code	Syriac	English
1198		And they were gathered
1817		with
2263		the elders
1532		and took
1384		counsel
1030		and gave
1209		money
1262		no
0686		little
2226		to the soldiers

MATTHEW CHAPTER 28

VERSE 13 — and said to them, "Say that his disciples came [and] stole him in the night while we were asleep.

Code	Aramaic	English
0116		and said
1261		to them
0116		Say
1304		that his disciples
0208		came
0436		[and] stole him
1299		in the night
1128		while
0544		asleep
0124		we were

VERSE 14 — And if this is heard before the governor, we will persuade him and we will not make trouble for you."

Code	Aramaic	English
0121		And if
2547		is heard
0598		this
2154		before
0586		the governor
0124		<we>
1955		will persuade
0124		we
1261		him
1261		and for you
1262		not
1072		trouble
1724		make
0124		we will

VERSE 15 — Now they, when they had received the money, did as they had instructed them. And this report has gone out among the Judeans up to today.

Code	Aramaic	English
0592		<they>
0518		Now
1128		when
1532		they had received
1209		the money
1724		they did
0060		as
1053		they had instructed
0592		them
1542		And has gone out
1364		report
0598		this
0266		among
3226		the Judeans
1747		up to
1037		today

VERSE 16 — Now the eleven disciples went to Galilee to the mountain where Jesus had arranged [for] them to meet.

Code	Aramaic	English
1304		the disciples
0518		Now
0724		eleven
0042		went
3153		to Galilee
0958		to the mountain
1108		where
0627		had arranged to meet
0592		[for] them
3257		Jesus

VERSE 17 — And when they saw him, they worshipped him. But some of them were doubting.

Code	Aramaic	English
1128		And when
0758		they saw him
1599		they worshipped
1261		him
1388		some of them
0518		But
1968		doubting
0603		were

VERSE 18 — And Jesus came near [and] spoke with them and said to them, "All authority is given to me in heaven and on earth. And as my Father sent me, I send you.

Code	Aramaic	English
2244		And came near
3257		Jesus
1362		[and] spoke
1817		with them

MATTHEW CHAPTER 28

0116	ܘܐܡܪ	and said		1817	ܥܡܟܘܢ	with you
1261	ܠܗܘܢ	to them		0124	ܐܢܐ	I am
1030	ܐܬܝܗܒ	is given		1168	ܟܠܗܘܢ	all
1261	ܠܝ	to me		1036	ܝܘܡܬܐ	the days
1168	ܟܠ	All		1747	ܥܕܡܐ	until
2527	ܫܘܠܛܢ	authority		2534	ܠܫܘܠܡܗ	the end
2543	ܒܫܡܝܐ	in heaven		1813	ܕܥܠܡܐ	of the world
0199	ܘܒܐܪܥܐ	and on earth		0110	ܐܡܝܢ	Amen
0061	ܘܐܝܟܢܐ	And as				
2458	ܕܫܕܪܢܝ	sent me				
0002	ܐܒܝ	my Father				
2458	ܡܫܕܪ	I send				
0124	ܐܢܐ	*				
1261	ܠܟܘܢ	you				

VERSE 19 Go, therefore, disciple all nations and baptize them in the name [of] the Father and the Son and the Holy Spirit.

0042	ܙܠܘ	Go
0596	ܗܟܝܠ	therefore
1302	ܬܠܡܕܘ	disciple
1168	ܟܠܗܘܢ	all
1818	ܥܡܡܐ	nations
1819	ܘܐܥܡܕܘ	and baptize
0592	ܐܢܘܢ	them
2539	ܒܫܡ	in the name [of]
0002	ܐܒܐ	the Father
0323	ܘܒܪܐ	and the Son
2323	ܘܪܘܚܐ	and the Holy Spirit
2164	ܕܩܘܕܫܐ	*

VERSE 20 And teach them to keep all that I commanded you. And behold, I am with you all the days until the end of the world." Amen.

1053	ܘܐܠܦܘ	And teach
0592	ܐܢܘܢ	them
1502	ܕܢܛܪܘܢ	to keep
1168	ܟܠ	all
1313	ܡܐ	that
2007	ܕܦܩܕܬܟܘܢ	I commanded you
0580	ܘܗܐ	And behold
0124	ܐܢܐ	<I>

221

MARK

CHAPTER 1

VERSE 1 — The beginning of the gospel of Jesus Christ, the Son of God.

2362		The beginning
0034		of the gospel
3257		of Jesus
1446		Christ
0323		the Son
0093		of God

VERSE 2 — As it is written in Isaiah the prophet: BEHOLD I WILL SEND MY MESSENGER BEFORE YOUR FACE THAT HE MIGHT PREPARE YOUR WAY.

0060		As
1247		it is written
3109		in Isaiah
1457		the prophet
0580		BEHOLD
2458		WILL SEND
0124		I
1375		MY MESSENGER
2154		BEFORE
2041		YOUR FACE
2699		THAT HE MIGHT PREPARE
0038		YOUR WAY

VERSE 3 — A VOICE THAT CRIES IN THE WILDERNESS: PREPARE THE WAY OF THE LORD AND MAKE STRAIGHT HIS PATHS.

2204		A VOICE
2239		THAT CRIES
0480		IN THE WILDERNESS
0950		PREPARE
0038		THE WAY
1426		OF THE LORD
2461		AND MAKE STRAIGHT
2434		HIS PATHS

VERSE 4 — John was in the wilderness, baptizing and preaching the baptism of repentance for the forgiveness of sins.

0603		was
3233		John
0480		in the wilderness
1819		baptizing
1230		and preaching
1821		the baptism
2651		of repentance
2441		for the forgiveness
0771		of sins

VERSE 5 — And the whole region of Judah went out to him and all the sons of Jerusalem, and he was baptizing them in the Jordan [river] as they confessed their sins.

1542		And went out
0603		*
1288		to him
1168		whole
1157		the region
3224		of Judah
1168		and all
0323		the sons
3022		of Jerusalem
1819		and baptizing
0603		he was
1261		them
3248		in the Jordan [River]
1128		as
1020		they confessed
0771		their sins

VERSE 6 — Now John was clothed with clothing of the hair of camels and was bound with a leather girdle around his loins and his food was locusts and wild honey.

0592		<he>
0518		Now
3233		John
1272		clothed
0603		was
1273		with clothing
1687		of the hair
0420		of camels
0160		and bound with

MARK   CHAPTER 1

0603	ܗܘܐ	was
1906	ܘܐܤܪ	a girdle
1449	ܕܡܫܟܐ	leather
0876	ܒܚܨܘܗܝ	around his loins
0079	ܘܡܐܟܘܠܬܗ	and his food
0069	ܐܝܬܝܗ	was
0603	ܗܘܐ	*
2213	ܩܡܨܐ	locusts
0484	ܘܕܒܫܐ	and honey
0320	ܕܒܪܐ	wild

VERSE 7   And he was preaching and said, "Behold, one comes after me who is more powerful than I, the straps of whose sandals I am not worthy to stoop [and] loosen.

1230	ܘܡܟܪܙ	And preaching
0603	ܗܘܐ	he was
0116	ܘܐܡܪ	and said
0580	ܗܐ	Behold
0208	ܐܬܐ	comes
0215	ܒܬܪܝ	after me
0788	ܕܚܝܠܬܢ	one who is more powerful
1388	ܡܢܝ	than I
0593	ܗܘ	whose
1262	ܠܐ	not
2461	ܫܘܐ	worthy
0124	ܐܢܐ	I am
0374	ܐܓܗܢ	to stoop
2597	ܐܫܪܐ	[and] loosen
1906	ܥܪܩܐ	the straps
1582	ܕܡܤܢܘܗܝ	of sandals

VERSE 8   I have baptized you with water, but he will baptize you with the Holy Spirit."

0124	ܐܢܐ	<I>
1819	ܐܥܡܕܬܟܘܢ	I have baptized you
1351	ܒܡܝܐ	with water
0592	ܗܘ	<he>
0518	ܕܝܢ	but
1819	ܢܥܡܕܟܘܢ	he will baptize you
2323	ܘܪܘܚܐ	with the Holy Spirit
2164	ܕܩܘܕܫܐ	*

VERSE 9   And it was in those days [that] Jesus came from Nazareth of Galilee and was baptized in the Jordan [river] by John.

0603	ܘܗܘܐ	And it was
1036	ܒܝܘܡܬܐ	in days
0593	ܗܢܘܢ	those
0208	ܐܬܐ	[that] came
3257	ܝܫܘܥ	Jesus
1388	ܡܢ	from
3354	ܢܨܪܬ	Nazareth
3153	ܕܓܠܝܠܐ	of Galilee
1819	ܘܐܬܥܡܕ	and was baptized
3248	ܒܝܘܪܕܢܢ	in the Jordan [River]
1388	ܡܢ	by
3233	ܝܘܚܢܢ	John

VERSE 10   And immediately when he came up from the water, he saw the heavens split and the Spirit, as a dove, came down on him.

0725	ܘܡܚܕܐ	And immediately
1658	ܕܤܠܩ	when he came up
1388	ܡܢ	from
1351	ܡܝܐ	the water
0758	ܚܙܐ	he saw
1606	ܐܤܬܕܩܘ	split
2543	ܫܡܝܐ	the heavens
2323	ܘܪܘܚܐ	and the Spirit
0060	ܐܝܟ	as
1038	ܝܘܢܐ	a dove
1499	ܕܢܚܬܬ	came down
1804	ܥܠܘܗܝ	on him

VERSE 11   And there was a voice from the heavens: "You are my beloved Son. I am pleased with you."

2204	ܘܩܠܐ	And a voice
0603	ܗܘܐ	there was
1388	ܡܢ	from
2543	ܫܡܝܐ	the heavens
0133	ܐܢܬ	You
0592	ܗܘ	are
0323	ܒܪܝ	my Son
0698	ܚܒܝܒܐ	beloved

Vertical Interlinear

MARK   CHAPTER 1

0217		with you
2077		I am pleased

VERSE 12 — And immediately the Spirit led him out into the wilderness.

0725		And immediately
1542		led him out
2323		the Spirit
0480		into the wilderness

VERSE 13 — And he was there in the wilderness [for] forty days, being tempted by Satan. And he was with the wild beasts and angels were ministering to him.

0603		And he was
2682		there
0480		in the wilderness
1036		days
0180		[for] forty
1128		being
1527		tempted
1388		by
1642		Satan
0069		And he
0603		was
1817		with
0783		the wild beasts
2554		and ministering
0603		were
1261		to him
1375		angels

VERSE 14 — Now after John was delivered up, Jesus came to Galilee and was preaching the gospel of the kingdom of God.

0215		after
2530		was delivered up
0518		Now
3233		John
0208		came
1261		<to him>
3257		Jesus
3153		to Galilee
1230		and preaching

0603		was
1593		the gospel
1385		of the kingdom
0093		of God

VERSE 15 — And he said, "The time is complete and the kingdom of God has arrived. Repent and believe in the gospel."

0116		And he said
2530		complete
1261		is
0633		The time
1346		and has arrived
1385		the kingdom
0093		of God
2649		Repent
0109		and believe
1593		in the gospel

VERSE 16 — And while walking round about the Sea of Galilee, he saw Simon and Andrew, his brother, who were casting nets into the sea, for they were fishermen.

1128		And while
0608		walking
0732		round about
1057		the Sea
3153		of Galilee
0758		he saw
3521		Simon
3061		and Andrew
0043		his brother
2372		who were casting
2090		nets
1057		into the sea
0069		they were
0603		*
0403		for
2091		fishermen

VERSE 17 — And Jesus said to them, "Follow me and I will make you fishermen of men."

0116		And said
1261		to them

Vertical Interlinear

MARK   CHAPTER 1

Code	Syriac	English
3257		Jesus
0208		Follow me
0215		*
1724		and I will make you
2091		fishermen
0323		of men
0131		*

VERSE 18 — And immediately they left their nets and followed him.

Code	Syriac	English
0725		And immediately
2440		they left
2090		their nets
0042		and followed him
0215		*

VERSE 19 — And as he passed on a little further, he saw James, the son of Zebedee, and John, his brother, and they also [were] in a boat mending their nets.

Code	Syriac	English
1128		And as
1733		he passed on
2203		a little further
0758		he saw
3255		James
0323		the son of
3185		Zebedee
3233		and John
0043		his brother
0169		and also
1261		they [were]
1692		in a boat
2699		mending
2090		their nets

VERSE 20 — And he called them and immediately they left Zebedee, their father, in the boat with the hired servants and followed him.

Code	Syriac	English
2239		And he called
0592		them
0725		and immediately
2440		they left
3185		Zebedee
0002		their father
1692		in the boat
1817		with
0017		the hired servants
0042		and followed him
0215		*

VERSE 21 — And when they entered Capernaum, immediately he was teaching on the Sabbaths in their synagogues.

Code	Syriac	English
1128		And when
1796		they entered
3268		Capernaum
0725		immediately
1053		teaching
0603		he was
2445		on the Sabbaths
1200		in their synagogues

VERSE 22 — And they were amazed at his teaching, for he was teaching them as an authority and not as their scribes.

Code	Syriac	English
2679		And they amazed
0603		were
1054		at his teaching
1053		teaching
0603		he was
1261		them
0403		for
0060		as
2526		an authority
1262		and not
0060		as
1699		their scribes

VERSE 23 — And in their synagogue there was a man in whom was an unclean spirit. And he called out

Code	Syriac	English
0069		And there
0603		was
1200		in their synagogue
0361		a man
0069		was
0217		in whom

Vertical Interlinear

MARK   CHAPTER 1

#	Aramaic	English
2323		spirit
0984		an unclean
2227		And he called out

VERSE 24 — and said, "What have we to do with you, Jesus, the Nazarene? Have you come to destroy us? I know who you [are]. You are the Holy [one] of God."

#	Aramaic	English
0116		and said
1313		What have we to do with you
1261		*
1261		*
3257		Jesus
3355		the Nazarene
0208		Have you come
0005		to destroy us
1023		I know
0124		*
1261		you [are]
1389		who
0133		You are
2162		the Holy [one]
0093		of God

VERSE 25 — And Jesus rebuked him and said, "Close your mouth and come out of him."

#	Aramaic	English
1113		And rebuked
0217		him
3257		Jesus
0116		and said
1653		Close
1936		your mouth
1542		and come out
1388		of him

VERSE 26 — And the unclean spirit threw him down and cried out with a loud voice and went out of him.

#	Aramaic	English
2455		And threw him down
2323		the spirit
0991		unclean
2227		and cried out
2204		with a voice
2336		loud
1542		and went out
1388		of him

VERSE 27 — And all of them were amazed and were asking each other and saying, "What is this? And what is this new teaching? For with authority he commands even the unclean spirits and they obey him."

#	Aramaic	English
0549		And were amazed
1168		all of them
0296		and asking
0603		were
0721		each other
1817		*
0721		*
0116		and saying
1393		What
0592		is
0598		this
1390		And what is
1054		teaching
0598		this
0735		new
2527		For with authority
0169		even
2323		the spirits
0991		unclean
2007		he commands
2547		and they obey
1261		him

VERSE 28 — And immediately his fame went out into all the land of Galilee.

#	Aramaic	English
0725		And immediately
1542		went out
0944		his fame
1168		into all
0214		the land
3153		of Galilee

VERSE 29 — And they went away from the synagogue and came to the house of Simon and of Andrew, with James and John.

#	Aramaic	English
1542		And they went away

MARK CHAPTER 1

#	Syriac	English
1388		from
1200		the synagogue
0208		and came
0243		to the house
3521		of Simon
3061		and of Andrew
1817		with
3255		James
3233		and John

VERSE 30 And the mother-in-law of Simon was sick with a fever and they told him about her.

#	Syriac	English
0823		And the mother-in-law
3521		of Simon
2372		sick
0603		was
0204		with a fever
0116		and they told
1261		him
1804		about her

VERSE 31 And he came near [and] took her by her hand and raised her up. And immediately her fever left her and she was ministering to them.

#	Syriac	English
2244		And he came near
0047		[and] took her
0057		by her hand
2168		and raised her up
0725		And immediately
2440		left her
0204		her fever
2554		and ministering
0603		she was
1261		to them

VERSE 32 Now in the evening at the setting of the sun, they brought to him all those who were very ill and possessed.

#	Syriac	English
2375		in the evening
0518		Now
1884		at the setting of
2557		the sun
0208		they brought
1288		to him
1168		all
0066		those
0221		who were very ill
1724		*
0515		and possessed

VERSE 33 And the entire city was gathered at the door.

#	Syriac	English
0499		And the city
1168		entire
1198		gathered
0603		was
1804		at
2718		the door

VERSE 34 And he healed many that were very ill with diverse sicknesses and he cast out many devils. And he did not allow the devils to speak, because they knew him.

#	Syriac	English
0136		And he healed
1596		many
0221		that very ill
1724		*
0603		were
1227		with sicknesses
0813		diverse
0514		and devils
1596		many
1542		he cast out
1262		And not
2440		allow
0603		he did
1261		<them>
0514		the devils
1362		to speak
1347		because
1023		they knew
0603		*
1261		him

MARK   CHAPTER 1

VERSE 35
And in the morning he got up very early and went to a desert place and was praying there.

2124	ܒܨܦܪܐ	And in the morning
2150	ܛܒ	early
2168	ܩܡ	he got up
0938	ܘܠܐ	very
0042	ܘܐܙܠ	and went
0214	ܠܐܬܪܐ	to a place
0892	ܚܘܪܒܐ	desert
2682	ܘܬܡܢ	and there
2106	ܡܨܠܐ	praying
0603	ܗܘܐ	was

VERSE 36
And Simon and those with him were searching for him.

0296	ܘܒܥܝܢ	And searching
0603	ܗܘܘ	were
1261	ܠܗ	for him
3521	ܫܡܥܘܢ	Simon
1817	ܘܕܥܡܗ	and those with him

VERSE 37
And when they found him, they said to him, "Everyone is searching for you."

1128	ܘܟܕ	And when
2510	ܐܫܟܚܘܗܝ	they found him
0116	ܐܡܪܝܢ	they said
1261	ܠܗ	to him
1168	ܟܠܗܘܢ	Everyone
0131	ܐܢܫܐ	*
0296	ܒܥܝܢ	is searching
1261	ܠܟ	for you

VERSE 38
He said to them, "Walk into the villages and into the cities that are nearby, for I will also preach there, for I have come to [do] this."

0116	ܐܡܪ	He said
1261	ܠܗܘܢ	to them
0608	ܗܠܟܘ	Walk
2251	ܠܩܘܪܝܐ	into the villages
0499	ܘܠܡܕܝܢܬܐ	and into the cities
2248	ܕܩܪܝܒܢ	that are nearby
0169	ܕܐܦ	for also
2682	ܬܡܢ	there
1230	ܐܟܪܙ	I will preach
0598	ܠܗܕܐ	to [do] this
0403	ܓܝܪ	for
0208	ܐܬܝܬ	I have come

VERSE 39
And he was preaching in all their synagogues in all of Galilee and cast out demons.

1230	ܘܡܟܪܙ	And preaching
0603	ܗܘܐ	he was
1168	ܒܟܠܗܝܢ	in all
1200	ܟܢܘܫܬܗܘܢ	their synagogues
1168	ܒܟܠܗ	in all of
3153	ܓܠܝܠܐ	Galilee
1542	ܘܡܦܩ	and cast out
2469	ܫܐܕܐ	demons

VERSE 40
And a leper came to him and fell at his feet and was begging him and said to him, "If you want to, you can cleanse me."

0208	ܘܐܬܐ	And came
1288	ܠܘܬܗ	to him
0456	ܓܪܒܐ	a leper
1538	ܘܢܦܠ	and fell
1804	ܥܠ	at
2293	ܪܓܠܘܗܝ	his feet
0296	ܘܒܥܐ	and begging
0603	ܗܘܐ	was
1388	ܡܢܗ	<from> him
0116	ܘܐܡܪ	and said
1261	ܠܗ	to him
0121	ܐܢ	If
2077	ܨܒܐ	want to
0133	ܐܢܬ	you
2510	ܡܫܟܚ	can
0133	ܐܢܬ	you
0521	ܠܡܕܟܝܘܬܝ	cleanse me

VERSE 41
And Jesus had compassion on him and stretched out his hand, touched him and said, "I want to. Be cleansed."

0592	ܗܘ	<he>
0518	ܕܝܢ	And

MARK — CHAPTER 1

Vertical Interlinear

#	Syriac	English
3257		Jesus
2342		had compassion
1804		on him
2054		and stretched out
0057		his hand
2244		touched
1261		him
0116		and said
2077		I want to
0124		*
0521		Be cleansed

VERSE 42 — And immediately his leprosy went away from him and he was cleansed.

#	Syriac	English
0217		And immediately
2573		*
0042		went away
0457		his leprosy
1388		from him
0521		and he was cleansed

VERSE 43 — And he charged him and sent him out

#	Syriac	English
1113		And he charged
0217		him
1542		and sent him out

VERSE 44 — and said to him, "See [that] you do not speak to anyone, but go, show yourself to the priests and offer an offering for your purification, as Moses commanded for their testimony."

#	Syriac	English
0116		and said
1261		to him
0758		See [that]
1316		not
0131		to anyone
0116		you do speak
0133		*
0090		but
0042		go
0739		show
1547		yourself
1135		to the priests
2244		and offer
2246		an offering
0812		for
0526		your purification
0061		as
2007		commanded
3305		Moses
1610		for their testimony

VERSE 45 — But when he went away, he began much preaching and made known the event, so that Jesus was not able to openly enter the city, but was outside in a deserted place. And they were coming to him from every place.

#	Syriac	English
0592		<he>
0518		But
1128		when
1542		he went away
2597		he began
0603		*
1230		preaching
1596		much
0943		and made known
1364		the event
0061		so that
1262		not
2510		able
0603		was
3257		Jesus
0412		openly
1796		to enter
0499		the city
0090		but
0322		outside
0603		was
0214		in a place
0892		deserted
0208		And they coming
0603		were
1288		to him
1388		from

MARK   CHAPTER 1

1168	ܟܠ	every
0494	ܕܘܟܐ	place

CHAPTER 2

VERSE 1   And Jesus again entered into Capernaum after [some] days. And when they heard that he was in the house,

1796	ܘܥܠ	And entered
2650	ܬܘܒ	again
3257	ܝܫܘܥ	Jesus
3268	ܠܟܦܪܢܚܘܡ	into Capernaum
1036	ܠܝܘܡܬܐ	after [some] days
1128	ܘܟܕ	And when
2547	ܫܡܥܘ	they heard
0243	ܕܒܒܝܬܐ	that in the house
0592	ܗܘ	he was

VERSE 2   many gathered, so that [the house] was not able to contain them, not even in front of the door. And he was speaking the word with them.

1198	ܐܬܟܢܫܘ	gathered
1596	ܣܓܝܐܐ	many
0061	ܐܝܟܢܐ	so that
1262	ܕܠܐ	not
2510	ܐܫܟܚ	[the house] was able
0047	ܐܚܕ	to contain
0592	ܐܢܘܢ	them
0170	ܐܦܠܐ	not even
2154	ܩܕܡ	in front of
2718	ܬܪܥܐ	the door
1362	ܘܡܡܠܠ	And speaking
0603	ܗܘܐ	he was
1817	ܥܡܗܘܢ	with them
1364	ܡܠܬܐ	the word

VERSE 3   And they came to him and brought him a paralytic, bearing him between four [men].

0208	ܘܐܬܘ	And they came
1288	ܠܘܬܗ	to him
0208	ܘܐܝܬܝܘ	and brought
1261	ܠܗ	him
2598	ܡܫܪܝܐ	a paralytic
1128	ܟܕ	bearing
2587	ܫܩܝܠܝܢ	*
1261	ܠܗ	him
0266	ܒܝܬ	between
0179	ܐܪܒܥܐ	four [men]

VERSE 4   And because they were not able to draw near to him because of the crowd, they climbed up to the roof and lifted the covering of the place where Jesus was and they lowered the bed on which the paralytic was laid.

1262	ܘܕܠܐ	And because not
2510	ܐܫܟܚܘ	they were able
2244	ܠܡܬܩܪܒܘ	to draw near
1288	ܠܘܬܗ	to him
1347	ܡܛܠ	because of
1201	ܟܢܫܐ	the crowd
1658	ܣܠܩܘ	they climbed up
1261	ܠܗܘܢ	*
0019	ܠܐܓܪܐ	to the roof
2331	ܘܐܪܝܡܘ	and lifted
0975	ܬܛܠܝܠܐ	the covering
0214	ܐܬܪ	of the place
0069	ܐܝܟܐ	where was
0603	ܗܘܐ	*
3257	ܝܫܘܥ	Jesus
2424	ܘܫܒܘܗ	and they lowered
1897	ܥܪܣܐ	the bed
2372	ܪܡܝܐ	laid
0603	ܗܘܐ	was
0217	ܒܗ	on which
2598	ܡܫܪܝܐ	the paralytic

VERSE 5   And when Jesus saw their faith, he said to that paralytic, "My son, your sins are forgiven you."

1128	ܟܕ	when
0758	ܚܙܐ	saw
0518	ܕܝܢ	And
3257	ܝܫܘܥ	Jesus
0113	ܗܝܡܢܘܬܗܘܢ	their faith
0116	ܐܡܪ	he said

230

MARK CHAPTER 2

0593	ܠܗܘ	to that
2598	ܡܫܪܝܐ	paralytic
0323	ܒܪܝ	My son
2440	ܫܒܝܩܝܢ	are forgiven
1261	ܠܟ	you
0771	ܚܛܗܝܟ	your sins

VERSE 6 Now there were there some scribes and Pharisees, who were sitting and reasoning in their heart[s],

0069	ܐܝܬ	there were
0603	ܗܘܘ	*
0518	ܕܝܢ	Now
2682	ܬܡܢ	there
1388	ܡܢ	some
1699	ܣܦܪܐ	scribes
3439	ܘܦܪܝܫܐ	and Pharisees
1093	ܕܝܬܒܝܢ	who were sitting
2381	ܘܡܬܪܥܝܢ	and reasoning
0603	ܗܘܘ	*
1268	ܒܠܒܗܘܢ	in their heart[s]

VERSE 7 "Why does this [man] speak blasphemy? Who is able to forgive sins, except one, God?"

1393	ܡܢܐ	Why
0598	ܗܢܐ	this [man]
1362	ܡܡܠܠ	does speak
0371	ܓܘܕܦܐ	blasphemy
1390	ܡܢܘ	Who is
2510	ܡܫܟܚ	able
2440	ܠܡܫܒܩ	to forgive
0771	ܚܛܗܐ	sins
0090	ܐܠܐ	except
0121	ܐܢ	*
0721	ܚܕ	one
0093	ܐܠܗܐ	God

VERSE 8 But Jesus knew in his spirit that they were reasoning these [things] in themselves and he said to them, "Why do you reason these [things] in your heart[s]?

3257	ܝܫܘܥ	Jesus
0518	ܕܝܢ	But
1023	ܝܕܥ	knew
2323	ܒܪܘܚܗ	in his spirit
0598	ܕܗܠܝܢ	that these [things]
2381	ܡܬܪܥܝܢ	they were reasoning
1547	ܒܢܦܫܗܘܢ	in themselves
0116	ܘܐܡܪ	and he said
1261	ܠܗܘܢ	to them
1393	ܡܢܐ	Why
2381	ܡܬܪܥܝܢ	do reason
0133	ܐܢܬܘܢ	you
0598	ܗܠܝܢ	these [things]
1268	ܒܠܒܟܘܢ	in your heart[s]

VERSE 9 Which is easier to say to the paralytic, 'Your sins are forgiven you' or to say, 'Rise, take up your bed and walk?'

0066	ܐܝܕܐ	Which
2061	ܦܫܝܩܐ	is easier
0116	ܠܡܐܡܪ	to say
2598	ܠܡܫܪܝܐ	to the paralytic
2440	ܫܒܝܩܝܢ	are forgiven
1261	ܠܟ	you
0771	ܚܛܗܝܟ	Your sins
0024	ܐܘ	or
0116	ܠܡܐܡܪ	to say
2168	ܩܘܡ	Rise
2587	ܫܩܘܠ	take up
1897	ܥܪܣܟ	your bed
0608	ܘܗܠܟ	and walk

VERSE 10 But that you might know that it is lawful [for] the Son of Man to forgive sins on earth," he said to the paralytic,

1023	ܕܬܕܥܘܢ	that you might know
0518	ܕܝܢ	But
2528	ܕܫܠܝܛ	that is lawful [for]
0592	ܗܘ	it
0323	ܠܒܪܗ	the Son of Man
0131	ܕܐܢܫܐ	*
0199	ܒܐܪܥܐ	on earth
2440	ܠܡܫܒܩ	to forgive
0771	ܚܛܗܐ	sins

231

MARK   CHAPTER 2

0116		he said
2598		to the paralytic
VERSE 11		"I say to you, Rise, take up your bed, and go to your house."
1261		to you
0116		say
0124		I
2168		Rise
2587		take up
1897		your bed
0042		and go
0243		to your house
VERSE 12		And he got up immediately and took his bed and went away in the sight of all, so that all of them were amazed and praised God, saying that they had never seen such.
2168		And he got up
0323		immediately
2573		*
2587		and took
1897		his bed
1542		and went away
1794		in the sight
1168		of all
0061		so that
0549		were amazed
1168		all of them
2428		and praised
0093		God
1128		saying
0116		*
1262		that never
1451		*
0758		they had seen
0597		such
VERSE 13		And he went again to the sea and all the crowds were coming to him and he was teaching them.
1542		And he went
2650		again
1288		to
1057		the sea
1168		and all
1201		the crowds
0208		coming
0603		were
1288		to him
1053		and teaching
0603		he was
1261		them
VERSE 14		And while passing by, he saw Levi the son of Alphaeus, who was sitting at the customs-house and he said to him, "Follow me." And he got up [and] followed him.
1128		And while
1733		passing by
0758		he saw
3280		Levi
0323		the son of
3196		Alphaeus
1093		who was sitting at
0243		the customs-house
1358		*
0116		and he said
1261		to him
0208		Follow me
0215		*
2168		And he got up
0042		[and] followed him
0215		*
VERSE 15		And it happened that when he was seated [to eat] in his house, many tax collectors and sinners were seated [to eat] with Jesus and with his disciples, for there were many and they followed him.
0603		And it happened
1128		that when
1664		he was seated [to eat]
0243		in his house
1596		many

MARK   CHAPTER 2

1358		tax collectors		2547		heard [this]
0772		and sinners		0518		But
1664		seated [to eat]		3257		Jesus
0603		were		0116		he said
1817		with		1261		to them
3257		Jesus		1262		not
1817		and with		1679		do have need
1304		his disciples		0808		The whole
0069		there		1804		for
0603		were		0137		a physician
0403		for		0090		but
1596		many		0066		those
0208		and they followed him		0220		who are very ill
0215		*		0220		*

VERSE 16   And the scribes and the Pharisees, when they saw that he was eating with the tax collectors and with sinners, said to his disciples, "Why does he eat and drink with tax collectors and sinners?"

				1724		*
				1262		not
				0208		I have come
1699		And the scribes		2239		to call
3439		and the Pharisees		0637		the just
1128		when		0090		but rather
0758		they saw		0772		the sinners

VERSE 18   Now the disciples of John and the Pharisees were fasting and came and said to him, "Why do the disciples of John and of the Pharisees fast and your disciples do not fast?"

1308		that he was eating				
1817		with				
1358		the tax collectors				
1817		and with		1304		the disciples
0772		sinners		0518		Now
0116		said		3233		of John
1304		to his disciples		3439		and the Pharisees
1395		Why		2093		fasting
1817		with		0603		were
1358		tax collectors		0208		and came
0772		and sinners		0116		and said
0075		does he eat		1261		to him
2620		and drink		1394		Why

VERSE 17   But when Jesus heard [this] he said to them, "The whole do not have need for a physician, but those who are very ill. I have not come to call the just, but rather the sinners."

				1304		the disciples
				3233		of John
				3439		and of the Pharisees
1128		when		2093		do fast

MARK CHAPTER 2

1304	ܬܠܡܝܕܝܟ	and disciples
0517	ܕܝܠܟ	your
1262	ܠܐ	not
2093	ܨܝܡܝܢ	do fast

VERSE 19 — Jesus said to them, "Are the guests of the wedding feast able to fast as long as the bridegroom is with them? No!

0116	ܐܡܪ	said
1261	ܠܗܘܢ	to them
3257	ܝܫܘܥ	Jesus
1316	ܠܡܐ	<?>
2510	ܡܫܟܚܝܢ	Are able
0323	ܒܢܘܗܝ	the guests of the wedding feast
0431	ܕܓܢܘܢܐ	*
1188	ܟܡܐ	as long as
0933	ܕܚܬܢܐ	the bridegroom
1817	ܥܡܗܘܢ	with them
0592	ܗܘ	is
2093	ܕܢܨܘܡܘܢ	to fast
1262	ܠܐ	No

VERSE 20 — But the days will come when the bridegroom will be taken away from them. Then they will fast in that day.

0208	ܢܐܬܘܢ	will come
0518	ܕܝܢ	But
1036	ܝܘܡܬܐ	the days
1313	ܕܡܐ	when
2587	ܕܡܫܬܩܠ	will be taken away
1388	ܡܢܗܘܢ	from them
0933	ܚܬܢܐ	the bridegroom
0594	ܘܗܝܕܝܢ	Then
2093	ܢܨܘܡܘܢ	they will fast
0593	ܒܗܘ	in that
1036	ܝܘܡܐ	day

VERSE 21 — No man lays a new patch and sews [it] on an old garment, lest the new addition takes away from the old and the tear becomes worse.

1262	ܠܐ	No
0131	ܐܢܫ	man
2372	ܪܡܐ	lays
2405	ܐܘܪܩܥܬܐ	a patch
0735	ܚܕܬܐ	new
0747	ܘܚܐܛ	and sews [it]
1804	ܥܠ	on
1320	ܢܚܬܐ	an garment
0275	ܒܠܝܐ	old
1262	ܕܠܐ	lest
1532	ܢܣܒܐ	takes away
1371	ܡܠܝܘܬܗ	the addition
0593	ܗܝ	<that>
0735	ܚܕܬܐ	new
1388	ܡܢ	from
0275	ܒܠܝܐ	the old
0603	ܘܗܘܐ	and becomes
1607	ܣܕܩܐ	the tear
1100	ܝܬܝܪ	worse

VERSE 22 — And no man puts new wine into old wineskins, lest the wine burst the wineskins and the wineskins are ruined and the wine is poured out. But they put new wine into new wineskins."

1262	ܘܠܐ	And no
0131	ܐܢܫ	man
2372	ܪܡܐ	puts
0831	ܚܡܪܐ	wine
0735	ܚܕܬܐ	new
0687	ܒܙܩܐ	into wineskins
0275	ܒܠܝܬܐ	old
1262	ܕܠܐ	lest
0831	ܚܡܪܐ	the wine
2129	ܡܨܪܐ	burst
0687	ܠܙܩܐ	the wineskins
0687	ܘܙܩܐ	and the wineskins
0005	ܐܒܕܢ	are ruined
0831	ܘܚܡܪܐ	and the wine
0201	ܡܬܐܫܕ	is poured out
0090	ܐܠܐ	But
2372	ܪܡܝܢ	they put
0831	ܚܡܪܐ	wine
0735	ܚܕܬܐ	new

MARK CHAPTER 2

0687		into wineskins		1724		did
0735		new		3159		David
VERSE 23		And it happened that when Jesus went [through] the sown fields on the Sabbath, his disciples were walking and picking the heads of grain.		1128		when
				1679		he had need
				1212		and was hungry
0603		And it happened		0592		[both] he
1128		that when		1817		and those with him
0042		went [through]		**VERSE 26**		how he entered the house of God, while Abiathar [was] high priest, and ate the bread of the table of the LORD, which was not lawful to eat except for the priests, and gave also to those who were with him?"
3257		Jesus				
2445		on the Sabbath				
0243		the sown fields				
0693		*				
1304		his disciples		0061		how
0608		walking		1796		he entered
0603		were		0243		the house
1376		and picking		0093		of God
2436		the heads of grain		1128		while
VERSE 24		And the Pharisees said to him, "See, why are they doing something that is not lawful [to do] on the Sabbath?"		3004		Abiathar [was]
				2271		high priest
				1135		*
0116		And said		1293		and the bread
1261		to him		2069		of the table
3439		the Pharisees		1426		of the LORD
0758		See		0075		ate
1393		why		0593		<that>
1724		are they doing		1262		which not
2445		on the Sabbath		2528		was lawful
1326		something		0075		to eat
1262		that not		0090		except
2528		is lawful [to do]		0121		*
VERSE 25		Jesus said to them, "Have you never read what David did when he had need and was hungry, [both] he and those with him,		1135		for the priests
				1030		and gave
				0169		also
0116		said		0066		to those
1261		to them		1817		who with him
3257		Jesus		0603		were
1262		never		**VERSE 27**		And he said to them, "The Sabbath was made for man and man was not [made] for the Sabbath.
1451		*				
2239		Have you read				
1393		what		0116		And he said

MARK CHAPTER 2

1261	ܠܗܘܢ	to them
2445	ܕܫܒܬܐ	The Sabbath
1347	ܡܛܠ	for
0325	ܒܪܢܫܐ	man
0328	ܐܬܒܪܝܬ	was made
1262	ܘܠܐ	and not
0603	ܗܘܐ	was [made]
0325	ܒܪܢܫܐ	man
1347	ܡܛܠ	for
2445	ܫܒܬܐ	the Sabbath

VERSE 28 So also, the Son of Man is the Lord of the Sabbath."

1426	ܡܪܗ	the Lord
0592	ܗܘ	is
0596	ܗܟܝܠ	So
0169	ܘܐܦ	also
2445	ܕܫܒܬܐ	of the Sabbath
0323	ܒܪܗ	the Son of Man
0131	ܕܐܢܫܐ	*

CHAPTER 3

VERSE 1 And again Jesus entered into the synagogue, and there was there a certain man whose hand was withered.

1796	ܘܥܠ	And entered
2650	ܬܘܒ	again
3257	ܝܫܘܥ	Jesus
1200	ܠܟܢܘܫܬܐ	into the synagogue
0069	ܘܐܝܬ	and there was
0603	ܗܘܐ	*
2682	ܬܡܢ	there
0361	ܓܒܪܐ	a man
0721	ܚܕ	certain
1018	ܕܝܒܝܫܐ	was withered
0057	ܐܝܕܗ	whose hand

VERSE 2 And they were watching him, so that if he healed him on the Sabbath, they might accuse him.

1502	ܘܢܛܪܝܢ	And watching
0603	ܗܘܘ	they were
1261	ܠܗ	him
0121	ܐܢ	so that if
0136	ܡܐܣܐ	he healed
1261	ܠܗ	him
2445	ܒܫܒܬܐ	on the Sabbath
2191	ܢܩܛܪܓܘܢܝܗܝ	they might accuse him

VERSE 3 And he said to that man whose hand was withered, "Stand up in the middle."

0116	ܘܐܡܪ	And he said
0593	ܠܗܘ	to that
0361	ܓܒܪܐ	man
1018	ܕܝܒܝܫܐ	was withered
0057	ܐܝܕܗ	whose hand
2168	ܩܘܡ	Stand up
1416	ܒܡܨܥܬܐ	in the middle

VERSE 4 And he also said to them, "Is it lawful on the Sabbath to do that which is good or that which is evil? To save life or to destroy [it]?" But they were silent.

0116	ܐܡܪ	he said
0518	ܕܝܢ	And
0169	ܐܦ	also
1261	ܠܗܘܢ	to them
2528	ܫܠܝܛ	Is it lawful
2445	ܒܫܒܬܐ	on the Sabbath
1724	ܠܡܥܒܕ	to do
0938	ܕܛܒ	that which is good
0024	ܐܘ	or
0220	ܕܒܝܫ	that which is evil
1547	ܢܦܫܐ	life
0780	ܠܡܚܐ	To save
0024	ܐܘ	or
0005	ܠܡܘܒܕܘ	to destroy [it]
0592	ܗܢܘܢ	<they>
0518	ܕܝܢ	But
2623	ܫܬܝܩܝܢ	silent
0603	ܗܘܘ	they were

VERSE 5 And he looked on them with anger, being saddened by the hardness of their heart[s]. And he said to that man, "Stretch out your hand." And he stretched [it] out and his hand was restored.

0756	ܘܚܪ	And he looked

MARK CHAPTER 3

Vertical Interlinear

#	Syriac	English
0217		on them
0838		with anger
1128		being saddened
1221		*
1261		*
1804		by
2267		the hardness
1268		of their heart[s]
0116		And he said
0593		to that
0361		man
2054		Stretch out
0057		your hand
2054		And he stretched [it] out
2699		and was restored
0057		his hand

VERSE 6 — And the Pharisees went out immediately with the Herodians and took counsel against him, how they might destroy him.

#	Syriac	English
1542		And went out
3439		the Pharisees
0323		immediately
2573		*
1817		with
0243		the Herodians
3179		*
1384		and counsel
1532		took
1804		against him
0061		how
0005		they might destroy him

VERSE 7 — And Jesus went with his disciples to the sea and many people were joining with him from Galilee and from Judah

#	Syriac	English
3257		And Jesus
1817		with
1304		his disciples
0042		went
1261		*
1288		to
1057		the sea
1818		and people
1596		many
1388		from
3153		Galilee
1565		joining him
0603		were
1388		and from
3224		Judah

VERSE 8 — and from Jerusalem and from Idumaea and from beyond Jordan and from Tyre and from Sidon. Many crowds who had heard all that he had done came to him.

#	Syriac	English
1388		and from
3022		Jerusalem
1388		and from
3009		Idumaea
1388		and from
1735		beyond
3248		Jordan
1388		and from
3450		Tyre
1388		and from
3452		Sidon
1201		crowds
1596		Many
2547		who had heard
0603		*
1168		all
1724		that he had done
0208		came
1288		to him

VERSE 9 — And he told his disciples to bring him a boat because of the crowds, so that they would not press on him.

#	Syriac	English
0116		And he told
1304		his disciples
2244		to bring
1261		him
1692		a boat
1347		because of

MARK   CHAPTER 3

#	Aramaic	English
1201		the crowds
1262		so that not
0711		they would press on him

VERSE 10 — For he had healed so many up until then that they were falling on him in order to touch him.

#	Aramaic	English
1596		so many
0403		For
0136		he had healed
0603		*
1747		up until then
0603		that they were
1538		falling
1804		on him
1347		in order
2244		to touch
1261		him

VERSE 11 — And those who had torments of unclean spirits, when they saw him, were falling down and crying out and saying, "You are the Son of God."

#	Aramaic	English
0066		And those
0069		who had
0603		*
1261		*
1342		torments
2323		of spirits
0991		unclean
1313		when
0758		they saw him
1538		falling down
0603		were
2227		and crying out
0116		and saying
0133		You are
0592		<he>
0323		the Son
0093		of God

VERSE 12 — And he severely rebuked them that they should not reveal him.

#	Aramaic	English
1596		And severely
1113		he rebuked
0603		*
0217		them
1262		that not
0409		they should reveal him

VERSE 13 — And he climbed up a mountain and called those whom he wanted and they came to him.

#	Aramaic	English
1658		And he climbed up
0958		a mountain
2239		and called
0066		those
2077		whom he wanted
0208		and they came
1288		to him

VERSE 14 — And he chose twelve to be with him and to send them to preach

#	Aramaic	English
0351		And he chose
2710		twelve
0603		to be
1817		with him
2458		and to send
0592		them
1230		to preach

VERSE 15 — and to be authorities to heal the sick and to cast out devils.

#	Aramaic	English
0603		and to be
2528		authorities
0136		to heal
1228		the sick
1542		and to cast out
0514		devils

VERSE 16 — And he named Simon the name Peter,

#	Aramaic	English
2540		And he named
3521		Simon
2539		the name
3258		Peter

MARK — CHAPTER 3

VERSE 17 — and to James the son of Zebedee and to John the brother of James, he gave them the name Boanerges, which is, sons of thunder.

Code	Syriac	Gloss
3255		And to James
0323		the son of
3185		Zebedee
3233		and to John
0043		the brother
3255		of James
1625		he gave
1261		them
2539		the name
3122		Boanerges
0069		which is
0323		sons of
2391		thunder

VERSE 18 — And [he chose] Andrew and Philip and Bartholomew and Matthew and Thomas and James, the son of Alphaeus, and Thaddeus and Simon the Canaanite,

Code	Syriac	Gloss
3061		And [he chose] Andrew
3420		and Philip
3133		and Bartholomew
3329		and Matthew
3528		and Thomas
3255		and James
0323		the son of
3196		Alphaeus
3530		and Thaddeus
3521		and Simon
3482		the Canaanite

VERSE 19 — and Judas Iscariot, who betrayed him. And they came to a house

Code	Syriac	Gloss
3228		and Judas
3370		Iscariot
0593		<he>
2530		who betrayed him
0208		And they came
0243		to a house

VERSE 20 — and the crowds gathered again, so that they were not able to eat bread.

Code	Syriac	Gloss
1198		and gathered
1201		the crowds
2650		again
0061		so
1262		that not
2510		they were able
0603		*
1293		bread
0075		to eat

VERSE 21 — And his relatives heard and went out to seize him, for they were saying that he had gone out of his mind.

Code	Syriac	Gloss
2547		And heard
0045		his relatives
1542		and went out
0047		to seize him
0116		saying
0603		they were
0403		for
1388		that out of
0605		his mind
1542		he had gone

VERSE 22 — And those scribes who had come down from Jerusalem were saying, "Beelzebub is in him, and he casts out devils by the chief of the devils."

Code	Syriac	Gloss
1699		And scribes
0066		those
1388		who from
3022		Jerusalem
1499		had come down
0116		saying
0603		were
3127		Beelzebub
0069		is
0217		in him
2362		and by the chief
0514		of devils
1542		he casts out

MARK CHAPTER 3

0514	ܕܝܘܐ	devils

VERSE 23 — And Jesus called them and in parables said to them, "How is Satan able to cast out Satan?

2239	ܘܩܪܐ	And called
0592	ܐܢܘܢ	them
3257	ܝܫܘܥ	Jesus
1454	ܘܒܡܬܠܐ	and in parables
0116	ܐܡܪ	said
1261	ܠܗܘܢ	to them
0061	ܐܝܟܢܐ	How
2510	ܡܫܟܚ	is able
1642	ܣܛܢܐ	Satan
1642	ܠܣܛܢܐ	Satan
1542	ܠܡܦܩܘ	to cast out

VERSE 24 — For if a kingdom will be divided against itself, that kingdom is not able to stand.

0121	ܐܢ	if
1385	ܡܠܟܘܬܐ	a kingdom
0403	ܓܝܪ	For
1804	ܥܠ	against
1547	ܢܦܫܗ	itself
1968	ܬܬܦܠܓ	will be divided
1262	ܠܐ	not
2510	ܡܫܟܚܐ	is able
2168	ܠܡܩܡ	to stand
1385	ܡܠܟܘܬܐ	kingdom
0593	ܗܝ	that

VERSE 25 — And if a house will be divided against itself, that house is not able to stand.

0121	ܐܢ	And if
0243	ܒܝܬܐ	a house
1804	ܥܠ	against
1547	ܢܦܫܗ	itself
1968	ܢܬܦܠܓ	will be divided
1262	ܠܐ	not
2510	ܡܫܟܚ	is able
0243	ܒܝܬܐ	house
0593	ܗܘ	that
2168	ܠܡܩܡ	to stand

VERSE 26 — And if Satan stands against himself and is divided, he is not able to stand, but is [at] his end.

0121	ܐܢ	And if
0592	ܗܘ	<he>
1642	ܣܛܢܐ	Satan
2168	ܩܡ	stands
1804	ܥܠ	against
1547	ܢܦܫܗ	himself
1968	ܘܐܬܦܠܓ	and is divided
1262	ܠܐ	not
2510	ܡܫܟܚ	he is able
2168	ܠܡܩܡ	to stand
0090	ܐܠܐ	but
0054	ܚܪܬܗ	[at] his end
0592	ܗܝ	is

VERSE 27 — No man is able to enter the house of a strong man and to grab his possessions, except he first binds the strong man and then robs his house.

1262	ܠܐ	No
0131	ܐܢܫ	man
2510	ܡܫܟܚ	is able
1796	ܕܢܥܘܠ	to enter
0243	ܠܒܝܬ	the house
0862	ܚܣܝܢܐ	of a strong man
0774	ܘܢܚܛܘܦ	and to grab
1320	ܡܐܢܘܗܝ	his possessions
0090	ܐܠܐ	except
0121	ܐܢ	*
2151	ܠܘܩܕܡ	first
0862	ܠܚܣܝܢܐ	the strong man
0160	ܢܐܣܘܪ	he binds
0594	ܘܗܝܕܝܢ	and then
0243	ܒܝܬܗ	his house
0244	ܢܒܘܙ	robs

VERSE 28 — Truly I say to you, all the sins and blasphemies that men will blaspheme will be forgiven them,

0110	ܐܡܝܢ	Truly
0116	ܐܡܪ	say

MARK CHAPTER 3

0124	ܐܢܐ	I
1261	ܠܟܘܢ	to you
1168	ܕܟܠܗܘܢ	all
0771	ܚܛܗܐ	the sins
0371	ܘܓܘܕܦܐ	and blasphemies
0370	ܕܢܓܕܦܘܢ	that will blaspheme
0323	ܒܢܝ	men
0131	ܐܢܫܐ	*
2440	ܢܫܬܒܩܘܢ	will be forgiven
1261	ܠܗܘܢ	them

VERSE 29 but he who blasphemes against the Holy Spirit has no forgiveness forever, but is guilty before the judgment that is eternal."

1389	ܡܢ	he who
0518	ܕܝܢ	but
0370	ܕܢܓܕܦ	blasphemes
1804	ܥܠ	against
2323	ܪܘܚܐ	the Holy Spirit
2164	ܕܩܘܕܫܐ	*
1264	ܠܝܬ	has no
1261	ܠܗ	*
2441	ܫܘܒܩܢܐ	forgiveness
1813	ܠܥܠܡ	forever
0090	ܐܠܐ	but
0742	ܡܚܝܒ	is guilty
0592	ܗܘ	<he>
0497	ܠܕܝܢܐ	before the judgment
1813	ܕܠܥܠܡ	that is eternal

VERSE 30 [This was] because they were saying, "He has an unclean spirit."

1347	ܡܛܠ	[This was] because
0116	ܕܐܡܪܝܢ	saying
0603	ܗܘܘ	they were
2323	ܕܪܘܚܐ	an spirit
0991	ܛܢܦܬܐ	unclean
0069	ܐܝܬ	He has
0217	ܒܗ	*

VERSE 31 And his mother and his brothers came, standing outside, and they sent [someone] to call him to them.

0208	ܘܐܬܘ	And came
0106	ܐܡܗ	his mother
0043	ܘܐܚܘܗܝ	and his brothers
2168	ܩܝܡܝܢ	standing
0322	ܠܒܪ	outside
2458	ܘܫܕܪܘ	and they sent [someone]
2239	ܕܢܩܪܘܢܝܗܝ	to call him
1261	ܠܗܘܢ	to them

VERSE 32 Now the crowd was sitting around him and they said to him, "Behold, your mother and your brothers [are] outside seeking you."

1093	ܝܬܒ	sitting
0603	ܗܘܐ	was
0518	ܕܝܢ	Now
0732	ܚܕܪܘܗܝ	around him
1201	ܟܢܫܐ	the crowd
0116	ܘܐܡܪܝܢ	and they said
1261	ܠܗ	to him
0580	ܗܐ	Behold
0106	ܐܡܟ	your mother
0043	ܘܐܚܝܟ	and your brothers
0322	ܠܒܪ	[are] outside
0296	ܒܥܝܢ	seeking
1261	ܠܟ	you

VERSE 33 And he answered and said to them, "Who is my mother? And who are my brothers?"

1838	ܘܥܢܐ	And he answered
0116	ܘܐܡܪ	and said
1261	ܠܗܘܢ	to them
1389	ܡܢ	Who
0592	ܗܝ	is
0106	ܐܡܝ	my mother
1389	ܘܡܢ	And who
0592	ܐܢܘܢ	are
0043	ܐܚܝ	my brothers

MARK　　　　　CHAPTER 3

VERSE 34 — And he looked at those who sat with him and said, "Behold, my mother, and behold, my brothers.

0756	ܚܙܐ	And he looked
0066	ܠܐܝܠܝܢ	at those
1093	ܕܝܬܒܝܢ	who sat
1288	ܠܘܬܗ	with him
0116	ܘܐܡܪ	and said
0580	ܗܐ	Behold
0106	ܐܡܝ	my mother
0580	ܘܗܐ	and behold
0043	ܐܚܝ	my brothers

VERSE 35 — For he who does the will of God is my brother and my sister and my mother."

1389	ܡܢ	he who
1724	ܕܢܥܒܕ	does
0403	ܓܝܪ	For
2079	ܨܒܝܢܗ	the will
0093	ܕܐܠܗܐ	of God
0592	ܗܘܝܘ	is
0043	ܐܚܝ	my brother
0046	ܘܚܬܝ	and my sister
0106	ܘܐܡܝ	and my mother

CHAPTER 4

VERSE 1 — And again he began to teach by the shore of the sea. And large crowds were gathered around him so that he boarded [and] sat in a boat on the sea. And the entire crowd was standing on the land by the shore of the sea.

2650	ܬܘܒ	again
0518	ܕܝܢ	And
2597	ܫܪܝ	he began
0603	ܗܘܐ	*
1053	ܠܡܠܦܘ	to teach
1804	ܥܠ	by
0057	ܝܕ	the shore of
1057	ܝܡܐ	the sea
1198	ܘܐܬܟܢܫܘ	And were gathered
1288	ܠܘܬܗ	around him
1201	ܟܢܫܐ	crowds
1596	ܣܓܝܐܐ	large

0060	ܐܝܟ	so that
1658	ܕܢܣܩ	he boarded
1093	ܢܬܒ	[and] sat
1261	ܠܗ	*
1692	ܒܣܦܝܢܬܐ	in a boat
1057	ܒܝܡܐ	on the sea
1168	ܘܟܠܗ	And entire
1201	ܟܢܫܐ	the crowd
2168	ܩܐܡ	standing
0603	ܗܘܐ	was
1804	ܥܠ	on
0199	ܐܪܥܐ	the land
1804	ܥܠ	by
0057	ܝܕ	the shore of
1057	ܝܡܐ	the sea

VERSE 2 — And he was teaching them in many parables and said in his teaching,

1053	ܘܡܠܦ	And teaching
0603	ܗܘܐ	he was
1261	ܠܗܘܢ	them
1454	ܒܡܬܠܐ	in parables
1596	ܣܓܝ	many
0116	ܘܐܡܪ	and said
0603	ܗܘܐ	*
1054	ܒܝܘܠܦܢܗ	in his teaching

VERSE 3 — "Listen. Behold, a sower went out to sow

2547	ܫܡܥܘ	Listen
0580	ܗܐ	Behold
1542	ܢܦܩ	went out
0692	ܙܪܘܥܐ	a sower
0691	ܠܡܙܪܥ	to sow

VERSE 4 — and while he sowed, one [seed] fell by the side of the road and a bird came and ate it.

1128	ܘܟܕ	and while
0691	ܙܪܥ	he sowed
0069	ܐܝܬ	one [seed]
1538	ܕܢܦܠ	fell
1804	ܥܠ	by
0057	ܝܕ	the side of

MARK — CHAPTER 4

0038		the road
0208		and came
2026		a bird
0075		and ate it

VERSE 5 — And another [seed] fell on rock where there was not much earth, and immediately it sprouted because there was no depth of earth.

0053		another [seed]
0518		And
1538		fell
1804		on
2477		rock
1108		where
1264		there was not
0199		earth
1596		much
0323		and immediately
2573		*
0280		it sprouted
1347		because
1264		there was no
0603		*
1831		depth
0199		of earth

VERSE 6 — But when the sun came up, [the plant] withered and because it had no root, it dried up.

1128		when
0555		came up
0518		But
2557		the sun
0821		[the plant] withered
1347		and because
1264		it had no
0603		*
1261		*
1877		root
1018		it dried up

VERSE 7 — And another [seed] fell among the thorns. And the thorns grew up and choked it and it did not bear fruit.

0053		And another [seed]
1538		fell
0266		among
1139		the thorns
1658		And grew up
1139		the thorns
0848		and choked it
2016		and fruit
1262		not
1030		it did bear

VERSE 8 — But another [seed] fell on good earth and grew up and matured and bore fruit, some thirty and some sixty and some one hundred[fold]."

0053		another [seed]
0518		But
1538		fell
1804		on
0199		earth
0938		good
1658		and grew up
2280		and matured
1030		and bore
2016		fruit
0069		some
2676		thirty
0069		and some
2616		sixty
0069		and some
1317		one hundred[fold]

VERSE 9 — And he said, "He who has ears to hear should hear."

0116		And he said
0603		*
1389		He who
0069		has
1261		*
0021		ears

MARK   CHAPTER 4

2547	ܕܢܫܡܥ	to hear
2547	ܢܫܡܥ	should hear

VERSE 10   Now when they were alone, those who were with him with his twelve asked him about that parable.

1128	ܟܕ	when
0603	ܗܘܘ	they were
0518	ܕܝܢ	Now
1041	ܒܠܚܘܕܝܗܘܢ	alone
2420	ܫܐܠܘܗܝ	asked him about
0592	ܗܢܘܢ	those
1817	ܕܥܡܗ	who were with him
1817	ܥܡ	with
2710	ܬܪܥܣܪܬܗ	his twelve
1454	ܡܬܠܐ	parable
0593	ܗܘ	that

VERSE 11   And Jesus said to them, "To you is given to know the mystery of the kingdom of God. But to [those] outside, everything is in parables,

0116	ܘܐܡܪ	And said
1261	ܠܗܘܢ	to them
3257	ܝܫܘܥ	Jesus
1261	ܠܟܘܢ	To you
1030	ܝܗܝܒ	is given
1023	ܠܡܕܥ	to know
0188	ܐܪܙܐ	the mystery
1385	ܕܡܠܟܘܬܗ	of the kingdom
0093	ܕܐܠܗܐ	of God
0321	ܠܒܪܝܐ	to [those] outside
0518	ܕܝܢ	But
1168	ܟܠ	everything
1326	ܡܕܡ	*
1454	ܒܡܬܠܐ	in parables
0603	ܗܘܐ	is

VERSE 12   so that WHEN THEY SEE, THEY WILL SEE YET NOT SEE, AND WHEN THEY HEAR, THEY WILL HEAR YET NOT UNDERSTAND, LEST THEY SHOULD RETURN AND THEIR SINS WOULD BE FORGIVEN THEM."

1128	ܕܟܕ	so that WHEN
0758	ܚܙܝܢ	THEY SEE
0758	ܢܚܙܘܢ	THEY WILL SEE
1262	ܘܠܐ	YET NOT
0758	ܢܚܙܘܢ	SEE
1128	ܘܟܕ	AND WHEN
2547	ܫܡܥܝܢ	THEY HEAR
2547	ܢܫܡܥܘܢ	THEY WILL HEAR
1262	ܘܠܐ	YET NOT
1647	ܢܣܬܟܠܘܢ	UNDERSTAND
1314	ܕܠܡܐ	LEST
1984	ܢܬܦܢܘܢ	THEY SHOULD RETURN
2440	ܘܢܫܬܒܩܘܢ	AND WOULD BE FORGIVEN
1261	ܠܗܘܢ	THEM
0771	ܚܛܗܝܗܘܢ	THEIR SINS

VERSE 13   And he said to them, "Do you not understand this parable? Then how will you understand all parables?

0116	ܐܡܪ ܠܗܘܢ	And he said
1261	ܠܗܘܢ	to them
1262	ܠܐ	not
1023	ܝܕܥܝܢ	Do understand
0133	ܐܢܬܘܢ	you
1261	ܠܗ	<it>
1454	ܠܡܬܠܐ	parable
0598	ܗܢܐ	this
0061	ܘܐܝܟܢܐ	Then how
1168	ܟܠܗܘܢ	all
1454	ܡܬܠܐ	parables
1023	ܬܕܥܘܢ	will you understand

VERSE 14   The sower, who sowed, sowed the word.

0692	ܙܪܘܥܐ	The sower
0691	ܕܙܪܥ	who sowed
1364	ܡܠܬܐ	the word
0691	ܙܪܥ	sowed

VERSE 15   And those [seed] that [were] by the side of the road are those in whom the word is sown. And when they have heard, immediately Satan comes and takes away the word that was sown in their heart[s].

0598	ܗܢܘܢ	those [seed]
0518	ܕܝܢ	And

MARK — CHAPTER 4

1804		that [were] by
0057		the side of
0038		the road
0598		those
0592		are
0691		is sown
0217		in whom
1364		the word
1313		And when
2547		they have heard
0725		immediately
0208		comes
1642		Satan
2587		and takes away
1261		<it>
1364		the word
0691		that was sown
1268		in their heart[s]

VERSE 16 And those that were sown on rock are those that when they have heard the word, immediately receive it with joy.

0593		And those
1804		that on
2477		rock
0691		were sown
0598		those
0592		are
1313		that when
2547		they have heard
1364		the word
0725		immediately
0727		with joy
2134		receive
1261		it

VERSE 17 And they have no root in themselves, but they are temporary. And when trouble or persecution happens on account of the word, they are quickly offended.

1264		And they have no
1261		*
1877		root
1547		in themselves
0090		but
0633		temporary
0592		they are
1313		And when
0603		happens
0103		trouble
0024		or
2306		persecution
1347		on account of
1364		the word
1738		quickly
1242		they are offended

VERSE 18 And those that were sown among thorns are those who have heard the word

0593		And those
0266		that among
1139		thorns
0691		were sown
0598		those
0592		are
0593		<those>
2547		who have heard
1364		the word

VERSE 19 and the care of this world and the deceit of riches and the rest of the other lusts enter [and] choke the word, and they are without fruit.

2377		and the care
1813		of world
0598		this
0994		and the deceit
1920		of riches
2611		and the rest
2288		of the lusts
0053		other
1796		enter
0848		[and] choke
1261		<it>

MARK   CHAPTER 4

1364	ܡܠܬܐ	the word
1262	ܘܕܠܐ	and without
2016	ܦܐܪܐ	fruit
0603	ܗܘܝܢ	they are

VERSE 20 — And those that were sown on good ground are those who have heard the word and receive [it] and bear fruit thirty and sixty and one hundred[fold]."

0593	ܘܗܢܘܢ	And those
0199	ܕܒܐܪܥܐ	that on ground
0938	ܛܒܬܐ	good
0691	ܐܙܕܪܥܘ	were sown
0598	ܗܢܘܢ	those
0592	ܐܢܘܢ	are
2547	ܕܫܡܥܝܢ	who have heard
1364	ܡܠܬܐ	the word
2134	ܘܡܩܒܠܝܢ	and receive [it]
1030	ܘܝܗܒܝܢ	and bear
2016	ܦܐܪܐ	fruit
2676	ܒܬܠܬܝܢ	thirty
2616	ܘܒܫܬܝܢ	and sixty
1317	ܘܒܡܐܐ	and one hundred[fold]

VERSE 21 — And he said to them, "Is there any profit for a lamp to be placed under a basket or under a couch? Should it not be placed on a lamp stand?

0116	ܘܐܡܪ	And he said
1261	ܠܗܘܢ	to them
1314	ܕܠܡܐ	<why>
0208	ܐܬܐ	Is there any profit
2607	ܫܪܓܐ	for a lamp
2660	ܬܚܝܬ	under
1583	ܣܐܬܐ	a basket
1625	ܡܬܬܣܝܡ	to be placed
0024	ܐܘ	or
2660	ܬܚܝܬ	under
1897	ܥܪܣܐ	a couch
1262	ܠܐ	not
0603	ܗܘܐ	<it>
1804	ܥܠ	on
1402	ܡܢܪܬܐ	a lamp stand

1625	ܡܬܬܣܝܡ	Should it be placed

VERSE 22 — For there is not anything that is hidden that will not be revealed or [anything] occurring in secret and is not revealed.

1264	ܠܝܬ	there is not
0403	ܓܝܪ	For
1326	ܡܕܡ	anything
1009	ܕܛܫܐ	that is hidden
1262	ܕܠܐ	that not
0409	ܢܬܓܠܐ	will be revealed
1262	ܘܠܐ	or [anything]
0603	ܗܘܐ	occurring
1010	ܒܛܘܫܝܐ	in secret
1262	ܘܠܐ	and not
0409	ܡܬܓܠܐ	is revealed

VERSE 23 — If a man has ears to hear, he should hear."

0121	ܐܢ	If
0131	ܐܢܫ	a man
0069	ܐܝܬ	has
1261	ܠܗ	*
0021	ܐܕܢܐ	ears
2547	ܕܢܫܡܥ	to hear
2547	ܢܫܡܥ	he should hear

VERSE 24 — And he said to them, "Notice what you hear. With that measure that you measure, it will be measured to you, and it is accumulated to you who hear.

0116	ܘܐܡܪ	And he said
1261	ܠܗܘܢ	to them
0758	ܚܙܘ	Notice
1393	ܡܢܐ	what
2547	ܫܡܥܝܢ	hear
0133	ܐܢܬܘܢ	you
0593	ܒܗܝ	With that
1144	ܟܝܠܬܐ	measure
1142	ܕܡܟܝܠܝܢ	that measure
0133	ܐܢܬܘܢ	you
1142	ܡܬܬܟܝܠ	it will be measured
1261	ܠܟܘܢ	to you
1064	ܘܡܬܬܘܣܦ	and it is accumulated

MARK — CHAPTER 4

Vertical Interlinear

Code		Gloss
1261		to you
0066		<those>
2547		who hear

VERSE 25 — For he who has, it will be given to him. And he who has not, even that which he has will be taken from him."

Code		Gloss
1389		he who
0069		has
1261		*
0403		For
1030		it will be given
1261		to him
1389		And he who
1264		has not
1261		*
0169		even
0593		that
0069		which he has
1261		*
2587		will be taken
1388		from him

VERSE 26 — And he was saying, "Such is the kingdom of God as a man who throws seed on the ground.

Code		Gloss
0116		And saying
0603		he was
0597		Such
0592		is
1385		the kingdom
0093		of God
0060		as
0131		a man
2372		who throws
0693		seed
0199		on the ground

VERSE 27 — And he will sleep and rise in the night and in the day, and the seed will grow and be tall, as he does not know [how],

Code		Gloss
0544		And he will sleep
2168		and rise
1299		in the night
0064		and in the day
0693		and the seed
2280		will grow
1084		and be tall
1128		as
0592		<he>
1262		not
1023		he does know [how]

VERSE 28 — for the ground brings forth the fruit. And first comes the plant, and after it the ear, and finally the full grain in the ear.

Code		Gloss
0199		the ground
0403		for
0208		brings forth
1261		<to it>
2016		the fruit
2151		And first
0603		comes
1845		the plant
0215		and after it
2436		the ear
0051		finally
0518		and
0779		the grain
1373		full
2436		in the ear

VERSE 29 — And when the fruit is ripe, immediately the sickle comes, because the harvest has arrived."

Code		Gloss
1313		when
2545		is ripe
0518		And
2016		the fruit
0725		immediately
0208		comes
1321		the sickle
1346		because has arrived
0879		the harvest

MARK   CHAPTER 4

VERSE 30 — And he said, "What is the kingdom of God like and with what parable can we compare it?

Code	Aramaic	English
0116		And he said
1394		What
0540		is like
1385		the kingdom
0093		of God
0066		and with what
1454		parable
1453		can we compare it

VERSE 31 — It is as a grain of mustard, which, when it is planted in the ground, is the least of all the small seeds that are on the earth.

Code	Aramaic	English
0060		as
2019		a grain
0592		It is
0895		of mustard
0593		which
1313		when
0691		it is planted
0199		in the ground
0686		the least
0592		is
1388		of
1168		all
0694		the small seeds
1804		that are on
0199		the earth

VERSE 32 — And when it is planted, it grows up and becomes greater than all the herbs and produces great branches, so that a bird is able to nest in its shade."

Code	Aramaic	English
1313		And when
0691		it is planted
1658		it grows up
0603		and becomes
2271		greater
1388		than
1168		all
1085		the herbs
1724		and produces
1623		branches
2271		great
0060		so that
2510		is able
0971		in its shade
2026		a bird
2511		to nest

VERSE 33 — With parables such as these, Jesus was speaking with them, parables such as they were able to hear.

Code	Aramaic	English
1454		With parables
0060		such as
0598		these
1362		speaking
0603		was
3257		Jesus
1817		with them
1454		parables
0060		such as
2510		able
0603		they were
2547		to hear

VERSE 34 — And without parables, he was not speaking with them. But he was explaining everything to his disciples privately.

Code	Aramaic	English
1262		And without
1454		parables
1262		not
1362		speaking
0603		he was
1817		with them
1304		to his disciples
0518		But
0266		privately
1261		*
2061		explaining
0603		he was
1173		everything

Vertical Interlinear

MARK CHAPTER 4

VERSE 35 — And he said to them on the same day at evening, "Let us cross over to the other shore."

Code	Syriac	English
0116		And he said
1261		to them
0593		on the same
1036		day
2375		at evening
1733		Let us cross over
1261		*
1735		to the other shore

VERSE 36 — And they left the crowds and conducted him away in a boat, and there were other boats with them.

Code	Syriac	English
2440		And they left
1201		the crowds
0477		and conducted him away
1128		<being>
1692		in a boat
0592		<he>
1692		and boats
0053		other
0069		there were
0603		*
1817		with them

VERSE 37 — And there was a great storm and wind, and waves were falling into the boat, and [the boat] was about to be filled.

Code	Syriac	English
0603		And there was
1816		a storm
2271		great
2323		and wind
0407		and waves
1538		falling
0603		were
1692		into the boat
2248		and [the boat] about
0603		was
1366		to be filled

VERSE 38 — And Jesus was asleep on a cushion in the stern of the boat, and they came [and] woke him and said to him, "Our Master, do you not care that we are being destroyed?"

Code	Syriac	English
0592		<he>
0518		And
3257		Jesus
1804		on
0285		a cushion
0544		asleep
0603		was
0054		in the stern
1692		of the boat
0208		and they came
2168		[and] woke him
0116		and said
1261		to him
2271		Our Master
1262		not
0253		do you care
1261		*
0005		that being destroyed
0124		we are

VERSE 39 — And he rose up and rebuked the wind and said to the sea, "Cease; be restrained." And the wind ceased and a great calm occurred.

Code	Syriac	English
2168		And he rose up
1113		and rebuked
2323		the wind
0116		and said
1057		to the sea
2516		Cease
0635		be restrained
0133		<you>
2516		And ceased
2323		the wind
0603		and occurred
1484		a calm
2271		great

MARK   CHAPTER 4

VERSE 40 — And he said to them, "Why are you fearful in this manner? And why do you not have faith?"

Code	Syriac	English
0116		And he said
1261		to them
1394		Why
0510		are fearful
0133		you
0597		in this manner
1394		And why
1264		do you not have
0217		*
0113		faith

VERSE 41 — And they feared a great fear and were saying one to another, "Who indeed is this [man] that the winds and sea obey him?"

Code	Syriac	English
0509		And they feared
0511		a fear
2271		great
0116		and saying
0603		were
0721		one to another
0721		*
1390		Who is
1163		indeed
0598		this [man]
2323		that the winds
1057		and sea
2547		obey
1261		him

CHAPTER 5

VERSE 1 — And he came to the opposite side of the sea to the region of the Gadarenes.

Code	Syriac	English
0208		And he came
1735		to the opposite side
1057		of the sea
0214		to the region
3147		of the Gadarenes

VERSE 2 — And when he disembarked from the boat, he met a man from the tombs who had an unclean spirit.

Code	Syriac	English
1128		And when
1542		he disembarked
1388		from
1692		the boat
1928		he met
0217		*
1388		from
0243		the tombs
2143		*
0361		a man
0069		who had
0217		*
2323		an spirit
0991		unclean

VERSE 3 — And he was living in the tombs and no man was able to bind him with chains,

Code	Syriac	English
1833		And living
0603		he was
0243		in the tombs
2143		*
2508		and with chains
0131		man
1262		no
2510		able
0603		was
0160		to bind him

VERSE 4 — because whenever he was bound with shackles and with chains, he would break the chains and would cut the shackles. And no man was able to subdue him.

Code	Syriac	English
1347		because
1168		whenever
0120		*
1641		with shackles
2508		and with chains
0160		bound
0603		he was

MARK — CHAPTER 5

Vertical Interlinear

2508		the chains
2634		break
0603		he would
1641		and the shackles
1992		cut
0603		would
1262		And no
0131		man
2510		able
0603		was
1126		to subdue him

VERSE 5 — And always in the night and in the day, he was in the tombs and in the mountains and he was crying and cutting himself with stones.

1168		And always
0633		*
1299		in the night
0064		and in the day
0243		in the tombs
2143		*
0958		and in the mountains
0069		he was
0603		*
2227		and crying
0603		he was
2113		and cutting
1547		himself
1119		with stones

VERSE 6 — And when he saw Jesus from a distance, he ran [and] worshipped him.

1128		when
0758		he saw
0518		And
3257		Jesus
1388		from
2354		a distance
2312		he ran
1599		[and] worshipped
1261		him

VERSE 7 — And he cried with a loud voice and said, "What have I to do with you, Jesus, Son of the Most High God? I urge you by God that you do not torment me."

2227		And he cried
2204		with a voice
2336		loud
0116		and said
1313		What have I to do with you
1261		*
1261		*
3257		Jesus
0323		Son
0093		of God
2333		the Most High
1059		urge
0124		I
1261		you
0093		by God
1262		that not
2565		you do torment me

VERSE 8 — For he was saying to him, "Come out from the man, unclean spirit."

0116		saying
0603		he was
1261		to him
0403		For
1542		Come out
1388		from
0325		the man
2323		spirit
0991		unclean

VERSE 9 — And he asked him, "What is your name?" He said to him, "Our name [is] Legion, because we are many."

2420		And he asked him
0061		What is
2539		your name
0116		He said
1261		to him
1275		Legion

MARK   CHAPTER 5

Vertical Interlinear

2539		Our name [is]
1347		because
1596		many
0124		we are

VERSE 10   And he was begging him very much not to send him out of the country.

0296		And begging
0603		he was
1388		him
1596		very much
1262		not
2458		to send him
0322		out
1388		of
0214		the country

VERSE 11   Now there was there near the mountain a large herd of pigs that were feeding.

0069		there was
0603		*
0518		Now
2682		there
1288		near
0958		the mountain
0319		a herd
2271		large
0766		of pigs
2381		that were feeding

VERSE 12   And those demons were begging him and saying, "Send us against those pigs that we may attack them."

0296		And begging
0603		were
1388		him
0593		those
2469		demons
0116		and saying
2458		Send us
1804		against
0593		those
0766		pigs
0217		that them
1796		we may attack

VERSE 13   And he allowed them. And those unclean spirits went away and attacked the pigs, and that herd ran to a steep place and fell into the sea and about two thousand [pigs] were drowned in the water.

1989		And he allowed
1261		them
1542		And went away
2323		spirits
0598		those
0991		unclean
1796		and attacked
0766		the pigs
2312		and ran
0593		that
0319		herd
2586		to a steep place
1538		and fell
1057		into the sea
0060		about
2709		two
0099		thousand [pigs]
0848		and were drowned
1351		in the water

VERSE 14   And those who were tending them fled and reported [it] in the city and also in the villages. And they came out to see what had happened.

0593		And those
2381		who tending
0603		were
1261		them
1904		fled
0116		and reported [it]
0499		in the city
0169		and also
2251		in the villages
1542		And they came out
0758		to see

MARK   CHAPTER 5

1326	ܡܕܡ	what		1388	ܗܘ	him
0603	ܕܗܘܐ	had happened		0042	ܕܢܐܙܠ	to leave

VERSE 15 — And they came to Jesus and saw him, the one possessed of demons, in whom Legion had been, dressed and sober and sitting. And they were afraid.

				1261	ܠܗ	<it>
				1388	ܢ	<from>
				2659	ܬܚܘܡܗܘܢ	their border

0208	ܘܐܬܘ	And they came
1288	ܠܘܬ	to
3257	ܝܫܘܥ	Jesus
0758	ܘܚܙܐܘܗܝ	and saw him
0593	ܠܗܘ	the one
2469	ܕܕܝܘܢܐ	possessed of demons
1128	ܟܕ	dressed
1272	ܠܒܝܫ	*
1517	ܘܡܢܟܦ	and sober
1093	ܘܝܬܒ	and sitting
0593	ܗܘ	<who>
0069	ܐܝܬܘܗܝ	had been
0603	ܗܘܐ	*
0217	ܒܗ	in whom
1275	ܠܓܝܘܢ	Legion
0509	ܘܕܚܠܘ	And they were afraid

VERSE 18 — And when he boarded a boat, he who had been possessed of demons was begging him that he might be with him,

1128	ܟܕ	And when
1658	ܣܠܩ	he boarded
1692	ܠܐܠܦܐ	a boat
0296	ܒܥܐ	was begging
0603	ܗܘܐ	*
1388	ܡܢܗ	him
0593	ܗܘ	he
2469	ܕܕܝܘܢܐ	who had been possessed of demons
1817	ܕܥܡܗ	that with him
0603	ܢܗܘܐ	he might be

VERSE 16 — And those who had seen related to them how it happened to the one possessed of demons and also about those pigs.

2569	ܘܐܫܬܥܝܘ	And related
1261	ܠܗܘܢ	to them
0593	ܗܢܘܢ	those
0758	ܕܚܙܘ	who had seen
0061	ܐܝܟܢܐ	how
0603	ܗܘܐ	it happened
0593	ܠܗܘ	to the one
2469	ܕܕܝܘܢܐ	possessed of demons
0169	ܘܐܦ	and also
1804	ܥܠ	about
0593	ܗܢܘܢ	those
0766	ܚܙܝܪܐ	pigs

VERSE 19 — yet he did not allow him. On the contrary, he said to him, "Go to your house to your people and tell them what the LORD did for you and how he had compassion on you."

1262	ܘܠܐ	yet not
2440	ܫܒܩܗ	he did allow him
0090	ܐܠܐ	On the contrary
0116	ܐܡܪ	he said
1261	ܠܗ	to him
0042	ܙܠ	Go
0243	ܠܒܝܬܟ	to your house
1288	ܠܘܬ	to
0131	ܐܢܫܝܟ	your people
2569	ܘܐܫܬܥܐ	and tell
1261	ܠܗܘܢ	them
1326	ܡܕܡ	what
1724	ܕܥܒܕ	did
1261	ܠܟ	for you
1426	ܡܪܝܐ	the LORD
2342	ܘܕܐܬܪܚܡ	and how he had compassion
1804	ܥܠܝܟ	on you

VERSE 17 — And they began begging him to leave their border.

2597	ܘܫܪܝܘ	And they began
0296	ܒܥܝܢ	begging

253

MARK　　CHAPTER 5

VERSE 20 — And he went and began preaching in the Decapolis what Jesus had done for him, and all of them were amazed.

0042	ܘܐܙܠ	And he went
2597	ܘܫܪܝ	and began
1230	ܡܟܪܙ	preaching
3402	ܒܥܣܪܬ-ܡܕܝܢܬܐ	in the Decapolis
1326	ܡܕܡ	what
1724	ܥܒܕ	had done
1261	ܠܗ	for him
3257	ܝܫܘܥ	Jesus
1168	ܘܟܠܗܘܢ	and all of them
2679	ܡܬܕܡܪܝܢ	amazed
0603	ܗܘܘ	were

VERSE 21 — And when Jesus had crossed over by boat to that other side, large crowds again were gathered around him while he was by the shore of the sea.

1128	ܘܟܕ	And when
1733	ܥܒܪ	had crossed over
3257	ܝܫܘܥ	Jesus
1692	ܒܣܦܝܢܬܐ	by boat
0593	ܠܗܘ	to that
1735	ܥܒܪܐ	other side
2650	ܬܘܒ	again
1198	ܐܬܟܢܫܘ	were gathered
1804	ܥܠܘܗܝ	around him
1201	ܟܢܫܐ	crowds
1596	ܣܓܝܐܐ	large
1128	ܟܕ	while
0069	ܐܝܬܘܗܝ	he was
1804	ܥܠ	by
0057	ܝܕ	the shore of
1057	ܝܡܐ	the sea

VERSE 22 — And a certain [man] whose name [was] Jairus came from the rulers of the synagogue. And when he saw him, he fell down at his feet.

0208	ܘܐܬܐ	And came
0721	ܚܕ	a certain [man]
2539	ܕܫܡܗ	whose name [was]
3231	ܝܘܐܪܫ	Jairus
1388	ܡܢ	from
2271	ܪܒܝ	the rulers of
1200	ܟܢܘܫܬܐ	the synagogue
1128	ܘܟܕ	And when
0758	ܚܙܝܗܝ	he saw him
1538	ܢܦܠ	he fell down
1288	ܠܘܬ	at
2293	ܪܓܠܘܗܝ	his feet

VERSE 23 — And he was begging him very much and said to him, "My daughter is very sick. Come [and] place your hand on her and she will be made whole and live."

0296	ܘܒܥܐ	And begging
0603	ܗܘܐ	he was
1388	ܡܢܗ	him
1596	ܣܓܝ	very much
0116	ܘܐܡܪ	and said
1261	ܠܗ	to him
0327	ܒܪܬܝ	My daughter
0221	ܒܝܫܐܝܬ	is very sick
1724	ܥܒܝܕܐ	*
0208	ܬܐ	Come
1625	ܣܝܡ	[and] place
0057	ܐܝܕܟ	your hand
1804	ܥܠܝܗ	on her
0807	ܘܬܬܚܠܡ	and she will be made whole
0780	ܘܬܚܐ	and live

VERSE 24 — And Jesus went away with him and a large crowd followed him and they were pressing on him.

0042	ܘܐܙܠ	And went away
1817	ܥܡܗ	with him
3257	ܝܫܘܥ	Jesus
0476	ܘܢܩܝܦ	and followed
0603	ܗܘܐ	*
1261	ܠܗ	him
1201	ܟܢܫܐ	a crowd
1596	ܣܓܝܐܐ	large
0711	ܘܚܒܨܝܢ	and pressing
0603	ܗܘܘ	they were
1261	ܠܗ	on him

MARK CHAPTER 5

VERSE 25 — And a certain woman, who had a flow of blood [for] twelve years,

Code	Syriac	Gloss
0135		a woman
0518		And
0721		certain
0069		who had
0603		*
2302		a flow
0539		of blood
2559		[for] years
2710		twelve

VERSE 26 — who had suffered much from many doctors and had spent everything that she had and was not some helped, but was afflicted even more,

Code	Syriac	Gloss
0066		who
1596		much
1584		had suffered
1388		from
0137		doctors
1596		many
1542		and had spent
1168		everything
1326		*
0069		that she had
1261		*
1326		and some
1262		not
1751		was helped
0090		but
0169		even
1101		more
0102		was afflicted

VERSE 27 — when she heard about Jesus, came through the press of the crowd [and] from behind him touched his clothing,

Code	Syriac	Gloss
1128		when
2547		she heard
1804		about
3257		Jesus
0208		came
0712		through the press
1201		of the crowd
1388		[and] from
0295		behind him
2244		touched
1273		his clothing

VERSE 28 — for she was saying, "If only I can touch his clothing, I will live."

Code	Syriac	Gloss
0116		saying
0603		she was
0403		for
0172		If only
1273		his clothing
2244		I can touch
0124		<I>
0780		I will live
0124		*

VERSE 29 — And immediately the flow of her blood dried up and she felt in her body that she had been healed of her sickness.

Code	Syriac	Gloss
0725		And immediately
1018		dried up
1795		the flow
0539		of her blood
2297		and she felt
1929		in her body
0136		that she had been healed
1388		of
1342		her sickness

VERSE 30 — Now Jesus immediately knew within himself that power had gone out of him. And he turned to the crowd and said, "Who touched my garments?"

Code	Syriac	Gloss
3257		Jesus
0518		Now
0725		immediately
1023		knew
1547		within himself
0786		that power
1542		had gone out
1388		of him

MARK   CHAPTER 5

1984		And he turned		1023		because she knew
1288		to		1313		what
1201		the crowd		0603		had happened
0116		and said		1261		to her
1390		Who		0208		came
2244		touched		1538		[and] fell down
1320		my garments		2154		before him

VERSE 31 And his disciples said to him, "Do you see the crowds that are pressing you, and you say, who touched me?"

				0116		and told
				1261		him
0116		And said		1168		all
1261		to him		2596		the truth

VERSE 34 And he said to her, "My daughter, your faith has given you life. Go in peace and be healed from your sickness."

1304		his disciples				
0758		see				
0133		Do you		0592		<he>
1201		the crowds		0518		And
0711		that are pressing		0116		he said
1261		you		1261		to her
0116		and say		0327		My daughter
0133		you		0113		your faith
1390		who		0780		has given you life
2244		touched		0042		Go
1261		me		2535		in peace

VERSE 32 And he was looking to see who had done this.

				0603		and be
				0808		healed
0756		And looking		1388		from
0603		he was		1342		your sickness
0758		to see				

VERSE 35 And while he was speaking they came from the house of the ruler of the synagogue and were saying, "Your daughter is dead. Why therefore are you troubling the teacher?"

1390		who				
0598		this				
1724		had done		1744		And while

VERSE 33 And that woman, being afraid and trembling, because she knew what had happened to her, came [and] fell down before him and told him all the truth.

				0592		he
				1362		was speaking
				0208		they came
				1388		from
0593		that		0243		the house of
0518		And		2271		the ruler of
0135		woman		1200		the synagogue
1128		being		0116		and were saying
0509		afraid				
2414		and trembling				

256

MARK CHAPTER 5

0327	ܒܪܬܟ	Your daughter
1334	ܡܝܬܬ	is dead
1394	ܠܡܢܐ	Why
1357	ܡܟܝܠ	therefore
1827	ܡܥܝܐ	troubling
0133	ܐܢܬ	are you
1055	ܠܡܠܦܢܐ	the teacher

VERSE 36 But Jesus heard the word that they said and said to the ruler of the synagogue, "Do not fear; only believe."

3257	ܝܫܘܥ	Jesus
0518	ܕܝܢ	But
2547	ܫܡܥ	heard
1364	ܠܡܠܬܐ	the word
0116	ܕܐܡܪܘ	that they said
0116	ܘܐܡܪ	and said
0593	ܠܗܘ	to <him>
2271	ܪܒ	the ruler of
1200	ܟܢܘܫܬܐ	the synagogue
1262	ܠܐ	not
0509	ܬܕܚܠ	Do fear
1041	ܒܠܚܘܕ	only
0109	ܗܝܡܢ	believe

VERSE 37 And he did not allow anyone to go with him, except Simon Peter and James and John, the brother of James.

1262	ܘܠܐ	And not
2440	ܫܒܩ	he did allow
0131	ܠܐܢܫ	anyone
0042	ܕܢܐܙܠ	to go
1817	ܥܡܗ	with him
0090	ܐܠܐ	except
3521	ܠܫܡܥܘܢ	Simon
3258	ܟܐܦܐ	Peter
3255	ܘܠܝܥܩܘܒ	and James
3233	ܘܠܝܘܚܢܢ	and John
0043	ܐܚܘܗܝ	the brother
3255	ܕܝܥܩܘܒ	of James

VERSE 38 And they came to the house of that ruler of the synagogue and saw that they were troubled and weeping and wailing.

0208	ܘܐܬܘ	And they came
0243	ܠܒܝܬܐ	to the house
0593	ܕܗܘ	of that
2271	ܪܒ	ruler of
1200	ܟܢܘܫܬܐ	the synagogue
0758	ܘܚܙܐ	and saw
2308	ܕܪܗܝܒܝܢ	that they were troubled
0267	ܘܒܟܝܢ	and weeping
1052	ܘܡܝܠܠܝܢ	and wailing

VERSE 39 And he entered and said to them, "Why are you troubled and weeping? The girl is not dead, but she is asleep,"

1796	ܘܥܠ	And he entered
0116	ܘܐܡܪ	and said
1261	ܠܗܘܢ	to them
1393	ܡܢܐ	Why
2308	ܪܗܝܒܝܢ	troubled
0133	ܐܢܬܘܢ	are you
0267	ܘܒܟܝܢ	and weeping
0978	ܛܠܝܬܐ	The girl
1262	ܠܐ	not
1334	ܡܝܬܬ	is dead
0090	ܐܠܐ	but
0544	ܕܡܟܐ	is asleep
0592	ܗܝ	she

VERSE 40 and they were laughing at him. But he sent all of them out and he took the father of the girl and her mother and those who were with him and entered where the girl was laid.

0400	ܘܓܚܟܝܢ	and laughing
0603	ܗܘܘ	they were
1804	ܥܠܘܗܝ	at him
0592	ܗܘ	<he>
0518	ܕܝܢ	But
1542	ܐܦܩ	he sent out
1168	ܠܟܠܗܘܢ	all of them
0477	ܘܕܒܪ	and he took
0002	ܠܐܒܘܗ	the father

MARK   CHAPTER 5

0978	ܕܛܠܝܬܐ	of the girl
0106	ܘܠܐܡܗ	and her mother
0593	ܘܠܐܝܠܝܢ	and those
1817	ܕܥܡܗ	who were with him
1796	ܘܥܠ	and entered
1108	ܐܝܟܐ	where
2372	ܕܪܡܝܐ	laid
0603	ܗܘܬ	was
0978	ܛܠܝܬܐ	the girl

VERSE 41   And he took the hand of the girl and said to her, "[Young] girl, rise."

0047	ܘܐܚܕ	And he took
0057	ܒܐܝܕܗ	the hand
0978	ܕܛܠܝܬܐ	of the girl
0116	ܘܐܡܪ	and said
1261	ܠܗ	to her
0978	ܛܠܝܬܐ	[Young] girl
2168	ܩܘܡܝ	rise

VERSE 42   And immediately the girl rose up and walked, for she was twelve years old. And they were amazed [with] great amazement.

0323	ܘܒܪ	And immediately
2573	ܫܥܬܗ	*
2168	ܩܡܬ	rose up
0978	ܛܠܝܬܐ	the girl
0608	ܘܡܗܠܟܐ	and walked
0603	ܗܘܬ	*
0069	ܐܝܬܝܗ	she was
0603	ܗܘܬ	*
0403	ܓܝܪ	for
0327	ܒܪܬ	years old
2559	ܫܢܝܢ	*
2710	ܬܪܬܥܣܪܐ	twelve
0549	ܘܐܬܕܡܪܘ	And amazed
0603	ܗܘܘ	they were
0550	ܕܘܡܪܐ	[with] amazement
2271	ܪܒܐ	great

VERSE 43   And he commanded them very much that no one should make this known. And he said that they should give her [something] to eat.

2007	ܘܦܩܕ	And he commanded
0592	ܐܢܘܢ	them
1596	ܣܓܝ	very much
1262	ܕܠܐ	that no
0131	ܐܢܫ	one
1023	ܢܕܥ	should make known
0598	ܗܕܐ	this
0116	ܘܐܡܪ	And he said
1030	ܕܢܬܠܘܢ	that they should give
1261	ܠܗ	her
1308	ܠܡܐܟܠ	[something] to eat

CHAPTER 6

VERSE 1   And he went away from there and came to his city and his disciples were following him.

1542	ܘܢܦܩ	And he went away
1388	ܡܢ	from
2682	ܬܡܢ	there
0208	ܘܐܬܐ	and came
0499	ܠܡܕܝܢܬܗ	to his city
0476	ܘܕܒܝܩܝܢ	and following
0603	ܗܘܘ	were
1261	ܠܗ	him
1304	ܬܠܡܝܕܘܗܝ	his disciples

VERSE 2   And when it was the Sabbath, he began to teach in the synagogue. And many who heard were amazed and were saying, "Where [did] this man [learn] these [things]? And what is [this] wisdom that was given to him, that miracles such as these might be done by his hand?"

1128	ܘܟܕ	And when
0603	ܗܘܬ	it was
2445	ܫܒܬܐ	the Sabbath
2597	ܫܪܝ	he began
1053	ܠܡܠܦܘ	to teach
1200	ܒܟܢܘܫܬܐ	in the synagogue
1596	ܘܣܓܝܐܐ	And many

258

MARK   CHAPTER 6

2547		who heard
0549		were amazed
0116		and saying
0603		were
1110		Where
1261		<him>
0598		these [things]
0598		[did] this man [learn]
0066		And what
0592		is
0792		[this] wisdom
1030		that was given
1261		to him
0786		that miracles
0060		such as
0598		these
0057		by his hand
0603		might be done

VERSE 3   Is this not the carpenter, the son of Mary and the brother of James and of Joses and of Judas and of Simon? And behold, are not his sisters here with us?" And they were offended at him.

1262		not
0603		Is
0598		this
1469		the carpenter
0323		the son
3325		of Mary
0043		and the brother
3255		of James
3244		and of Joses
3228		and of Judas
3521		and of Simon
1262		And not
0580		behold
0046		are his sisters
2694		here
1288		with us
1242		And offended

0603		they were
0217		at him

VERSE 4   And Jesus said to them, "There is no prophet who is dishonored, except in his own city and among his own relatives and in his own house."

0116		And said
1261		to them
3257		Jesus
1264		There is no
1457		prophet
2119		who is dishonored
0090		except
0121		*
0499		in his own city
0243		and among
0045		his own relatives
0243		and in his own house

VERSE 5   And he was not able to do even one miracle there, except that he laid his hand on a few sick and healed [them].

1262		And not
2510		able
0603		he was
1724		to do
2682		there
0169		even
1262		<not>
0721		one
0786		miracle
0090		except
0121		*
1804		that on
1228		sick
2203		a few
1625		he laid
0057		his hand
0136		and healed [them]

MARK CHAPTER 6

VERSE 6 — And he was amazed by the lack of their faith. And he was traveling in the villages while teaching.

Number	Syriac	English
0549		And amazed
0603		he was
0868		by the lack
0113		of their faith
1236		And traveling
0603		he was
2251		in the villages
1128		while
1053		teaching

VERSE 7 — And he called his twelve and began to send them in pairs. And he gave them authority over unclean spirits, to cast [them] out.

Number	Syriac	English
2239		And he called
2710		his twelve
2597		and began
2458		to send
0592		them
2709		in pairs
2709		*
1030		And he gave
1261		them
2527		authority
1804		over
2323		spirits
0991		unclean
1542		to cast [them] out

VERSE 8 — And he commanded them that they should not carry anything for the journey, except only a staff, no bag and no bread and no brass in their purses,

Number	Syriac	English
2007		And he commanded
0592		them
1262		that not
2587		they should carry
1326		anything
0038		for the journey
0090		except
0121		*
2433		a staff
1041		only
1262		no
2712		bag
1262		and no
1293		bread
1262		and no
1498		brass
1165		in their purses

VERSE 9 — but [that] they should wear sandals and not wear two coats.

Number	Syriac	English
0090		but
1581		[that] they should wear
0981		sandals
1262		and not
1272		wear
2709		two
1256		coats

VERSE 10 — And he said to them, "Into that house, which you enter, there be until you leave there.

Number	Syriac	English
0116		And he said
1261		to them
0066		Into that
0243		house
1796		which enter
0133		you
2682		there
0603		be
1747		until
1542		leave
0133		you
1388		<from>
2682		there

VERSE 11 — And whoever does not receive you and does not hear you when you leave from there, shake off the dust that is under the sole of your feet for their witness. And truly I say to you, it will be [more] pleasant for Sodom and for Gomorrah in the day of judgment than for that city.

Number	Syriac	English
1168		And whoever

MARK   CHAPTER 6

1389		*
1262		not
2134		does receive you
1262		and not
2547		does hear you
1313		when
1542		leave
0133		you
1388		from
2682		there
1541		shake off
0795		the dust
2662		that is under the sole
2293		of your feet
1610		for their witness
0110		And truly
0116		say
0124		I
1261		to you
0603		it will be
1483		[more] pleasant
3362		for Sodom
3398		and for Gomorrah
1036		in the day
0497		of judgment
0024		than
0499		for city
0593		that

VERSE 12   And they went out and preached that [men] should repent.

1542		And they went out
0603		*
1230		and preached
2649		that [men] should repent

VERSE 13   And many demons were cast out. And they were anointing with oil many sick [people] and were healing [them].

2469		And demons
1596		many
1542		cast out
0603		were
1443		And anointing
0603		they were
1445		with oil
1228		sick [people]
1596		many
0136		and healing [them]
0603		were

VERSE 14   And Herod, the king, heard about Jesus, for his name was made known to him. And he was saying [that] John the baptizer had risen from the dead, [and] because of this, miracles are done by him.

2547		And heard
3179		Herod
1383		the king
1804		about
3257		Jesus
1023		made known
0603		was
1261		to him
0403		for
2539		his name
0116		And saying
0603		he was
3233		[that] John
1820		the baptizer
2168		had risen
1388		from
0243		the dead
1338		*
1347		[and] because of
0598		this
0786		miracles
1684		are done
0217		by him

VERSE 15   Others were saying that he was Elijah, and others that he was a prophet like one of the prophets.

0053		Others

261

MARK   CHAPTER 6

0116		saying
0603		were
3047		that Elijah
0592		he was
0053		and others
1457		that a prophet
0592		he was
0060		like
0721		one
1388		of
1457		the prophets

VERSE 16   Now when Herod heard [this] he said, "[It is] John, the one whose head I cut off. He has risen from the dead."

1128		when
2547		heard [this]
0518		Now
3179		Herod
0116		he said
3233		[It is] John
0593		the one
0124		<I>
1992		I cut off
2362		whose head
0592		<he>
2168		He has risen
1388		from
0243		the dead
1338		*

VERSE 17   For Herod had sent [and] arrested John and bound him [in] prison because of Herodias, the wife of Philip, his brother, whom he had taken.

0592		<he>
0403		For
3179		Herod
2458		had sent
0603		*
0047		[and] arrested <him>
3233		John
0160		and bound him
0243		[in] prison
0163		*
1347		because of
3178		Herodias
0135		the wife of
3420		Philip
0043		his brother
0593		whom
1532		he had taken

VERSE 18   For John had told Herod, "It is unlawful for you to take the wife of your brother."

0116		had told
0603		*
0403		For
3233		John
3179		Herod
1262		It is unlawful
2528		*
1261		for you
1532		to take
0135		the wife of
0043		your brother

VERSE 19   Now Herodias was threatened by him and she wanted to kill him and was not able,

0592		<she>
0518		Now
3178		Herodias
1291		threatened
0603		was
1261		by him
2077		and she wanted
0603		*
2179		to kill him
1262		and not
2510		able
0603		was

MARK   CHAPTER 6

VERSE 20   for Herod was afraid of John, because he knew that he was a just and holy man. And he observed him, and [in] many [things] heard him and did [these things], and gladly heard him.

3179	ܗܪܘܕܣ	Herod
0403	ܓܝܪ	for
0509	ܕܚܠ	afraid
0603	ܗܘܐ	was
1388	ܡܢ	of
3233	ܝܘܚܢܢ	John
1804	ܥܠ	because
1023	ܕܝܕܥ	he knew
0603	ܗܘܐ	*
0361	ܕܓܒܪܐ	that a man
0592	ܗܘ	he was
0637	ܙܕܝܩܐ	just
2162	ܘܩܕܝܫܐ	and holy
1502	ܘܡܢܛܪ	And he observed
0603	ܗܘܐ	*
1261	ܠܗ	him
1596	ܘܣܓܝܐܬܐ	and [in] many [things]
2547	ܫܡܥ	heard
0603	ܗܘܐ	*
1261	ܠܗ	him
1724	ܘܥܒܕ	and did [these things]
0289	ܘܒܣܝܡܐܝܬ	and gladly
2547	ܫܡܥ	heard
0603	ܗܘܐ	*
1261	ܠܗ	him

VERSE 21   And there was a notable day when Herod made a banquet on his birthday for his nobles and chiliarchs and rulers of Galilee.

0603	ܘܗܘܐ	And there was
1036	ܝܘܡܐ	a day
1025	ܝܕܝܥܐ	notable
1128	ܟܕ	when
3179	ܗܪܘܕܣ	Herod
0243	ܒܒܝܬ	on his birthday
1047	ܝܠܕܗ	*
0928	ܚܫܡܝܬܐ	a banquet
1724	ܥܒܕ	made
0603	ܗܘܐ	*
2271	ܠܪܘܪܒܢܘܗܝ	for his nobles
1184	ܘܠܟܝܠܝܪܟܐ	and chiliarchs
2362	ܘܠܪܫܐ	and rulers
3153	ܕܓܠܝܠܐ	of Galilee

VERSE 22   And the daughter of Herodias entered [and] danced and pleased Herod and those who were sitting to eat with him. And the king said to the girl, "Ask me anything that you want and I will give [it] to you."

1796	ܘܥܠܬ	And entered
0327	ܒܪܬܗ	the daughter
3178	ܕܗܪܘܕܝܐ	of Herodias
2403	ܘܪܩܕܬ	[and] danced
2580	ܘܫܦܪܬ	and pleased
1261	ܠܗ	<him>
3179	ܠܗܪܘܕܣ	Herod
0066	ܘܠܐܝܠܝܢ	and those
1664	ܕܣܡܝܟܝܢ	who were sitting to eat
1817	ܥܡܗ	with him
0116	ܘܐܡܪ	And said
1383	ܡܠܟܐ	the king
0978	ܠܛܠܝܬܐ	to the girl
2420	ܫܐܠܝ	Ask
1388	ܡܢܝ	me
1326	ܡܕܡ	anything
2077	ܕܨܒܝܐ	that want
0133	ܐܢܬܝ	you
1030	ܘܐܬܠ	and I will give [it]
1261	ܠܟܝ	to you

VERSE 23   And he swore to her, "Whatever you ask, I will give to you, up to half of my kingdom."

1059	ܘܝܡܐ	And he swore
1261	ܠܗ	to her
1326	ܕܡܕܡ	Whatever
2420	ܕܬܫܐܠܝܢ	you ask
1030	ܐܬܠ	I will give

MARK   CHAPTER 6

1261	ܠܟ	to you
1747	ܥܕܡܐ	up to
1971	ܠܦܠܓܗ	half
1385	ܕܡܠܟܘܬܝ	of my kingdom
VERSE 24		And she went away and said to her mother, "What should I ask of him?" She said to her, "The head of John the baptizer."
0592	ܗܝ	<she>
0518	ܕܝܢ	And
1542	ܢܦܩܬ	she went away
0116	ܘܐܡܪܐ	and said
0106	ܠܐܡܗ	to her mother
1393	ܡܢܐ	What
2420	ܐܫܐܠܝܘܗܝ	should I ask of him
0116	ܐܡܪܐ	She said
1261	ܠܗ	to her
2362	ܪܫܗ	The head
3233	ܕܝܘܚܢܢ	of John
1820	ܡܥܡܕܢܐ	the baptizer
VERSE 25		And immediately she entered with care to the king and said to him, "I desire right now that you would give me on a platter the head of John the baptizer."
0725	ܘܒܪܫܥܬܗ	And immediately
1796	ܥܠܬ	she entered
0256	ܒܒܛܝܠܘܬܐ	with care
1288	ܠܘܬ	to
1383	ܡܠܟܐ	the king
0116	ܘܐܡܪܐ	and said
1261	ܠܗ	to him
2077	ܨܒܝܐ	I desire
0124	ܐܢܐ	*
0598	ܕܗܫܐ	right now
2573	ܬܬܠ	*
1030	ܬܬܠ	that you would give
1261	ܠܝ	me
1804	ܥܠ	on
1954	ܦܝܢܟܐ	a platter
2362	ܪܫܗ	the head
3233	ܕܝܘܚܢܢ	of John
1820	ܡܥܡܕܢܐ	the baptizer
VERSE 26		And it made the king very sad, but because of the oaths and because of the guests, he did not want to deny her.
1221	ܘܟܪܝܬ	And it made sad
1261	ܠܗ	*
1596	ܣܓܝ	very
1383	ܠܡܠܟܐ	the king
1347	ܡܛܠ	because of
0518	ܕܝܢ	but
1060	ܡܘܡܬܐ	the oaths
1347	ܘܡܛܠ	and because of
1665	ܣܡܝܟܐ	the guests
1262	ܠܐ	not
2077	ܨܒܐ	he did want
0417	ܕܢܓܠܙܝܗ	to deny her
VERSE 27		But immediately the king sent the executioner and commanded that he should bring the head of John. And he went [and] cut off the head of John [in] prison.
0090	ܐܠܐ	But
0725	ܒܪܫܥܬܗ	immediately
2458	ܫܕܪ	sent
1383	ܡܠܟܐ	the king
0156	ܐܣܦܘܩܠܛܪܐ	the executioner
2007	ܘܦܩܕ	and commanded
0208	ܕܢܝܬܐ	that he should bring
2362	ܪܫܗ	the head
3233	ܕܝܘܚܢܢ	of John
0042	ܘܐܙܠ	And he went
1992	ܦܣܩܗ	[and] cut off
2362	ܪܫܗ	the head
3233	ܕܝܘܚܢܢ	of John
0243	ܒܝܬ	[in] prison
0163	ܐܣܝܪܐ	*
VERSE 28		And he brought [it] on a platter and gave [it] to the girl, and the girl gave [it] to her mother.
0208	ܘܐܝܬܝ	And he brought [it]
1954	ܒܦܝܢܟܐ	on a platter
1030	ܘܝܗܒ	and gave [it]

MARK   CHAPTER 6

0978		to the girl
0592		and <she>
0978		the girl
1030		gave [it]
0106		to her mother

VERSE 29 And his disciples heard and came [and] took his body and placed [it] in a grave.

2547		And heard
1304		his disciples
0208		and came
2587		[and] took
2520		his body
1625		and placed [it]
0243		in a grave
2143		*

VERSE 30 And the apostles were gathered around Jesus and told him everything they had done and everything they had learned.

1198		And were gathered
2522		the apostles
1288		around
3257		Jesus
0116		and told
1261		him
1168		everything
1313		*
1724		they had done
1168		and everything
1313		*
1053		they had learned

VERSE 31 And he said to them, "Come, let us go into the desert by ourselves and rest a little," for there were many who were going and coming and they had no opportunity even to eat.

0116		And he said
1261		to them
0208		Come
1261		<to you>
0042		let us go
0478		into the desert
1041		by ourselves
1483		and rest
2203		a little
0069		there were
0603		*
0403		for
1596		many
0042		who were going
0208		and coming
1264		and they had no
0603		*
1261		*
0214		opportunity
0169		even
1262		<not>
0075		to eat

VERSE 32 And they went away to a deserted place in a boat by themselves.

0042		And they went away
0214		to a place
0892		deserted
1692		in a boat
1041		by themselves

VERSE 33 And many saw them as they were going away and recognized them. And they ran by land before him, from all the cities, to the place.

0758		And saw
0592		them
1596		many
1128		as
0042		they were going away
1023		and recognized
0592		them
1019		And by land
2312		they ran
1388		from
1168		all
0499		the cities
2154		before him

MARK   CHAPTER 6

2682	ܠܐܬܪܐ	to the place

VERSE 34 — And Jesus disembarked [and] saw the large crowds and had compassion on them because they were like sheep that did not have a shepherd. And he began to teach them many [things].

1542	ܘܢܦܩ	And disembarked
3257	ܝܫܘܥ	Jesus
0758	ܚܙܐ	[and] saw
1201	ܟܢܫܐ	the crowds
1596	ܣܓܝܐܐ	large
2342	ܘܐܬܪܚܡ	and had compassion
1804	ܥܠܝܗܘܢ	on them
0540	ܕܐܝܟ	because like
0603	ܗܘܘ	they were
1887	ܠܥܢܐ	sheep
1264	ܕܠܝܬ	that did not have
1261	ܠܗܘܢ	*
2383	ܪܥܝܐ	a shepherd
2597	ܘܫܪܝ	And he began
0603	ܗܘܐ	*
1053	ܠܡܠܦܘ	to teach
0592	ܐܢܘܢ	them
1596	ܣܓܝܐܬܐ	many [things]

VERSE 35 — And when the time grew late, his disciples came to him and said to him, "This is a barren place and the time is late.

1128	ܘܟܕ	And when
0603	ܗܘܐ	grew
1750	ܥܕܢܐ	the time
1596	ܣܓܝܐܐ	late
2244	ܩܪܒܘ	came
1288	ܠܘܬܗ	to him
1304	ܬܠܡܝܕܘܗܝ	his disciples
0116	ܘܐܡܪܝܢ	and said
1261	ܠܗ	to him
0598	ܕܗܢܐ	This is
0214	ܐܬܪܐ	a place
0892	ܚܘܪܒܐ	barren
0592	ܗܘ	<it>

1750	ܘܥܕܢܐ	and the time
1596	ܣܓܝ	is late

VERSE 36 — Dismiss them to go to the surrounding fields and villages and let them buy bread for themselves, for they do not have anything to eat."

2597	ܫܪܝ	Dismiss
0592	ܐܢܘܢ	them
0042	ܕܢܐܙܠܘܢ	to go
0014	ܠܐܓܘܪܣܐ	to the fields
0732	ܕܚܕܪܝܢ	surrounding
2251	ܘܠܩܘܪܝܐ	and villages
0632	ܘܢܙܒܢܘܢ	and let them buy
1261	ܠܗܘܢ	for themselves
1293	ܠܚܡܐ	bread
1264	ܠܝܬ	they do not have
1261	ܠܗܘܢ	*
0403	ܓܝܪ	for
1326	ܡܕܡ	anything
0075	ܠܡܐܟܠ	to eat

VERSE 37 — But he said to them, "Give them to eat." They said to him, "Should we go [and] buy bread [worth] two hundred denarii and give them to eat?"

0592	ܗܘ	<he>
0518	ܕܝܢ	But
0116	ܐܡܪ	he said
1261	ܠܗܘܢ	to them
1030	ܗܒܘ	Give
1261	ܠܗܘܢ	them
0133	ܐܢܬܘܢ	<you>
1308	ܠܡܐܟܠ	to eat
0116	ܐܡܪܝܢ	They said
1261	ܠܗ	to him
0042	ܢܐܙܠ	Should we go
0632	ܢܙܒܢ	[and] buy
1318	ܕܡܐܬܝܢ	two hundred
0519	ܕܝܢܪܝܢ	denarii
1293	ܠܚܡܐ	bread [worth]
1030	ܘܢܬܠ	and give
1261	ܠܗܘܢ	them

MARK CHAPTER 6

#	Syriac	English
1308		to eat
VERSE 38		And he said to them, "Go [and] see how much bread you have here." And when they saw, they said to him, "Five [loaves of] bread and two fish."
0592		\<he\>
0518		And
0116		he said
1261		to them
0042		Go
0758		[and] see
1188		how much
1293		bread
0069		you have
1261		*
0600		here
1128		And when
0758		they saw
0116		they said
1261		to him
0833		Five
1293		[loaves of] bread
2709		and two
1490		fish
VERSE 39		And he commanded them to seat everyone by groups on the grass.
2007		And he commanded
1261		them
1664		to seat
1175		everyone
1666		by groups
1666		*
1804		on
1845		the grass
VERSE 40		And they sat [to eat] by groups of hundreds and fifties.
1664		And they sat [to eat]
1666		by groups
1666		*
1317		of hundreds
1317		*
0834		and fifties
0834		*
VERSE 41		And he took those five [loaves of] bread and two fish, and looked into heaven and blessed and broke the bread, and gave [it] to his disciples to place before them. And they distributed those two fish to all.
1532		And he took
0593		those
0833		five
1293		[loaves of] bread
2709		and two
1490		fish
0756		and looked
2543		into heaven
0335		and blessed
2234		and broke
1293		the bread
1030		and gave [it]
1304		to his disciples
1625		to place
1261		before them
0593		those
2709		two
1490		fish
1968		they distributed
1168		to all
VERSE 42		And all ate and were full.
0075		And ate
1168		all
1585		and were full
VERSE 43		And they took up the fragments [of bread] and of fish, twelve baskets full.
2587		And they took up
2235		the fragments [of bread]
2710		twelve
2176		baskets
1128		full
1366		*
1388		and of

MARK CHAPTER 6

1490	ܢܘܢܐ	fish
VERSE 44		And those who ate bread were five thousand men.
0069	ܐܝܬܝܗܘܢ	were
0603	ܗܘܘ	*
0518	ܕܝܢ	And
0075	ܕܐܟܠܘ	those who ate
1293	ܠܚܡܐ	bread
0833	ܚܡܫܐ	five
0099	ܐܠܦܝܢ	thousand
0361	ܓܒܪܝܢ	men
VERSE 45		And immediately he pressed his disciples to board a boat and to precede him to the opposite shore to Bethsaida while he dismissed the crowds.
0725	ܘܡܚܕܐ	And immediately
0102	ܐܠܨ	he pressed
1304	ܠܬܠܡܝܕܘܗܝ	his disciples
1658	ܕܢܣܩܘܢ	to board
1692	ܠܣܦܝܢܬܐ	a boat
0042	ܘܢܐܙܠܘܢ	and to precede him
2154	ܩܕܡܘܗܝ	*
1735	ܠܥܒܪܐ	to the opposite shore
3118	ܠܒܝܬܨܝܕܐ	to Bethsaida
1744	ܥܕ	while
2597	ܫܪܐ	he dismissed
0592	ܗܘ	*
1201	ܠܟܢܫܐ	the crowds
VERSE 46		And when he had dismissed them, he went to a mountain to pray.
1128	ܘܟܕ	And when
2597	ܫܪܐ	he had dismissed
0592	ܐܢܘܢ	them
0042	ܐܙܠ	he went
0958	ܠܛܘܪܐ	to a mountain
2106	ܠܡܨܠܝܘ	to pray
VERSE 47		And when evening came, the boat was in the middle of the sea and he [was] alone on the land.
1128	ܟܕ	when
0603	ܗܘܐ	came
0518	ܕܝܢ	And
2375	ܪܡܫܐ	evening
1692	ܣܦܝܢܬܐ	the boat
0069	ܐܝܬܝܗ	was
0603	ܗܘܬ	*
1416	ܒܡܨܥܬ	in the middle of
1057	ܝܡܐ	the sea
0592	ܘܗܘ	and he [was]
1041	ܒܠܚܘܕܘܗܝ	alone
1804	ܥܠ	on
0199	ܐܪܥܐ	the land
VERSE 48		And he saw them straining while rowing, for the wind was against them. And in the fourth watch of the night, Jesus came to them, walking on the water. And he wanted to pass by them.
0758	ܘܚܙܐ	And he saw
0592	ܐܢܘܢ	them
2565	ܕܡܫܬܢܩܝܢ	straining
1128	ܟܕ	while
2299	ܪܕܝܢ	rowing
2323	ܪܘܚܐ	the wind
0403	ܓܝܪ	for
2135	ܠܩܘܒܠܗܘܢ	against them
0603	ܗܘܬ	was
1503	ܘܒܡܛܪܬܐ	And in the watch
0184	ܪܒܝܥܝܬܐ	fourth
1299	ܕܠܠܝܐ	of the night
0208	ܐܬܐ	came
1288	ܠܘܬܗܘܢ	to them
3257	ܝܫܘܥ	Jesus
1128	ܟܕ	walking
0608	ܡܗܠܟ	*
1804	ܥܠ	on
1351	ܡܝܐ	the water
2077	ܘܨܒܐ	And he wanted
0603	ܗܘܐ	*
1733	ܕܢܥܒܪ	to pass by
0592	ܐܢܘܢ	them

MARK   CHAPTER 6

VERSE 49 — But they saw him walking on the water, and they thought to themselves that it was a false vision, and they cried out,

Code	Syriac	English
0593		\<those\>
0518		But
0758		they saw him
0608		walking
1804		on
1351		the water
1588		and they thought
1261		to themselves
0759		that a vision
0592		it was
0486		false
2227		and they cried out

VERSE 50 — for all of them saw him and were afraid. And immediately he spoke with them and said to them, "Take courage, it is I. Do not be afraid."

Code	Syriac	English
1168		all of them
0403		for
0758		saw him
0509		and were afraid
0323		And immediately
2573		*
1362		he spoke
1817		with them
0116		and said
1261		to them
1267		Take courage
0124		it is I
0124		*
1262		not
0509		Do be afraid

VERSE 51 — And he climbed into the boat with them and the wind ceased. And they were greatly amazed and astonished among themselves,

Code	Syriac	English
1658		And he climbed
1288		with them
1692		into the boat
2516		and ceased
2323		the wind
0938		And greatly
0549		amazed
0603		they were
2644		and astonished
1547		among themselves

VERSE 52 — for they had not gained insight from that bread, because their heart was hardened.

Code	Syriac	English
1262		not
0403		for
1647		they had gained insight
0603		*
1388		from
1293		bread
0593		that
1347		because
1268		their heart
1722		hardened
0603		was

VERSE 53 — And when they had crossed to the other side, they came to the land of Gennesaret.

Code	Syriac	English
1128		And when
1733		they had crossed to
1735		the other side
0208		they came
0199		to the land
3156		of Gennesaret

VERSE 54 — And after they had disembarked from the boat, immediately the people of the place recognized him.

Code	Syriac	English
1128		And after
1542		they had disembarked
1388		from
1692		the boat
0323		immediately
2573		*
1647		recognized him
0131		the people
0214		of the place

MARK   CHAPTER 6

VERSE 55 — And they ran into that entire region and began to bring those who were very ill, carrying them on pallets to where they heard that he was.

2312		And they ran
1168		into entire
0199		region
0593		that
2597		and began
0208		to bring
0066		those
0221		who were very ill
1724		*
1128		carrying
2587		*
1261		them
1897		on pallets
1108		to where
2547		that they heard
0603		*
0069		he was

VERSE 56 — And wherever he entered into the villages and cities, the sick were placed in the streets. And they were begging him that they might touch even the border of his clothes. And all those who touched him were healed.

1108		And wherever
1796		he entered
0603		*
2251		into the villages
0499		and cities
2481		in the streets
1625		placed
0603		were
1228		the sick
0296		And begging
0603		they were
1388		him
0172		that even
1197		the border
1273		of his clothes
2244		they might touch
1168		And all
0066		those
2244		who touched
0603		*
1261		him
0136		healed
0603		were

CHAPTER 7

VERSE 1 — And the Pharisees and scribes gathered around him who came from Jerusalem.

1198		And gathered
1288		around him
3439		the Pharisees
1699		and scribes
0208		who came
1388		from
3022		Jerusalem

VERSE 2 — And they saw some of his disciples who were eating bread while their hands were not washed, and they complained.

0758		And they saw
0131		some
1388		of
1304		his disciples
0075		who were eating
1293		bread
1128		while
1262		not
2466		were washed
0057		their hands
1748		and they complained

VERSE 3 — For all the Judeans and the Pharisees do not eat unless they wash their hands carefully, because they hold to the tradition of the elders.

1168		all
0403		For
3226		the Judeans
3439		and the Pharisees
0121		unless

MARK CHAPTER 7

#	Aramaic	Gloss	#	Aramaic	Gloss
0592		<it>	3439		and the Pharisees
0255		carefully	1394		Why
1262		*	1304		your disciples
2466		they wash	1262		not
0057		their hands	0608		do walk
1262		not	0060		according to
1308		do eat	2533		the tradition
1347		because	2263		of the elders
0047		they hold to	0090		but
2533		the tradition	1128		while
2263		of the elders	1262		not

VERSE 4 And they do not eat [things] from the marketplace unless they are washed. And there are many other [traditions] that they have received to observe, washings of cups and of pots and of brass vessels and of beds.

#	Aramaic	Gloss	#	Aramaic	Gloss
			2466		are washed
			0057		their hands
			0075		they eat
			1293		bread

VERSE 6 And he said to them, "Well did Isaiah the prophet prophesy concerning you. Hypocrites! As it is written: THIS PEOPLE HONORS ME WITH ITS LIPS BUT THEIR HEART IS VERY FAR FROM ME.

#	Aramaic	Gloss	#	Aramaic	Gloss
1388		And [things] from			
2481		the marketplace			
0090		unless			
1819		they are washed			
1262		not	0592		<he>
1308		they do eat	0518		But
1596		And many	0116		he said
0053		other [traditions]	1261		to them
0069		there are	2583		Well
0066		<those>	1456		did prophesy
2134		that they have received	1804		concerning you
1502		to observe	3109		Isaiah
1821		washings	1457		the prophet
1205		of cups	1532		Hypocrites
2225		and of pots	0173		*
1320		and of vessels	0060		As
1498		brass	1247		it is written
1897		and of beds	1818		PEOPLE

VERSE 5 And the scribes and the Pharisees asked him, "Why do your disciples not walk according to the tradition of the elders, but they eat bread while their hands are not washed?"

#	Aramaic	Gloss
0598		THIS
1701		WITH ITS LIPS
0592		<IT>
2420		And asked him
1699		the scribes
1076		HONORS
1261		ME
1268		THEIR HEART

MARK CHAPTER 7

0518		BUT
1596		VERY
2355		IS FAR
1388		FROM ME
VERSE 7		AND WITHOUT RESULTS THEY REVERENCE ME WHILE TEACHING THE TEACHINGS OF THE COMMANDMENTS OF MEN.
1715		AND WITHOUT RESULTS
0509		THEY REVERENCE
1261		ME
1128		WHILE
1053		TEACHING
1054		THE TEACHINGS
2009		OF THE COMMANDMENTS
0323		OF MEN
0131		*
VERSE 8		For you have left the commandment of God and you have held to the tradition of men, washings of cups and of pots and many [things] that resemble these."
2440		you have left
0403		For
2009		the commandment
0093		of God
0047		and have held to
0133		you
2533		the tradition
0323		of men
0131		*
1821		washings
1205		of cups
2225		and of pots
1596		and many [things]
0066		<those>
0598		that these
0540		resemble
VERSE 9		He said to them, "Well did you reject the commandment of God that you might establish your tradition.
0116		He said
1261		to them

2583		Well
0979		did reject
0133		you
2009		the commandment
0093		of God
2168		that you might establish
2533		your tradition
VERSE 10		For Moses said: HONOR YOUR FATHER AND YOUR MOTHER. And HE WHO REVILES FATHER AND MOTHER SHOULD INDEED DIE.
3305		Moses
0403		For
0116		said
1076		HONOR
0002		YOUR FATHER
0106		AND YOUR MOTHER
1389		And HE WHO
2101		REVILES
0002		FATHER
0106		AND MOTHER
1335		SHOULD INDEED DIE
1334		*
VERSE 11		But you say [that] if a man should say to his father or to his mother, 'My offering [is] what you have gained from me,'
0133		<you>
0518		But
0116		say [that]
0133		you
0121		if
0116		should say
0361		a man
0002		to his father
0024		or
0106		to his mother
2246		My offering
1326		[is] what
1388		from me
1098		you have gained

MARK CHAPTER 7

VERSE 12 — then you allow him not to do anything for his father or his mother.

1262	ܘܠܐ	then not
2440	ܫܒܩܝܢ	allow
0133	ܐܢܬܘܢ	you
1261	ܠܗ	him
1724	ܕܢܥܒܕ	to do
1326	ܡܕܡ	anything
0002	ܠܐܒܘܗܝ	for his father
0024	ܐܘ	or
0106	ܠܐܡܗ	his mother

VERSE 13 — And you despise the word of God because of the tradition that you have handed down and you do many [things] that resemble these.

1655	ܘܛܠܡܝܢ	And despise
0133	ܐܢܬܘܢ	you
1364	ܡܠܬܐ	the word
0093	ܕܐܠܗܐ	of God
1347	ܡܛܠ	because of
2533	ܡܫܠܡܢܘܬܐ	the tradition
2530	ܕܐܫܠܡܬܘܢ	that you have handed down
0540	ܘܕܕܡܝܢ	and that resemble
0598	ܠܗܠܝܢ	these
1596	ܣܓܝܐܬܐ	many [things]
1724	ܥܒܕܝܢ	do
0133	ܐܢܬܘܢ	you

VERSE 14 — And Jesus called to the entire crowd and said to them, "Hear me, all of you, and understand.

2239	ܘܩܪܐ	And called
3257	ܝܫܘܥ	Jesus
1201	ܠܟܢܫܐ	to the crowd
1168	ܟܠܗ	entire
0116	ܘܐܡܪ	and said
1261	ܠܗܘܢ	to them
2547	ܫܘܡܥܘܢܝ	Hear me
1168	ܟܠܟܘܢ	all of you
1647	ܘܐܣܬܟܠܘ	and understand

VERSE 15 — There is nothing that is outside of a man that enters him that is able [to] defile him. But what goes out from him, that defiles a man.

1264	ܠܝܬ	There is nothing
1326	ܡܕܡ	*
0322	ܕܠܒܪ	that is outside
1388	ܡܢ	of
0325	ܒܪܢܫܐ	a man
0592	ܗܘ	<he>
1796	ܘܥܐܠ	that enters
1261	ܠܗ	him
2510	ܘܡܫܟܚ	that is able
1613	ܡܣܝܒ	[to] defile
1261	ܠܗ	him
0090	ܐܠܐ	But
1326	ܡܕܡ	what
1542	ܕܢܦܩ	goes out
1388	ܡܢܗ	from him
0593	ܗܘ	that
0592	ܗܘ	<it>
1613	ܡܣܝܒ	defiles
0323	ܠܒܪ	a man
0131	ܐܢܫܐ	*

VERSE 16 — He who has ears to hear should hear."

1389	ܡܢ	He who
0069	ܐܝܬ	has
1261	ܠܗ	*
0021	ܐܕܢܐ	ears
2547	ܕܢܫܡܥ	to hear
2547	ܢܫܡܥ	should hear

VERSE 17 — And when Jesus entered the house [away] from the crowd, his disciples asked him about that saying.

1128	ܟܕ	when
0518	ܕܝܢ	And
1796	ܥܠ	entered
3257	ܝܫܘܥ	Jesus
0243	ܠܒܝܬܐ	the house
1388	ܡܢ	[away] from

MARK — CHAPTER 7

Vertical Interlinear

Code	Syriac	English
1201		the crowd
2420		asked him
1304		his disciples
1804		about
1454		saying
0593		that

VERSE 18 — He said to them, "Are you likewise also slow to understand? Do you not know that everything that enters a man from the outside cannot defile him,

Code	Syriac	English
0116		He said
1261		to them
0597		likewise
0169		also
0133		<you>
1788		slow to understand
0133		Are you
1262		not
1023		Do know
0133		you
1168		that everything
1326		*
1388		that from
0322		the outside
1796		enters
0323		a man
0131		*
1262		cannot
2510		*
1613		defile
1261		him

VERSE 19 — because it does not enter his heart but into his stomach and is cast off by excretion, which purifies all the food?

Code	Syriac	English
1262		because not
0603		it does
1268		his heart
1796		enter
0090		but
1241		into his stomach
2455		and is cast off
0526		by excretion
0521		which purifies
1168		all
0079		the food

VERSE 20 — But anything that goes out from a man, that defiles the man.

Code	Syriac	English
1326		anything
0518		But
1542		that goes out
1388		from
0325		a man
0593		that
0592		<it>
1613		defiles
0323		the man
0131		*

VERSE 21 — For from within, from the heart of men, evil thoughts proceed: adultery, fornication, theft, murder,

Code	Syriac	English
1388		from
0379		within
0403		For
1388		from
1268		the heart
0323		of men
0131		*
1542		proceed
0917		thoughts
0220		evil
0386		adultery
0681		fornication
0438		theft
2181		murder

VERSE 22 — injustice, wickedness, deceit, filthiness, an evil eye, blasphemy, boastfulness, foolishness.

Code	Syriac	English
1809		injustice
0222		wickedness
1513		deceit
2104		filthiness
1794		an eye

MARK   CHAPTER 7

0220		evil
0371		blasphemy
0233		boastfulness
2500		foolishness

VERSE 23 — All these evils proceed from within and defile a man."

0598		these
1168		All
0220		evils
1388		from
0379		within
0592		<it>
1542		proceed
1613		and defile
1261		<him>
0325		a man

VERSE 24 — From there Jesus rose up and came to the border of Tyre and Sidon. And he entered a certain house. And he did not want anyone to know about him, yet he was not able to conceal [himself],

1388		From
2682		there
2168		rose up
3257		Jesus
0208		and came
2659		to the border
3450		of Tyre
3452		and Sidon
1796		And he entered
0243		a house
0721		certain
1262		And not
2077		want
0603		he did
0131		anyone
1023		to know
0217		about him
1262		yet not
2510		he was able
1009		to conceal [himself]

VERSE 25 — for immediately a certain woman, whose daughter had an unclean spirit, heard about him and came [and] fell down before his feet.

0725		immediately
0403		for
2547		heard
0135		a woman
0721		certain
1347		about him
0069		had
0603		*
0327		whose daughter
2323		an spirit
0991		unclean
0208		and came
1538		[and] fell down
2154		before
2293		his feet

VERSE 26 — Now the woman was a foreigner from Phoenicia of Syria, and she was begging him to cast out the demon from her daughter.

0592		<she>
0518		Now
0135		the woman
0069		was
0603		*
0847		a foreigner
1388		from
3410		Phoenicia
3367		of Syria
0296		and begging
0603		she was
1388		him
1542		to cast out
2469		the demon
1388		from
0327		her daughter

MARK CHAPTER 7

VERSE 27
And Jesus said to her, "Allow first the children to be satisfied, for it is not proper to take the bread of the children and to throw [it] to the dogs."

Code	Syriac	English
0116		And said
1261		to her
3257		Jesus
2440		Allow
2151		first
1585		to be satisfied
0323		the children
1262		not
0603		it is
0403		for
2583		proper
1532		to take
1293		the bread
0323		of the children
2372		and to throw [it]
1183		to the dogs

VERSE 28
And she answered and said to him, "Yes, my Lord. Yet even the dogs eat the crumbs of the children from under the tables."

Code	Syriac	English
0592		<she>
0518		And
1838		she answered
0116		and said
1261		to him
0065		Yes
1426		my Lord
0169		Yet even
1183		the dogs
1388		from
2660		under
2069		the tables
0075		eat
2052		the crumbs
0323		of the children

VERSE 29
Jesus said to her, "Go! Because of this saying, the demon has gone out from your daughter."

Code	Syriac	English
0116		said
1261		to her
3257		Jesus
0042		Go
1347		Because of
0598		this
1364		saying
1542		has gone out
1261		*
2469		the demon
1388		from
0327		your daughter

VERSE 30
And she went to her house and found her daughter lying on a pallet and her demon had left her.

Code	Syriac	English
0042		And she went
0243		to her house
2510		and found
0327		her daughter
1128		lying
2372		*
1897		on a pallet
1542		and had left
1388		her
2469		her demon

VERSE 31
Again Jesus went out from the border of Tyre and Sidon and came to the Sea of Galilee, on the border of the Decapolis.

Code	Syriac	English
2650		Again
1542		went out
3257		Jesus
1388		from
2659		the border
3450		of Tyre
3452		and Sidon
0208		and came
1057		to the Sea
3153		of Galilee

MARK — CHAPTER 7

#	Syriac	English
2659		on the border
3402		of the Decapolis

VERSE 32 — And they brought him a certain deaf man, a stammerer, and were asking him to place a hand on him.

#	Syriac	English
0208		And they brought
1261		him
0907		a deaf man
0721		certain
2006		a stammerer
0296		and asking
0603		were
1388		him
1625		to place
1804		on him
0057		a hand

VERSE 33 — And he led him away from the crowd privately and placed his fingers in his ears and he spit and touched his tongue.

#	Syriac	English
1461		And he led him away
1388		from
1201		the crowd
1041		privately
2372		and placed
2081		his fingers
0021		in his ears
2400		and he spit
2244		and touched
1312		his tongue

VERSE 34 — And he looked into heaven and sighed and said to him, "Be opened."

#	Syriac	English
0756		And he looked
2543		into heaven
0125		and sighed
0116		and said
1261		to him
2070		Be opened

VERSE 35 — And immediately his ears were opened and the restriction of his tongue was loosed and he spoke plainly.

#	Syriac	English
0217		And immediately
2573		*
2070		were opened
0021		his ears
2597		and was loosed
0164		the restriction
1312		of his tongue
1362		and he spoke
2063		plainly

VERSE 36 — And he admonished them not to tell anyone. And the more that he was admonishing them, the more they were proclaiming.

#	Syriac	English
0645		And he admonished
0592		them
0131		anyone
1262		not
0116		to tell
1188		And the more
0592		that <he>
0645		admonishing
0603		he was
1261		them
0592		<they>
1100		the more
1230		proclaiming
0603		they were

VERSE 37 — And they were exceedingly amazed and were saying, "He does everything well. He makes the deaf to hear, and those not speaking to speak."

#	Syriac	English
1101		And exceedingly
0549		amazed
0603		they were
0116		and were saying
1168		everything
1326		*
2583		well
1724		He does
0907		the deaf
1724		He makes
2547		to hear
1262		and those not

277

MARK   CHAPTER 7

| 1362 | ܡܡܠܠܝܢ | speaking |
| 1362 | ܢܡܠܠܘܢ | to speak |

CHAPTER 8

VERSE 1 — Now in those days when there was a large crowd and there was nothing to eat, he called his disciples and said to them,

0593		in those
0518		Now
1036		days
1128		when
1201		a crowd
1596		large
0069		there was
0603		*
1262		and nothing
0069		there was
0603		*
1326		<what>
0075		to eat
2239		he called
1304		his disciples
0116		and said
1261		to them

VERSE 2 — "I have compassion on this crowd because, behold, they have remained with me three days and they do not have anything to eat.

2342		have compassion
0124		I
1804		on
1201		crowd
0598		this
0580		because behold
2674		three
1036		days
2165		they have remained
1288		with me
1264		and they do not have
1261		*
1393		anything

| 0075 | | to eat |

VERSE 3 — And if I dismiss them to their homes while they are fasting, they will faint along the road, for some of them have come from far away."

0121		And if
0592		<it>
2597		dismiss
0124		I
1261		them
1128		while
2093		they are fasting
0243		to their homes
1770		they will faint
0038		along the road
0131		some
0403		for
1388		of them
1388		from
2354		far away
0208		have come

VERSE 4 — His disciples said to him, "[From] where can a man find here in the wilderness bread to satisfy all these [people]?"

0116		said
1261		to him
1304		His disciples
1110		[From] where
2510		can find
0131		a man
0600		here
0892		in the wilderness
1585		to satisfy
1293		bread
0598		these
1168		all [people]

VERSE 5 — And he asked them, "How many [loaves of] bread do you have?" They told him, "Seven."

| 2420 | | And he asked |
| 0592 | | them |

MARK — CHAPTER 8

#	Syriac	Gloss
0592	ܗܘ	<he>
1188	ܟܡܐ	How many
1293	ܠܚܡܝܢ	[loaves of] bread
0069	ܐܝܬ	do you have
1261	ܠܟܘܢ	*
0116	ܐܡܪܝܢ	They told
1261	ܠܗ	him
2437	ܫܒܥܐ	Seven

VERSE 6 — And he commanded the crowds to recline on the ground, and he took those seven [loaves of] bread and blessed and broke [them] and gave [them] to his disciples to set out, and they set [the food] before the crowds.

#	Syriac	Gloss
2007	ܘܦܩܕ	And he commanded
1201	ܠܟܢܫܐ	the crowds
1664	ܕܢܣܬܡܟܘܢ	to recline
1804	ܥܠ	on
0199	ܐܪܥܐ	the ground
1532	ܘܫܩܠ	and he took
0593	ܗܢܘܢ	those
2437	ܫܒܥܐ	seven
1293	ܠܚܡܝܢ	[loaves of] bread
0335	ܘܒܪܟ	and blessed
2234	ܘܩܨܐ	and broke [them]
1030	ܘܝܗܒ	and gave [them]
1304	ܠܬܠܡܝܕܘܗܝ	to his disciples
1625	ܕܢܣܝܡܘܢ	to set out
1625	ܘܣܡܘ	and they set [the food]
1201	ܠܟܢܫܐ	before the crowds

VERSE 7 — And there were a few fish and he also blessed them, and said to set them out.

#	Syriac	Gloss
0069	ܘܐܝܬ	And there were
0603	ܗܘܐ	*
1490	ܢܘܢܐ	fish
2203	ܩܠܝܠ	a few
0169	ܘܐܦ	and also
1804	ܥܠܝܗܘܢ	them
0335	ܒܪܟ	he blessed
0116	ܘܐܡܪ	and said
1625	ܕܢܣܝܡܘܢ	to set out

#	Syriac	Gloss
0592	ܐܢܘܢ	them

VERSE 8 — And they ate and were satisfied. And they took up the remains of the fragments, seven baskets.

#	Syriac	Gloss
0075	ܘܐܟܠܘ	And they ate
1585	ܘܣܒܥܘ	and were satisfied
2587	ܘܫܩܠܘ	And they took up
1106	ܬܘܬܪܐ	the remains
2235	ܕܩܨܝܐ	of the fragments
2437	ܫܒܥܐ	seven
0159	ܐܣܦܪܝܕܝܢ	baskets

VERSE 9 — And the men who ate were about four thousand.

#	Syriac	Gloss
0069	ܐܝܬܝܗܘܢ	were
0603	ܗܘܘ	*
0518	ܕܝܢ	And
0131	ܐܢܫܐ	the men
0075	ܕܐܟܠܘ	who ate
0060	ܐܝܟ	about
0179	ܐܪܒܥܐ	four
0099	ܐܠܦܝܢ	thousand

VERSE 10 — And he dismissed them, and immediately boarded a boat with his disciples, and came to the region of Dalmanutha.

#	Syriac	Gloss
2597	ܘܫܪܐ	And he dismissed
0592	ܐܢܘܢ	them
1658	ܘܣܠܩ	and boarded
0725	ܒܪܫܥܬܗ	immediately
1692	ܠܣܦܝܢܬܐ	a boat
1817	ܥܡ	with
1304	ܠܬܠܡܝܕܘܗܝ	his disciples
0208	ܘܐܬܐ	and came
0214	ܠܐܬܪܐ	to the region
3164	ܕܕܠܡܢܘܬܐ	of Dalmanutha

VERSE 11 — And the Pharisees came out and began to dispute with him. And they were asking him [for] a sign from heaven, tempting him.

#	Syriac	Gloss
1542	ܘܢܦܩܘ	And came out
3439	ܦܪܝܫܐ	the Pharisees
2597	ܘܫܪܝܘ	and began

MARK   CHAPTER 8

0296		to dispute
1817		with him
2420		And asking
0603		they were
1261		him
0206		[for] a sign
1388		from
2543		heaven
1128		tempting
1527		*
1261		him

VERSE 12   And he sighed in his spirit and said, "Why does this generation seek a sign? Truly I say to you, a sign will not be given to this generation."

0125		And he sighed
2323		in his spirit
0116		and said
1393		Why
0296		does seek
0206		a sign
2605		generation
0598		this
0110		Truly
0116		say
0124		I
1261		to you
1262		not
1030		will be given
1261		<to it>
0206		a sign
2605		to generation
0598		this

VERSE 13   And he left them and boarded a boat and they went to the other side.

2440		And he left
0592		them
1658		and boarded
1692		a boat
0042		and they went

0593		to <it>
1735		the other side

VERSE 14   And they forgot to take bread. And except [for] one loaf, there was nothing with them in the boat.

0993		And they forgot
1532		to take
1293		bread
0090		And except [for]
0721		one
0462		loaf
1264		there was nothing
0603		*
1817		with them
1692		in the boat

VERSE 15   And he commanded them and said to them, "Watch out! Beware of the leaven of the Pharisees and of the leaven of Herod."

2007		And he commanded
0592		them
0116		and said
1261		to them
0758		Watch out
0645		Beware
1388		of
0832		the leaven
3439		of the Pharisees
1388		and of
0832		the leaven
3179		of Herod

VERSE 16   And they were reasoning with each other and saying, "[It is] because we have no bread."

0914		And reasoning
0603		they were
0721		with each other
1817		*
0721		*
0116		and saying
1293		[It is] because bread

MARK — CHAPTER 8

Vertical Interlinear

#	Syriac	English
1264		we have no
1261		*

VERSE 17 — But Jesus knew [this] and said to them, "Why are you thinking [it is] because you have no bread? Do you still not know and do you not understand? How long will you have a hard heart?"

#	Syriac	English
3257		Jesus
0518		But
1023		knew [this]
0116		and said
1261		to them
1393		Why
2376		are thinking
0133		you
1293		[It is] because bread
1264		you have no
1261		*
1262		not
1747		still
0602		*
1023		Do know
0133		you
1262		and not
1647		do understand
0133		you
1745		How long
1268		a heart
2265		hard
0069		will you have
1261		*

VERSE 18 — And you have eyes and you do not see, and you have ears and you do not hear, and you do not remember.

#	Syriac	English
1794		And eyes
0069		you have
1261		*
1262		and not
0758		do see
0133		you
0021		and ears
0069		you have
1261		*
1262		and not
2547		do hear
0133		you
1262		and not
1756		do remember
0133		you

VERSE 19 — When I broke those five [loaves of] bread for the five thousand, how many baskets full of fragments did you take up?" They told him, "Twelve."

#	Syriac	English
1128		When
0598		those
0833		five
1293		[loaves of] bread
2234		I broke
0833		for the five
0099		thousand
1188		how many
2176		baskets
2235		of fragments
1128		full
1366		*
2587		did you take up
0116		They told
1261		him
2710		Twelve

VERSE 20 — He said to them, "And when seven [loaves] to the four thousand, how many baskets full of fragments did you take up?" They said, "Seven."

#	Syriac	English
0116		He said
1261		to them
1128		And when
2437		seven [loaves]
0179		to the four
0099		thousand
1188		how many
0159		baskets
2235		of fragments

MARK   CHAPTER 8

#		word		#		word
1128		full		1625		and laid
1366		*		0057		his hand [on him]
2587		did you take up		2420		and asked him
0116		They said		1393		what
2437		Seven		0758		he saw

VERSE 21   He said to them, "Why is it [that] still you do not understand?"

VERSE 24   And he looked and said, "I see men as trees that are walking."

#		word		#		word
0116		He said		0756		And he looked
1261		to them		0116		and said
1109		Why is it [that]		0758		see
1262		not		0124		I
1747		still		0323		men
0602		*		0131		*
1647		do understand		0060		as
0133		you		0063		trees
				0608		that are walking

VERSE 22   And he came to Bethsaida. And they brought him a blind man and were begging him to touch him.

VERSE 25   Again he laid his hand on his eyes and he was restored and was seeing everything clearly.

#		word		#		word
0208		And he came		2650		Again
3118		to Bethsaida		1625		he laid
0208		And they brought		0057		his hand
1261		him		1804		on
1662		a blind man		1794		his eyes
0296		and begging		2699		and he was restored
0603		were		0758		and seeing
1388		him		0603		was
2244		to touch		1168		everything
1261		him		1326		*
				1476		clearly

VERSE 23   And he took the hand of the blind man and led him outside of the village. And he spat on his eyes and laid his hand [on him] and asked him what he saw.

VERSE 26   And he sent him to his house and said, "Neither enter the village nor tell anyone in the village."

#		word		#		word
0047		And he took		2458		And he sent him
0057		the hand		0243		to his house
1662		of the blind man		0116		and said
1542		and led him		0169		Neither
0322		outside		1262		*
1388		of		2251		the village
2251		the village		1796		enter
2400		And he spat		1262		nor
1794		on his eyes				

Vertical Interlinear

MARK   CHAPTER 8

0116		tell
0131		anyone
2251		in the village

VERSE 27 — And Jesus and his disciples went out to the villages of Caesarea Philippi. And he was asking his disciples along the way and said to them, "What do men say about me, who I am?"

1542		And went out
3257		Jesus
1304		and his disciples
2251		to the villages
3485		of Caesarea Philippi
2420		And asking
0603		he was
1304		his disciples
0038		along the way
0116		and said
1261		to them
1390		What
0116		do say
1804		about me
0131		men
0069		who I am

VERSE 28 — And they said, "John the baptizer, and others Elijah, and others, one of the prophets.

0592		<they>
0518		And
0116		they said
3233		John
1820		the baptizer
0053		and other
3047		Elijah
0053		and others
0721		one
1388		of
1457		the prophets

VERSE 29 — Jesus said to them, "But what do you say about me, who I am?" Simon answered and said to him, "You are the Messiah, the Son of the living God."

0116		said
1261		to them
3257		Jesus
0133		<you>
0518		But
1390		what
0116		do say
0133		you
1804		about me
0069		who I am
1838		answered
3521		Simon
0116		and said
1261		to him
0133		You
0592		are
1446		the Messiah
0323		the Son
0093		of God
0781		the living

VERSE 30 — And he charged them not to tell anyone about him.

1113		And he charged
0217		them
0131		anyone
1262		not
0116		to tell
1804		about him

VERSE 31 — And he began to teach them that the Son of Man would suffer much, and be rejected by the elders and by the chief priests and by the scribes, and be killed and after three days, rise up.

2597		And he began
0603		*
1053		to teach
0592		them
1914		that would

MARK   CHAPTER 8

0592	ܗܘ	<he>
0323	ܒܪܗ	the Son
0131	ܕܐܢܫܐ	of Man
0911	ܢܚܫ	suffer
1596	ܣܓܝ	much
1655	ܘܢܣܬܠܐ	and be rejected
1388	ܡܢ	by
2263	ܩܫܝܫܐ	the elders
1388	ܘܡܢ	and by
2271	ܪܒܝ	the chief priests
1135	ܟܗܢܐ	*
1388	ܘܡܢ	and by
1699	ܣܦܪܐ	the scribes
2179	ܘܢܬܩܛܠ	and be killed
2674	ܘܠܬܠܬܐ	and after three
1036	ܝܘܡܝܢ	days
2168	ܢܩܘܡ	rise up

VERSE 32   And he was speaking publicly [about this] matter. And Peter took him and began to rebuke him.

1794	ܘܥܝܢ	And publicly
0411	ܒܓܠܐ	*
1364	ܡܠܬܐ	[about this] matter
1362	ܡܡܠܠ	speaking
0603	ܗܘܐ	he was
0477	ܘܕܒܪܗ	And took him
3258	ܟܐܦܐ	Peter
2597	ܘܫܪܝ	and began
1113	ܠܡܟܐܐ	to rebuke
0217	ܒܗ	him

VERSE 33   But he turned and looked at his disciples and rebuked Simon and said, "Go behind me, Satan, because you do not think about [the things] of God, but [the things] of men!"

0592	ܗܘ	<he>
0518	ܕܝܢ	But
1984	ܐܬܦܢܝ	he turned
0756	ܘܚܪ	and looked
1304	ܒܬܠܡܝܕܘܗܝ	at his disciples
1113	ܘܟܐܐ	and rebuked
3521	ܒܫܡܥܘܢ	Simon
0116	ܘܐܡܪ	and said
0042	ܙܠ	Go
1261	ܠܟ	*
0295	ܠܒܣܬܪܝ	behind me
1642	ܣܛܢܐ	Satan
1262	ܠܐ	because not
2376	ܪܢܐ	do think about
0133	ܐܢܬ	you
0093	ܕܐܠܗܐ	[the things] of God
0090	ܐܠܐ	but [the things]
0323	ܕܒܢܝ	of men
0131	ܐܢܫܐ	*

VERSE 34   And Jesus called the crowds with his disciples and said to them, "He who wants to follow me should deny himself and take up his cross and follow me.

2239	ܘܩܪܐ	And called
3257	ܝܫܘܥ	Jesus
1201	ܠܟܢܫܐ	the crowds
1817	ܥܡ	with
1304	ܬܠܡܝܕܘܗܝ	his disciples
0116	ܘܐܡܪ	and said
1261	ܠܗܘܢ	to them
1389	ܡܢ	He who
2077	ܕܨܒܐ	wants
0208	ܕܢܐܬܐ	to follow me
0215	ܒܬܪܝ	*
1215	ܢܟܦܘܪ	should deny
1547	ܒܢܦܫܗ	himself
2587	ܘܢܫܩܘܠ	and take up
0689	ܨܠܝܒܗ	his cross
0208	ܘܢܐܬܐ	and follow me
0215	ܒܬܪܝ	*

VERSE 35   For everyone who wants to save his soul will lose it. And anyone who will lose his soul because of me and because of my gospel will save it.

1168	ܟܠ	everyone
1389	ܡܢ	*
2077	ܕܨܒܐ	who wants

MARK — CHAPTER 8

#	Syriac	Gloss
0403		For
0780		to save
1547		his soul
0005		will lose it
1168		And anyone
0005		who will lose
1547		his soul
1347		because of me
1347		and because of
1593		my gospel
0780		will save it

VERSE 36 — For what is a man profited if he should gain the entire world and should lose his soul?

#	Syriac	Gloss
1393		what
0403		For
1751		is profited
0325		a man
0121		if
1813		the world
1168		entire
1098		he should gain
1547		and his soul
0865		should lose

VERSE 37 — Or what will a man give in exchange of his soul?

#	Syriac	Gloss
0024		Or
1393		what
1030		will give
0325		a man
0815		in exchange
1547		of his soul

VERSE 38 — For anyone who is ashamed of me and my words in this sinful and adulterous generation, the Son of Man will also be ashamed of him when he comes in the glory of his Father with his holy angels."

#	Syriac	Gloss
1168		anyone
0403		For
0235		who is ashamed
0217		of me
1364		and my words
2605		in generation
0598		this
0772		sinful
0388		and adulterous
0169		<and> also
0323		the Son
0131		of Man
0235		will be ashamed
0217		of him
1313		when
0208		he comes
2431		in the glory
0002		of his Father
1817		with
1375		his angels
2162		holy

CHAPTER 9

VERSE 1 — And he was saying to them, "Truly I say to you, there are some that are standing here who will not taste death until they see the kingdom of God that has come in power."

#	Syriac	Gloss
0116		And saying
0603		he was
1261		to them
0110		Truly
0116		say
0124		I
1261		to you
0069		there are
0131		some
2168		that are standing
2694		here
1262		who not
0998		will taste
1335		death
1747		until
0758		they see
1385		the kingdom

Vertical Interlinear

MARK CHAPTER 9

0093	ܐܠܗܐ	of God
0208	ܕܐܬܬ	that has come
0786	ܒܚܝܠܐ	in power

VERSE 2 — And after six days, Jesus led Peter and James and John and took them up into a high mountain privately and he was changed before their eyes.

0215	ܘܒܬܪ	And after
2615	ܫܬܐ	six
1036	ܝܘܡܝܢ	days
0477	ܕܒܪ	led
3257	ܝܫܘܥ	Jesus
3258	ܠܟܐܦܐ	Peter
3255	ܘܠܝܥܩܘܒ	and James
3233	ܘܠܝܘܚܢܢ	and John
1658	ܘܐܣܩ	and took up
0592	ܐܢܘܢ	them
0958	ܠܛܘܪܐ	into a mountain
2336	ܪܡܐ	high
1041	ܒܠܚܘܕܝܗܘܢ	privately
0811	ܘܐܫܬܚܠܦ	and he was changed
1794	ܠܥܢܝܗܘܢ	before their eyes

VERSE 3 — And his clothing was bright and became very white like snow, such that men are not able to make white on earth.

0645	ܘܡܒܪܩ	And bright
0603	ܗܘܐ	was
1273	ܠܒܘܫܗ	his clothing
0754	ܘܡܚܘܪ	and became white
0938	ܛܒ	very
0060	ܐܝܟ	like
2673	ܬܠܓܐ	snow
0061	ܐܝܟܢܐ	such
0323	ܕܒܢܝ	that men
0131	ܐܢܫܐ	*
0754	ܠܡܚܘܪܘ	to make white
0199	ܒܐܪܥܐ	on earth
1262	ܠܐ	not
2510	ܡܫܟܚܝܢ	are able

VERSE 4 — And Elijah and Moses were seen by them, speaking with Jesus.

0758	ܘܐܬܚܙܝܘ	And were seen
1261	ܠܗܘܢ	by them
3047	ܐܠܝܐ	Elijah
3305	ܘܡܘܫܐ	and Moses
1128	ܟܕ	speaking
1362	ܡܡܠܠܝܢ	*
1817	ܥܡ	with
3257	ܝܫܘܥ	Jesus

VERSE 5 — And Peter said to him, "My Master, it is good for us to be here. And let us make three booths, one for you and one for Moses and one for Elijah."

0116	ܘܐܡܪ	And said
1261	ܠܗ	to him
3258	ܟܐܦܐ	Peter
2275	ܪܒܝ	My Master
2583	ܫܦܝܪ	good
0592	ܗܘ	it is
1261	ܠ	for us
0600	ܕܗܪܟܐ	here
0603	ܢܗܘܐ	to be
1724	ܘܢܥܒܕ	And let us make
2674	ܬܠܬ	three
0974	ܡܛܠܠܝܢ	booths
1261	ܠܟ	for you
0721	ܚܕ	one
3305	ܘܠܡܘܫܐ	and for Moses
0721	ܚܕ	one
3047	ܘܠܐܠܝܐ	and for Elijah
0721	ܚܕ	one

VERSE 6 — And he did not know what he was saying, for they were in fear.

1262	ܠܐ	not
0518	ܕܝܢ	And
1023	ܝܕܥ	he did know
0603	ܗܘܐ	*
1393	ܡܢܐ	what
0116	ܐܡܪ	he was saying
0069	ܐܝܬܝܗܘܢ	they were

MARK — CHAPTER 9

Vertical Interlinear

#	Syriac	Gloss
0603	ܗܘܘ	*
0403	ܓܝܪ	for
0511	ܒܕܚܠܬܐ	in fear

VERSE 7 — And a cloud came and overshadowed them, and a voice [came] from the cloud that said, "This is my beloved Son; hear him."

#	Syriac	Gloss
0603	ܘܗܘܬ	And came
1844	ܥܢܢܐ	a cloud
0970	ܘܡܛܠܐ	and overshadowed
0603	ܗܘܬ	*
1804	ܠܗܘܢ	them
2204	ܘܩܠܐ	and a voice [came]
1388	ܡܢ	from
1844	ܥܢܢܐ	the cloud
0116	ܕܐܡܪ	that said
0599	ܗܢܘ	This is
0323	ܒܪܝ	my Son
0698	ܚܒܝܒܐ	beloved
1261	ܠܗ	him
2547	ܫܡܥܘ	hear

VERSE 8 — And suddenly, when the disciples looked up, they did not see anyone except Jesus only with them.

#	Syriac	Gloss
1388	ܘܡܢ	And suddenly
2519	ܫܠܝܐ	*
1128	ܟܕ	when
0756	ܚܪܘ	looked up
1304	ܬܠܡܝܕܐ	the disciples
0131	ܠܐܢܫ	anyone
1262	ܠܐ	not
0758	ܚܙܘ	they did see
0090	ܐܠܐ	except
3257	ܠܝܫܘܥ	Jesus
1041	ܒܠܚܘܕܘܗܝ	only
1817	ܥܡܗܘܢ	with them

VERSE 9 — And while they were descending from the mountain, he was commanding them that they should not tell anyone what they saw until after the Son of Man had risen from the dead.

#	Syriac	Gloss
1128	ܘܟܕ	And while
1499	ܢܚܬܝܢ	they were descending
1388	ܡܢ	from
0958	ܛܘܪܐ	the mountain
2007	ܡܦܩܕ	commanding
0603	ܗܘܐ	he was
1261	ܠܗܘܢ	them
0131	ܕܠܐܢܫ	that anyone
1262	ܠܐ	not
0116	ܢܐܡܪܘܢ	they should tell
1326	ܡܕܡ	what
0758	ܕܚܙܘ	they saw
0090	ܥܕܡܐ	until
0121	*	*
1313	*	*
2168	ܕܢܩܘܡ	after had risen
0323	ܒܪܗ	the Son
0131	ܕܐܢܫܐ	of Man
1388	ܡܢ	from
1338	ܡܝܬܐ	the dead

VERSE 10 — And they kept the saying to themselves and were inquiring, "What is this saying, 'When he is raised from the dead?'"

#	Syriac	Gloss
0047	ܘܐܚܕܘܗ	And they kept
1364	ܠܡܠܬܐ	the saying
1547	ܒܢܦܫܗܘܢ	to themselves
0296	ܘܒܥܝܢ	and inquiring
0603	ܗܘܘ	were
1393	ܕܡܢܐ	What
0592	ܗܝ	is
0598	ܗܕܐ	this
1364	ܡܠܬܐ	saying
1313	ܕܡܐ	When
2168	ܕܢܩܘܡ	he is raised
1388	ܡܢ	from
0243	ܒܝܬ	the dead
1338	ܡܝܬܐ	*

VERSE 11 — And they were asking him and saying, "Why then do the scribes say that Elijah must come first?"

#	Syriac	Gloss
2420	ܘܡܫܐܠܝܢ	And asking

MARK   CHAPTER 9

ID	Syriac	English
0603	ܗܘܘ	they were
1261	ܠܗ	him
0116	ܘܐܡܪܝܢ	and saying
1393	ܠܡܢܐ	Why
0596	ܗܟܝܠ	then
0116	ܐܡܪܝܢ	do say
1699	ܣܦܪܐ	the scribes
3047	ܕܐܠܝܐ	that Elijah
0626	ܘܠܐ	must
0208	ܕܢܐܬܐ	come
2151	ܠܘܩܕܡ	first

VERSE 12   He said to them, "Elijah will come first in order to prepare everything and as it is written about the Son of Man: HE WILL SUFFER MUCH AND BE REJECTED.

ID	Syriac	English
0116	ܐܡܪ	He said
1261	ܠܗܘܢ	to them
3047	ܐܠܝܐ	Elijah
0208	ܐܬܐ	will come
2151	ܠܘܩܕܡ	first
1173	ܕܟܠܡܕܡ	in order everything
2699	ܢܬܩܢ	to prepare
0061	ܘܐܝܟܢܐ	and as
1247	ܟܬܝܒ	it is written
1804	ܥܠ	about
0323	ܒܪܗ	the Son
0131	ܕܐܢܫܐ	of Man
1596	ܕܣܓܝ	MUCH
0911	ܢܚܫ	HE WILL SUFFER
1655	ܘܢܣܬܠܐ	AND BE REJECTED

VERSE 13   But I say to you, indeed Elijah has come and they did with him whatever they desired, as it was written about him."

ID	Syriac	English
0090	ܐܠܐ	But
0116	ܐܡܪ	say
0124	ܐܢܐ	I
1261	ܠܟܘܢ	to you
0169	ܕܐܦ	indeed
3047	ܐܠܝܐ	Elijah
0208	ܐܬܐ	has come
1724	ܘܥܒܕܘ	and they did
0217	ܒܗ	with him
1168	ܟܠ	whatever
1313	ܡܐ	*
2077	ܕܨܒܘ	they desired
0061	ܐܝܟܢܐ	as
1247	ܕܟܬܝܒ	it was written
1804	ܥܠܘܗܝ	about him

VERSE 14   And when he came to the disciples, he saw a large crowd with them and the scribes disputing with them.

ID	Syriac	English
1128	ܘܟܕ	And when
0208	ܐܬܐ	he came
1288	ܠܘܬ	to
1304	ܬܠܡܝܕܐ	the disciples
0758	ܚܙܐ	he saw
1288	ܠܘܬܗܘܢ	with them
1201	ܟܢܫܐ	a crowd
1596	ܣܓܝܐܐ	large
1699	ܘܣܦܪܐ	and the scribes
1128	ܟܕ	disputing
0576	ܕܪܫܝܢ	*
1817	ܥܡܗܘܢ	with them

VERSE 15   And immediately all the crowds saw him and were amazed, and they ran [and] greeted him.

ID	Syriac	English
0323	ܘܒܪ	And immediately
2573	ܫܥܬܗ	*
1168	ܟܠܗ	all
1201	ܟܢܫܐ	the crowds
0758	ܚܙܐܘܗܝ	saw him
2653	ܘܬܘܗܘ	and were amazed
2312	ܘܪܗܛܘ	and they ran
2420	ܫܐܠܘ	[and] greeted him
2535	ܒܫܠܡܗ	*

VERSE 16   And he asked the scribes, "What are you disputing with them?"

ID	Syriac	English
2420	ܘܫܐܠ	And he asked
0603	ܗܘܐ	*
1699	ܠܣܦܪܐ	the scribes
1393	ܡܢܐ	What
0576	ܕܪܫܝܢ	are disputing

Vertical Interlinear

MARK   CHAPTER 9

0133	ܐܢܬܘܢ	you
1817	ܥܡܗܘܢ	with them

VERSE 17 — And one of the crowd answered and said, "Teacher, I brought my son to you, because he has a spirit that does not speak.

1838	ܘܥܢܐ	And answered
0721	ܚܕ	one
1388	ܡܢ	of
1201	ܟܢܫܐ	the crowd
0116	ܘܐܡܪ	and said
1055	ܡܠܦܢܐ	Teacher
0208	ܐܝܬܝܬ	I brought
0323	ܒܪܝ	my son
1288	ܠܘܬܟ	to you
0069	ܐܝܬ	because he has
1261	ܠܗ	*
2323	ܪܘܚܐ	a spirit
1262	ܕܠܐ	that not
1362	ܡܡܠܠܐ	does speak

VERSE 18 — And sometimes it grabs him, it knocks him down and he foams and gnashes his teeth and he languishes. And I asked your disciples to cast it out, and they were not able."

1108	ܘܐܝܟܐ	And sometimes
0572	ܕܡܕܪܟܐ	it grabs
1261	ܠܗ	him
0701	ܣܚܦܐ	it knocks down
1261	ܠܗ	him
2340	ܘܡܪܥܬ	and he foams
0904	ܘܡܚܪܩ	and gnashes
2558	ܫܢܘܗܝ	his teeth
1018	ܘܝܒܫ	and he languishes
0116	ܘܐܡܪܬ	And I asked
1304	ܠܬܠܡܝܕܝܟ	your disciples
1542	ܕܢܦܩܘܢܝܗܝ	to cast it out
1262	ܘܠܐ	and not
2510	ܐܫܟܚܘ	they were able

VERSE 19 — Jesus answered and said to him, "Oh faithless generation! How long must I be with you and how long must I endure you? Bring him to me."

1838	ܥܢܐ	answered
3257	ܝܫܘܥ	Jesus
0116	ܘܐܡܪ	and said
1261	ܠܗ	to him
0033	ܐܘ	Oh
2605	ܫܪܒܬܐ	generation
1262	ܕܠܐ	faithless
0114	ܡܗܝܡܢܐ	*
1747	ܥܕܡܐ	How long
0120	ܠܐܡܬܝ	*
0603	ܐܗܘܐ	must I be
1288	ܠܘܬܟܘܢ	with you
1747	ܘܥܕܡܐ	and how long
0120	ܠܐܡܬܝ	*
1588	ܐܣܝܒܪܟܘܢ	must I endure you
0208	ܐܝܬܐܘܗܝ	Bring him
1288	ܠܘܬܝ	to me

VERSE 20 — And they brought him to him. And when the spirit saw him, immediately it knocked him down and he fell on the ground and was violently shaken, and he foamed.

0208	ܘܐܝܬܝܘܗܝ	And they brought him
1288	ܠܘܬܗ	to him
1128	ܘܟܕ	And when
0758	ܚܙܬܗ	saw him
2323	ܪܘܚܐ	the spirit
0323	ܒܪ	immediately
2573	ܫܥܬܗ	*
0701	ܣܚܦܬܗ	it knocked him down
1538	ܘܢܦܠ	and he fell
1804	ܥܠ	on
0199	ܐܪܥܐ	the ground
0310	ܘܡܬܒܥܨ	and violently shaken
0603	ܗܘܐ	was
2340	ܘܡܪܥܬ	and he foamed

Vertical Interlinear

MARK   CHAPTER 9

VERSE 21   And Jesus asked his father, "How long [has it been] since [he was] this way?" He said to him, "Since his youth.

2420	ܘܫܐܠ	And asked
3257	ܝܫܘܥ	Jesus
0002	ܠܐܒܘܗܝ	his father
1188	ܕܟܡܐ	How long [has it been]
1261	ܠܗ	*
0633	ܙܒܢܐ	*
0580	ܗܐ	since
1388	ܡܢ	*
0597	ܕܗܟܢܐ	[he was] this way
0592	ܗܘ	<he>
0116	ܐܡܪ	He said
1261	ܠܗ	to him
0580	ܗܐ	Since
1388	ܡܢ	*
0977	ܛܠܝܘܬܗ	his youth

VERSE 22   And many times it has thrown him into the fire and into the water to destroy him, but whatever you are able [to do], help me and have compassion on us."

0633	ܘܙܒܢܝܢ	And times
1596	ܣܓܝܐܢ	many
2372	ܐܪܡܝܬܗ	it has thrown him
1494	ܒܢܘܪܐ	into the fire
1351	ܘܒܡܝܐ	and into the water
0005	ܕܬܘܒܕܝܘܗܝ	to destroy him
0090	ܐܠܐ	but
1326	ܡܕܡ	whatever
2510	ܕܡܫܟܚ	are able [to do]
0133	ܐܢܬ	you
1751	ܥܕܪܝܢܝ	help me
2342	ܘܐܬܪܚܡ	and have compassion
1804	ܥܠܝܢ	on us

VERSE 23   Jesus said to him, "If you are able to believe, everything will be possible to him who believes."

0116	ܐܡܪ	said
1261	ܠܗ	to him
3257	ܝܫܘܥ	Jesus
0121	ܐܢ	If
2510	ܡܫܟܚ	are able
0133	ܐܢܬ	you
0109	ܕܬܗܝܡܢ	to believe
1168	ܟܠ	everything
1326	ܡܕܡ	*
2510	ܡܫܟܚ	possible
0603	ܕܢܗܘܐ	will be
1389	ܠܗ	to him
0109	ܕܡܗܝܡܢ	who believes

VERSE 24   And immediately the father of the boy cried out, mourning, and said, "I believe, my Lord! Help the lack of my faith."

0323	ܘܒܪ	And immediately
2573	ܫܥܬܗ	*
2227	ܩܥܐ	cried out
0002	ܐܒܘܗܝ	the father
0976	ܕܛܠܝܐ	of the boy
1128	ܟܕ	mourning
0267	ܒܟܐ	*
0116	ܘܐܡܪ	and said
0109	ܡܗܝܡܢ	believe
0124	ܐܢܐ	I
1426	ܡܪܝ	my Lord
1751	ܥܕܪ	Help
0868	ܠܚܣܝܪܘܬ	the lack of
0113	ܗܝܡܢܘܬܝ	my faith

VERSE 25   And when Jesus saw that the people ran and gathered about him, he rebuked that unclean spirit and said to it, "Dumb spirit that does not speak, I command you, come out of him and do not enter him again."

1128	ܟܕ	when
0758	ܚܙܐ	saw
0518	ܕܝܢ	And
3257	ܝܫܘܥ	Jesus
2312	ܕܪܗܛ	that ran
1818	ܥܡܐ	the people
1198	ܘܡܬܟܢܫ	and gathered
1288	ܠܘܬܗ	about him

290

MARK   CHAPTER 9

1113		he rebuked
0593		that
2323		spirit
0991		unclean
0116		and said
1261		to it
2323		spirit
0907		Dumb
1262		that not
1362		does speak
0124		<I>
2007		command
0124		I
1261		you
1542		come out
1388		of him
2650		and again
1262		not
1796		do enter
1261		him

VERSE 26   And that demon cried out and he bruised him much and came out. And he was like a dead man, so that many said, "He is dead."

2227		And cried out
2469		demon
0593		that
1596		much
2494		and he bruised him
1542		and came out
0603		And he was
0060		like
1338		a dead man
0060		so that
1596		many
0116		said
1334		He is dead
1261		*

VERSE 27   But Jesus took him by his hand and raised him up.

0592		<he>
0518		But
3257		Jesus
0047		took him
0057		by his hand
2168		and raised him up

VERSE 28   Now when Jesus entered the house, his disciples asked him privately, "Why were we not able to cast it out?"

1128		when
1796		entered
0518		Now
0243		the house
3257		Jesus
2420		asked him
1304		his disciples
1041		privately
1394		Why
0124		we
1262		not
2510		were able
1542		to cast it out

VERSE 29   He said to them, "This kind cannot be cast out by anything except by fasting and by prayer."

0116		He said
1261		to them
0598		This
0444		kind
1326		by anything
1262		cannot
2510		*
1542		be cast out
0090		except
2094		by fasting
2107		and by prayer

MARK   CHAPTER 9

VERSE 30
And when he went away from there, they were passing through Galilee. And he did not want anyone to know about him,

1128	And when
1542	he went away
1388	from
2682	there
1733	passing
0603	they were
3153	through Galilee
1262	And not
2077	he did want
0603	*
0131	anyone
1023	to know
0217	about him

VERSE 31
For he was teaching his disciples and said to them, "The Son of Man will be delivered into the hands of man, and they will kill him, and after he has been killed, on the third day he will rise up."

1053	teaching
0603	he was
0403	For
1304	his disciples
0116	and said
1261	to them
0323	The Son
0131	of Man
2530	will be delivered
0057	into the hands of
0131	man
2179	and they will kill him
1313	and after
2179	he has been killed
1036	on the day
2674	third
2168	he will rise up

VERSE 32
And they did not understand the meaning, yet were afraid to ask him.

0592	<they>
0518	And
1262	not
1023	they did not understand
0603	*
1261	<it>
1364	the meaning
0509	yet afraid
0603	were
2420	to ask him

VERSE 33
And they came to Capernaum and when they had entered the house, he asked them, "What were you discussing among yourselves on the way?"

0208	And they came
3268	to Capernaum
1128	and when
1796	they had entered
0243	the house
2420	he asked
0603	*
1261	them
1393	What
0914	discussing
0603	were you
0038	on the way
0266	among yourselves

VERSE 34
But they were silent, for they were arguing on the way with each other, who was the greater among them.

0592	<they>
0518	But
2623	silent
0603	they were
0889	arguing
0603	they were
0403	for
0038	on the way
0721	with each other
1817	*
0721	*
1390	who was

MARK CHAPTER 9

Vertical Interlinear

2271		the greater
0217		among them
VERSE 35		And Jesus sat down and called the twelve and said to them, "He who wants to be first should be the last of all men and a servant of all men."
1093		And sat down
3257		Jesus
2239		and called
2710		the twelve
0116		and said
1261		to them
1389		He who
2077		wants
0603		to be
2157		first
0603		should be
0051		the last
1168		of all
0131		men
2555		and a servant
1168		of all
0131		men
VERSE 36		And he took a certain child and set him in the middle [of them] and took him into his arms and said to them,
1532		And he took
0976		a child
0721		certain
2168		and set him
1416		in the middle [of them]
2587		and took him
1804		into
0575		his arms
0116		and said
1261		to them
VERSE 37		Whoever receives like this child in my name receives me. And he who receives me does not receive me, but him who sent me.
1168		Whoever
1389		*

2134		receives
0060		like
0598		this
0976		child
2539		in my name
1261		me
0592		<he>
2134		receives
1389		And he
1261		who me
2134		receives
1262		not
0603		does
1261		me
2134		receive
0090		but
1389		him
2458		who sent me
VERSE 38		John said to him, "My Master, we saw a man who was casting out demons in your name and we stopped him, because he did not follow us."
0116		said
1261		to him
3233		John
2275		My Master
0758		we saw
0131		a man
1542		who was casting out
2469		demons
2539		in your name
1180		and we stopped him
1804		because
1262		not
1565		he did follow
1261		us
VERSE 39		Jesus said to them, "Do not stop him, for there is no one who does miracles in my name and is readily able [to] speak wickedly about me.
0116		said

293

MARK CHAPTER 9

Vertical Interlinear

#	Aramaic	English
1261		to them
3257		Jesus
1262		not
1180		Do stop him
1264		there is no
0403		for
0131		one
1724		who does
0786		miracles
2539		in my name
2510		and is able
1738		readily
0116		[to] speak
1804		about me
0220		wickedly

VERSE 40 — Therefore, he who is not against you is for you.

#	Aramaic	English
1389		he who
1262		not
0603		is
0596		Therefore
2135		against you
0812		for you
0592		is

VERSE 41 — But anyone who gives you only a cup of water to drink because you are in the name of the Messiah, truly I say to you, 'he will not lose his reward.'

#	Aramaic	English
1168		anyone
0518		But
2585		who gives you to drink
1205		a cup
1351		of water
1041		only
2539		in the name
1446		because of the Messiah
0133		you are
0110		truly
0116		say
0124		I
1261		to you
1262		not
0005		He will lose
0018		his reward

VERSE 42 — And whoever causes one of these little ones who believe in me to stumble, it would be better for him if the millstone of a donkey were placed on his neck and he were thrown into the sea.

#	Aramaic	English
1168		And whoever
1389		*
1242		causes to stumble
0721		one
1388		of
0598		these
0686		little ones
0109		who believe
0217		in me
2010		it would be better
0603		*
1261		for him
0097		if
2372		were placed
0603		*
2341		the millstone
0830		of a donkey
2097		on his neck
2455		and he were thrown
1057		into the sea

VERSE 43 — Now if your hand offends you, cut it off. It is better for you to enter life maimed, than although you have two hands, to go to Gehenna,

#	Aramaic	English
0121		if
0518		Now
1242		offends
1261		you
0057		your hand
1992		cut it off
2010		It is better
0592		*

MARK   CHAPTER 9

1261		for you
2058		maimed
1796		to enter
0782		life
0024		than
1128		although
0069		you have
1261		*
2709		two
0057		hands
0042		to go
3148		to Gehenna

VERSE 44   where their worm does not die and their fire does not go out.

1108		where
2655		their worm
1262		not
1334		does die
1494		and their fire
1262		not
0558		does go out

VERSE 45   And if your foot offends you, cut if off. It is better for you to enter life lame, than although you have two feet, to fall in Gehenna,

0121		And if
2293		your foot
1242		offends
1261		you
1992		cut it off
2010		It is better
0592		*
1261		for you
1796		to enter
0782		life
0718		lame
0024		than
1128		although
0069		you have
1261		*
2709		two
2293		feet
1538		to fall
3148		in Gehenna

VERSE 46   where their worm does not die and their fire does not go out.

1108		where
2655		their worm
1262		not
1334		does die
1494		and their fire
1262		not
0558		does go out

VERSE 47   And if your eye offends you, pick it out. It is better for you to enter into the kingdom of God with one of your eye[s], than although you have two eyes, to fall in the Gehenna of fire,

0121		And if
1794		your eye
1242		offends
1261		you
0877		pick it out
2010		It is better
0592		*
1261		for you
0721		with one of
1794		your eye[s]
1796		to enter
1385		into the kingdom
0093		of God
0024		than
1128		although
0069		you have
1261		*
2709		two
1794		eyes
1538		to fall
3148		in the Gehenna
1494		of fire

MARK CHAPTER 9

VERSE 48 — where their worm does not die and their fire does not go out.

#	Aramaic	English
1108		where
2655		their worm
1262		not
1334		does die
1494		and their fire
1262		not
0558		does go out

VERSE 49 — For everything will be salted with fire and every sacrifice will be salted with salt.

#	Aramaic	English
1168		everything
0403		For
1494		with fire
1377		will be salted
1168		and every
0474		sacrifice
1378		with salt
1377		will be salted

VERSE 50 — Salt is good, but if the salt should lose its flavor, with what will it be salted? Let salt be in you and be in harmony with each other."

#	Aramaic	English
2583		good
0592		is
1378		Salt
0121		if
0518		but
1378		the salt
1962		should lose its flavor
1393		with what
1377		will it be salted
0603		Let be
0217		in you
1378		salt
2505		and in harmony
0603		be
0721		with each other
1817		*
0721		*

CHAPTER 10

VERSE 1 — And he rose up from there and came to the border of Judea to the crossing of the Jordan and large crowds went there with him. And he was teaching them again, as he was accustomed.

#	Aramaic	English
2168		And he rose up
1388		from
2682		there
0208		and came
2659		to the border
3224		of Judea
1735		to the crossing
3248		of the Jordan
0042		and went
2682		there
1288		with him
1201		crowds
1596		large
1053		And teaching
0603		he was
1261		them
2650		again
0060		as
1761		accustomed
0603		he was

VERSE 2 — And the Pharisees approached, tempting him, and were asking if it was lawful for a man to divorce his wife.

#	Aramaic	English
2244		And approached
3439		the Pharisees
1527		tempting
1261		him
2420		and were asking
0121		if
2528		it was lawful
0361		for a man
2440		to divorce
0135		his wife

MARK CHAPTER 10

Vertical Interlinear

VERSE	3		He said to them, "What did Moses command you?"
0116			He said
1261			to them
1393			What
2007			did command you
3305			Moses
VERSE	4		And they said, "Moses allowed us to write a decree of divorce and to send [her] away."
0592			<they>
0518			And
0116			they said
3305			Moses
1989			allowed
1261			us
1247			to write
1248			a decree
2441			of divorce
2597			and to send [her] away
VERSE	5		Jesus answered and said to them, "In contrast to the hardness of your heart, he wrote this commandment for you,
1838			answered
3257			Jesus
0116			and said
1261			to them
2135			In contrast to
2267			the hardness
1268			of your heart
1247			he wrote
1261			for you
2009			commandment
0598			this
VERSE	6		but from the beginning GOD MADE THEM MALE AND FEMALE.
1388			from
2363			the beginning
0518			but
0529			MALE
1561			AND FEMALE
1724			MADE
0592			THEM
0093			GOD
VERSE	7		Because of this, A MAN WILL LEAVE HIS FATHER AND HIS MOTHER AND JOIN TO HIS WIFE
1347			Because of
0598			this
2440			WILL LEAVE
0361			A MAN
0002			HIS FATHER
0106			AND HIS MOTHER
1565			AND JOIN
0135			TO HIS WIFE
VERSE	8		AND THE TWO OF THEM WILL BECOME ONE FLESH. So then, they are not two, but one flesh.
0603			AND WILL BECOME
2709			THE TWO OF THEM
0721			ONE
0294			FLESH
1357			So then
1262			not
0603			they are
2709			two
0090			but
0721			one
0294			flesh
VERSE	9		Therefore, that which God has joined together, man should not separate."
1326			that which
0093			God
0596			Therefore
0647			has joined together
0325			man
1262			not
2046			should separate
VERSE	10		And his disciples asked him again in the house about this [matter].
2420			And asked him
2650			again

297

MARK　　　　　CHAPTER 10

Vertical Interlinear

1304		his disciples
0243		in the house
1804		about
0598		this [matter]

VERSE 11 And he said to them, "Whoever dismisses his wife and takes another commits adultery.

0116		And he said
1261		to them
1168		Whoever
1389		*
2597		dismisses
0135		his wife
1532		and takes
0053		another
0385		commits adultery

VERSE 12 And if a woman should dismiss her husband and be [a wife] to another, she commits adultery."

0121		And if
0135		a woman
2597		should dismiss
0306		her husband
0603		and be [a wife]
0053		to another
0385		she commits adultery

VERSE 13 And children were approaching him so that he would touch them, but his disciples were rebuking those who were bringing them.

2244		And approaching
0603		were
1261		him
0976		children
2244		so that he would touch
1261		them
1304		his disciples
0518		but
1113		rebuking
0603		were
0598		those
2244		who were bringing
1261		them

VERSE 14 And Jesus saw [it] and was offended and said to them, "Allow the children [to] come to me and do not hinder them, for because of those who are as these are, the kingdom of God exists.

3257		Jesus
0518		And
0758		saw [it]
0219		and was offended
1261		*
0116		and said
1261		to them
2440		Allow
0976		the children
0208		[to] come
1288		to me
1262		and not
1180		do hinder
0592		them
0066		because of those
0403		for
0060		who are as
0598		these
0592		are
0069		exists
1385		the kingdom
0093		of God

VERSE 15 Truly I say to you, anyone who does not receive the kingdom of God like a child will not enter it."

0110		Truly
0116		say
0124		I
1261		to you
1168		anyone
1262		who not
2134		does receive
1385		the kingdom
0093		of God

MARK   CHAPTER 10

0060		like
0976		a child
1262		not
1796		will enter
1261		it

VERSE 16   And he took them into his arms and placed his hand on them and blessed them.

2587		And he took
0592		them
1804		into
0575		his arms
1625		and placed
0057		his hand
1804		on them
0335		and blessed
0592		them

VERSE 17   And while he was traveling on the road, a certain [man] ran [and] fell on his knees and asked him and said, "Good teacher, what should I do to gain eternal life?"

1128		And while
2299		he was traveling
0038		on the road
2312		ran
0721		a certain [man]
1538		[and] fell
1804		on
0336		his knees
2420		and asked
0603		*
1261		him
0116		and said
1055		teacher
0938		Good
1393		what
1724		should I do
1098		to gain
0782		life
1813		eternal

VERSE 18   Jesus said to him, "Why do you call me good? There is no [one] good, except one, God.

0116		said
1261		to him
3257		Jesus
1393		Why
2239		do call
0133		you
1261		me
0938		good
1264		There is no [one]
0938		good
0090		except
0121		*
0721		one
0093		God

VERSE 19   You know the commandments: DO NOT COMMIT ADULTERY, DO NOT STEAL, DO NOT KILL AND DO NOT BEAR FALSE WITNESS, DO NOT DEFRAUD, HONOR YOUR FATHER AND YOUR MOTHER."

2009		the commandments
1023		know
0133		You
1262		NOT
0385		DO COMMIT ADULTERY
1262		NOT
0436		DO STEAL
1262		NOT
2179		DO KILL
1262		AND NOT
1608		DO BEAR
1610		WITNESS
0486		FALSE
1262		NOT
0979		DO DEFRAUD
1076		HONOR
0002		YOUR FATHER
0106		AND YOUR MOTHER

MARK CHAPTER 10

VERSE 20 — And he answered and said to him, "Teacher, I have kept all of these [things] from my youth."

Num	Syriac	Gloss
0592	ܗܘ	<he>
0518	ܕܝܢ	And
1838	ܥܢܐ	he answered
0116	ܘܐܡܪ	and said
1261	ܠܗ	to him
1055	ܡܠܦܢܐ	Teacher
0598	ܗܠܝܢ	these [things]
1168	ܟܠܗܝܢ	all of
1502	ܢܛܪܬ	I have kept
0592	ܐܢܝܢ	<them>
1388	ܡܢ	from
0977	ܛܠܝܘܬܝ	my youth

VERSE 21 — And Jesus looked at him and loved him and said to him, "You lack one [thing]. Go [and] sell everything that you have and give to the poor and you will have treasure in heaven and take up a cross and follow me."

Num	Syriac	Gloss
3257	ܝܫܘܥ	Jesus
0518	ܕܝܢ	And
0756	ܚܪ	looked
0217	ܒܗ	at him
0696	ܘܐܚܒܗ	and loved him
0116	ܘܐܡܪ	and said
1261	ܠܗ	to him
0721	ܚܕܐ	one [thing]
0867	ܚܣܝܪܐ ܠܟ	You lack
1261	ܠܟ	*
0042	ܙܠ	Go
0632	ܘܙܒܢ	[and] sell
1168	ܟܠ	everything
1326	ܡܕܡ	*
0069	ܕܐܝܬ	that you have
1261	ܠܟ	*
1030	ܘܗܒ	and give
1406	ܠܡܣܟܢܐ	to the poor
0603	ܘܗܘܐ	and you will have
1261	ܠܟ	*
1627	ܣܝܡܬܐ	treasure
2543	ܒܫܡܝܐ	in heaven
1532	ܘܫܩܘܠ	and take up
2109	ܨܠܝܒܐ	a cross
0208	ܘܬܐ	and follow me
0215	ܒܬܪܝ	*

VERSE 22 — And he was sad at this saying and went away, being grieved, for he had many possessions.

Num	Syriac	Gloss
0592	ܗܘ	<he>
0518	ܕܝܢ	And
1192	ܐܬܟܡܪ	he was sad
1364	ܒܡܠܬܐ	at saying
0598	ܗܕܐ	this
0042	ܘܐܙܠ	and went away
1128	ܟܕ	being
1772	ܥܝܝܩܐ	grieved
1261	ܠܗ	<to him>
0069	ܐܝܬ	he had
0603	ܗܘܐ	*
1261	ܠܗ	*
0403	ܓܝܪ	for
1515	ܢܟܣܐ	possessions
1596	ܣܓܝܐܐ	many

VERSE 23 — And Jesus looked at his disciples and said to them, "How difficult [it is] for those who have possessions to enter the kingdom of God."

Num	Syriac	Gloss
0756	ܚܪ	looked
0518	ܕܝܢ	And
3257	ܝܫܘܥ	Jesus
1304	ܒܬܠܡܝܕܘܗܝ	at his disciples
0116	ܘܐܡܪ	and said
1261	ܠܗܘܢ	to them
1188	ܟܡܐ	How
1788	ܥܛܠܐ	difficult [it is]
0066	ܠܐܝܠܝܢ	for those
0069	ܐܝܬ	who have
1261	ܠܗܘܢ	*
1515	ܢܟܣܐ	possessions
1796	ܕܢܥܠܘܢ	to enter

Vertical Interlinear

MARK — CHAPTER 10

1385		the kingdom
0093		of God

VERSE 24 — And the disciples were wondering at his words, and Jesus answered again and said to them, "My sons, how difficult [it is] for those who trust in their possessions to enter the kingdom of God.

1304		the disciples
0518		And
0549		wondering
0603		were
1804		at
1364		his words
1838		and answered
2650		again
3257		Jesus
0116		and said
1261		to them
0323		My sons
1188		how
1788		difficult [it is]
0066		for those
2665		who trust
1804		in
1515		their possessions
1796		to enter
1385		the kingdom
0093		of God

VERSE 25 — It is easier for a camel to enter through the eye of the needle than [for] a rich man to enter the kingdom of God."

2061		is easier
0592		It
0420		for a camel
1796		to enter
0888		through the eye
0748		of the needle
0024		than [for]
1921		a rich man
1385		the kingdom

0093		of God
1796		to enter

VERSE 26 — And they were all the more wondering and saying among themselves, "Who is able to [gain] life?"

0592		<they>
0518		And
1101		all the more
0549		wondering
0603		they were
0116		and saying
0266		among themselves
1390		Who
2510		is able
0780		to [gain] life

VERSE 27 — And Jesus looked at them and said to them, "With men this is not possible, but with God [it is]. For everything is possible with God."

0756		looked
0518		And
0217		at them
3257		Jesus
0116		and said
1261		to them
1288		With
0323		men
0131		*
0598		this
1262		not
2510		is possible
0090		but
1288		with
0093		God [it is]
1168		everything
1326		*
0403		For
2510		is possible
1288		with
0093		God

MARK   CHAPTER 10

VERSE 28 — And Peter began to say, "Behold, we have left everything and followed you."

Strongs	Aramaic	English
2597		And began
3258		Peter
0116		to say
0580		Behold
0124		<we>
2440		we have left
1168		everything
1326		*
1565		and followed you

VERSE 29 — Jesus answered and said, "Truly I say to you, there is no man who has left houses or brothers or sisters or father or mother or wife or children or fields because of me and because of my gospel,

Strongs	Aramaic	English
1838		answered
3257		Jesus
0116		and said
0110		Truly
0116		say
0124		I
1261		to you
1264		there is no
0131		man
2440		who has left
0243		houses
0024		or
0043		brothers
0024		or
0046		sisters
0024		or
0002		father
0024		or
0106		mother
0024		or
0135		wife
0024		or
0323		children
0024		or
2251		fields
1347		because of me
1347		and because of
1593		my gospel

VERSE 30 — and will not receive a hundredth part now in this time, houses and brothers and sisters and mothers and children and fields with persecution. Yet in the age to come, [he will receive] eternal life.

Strongs	Aramaic	English
1262		and not
2134		will receive
0721		a hundredth part
1317		*
0602		now
0633		in time
0598		this
0243		houses
0043		and brothers
0046		and sisters
0106		and mothers
0323		and children
2251		and fields
1817		with
2306		persecution
1813		Yet in the age
0208		to come
0782		[he will receive] life
1813		eternal

VERSE 31 — And [there will be] many first who will be last, and last, first."

Strongs	Aramaic	English
1596		[there will be] many
0518		And
2157		first
0603		who will be
0051		last
0051		and last
2157		first

MARK — CHAPTER 10

Vertical Interlinear

VERSE 32 — And while they were climbing up on the road to Jerusalem, Jesus was before them. And they were amazed and were following him, although they were afraid. And he took his twelve and began to tell them what would happen to him.

Number	Syriac	English
1128		while
1658		climbing up
0603		they were
0518		And
0038		on the road
3022		to Jerusalem
0592		<he>
3257		Jesus
2153		before
0603		was
1261		them
2679		And amazed
0603		they were
0042		and were following him
0603		*
0215		*
1128		although
0509		they were afraid
0477		And he took
2710		his twelve
2597		and began
0116		to tell
1261		them
1326		what
1914		would
0603		happen
1261		to him

VERSE 33 — "Behold, we will go up to Jerusalem, and the Son of Man will be delivered to the chief priests and to the scribes, and they will condemn him to death and deliver him to the Gentiles.

Number	Syriac	English
0580		Behold
1658		will go up
0124		we
3022		to Jerusalem
0323		and the Son
0131		of Man
2530		will be delivered
2271		to the chief priests
1135		*
1699		and to the scribes
0742		and they will condemn him
1335		to death
2530		and deliver him
1818		to the Gentiles

VERSE 34 — And they will mock him and beat him and spit in his face and kill him and on the third day, he will rise up."

Number	Syriac	English
0246		And they will mock
0217		him
1461		and beat him
2400		and spit
0173		in his face
2179		and kill him
1036		and on the day
2674		third
2168		he will rise up

VERSE 35 — And James and John, the sons of Zebedee, approached him and said to him, "Teacher, we want you to do for us all that we ask."

Number	Syriac	English
2244		And approached
1288		him
3255		James
3233		and John
0323		the sons of
3185		Zebedee
0116		and said
1261		to him
1055		Teacher
2077		want
0124		we
1168		all
2420		that we ask
1724		you to do
1261		for us

MARK CHAPTER 10

VERSE 36 He said to them, "What do you want me to do for you?"

0116	He said
1261	to them
1393	What
2077	do want
0133	you
1724	me to do
1261	for you

VERSE 37 They said to him, "Grant us that one sit on your right and one on your left in your glory."

0116	They said
1261	to him
1030	Grant
1261	us
0721	that one
1093	sit
1388	on
1061	your right
0721	and one
1388	on
1668	your left
2431	in your glory

VERSE 38 But he said to them, "You do not know what you ask. Are you able to drink the cup that I drink and to be baptized with the baptism [with] which I am baptized?"

0592	<he>
0518	But
0116	he said
1261	to them
1262	not
1023	do know
0133	You
1393	what
2420	ask
0133	you
2510	Are able
0133	you
2620	to drink

1205	the cup
0124	that <I>
2620	drink
0124	I
1821	and the baptism
0124	[with] which <I>
1819	am baptized
0124	I
1819	to be baptized

VERSE 39 They said to him, "We are able." Jesus said to them, "The cup that I drink, you will drink, and the baptism [with] which I am baptized, you will be baptized,

0116	They said
1261	to him
2510	We are able
0116	said
1261	to them
3257	Jesus
1205	The cup
2620	that drink
0124	I
2620	you will drink
1821	and the baptism
1819	[with] which am baptized
0124	I
1819	you will be baptized

VERSE 40 but that you may sit at my right and at my left is not mine to give, except to those for whom it is prepared."

1093	that you may sit
0518	but
1388	at
1061	my right
1388	and at
1668	my left
1262	not
0603	is
0517	mine
1030	to give
0090	except

MARK   CHAPTER 10

0066		to those
0950		for whom it is prepared

VERSE 41 — And when the ten heard [it], they began murmuring against James and John.

1128		And when
2547		heard [it]
1848		the ten
2597		they began
2360		murmuring
1804		against
3255		James
3233		and John

VERSE 42 — And Jesus called them and said to them, "You know that those who are counted as chiefs of the nations are their lords and their great men are in authority over them.

2239		And called
0592		them
3257		Jesus
0116		and said
1261		to them
1023		know
0133		You
0066		that those
1588		who are counted as
2362		chiefs
1818		of the nations
1426		their lords
0592		are
2271		and their great men
2528		are in authority
1804		over them

VERSE 43 — But it should not be so among you, but rather he who wants to be great among you should be a minister to you.

1262		not
0518		But
0597		so
0603		it should be
0266		among you
0090		but rather
1389		he who
2077		wants
0217		among you
0603		to be
2271		great
0603		should be
1261		to you
2555		a minister

VERSE 44 — And whoever of you wants to be first should be a servant of everyone.

0066		And whoever
1388		of you
2077		wants
0603		to be
2157		first
0603		should be
1727		a servant
1175		of everyone

VERSE 45 — For even the Son of Man did not come to be served, but rather to serve and to give himself [as] a ransom for many."

0169		even
0323		the Son
0403		For
0131		of Man
1262		not
0208		did come
2554		to be served
0090		but rather
2554		to serve
1030		and to give
1547		himself [as]
2043		a ransom
0812		for
1596		many

MARK CHAPTER 10

VERSE 46 — And they came to Jericho. And when Jesus went out from Jericho and his disciples and a large crowd, Timaeus, the son of Timaeus, a blind man, was sitting by the side of the road and begging.

Code	Syriac	English
0208		And they came
3039		to Jericho
1128		And when
1542		went out
3257		Jesus
1388		from
3039		Jericho
0592		<he>
1304		and his disciples
1201		and a crowd
1596		large
3212		Timaeus
3129		the son of Timaeus
1662		a blind man
1093		sitting
0603		was
1804		by
0057		the side of
0038		the road
0730		and begging

VERSE 47 — And he heard that it was Jesus the Nazarene and he began to cry out and to say, "Son of David, have compassion on me."

Code	Syriac	English
2547		And he heard
3257		that Jesus
0592		it was
3355		the Nazarene
2597		and he began
2227		to cry out
0116		and to say
0323		Son
3159		of David
2342		have compassion
1804		on me

VERSE 48 — Many were reproving him to be silent, but he was crying out all the more and said, "Son of David, have compassion on me."

Code	Syriac	English
1113		And reproving
0603		were
0217		him
1596		Many
2623		to be silent
0592		<he>
0518		but
1101		all the more
2227		crying out
0603		he was
0116		and said
0323		Son
3159		of David
2342		have compassion
1804		on me

VERSE 49 — And Jesus stopped and commanded that they call him. And they called the blind man and said to him, "Take courage [and] rise up. He calls you."

Code	Syriac	English
2168		And stopped
3257		Jesus
2007		and commanded
2239		that they call him
2239		And they called
1662		the blind man
0116		and said
1261		to him
1267		Take courage
2168		[and] rise up
2239		He calls
1261		you

VERSE 50 — And the blind man threw off his garment and rose up [and] came to Jesus.

Code	Syriac	English
0592		<he>
0518		And
1662		the blind man
2455		threw off

MARK   CHAPTER 10

#	Syriac	English
1274		his garment
2168		and rose up
0208		[and] came
1288		to
3257		Jesus

VERSE 51 — Jesus said to him, "What do you want me to do for you?" And the blind man said to him, "My Master, that I may see."

#	Syriac	English
0116		said
1261		to him
3257		Jesus
1393		What
2077		do want
0133		you
1724		me to do
1261		for you
0592		<he>
0518		And
1662		the blind man
0116		said
1261		to him
2275		My Master
0758		that I may see

VERSE 52 — And Jesus said to him, "See! Your faith has made you whole." And immediately he received sight and went on [his] way.

#	Syriac	English
3257		And Jesus
0116		said
1261		to him
0758		See
0113		Your faith
0780		has made you whole
0725		And immediately
0758		he received sight
1261		*
0042		and went
0603		*
0038		on [his] way

CHAPTER 11

VERSE 1 — And when he came near to Jerusalem by the side of Bethphage and Bethany toward the Mount of Olives, he sent two of his disciples

#	Syriac	English
1128		And when
2244		he came near
3022		to Jerusalem
1804		by
0439		the side of
3117		Bethphage
3116		and Bethany
1288		toward
0958		the Mount
0663		of Olives
2458		he sent
2709		two
1388		of
1304		his disciples

VERSE 2 — and said to them, "Go to that village opposite us. And immediately when you enter it, you will find a colt that is tied that no man has ridden. Untie [it] [and] bring it.

#	Syriac	English
0116		and said
1261		to them
0042		Go
2251		to village
0593		that
2135		opposite us
0323		And immediately
2573		*
1796		when enter
0133		you
1261		it
2510		will find
0133		you
1793		a colt
0160		that is tied
0131		that man
1388		<of>

MARK CHAPTER 11

0325		<men>
1262		no
2367		has ridden
2597		Untie [it]
0208		[and] bring it

VERSE 3 — And if anyone should say to you, 'Why are you doing this?' say to him, 'It is necessary for our Lord,' and immediately he will send it here."

0121		and if
0131		anyone
0116		should say
1261		to you
1393		Why
1724		are doing
0133		you
0598		this
0116		say
1261		to him
1426		for our Lord
0296		It is necessary
0725		And immediately
2458		he will send
1261		it
1111		here

VERSE 4 — And they went [and] found a colt that was tied at the door outside on the street. And while they were untying it,

0042		And they went
2510		[and] found
1793		a colt
0160		that was tied
1804		at
2718		the door
0322		outside
2481		on the street
1128		And while
2597		they were untying
1261		it

VERSE 5 — some of those who were standing [there] said to them, "What are you doing untying the colt?"

0131		some
1388		of
0066		those
2168		who were standing [there]
0116		said
1261		to them
1393		What
1724		are doing
0133		you
2597		untying
0133		<you>
1793		the colt

VERSE 6 — And they said to them as Jesus had commanded and they allowed them.

0592		<they>
0518		And
0116		they said
1261		to them
0060		as
2007		had commanded
0592		them
3257		Jesus
2440		and they allowed
0592		them

VERSE 7 — And they brought the colt to Jesus and placed their garments on it and Jesus rode on it.

0208		And they brought
1793		the colt
1288		to
3257		Jesus
2372		and placed
1804		on it
1320		their garments
2367		and rode
1804		on it
3257		Jesus

MARK — CHAPTER 11

VERSE 8 — And many were spreading their garments on the road and others were cutting branches from trees and spreading [them] on the road.

1596		many
0518		And
2461		spreading
0603		were
1501		their garments
0038		on the road
0053		and others
1992		cutting
0603		were
1623		branches
1388		from
0063		trees
2461		and spreading [them]
0038		on the road

VERSE 9 — And those who were before him and those who were behind him were crying out and saying: "HOSANNA! BLESSED IS HE WHO COMES IN THE NAME OF THE LORD.

0593		And those
2154		who were before him
0593		and those
0215		who were behind him
2227		crying out
0603		were
0116		and saying
0041		HOSANNA
0338		BLESSED
0592		IS
0208		HE WHO COMES
2539		IN THE NAME
1426		OF THE LORD

VERSE 10 — And BLESSED IS THE KINGDOM OF OUR FATHER DAVID THAT IS COMING! HOSANNA ON HIGH!

0338		And BLESSED
0592		IS
1385		THE KINGDOM
0208		THAT IS COMING
0002		OF OUR FATHER
3159		DAVID
0041		HOSANNA
2332		ON HIGH

VERSE 11 — And Jesus entered Jerusalem [and] the temple and saw everything. And when evening time came, he went out to Bethany with the twelve.

1796		And entered
3257		Jesus
3022		Jerusalem
0607		[and] the temple
0758		and saw
1173		everything
1128		when
0603		came
0518		And
1750		time
2375		evening
1542		he went out
3116		to Bethany
1817		with
2710		the twelve

VERSE 12 — And on the next day, when he went out from Bethany, he was hungry.

1036		And on the day
0053		next
1128		when
1542		he went out
1388		from
3116		Bethany
1212		he was hungry

VERSE 13 — And he saw a certain fig tree from a distance that had leaves on it. And he came to it [to see] if he could find anything on it. And when he arrived, he did not find [anything] on it except leaves, for the time of figs had not [yet] come.

0758		And he saw
2628		a fig tree
0721		certain

MARK CHAPTER 11

#	Syriac	English
1388		from
2354		a distance
0069		that had
0217		on it
1008		leaves
0208		And he came
1288		to it
0121		[to see] if
2510		he could find
0217		on it
1326		anything
1128		And when
0208		he arrived
1262		not
2510		he did find
0217		[anything] on it
0090		except
0121		*
1008		leaves
0633		the time
0403		for
1262		not
0603		had [yet] come
0603		*
2628		of figs

VERSE 14 And he said to it, "Now and forever man will not eat fruit from you." And his disciples heard [it]. And they came to Jerusalem.

#	Syriac	English
0116		And he said
1261		to it
1357		Now
1813		and forever
0131		man
1388		from you
2016		fruit
1262		not
0075		will eat
2547		And heard [it]
1304		his disciples

#	Syriac	English
0208		And they came
3022		to Jerusalem

VERSE 15 And Jesus entered the temple of God and began to drive out those who were buying and selling in the temple. And he turned over the tables of the moneychangers and the seats of those who were selling doves.

#	Syriac	English
1796		And entered
3257		Jesus
0607		the temple
0093		of God
2597		and began
1542		to drive out
0066		those
0632		who were buying
0632		and selling
0607		in the temple
0616		And he turned over
2069		the table
1899		of the moneychangers
1159		and the seats
0593		of those
0632		who were selling
1038		doves

VERSE 16 And he did not allow anyone to carry goods inside the temple.

#	Syriac	English
1262		And not
2440		he did allow
0603		*
0131		anyone
1733		to carry
1320		goods
0376		inside
0607		the temple

VERSE 17 And he was teaching and said to them, "Is it not written: MY HOUSE WILL BE CALLED A HOUSE OF PRAYER FOR ALL NATIONS? But you have made it a den of robbers."

#	Syriac	English
1053		And teaching
0603		he was
0116		and said

MARK CHAPTER 11

Num	Aramaic	English
1261		to them
1262		not
1247		Is it written
0243		MY HOUSE
0243		A HOUSE OF
2107		PRAYER
2239		WILL BE CALLED
1168		FOR ALL
1818		NATIONS
0133		<you>
0518		But
1724		you have made it
1775		a den
1306		of robbers

VERSE 18 And the chief priests and scribes heard [it] and were seeking how they might destroy him, for they were afraid of him because all the people were astonished at his teaching.

Num	Aramaic	English
2547		And heard [it]
2271		the chief priests
1135		*
1699		and scribes
0296		and seeking
0603		were
0061		how
0005		they might destroy him
0509		afraid
0603		they were
0403		for
1388		of him
1347		because
1168		all
1818		the people
2679		astonished
0603		were
1054		at his teaching

VERSE 19 And when it was evening, they went out of the city.

Num	Aramaic	English
1128		And when
0603		it was
2375		evening
1542		they went
0322		out
1388		of
0499		the city

VERSE 20 And in the morning while they were passing by, they saw that fig tree dried up from its root.

Num	Aramaic	English
2124		And in the morning
1128		while
1733		they were passing by
0758		they saw
2628		fig tree
0593		that
1128		dried up
1018		*
1388		from
1877		its root

VERSE 21 And Simon remembered and said to him, "My Master, behold, that fig tree that you cursed has dried up."

Num	Aramaic	English
0527		And remembered
3521		Simon
0116		and said
1261		to him
2275		My Master
0580		behold
2628		fig tree
0593		that
1284		that you cursed
1018		has dried up

VERSE 22 And Jesus answered and said to them, "You should have faith of God.

Num	Aramaic	English
1838		And answered
3257		Jesus
0116		and said
1261		to them
0603		You should have
0217		*
0113		faith
0093		of God

MARK   CHAPTER 11

VERSE 23
For truly I say to you, whoever says to this mountain, 'Be lifted up and fall into the sea,' and is not divided in his heart, but believes that what he said will happen, he will have what he said.

Code	Syriac	Gloss
0110		truly
0403		For
0116		say
0124		I
1261		to you
1389		whoever
0116		says
0958		to mountain
0598		this
2587		Be lifted up
1538		and fall
1057		into the sea
1262		and not
1968		is divided
1268		in his heart
0090		but
0109		believes
0603		that will happen
0593		<that>
1326		what
0116		he said
0603		he will have
1261		*
1326		what
0116		he said

VERSE 24
Because of this, I say to you, everything that you pray and you ask [for], believe that you will receive [it], and you will have [it].

Code	Syriac	Gloss
1347		Because of
0598		this
0116		say
0124		I
1261		to you
1168		everything
1326		*
2106		that pray
0133		you
2420		and ask [for]
0133		you
0109		believe
1532		that will receive [it]
0133		you
0603		and you will have [it]
1261		*

VERSE 25
And when you stand to pray, forgive anything that you have against anyone, so that your Father, who is in heaven, will also forgive you your transgressions.

Code	Syriac	Gloss
1313		And when
2168		stand
0133		you
2106		to pray
2440		forgive
1326		anything
0069		that you have
1261		*
1804		against
0131		anyone
0169		so that also
0002		your Father
2543		who is in heaven
2440		will forgive
1261		you
1652		your transgressions

VERSE 26
And if you do not forgive, neither will your Father who is in heaven forgive you your transgressions."

Code	Syriac	Gloss
0121		if
0518		And
0133		<you>
1262		not
2440		do forgive
0133		you
0170		neither
0002		your Father
2543		who is in heaven

MARK — CHAPTER 11

Vertical Interlinear

#	Syriac	English
2440		will forgive
1261		you
1652		your transgressions

VERSE 27 — And they came again to Jerusalem. And while he was walking in the temple, the chief priests and scribes and elders came to him.

#	Syriac	English
0208		And they came
2650		again
3022		to Jerusalem
1128		And while
0608		walking
0603		he was
0607		in the temple
0208		came
1288		to him
2271		the chief priests
1135		*
1699		and scribes
2263		and elders

VERSE 28 — And they said to him, "With what authority do you do these [things]? And who gave you this authority to do these [things]?"

#	Syriac	English
0116		And they said
1261		to him
0066		With what
2527		authority
0598		these [things]
1724		do you do
0133		*
1390		And who
1030		gave
1261		you
2527		authority
0598		this
0598		these [things]
1724		to do

VERSE 29 — And Jesus said to them, "I will ask you also a certain question that you might answer me. And I will tell you with what authority I do these [things].

#	Syriac	English
0592		\<he\>
0518		And
3257		Jesus
0116		said
1261		to them
2420		I will ask you
0169		also
0124		\<I\>
1364		a question
0721		certain
0116		that you might answer
1261		me
0124		And \<I\>
0116		will tell
0124		I
1261		you
0066		with what
2527		authority
0598		these [things]
1724		do
0124		I

VERSE 30 — The baptism of John, from where was it, from heaven or from men? Tell me."

#	Syriac	English
1821		The baptism
3233		of John
1388		from
1110		where
0592		was it
1388		from
2543		heaven
0024		or
1388		from
0323		men
0131		*
0116		Tell
1261		me

MARK　　CHAPTER 11

VERSE 31 — And they reasoned among themselves and said, "If we say to him that [it was] from heaven, he will say to us, 'Then why did you not believe him?'

Code	Syriac	English
0914		And they reasoned
1547		among themselves
0116		and said
0121		If
0116		we say
1261		to him
1388		that [it was] from
2543		heaven
0116		he will say
1261		to us
1394		Then why
1262		not
0109		did you believe him

VERSE 32 — And [if] we say from men, there is the fear of the people, for all of them were regarding John to be truly a prophet."

Code	Syriac	English
0116		And [if] we say
1388		from
0323		men
0131		*
0511		the fear
0592		there is
1388		of
1818		the people
1168		all of them
0403		for
0047		regarding
0603		were
1261		<him>
3233		John
2594		truly
1457		a prophet
0592		to be

VERSE 33 — And they answered and said to Jesus, "We do not know." He said to them, "Neither will I tell you by what authority I do these [things]."

Code	Syriac	English
1838		And they answered
0116		and said
1261		<to him>
3257		to Jesus
1262		not
1023		We do know
0116		He said
1261		to them
0169		Neither
1262		*
0124		<I>
0116		will tell
0124		I
1261		you
0066		by what
2527		authority
0598		these [things]
1724		do
0124		I

CHAPTER 12

VERSE 1 — And he began to speak with them in parables. "A certain man planted a vineyard and surrounded it [with] a hedge, and dug a wine press in it, and built a tower in it, and handed it over to workers and went on a journey.

Code	Syriac	English
2597		And he began
1362		to speak
1817		with them
1454		in parables
0361		A man
0721		certain
1554		planted
1240		a vineyard
0730		and surrounded it [with]
1617		a hedge
0875		and dug
0217		in it
1866		a wine press
0281		and built
0217		in it
0369		a tower

MARK CHAPTER 12

0047	ܘܐܘܟܠܗ	and handed it over
1977	ܠܦܠܚܐ	to workers
0768	ܘܚܙܩ	and went on a journey

VERSE 2 — And in time he sent his servant to the workers to receive from the fruit of the vineyard.

2458	ܘܫܕܪ	And he sent
1288	ܠܘܬ	to
1977	ܦܠܚܐ	the workers
1727	ܥܒܕܗ	his servant
0633	ܒܙܒܢܐ	in time
1388	ܡܢ	from
2016	ܦܐܪܐ	the fruit
1240	ܕܟܪܡܐ	of the vineyard
1532	ܢܣܒ	to receive

VERSE 3 — But they beat him and sent him away empty.

0592	ܗܢܘܢ	<they>
0518	ܕܝܢ	But
1341	ܡܚܐܘܗܝ	they beat him
2458	ܘܫܕܪܘܗܝ	and sent him away
1128	ܣܪܝܩܐ	empty
1695	ܘܩܦܣ	*

VERSE 4 — And he sent again to them another servant and they also stoned and wounded that one and they sent him away in shame.

2458	ܘܫܕܪ	And he sent
2650	ܬܘܒ	again
1288	ܠܘܬܗܘܢ	to them
1727	ܥܒܕܐ	servant
0053	ܐܚܪܢܐ	another
0169	ܘܐܦ	and also
0593	ܠܗܘ	that one
2296	ܪܓܡܘܗܝ	they stoned
2113	ܘܨܠܦܘܗܝ	and wounded
2458	ܘܫܕܪܘܗܝ	and they sent him away
2121	ܒܒܗܬܬܐ	in shame

VERSE 5 — And he sent again another also, whom they killed. And he sent many other servants and they beat some and killed some.

2458	ܘܫܕܪ	And he sent
2650	ܬܘܒ	again
0053	ܐܚܪܢܐ	another
0169	ܐܦ	also
0593	ܠܗܘ	whom
2179	ܩܛܠܘܗܝ	they killed
1596	ܘܣܓܝܐܐ	And many
1727	ܥܒܕܐ	servants
0053	ܐܚܪܢܐ	other
2458	ܫܕܪ	he sent
1388	ܘܡܢܗܘܢ	and some
1341	ܡܚܘ	they beat
1388	ܘܡܢܗܘܢ	some
0518	ܕܝܢ	and
2179	ܩܛܠܘ	killed

VERSE 6 — And [at] the end, he had one beloved son and he sent him to them finally, for he said, 'Perhaps they will respect my son.'

0054	ܚܪܬܐ	[at] the end
0518	ܕܝܢ	And
0721	ܚܕ	one
0323	ܒܪܐ	son
0698	ܚܒܝܒܐ	beloved
0069	ܐܝܬ	he had
0603	ܗܘܐ	*
1261	ܠܗ	*
2458	ܘܫܕܪܗ	and he sent him
1288	ܠܘܬܗܘܢ	to them
0051	ܐܚܪܝܬ	finally
0116	ܐܡܪ	he said
0403	ܓܝܪ	for
1124	ܟܒܪ	Perhaps
0235	ܢܒܗܬܘܢ	they will respect
1388	ܡܢ	<from>
0323	ܒܪܝ	my son

MARK CHAPTER 12

VERSE 7 — But those workers said among themselves, 'This is the heir. Come, let us kill him and the inheritance will be ours.'

0593	ܗܢܘܢ	those
0518	ܕܝܢ	But
1977	ܦܠܚܐ	workers
0116	ܐܡܪܘ	said
1547	ܒܢܦܫܗܘܢ	among themselves
0599	ܗܢܐ	This is
1089	ܝܪܬܐ	the heir
0208	ܬܘ	Come
2179	ܢܩܛܠܝܘܗܝ	let us kill him
0603	ܘܬܗܘܐ	and will be
0517	ܕܝܠܢ	ours
1090	ܝܪܬܘܬܐ	the inheritance

VERSE 8 — And they took [and] killed him and they drove him outside of the vineyard.

1532	ܘܢܣܒܘ	And they took
2179	ܩܛܠܘܗܝ	[and] killed him
1542	ܘܐܦܩܘܗܝ	and they drove him
0322	ܠܒܪ	outside
1388	ܡܢ	of
1240	ܟܪܡܐ	the vineyard

VERSE 9 — What then will the lord of the vineyard do? He will come to destroy those workers and give the vineyard to others.

1393	ܡܢܐ	What
0596	ܗܟܝܠ	then
1724	ܢܥܒܕ	will do
1426	ܡܪܐ	the lord of
1240	ܟܪܡܐ	the vineyard
0208	ܢܐܬܐ	He will come
0005	ܘܢܘܒܕ	to destroy
0593	ܠܗܢܘܢ	those
1977	ܦܠܚܐ	workers
1030	ܘܢܬܠܝܘܗܝ	and give
1240	ܟܪܡܐ	the vineyard
0053	ܠܐܚܪܢܐ	to others

VERSE 10 — And have you not even read this scripture: THE STONE THAT THE BUILDERS REJECTED HAS BECOME THE HEAD OF THE CORNER?

0170	ܘܐܦܠܐ	And not even
1248	ܟܬܒܐ	scripture
0598	ܗܢܐ	this
2239	ܩܪܝܬܘܢ	have you read
1119	ܕܟܐܦܐ	THE STONE
1655	ܐܣܠܝܘ	THAT REJECTED
0282	ܒܢܝܐ	THE BUILDERS
0592	ܗܝ	<IT>
0603	ܗܘܬ	HAS BECOME
2362	ܠܪܝܫ	THE HEAD
0654	ܕܙܘܝܬܐ	OF THE CORNER

VERSE 11 — THIS CAME FROM THE PRESENCE OF THE LORD AND IT IS A WONDER IN OUR EYES."

1388	ܡܢ	FROM
1288	ܠܘܬ	THE PRESENCE OF
1426	ܡܪܝܐ	THE LORD
0603	ܗܘܬ	CAME
0598	ܗܕܐ	THIS
0069	ܘܐܝܬܝܗ	AND IT IS
0551	ܬܕܡܘܪܬܐ	A WONDER
1794	ܒܥܝܢܝܢ	IN OUR EYES

VERSE 12 — And they sought to arrest him, yet they were afraid of the people, for they knew that he spoke this parable about them, and they left him and went away.

0296	ܘܒܥܝܢ	And they sought
0603	ܗܘܘ	*
0047	ܠܡܐܚܕܗ	to arrest him
0509	ܘܕܚܠܘ	yet they were afraid
1388	ܡܢ	of
1818	ܥܡܐ	the people
1023	ܝܕܥܘ	they knew
0403	ܓܝܪ	for
1804	ܕܥܠܝܗܘܢ	that about them
0116	ܐܡܪ	he spoke
1454	ܡܬܠܐ	parable
0598	ܗܢܐ	this

MARK — CHAPTER 12

2440	ܫܒܩܘܗܝ	and they left him
0042	ܘܐܙܠܘ	and went away

VERSE 13 And they sent him some of the scribes and [some] of the Herodians to ensnare him in speech.

2458	ܘܫܕܪܘ	And they sent
1288	ܠܘܬܗ	him
0131	ܐܢܫܐ	some
1388	ܡܢ	of
1699	ܣܦܪܐ	the scribes
1388	ܘܡܢ	and [some] of
0243	ܗܪܘܕܣ	the Herodians
3179	ܕܢܨܘܕܘܢܝܗܝ	*
2089	ܕܢܨܘܕܘܢܝܗܝ	to ensnare him
1364	ܒܡܠܬܐ	in speech

VERSE 14 And they came and asked him, "Teacher, we know that you are true and [that] you are not moved by anyone, for you do not look on the faces of men, but in truth you teach the way of God. Is it lawful to give the poll tax to Caesar or not? Should we give or should we not give [it]?"

0592	ܗܢܘܢ	<they>
0518	ܕܝܢ	And
0208	ܐܬܘ	they came
2420	ܘܫܐܠܘܗܝ	and asked him
1055	ܡܠܦܢܐ	Teacher
1023	ܝܕܥܝܢ	know
0124	ܚܢܢ	we
2593	ܕܫܪܝܪ	that true
0133	ܐܢܬ	you are
1262	ܘܠܐ	and [that] not
2587	ܫܩܝܠ	you are moved
0133	ܐܢܬ	*
1072	ܨܦܬܐ	*
0131	ܠܐܢܫ	by anyone
1262	ܠܐ	not
0403	ܓܝܪ	for
0756	ܚܐܪ	do look
0133	ܐܢܬ	you
2041	ܒܦܪܨܘܦܐ	on the faces
0323	ܕܒܢܝܢܫܐ	of men
0131	ܐܢܫܐ	*
0090	ܐܠܐ	but
2596	ܒܫܪܪܐ	in truth
0038	ܐܘܪܚܐ	the way
0093	ܕܐܠܗܐ	of God
1053	ܡܠܦ	teach
0133	ܐܢܬ	you
2528	ܫܠܝܛ	Is it lawful
1030	ܠܡܬܠ	to give
1209	ܟܣܦ	the poll tax
2362	ܪܫܐ	*
3483	ܠܩܣܪ	to Caesar
0024	ܐܘ	or
1262	ܠܐ	not
1030	ܢܬܠ	Should we give
0024	ܐܘ	or
1262	ܠܐ	not
1030	ܢܬܠ	should we give [it]

VERSE 15 But he knew their trickery and said to them, "Why do you tempt me? Bring me a denarius to see."

0592	ܗܘ	<he>
0518	ܕܝܢ	But
1023	ܝܕܥ	he knew
1513	ܢܟܠܗܘܢ	their trickery
0116	ܘܐܡܪ	and said
1261	ܠܗܘܢ	to them
1393	ܡܢܐ	Why
1527	ܡܢܣܝܢ	do tempt
0133	ܐܢܬܘܢ	you
1261	ܠܝ	me
0208	ܐܝܬܘ	Bring
1261	ܠܝ	me
0519	ܕܝܢܪܐ	a denarius
0758	ܐܚܙܐ	to see

VERSE 16 And they brought [one] to him. He said to them, "Whose image and inscription is this?" And they said, "Caesar's."

0208	ܘܐܝܬܝܘ	And they brought [one]

317

MARK CHAPTER 12

ID	Syriac	English
1261		to him
0116		He said
1261		to them
1390		Whose
2112		image
0598		is this
1248		and inscription
0592		<they>
0518		And
0116		they said
3483		Caesar's

VERSE 17 Jesus said to them, "That which is of Caesar give to Caesar and that which is of God to God." And they were marveling at him.

ID	Syriac	English
0116		said
1261		to them
3257		Jesus
3483		That which is of Caesar
1030		give
3483		to Caesar
0093		and that which is of God
0093		to God
2679		And marveling
0603		they were
0217		at him

VERSE 18 And the Sadducees came to him, those who say that there is no resurrection, and were asking him and saying,

ID	Syriac	English
0208		And came
3188		the Sadducees
1288		to him
0593		those
0116		who say
2173		that resurrection
1264		there is no
2420		and asking
0603		were
1261		him
0116		and saying

VERSE 19 "Teacher, Moses wrote to us: IF THE BROTHER OF A MAN DIES AND LEAVES A WIFE AND DOES NOT LEAVE SONS, HIS BROTHER SHOULD TAKE HIS WIFE AND RAISE UP SEED FOR HIS BROTHER.

ID	Syriac	English
1055		Teacher
3305		Moses
1247		wrote
1261		to us
0121		IF
1334		DIES
0043		THE BROTHER
0131		OF A MAN
2440		AND LEAVES
0135		A WIFE
0323		AND SONS
1262		NOT
2440		DOES LEAVE
1532		SHOULD TAKE
0043		HIS BROTHER
0135		HIS WIFE
2168		AND RAISE UP
0693		SEED
0043		FOR HIS BROTHER

VERSE 20 There were seven brothers. The first took a wife and died and did not leave [any] seed.

ID	Syriac	English
2437		seven
0043		brothers
0069		There were
0603		*
2157		The first
1532		took
0135		a wife
1334		and died
1262		and not even
2440		did leave
0693		[any] seed

MARK — CHAPTER 12

VERSE 21
And the second took her and died, although also he did not leave [any] seed, and the third likewise.

2709		And the second
1532		took her
1334		and died
1128		although
0169		also
1262		not
0592		he
2440		did leave
0693		[any] seed
2674		and the third
0595		likewise

VERSE 22
And the seven of them took her and did not leave [any] seed. Last of all of them, the wife also died.

2437		And the seven of them
1532		took her
1262		and not
2440		did leave
0693		[any] seed
0051		Last of
1168		all of them
1334		died
0169		also
0592		<she>
0135		the wife

VERSE 23
Therefore, in the resurrection, whose wife will she be? For the seven of them took her."

2173		in the resurrection
0596		Therefore
0066		whose
1388		<from them>
0603		will she be
0135		wife
2437		the seven of them
0403		For
1532		took her

VERSE 24
Jesus said to them, "Is it not because of this you err? For you do not know the scriptures nor the power of God.

0116		said
1261		to them
3257		Jesus
1262		not
0603		Is it
1347		because of
0598		this
0993		err
0133		you
1262		For not
1023		do know
0133		you
1248		the scriptures
1262		nor
0786		the power
0093		of God

VERSE 25
For when they rise up from the dead, they do not marry women nor are women with men, but rather they are as the angels that are in heaven.

1313		when
0403		For
2168		they rise up
1388		from
1338		the dead
1262		not
1532		they do marry
0135		women
0169		nor
1262		*
0135		women
0603		are
0361		with men
0090		but rather
0069		they are
0060		as
1375		the angels
2543		that are in heaven

Vertical Interlinear

MARK   CHAPTER 12

VERSE 26   Now about the dead who will rise up, have you not read in the book of Moses how God spoke to him from the bush: I AM THE GOD OF ABRAHAM AND THE GOD OF ISAAC AND THE GOD OF JACOB?

1804		about
1338		the dead
0518		Now
2168		who will rise up
1262		not
2239		have you read
1248		in the book
3305		of Moses
0061		how
1388		from
1678		the bush
0116		spoke
1261		to him
0093		God
0124		I AM
0124		*
0093		THE GOD
3005		OF ABRAHAM
0093		AND THE GOD
3033		OF ISAAC
0093		AND THE GOD
3255		OF JACOB

VERSE 27   And he is not the God of the dead, but of the living. Therefore you err greatly."

1262		And not
0603		he is
0093		the God
1338		of the dead
0090		but
0781		of the living
0133		<you>
0596		Therefore
1596		greatly
0993		err
0133		you

VERSE 28   And one of the scribes approached and heard them disputing and saw that he answered the matter well for them. And he asked, "What is the most important commandment?"

2244		And approached
0721		one
1388		of
1699		the scribes
2547		and heard
0592		them
0576		disputing
0758		and saw
2583		that well
2649		he answered
1261		for them
2068		the matter
2420		And he asked
0067		What is
2009		the commandment
2157		most important
1168		*

VERSE 29   Jesus said to him, "The most important of all the commandments [is]: HEAR, ISRAEL, THE LORD OUR GOD IS ONE LORD

0116		said
1261		to him
3257		Jesus
2157		The most important
1388		of
1168		all
2009		the commandments [is]
2547		HEAR
3035		ISRAEL
1426		THE LORD
0093		OUR GOD
1426		LORD
0721		ONE
0592		IS

MARK — CHAPTER 12

VERSE 30 — and YOU SHOULD LOVE THE LORD YOUR GOD WITH ALL YOUR HEART AND WITH ALL YOUR SOUL AND WITH ALL YOUR MIND AND WITH ALL YOUR MIGHT. This is the most important commandment.

#	Aramaic	English
2342		and YOU SHOULD LOVE
1426		THE LORD
0093		YOUR GOD
1388		WITH
1168		ALL
1268		YOUR HEART
1388		AND WITH
1168		ALL
1547		YOUR SOUL
1388		AND WITH
1168		ALL
2385		YOUR MIND
1388		AND WITH
1168		ALL
0786		YOUR MIGHT
0599		This is
2009		the commandment
2157		most important

VERSE 31 — And the second that is like it [is]: YOU SHOULD LOVE YOUR NEIGHBOR AS YOURSELF. There is no other commandment that is greater than these."

#	Aramaic	English
2709		And the second
0540		that is like
1261		it [is]
0696		YOU SHOULD LOVE
2248		YOUR NEIGHBOR
0060		AS
1547		YOURSELF
2009		commandment
0053		other
2271		that is greater
1388		than
0598		these
1264		There is no

VERSE 32 — The scribe said to him, "Well [said], my Master. You have spoken in truth, because he is one and there are no others outside of him.

#	Aramaic	English
0116		said
1261		to him
0593		<that>
1699		The scribe
2583		Well [said]
2275		my Master
2596		in truth
0116		You have spoken
0721		because one
0592		he is
1264		and there are no
0053		others
0322		outside
1388		of him

VERSE 33 — And that a man should love him with all the heart and with all the mind and with all the soul and with all might, and that he should love his neighbor as himself, greater is [this] than all the burnt offerings and sacrifices."

#	Aramaic	English
2342		And that should love him
0131		a man
1388		with
1168		all
1268		the heart
1388		and with
1168		all
2385		the mind
1388		and with
1168		all
1547		the soul
1388		and with
1168		all
0786		might
2342		and that he should love
2248		his neighbor
0060		as
1547		himself

MARK   CHAPTER 12

1100		greater
0592		is [this]
1388		than
1168		all
1074		the burnt offerings
0474		and sacrifices

VERSE 34   And Jesus saw that he responded to the matter wisely. He answered and said to him, "You are not far from the kingdom of God." And no man dared to question him again.

3257		Jesus
0518		And
0758		saw
0791		that wisely
1984		he responded to
2068		the matter
1838		He answered
0116		and said
1261		to him
1262		not
0603		You are
2355		far
1388		from him
1385		the kingdom
0093		of God
1262		And no
0131		man
2650		again
1435		dared
2420		to question him

VERSE 35   And Jesus answered and said while [he was] teaching in the temple, "In what way do the scribes say that the Messiah is the Son of David?

1838		And answered
3257		Jesus
0116		and said
1128		while
1053		[he was] teaching
0607		in the temple
0061		In what way
0116		do say
1699		the scribes
1446		that the Messiah
0323		the Son
0592		is
3159		of David

VERSE 36   For David spoke by the Holy Spirit: THE LORD SAID TO MY LORD, SIT ON MY RIGHT [HAND] UNTIL I PLACE YOUR ENEMIES [AS] A FOOTSTOOL UNDER YOUR FEET.

0592		\<he\>
0403		For
3159		David
0116		spoke
2323		by the Holy Spirit
2164		*
0116		SAID
1426		THE LORD
1426		TO MY LORD
1093		SIT
1261		\<you\>
1388		ON
1061		MY RIGHT [HAND]
1747		UNTIL
1625		I PLACE
0307		YOUR ENEMIES
1127		[AS] A FOOTSTOOL
2660		UNDER
2293		YOUR FEET

VERSE 37   Since David called him, 'My Lord,' then how is he his Son?" And the whole crowd was hearing him gladly.

0592		\<he\>
0596		Since
3159		David
2239		called
1261		him
1426		My Lord
0061		then how

MARK CHAPTER 12

0323		his Son
0069		is he
1168		And the whole
1201		crowd
2547		hearing
0603		was
1261		him
0289		gladly

VERSE 38 And in his teaching he was saying to them, "Beware of the scribes who want to walk in robes and love a greeting in the streets

1054		And in his teaching
0116		saying
0603		he was
1261		to them
0645		Beware
1388		of
1699		the scribes
2077		who want
0146		in robes
0608		to walk
2342		and love
2535		a greeting
2481		in the streets

VERSE 39 and the chief seats in the synagogues and the chief places at banquets,

2362		and the chief
1094		seats
1200		in the synagogues
2362		and the chief
1666		places
0928		at banquets

VERSE 40 those who devour the house of widows with the pretext that they lengthen their prayers. Those will receive the greater judgment."

0593		those
0075		who devour
0243		the house
0195		of widows
1801		with the pretext
0192		that they lengthen
2107		their prayers
0592		Those
2134		will receive
0497		the judgment
1100		greater

VERSE 41 And when Jesus sat near the treasury, he considered how the crowds were putting money into the treasury. And many rich men were putting in much.

1128		And when
1093		sat
3257		Jesus
2135		near
0243		the treasury
0393		*
0756		he considered
0603		*
0061		how
1201		the crowds
2372		were putting into
1900		money
0243		the treasury
0393		*
1596		And many
1921		rich men
2372		putting in
0603		were
1596		much

VERSE 42 And a certain poor widow came [and] put in two lepta that are very small coins.

0208		And came
0195		a widow
0721		certain
1406		poor
2372		[and] put in
2709		two
1397		lepta
0069		that are

Vertical Interlinear

MARK   **CHAPTER 12**

2541	ܫܡܘܢܐ	very small coins
VERSE 43		And Jesus called his disciples and said to them, "Truly I say to you, this poor widow has put in more than everyone who put in the treasury.
2239	ܘܩܪܐ	And called
3257	ܝܫܘܥ	Jesus
1304	ܠܬܠܡܝܕܘܗܝ	his disciples
0116	ܘܐܡܪ	and said
1261	ܠܗܘܢ	to them
0110	ܐܡܝܢ	truly
0116	ܐܡܪ	say
0124	ܐܢܐ	I
1261	ܠܟܘܢ	to you
0598	ܕܗܕܐ	this
0195	ܐܪܡܠܬܐ	widow
1406	ܡܣܟܢܬܐ	poor
1100	ܝܬܝܪ	more
1388	ܡܢ	than
1168	ܟܠܗܘܢ	everyone
0131	ܐܢܫܐ	*
2372	ܕܪܡܝܢ	who put in
2372	ܐܪܡܝܬ	has put in
0243	ܒܝܬ	the treasury
0393	ܓܙܐ	*
VERSE 44		For all of them put in from what abounded to them, but this one, from her need, put in everything that she had, her entire wealth."
1168	ܟܠܗܘܢ	all of them
0403	ܓܝܪ	For
1388	ܡܢ	from
1326	ܡܕܡ	what
1100	ܕܝܬܝܪ	abounded
1261	ܠܗܘܢ	to them
2372	ܐܪܡܝܘ	put in
0598	ܗܕܐ	this one
0518	ܕܝܢ	but
1388	ܡܢ	from
0868	ܚܣܝܪܘܬܗ	her need
1168	ܟܠ	everything
2541	*	very small coins
0069	ܐܝܬ	that she had
0603	ܗܘܐ	*
1261	ܠܗ	*
2372	ܐܪܡܝܬܗ	put in
1168	ܟܠܗ	entire
2217	ܩܢܝܢܗ	her wealth

CHAPTER 13

VERSE 1		And when Jesus went out from the temple, one of his disciples said to him, "Teacher, behold, look at those stones and those buildings."
1128	ܘܟܕ	And when
1542	ܢܦܩ	went out
3257	ܝܫܘܥ	Jesus
1388	ܡܢ	from
0607	ܗܝܟܠܐ	the temple
0116	ܐܡܪ	said
1261	ܠܗ	to him
0721	ܚܕ	one
1388	ܡܢ	of
1304	ܬܠܡܝܕܘܗܝ	his disciples
1055	ܡܠܦܢܐ	Teacher
0580	ܗܐ	behold
0758	ܚܙܝ	look at
0066	ܗܠܝܢ	those
1119	ܟܐܦܐ	stones
0066	ܘܗܠܝܢ	and those
0283	ܒܢܝܢܐ	buildings
VERSE 2		But Jesus said to him, "Do you see these great buildings? One stone on another will not be left here that will not be torn down."
3257	ܝܫܘܥ	Jesus
0518	ܕܝܢ	But
0116	ܐܡܪ	said
1261	ܠܗ	to him
0758	ܚܙܐ	Do see
0133	ܐܢܬ	you
0598	ܗܠܝܢ	these
0283	ܒܢܝܢܐ	buildings

MARK　　　CHAPTER 13

2271	ܪܘܪܒܐ	great
1262	ܠܐ	not
2440	ܬܫܬܒܩ	will be left
0600	ܗܪܟܐ	here
1119	ܟܐܦ	One stone
1804	ܥܠ	on
1119	ܟܐܦ	another
1262	ܕܠܐ	that not
1719	ܬܣܬܬܪ	will be torn down

VERSE 3 And while Jesus sat on the Mount of Olives opposite the temple, Peter and James and John and Andrew asked him privately,

1128	ܘܟܕ	And while
1093	ܝܬܒ	sat
3257	ܝܫܘܥ	Jesus
0958	ܒܛܘܪܐ	on the Mount
0663	ܕܙܝܬܐ	of Olives
2135	ܠܘܩܒܠ	opposite
0607	ܗܝܟܠܐ	the temple
2420	ܫܐܠܘܗܝ	asked him
3258	ܟܐܦܐ	Peter
3255	ܘܝܥܩܘܒ	and James
3233	ܘܝܘܚܢܢ	and John
3061	ܘܐܢܕܪܐܘܣ	and Andrew
1041	ܒܠܚܘܕܝܗܘܢ	privately

VERSE 4 Tell us when these [things] will be. And what [is] the sign when all these [things] are close to being fulfilled?

0116	ܐܡܪ	Tell
1261	ܠܢ	us
0120	ܐܡܬܝ	when
0598	ܗܠܝܢ	these [things]
0603	ܢܗܘܝܢ	will be
1393	ܘܡܢܐ	And what [is]
0206	ܐܬܐ	the sign
1313	ܡܐ	when
2248	ܕܩܪܝܒܢ	are close
0598	ܗܠܝܢ	these [things]
1168	ܟܠܗܝܢ	all
2530	ܠܡܫܬܠܡܘ	to being fulfilled

VERSE 5 And Jesus began to say to them, "Beware, so that no one will deceive you.

0592	ܗܘ	<he>
0518	ܕܝܢ	And
3257	ܝܫܘܥ	Jesus
2597	ܫܪܝ	began
0116	ܠܡܐܡܪ	to say
1261	ܠܗܘܢ	to them
0758	ܚܙܘ	Beware
1314	ܕܠܡܐ	so that no
0131	ܐܢܫ	one
0993	ܢܛܥܝܟܘܢ	will deceive you

VERSE 6 For many will come in my name and say, 'I am [he],' and will deceive many.

1596	ܣܓܝܐܐ	many
0403	ܓܝܪ	For
0208	ܢܐܬܘܢ	will come
2539	ܒܫܡܝ	in my name
0116	ܘܢܐܡܪܘܢ	and say
0124	ܐܢܐ	I am [he]
0124	ܐܢܐ	*
1596	ܘܠܣܓܝܐܐ	and many
0993	ܢܛܥܘܢ	will deceive

VERSE 7 But when you hear of wars and a rumor of battles, do not be afraid, for it is about to occur, but the end [is] not yet.

1313	ܡܐ	when
0518	ܕܝܢ	But
2547	ܕܫܡܥܬܘܢ	you hear of
2247	ܩܪܒܐ	wars
0944	ܘܛܒܐ	and a rumor
2131	ܕܩܪܒܐ	of battles
1262	ܠܐ	not
0509	ܬܕܚܠܘܢ	do be afraid
1914	ܥܬܝܕ	is about
0592	ܗܘ	it
0603	ܕܢܗܘܐ	for to occur
0090	ܐܠܐ	but
1262	ܠܐ	not
1745	ܥܕܟܝܠ	yet

MARK CHAPTER 13

0054	ܫܘܠܡܐ	the end [is]

VERSE 8 For people will rise up against people and kingdom against kingdom. And there will be earthquakes in various places and there will be famines and riots. These [things] are the beginning of sorrows.

2168	ܢܩܘܡ	will rise up
0403	ܓܝܪ	For
1818	ܥܡܐ	people
1804	ܥܠ	against
1818	ܥܡܐ	people
1385	ܘܡܠܟܘ	and kingdom
1804	ܥܠ	against
1385	ܡܠܟܘ	kingdom
0603	ܘܢܗܘܘܢ	And there will be
0658	ܙܘܥܐ	earthquakes
0494	ܕܘܟܐ	in various places
0494	ܕܘܟܐ	*
0603	ܘܢܗܘܘܢ	And there will be
1213	ܟܦܢܐ	famines
2454	ܘܫܓܘܫܝܐ	and riots
0598	ܗܠܝܢ	These [things]
2362	ܪܫܐ	the beginning
0592	ܐܢܝܢ	are
0704	ܕܚܒܠܐ	of sorrows

VERSE 9 But watch out for yourselves, for they will deliver you to the judges, and in the synagogues you will be beaten, and you will stand before kings and governors because of me, as a testimony to them.

0758	ܚܙܘ	watch out for
0518	ܕܝܢ	But
0133	ܐܢܬܘܢ	<you>
1547	ܢܦܫܟܘܢ	yourselves
2530	ܢܫܠܡܘܢܟܘܢ	they will deliver you
0403	ܓܝܪ	for
0498	ܠܕܝܢܐ	to the judges
1200	ܘܒܟܢܘܫܬܗܘܢ	and in the synagogues
1461	ܬܬܢܓܕܘܢ	you will be beaten
2154	ܘܩܕܡ	and before
1383	ܡܠܟܐ	kings
0586	ܘܗܓܡܘܢܐ	and governors
2168	ܬܩܘܡܘܢ	you will stand
1347	ܡܛܠܬܝ	because of me
1610	ܠܣܗܕܘܬܗܘܢ	as a testimony to them

VERSE 10 But first my gospel will be preached among all the nations.

2151	ܠܘܩܕܡ	first
0518	ܕܝܢ	But
1914	ܥܬܝܕܐ	will
1230	ܕܬܬܟܪܙ	be preached
1593	ܣܒܪܬܝ	my gospel
1168	ܒܟܠܗܘܢ	among all
1818	ܥܡܡܐ	the nations

VERSE 11 And when they bring you to deliver you up, do not be anxious beforehand about what you will say or think, but what is given to you at that moment, that speak. For you are not speaking, but the Holy Spirit.

1313	ܡܐ	when
2244	ܕܡܩܪܒܝܢ	they bring
1261	ܠܟܘܢ	you
0518	ܕܝܢ	And
2530	ܕܢܫܠܡܘܢܟܘܢ	to deliver you up
1262	ܠܐ	not
2150	ܬܩܕܡܘܢ	beforehand
1069	ܬܐܨܦܘܢ	do be anxious about
1393	ܡܢܐ	what
1362	ܬܡܠܠܘܢ	you will say
1262	ܘܠܐ	or
2376	ܬܪܢܘܢ	think
0090	ܐܠܐ	but
1326	ܡܕܡ	what
1030	ܕܡܬܝܗܒ	is given
1261	ܠܟܘܢ	to you
0593	ܒܗܝ	at that
2573	ܫܥܬܐ	moment
0593	ܗܝ	that
1362	ܡܠܠܘ	speak
1262	ܠܐ	not
0603	ܗܘܐ	are

MARK CHAPTER 13

0403		For
0133		you
1362		speaking
0090		but
2323		the Holy Spirit
2164		*

VERSE 12 — And brother will deliver his brother to death and a father his son and children will rise up against their parents and will put them to death.

2530		will deliver
0518		And
0043		brother
0043		his brother
1335		to death
0002		and a father
0323		his son
2168		and will rise up
0323		children
1804		against
0002		their parents
1334		and will put to death
0592		them

VERSE 13 — And you will be hated by all men because of my name. But he who endures until the end will live.

0603		And you will be
1675		hated
1388		by
1175		all men
1347		because of
2539		my name
1389		he who
0518		But
1588		endures
1747		until
0054		the end
0592		<he>
0780		will live

VERSE 14 — And when you see the abominable sign of desecration that was spoken of by Daniel the prophet that will stand where it should not be (he who reads should understand) then those who are in Judah should flee to the mountain.

1313		when
0518		And
0758		you see
0206		the sign
0991		abominable
0892		of desecration
0593		that
0116		was spoken of
3167		by Daniel
1457		the prophet
2168		that will stand
1108		where
1262		not
0626		it should be
0593		he
2239		who reads
1647		should understand
0594		then
0066		those
3224		who are in Judah
0592		<they>
1904		should flee
0958		to the mountain

VERSE 15 — And he who is on the roof should not come down nor enter to take anything from his house.

1389		And <he>
0019		who is on the roof
0592		<he>
1262		not
1499		he should come down
1262		nor
1796		enter
2587		to take
1326		anything

MARK   CHAPTER 13

1388		from		1388		from
0243		his house		2362		the beginning of
VERSE 16		And he who is in the field should not turn back to pick up his clothing.		0331		the creation
				0328		that created
1389		And <he>		0093		God
0884		who is in the field		1747		until
0592		<he>		0602		now
1262		not		1262		nor
0616		he should turn		0603		will be [again]
0295		back		**VERSE 20**		And if the LORD had not shortened those days, no flesh would live. But because of the chosen [ones] that he chose, he shortened those days.
2587		to pick up				
1274		his clothing				
VERSE 17		And woe to pregnant women and to those who are nursing in those days!		0097		And if
				1262		not
0625		woe		1426		the LORD
0518		And		1221		had shortened
0260		to pregnant women		1036		days
0066		and to those		0593		those
1063		who are nursing		1262		no
0593		in those		0780		would live
1036		days		0603		*
VERSE 18		Now pray, so that your flight will not be in winter.		1168		<all>
				0294		flesh
2106		pray		0090		But
0518		Now		1347		because of
1262		so that not		0353		the chosen [ones]
0603		will be		0351		that he chose
1905		your flight		1221		he shortened
1718		in winter		1036		days
VERSE 19		For an ordeal will come in those days such as has not occurred from the beginning of the creation that God created until now, nor will be [again].		0593		those
				VERSE 21		Then, if anyone says to you, 'Behold, here is the Messiah and behold, [over] here,' do not believe [him].
0603		will come		0594		Then
0403		For		0121		if
1036		in days		0131		anyone
0593		those		0116		says
0103		an ordeal		1261		to you
1262		such as not		0580		Behold
0603		has occurred		0600		here
0072		*				

MARK — CHAPTER 13

Code	Aramaic	English
0592		is
1446		the Messiah
0580		and behold
0601		[over] here
1262		not
0109		do believe [him]

VERSE 22 — For false messiahs and lying prophets will rise up and they will produce signs and wonders and will deceive even the chosen [ones], if possible.

Code	Aramaic	English
2168		will rise up
0403		For
1446		messiahs
0487		false
1457		and prophets
1132		lying
1030		and they will produce
0206		signs
0551		and wonders
0993		and will deceive
0121		if
2510		possible
0169		even
0353		the chosen [ones]

VERSE 23 — But watch out! Behold, I have told you everything beforehand.

Code	Aramaic	English
0133		<you>
0518		But
0645		watch out
0580		Behold
2150		beforehand
0116		I have told
1261		you
1168		everything
1326		*

VERSE 24 — And in those days after that ordeal, THE SUN WILL DARKEN AND THE MOON WILL NOT GIVE ITS LIGHT.

Code	Aramaic	English
0593		in those
0518		And
1036		days
0215		after
0103		ordeal
0593		that
2557		THE SUN
0922		WILL DARKEN
1611		AND THE MOON
1262		NOT
1030		WILL GIVE
1477		ITS LIGHT

VERSE 25 — AND THE STARS WILL FALL FROM HEAVEN AND THE POWERS OF HEAVEN WILL BE SHAKEN.

Code	Aramaic	English
1141		AND THE STARS
1538		WILL FALL
1388		FROM
2543		HEAVEN
0786		AND THE POWERS
2543		OF HEAVEN
0657		WILL BE SHAKEN

VERSE 26 — And then they will see THE SON OF MAN COMING IN THE CLOUDS WITH GREAT POWER AND WITH GLORY.

Code	Aramaic	English
0594		And then
0758		they will see
0323		THE SON
0131		OF MAN
1128		COMING
0208		*
1844		IN THE CLOUDS
1817		WITH
0786		POWER
2271		GREAT
1817		AND WITH
2431		GLORY

VERSE 27 — Then he will send his angels and gather his chosen [ones] from the four winds, from one end of the earth to the end of heaven.

Code	Aramaic	English
0594		Then
2458		he will send
1375		his angels

MARK   CHAPTER 13

#		word		#		word
1198		and gather		0592		it is
0353		his chosen [ones]		1804		at
1388		from		2718		the door

VERSE 30   Truly I say to you, this generation will not pass away until all these [things] occur.

0179		the four
2323		winds
1388		from
2362		one end
0199		of the earth
1747		<and up to>
2362		to the end
2543		of heaven

0110		Truly
0116		say
0124		I
1261		to you
1262		not
1733		will pass away
2605		generation
0598		this
1747		until
0598		these [things]
1168		all
0603		occur

VERSE 28   Now learn an illustration from the fig tree that when its branches are tender and its leaves bud, you know that summer has arrived.

1388		from
2628		the fig tree
0518		Now
1053		learn
1967		an illustration
1313		that when
2366		are tender
1623		its branches
2037		and bud
1008		its leaves
1023		know
0133		you
1346		that has arrived
2194		summer

VERSE 31   Heaven and earth will pass away, yet my words will not pass away.

2543		Heaven
0199		and earth
1733		will pass away
1364		yet my words
1262		not
1733		will pass away

VERSE 32   But about that day and about that hour, no man knows, not even the angels of heaven, nor the Son, but only the Father.

1804		about
0518		But
1036		day
0593		that
1804		and about
2573		hour
0593		that
0131		man
1262		no
1023		knows
0170		not even
1375		the angels

VERSE 29   So also, when you have seen these [things] that are going to be, know that it is near, at the door.

0597		So
0169		also
0133		<you>
1313		when
0758		you have seen
0598		these [things]
0603		that are going to be
1023		know
2248		that near

MARK — CHAPTER 13

2543		of heaven
1262		nor
0323		the Son
0090		but
0121		only
0002		the Father

VERSE 33 — Watch, be alert and pray, for you do not know when the time is.

0758		Watch
1880		be alert
2106		and pray
1262		not
0403		for
1023		do know
0133		you
0120		when
0592		is
0633		the time

VERSE 34 — For [it is] like a man who went on a journey and left his house and gave authority to his servants and to each man his work and commanded the porter to be alert.

0060		[it is] like
0361		a man
0592		<he>
0403		For
0768		who went on a journey
2440		and left
0243		his house
1030		and gave
2527		authority
1727		to his servants
0131		and to each man
0131		*
1728		his work
2719		and the porter
2007		commanded
0603		to be
1880		alert

VERSE 35 — Be alert, therefore, because you do not know when the lord of the house will come, in the evening or in the middle of the night or at the rooster crow or in the morning,

1880		Be alert
0596		therefore
1262		because not
1023		do know
0133		you
0120		when
0208		will come
1426		the lord
0243		of the house
2375		in the evening
0024		or
1971		in the middle
1299		of the night
0024		or
2240		at the crow
2713		rooster
0024		or
2124		in the morning

VERSE 36 — lest he comes suddenly and finds you sleeping.

1314		lest
0208		he comes
1388		suddenly
2519		*
2510		and finds you
1128		sleeping
0544		*
0133		<you>

VERSE 37 — Now what I say to you, I say to all of you, 'Be alert.'"

1326		what
1261		to you
0518		Now
0116		say
0124		I
1168		to all of you

MARK   CHAPTER 13

0592	ܗܘ	\<it\>
0116	ܐܡܪ	say
0124	ܐܢܐ	I
0603	ܗܘܘܢ	Be
1880	ܥܝܪܝܢ	alert

CHAPTER 14

VERSE 1 — Now after two days was the Passover of the unleavened bread, and the chief priests and scribes were seeking how they might arrest [him] with trickery and kill him.

0215	ܒܬܪ	after
0518	ܕܝܢ	Now
2709	ܬܪܝܢ	two
1036	ܝܘܡܝܢ	days
0603	ܗܘܐ	was
0603	ܗܘܐ	*
3433	ܦܨܚܐ	the Passover
1951	ܕܦܛܝܪܐ	of the unleavened bread
0296	ܘܒܥܝܢ	and seeking
0603	ܗܘܘ	were
2271	ܪܒܝ	the chief priests
1135	ܟܗܢܐ	*
1699	ܘܣܦܪܐ	and scribes
0061	ܐܝܟܢܐ	how
1513	ܒܢܟܠܐ	with trickery
0047	ܢܐܚܕܘܢ	they might arrest [him]
2179	ܘܢܩܛܠܘܢܝܗܝ	and kill him

VERSE 2 — And they were saying, "Not during the feast, so that a riot will not occur among the people."

0116	ܘܐܡܪܝܢ	And saying
0603	ܗܘܘ	they were
1262	ܠܐ	Not
1721	ܒܥܕܥܐܕܐ	during the feast
1314	ܕܠܐ	so that not
0603	ܢܗܘܐ	will occur
2454	ܫܓܘܫܝܐ	a riot
1818	ܒܥܡܐ	among the people

VERSE 3 — And while he was in Bethany in the house of Simon the leper while reclining, a woman came who had near her an alabaster box of perfume of spikenard, the best, very costly, and she opened it and poured it on the head of Jesus.

1128	ܘܟܕ	And while
0592	ܗܘ	he was
0069	ܐܝܬܘܗܝ	*
3116	ܒܒܝܬܥܢܝܐ	in Bethany
0243	ܒܒܝܬܗ	in the house
3521	ܕܫܡܥܘܢ	of Simon
0456	ܓܪܒܐ	the leper
1128	ܟܕ	while
1664	ܣܡܝܟ	reclining
0208	ܐܬܬ	came
0135	ܐܢܬܬܐ	a woman
0069	ܐܝܬ	who had
1804	ܥܠܝܗ	near her
2502	ܫܛܝܦܬܐ	an alabaster box
0291	ܕܒܣܡܐ	of perfume
1570	ܕܢܪܕܝܢ	of spikenard
2365	ܪܫܝܐ	the best
1596	ܣܓܝ	very
0543	ܕܡܝܐ	costly
2070	ܘܦܬܚܬܗ	and she opened it
2577	ܘܐܫܦܥܬܗ	and poured it
1804	ܥܠ	on
2362	ܪܝܫܗ	the head
3257	ܕܝܫܘܥ	of Jesus

VERSE 4 — And there were some of the disciples who were offended among themselves and said, "Why was [there] the waste of this perfume?

0069	ܐܝܬ	there were
0603	ܗܘܘ	*
0518	ܕܝܢ	And
0131	ܐܢܫܐ	some
1388	ܡܢ	of
1304	ܬܠܡܝܕܐ	the disciples
0219	ܐܬܒܐܫ	who were offended

MARK   CHAPTER 14

1261		<to them>
1547		among themselves
0116		and said
1394		Why
0603		was [there]
0006		the waste
0598		of this
0291		perfume

VERSE 5   For it was possible to be sold [for] more than three hundred denarii and be given to the poor." And they were angry with him.

2510		possible
0603		it was
0403		For
0632		to be sold
1100		[for] more
1388		than
2677		three hundred
0519		denarii
1030		and be given
1406		to the poor
0682		And angry
0603		they were
0217		with him

VERSE 6   But Jesus said, "Leave her alone. Why are you troubling her? She has done a proper act for me.

0592		<he>
0518		But
3257		Jesus
0116		said
2440		Leave her alone
1393		Why
0621		are troubling
0133		you
1261		her
1728		act
2583		a proper
1724		She has done
1288		for me

VERSE 7   For you always have the poor with you, and whenever you want, you are able to do for them what is proper, but I am not always with you.

1170		always
0403		For
1406		the poor
0069		you have
1261		*
1817		with you
0120		and whenever
2077		want
0133		you
2510		are able
0133		you
1724		to do
1261		for them
2583		what is proper
0124		I
0518		but
1262		not
1170		always
0069		am
1288		with you

VERSE 8   She did this of what she had and she has perfumed my body as for burial beforehand.

0593		of what
0069		she had
0603		*
1261		*
0598		this
1724		She did
2150		and beforehand
0060		as
2145		for burial
0286		she has perfumed
0389		my body

MARK   CHAPTER 14

VERSE 9 — And truly I say to you, wherever this, my gospel, is preached in all the world, also the thing that she has done will be spoken for her remembrance."

Code	Syriac	English
0110		And truly
0116		say
0124		I
1261		to you
1168		wherever
1108		*
1230		is preached
1593		my gospel
0598		this
1168		in all
1813		the world
0169		also
1326		the thing
1724		that she has done
0598		<this>
1362		will be spoken
0528		for her remembrance

VERSE 10 — And Judas Iscariot, one of the twelve, went to the chief priests to betray Jesus to them.

Code	Syriac	English
3228		Judas
0518		And
3370		Iscariot
0721		one
1388		of
2710		the twelve
0042		went
1288		to
2271		the chief priests
1135		*
0060		<as>
2530		to betray <him>
1261		to them
3257		Jesus

VERSE 11 — And they, when they heard [him], rejoiced and promised to give him money. And he was seeking for himself an opportunity to betray him.

Code	Syriac	English
0592		they
0518		And
1128		when
2547		they heard [him]
0726		rejoiced
1020		and promised
1209		money
1030		to give
1261		him
0296		And seeking
0603		he was
1261		for himself
1982		an opportunity
2530		to betray him

VERSE 12 — And on the first day of unleavened bread on which the Judeans slay the Passover, his disciples were saying to him, "Where do you want us to go to prepare for you to eat the Passover?"

Code	Syriac	English
1036		And on the day
2157		first
1951		of unleavened bread
0217		on which
0471		slay
3226		the Judeans
3433		the Passover
0116		were saying
1261		to him
1304		his disciples
1108		Where
2077		do want
0133		you
0042		us to go
0950		to prepare
1261		for you
0075		to eat
3433		the Passover

Vertical Interlinear

MARK   CHAPTER 14

VERSE	**13**		And he sent two of his disciples and said to them, "Go to the city and behold, a man who is carrying a vessel of water will meet you. Follow him.
2458			And he sent
2709			two
1388			of
1304			his disciples
0116			and said
1261			to them
0042			Go
0499			to the city
0580			and behold
1928			will meet
0217			you
0361			a man
2587			who is carrying
1320			a vessel
1351			of water
0042			Follow him
0215			*
VERSE	**14**		And wherever he enters, say to the lord of the house, 'Our Master said, Where is the guest house where I may eat the Passover with my disciples?'
1108			And wherever
1796			he enters
0116			say
1426			to the lord of
0243			the house
2271			Our Master
0116			said
1109			Where is
0243			the house
2599			guest
1108			where
0075			I may eat
1817			with
1304			my disciples
3433			the Passover

VERSE	**15**		And behold, he will show you a large upper room that is furnished and prepared. There make ready for us."
0580			And behold
0739			he will show
1261			you
1805			upper room
2271			a large
2461			that is furnished
0950			and prepared
2682			There
2699			make ready
1261			for us
VERSE	**16**		And his disciples went out and came to the city and found as he had said to them and they prepared the Passover.
1542			And went out
1304			his disciples
0208			and came
0499			to the city
2510			and found
0061			as
0116			he had said
1261			to them
0950			and they prepared
3433			the Passover
VERSE	**17**		And when evening came, he came with his twelve.
1128			And when
0603			came
2375			evening
0208			he came
1817			with
2710			his twelve
VERSE	**18**		And while they were reclining and eating, Jesus said, "Truly I say to you, one of you who eats with me will betray me."
1128			And while
1664			they were reclining
1308			and eating
0116			said

MARK   CHAPTER 14

3257		Jesus
0110		Truly
0116		say
0124		I
1261		to you
0721		one
1388		of you
0075		who eats
1817		with me
0592		\<he\>
2530		will betray me

VERSE 19   And they began to be grieved and were saying to him, one by one, "Is it I?"

0592		\<they\>
0518		And
2597		they began
1771		to be grieved
0116		and were saying
1261		to him
0721		one by one
0721		*
1316		\<?\>
0124		Is it I

VERSE 20   And he said to them, "[It is] one of the twelve who dips with me in the dish.

0592		\<he\>
0518		And
0116		he said
1261		to them
0721		[It is] one
1388		of
2710		the twelve
2080		who dips
1817		with me
1276		in the dish

VERSE 21   And the Son of Man will die as it is written about him. But woe to that man by whose hand the Son of Man is delivered up! It would be better for that man if he had not been born."

0323		And the Son
0131		of Man
0042		will die
0061		as
1247		it is written
1804		about him
0625		woe
0518		But
0361		to man
0593		that
0057		by whose hand
2530		is delivered up
0323		the Son
0131		of Man
2010		It would be better
0603		*
1261		\<for him\>
0361		for man
0593		that
0097		if
1262		not
1046		he had been born

VERSE 22   And while they were eating, Jesus took bread and blessed [it] and broke [it] and gave [it] to them. And he said to them, "Take, this is my body."

1128		And while
0592		they
1308		were eating
1532		took
3257		Jesus
1293		bread
0335		and blessed [it]
2234		and broke [it]
1030		and gave [it]
1261		to them
0116		And he said
1261		to them
1532		Take
0598		this
0069		is

MARK — CHAPTER 14

1929		my body
VERSE 23		And he took a cup and gave thanks and blessed [it] and gave [it] to them, and they all drank from it.
1532		And he took
1205		a cup
1020		and gave thanks
0335		and blessed [it]
1030		and gave [it]
1261		to them
2620		and they drank
1388		from it
1168		all
VERSE 24		And he said to them, "This is my blood of the new covenant that is shed on behalf of many.
0116		And he said
1261		to them
0599		This is
0539		my blood
0520		of the covenant
0735		new
0812		that on behalf of
1596		many
0201		is shed
VERSE 25		Truly I say to you, I will not drink again from the fruit of the vine until that day in which I will drink it anew in the kingdom of God."
0110		Truly
0116		say
0124		I
1261		to you
2650		again
1262		not
2620		I will drink
1388		from
1047		the fruit
0452		of the vine
1747		until
1036		day
0593		that
0217		in which
2620		I will drink it
0736		anew
1385		in the kingdom
0093		of God
VERSE 26		And they offered praise and went out to the Mount of Olives.
2428		And they offered praise
1542		and went out
0958		to the Mount of
0663		Olives
VERSE 27		And Jesus said to them, "All of you will be offended at me in this night, for it is written: I WILL STRIKE THE SHEPHERD AND HIS LAMBS WILL BE SCATTERED.
0116		And said
1261		to them
3257		Jesus
1168		All of you
1242		will be offended
0217		at me
0598		in this
1299		night
1247		it is written
0403		for
1341		I WILL STRIKE
2383		THE SHEPHERD
0229		AND WILL BE SCATTERED
0117		HIS LAMBS
VERSE 28		But when I have risen, I will go before you into Galilee."
0090		But
1313		when
2168		I have risen
2150		go before
0124		I will
1261		you
3153		into Galilee

MARK CHAPTER 14

VERSE 29 — Peter said to him, "Though all of them be offended, I [will] not [be]."

0116	ܐܡܪ	said
1261	ܠܗ	to him
3258	ܟܐܦܐ	Peter
0121	ܐܢ	Though
1168	ܟܠܗܘܢ	all of them
1242	ܢܬܟܫܠܘܢ	be offended
0090	ܐܠܐ	<but>
1262	ܠܐ	not [be]
0124	ܐܢܐ	I [will]

VERSE 30 — Jesus said to him, "Truly I say to you, today in this night, before the rooster will crow two times, you will deny me three [times]."

0116	ܐܡܪ	said
1261	ܠܗ	to him
3257	ܝܫܘܥ	Jesus
0110	ܐܡܝܢ	Truly
0116	ܐܡܪ	say
0124	ܐܢܐ	I
1261	ܠܟ	to you
0133	ܐܢܬ	<you>
1037	ܕܝܘܡܢܐ	today
1299	ܒܠܠܝܐ	in night
0598	ܗܢܐ	this
2154	ܩܕܡ	before
2239	ܢܩܪܐ	will crow
2713	ܬܪܢܓܠܐ	the rooster
2709	ܬܪܬܝܢ	two
0633	ܙܒܢܝܢ	times
2674	ܬܠܬ	three [times]
1215	ܬܟܦܘܪ	you will deny
0217	ܒܝ	me

VERSE 31 — And all the more he was saying, "If I must die with you, I will not deny you, my Lord." And all of them also spoke likewise.

0592	ܗܘ	<he>
0518	ܕܝܢ	And
1101	ܝܬܝܪܐܝܬ	all the more
0116	ܐܡܪ	saying
0603	ܗܘܐ	he was
0121	ܐܢ	If
0603	ܢܗܘܐ	I must
1261	ܠܝ	*
1334	ܠܡܡܬ	die
1817	ܥܡܟ	with you
1262	ܠܐ	not
1215	ܐܟܦܘܪܟ	I will deny
0217	ܒܟ	you
1426	ܡܪܝ	my Lord
0072	ܘܗܟܘܬ	And likewise
0169	ܐܦ	also
1168	ܟܠܗܘܢ	all of them
0116	ܐܡܪܘ	spoke

VERSE 32 — And they came to a place that was called Gethsemane, and he said to his disciples, "Sit here while I pray."

0208	ܘܐܬܘ	And they came
0494	ܠܕܘܟܬܐ	to a place
0066	ܐܝܕܐ	that
2239	ܕܡܬܩܪܝܐ	was called
3145	ܓܕܣܡܢ	Gethsemane
0116	ܘܐܡܪ	and he said
1304	ܠܬܠܡܝܕܘܗܝ	to his disciples
1093	ܬܒܘ	Sit
0600	ܗܪܟܐ	here
1744	ܥܕ	while
2106	ܐܨܠܐ	pray
0124	ܐܢܐ	I

VERSE 33 — And he took with him Peter and James and John and began to be sad and to grieve.

0477	ܘܕܒܪ	And he took
1817	ܥܡܗ	with him
3258	ܠܟܐܦܐ	Peter
3255	ܘܠܝܥܩܘܒ	and James
3233	ܘܠܝܘܚܢܢ	and John
2597	ܘܫܪܝ	and began
1192	ܠܡܬܟܡܪܘ	to be sad

MARK — CHAPTER 14

#	Syriac	English
1771		and to grieve

VERSE 34 — And he said to them, "It is grievous to my soul unto death. Remain here and be watchful."

#	Syriac	English
0116		And he said
1261		to them
1221		It is grievous
0592		*
1261		<to it>
1547		to my soul
1747		unto
1335		death
2165		Remain
0600		here
1880		and be watchful

VERSE 35 — And he went on a little and fell on the ground and was praying that if it was possible, [this] hour might pass from him.

#	Syriac	English
2244		And he went on
2203		a little
1538		and fell
1804		on
0199		the ground
2106		and praying
0603		was
0121		that if
2510		it was possible
1733		might pass
1388		from him
2573		[this] hour

VERSE 36 — And he said, "Father, my Father, you can [do] everything. Make this cup pass from me. Yet not my own will, but yours."

#	Syriac	English
0116		and he said
0002		Father
0002		my Father
1168		everything
1326		*
2510		can [do]
0133		you
1733		Make pass
1388		from me
1205		cup
0598		this
0090		Yet
1262		not
2079		my will
0517		own
0090		but
0517		yours

VERSE 37 — And he came [and] found them sleeping. And he said to Peter, "Simon, are you sleeping? Are you not able to be watchful for one hour?

#	Syriac	English
0208		And he came
2510		[and] found
0592		them
1128		sleeping
0544		*
0116		And he said
3258		to Peter
3521		Simon
0544		are you sleeping
1261		*
1262		not
2510		Are you able
0721		for one
2573		hour
1880		to be watchful

VERSE 38 — Be watchful and pray, so that you might not enter into temptation. The spirit is willing and ready, but the body is weak."

#	Syriac	English
1880		Be watchful
2106		and pray
1262		so that not
1796		you might enter
1528		into temptation
2323		The spirit
2077		is willing
0950		and ready
0090		but
1929		the body

MARK   CHAPTER 14

1226		is weak
VERSE 39		And he went again [and] prayed and he said the same thing.
0042		And he went
2650		again
2106		[and] prayed
0592		and the same
1364		thing
0116		he said
VERSE 40		And he returned [and] came [and] again found them sleeping, because their eyes were heavy, and they did not know what to say to him.
0616		And he returned
0208		[and] came
2650		again
2510		[and] found
0592		them
1128		sleeping
0544		*
1347		because
1794		their eyes
1079		were heavy
0603		*
1262		and not
1023		know
0603		they did
1393		what
0116		to say
1261		to him
VERSE 41		And he came a third time and said to them, "Sleep now, and rest. The end has arrived and the hour has come and behold, the Son of Man is delivered into the hands of sinners.
0208		And he came
2674		a third
0633		time
0116		and said
1261		to them
0544		Sleep
1357		now
1483		and rest
1346		has arrived
0054		The end
0208		and has come
2573		the hour
0580		and behold
2530		is delivered
0323		the Son
0131		of Man
0057		into the hands
0772		of sinners
VERSE 42		Rise up, let us go. Behold, he who has delivered me draws near."
2168		Rise up
0042		let us go
0580		Behold
2244		draws near
0593		he
2530		who has delivered
1261		me
VERSE 43		And while he was speaking, Judas Iscariot, one of the twelve, and many people with swords and rods, came from being with the chief priests and scribes and elders.
1744		And while
0592		he
1362		was speaking
0208		came
3228		Judas
3370		Iscariot
0721		one
1388		of
2710		the twelve
1818		and people
1596		many
1817		with
1693		swords
0778		and rods
1388		from
1288		being with

340

MARK — CHAPTER 14

Vertical Interlinear

Code	Syriac	English
2271		the chief priests
1135		*
1699		and scribes
2263		and elders

VERSE 44 — And the traitor who betrayed [him] had given them a sign and had said, "Whomever I kiss is he. Arrest him securely and take him away."

Code	Syriac	English
1030		And had given
1261		them
0206		a sign
2531		the traitor
0593		<who>
2530		who betrayed [him]
0116		and had said
0593		Whomever
1573		kiss
0124		I
0592		is he
0047		Arrest him
0646		securely
1015		and take him away

VERSE 45 — And immediately he drew near and said to him, "My Master, my Master," and he kissed him.

Code	Syriac	English
0323		And immediately
2573		*
2244		he drew near
0116		and said
1261		to him
2275		My Master
2275		my Master
1573		and he kissed him

VERSE 46 — And they placed [their] hands on him and arrested him.

Code	Syriac	English
0592		<they>
0518		And
2372		they placed
1804		on him
0057		[their] hands
0047		and arrested him

VERSE 47 — And one of those who were standing [there] drew a sword and struck the servant of the high priest and took off his ear.

Code	Syriac	English
0721		one
0518		And
1388		of
0593		those
2168		who were standing [there]
2542		drew
1645		a sword
1341		and struck
1727		the servant
2271		of the high priest
1135		*
2587		and took off
0021		his ear

VERSE 48 — And Jesus answered and said to them, "Do you come out as against a robber with swords and rods to arrest me?

Code	Syriac	English
0592		<he>
0518		And
3257		Jesus
1838		answered
0116		and said
1261		to them
0060		as
1804		against
0402		a robber
1542		Do you come out
1645		with swords
0778		and rods
0047		to arrest me

VERSE 49 — Every day I was with you while I was teaching in the temple and you did not arrest me. But this has occurred that the scriptures would be fulfilled."

Code	Syriac	English
1172		Every day
1288		with you
0603		I was
1128		while
1053		I was teaching

MARK CHAPTER 14

0124	ܐܢܐ	*
0607	ܒܗܝܟܠܐ	in the temple
1262	ܘܠܐ	and not
0047	ܐܚܕܬܘܢܢܝ	you did arrest me
0090	ܐܠܐ	But
2530	ܕܢܫܠܡܘܢ	that would be fulfilled
1248	ܟܬܒܐ	the scriptures
0603	ܗܘܐ	has occurred
0598	ܗܢܐ	this

VERSE 50 Then his disciples left him and fled.

0594	ܗܝܕܝܢ	Then
2440	ܫܒܩܘܗܝ	left him
1304	ܬܠܡܝܕܘܗܝ	his disciples
1904	ܘܥܪܩܘ	and fled

VERSE 51 And a certain young man followed him, and a linen cloth was wrapped around [his] naked [body], and they grabbed him.

1811	ܘܥܠܝܡܐ	And a young man
0721	ܚܕ	certain
0208	ܐܬܐ	followed him
0603	ܗܘܐ	*
0215	ܒܬܪܗ	*
1790	ܘܥܛܝܦ	and was wrapped around
1605	ܣܕܘܢܐ	a linen cloth
1889	ܥܪܛܠ	[his] naked [body]
0047	ܘܐܚܕܘܗܝ	and they grabbed him

VERSE 52 And he left the linen cloth and fled naked.

0592	ܗܘ	<he>
0518	ܕܝܢ	And
2440	ܫܒܩ	he left
1605	ܣܕܘܢܐ	the linen cloth
1904	ܘܥܪܩ	and fled
1889	ܥܪܛܠ	naked

VERSE 53 And they took Jesus to Caiaphas, the high priest, and all the chief priests and scribes and elders were gathered with him.

1015	ܘܐܘܒܠܘܗܝ	And they took
3257	ܠܝܫܘܥ	Jesus
1288	ܠܘܬ	to
3473	ܩܝܦܐ	Caiaphas
2271	ܪܒ	the high priest
1135	ܟܗܢܐ	*
1198	ܘܐܬܟܢܫܘ	and were gathered
1288	ܠܘܬܗ	with him
1168	ܟܠܗܘܢ	all
2271	ܪܒܝ	the chief priests
1135	ܟܗܢܐ	*
1699	ܘܣܦܪܐ	and scribes
2263	ܘܩܫܝܫܐ	and elders

VERSE 54 And Simon was following him from a distance as far as the inside of the courtyard of the high priest. And he was sitting with the servants and was warming [himself] near the fire.

3521	ܫܡܥܘܢ	Simon
0518	ܕܝܢ	And
1388	ܡܢ	from
2354	ܪܘܚܩܐ	a distance
0208	ܐܬܐ	was following him
0603	ܗܘܐ	*
0215	ܒܬܪܗ	*
1747	ܠܓܘ	as far as
0379	ܠܓܘ	the inside
0505	ܕܪܬܐ	of the courtyard
2271	ܪܒ	of the high priest
1135	ܟܗܢܐ	*
1093	ܘܝܬܒ	And sitting
0603	ܗܘܐ	he was
1817	ܥܡ	with
2555	ܡܫܡܫܢܐ	the servants
2492	ܘܫܚܢ	and was warming [himself]
2135	ܠܘܩܒܠ	near
1494	ܢܘܪܐ	the fire

VERSE 55 And the chief priests and all their assembly were seeking testimony against Jesus, so that they might kill him, but they did not find [any].

2271	ܪܒܝ	the chief priests
1135	ܟܗܢܐ	*

MARK　　　　　CHAPTER 14

0518		And		2597		I will destroy
1168		and all		0124		*
1201		their assembly		0607		temple
0296		seeking		0598		this
0603		were		1724		that was made
1804		against		0057		with hands
3257		Jesus		2674		and after three
1610		testimony		1036		days
1334		so that they might kill him		0281		I will build
1262		but		0124		*
2510		they did not find [any]		0053		another

VERSE 56 For although many were testifying against him, their testimony was not agreeing.

1128		although
1596		many
0403		For
1608		testifying
0603		were
1804		against him
1262		not
2461		agreeing
0603		was
1610		their testimony

1262		that not
1724		is made
0057		with hands

VERSE 59 But even so, their testimony was not agreeing.

0170		even not
0518		But
0597		so
2461		agreeing
0603		was
1610		their testimony

VERSE 60 And the high priest stood up in the middle [of them] and questioned Jesus and said, "Do you not answer the accusation? Why are they testifying these [things] against you?"

VERSE 57 And some false witnesses stood up against him and said,

0131		some
0518		And
2168		stood up
1804		against him
1609		witnesses
2482		false
0116		and said

VERSE 58 "We heard him when he said, 'I will destroy this temple that was made with hands, and after three days I will build another that is not made with hands.'"

0124		We
2547		heard him
0116		when he said
0124		<I>

2168		And stood up
2271		the high priest
1135		*
1416		in the middle [of them]
2420		and questioned
3257		Jesus
0116		and said
1262		not
1984		Do answer
0133		you
2068		the accusation
1393		Why
1608		are they testifying
1804		against you

343

MARK   CHAPTER 14

0598	ܗܠܝܢ	these [things]
VERSE 61		But he was silent and did not answer him anything. And again the high priest questioned him and said, "Are you the Messiah, the Son of the Blessed One?"
0592	ܗܘ	\<he\>
0518	ܕܝܢ	But
2623	ܫܬܝܩ	silent
0603	ܗܘܐ	he was
1326	ܘܡܕܡ	and anything
1262	ܠܐ	not
1838	ܦܢܝܗ	did answer him
2650	ܘܬܘܒ	And again
2420	ܫܐܠܗ	questioned him
2271	ܪܒ	the high priest
1135	ܟܗܢܐ	*
0116	ܘܐܡܪ	and said
0133	ܐܢܬ	Are you
0592	ܗܘ	\<he\>
1446	ܡܫܝܚܐ	the Messiah
0323	ܒܪܗ	the Son
0335	ܕܡܒܪܟܐ	of the Blessed One
VERSE 62		And Jesus said to him, "I am. And you will see THE SON OF MAN WHEN HE SITS ON THE RIGHT [HAND] OF POWER and COMES ON THE CLOUDS OF HEAVEN."
0592	ܗܘ	\<he\>
0518	ܕܝܢ	And
3257	ܝܫܘܥ	Jesus
0116	ܐܡܪ	said
1261	ܠܗ	to him
0124	ܐܢܐ	I am
0124	ܐܢܐ	*
0758	ܘܬܚܙܘܢ	And you will see
0323	ܠܒܪܗ	THE SON
0131	ܕܐܢܫܐ	OF MAN
1093	ܕܝܬܒ	WHEN HE SITS
1388	ܡܢ	ON
1061	ܝܡܝܢܐ	THE RIGHT [HAND]
0786	ܕܚܝܠܐ	OF POWER
0208	ܘܐܬܐ	and COMES
1804	ܥܠ	ON
1844	ܥܢܢܝ	THE CLOUDS OF
2543	ܫܡܝܐ	HEAVEN
VERSE 63		And the high priest tore his robe and said, "Why now are we seeking witnesses?
2271	ܪܒ	the high priest
1135	ܟܗܢܐ	*
0518	ܕܝܢ	And
2129	ܨܪܐ	tore
1256	ܟܘܬܝܢܗ	his robe
0116	ܘܐܡܪ	and said
1393	ܡܢܐ	Why
1357	ܡܟܝܠ	now
0296	ܒܥܝܢܢ	are we seeking
1261	ܠܢ	*
1609	ܣܗܕܐ	witnesses
VERSE 64		Behold, from his mouth you have heard blasphemy. What do you think?" And all of them judged that he was deserving of death.
0580	ܗܐ	Behold
1388	ܡܢ	from
1936	ܦܘܡܗ	his mouth
2547	ܫܡܥܬܘܢ	you have heard
0371	ܓܘܕܦܐ	blasphemy
1393	ܡܢܐ	What do you think
0758	ܡܬܚܙܐ	*
1261	ܠܟܘܢ	*
0592	ܗܢܘܢ	\<they\>
0518	ܕܝܢ	And
1168	ܟܠܗܘܢ	all of them
0496	ܕܢܘ	judged
0745	ܕܚܝܒ	that he was deserving of
0592	ܗܘ	\<it\>
1335	ܡܘܬܐ	death

MARK   CHAPTER 14

VERSE 65 — And some began spitting in his face. And they covered his face and were striking him and saying, "Prophesy!" And the guards were striking him on his cheeks.

2597	And began
0131	some
2400	spitting
2041	in his face
0869	And they covered
0173	his face
2230	and were striking
1261	him
0116	and saying
1456	Prophesy
0513	And the guards
1341	striking
0603	were
1261	him
1804	on
1961	his cheeks

VERSE 66 — And while Simon was below in the courtyard, a certain maiden of the high priest came.

1128	And while
3521	Simon
2660	was below
0505	in the courtyard
0208	came
1812	a maiden
0721	certain
2271	of the high priest
1135	*

VERSE 67 — She saw him while he was warming [himself] and she looked at him and said to him, "And you also were with Jesus the Nazarene."

0758	She saw him
2492	while he was warming [himself]
0756	and she looked
0217	at him
0116	and said
1261	to him
0169	And also
0133	<you>
1817	with
3257	Jesus
0603	you were
3355	the Nazarene

VERSE 68 — But he denied [it] and said, "I do not know what you are saying." And he went outside to the porch and the rooster crowed.

0592	<he>
0518	But
1215	he denied [it]
0116	and said
1262	not
1023	I do know
0124	*
1393	what
0116	are saying
0133	you
1542	And he went
0322	outside
1689	to the porch
2239	and crowed
2713	the rooster

VERSE 69 — And again the maiden saw him and she began to tell those who were standing [there], "This one also is one of them."

0758	And saw him
2650	again
1812	the maiden
0593	<that>
2597	and she began
0116	to tell
0066	those
2168	who were standing [there]
0169	also
0598	This one
1388	one of them
0592	is

345

MARK   CHAPTER 14

VERSE 70   But again he denied [it]. And after a little [time] again those who were standing [there] said to Peter, "Truly you are one of them, for you are also a Galilean and your speech is like [theirs]."

0592		<he>
0518		But
2650		again
1215		he denied [it]
0215		And after
2203		a little [time]
2650		again
0593		those
2168		who were standing [there]
0116		said
3258		to Peter
2594		Truly
1388		one of them
0133		you are
0169		also
0403		for
3154		a Galilean
0133		you are
1365		and your speech
0540		is like [theirs]

VERSE 71   And he began to curse and swore, "I do not know this man of whom you speak!"

0592		<he>
0518		And
2597		he began
0603		*
0897		to curse
1059		and swore
1262		not
1023		do know
0124		I
0361		man
0598		this
0116		of whom speak
0133		you

VERSE 72   And immediately, the rooster crowed the second time, and Simon remembered the saying of Jesus, who had said to him, "Before the rooster crows two times, you will deny me three [times]," and he began to cry.

0217		And immediately
2573		*
2239		crowed
2713		the rooster
2709		the second
0633		time
0527		and remembered
3521		Simon
1364		the saying
3257		of Jesus
0116		who had said
0603		*
1261		to him
2154		Before
2239		crows
2713		the rooster
2709		two
0633		times
2674		three [times]
1215		you will deny
0217		me
2597		and he began
0267		to cry

CHAPTER 15

VERSE 1   And immediately in the morning the chief priests took counsel with the elders and with the scribes and with the entire assembly. And they bound Jesus and led him away. And they delivered him to Pilate.

0725		And immediately
2124		in the morning
1724		took
1384		counsel
2271		the chief priests
1135		*
1817		with

MARK CHAPTER 15

2263		the elders		3417		Pilate
1817		and with		2650		again
1699		the scribes		2420		asked him
1817		and with		0116		and said
1168		entire		1261		to him
1200		the assembly		1262		not
0160		And they bound		1984		Will answer
3257		Jesus		0133		you
1015		and led him away		2068		the accusation
2530		And they delivered him		0758		See
3417		to Pilate		1188		how many

VERSE 2 — And Pilate asked him, "Are you the king of the Judeans?" And he answered and said to him, "You have said [it]."

1608		are testifying
1804		against you

VERSE 5 — But Jesus did not give any answer, so that Pilate was amazed.

2420		And asked him
3417		Pilate
0133		Are you
0592		<him>
1383		the king
3226		of the Judeans
0592		<he>
0518		And
1838		he answered
0116		and said
1261		to him
0133		<you>
0116		You have said [it]

0592		<he>
0518		But
3257		Jesus
1326		any
2068		answer
1262		not
1030		did give
0061		so that
0549		was amazed
3417		Pilate

VERSE 3 — And the chief priests were accusing him of many [things].

0075		And were accusing him
0603		*
2257		*
2271		the chief priests
1135		*
1596		of many [things]

VERSE 6 — Now he was accustomed during every feast to release one prisoner to them, whomever they requested.

1761		he was accustomed
0603		*
0518		Now
1168		during every
1720		feast
2597		to release
1261		to them
0163		prisoner
0721		one
0066		whomever
2420		they requested

VERSE 4 — And Pilate again asked him and said to him, "Will you not answer the accusation? See how many are testifying against you!"

0592		<he>
0518		And

MARK CHAPTER 15

VERSE 7 — And there was one who was called Barabbas who was a prisoner with the ones who had caused an insurrection, those who had committed murder in the insurrection.

0069	ܐܝܬ ܗܘܐ	And there was
0603	ܗܘܐ	*
0721	ܚܕ	one
2239	ܕܡܬܩܪܐ	who was called
3128	ܒܪ ܐܒܐ	Barabbas
0160	ܐܣܝܪܐ	who a prisoner
0603	ܗܘܐ	was
1817	ܥܡ	with
1724	ܥܒܕܝ	the ones who had caused
0147	ܐܣܛܣܝܣ	an insurrection
0593	ܗܢܘܢ	those
2181	ܕܩܛܠܐ	who murder
0147	ܒܐܣܛܣܝܣ	in the insurrection
1724	ܥܒܕܘ	had committed

VERSE 8 — And the people cried out and began to request he do [this] for them as he was accustomed.

2227	ܘܩܥܐ	And cried out
1818	ܥܡܐ	the people
2597	ܘܫܪܝܘ	and began
2420	ܠܡܫܐܠ	to request
0060	ܐܝܟ	as
1761	ܕܡܥܕ	he was accustomed
0603	ܗܘܐ	*
1724	ܕܢܥܒܕ	he do [this]
1261	ܠܗܘܢ	for them

VERSE 9 — But Pilate answered and said, "Do you want me to release to you the king of the Judeans?"

0592	ܗܘ	<he>
0518	ܕܝܢ	But
3417	ܦܝܠܛܘܣ	Pilate
1838	ܥܢܐ	answered
0116	ܘܐܡܪ	and said
2077	ܨܒܝܢ	Do want
0133	ܐܢܬܘܢ	you
2597	ܐܫܪܐ	me to release
1261	ܠܟܘܢ	to you
1383	ܡܠܟܐ	the king
3226	ܕܝܗܘܕܝܐ	of the Judeans

VERSE 10 — (For Pilate knew that the chief priests had delivered him up out of envy.)

1023	ܝܕܥ	knew
0603	ܗܘܐ	*
0403	ܓܝܪ	For
3417	ܦܝܠܛܘܣ	Pilate
1388	ܕܡܢ	that out of
0860	ܚܣܡܐ	envy
2530	ܐܫܠܡܘܗܝ	had delivered him up
2271	ܪܒܝ	the chief priests
1135	ܟܗܢܐ	*

VERSE 11 — And the chief priests all the more exhorted the crowds [to ask] that he should release Barabbas to them.

2271	ܪܒܝ	the chief priests
1135	ܟܗܢܐ	*
0518	ܕܝܢ	And
1101	ܝܬܝܪܐܝܬ	all the more
0871	ܚܦܛܘ	exhorted
1201	ܠܟܢܫܐ	the crowds [to ask]
3128	ܕܠܒܪ ܐܒܐ	that Barabbas
2597	ܢܫܪܐ	he should release
1261	ܠܗܘܢ	to them

VERSE 12 — And Pilate said to them, "What then do you want me to do to this one whom you call king of the Judeans?"

0592	ܗܘ	<he>
0518	ܕܝܢ	And
3417	ܦܝܠܛܘܣ	Pilate
0116	ܐܡܪ	said
1261	ܠܗܘܢ	to them
1393	ܡܢܐ	What
0596	ܗܟܝܠ	then
2077	ܨܒܝܢ	do want
0133	ܐܢܬܘܢ	you
1724	ܐܥܒܕ	me to do
0598	ܠܗܢܐ	to this one
2239	ܕܩܪܝܢ	whom you call

MARK   CHAPTER 15

0133	ܐܬܐ	*
1383	ܡܠܟܐ	king
3226	ܕܝܗܘܕܝܐ	of the Judeans

VERSE 13 — And again they cried out, "Crucify him!"

0592	ܗܢܘܢ	<they>
0518	ܕܝܢ	And
2650	ܬܘܒ	again
2227	ܩܥܘ	they cried out
0688	ܙܩܘܦܝܗܝ	Crucify him

VERSE 14 — And Pilate said to them, "What evil has he done?" And they were crying out all the more, "Crucify him!"

0592	ܗܘ	<he>
0518	ܕܝܢ	And
3417	ܦܝܠܛܘܣ	Pilate
0116	ܐܡܪ	said
1261	ܠܗܘܢ	to them
1393	ܡܢܐ	What
0403	ܓܝܪ	<for>
0220	ܕܒܝܫ	evil
1724	ܥܒܕ	has he done
0592	ܘܗܢܘܢ	And <they>
1101	ܝܬܝܪܐܝܬ	all the more
2227	ܩܥܝܢ	crying out
0603	ܗܘܘ	they were
0688	ܙܩܘܦܝܗܝ	Crucify him

VERSE 15 — And Pilate wanted to do the will of the crowds and he released Barabbas to them and he delivered Jesus to them, after he had scourged [him], to be crucified.

3417	ܦܝܠܛܘܣ	Pilate
0518	ܕܝܢ	And
2077	ܨܒܐ	wanted
1724	ܕܢܥܒܕ	to do
2079	ܨܒܝܢܐ	the will
1201	ܕܟܢܫܐ	of the crowds
2597	ܘܫܪܐ	and he released
1261	ܠܗܘܢ	to them
3128	ܠܒܪܐܒܐ	Barabbas
2530	ܘܐܫܠܡ	and he delivered
1261	ܠܗܘܢ	to them
3257	ܠܝܫܘܥ	Jesus
1128	ܟܕ	after
1461	ܡܢܓܕ	he had scourged [him]
0688	ܕܢܙܕܩܦ	to be crucified

VERSE 16 — And the soldiers led him away inside the hall that was the Praetorium and they called the whole company of soldiers.

0150	ܐܣܛܪܛܝܘܛܐ	the soldiers
0518	ܕܝܢ	And
1015	ܐܘܒܠܘܗܝ	led him away
0379	ܠܓܘ	inside
0505	ܕܪܬܐ	the hall
0069	ܐܝܬܝܗ	that was
2027	ܦܪܛܘܪܝܢ	the Praetorium
2239	ܘܩܪܘ	and they called
1168	ܠܟܠܗ	the whole
0157	ܐܣܦܝܪ	company of soldiers

VERSE 17 — And they put purple clothes on him and wove [and] placed on him a crown of thorns.

1272	ܘܐܠܒܫܘܗܝ	And they put on him
0186	ܐܪܓܘܢܐ	purple clothes
0367	ܘܓܕܠܘ	and wove
1625	ܣܡܘ	[and] placed
1261	ܠܗ	on him
1178	ܟܠܝܠܐ	a crown
1139	ܕܟܘܒܐ	of thorns

VERSE 18 — And they began to salute him [with], "Hail, king of the Judeans."

2597	ܘܫܪܝܘ	And they began
2420	ܠܡܫܐܠ	to salute him [with]
2535	ܒܫܠܡܗ	*
2535	ܫܠܡ	Hail
1383	ܡܠܟܐ	king
3226	ܕܝܗܘܕܝܐ	of the Judeans

VERSE 19 — And they were striking him on his head with a reed and were spitting in his face and were kneeling on their knees and bowing to him.

1341	ܘܡܚܝܢ	And striking
0603	ܗܘܘ	they were

MARK CHAPTER 15

1261		him
1804		on
2362		his head
2224		with a reed
2400		and spitting
0603		were
0173		in his face
0335		and kneeling
0603		were
1804		on
0336		their knees
1599		and bowing
1261		to him

VERSE 20 And after they had mocked him, they stripped off the purple clothes and put on his own garments and took him out to crucify him.

1128		And after
0246		they had mocked
0217		him
2521		they stripped off
0186		the purple clothes
1272		and put on <him>
1320		his own garments
1542		and took him out
0688		to crucify him

VERSE 21 And they compelled one who was passing by, Simon, a Cyrenian, who had come from the country, the father of Alexander and of Rufus, to carry his cross.

2496		And they compelled
0721		one
1733		who was passing by
0603		*
3521		Simon
3465		a Cyrenian
0208		who had come
0603		*
1388		from
2251		the country
0002		the father
3053		of Alexander
3498		and of Rufus
2587		to carry
0689		his cross

VERSE 22 And they brought him to Golgotha, the place that is interpreted, The Skull.

0208		And they brought him
3143		to Golgotha
0494		the place
2061		that is interpreted
2259		The Skull

VERSE 23 And they gave him wine in which was mixed myrrh to drink, but he did not take [it].

1030		And they gave
1261		him
2620		to drink
0831		wine
0802		was mixed
0217		in which
1331		myrrh
0592		<he>
0518		but
1262		not
1532		he did take [it]

VERSE 24 And after they had crucified him, they divided his garments and cast lots for them, what each should take.

1128		And after
0688		they had crucified him
1968		they divided
1320		his garments
2372		and cast
1804		for them
1991		lots
1390		what
1393		each
1532		should take

MARK — CHAPTER 15

VERSE 25
And it was the third hour when they crucified him.

0069		it was
0603		*
0518		And
2573		the hour
2674		third
1128		when
0688		they crucified him

VERSE 26
And the cause of his death was written in the inscription, "This is the king of the Judeans."

1247		And was written
0603		*
1801		the cause
1335		of his death
1248		in the inscription
0598		This
0592		is
1383		the king
3226		of the Judeans

VERSE 27
And they crucified with him two robbers, one on his right and one on his left.

0688		And they crucified
1817		with him
2709		two
1306		robbers
0721		one
1388		on
1061		his right
0721		and one
1388		on
1668		his left

VERSE 28
And the scripture was fulfilled that said: HE WAS COUNTED WITH THE WICKED.

2530		And was fulfilled
1248		the scripture
0116		that said
1817		WITH
1767		THE WICKED
0914		HE WAS COUNTED

VERSE 29
And also those who were passing by were reviling him and shaking their heads and saying, "Oh indeed! [He said] he will destroy the temple and build it after three days.

0169		also
0066		those
0518		And
1733		who passing by
0603		were
0370		reviling
0603		were
1804		him
1481		and shaking
2362		their heads
0116		and saying
0033		Oh indeed
2597		[He said] he will destroy
0607		the temple
0281		and build
1261		it
2674		after three
1036		days

VERSE 30
Save yourself and come down from the cross."

2002		Save
1547		yourself
1499		and come down
1388		from
0689		the cross

VERSE 31
And likewise also the chief priests and the scribes were laughing with each other and saying, "Others he saved. Himself he is not able to save.

0597		And likewise
0169		also
2271		the chief priests
1135		*
0400		laughing
0603		were
0721		with each other

MARK — CHAPTER 15

Vertical Interlinear

Code	Aramaic	English
1817		*
0721		*
1699		and the scribes
0116		and saying
0053		Others
0780		he saved
1547		Himself
1262		not
2510		he is able
0780		to save

VERSE 32 — Let the Messiah, the King of Israel, come down now from the cross that we might see and believe in him." And those also who were crucified with him were reviling him.

Code	Aramaic	English
1446		the Messiah
1383		the King
3035		of Israel
1499		Let come down
0602		now
1388		from
0689		the cross
0758		that we might see
0109		and believe
0217		in him
0169		also
0593		those
0518		And
0688		who were crucified
0603		*
1817		with him
0855		reviling
0603		were
1261		him

VERSE 33 — And when the sixth hour came, there was darkness over all the land until the ninth hour.

Code	Aramaic	English
1128		And when
0603		came
2615		sixth
2573		the hour
0603		there was
0923		darkness
1804		over
1168		all
0199		the land
1747		until
2573		the hour
2723		ninth

VERSE 34 — And in the ninth hour Jesus cried out with a loud voice and said, "Eil, Eil, lmana shavaqtani," which is [interpreted], "MY GOD, MY GOD, WHY HAVE YOU LEFT ME?"

Code	Aramaic	English
2723		And in the ninth
2573		hour
2227		cried out
3257		Jesus
2204		with a voice
2336		loud
0116		and said
3031		Eil
3031		Eil
1394		Imana
2440		shavaqtani
0069		which is [interpreted]
0093		MY GOD
0093		MY GOD
1394		WHY
2440		HAVE YOU LEFT ME

VERSE 35 — And some of those who were standing [there] who heard were saying, "He calls to Elijah."

Code	Aramaic	English
0131		And some
2547		who heard
1388		of Israel
0593		those
2168		who were standing [there]
0116		saying
0603		were
3047		to Elijah
2239		He calls

MARK CHAPTER 15

VERSE 36
And one ran and filled a sponge [with] vinegar and fastened [it] on a reed to give him to drink. And they said, "Leave [him]! Let us see if Elijah will come to take him down."

2312	ܪܗܛ	ran
0518	ܕܝܢ	And
0721	ܚܕ	one
1366	ܘܡܠܐ	and filled
0155	ܐܣܦܘܓܐ	a sponge
0794	ܚܠܐ	[with] vinegar
0160	ܘܩܛܪ	and fastened [it]
2224	ܒܩܢܝܐ	on a reed
2585	ܕܢܫܩܝܘܗܝ	to give him to drink
0116	ܘܐܡܪܝܢ	And they said
2440	ܫܒܘܩܘ	Leave [him]
0758	ܢܚܙܐ	Let us see
0121	ܐܢ	if
0208	ܐܬܐ	will come
3047	ܐܠܝܐ	Elijah
1499	ܡܚܬ	to take down
1261	ܠܗ	him

VERSE 37
And Jesus cried out with a loud voice and died.

0592	ܗܘ	<he>
0518	ܕܝܢ	And
3257	ܝܫܘܥ	Jesus
2227	ܩܥܐ	cried out
2204	ܒܩܠܐ	with a voice
2336	ܪܡܐ	loud
2530	ܘܡܝܬ	and died

VERSE 38
And the veil of the temple was torn into two [pieces], from the top to the bottom.

0173	ܘܐܦܝ	And the veil
2718	ܬܪܥܐ	*
0607	ܕܗܝܟܠܐ	of the temple
2129	ܐܨܛܪܝ	was torn
2709	ܠܬܪܬܝܢ	into two [pieces]
1388	ܡܢ	from
1803	ܠܥܠ	the top
1747	ܠܬܚܬ	to

2660	ܬܚܬ	the bottom

VERSE 39
Now when the centurion who was standing near him saw that he cried out so and died, he said, "Truly this man was the Son of God."

1128	ܟܕ	when
0758	ܚܙܐ	saw
0518	ܕܝܢ	Now
2223	ܩܢܛܪܘܢܐ	the centurion
0593	ܗܘ	<he>
2168	ܕܩܐܡ	who standing
0603	ܗܘܐ	was
1288	ܠܘܬܗ	near him
0597	ܕܗܟܢܐ	that so
2227	ܩܥܐ	he cried out
2530	ܘܡܝܬ	and died
0116	ܐܡܪ	he said
2594	ܫܪܝܪܐܝܬ	Truly
0598	ܗܢܐ	this
0361	ܓܒܪܐ	man
0323	ܒܪܗ	the Son
0603	ܗܘܐ	was
0093	ܕܐܠܗܐ	of God

VERSE 40
And there were also women who were watching from afar, Mary Magdalene and Mary the mother of James the less and of Joses and Salome,

0069	ܐܝܬ	there were
0603	ܗܘܝ	*
0518	ܕܝܢ	And
0169	ܐܦ	also
0135	ܢܫܐ	women
1388	ܡܢ	from
2354	ܪܘܚܩܐ	afar
0758	ܕܚܙܝܢ	who watching
0603	ܗܘܝ	were
3325	ܡܪܝܡ	Mary
3297	ܡܓܕܠܝܬܐ	Magdalene
3325	ܘܡܪܝܡ	and Mary
0106	ܐܡܗ	the mother
3255	ܕܝܥܩܘܒ	of James

MARK   CHAPTER 15

#	Syriac	English
0686		the less
3244		and of Joses
3515		and Salome

VERSE 41 — those who, when he was in Galilee, were following him and ministering to him, and many others who had gone up with him to Jerusalem.

#	Syriac	English
0593		those
1128		who when
0592		he was
3153		in Galilee
1566		following
0603		were
1261		him
2554		and ministering
1261		to him
0053		and others
1596		many
1658		who had gone up
0603		*
1817		with him
3022		to Jerusalem

VERSE 42 — And when the evening of the preparation had come, that was before the Sabbath,

#	Syriac	English
1128		And when
0603		had come
2375		the evening
1886		of the preparation
0069		that was
2154		before
2445		the Sabbath

VERSE 43 — Joseph who was from Arimathaea, an honorable counselor who also was waiting for the kingdom of God, came and was bold and approached Pilate and requested the body of Jesus.

#	Syriac	English
0208		came
3246		Joseph
0593		<who>
1388		who was from
3502		Arimathaea
1081		an honorable
0237		counselor
0066		who
0169		also
0592		<he>
1646		waiting
0603		was
1385		for the kingdom
0093		of God
1435		and was bold
1796		and approached
1288		*
3417		Pilate
2420		and requested
1929		the body
3257		of Jesus

VERSE 44 — And Pilate marveled that he had already died. And he called the centurion and asked him if he had already died.

#	Syriac	English
3417		Pilate
0518		And
2679		marveled
0121		that already
1388		*
1129		*
1334		he had died
2239		And he called
2223		the centurion
2420		and asked him
0121		if
1388		already
2154		*
1750		*
1334		he had died

VERSE 45 — And when he learned [it], he gave his body to Joseph.

#	Syriac	English
1128		And when
1053		he learned [it]
1030		he gave
1929		his body

MARK CHAPTER 15

Code	Syriac	English
3246		to Joseph
VERSE 46		And Joseph bought linen cloth and took him down and wrapped him in it and placed him in a grave that was hewn out in the rock and he rolled a stone on the door of the grave.
0632		And bought
3246		Joseph
1255		linen cloth
1499		and took him down
1236		and wrapped him
0217		in it
1625		and placed him
2146		in a grave
1567		that was hewn out
0603		*
2477		in the rock
1737		and he rolled
1119		a stone
1804		on
2718		the door
2146		of the grave
VERSE 47		And Mary Magdalene and Mary the [mother] of Joses saw where he was laid.
3325		Mary
0518		And
3297		Magdalene
3325		and Mary
0593		<who>
3244		[the mother] of Joses
0758		saw
1108		where
1625		he was laid

CHAPTER 16

Code	Syriac	English
VERSE 1		And when the Sabbath had passed, Mary Magdalene and Mary [the mother] of James and Salome bought spices that they might come to anoint him.
1128		And when
1733		had passed
2445		the Sabbath
3325		Mary
3297		Magdalene
3325		and Mary [the mother]
3255		of James
3515		and Salome
0632		bought
0622		spices
0208		that they might come
1443		to anoint him
VERSE 2		And early on the first [day] of the week, they came to the tomb while the sun was rising.
2582		early
0518		And
0721		on the first [day]
2445		of the week
0208		they came
0243		to the tomb
2143		*
1128		while
0555		was rising
2557		the sun
VERSE 3		And they were saying among themselves, "Who [will] roll the stone from the door of the tomb for us?"
0116		And saying
0603		they were
1547		among themselves
1389		Who
0518		<and>
1737		[will] roll
1261		for us
1119		the stone
1388		from
2718		the door
0243		of the tomb
2143		*
VERSE 4		And they looked [and] saw that the stone was rolled away, for it was very great.
0756		And they looked

355

MARK CHAPTER 16

0758		[and] saw		1261		<to him>
1737		that was rolled away		1262		not
0593		<that>		0603		He is
1119		the stone		2694		here
2271		great		0580		Behold
0603		it was		0494		the place
0403		for		1108		where
0938		very		1625		laid

VERSE 5 — And they entered the tomb and saw a young man who was sitting on the right [side] and wrapped around [him] was a white robe, and they were amazed.

				0603		he was

VERSE 7 — But go [and] tell his disciples and Peter that behold, [he goes] before you to Galilee. There you will see him as he said to you."

1796		And they entered		0090		But
0243		the tomb		0042		go
2143		*		0116		[and] tell
0758		and saw		1304		his disciples
1811		a young man		3258		and Peter
1093		who was sitting		0580		that behold
1388		on		2150		[he goes] before
1061		the right [side]		1261		you
1790		and wrapped around [him]		3153		to Galilee
0146		was a robe		2682		There
0755		white		0758		you will see him
2679		and they were amazed		0061		as
				0116		he said
				1261		to you

VERSE 6 — And he said to them, "Do not be afraid. You seek Jesus the Nazarene who was crucified. He has risen. He is not here. Behold the place where he was laid.

VERSE 8 — And when they had heard, they fled and went out of the grave, for amazement and trembling had taken hold on them and they did not speak anything to anyone, for they were afraid.

0592		<he>				
0518		And		1128		And when
0116		he said		2547		they had heard
1261		to them		1904		they fled
1262		not		1542		and went out
0509		Do be afraid		1388		of
3257		Jesus		2146		the grave
3355		the Nazarene		0047		had taken hold
0296		seek		0603		*
0133		You		1261		on them
0593		<he>				
0688		who was crucified				
2168		He has risen				

MARK   CHAPTER 16

0403		for
2645		amazement
2414		and trembling
0131		and to anyone
1326		anything
1262		not
0116		they did speak
0509		they were afraid
0603		*
0403		for

VERSE 9   And early on the first of the week he had risen and appeared first to Mary Magdalene from whom he had cast out seven demons.

2582		early
0518		And
0721		on the first
2445		of the week
2168		he had risen
0758		and appeared
2151		first
3325		to Mary
3297		Magdalene
0593		<who>
2437		seven
2469		demons
1542		he had cast out
0603		*
1388		from whom

VERSE 10   And she went [and] brought hope to those who had been with him who were mourning and weeping.

0592		And <she>
0042		she went
1588		[and] brought hope
0593		to those
1817		who with him
0603		had been
0010		who mourning
0603		were
0267		and weeping

VERSE 11   And when they heard what they were saying, that he was alive and had appeared to them, they did not believe them.

0592		And <they>
1128		when
2547		they heard
0116		what they were saying
0781		that he was alive
0758		and had appeared
1261		to them
1262		not
0109		they did believe
0592		them

VERSE 12   After these [things] he appeared to two of them in another form while they were walking and traveling to a village.

0215		After
0598		these [things]
0758		he appeared
2709		to two
1388		of them
0542		in form
0053		another
1128		while
0608		they were walking
0042		and traveling
2251		to a village

VERSE 13   And those went [and] told the rest. They did not even believe them.

0592		And those
0042		went
0116		[and] told
2611		the rest
0169		even
1262		not
0593		them
0109		They did believe

MARK   CHAPTER 16

VERSE 14 — And finally he appeared to the eleven while they were eating. And he reproved the lack of their faith and the hardness of their heart, since they had not believed those who had seen that he had risen.

0051		finally
0518		And
0758		he appeared
0724		to the eleven
1128		while
1664		they were eating
0855		And he reproved
0868		the lack
0113		of their faith
2267		and the hardness
1268		of their heart
0593		since those
0758		who had seen
2168		that he had risen
1262		not
0109		they had believed

VERSE 15 — And he said to them, "Go to all the world and preach my gospel in all of creation.

0116		And he said
1261		to them
0042		Go
1813		to the world
1168		all
1230		and preach
1593		my gospel
1168		in all of
0331		creation

VERSE 16 — Whoever believes and is baptized will live, and whoever does not believe is condemned.

0066		Whoever
0109		believes
1819		and is baptized
0780		will live
0066		and whoever
1262		not
0109		does believe
0742		is condemned

VERSE 17 — And these signs will follow those who believe. In my name they will cast out demons and they will speak with new tongues.

0206		signs
0518		And
0066		those
0109		who believe
0598		these
1565		will follow
2539		In my name
2469		demons
1542		they will cast out
1312		and with tongues
0735		new
1362		they will speak

VERSE 18 — And they will capture snakes, and if they should drink a deadly poison, it will harm not them and they will place their hands on the sick and they will be made whole."

0740		And snakes
2587		they will capture
0121		and if
1660		a poison
1335		deadly
2620		they should drink
1262		not
0621		it will harm
0592		them
0057		and their hands
1625		they will place
1804		on
1228		the sick
0807		and they will be made whole

VERSE 19 — And Jesus, our Lord, after speaking with them, went up to heaven and sat on the right hand of God.

3257		Jesus
0518		And
1426		our Lord

MARK CHAPTER 16

1388	ܡܢ	after
0215	ܒܬܪ	*
1362	ܕܡܠܠ	speaking
1817	ܥܡܗܘܢ	with them
2543	ܠܫܡܝܐ	to heaven
1658	ܣܠܩ	went up
1093	ܘܝܬܒ	and sat
1388	ܡܢ	on
1061	ܝܡܝܢܐ	the right hand
0093	ܕܐܠܗܐ	of God

VERSE 20 And they went out and preached in every place and our Lord was helping them and establishing their words by the signs that they were doing.

0592	ܗܢܘܢ	<they>
0518	ܕܝܢ	And
1542	ܢܦܩܘ	they went out
1230	ܘܐܟܪܙܘ	and preached
1168	ܒܟܠ	in every
0494	ܕܘܟܐ	place
1426	ܘܡܪܢ	and our Lord
1751	ܡܥܕܪ	helping
0603	ܗܘܐ	was
1261	ܠܗܘܢ	them
2591	ܘܡܫܪܪ	and establishing
1364	ܡܠܝܗܘܢ	their words
0206	ܒܐܬܘܬܐ	by the signs
1724	ܕܥܒܕܝܢ	that doing
0603	ܗܘܘ	they were

LUKE

CHAPTER 1

VERSE 1 — Because many have wanted to write the accounts of the works of which we are persuaded,

Code	Syriac	English
1347		Because
1596		many
2077		have wanted
1247		to write
2572		the accounts
1685		of the works
0066		<those>
0124		<we>
1955		are persuaded
0124		we
0217		of which

VERSE 2 — according to what they delivered to us, those who were eye-witnesses and ministers of the word at the first,

Code	Syriac	English
0060		according to
1326		what
2530		they delivered
1261		to us
0593		those
1388		who at
2153		the first
0603		were
0762		eye-witnesses
2555		and ministers
0517		<his own>
1364		of the word

VERSE 3 — it seemed [good] to me also, because I had carefully attended to all of them that I should write down everything in order for you, noble Theophilus,

Code	Syriac	English
0758		it seemed [good]
0169		also
1261		to me
1347		because
2248		attended
0603		I had
1070		carefully
1168		to all of them
1168		that everything
1326		*
0968		in order
1247		I should write down
1261		for you
1557		noble
3529		Theophilus

VERSE 4 — that you would know the truth of the words by which you were taught.

Code	Syriac	English
1023		that you would know
2596		the truth
1364		of the words
1302		you were taught
1261		by which

VERSE 5 — In the days of Herod, the king of Judea, there was a certain priest, whose name was Zachariah, from the course of the house of Abia, and his wife, from the daughters of Aaron, whose name was Elizabeth.

Code	Syriac	English
0603		there was
1036		In the days
3179		of Herod
1383		the king
3224		of Judea
1135		a priest
0721		certain
2539		whose name
0603		was
3191		Zachariah
1388		from
2556		the course
0243		of the house of
3001		Abia
0135		and his wife
1388		from
0327		the daughters
3013		of Aaron
2539		whose name
0603		was

Vertical Interlinear

LUKE — CHAPTER 1

#	Syriac	Gloss
3051		Elizabeth

VERSE 6 — Now both of them were just before God and were walking in all his commandments and in the uprightness of the LORD without blame.

#	Syriac	Gloss
2709		both of them
0518		Now
0637		just
0603		were
2154		before
0093		God
0608		and were walking
1168		in all
2009		his commandments
1152		and in the uprightness
1426		of the LORD
1262		without
1749		blame

VERSE 7 — But they had no son because Elizabeth was barren and both of them were advanced in their days.

#	Syriac	Gloss
0323		son
0518		But
1264		they had no
0603		*
1261		*
1347		because
3051		Elizabeth
1878		barren
0603		was
2709		and both of them
1596		advanced
1036		in their days
0603		were

VERSE 8 — And it happened, while he was serving as priest in the order of his ministering before God,

#	Syriac	Gloss
0603		it happened
0603		*
0518		And
1128		while
1134		serving as priest
0603		he was
0968		in the order
2556		of his ministering
2154		before
0093		God

VERSE 9 — in the custom of the priesthood, it arrived that he was to place the incense. And he entered the temple of the LORD

#	Syriac	Gloss
1762		in the custom
1136		of the priesthood
1346		it arrived
1625		that he was to place
0291		the incense
1796		And he entered
0607		the temple
1426		of the LORD

VERSE 10 — and the whole assembly of people was praying outside at the time of the incense.

#	Syriac	Gloss
1168		and whole
1201		the assembly
1818		of people
2106		praying
0603		was
0322		outside
1750		at the time
0291		of the incense

VERSE 11 — And an angel of the LORD appeared to Zachariah, who stood on the right [side] of the altar of incense,

#	Syriac	Gloss
0758		And appeared
1261		<to him>
3191		to Zachariah
1375		an angel
1426		of the LORD
2168		who stood
1388		on
1061		the right [side]
0475		of the altar
0291		of incense

Vertical Interlinear

LUKE   CHAPTER 1

VERSE 12   and Zachariah was agitated when he saw him, and fear fell on him.

2452	ܘܐܬܪܗܒ	and was agitated
3191	ܙܟܪܝܐ	Zachariah
1128	ܟܕ	when
0758	ܚܙܝܗܝ	he saw him
0511	ܘܕܚܠܬܐ	and fear
1538	ܢܦܠܬ	fell
1804	ܥܠܘܗܝ	on him

VERSE 13   And the angel said to him, "Do not fear, Zachariah, because your prayer has been heard, and your wife, Elizabeth, will bear you a son, and you will call his name John,

0116	ܘܐܡܪ	And said
1261	ܠܗ	to him
1375	ܡܠܐܟܐ	the angel
1262	ܠܐ	not
0509	ܬܕܚܠ	Do fear
3191	ܙܟܪܝܐ	Zachariah
1347	ܡܛܠ	because
2547	ܕܐܫܬܡܥܬ	has been heard
2107	ܨܠܘܬܟ	your prayer
0135	ܘܐܢܬܬܟ	and your wife
3051	ܐܠܝܫܒܥ	Elizabeth
1046	ܬܐܠܕ	will bear
1261	ܠܟ	you
0323	ܒܪܐ	a son
2239	ܘܬܩܪܐ	and you will call
2539	ܫܡܗ	his name
3233	ܝܘܚܢܢ	John

VERSE 14   and you will have joy and gladness, and many will rejoice at his birth.

0603	ܘܬܗܘܐ	and you will have
1261	ܠܟ	*
0727	ܚܕܘܬܐ	joy
2321	ܘܐܪܘܙܐ	and gladness
1596	ܘܣܓܝܐܐ	and many
0726	ܢܚܕܘܢ	will rejoice
1051	ܒܡܘܠܕܗ	at his birth

VERSE 15   For he will be great before the LORD, and he will not drink wine or strong drink, and he will be filled with the Holy Spirit while he is in the womb of his mother,

0603	ܢܗܘܐ	he will be
0403	ܓܝܪ	For
2271	ܪܒ	great
2154	ܩܕܡ	before
1426	ܡܪܝܐ	the LORD
0831	ܘܚܡܪܐ	and wine
2515	ܘܫܟܪܐ	or strong drink
1262	ܠܐ	not
2620	ܢܫܬܐ	he will drink
2323	ܘܪܘܚܐ	and the Holy Spirit
2164	ܕܩܘܕܫܐ	*
1366	ܢܬܡܠܐ	he will be filled with
1744	ܥܕ	while
0592	ܗܘ	he is
1241	ܒܟܪܣܐ	in the womb
0106	ܕܐܡܗ	of his mother

VERSE 16   and he will turn many of the sons of Israel to the LORD their God,

1596	ܘܣܓܝܐܐ	and many
1388	ܡܢ	of
0323	ܒܢܝ	the sons
3035	ܐܝܣܪܐܝܠ	of Israel
1984	ܢܦܢܐ	he will turn
1288	ܠܘܬ	to
1426	ܡܪܝܐ	the LORD
0093	ܐܠܗܗܘܢ	their God

VERSE 17   and he will go before him in the spirit and in the power of Elijah the prophet, that he might turn the heart of the parents to the children and those who are disobedient to the knowledge of the upright, and he will prepare a mature people for the LORD."

0592	ܘܗܘ	and <he>
0042	ܢܐܙܠ	he will go
2154	ܩܕܡܘܗܝ	before him
2323	ܒܪܘܚܐ	in the spirit
0786	ܘܒܚܝܠܐ	and in the power

Vertical Interlinear

LUKE　　　CHAPTER 1

#	Aramaic	English
3047		of Elijah
1457		the prophet
1984		that he might turn
1268		the heart
0002		of the parents
1804		to
0323		the children
0066		and those
1262		who are disobedient
1955		*
1027		to the knowledge
1150		of the upright
0950		and he will prepare
1426		for the LORD
1818		a people
0426		mature

VERSE 18 And Zachariah said to the angel, "How will I know this? For I am old and my wife is advanced in her days."

#	Aramaic	English
0116		And said
3191		Zachariah
1375		to the angel
0061		How
1023		will I know
0598		this
0124		<I>
0403		For
0069		I am
1578		old
0135		and my wife
1596		advanced
1036		in her days
0592		is

VERSE 19 And the angel answered and said to him, "I am Gabriel, for I stand before God. And I have been sent to speak with you and to declare to you these [things].

#	Aramaic	English
1838		And answered
1375		the angel
0116		And said
1261		to him
0124		I
0124		am
3142		Gabriel
2168		for stand
0124		I
2154		before
0093		God
2521		And I have been sent
1362		to speak
1817		with you
1588		and to declare to you
0598		these [things]

VERSE 20 From now on, you will be silent and not able to speak until the day that these [things] occur, because you did not believe my words that will be fulfilled in their season."

#	Aramaic	English
1357		From now on
0603		you will be
2623		silent
1262		and not
2510		able
1362		to speak
1747		until
1036		the day
0598		that these [things]
0603		occur
1804		<on>
1262		because not
0109		you did believe
1364		my words
0598		<these>
1366		that will be fulfilled
0633		in their season

VERSE 21 Now the people were standing and waiting for Zachariah and they were wondering about his delay in the temple.

#	Aramaic	English
1818		the people
0518		Now
2168		standing

LUKE CHAPTER 1

#	Aramaic	English
0603		were
1646		and waiting
3191		for Zachariah
2679		and wondering
0603		they were
1804		about
0056		his delay
0607		in the temple

VERSE 22 — And when Zachariah came out, he was not able to speak with them and they perceived that he had seen a vision in the temple. And he continually made signs to them, yet remained mute.

#	Aramaic	English
1128		when
1542		came out
0518		And
3191		Zachariah
1262		not
2510		able
0603		he was
1362		to speak
1817		with them
1647		and they perceived
0759		that a vision
0758		he had seen
0607		in the temple
0592		and <he>
2374		he continually made signs
2374		*
0603		*
1261		to them
2165		yet remained
1128		mute
0906		*

VERSE 23 — And when the days of his service were completed, he went to his house.

#	Aramaic	English
1128		And when
1366		were completed
1036		the days
2556		of his service
0042		he went
0243		to his house

VERSE 24 — And it happened after those days [that] Elizabeth, his wife, conceived. And she hid herself [for] five months, and she said,

#	Aramaic	English
0603		And it happened
1388		after
0215		*
1036		days
0593		those
0259		[that] conceived
3051		Elizabeth
0135		his wife
1009		And she hid
0603		*
1547		herself
1083		[for] months
0833		five
0116		and she said
0603		*

VERSE 25 — "These [things] the LORD has done for me in the days that he looked on me to remove my reproach that was among men."

#	Aramaic	English
0598		These [things]
1724		has done
1261		for me
1426		the LORD
1036		in the days
0756		that he looked
0217		on me
1532		to remove
0856		my reproach
0266		that was among
0323		men
0131		*

VERSE 26 — Now in the sixth month, the angel Gabriel was sent from before God to Galilee, to a city by the name of Nazareth,

#	Aramaic	English
1083		in the month
0518		Now

LUKE CHAPTER 1

Number	Syriac	English
2615		sixth
2521		was sent
3142		Gabriel
1375		the angel
1388		From
1288		before
0093		God
3153		to Galilee
0499		to a city
2539		by the name of
3354		Nazareth

VERSE 27 — to a virgin who was engaged to a man whose name [was] Joseph from the house of David. And the name of the virgin [was] Mary.

Number	Syriac	English
1288		to
0347		a virgin
1361		who was engaged
0361		to a man
2539		whose name
3246		[was] Joseph
1388		from
0243		the house
3159		of David
2539		And the name
0347		of the virgin
3325		[was] Mary

VERSE 28 — And the angel approached her and said to her, "Peace to you, [one] full of grace! Our Lord [is] with you, blessed [one] of women."

Number	Syriac	English
1796		And approached
1288		her
1375		the angel
0116		and said
1261		to her
2535		Peace
1261		to you
1366		[one] full of
0942		grace
1426		Our Lord [is]
1817		with you
0338		blessed [one] of
0135		women

VERSE 29 — Now when she saw [him], she was shocked at his saying and wondered, "What is this greeting?"

Number	Syriac	English
0592		<she>
0518		Now
1128		when
0758		she saw [him]
2308		she was shocked
1364		at his saying
0914		and wondered
0603		*
1393		What
0592		is
2535		greeting
0598		this

VERSE 30 — And the angel said to her, "Do not be afraid, Mary, for you have found grace with God.

Number	Syriac	English
0116		And said
1261		to her
1375		the angel
1262		not
0509		Do be afraid
3325		Mary
2510		you have found
0403		for
0942		grace
1288		with
0093		God

VERSE 31 — For behold, you will conceive and give birth to a son and you will call his name Jesus.

Number	Syriac	English
0580		behold
0403		For
2134		you will conceive
0261		*
1046		and give birth to
0323		a son

LUKE   CHAPTER 1

Vertical Interlinear

2239		and you will call
2539		his name
3257		Jesus

VERSE 32 — He will be great, and he will be called the Son of the Most High, and the LORD God will give to him the throne of David, his father,

0598		He
0603		will be
2271		great
0323		and the Son
3395		of the Most High
2239		he will be called
1030		and will give
1261		to him
1426		the LORD
0093		God
1159		the throne
3159		of David
0002		his father

VERSE 33 — and he will reign over the house of Jacob forever, and there will not be a boundary to his kingdom."

1381		and he will reign
1804		over
0243		the house
3255		of Jacob
1813		forever
1385		and to his kingdom
1631		a boundary
1262		not
0603		there will be

VERSE 34 — Mary said to the angel, "How can this be? Because no man has known me."

0116		said
3325		Mary
1375		to the angel
0061		How
0603		can be
0598		this
0361		Because man

1262		no
0789		has known
1261		me

VERSE 35 — The angel answered and said to her, "The Holy Spirit will come and the power of the Most High will overshadow you. Because of this, the one who is begotten in you will be holy and will be called the Son of God.

1838		answered
1375		The angel
0116		and said
1261		to her
2323		The Holy Spirit
2164		*
0208		will come
0786		and the power
3395		of the Most High
0430		will overshadow
1804		you
1347		Because of
0598		this
0593		the one
1046		who is begotten
0217		in you
2162		holy
0592		will be
0323		and the Son
0093		of God
2239		will be called

VERSE 36 — And behold, Elizabeth, your kinswoman, is also pregnant with a son in her old age and this [is] the sixth month for her who was called barren,

0580		And behold
3051		Elizabeth
0045		your kinswoman
0169		also
0592		is
0260		pregnant with
0323		a son
1579		in her old age

366

LUKE   CHAPTER 1

0598	and this [is]
1083	the month
2615	sixth
1261	for her
0593	<she>
2239	who was called
1878	barren

VERSE 37 because nothing [is] difficult for God."

1347	because
1262	nothing
1788	[is] difficult
0093	for God
1326	<thing>

VERSE 38 Mary said, "Behold, I am the handmaid of the LORD. It will happen to me according to your word." And the angel left her.

0116	said
3325	Mary
0580	Behold
0124	I am
0118	the handmaid
1426	of the LORD
0603	It will happen
1261	to me
0060	according to
1364	your word
0042	And left
1375	the angel
1388	<from>
1288	her

VERSE 39 And Mary rose up in those days and went quickly to a mountain, to a city of Judea.

2168	rose up
0518	And
3325	Mary
0217	<in them>
1036	in days
0593	those
0042	and went
0255	quickly
0958	to a mountain
0499	to a city
3224	of Judea

VERSE 40 And she entered the house of Zachariah and greeted Elizabeth.

1796	And she entered
0243	the house
3191	of Zachariah
2420	and greeted
2535	*
3051	Elizabeth

VERSE 41 And it happened that when Elizabeth heard the greeting of Mary, the baby leaped in her womb, and Elizabeth was filled with the Holy Spirit

0603	And it happened
1128	that when
2547	heard
3051	Elizabeth
2535	the greeting
3325	of Mary
0500	leaped
1769	the baby
1241	in her womb
1366	and was filled
3051	Elizabeth
2323	the Holy Spirit
2164	*

VERSE 42 and she cried out in a loud voice and said to Mary, "You are blessed among women, and blessed is the fruit that is in your womb.

2227	and she cried out
2204	with a voice
2336	loud
0116	and said
3325	to Mary
0335	blessed
0133	You are

Vertical Interlinear

LUKE — CHAPTER 1

0135		among women
0335		and blessed
0592		is
2016		the fruit
1241		that is in your womb

VERSE 43 — How did this [happen] to me that the mother of my Lord would come to me?

1110		How
1261		to me
0598		did this [happen]
0106		that the mother
1426		of my Lord
0208		would come
1288		to me

VERSE 44 — For behold, when the sound of your greeting fell on my ears, the baby in my womb leaped with great joy.

0580		behold
0403		For
1128		when
1538		fell
2204		the sound
2535		of your greeting
0021		on my ears
0727		with joy
2271		great
0500		leaped
1769		the baby
1241		in my womb

VERSE 45 — And blessed [is] she who believed, because there will be a completion of those [things] that were spoken with her in the presence of the LORD."

0940		And blessed [is]
0066		she
0109		who believed
0603		because there will be
2534		a completion
0066		of those [things]
1362		that were spoken
1817		with her
1388		in the presence of
1288		*
1426		the LORD

VERSE 46 — And Mary said, "My soul magnifies the LORD

0116		And said
3325		Mary
1082		magnifies
1547		My soul
1426		the LORD

VERSE 47 — and my spirit has rejoiced in God, my Life-giver,

0726		and has rejoiced
2323		my spirit
0093		in God
0785		my Life-giver

VERSE 48 — because he has looked at the humiliation of his handmaid. For behold, from now on, all generations will give me a blessing,

0756		because he has looked
1354		at the humiliation
0118		of his handmaid
0580		behold
0403		For
1388		from
0602		now on
0940		a blessing
1030		will give
1261		me
2605		generations
1168		all

VERSE 49 — because he who is mighty has done great [things] with me and his name [is] holy

1724		because he has done
1288		with me
2271		great [things]
0593		<he>
0788		who is mighty
2162		and holy [is]
2539		his name

Vertical Interlinear

LUKE CHAPTER 1

VERSE	50		and his mercy [is] on those who fear him for ages and generations.
0841		ܘܪܚܡܗ	and his mercy
0504		ܠܥܠܡ	for ages
2605		ܘܫܪܒܬܐ	and generations
1804		ܥܠ	[is] on
0066		ܐܝܠܝܢ	those
0509		ܕܕܚܠܝܢ	who fear
1261		ܠܗ	him

VERSE	51		He has accomplished victory with his arm and has scattered the proud in the thought of their heart[s].
1724		ܥܒܕ	He has accomplished
0665		ܙܟܘܬܐ	victory
0575		ܒܕܪܥܗ	with his arm
0229		ܘܒܕܪ	and has scattered
0935		ܚܬܝܪܝ	the proud
2387		ܒܬܪܥܝܬܐ	in the thought
1268		ܕܠܒܗܘܢ	of their heart[s]

VERSE	52		He has thrown down the mighty from the seats and elevated the humble.
1636		ܣܚܦ	He has thrown down
2702		ܬܩܝܦܐ	the mighty
1388		ܡܢ	from
1159		ܟܘܪܣܘܬܐ	the seats
2331		ܘܐܪܝܡ	and elevated
1355		ܡܟܝܟܐ	the humble

VERSE	53		The hungry he has satisfied with good [things] and the rich he has sent away empty-handed.
1214		ܟܦܢܐ	The hungry
1585		ܣܒܥ	he has satisfied with
0938		ܛܒܬܐ	good [things]
1921		ܘܥܬܝܪܐ	and the rich
2597		ܫܪܐ	he has sent away
1696		ܣܦܝܩܐܝܬ	empty-handed

VERSE	54		He has aided Israel his servant and remembered his mercy,
1751		ܥܕܪ	He has aided
3035		ܠܐܝܣܪܐܝܠ	Israel
1727		ܥܒܕܗ	his servant
0527		ܘܐܬܕܟܪ	and remembered

0841		ܪܚܡܘܗܝ	his mercy

VERSE	55		as he spoke with our fathers, with Abraham and with his seed forever."
0060		ܐܝܟ	as
1362		ܕܡܠܠ	he spoke
1817		ܥܡ	with
0002		ܐܒܗܝܢ	our fathers
1817		ܥܡ	with
3005		ܐܒܪܗܡ	Abraham
1817		ܘܥܡ	and with
0693		ܙܪܥܗ	his seed
1813		ܠܥܠܡ	forever

VERSE	56		And Mary stayed with Elizabeth for three months and she returned to her house.
2165		ܩܘܝܬ	stayed
0518		ܕܝܢ	And
3325		ܡܪܝܡ	Mary
1288		ܠܘܬ	with
3051		ܐܠܝܫܒܥ	Elizabeth
0060		ܐܝܟ	for
1083		ܝܪܚܐ	months
2674		ܬܠܬܐ	three
0616		ܘܗܦܟܬ	and she returned
0243		ܠܒܝܬܗ	to her house

VERSE	57		Now [concerning] Elizabeth, the time came that she should give birth and she bore a son.
3051		ܐܠܝܫܒܥ	[concerning] Elizabeth
0518		ܕܝܢ	Now
0603		ܗܘܐ	came
0603		ܗܘܐ	*
1261		ܠܗ	to her
0633		ܙܒܢܐ	the time
1046		ܕܬܐܠܕ	that she should give birth
1046		ܘܝܠܕܬ	and she bore
0323		ܒܪܐ	a son

VERSE	58		And her neighbors and her relatives heard that God had increased his mercy toward her and they rejoiced with her.
2547		ܘܫܡܥܘ	And heard
2425		ܫܒܒܝܗ	her neighbors

Vertical Interlinear

LUKE   CHAPTER 1

0323		and her relatives
0952		*
1595		that had increased
0093		God
0841		his mercy
1288		toward her
0726		and they rejoiced
0603		*
1817		with her

VERSE 59 And it happened on the eighth day and they came to circumcise the young boy and they were going to call him by the name of his father, Zachariah.

0603		And it happened
1036		on the day
2683		eighth
0208		and they came
0396		to circumcise
0976		the young boy
2239		and going to call
0603		they were
1261		him
2539		by the name
0002		of his father
3191		Zachariah

VERSE 60 But his mother answered and said to them, "Not so, but he will be called John."

1838		But answered
0106		his mother
0116		and said
1261		to them
1262		Not
0597		so
0090		but
2239		he will be called
3233		John

VERSE 61 And they said to her, "There is no man in your tribe who is called by this name."

0116		And they said
1261		to her
1264		There is no
0131		man
2605		in your tribe
2239		who is called
2539		by name
0598		this

VERSE 62 And they made signs to his father as to what he wanted to name him.

2374		And they made signs
0002		to his father
0061		as to what
2077		he wanted
2540		to name him

VERSE 63 And he asked for a writing tablet and wrote and said, "His name is John." And everyone marveled.

2420		And he asked for
1988		a writing tablet
1247		and wrote
0116		and said
3233		John
0592		is
2539		His name
0549		And marveled
1175		everyone

VERSE 64 And immediately his mouth was opened and his tongue [was loosed] and he spoke and blessed God.

0725		And immediately
2070		was opened
1936		his mouth
1312		and his tongue [was loosed]
1362		and he spoke
0335		and blessed
0093		God

VERSE 65 And fear came over all their neighbors, and in all the mountain of Judea these [things] were spoken.

0603		And came
0511		fear
1804		over
1168		all

LUKE — CHAPTER 1

Vertical Interlinear

Code	Aramaic	English
2425		their neighbors
1168		and in all
0958		the mountain
3224		of Judea
0598		these [things]
1362		spoken
0603		were

VERSE 66 And all that heard were pondering in their heart[s] and saying, "What indeed will this child be?" And the hand of the LORD was with him.

Code	Aramaic	English
1168		And all
2547		that heard
0914		pondering
0603		were
1268		in their heart[s]
0116		and saying
1393		What
1163		indeed
0603		will be
0976		child
0598		this
0057		And the hand
1426		of the LORD
0069		was
0603		*
1817		with him

VERSE 67 And Zachariah, his father, was filled with the Holy Spirit and prophesied and said,

Code	Aramaic	English
1366		and was filled with
3191		Zachariah
0002		his father
2323		the Holy Spirit
2164		*
1456		and prophesied
0116		and said

VERSE 68 "The LORD is blessed, the God of Israel, who has visited his nation and brought redemption for it.

Code	Aramaic	English
0335		blessed
0592		is
1426		The LORD
0093		the God
3035		of Israel
1684		who has visited
1818		his nation
1724		and brought
1261		for it
2043		redemption

VERSE 69 And he has raised up for us a horn of redemption in the house of David his servant,

Code	Aramaic	English
2168		And he has raised up
1261		for us
2255		a horn
2043		of redemption
0243		in the house
3159		of David
1727		his servant

VERSE 70 as he spoke by the mouth of his holy prophets who were from old,

Code	Aramaic	English
0060		as
1362		he spoke
1936		by the mouth
1457		of his prophets
2162		holy
1388		who were from
1813		old

VERSE 71 that he would redeem us from our enemies and from the hand of all our adversaries.

Code	Aramaic	English
2042		that he would redeem us
1388		from
0307		our enemies
1388		and from
0057		the hand
1168		of all
1674		our adversaries

VERSE 72 And he has performed his mercy with our fathers and has remembered his holy covenants

Code	Aramaic	English
1724		And he has performed
0841		his mercy

LUKE — CHAPTER 1

Vertical Interlinear

#	Aramaic	English
1817		with
0002		our fathers
1756		and has remembered
0520		his covenants
2162		holy

VERSE 73 — and the oaths that he swore to Abraham, our father, that he would give to us,

#	Aramaic	English
1060		and the oaths
1059		that he swore
3005		to Abraham
0002		our father
1030		that he would give
1261		to us

VERSE 74 — so that we would be redeemed from the hand of our enemies and [that] without fear we might serve before him

#	Aramaic	English
2042		so that we would be redeemed
1388		from
0057		the hand
0307		of our enemies
1262		and [that] without
0511		fear
1974		we might serve
2154		before him

VERSE 75 — all our days in uprightness and justification.

#	Aramaic	English
1168		all
1036		our days
1152		in uprightness
0639		and justification

VERSE 76 — And you, [oh] child, will be called the prophet of the Most High, for you will go before the face of the LORD to prepare his way,

#	Aramaic	English
0133		And <you>
0976		[oh] child
1457		the prophet
3395		of the Most High
2239		you will be called
0042		you will go
0403		for
2154		before
2041		the face
1426		of the LORD
0950		to prepare
0038		his way

VERSE 77 — so that he may give the knowledge of life to his people in the forgiveness of their sins,

#	Aramaic	English
1030		so that he may give
1028		the knowledge
0782		of life
1818		to his people
2441		in the forgiveness
0771		of their sins

VERSE 78 — by the bowels of mercy of our God, by which the dawn from on high will visit us,

#	Aramaic	English
2346		by the bowels
0841		of mercy
0093		of our God
0217		by which
1684		will visit us
0556		the dawn
1388		from
2334		on high

VERSE 79 — to enlighten those who sit in darkness and in the shadows of death, that he may direct our feet in the way of peace."

#	Aramaic	English
1474		to enlighten
0066		those
0923		who in darkness
0971		and in the shadows
1335		of death
1093		sit
2720		that he may direct
2293		our feet
0038		in the way
2535		of peace

LUKE   CHAPTER 1

VERSE 80 — And the child grew and was strengthened by the Spirit and he was in the wilderness until the day of his appearance to Israel.

0976	the child
0518	And
2280	grew
0603	*
0787	and was strengthened
2323	by the Spirit
0892	and in the wilderness
0069	he was
0603	*
1747	until
1036	the day
0741	of his appearance
1288	to
3035	Israel

CHAPTER 2

VERSE 1 — And it happened [that] in those days a decree went out from Caesar Augustus that every nation of his jurisdiction should be enrolled.

0603	it happened
0518	And
1036	[that] in days
0593	those
1542	<and> went out
2009	a decree
1388	from
3007	Augustus
3483	Caesar
1247	that should be enrolled
1168	every
1818	nation
0049	of his jurisdiction

VERSE 2 — This was the first enrollment during the governorship of Quirinius in Syria.

0598	This
1252	enrollment
2157	the first
0603	was
0587	during the governorship
3466	of Quirinius
3367	in Syria

VERSE 3 — And everyone went to his city to be enrolled.

0042	And went
0603	*
1175	everyone
1247	to be enrolled
0499	to his city

VERSE 4 — And Joseph also went up from Nazareth, a city of Galilee, into Judea to the city of David that is called Bethlehem, because he was from the house and from the tribe of David,

1658	went up
0603	*
0518	And
0169	also
3246	Joseph
1388	from
3354	Nazareth
0499	a city
3153	of Galilee
3224	into Judea
0499	to the city
3159	of David
2239	that is called
3114	Bethlehem
1347	because
0069	he was
0603	*
1388	from
0243	the house
1388	and from
2605	the tribe
3159	of David

VERSE 5 — with Mary, his pregnant wife, to be enrolled there.

| 1817 | with |

LUKE   CHAPTER 2

3325		Mary
1361		his wife
1128		pregnant
0260		*
2682		there
1247		to be enrolled

VERSE 6   And it happened that while they were there, her days were fulfilled that she should give birth,

0603		And it happened
1128		that while
2682		there
0592		they were
1366		were fulfilled
1036		her days
1046		that she should give birth

VERSE 7   and she bore her firstborn son and wrapped him in swaddling clothes and laid him in a manger, because they had no place where they were staying.

1046		and she bore
0323		her son
0271		firstborn
1236		and wrapped him
1785		in swaddling clothes
2372		and laid him
0039		in a manger
1347		because
1264		they had no
0603		*
1261		*
0494		place
1108		where
2597		staying
0603		they were

VERSE 8   And there were shepherds in that region who were abiding there and keeping watch over their flocks at night.

2383		shepherds
0518		And
0069		there were
0603		*
0217		in that
0214		<in> region
2597		who abiding
0603		were
2682		there
1502		and keeping
1503		watch
1299		at night
1804		over
2382		their flocks

VERSE 9   And behold, an angel of God came to them and the glory of the LORD shone on them and they were very afraid.

0580		And behold
1375		an angel
0093		of God
0208		came
1288		to them
2432		and the glory
1426		of the LORD
1474		shone
1804		on them
0509		and they were afraid
0511		<fear>
2271		very

VERSE 10   And the angel said to them, "Do not be afraid, for behold, I announce to you great joy that will be to all the world.

0116		And said
1261		to them
1375		the angel
1262		not
0509		Do be afraid
0580		behold
0403		for
1588		announce
0124		I
1261		to you
0727		joy

LUKE — CHAPTER 2

Vertical Interlinear

2271		great
0603		that will be
1168		to all
1813		the world

VERSE 11 — For today the deliverer, who is the LORD the Messiah, is born to you in the city of David.

1046		is born
1261		to you
0403		For
1037		today
2044		the deliverer
0069		who is
1426		the LORD
1446		the Messiah
0499		in the city
3159		of David

VERSE 12 — And this [is] a sign to you, you will find a baby who is wrapped in swaddling clothes and laid in a manger."

0598		And this [is]
1261		to you
0206		a sign
2510		will find
0133		you
1769		a baby
1236		who is wrapped
1785		in swaddling clothes
1625		and laid
0039		in a manger

VERSE 13 — And suddenly the great hosts of heaven appeared with the angel, praising God and saying,

1388		And suddenly
2519		*
0758		appeared
1817		with
1375		the angel
0786		the hosts
1596		great
2543		of heaven
1128		praising
2428		*
0093		God
0116		and saying

VERSE 14 — "Glory to God in the highest and on earth, peace and a good hope to men."

2432		Glory
0093		to God
2332		in the highest
1804		and on
0199		earth
2535		peace
1592		and hope
0938		good
0323		to men
0131		*

VERSE 15 — And it happened that after the angels had gone away from them to heaven, the shepherds spoke with each other and said, "Let us journey to Bethlehem and see this matter that has happened as the LORD has made known to us."

0603		And it happened
1128		that after
0042		had gone away
1388		from
1288		them
1375		the angels
2543		to heaven
1362		spoke
2383		the shepherds
0721		with each other
1817		*
0721		*
0116		and said
2299		Let us journey
1747		to
3114		Bethlehem
0758		and see
1364		matter
0598		this

Vertical Interlinear

LUKE   CHAPTER 2

0603		that has happened
0060		as
1426		the LORD
1023		has made known
1261		to us

VERSE 16   And they came quickly and found Mary and Joseph and the baby, who was laid in the manger.

0208		And they came
2309		quickly
2510		and found
3325		Mary
3246		and Joseph
1769		and the baby
1625		who was laid
0039		in the manger

VERSE 17   And after they had seen [him], they made known the message that had been told to them about the child.

1128		And after
0758		they had seen [him]
1023		they made known
1364		the message
1362		that had been told
1817		to them
1804		about <him>
1804		<about>
0976		the child

VERSE 18   And all who heard [it] marveled at those [things] that were spoken to them by the shepherds.

1168		And all
2547		who heard [it]
0549		marveled
1804		at
0066		those [things]
1362		that were spoken
1261		to them
1388		by
2383		the shepherds

VERSE 19   But Mary kept all those words and was pondering [them] in her heart.

3325		Mary
0518		But
1502		kept
0603		*
1168		all
1364		words
0598		those
1944		and was pondering [them]
1268		in her heart

VERSE 20   And those shepherds returned, glorifying and praising God for all that they had seen and heard as it was told to them.

0616		And returned
2383		shepherds
0593		those
1128		glorifying
2428		*
0610		and praising
0093		God
1804		for
1168		all
0758		that they had seen
2547		and heard
0061		as
1362		it was told
1817		to them

VERSE 21   And when eight days were completed so that the boy could be circumcised, his name was called Jesus as he had been named by the angel before he was conceived in the womb.

1128		And when
1366		were completed
2683		eight
1036		days
0396		so that could be circumcised
0976		the boy
2239		was called
2539		his name

Vertical Interlinear

LUKE   CHAPTER 2

3257		Jesus
2239		as he had been named
1388		by
1375		the angel
2154		before
0259		he was conceived
1241		in the womb

VERSE 22 — And when the days of their purification were fulfilled according to the law of Moses, they took him up to Jerusalem to present him to the LORD,

1128		And when
1366		were fulfilled
1036		the days
0526		of their purification
0060		according to
1524		the law
3305		of Moses
1658		they took him up
3022		to Jerusalem
2168		to present him
2154		to
1426		the LORD

VERSE 23 — according to what was written in the law of the LORD: EVERY MALE [WHO] OPENS THE WOMB WILL BE CALLED A HOLY ONE OF THE LORD,

0060		according to
1247		what was written
1524		in the law
1426		of the LORD
1168		EVERY
0529		MALE
2070		[WHO] OPENS
2285		THE WOMB
2162		A HOLY ONE
1426		OF THE LORD
2239		WILL BE CALLED

VERSE 24 — and to give a sacrifice, as is said in the law of the LORD, A PAIR OF TURTLEDOVES OR TWO CHICKS OF A DOVE.

1030		and to give
0474		a sacrifice
0061		as
0116		is said
1524		in the law
1426		of the LORD
0648		A PAIR
2480		OF TURTLEDOVES
0024		OR
2709		TWO
2022		CHICKS
1038		OF A DOVE

VERSE 25 — Now there was a certain man in Jerusalem whose name was Simeon. And this man was upright and just and was waiting for the comfort of Israel and the Holy Spirit was on him.

0361		a man
0518		Now
0721		certain
0069		there was
0603		*
3022		in Jerusalem
2539		whose name
0603		was
3521		Simeon
0361		And man
0598		this
1150		upright
0603		was
0637		and just
1646		and waiting
0603		was
0263		for the comfort
3035		of Israel
2323		and the Holy Spirit
2164		*

LUKE CHAPTER 2

0069		was
0603		*
1804		on him

VERSE 26 — And it had been spoken to him by the Holy Spirit that he would not see death until he would see the Messiah of the LORD.

0116		And it had been spoken
0603		*
1261		to him
1388		by
2323		the Holy Spirit
2164		*
1262		that not
0758		he would see
1335		death
1747		until
0758		he would see
1446		the Messiah
1426		of the LORD

VERSE 27 — This [man] came by the Spirit to the temple and when his parents brought the child Jesus to do for him as was commanded in the law,

0592		<he>
0598		This [man]
0208		came
0603		*
2323		by the Spirit
0607		to the temple
1128		and when
1796		brought
1261		<him>
0002		his parents
3257		Jesus
0976		the child
1724		to do
0812		for him
0061		as
2007		was commanded
1524		in the law

VERSE 28 — he took him up in his arms and blessed God and said,

2134		he took him up
1804		in
0575		his arms
0335		and blessed
0093		God
0116		and said

VERSE 29 — "Now, my Lord, dismiss your servant in peace according to your word.

1357		Now
2597		dismiss
0133		*
1261		<him>
1727		your servant
1426		my Lord
0060		according to
1364		your word
2535		in peace

VERSE 30 — For behold, my eyes have seen your mercy

0580		For behold
0758		have seen
1794		my eyes
0841		your mercy

VERSE 31 — that you have prepared in the presence of all nations,

0593		<who>
0950		that you have prepared
2041		in the presence
1168		of all
0107		nations

VERSE 32 — a light for a revelation to the Gentiles and a glory to your people, Israel."

1477		a light
0414		for a revelation
1818		to the Gentiles
2431		and a glory
1818		to your people
3035		Israel

LUKE — CHAPTER 2

VERSE 33
And Joseph and his mother marveled at these [things] that were spoken about him.

Code	Syriac	English
3246		Joseph
0518		And
0106		and his mother
2679		marveled
0603		*
1804		at
0066		these [things]
1362		that were spoken
0603		*
1804		about him

VERSE 34
And Simeon blessed them and said to Mary his mother, "Behold, this [man] is set for the fall and the rising of many in Israel and for a sign of contention,

Code	Syriac	English
0335		And blessed
0592		them
3521		Simeon
0116		and said
3325		to Mary
0106		his mother
0580		Behold
0598		this [man]
1625		is set
1539		for the fall
2173		and the rising
1596		of many
3035		in Israel
0206		and for a sign
0890		of contention

VERSE 35
(and a spear will pass through your soul) so that the thoughts of many hearts may be revealed."

Code	Syriac	English
1547		<and> through your soul
0518		And
0517		<your>
1733		will pass
2338		a spear
0060		so that
0409		may be revealed
0917		the thoughts
1268		of hearts
1596		many

VERSE 36
And Anna, a prophetess, the daughter of Phanuel, from the tribe of Asher, was also advanced in her years. And she had lived [for] seven years with her husband from her maidenhood.

Code	Syriac	English
3198		<and> Anna
0518		And
1457		a prophetess
0327		the daughter
3429		of Phanuel
1388		from
2433		the tribe
3108		of Asher
0169		also
0592		<she>
2263		advanced
1036		in her days
0603		was
2437		And [for] seven
2559		years
1817		with
0306		her husband
0780		she had lived
1388		from
0346		her maidenhood

VERSE 37
And she was a widow for about eighty-four years and she did not go out of the temple and she served in fasting and in prayer both day and night.

Code	Syriac	English
0603		And she was
0195		a widow
0060		for about
2559		years
2685		eighty-
0179		<and> four
1262		and not
2042		she did go out

Vertical Interlinear

LUKE CHAPTER 2

0603	ܗܘܐ	*
1388	ܡܢ	of
0607	ܗܝܟܠܐ	the temple
2094	ܘܒܨܘܡܐ	and in fasting
2107	ܘܒܨܠܘܬܐ	and in prayer
1974	ܦܠܚܐ	she served
0603	ܗܘܐ	*
0064	ܒܐܝܡܡܐ	both day
1299	ܘܒܠܠܝܐ	and night

VERSE 38 — And she also stood up immediately and gave thanks to the LORD and spoke about him to everyone who waited for the redemption of Jerusalem.

0169	ܘܐܦ	And also
0592	ܗܝ	<she>
2168	ܩܡܬ	she stood up
0217	ܒܗ	immediately
2573	ܒܫܥܬܐ	*
1020	ܘܐܘܕܝܬ	and gave thanks
1426	ܠܡܪܝܐ	to the LORD
1362	ܘܡܡܠܠܐ	and spoke
0603	ܗܘܐ	*
1804	ܥܠܘܗܝ	about him
1817	ܥܡ	to
1175	ܟܠܢܫ	everyone
1646	ܕܡܣܟܐ	who waited
0603	ܗܘܐ	*
2043	ܠܦܘܪܩܢܗ	for the redemption
3022	ܕܐܘܪܫܠܡ	of Jerusalem

VERSE 39 — And when they had completed everything according to in the law of the LORD, they returned to Galilee, to their city Nazareth.

1128	ܘܟܕ	And when
2530	ܫܠܡܘ	they had completed
1168	ܟܠ	everything
1326	ܡܕܡ	*
0060	ܐܝܟ	according to
1524	ܕܒܢܡܘܣܐ	the law
1426	ܕܡܪܝܐ	of the LORD
0616	ܗܦܟܘ	they returned
3153	ܠܓܠܝܠܐ	to Galilee
3354	ܠܢܨܪܬ	to Nazareth
0499	ܡܕܝܢܬܗܘܢ	their city

VERSE 40 — And the child grew and was strengthened by the Spirit and was filled with wisdom and the grace of God was on him.

0976	ܛܠܝܐ	the child
0518	ܕܝܢ	And
2280	ܪܒܐ	grew
0603	ܗܘܐ	*
0787	ܘܡܬܚܝܠ	and was strengthened
2323	ܒܪܘܚܐ	by the Spirit
1366	ܘܡܬܡܠܐ	and was filled with
0792	ܚܟܡܬܐ	wisdom
0942	ܘܛܝܒܘܬܐ	and the grace
0093	ܕܐܠܗܐ	of God
0069	ܐܝܬ	was
0603	ܗܘܐ	*
1804	ܥܠܘܗܝ	on him

VERSE 41 — And his relatives, during every year, went to Jerusalem for the celebration of the feast of Passover.

0131	ܘܐܢܫܘܗܝ	And his relatives
1168	ܒܟܠ	during every
2559	ܫܢܐ	year
0042	ܐܙܠܝܢ	went
0603	ܗܘܘ	*
3022	ܠܐܘܪܫܠܡ	to Jerusalem
1721	ܒܥܕܥܕܐ	for the celebration
3433	ܕܦܨܚܐ	of the feast of Passover

VERSE 42 — And when he was twelve years old, they went up, as they were accustomed, for the celebration.

1128	ܘܟܕ	And when
0603	ܗܘܐ	he was
0323	ܒܪ	twelve years old
2559	ܫܢܝܢ	*
2710	ܬܪܬܥܣܪܐ	*
1658	ܣܠܩܘ	they went up
0061	ܐܝܟ	as

380

LUKE — CHAPTER 2

#	Syriac	English
1761		they were accustomed
0603		*
1721		for the celebration

VERSE 43 — And after the [feast] days were completed, they returned. But the child Jesus remained in Jerusalem and Joseph and his mother did not know [it],

#	Syriac	English
1128		And after
2530		were completed
1036		the [feast] days
0616		they returned
1261		<to them>
3257		Jesus
0518		But
0976		the child
1938		remained
1261		<to him>
3022		in Jerusalem
3246		and Joseph
0106		and his mother
1262		not
1023		did know [it]

VERSE 44 — for they thought that he was with their companions. And after they had journeyed one day, they searched for him among their relatives and among anyone who knew them

#	Syriac	English
1588		they thought
0603		*
0403		for
1817		that with
0323		their companions
1282		*
0592		he was
1128		And after
0208		they journeyed
2300		*
1036		day
0721		one
0296		they searched for him
1288		among
0132		their relatives
1288		and among
1389		anyone
1023		who knew
1261		them

VERSE 45 — and they did not find him. So they returned again to Jerusalem and searched for him.

#	Syriac	English
1262		and not
2510		they did find him
0616		So they returned
1261		<to them>
2650		again
3022		to Jerusalem
0296		and searched
0603		*
1261		for him

VERSE 46 — And after three days, they found him in the temple, sitting in the middle of the teachers. And he was listening to them and questioning them.

#	Syriac	English
1388		And after
0215		*
2674		three
1036		days
2510		they found him
0607		in the temple
1128		sitting
1093		*
1416		in the middle of
1055		the teachers
2547		And he was listening
1388		to them
2420		and questioning
1261		them

VERSE 47 — And all those who heard him were amazed by his wisdom and his answers.

#	Syriac	English
2679		And were amazed
0603		*
1168		all
0066		those

LUKE CHAPTER 2

#	Aramaic	English
2547		who heard
0603		*
1261		him
0792		by his wisdom
2068		and his answers

VERSE 48 And when they saw him, they were amazed and his mother said to him, "My son, why have you acted toward us in this manner? For behold, your father and I have been searching for you with much anxiety."

#	Aramaic	English
1128		And when
0758		they saw him
2679		they were amazed
0116		and said
1261		to him
0106		his mother
0323		My son
1394		why
1724		have you acted
1261		toward us
0597		in this manner
0580		For behold
0002		your father
0124		and I
1007		with anxiety
1596		much
0296		searching
0603		have been
1261		for you

VERSE 49 He said to them, "Why were you searching for me? Do you not know that it is necessary for me to be in the house of my Father?"

#	Aramaic	English
0116		He said
1261		to them
1393		Why
0296		searching
0603		were you
1261		for me
1262		not
1023		Did know

#	Aramaic	English
0133		you
0243		that in the house of
0002		my Father
0626		it is necessary
1261		for me
0603		to be

VERSE 50 But they did not understand the saying that he had told them.

#	Aramaic	English
0592		<they>
0518		But
1262		not
1023		they did understand
1364		the saying
0116		that he had told
1261		them

VERSE 51 And he went down with them and came to Nazareth and was subject to them. And his mother kept all the words in her heart.

#	Aramaic	English
1499		And he went down
1817		with them
0208		and came
3354		to Nazareth
1724		and was subject
0603		*
1261		to them
0106		his mother
0518		And
1502		kept
0603		*
1168		all
1364		the words
1268		in her heart

VERSE 52 And Jesus grew in his stature and in his wisdom and in favor with God and men.

#	Aramaic	English
3257		Jesus
0518		And
2280		grew
0603		*
2171		in his stature
0792		and in his wisdom

Vertical Interlinear

LUKE — CHAPTER 2

0942	ܘܒܛܝܒܘܬܐ	and in favor
1288	ܠܘܬ	with
0093	ܐܠܗܐ	God
0325	ܘܒܢܝܢܫܐ	and men

CHAPTER 3

VERSE 1 — Now in the fifteenth year of the reign of Tiberius Caesar, in the governorship of Pontius Pilate in Judea, while Herod [was] tetrarch in Galilee and Philip, his brother, [was] tetrarch in Ituraea and in the region of Trachonitis, and Lysanias [was] tetrarch of Abilene,

2559	ܒܫܢܬ	in the year
0836	ܚܡܫܥܣܪܐ	fifteenth
0518	ܕܝܢ	Now
1385	ܕܡܠܟܘܬܗ	of the reign
3209	ܕܛܒܪܝܘܣ	of Tiberius
3483	ܩܣܪ	Caesar
0587	ܒܗܓܡܘܢܘܬܐ	in the governorship
3417	ܕܦܢܛܝܘܣ ܦܝܠܛܘܣ	of Pontius Pilate
3224	ܒܝܗܘܕ	in Judea
1128	ܟܕ	while
2362	ܪܫܐ	[was] tetrarch
0184	ܪܒܥܝܐ	*
3179	ܗܪܘܕܣ	Herod
3153	ܒܓܠܝܠܐ	in Galilee
3420	ܘܦܝܠܝܦܘܣ	and Philip
0043	ܐܚܘܗܝ	his brother
2362	ܪܫܐ	[was] tetrarch
0184	ܪܒܥܝܐ	*
3027	ܒܐܝܛܘܪܝܐ	in Ituraea
0214	ܘܒܐܬܪܐ	and in the region
3221	ܕܛܪܟܘܢܐ	of Trachonitis
3284	ܘܠܘܣܢܝܐ	and Lysanias
2362	ܪܫܐ	[was] tetrarch
0184	ܪܒܥܝܐ	*
3003	ܕܐܒܝܠܝܢܐ	of Abilene

VERSE 2 — during the high priesthood of Annas and Caiaphas, the word of God came to John, the son of Zachariah, in the wilderness.

2273	ܒܪܒܟܗܢܘܬܐ	during the high priesthood
1136	ܕܚܢܢ	*
3200	ܕܚܢܢ	of Annas
3473	ܘܕܩܝܦܐ	and Caiaphas
0603	ܗܘܬ	came
1364	ܡܠܬܐ	the word
0093	ܕܐܠܗܐ	of God
1804	ܥܠ	to
3233	ܝܘܚܢܢ	John
0323	ܒܪ	the son
3191	ܕܙܟܪܝܐ	of Zachariah
0892	ܒܚܘܪܒܐ	in the wilderness

VERSE 3 — And he came into all the region that was around the Jordan, proclaiming the baptism of repentance for the forgiveness of sins,

0208	ܘܐܬܐ	And he came
1168	ܒܟܠܗ	into all
0214	ܐܬܪܐ	the region
0732	ܕܚܕܪܝ	that was around
3248	ܝܘܪܕܢܢ	the Jordan
1128	ܟܕ	proclaiming
1230	ܡܟܪܙ	*
1821	ܡܥܡܘܕܝܬܐ	the baptism
2651	ܕܬܝܒܘܬܐ	of repentance
2441	ܠܫܘܒܩܢܐ	for the forgiveness
0771	ܕܚܛܗܐ	of sins

VERSE 4 — as it is written in the book of the words of Isaiah the prophet who said: THE VOICE THAT CALLS IN THE WILDERNESS: PREPARE THE WAY OF THE LORD AND MAKE STRAIGHT PATHS IN THE PLAIN FOR OUR GOD.

0061	ܐܝܟܢܐ	as
1247	ܕܟܬܝܒ	it is written
1248	ܒܟܬܒܐ	in the book
1364	ܕܡܠܐ	of the words
3109	ܕܐܫܥܝܐ	of Isaiah
1457	ܢܒܝܐ	the prophet
0116	ܕܐܡܪ	who said
2204	ܩܠܐ	THE VOICE
2239	ܕܩܪܐ	THAT CALLS
0892	ܒܚܘܪܒܐ	IN THE WILDERNESS

LUKE CHAPTER 3

Code	Aramaic	English
0950		PREPARE
0038		THE WAY
1426		OF THE LORD
2720		AND MAKE STRAIGHT
2014		IN THE PLAIN
2434		PATHS
0093		FOR OUR GOD

VERSE 5 ALL THE VALLEYS WILL BE FILLED AND ALL THE MOUNTAINS AND HILLS WILL BE LEVELED AND THE RUGGED [PLACE] WILL BE CLEARED AND THE ROUGH LAND, A PLAIN.

Code	Aramaic	English
1168		ALL
1495		THE VALLEYS
1366		WILL BE FILLED
1168		AND ALL
0958		THE MOUNTAINS
2337		AND HILLS
1353		WILL BE LEVELED
0603		AND WILL
1896		THE RUGGED [PLACE]
2574		BE CLEARED
0214		AND THE LAND
1847		ROUGH
2014		A PLAIN

VERSE 6 AND ALL FLESH WILL SEE THE LIFE OF GOD.

Code	Aramaic	English
0758		AND WILL SEE
1168		ALL
0294		FLESH
0782		THE LIFE
0093		OF GOD

VERSE 7 And he said to those crowds that had come to him to be baptized, "Generation of vipers, who has shown you to flee from the wrath that is to come?

Code	Aramaic	English
0116		And he said
0603		*
1201		to crowds
0066		those
0208		that come
0603		had
1288		to him
1819		to be baptized
1047		Generation
0071		of vipers
1390		who
0739		has shown you
1904		to flee
1388		from
2291		the wrath
1914		that is to come

VERSE 8 Produce therefore fruit that is worthy for repentance and do not begin to say within yourselves, 'We have Abraham [for] a father.' For I say to you, 'From these stones, God is able to raise up sons to Abraham.'

Code	Aramaic	English
1724		Produce
0596		therefore
2016		fruit
2461		that is worthy
2651		for repentance
1262		and not
2597		do begin
0116		to say
1547		within yourselves
0002		[for] a father
0069		We have
1261		*
3005		Abraham
0116		say
0124		I
1261		to you
0403		For
1388		From
0598		these
1119		stones
2510		is able
0093		God
2168		to raise up
0323		sons
3005		to Abraham

Vertical Interlinear

LUKE   CHAPTER 3

VERSE 9 — And behold, the ax is laid on the root of the trees. Therefore, every tree that does not produce good fruit will be cut off and will fall into the fire."

Code	Syriac	English
0580		behold
0518		And
1569		the ax
1625		is laid
1804		on
1877		the root
0063		of the trees
1168		every
0063		tree
0596		Therefore
2016		that fruit
0938		good
1262		not
1724		does produce
1992		will be cut off
1494		and into the fire
1538		will fall

VERSE 10 — And the crowds were asking him and saying, "What then should we do?"

Code	Syriac	English
2420		And asking
0603		were
1261		him
1201		the crowds
0116		and saying
1393		What
0596		then
1724		should we do

VERSE 11 — He answered and said to them, "He who has two coats should give to him who does not have [any] and he who has food should do likewise."

Code	Syriac	English
1838		He answered
0116		and said
1261		to them
1389		He
0069		who has
1261		*
2709		two
1256		coats
1030		should give
1389		to him
1264		who does not have [any]
1261		*
1389		and he
0069		who has
1261		*
1594		food
0597		likewise
1724		should do

VERSE 12 — And the tax collectors also came to be baptized and were saying to him, "Teacher, what should we do?"

Code	Syriac	English
0208		And came
0169		also
1358		the tax collectors
1819		to be baptized
0116		and were saying
1261		to him
1055		Teacher
1393		what
1724		should we do

VERSE 13 — And he said to them, "Do not require anything more than what is commanded to you to require."

Code	Syriac	English
0592		\<he\>
0518		And
0116		he said
1261		to them
1262		not
2631		Do require
1326		anything
1100		more than
1804		*
1313		what
2007		is commanded
1261		you
2631		to require

Vertical Interlinear

LUKE CHAPTER 3

VERSE 14 And the soldiers were asking him and said, "What should we also do?" He said to them, "Do not deal harshly with anyone and do not accuse anyone and let your rations be sufficient for you."

Code	Syriac	English
2420		And asking
0603		were
1261		him
1976		the soldiers
0148		*
0116		and said
1393		What
1724		should we do
0169		also
0124		<we>
0116		He said
1261		to them
1262		not
0131		with anyone
0947		Do deal harshly
0131		and anyone
1262		not
1910		do accuse
1694		and let be sufficient
1261		for you
0177		your rations

VERSE 15 And as the nation was thinking about John and all were considering in their heart that perhaps he was the Messiah,

Code	Syriac	English
1128		as
0518		And
1588		thinking
0603		was
1818		the nation
1804		about
3233		John
1168		and all
0914		considering
0603		were
1268		in their heart
1314		that perhaps
0592		he was
1446		the Messiah

VERSE 16 John answered and said to them, "Behold, I baptize you with water, but one who is greater than I will come, the straps of whose sandals I am not worthy to loosen. He will baptize you with the Holy Spirit and with fire,

Code	Syriac	English
1838		answered
3233		John
0116		and said
1261		to them
0124		<I>
0580		Behold
1819		baptize
0124		I
1261		you
1351		with water
0208		will come
0518		but
0593		one
0788		who is greater
1388		than I
0593		<who>
1262		not
2461		am worthy
0124		I
2597		to loosen
1906		the straps
1582		of whose sandals
0592		<he>
1819		He will baptize you
2323		with the Holy Spirit
2164		*
1494		and with fire

VERSE 17 he who holds a winnowing fan in his hand and has cleaned his threshing floors. And he will gather the wheat into his granaries and he will burn the chaff with a fire that will not go out."

Code	Syriac	English
0593		he
0047		who holds

LUKE   CHAPTER 3

Code	Syriac	English
2396		a winnowing fan
0057		in his hand
0521		and has cleaned
0022		his threshing floors
0779		And the wheat
1198		he will gather
0035		into his granaries
2630		and the chaff
1073		he will burn
1494		with a fire
1262		that not
0558		does go out

VERSE 18 Now also many other [things] he was teaching and declaring to the people.

Code	Syriac	English
0169		also
0053		other [things]
0518		Now
1596		many
1053		teaching
0603		he was
1588		and declaring
1818		to the people

VERSE 19 But Herod, the tetrarch, because he had been reproved by John on account of Herodias, the wife of Philip, his brother, and on account of all the evil [things] that he had done,

Code	Syriac	English
3179		Herod
0518		But
0961		the tetrarch
1347		because
1203		he had been reproved
0603		*
1388		by
3233		John
1804		on account of
3178		Herodias
0135		the wife of
3420		Philip
0043		his brother
1804		and on account of
1168		all
0220		the evil [things]
1724		that he had done
0603		*

VERSE 20 added this also above all of them, that he shut up John [in] prison.

Code	Syriac	English
1064		added
0169		also
0598		this
1804		above
1168		all of them
0716		that he shut up
3233		John
0243		[in] prison
0163		*

VERSE 21 Now it happened while he baptized all the people, he also baptized Jesus. And while he prayed, the sky opened,

Code	Syriac	English
0603		it happened
0518		Now
1128		while
1819		he baptized
1168		all
1818		the people
0169		also
3257		Jesus
1819		he baptized
1128		And while
2106		he prayed
2070		opened
2543		the sky

VERSE 22 and the Holy Spirit came down on him in the likeness of the form of a dove. And a voice came from heaven that said, "You are my beloved Son in whom I am pleased."

Code	Syriac	English
1499		and came down
2323		the Holy Spirit
2164		*
1804		on him
0542		in the likeness of

LUKE CHAPTER 3

0389	ܕܡܘܬܐ	the form
1038	ܕܝܘܢܐ	of a dove
2204	ܘܩܠܐ	And a voice
0603	ܗܘܐ	came
1388	ܡܢ	from
2543	ܫܡܝܐ	heaven
0116	ܕܐܡܪ	that said
0133	ܐܢܬ	You
0592	ܗܘ	are
0323	ܒܪܝ	my Son
0698	ܚܒܝܒܐ	beloved
0217	ܕܒܟ	in whom
2077	ܐܨܛܒܝܬ	I am pleased

VERSE 23 And Jesus was about thirty years old and was thought [to be] the son of Joseph, the son of Heli,

0592	ܗܘ	\<he\>
0518	ܕܝܢ	And
3257	ܝܫܘܥ	Jesus
0069	ܐܝܬܘܗܝ	was
0603	ܗܘܐ	*
0060	ܐܝܟ	about
0323	ܒܪ	thirty years old
2559	ܫܢܝܢ	*
2676	ܬܠܬܝܢ	*
1588	ܘܡܣܬܒܪ	and thought [to be]
0603	ܗܘܐ	was
0323	ܒܪ	the son of
3246	ܝܘܣܦ	Joseph
0323	ܒܪ	the son of
3176	ܗܠܝ	Heli

VERSE 24 the son of Matthat, the son of Levi, the son of Melki, the son of Janni, the son of Joseph,

0323	ܒܪ	the son of
3308	ܡܛܬ	Matthat
0323	ܒܪ	the son of
3280	ܠܘܝ	Levi
0323	ܒܪ	and son of
3316	ܡܠܟܝ	Melki

0323	ܒܪ	the son of
3223	ܝܐܢܝ	Janni
0323	ܒܪ	the son of
3246	ܝܘܣܦ	Joseph

VERSE 25 the son of Mattathias, the son of Amos, the son of Nahum, the son of Esli, the son of Naggai,

0323	ܒܪ	the son of
3333	ܡܬܬܐ	Mattathias
0323	ܒܪ	the son of
3397	ܥܡܘܨ	Amos
0323	ܒܪ	the son of
3342	ܢܚܘܡ	Nahum
0323	ܒܪ	the son of
3202	ܚܣܠܝ	Esli
0323	ܒܪ	the son of
3338	ܢܓܝ	Naggai

VERSE 26 the son of Maath, the son of Mattathias, the son of Semein, the son of Joseph, the son of Judah,

0323	ܒܪ	the son of
3294	ܡܐܬ	Maath
0323	ܒܪ	the son of
3306	ܡܛܠܬ	Mattathias
0323	ܒܪ	the son of
3522	ܫܡܥܝ	Semein
0323	ܒܪ	the son of
3246	ܝܘܣܦ	Joseph
0323	ܒܪ	the son of
3228	ܕܝܗܘܕܐ	of Judah

VERSE 27 the son of Joanan, the son of Rhesa, the son of Zerabbabel, the son of Shealtiel, the son of Neri,

0323	ܒܪ	the son of
3233	ܝܘܚܢܢ	Joanan
0323	ܒܪ	the son of
3503	ܪܣܐ	Rhesa
0323	ܒܪ	the son of
3189	ܙܘܪܒܒܠ	Zerubbabel
0323	ܒܪ	the son of
3519	ܫܠܬܐܝܠ	Shealtiel

LUKE — CHAPTER 3

0323	ܒܪ	the son of
3356	ܢܪܝ	Neri

VERSE 28 — the son of Melki, the son of Addi, the son of Cosam, the son of Elmodam, the son of Er,

0323	ܒܪ	the son of
3316	ܡܠܟܝ	Melki
0323	ܒܪ	the son of
3010	ܐܕܝ	Addi
0323	ܒܪ	the son of
3461	ܩܘܣܡ	Cosam
0323	ܒܪ	the son of
3056	ܐܠܡܘܕܕ	Elmodam
0323	ܒܪ	the son of
3393	ܥܝܪ	Er

VERSE 29 — the son of Jose, the son of Eliezer, the son of Jorim, the son of Matthat, the son of Levi,

0323	ܒܪ	the son of
3243	ܝܘܣܐ	Jose
0323	ܒܪ	the son of
3049	ܐܠܝܥܙܪ	Eliezer
0323	ܒܪ	the son of
3249	ܝܘܪܝܡ	Jorim
0323	ܒܪ	the son of
3331	ܡܬܬܐ	Matthat
0323	ܒܪ	the son of
3280	ܠܘܝ	Levi

VERSE 30 — the son of Simeon, the son of Juda, the son of Joseph, the son of Jonam, the son of Eliakim,

0323	ܒܪ	the son of
3521	ܫܡܥܘܢ	Simeon
0323	ܒܪ	the son of
3228	ܝܗܘܕܐ	Juda
0323	ܒܪ	the son of
3246	ܝܘܣܦ	of Joseph
0323	ܒܪ	the son of
3241	ܝܘܢܡ	Jonam
0323	ܒܪ	the son of
3050	ܐܠܝܩܝܡ	Eliakim

VERSE 31 — the son of Melea, the son of Menna, the son of Mattatha, the son of Nathan, the son of David,

0323	ܒܪ	the son of
3313	ܡܠܐܐ	Melea
0323	ܒܪ	the son of
3293	ܡܢܢ	Menna
0323	ܒܪ	the son of
3307	ܡܬܬܐ	Mattatha
0323	ܒܪ	the son of
3358	ܢܬܢ	Nathan
0323	ܒܪ	the son of
3159	ܕܘܝܕ	David

VERSE 32 — the son of Jesse, the son of Obed, the son of Boaz, the son of Salmon, the son of Nahshon,

0323	ܒܪ	the son of
3040	ܐܝܫܝ	Jesse
0323	ܒܪ	the son of
3389	ܥܘܒܝܕ	Obed
0323	ܒܪ	the son of
3125	ܒܥܙ	Boaz
0323	ܒܪ	the son of
3373	ܣܠܡܘܢ	Salmon
0323	ܒܪ	the son of
3344	ܢܚܫܘܢ	Nahshon

VERSE 33 — the son of Aminadab, the son of Aram, the son of Hezron, the son of Perez, the son of Judah,

0323	ܒܪ	the son of
3399	ܥܡܝܢܕܒ	Aminadab
0323	ܒܪ	the son of
3099	ܐܪܡ	Aram
0323	ܒܪ	the son of
3203	ܚܨܪܘܢ	Hezron
0323	ܒܪ	the son of
3445	ܦܪܨ	Perez
0323	ܒܪ	the son of
3228	ܝܗܘܕܐ	Judah

LUKE CHAPTER 3

VERSE 34
the son of Jacob, the son of Isaac, the son of Abraham, the son of Terah, the son of Nahor,

Code	Syriac	Translation
0323		the son of
3255		Jacob
0323		the son of
3033		Isaac
0323		the son of
3005		Abraham
0323		the son of
3536		Terah
0323		the son of
3343		Nahor

VERSE 35
the son of Serug, the son of Reu, the son of Peleg, the son of Eber, the son of Shelah,

Code	Syriac	Translation
0323		the son of
3383		Serug
0323		the son of
3106		Reu
0323		the son of
3426		Peleg
0323		the son of
3386		Eber
0323		the son of
3516		Shelah

VERSE 36
the son of Cainan, the son of Arphaxad, the son of Shem, the son of Noah, the son of Lamech,

Code	Syriac	Translation
0323		the son of
3472		Cainan
0323		the son of
3107		Arphaxad
0323		the son of
3511		Shem
0323		the son of
3339		Noah
0323		the son of
3291		Lamech

VERSE 37
the son of Methuselah, the son of Enoch, the son of Jared, the son of Mahalalel, the son of Kenan,

Code	Syriac	Translation
0323		the son of
3328		Methuselah
0323		the son of
3199		Enoch
0323		the son of
3256		Jared
0323		the son of
3302		Mahalalel
0323		the son of
3472		Kenan

VERSE 38
the son of Enosh, the son of Seth, the son of Adam, who [was] from God.

Code	Syriac	Translation
0323		the son of
3063		Enosh
0323		the son of
3512		Seth
0323		the son of
3011		Adam
1388		who [was] from
0093		God

CHAPTER 4

VERSE 1
And Jesus, being full of the Holy Spirit, returned from the Jordan. And the Spirit led him to the wilderness

Code	Syriac	Translation
3257		Jesus
0518		And
1128		being
1366		full of
2323		the Holy Spirit
2164		*
0616		returned
1388		from
3248		the Jordan
0477		and led him
2323		the Spirit
0892		to the wilderness

LUKE — CHAPTER 4

VERSE 2 — [for] forty days to be tempted by the Accuser. And he did not eat anything in those days, and when he had completed them, at the end he was hungry.

#	Syriac	Gloss
1036		[for] days
0180		forty
1527		to be tempted
1388		by
0078		the Accuser
1262		And not
1308		he did eat
1326		anything
0593		in those
1036		days
1128		and when
2530		he had completed
0592		them
0054		at the end
1212		he was hungry

VERSE 3 — And the Accuser said to him, "If you are the Son of God, tell this stone to become bread."

#	Syriac	Gloss
0116		And said
1261		to him
0078		the Accuser
0121		If
0323		the Son
0133		you are
0093		of God
0116		tell
1119		stone
0598		this
0603		to become
1293		bread

VERSE 4 — Jesus answered and said to him, "It is written: MAN SHOULD NOT LIVE BY BREAD ALONE, BUT BY EVERY ANSWER OF GOD."

#	Syriac	Gloss
1838		answered
3257		Jesus
0116		and said
1261		to him
1247		It is written
0592		<he>
1262		NOT
0603		*
1293		BY BREAD
1041		ALONE
0780		SHOULD LIVE
0325		MAN
0090		BUT
1168		BY EVERY
2068		ANSWER
0093		OF GOD

VERSE 5 — And Satan took him up to a high mountain and showed him all the kingdoms of the earth in a short period of time.

#	Syriac	Gloss
1658		And took him up
1642		Satan
0958		to a mountain
2336		high
0739		and showed him
1168		all
1385		the kingdoms
0199		of the earth
1750		in a period of time
0686		short

VERSE 6 — And the Accuser said to him, "I will give you all this authority and its glory that is delivered to me and to whom I want, I give it.

#	Syriac	Gloss
0116		And said
1261		to him
0078		the Accuser
1261		you
1030		I will give
2527		authority
0598		this
1168		all
2431		and its glory
1261		that to me
2530		is delivered

Vertical Interlinear

LUKE — CHAPTER 4

#	Syriac	English		#	Syriac	English
1389		and to whom		1261		to him
2077		I want		0121		If
1030		give		0323		the Son
0124		I		0133		you are
1261		it		0093		of God

VERSE 7 — Therefore, if you worship before me, all of it will be yours."

#	Syriac	English
0121		if
0596		Therefore
1599		you worship
2154		before me
0517		yours
0603		will be
1168		all of it

#	Syriac	English
2372		throw down
1547		yourself
1112		from here
2660		to the bottom

VERSE 10 — For it is written: HE WILL COMMAND HIS ANGELS CONCERNING YOU TO KEEP YOU

#	Syriac	English
1247		It is written
0403		For
1375		HIS ANGELS
2007		HE WILL COMMAND
1804		CONCERNING YOU
1502		TO KEEP YOU

VERSE 8 — Jesus answered and said to him, "It is written: YOU SHOULD WORSHIP THE LORD YOUR GOD AND YOU SHOULD SERVE HIM ALONE."

#	Syriac	English
1838		answered
3257		Jesus
0116		and said
1261		to him
1247		It is written
0592		<him>
1426		THE LORD
0093		YOUR GOD
1599		YOU SHOULD WORSHIP
1261		AND HIM
1041		ALONE
1974		YOU SHOULD SERVE

VERSE 11 — AND BEAR YOU IN THEIR ARMS, SO THAT YOUR FOOT WILL NOT STUMBLE ON A STONE."

#	Syriac	English
1804		AND IN
0575		THEIR ARMS
2587		BEAR YOU
1262		SO THAT NOT
2697		WILL STUMBLE
2293		YOUR FOOT
1119		ON A STONE

VERSE 9 — And he brought him to Jerusalem and placed him on the edge of the temple and said to him, "If you are the Son of God, throw yourself down from here to the bottom.

#	Syriac	English
0208		And he brought him
3022		to Jerusalem
2168		and placed him
1804		on
1197		the edge
0607		of the temple
0116		and said

VERSE 12 — And Jesus answered and said to him, "It is said: YOU SHOULD NOT TEMPT THE LORD YOUR GOD."

#	Syriac	English
1838		answered
0518		And
3257		Jesus
0116		and said
1261		to him
0116		It is said
0592		<him>
1262		NOT
1527		YOU SHOULD TEMPT
1426		THE LORD

LUKE CHAPTER 4

| 0093 | ܐܠܗܟ | YOUR GOD |

VERSE 13 — And after the Accuser had finished all his temptations, he left his presence for a while.

1128		And after
2530		had finished
0078		the Accuser
1168		all
1528		his temptations
2042		he left
1388		<from>
1288		his presence
1744		for a while
0633		*

VERSE 14 — And Jesus returned in the power of the Spirit to Galilee and a report about him went out into every region around them.

0616		And returned
3257		Jesus
0786		in the power
2323		of the Spirit
3153		to Galilee
1542		and went out
1804		about him
0944		a report
1168		into every
0214		region
0732		around them

VERSE 15 — And he was teaching in their synagogues and was being praised by everyone.

0592		And <he>
1053		teaching
0603		he was
1200		in their synagogues
2428		and being praised
0603		was
1388		by
1168		everyone
0131		*

VERSE 16 — And he came to Nazareth where he had been raised. And he entered into the synagogue as he was accustomed on the day of the Sabbath and stood up to read.

0208		And he came
3354		to Nazareth
1108		where
2280		he had been raised
1796		And he entered
0061		as
1761		he was accustomed
0603		*
1200		into the synagogue
1036		on the day
2445		of the Sabbath
2168		and stood up
2239		to read

VERSE 17 — And the scroll of Isaiah the prophet was given to him and Jesus opened the scroll and found the place where it was written:

1030		And was given
1261		to him
1698		the scroll
3109		of Isaiah
1457		the prophet
2070		and opened
3257		Jesus
1698		the scroll
2510		and found
0494		the place
1108		where
1247		it was written

VERSE 18 — THE SPIRIT OF THE LORD [IS] ON ME AND BECAUSE OF THIS, HE HAS ANOINTED ME TO PREACH TO THE POOR AND HAS SENT ME TO HEAL THE BROKEN-HEARTED AND TO PREACH FORGIVENESS TO THE CAPTIVES AND SIGHT TO THE BLIND AND TO STRENGTHEN THE BROKEN WITH FORGIVENESS

| 2323 | | THE SPIRIT |
| 1426 | | OF THE LORD |

LUKE   CHAPTER 4

Vertical Interlinear

1804		[IS] ON ME
1347		AND BECAUSE OF
0598		THIS
1443		HE HAS ANOINTED ME
1588		TO PREACH
1406		TO THE POOR
2521		AND HAS SENT ME
0136		TO HEAL
2635		THE BROKEN-HEARTED
1268		*
1230		AND TO PREACH
2427		TO THE CAPTIVES
2441		FORGIVENESS
1776		AND TO THE BLIND
0761		SIGHT
2591		AND TO STRENGTHEN
2635		THE BROKEN
2441		WITH FORGIVENESS
VERSE 19		**AND TO PREACH THE ACCEPTABLE YEAR OF THE LORD."**
1230		AND TO PREACH
2559		THE YEAR
2136		ACCEPTABLE
1426		OF THE LORD
VERSE 20		**And he rolled up the scroll and gave it to the minister and went [and] sat down. And the eyes of all of them in the synagogue were fixed on him.**
1236		And he rolled up
1698		the scroll
1030		and gave it
2555		to the minister
0042		and went [and]
1093		sat down
1168		all of them
0518		And
1200		in the synagogue
1794		the eyes of <them>
0756		fixed
0603		were
0217		on him
VERSE 21		**And he began to speak to them, "Today this scripture is fulfilled in your ears."**
2597		And he began
0116		to speak
1288		to them
1037		Today
2530		is fulfilled
1248		scripture
0598		this
0021		in your ears
VERSE 22		**And all were witnessing to him and were amazed at the words of blessing that were coming out of his mouth. And they were saying, "Is not this [man] the son of Joseph?"**
1608		And witnessing
0603		were
1261		to him
1168		all
0549		and amazed
0603		were
1364		at the words
0942		of blessing
1542		that were coming out
0603		*
1388		of
1936		his mouth
0116		And saying
0603		they were
1262		not
0603		Is
0598		this [man]
0323		the son of
3246		Joseph
VERSE 23		**Jesus said to them, "Perhaps you will tell me this proverb: 'Physician, heal yourself,' and all that we have heard that you did in Capernaum, do also here in your city."**
0116		said
1261		to them

394

LUKE — CHAPTER 4

Vertical Interlinear

#	Syriac	English
3257		Jesus
1124		Perhaps
0116		you will tell
1261		me
1454		proverb
0598		this
0137		Physician
0136		heal
1547		yourself
1168		and all
2547		that we have heard
1724		that you did
3268		in Capernaum
1724		do
0169		also
0600		here
0499		in your city

VERSE 24 But he said, "Truly, I say to you, there is no prophet that is received in his city.

#	Syriac	English
0592		<he>
0518		But
0116		he said
0110		Truly
0116		say
0124		I
1261		to you
1264		there is no
1457		prophet
2134		that is received
0499		in his city

VERSE 25 For I tell you the truth, that there were many widows in Israel in the days of Elijah the prophet, while the heavens were closed [for] three years and six months and a great famine was in all the land.

#	Syriac	English
2596		the truth
0403		For
0116		tell
0124		I
1261		you
1596		that many
0195		widows
0069		there were
0603		*
3035		in Israel
1036		in the days of
3047		Elijah
1457		the prophet
1128		while
0047		were closed
2543		the heavens
2559		[for] years
2674		three
1083		and months
2615		six
0603		and was
1213		a famine
2271		great
1168		in all
0199		the land

VERSE 26 And Elijah was not sent to one of them, except to Zarephath of Sidon, to a widow woman.

#	Syriac	English
1288		And to
0721		one
1388		of them
1262		not
2458		was sent
3047		Elijah
0090		except
3454		to Zarephath
3452		of Sidon
1288		to
0135		woman
0195		widow

VERSE 27 And there were many lepers [in] Israel in the days of Elisha the prophet, yet not one of them was cleansed, except Naaman the Syrian."

#	Syriac	English
1596		And many
0456		lepers

LUKE CHAPTER 4

Code	Syriac	English
0069		there were
0603		*
0243		[in] Israel
3035		*
1036		in the days of
3052		Elisha
1457		the prophet
0721		yet one
1388		of them
1262		not
0521		was cleansed
0090		except
0121		*
3351		Naaman
3101		the Syrian

VERSE 28 And when they heard these [things], all that were in the synagogue were filled with anger.

Code	Syriac	English
1128		And when
2547		they heard
0598		these [things]
0593		<they>
1200		that were in the synagogue
1366		were filled with
0838		anger
1168		all

VERSE 29 And they rose up [and] threw him outside of the city. And they brought him up to the top of the mountain on which their city was built to throw him down from the steep place.

Code	Syriac	English
2168		And they rose up
1542		[and] threw him
0322		outside
1388		of
0499		the city
0208		And they brought him
1747		up to
0359		the top
0958		of the mountain
0593		<that>
0499		their city
0281		built
0603		was
1804		on which
2455		to throw him down
1388		from
2586		the steep place

VERSE 30 But he passed through them and went away.

Code	Syriac	English
0592		<he>
0518		But
1733		he passed
0266		through them
0042		and went away

VERSE 31 And he went down to Capernaum, a city of Galilee, and taught them on the Sabbaths.

Code	Syriac	English
1499		And he went down
3268		to Capernaum
0499		a city
3153		of Galilee
1053		and taught
0603		*
1261		them
2445		on the Sabbaths

VERSE 32 And they were astonished at his teaching, because his message had power.

Code	Syriac	English
2679		And astonished
0603		they were
1054		at his teaching
2526		because power
0603		had
1364		his message

VERSE 33 And there was in the synagogue a man who had the spirit of an unclean demon and he cried out with a loud voice

Code	Syriac	English
0069		And there was
0603		*
1200		in the synagogue
0361		a man
0069		who had

LUKE CHAPTER 4

0603		*
0217		\<in him\>
2323		the spirit
2469		of demon
0991		an unclean
0683		and he cried out
2204		with a voice
2336		loud

VERSE 34 — and said, "Leave me. What do we have in common, Jesus the Nazarene? Have you come to destroy us? I know you, who you are, the Holy [one] of God."

0116		and said
2440		Leave me
1313		What
1261		do we have in common
1261		*
3257		Jesus
3355		the Nazarene
0208		Have you come
0005		to destroy us
1023		know
0124		I
1261		you
1389		who
0133		you are
2162		the Holy [one]
0093		of God

VERSE 35 — And Jesus rebuked him and said, "Shut your mouth and go out of him." And the demon threw him down in the middle and went out of him, not harming him at all.

1113		And rebuked
0217		him
3257		Jesus
0116		and said
1653		Shut
1936		your mouth
1542		and go out
1388		of him
2455		And threw him
2469		the demon
1416		in the middle
1542		and went out
1388		of him
1128		\<while\>
1262		not
1710		harming
0217		him
1326		at all

VERSE 36 — And great amazement took hold of everyone and they were speaking with each other and saying, "What indeed is this message, because with authority and power he commands the unclean spirits and they go out?"

2680		And amazement
2271		great
0047		took hold
1175		of everyone
1362		and speaking
0603		they were
1817		with
0723		each other
0116		and saying
1393		What
0592		is
1163		indeed
1364		message
0598		this
2527		because with authority
0786		and power
2007		he commands
2323		the spirits
0991		unclean
1542		and they go out

VERSE 37 — And a report went out about him into the entire region surrounding them.

1542		And went out
1804		about him
0944		a report

LUKE CHAPTER 4

1168		into the entire
0214		region
0732		surrounding them

VERSE 38 — And after Jesus went out of the synagogue, he entered the house of Simon, and the mother-in-law of Simon was tormented with a great fever, and they begged him on account of her.

1128		And after
1542		went out
3257		Jesus
1388		of
1200		the synagogue
1796		he entered
0243		the house
3521		of Simon
0823		and the mother-in-law
3521		of Simon
0104		tormented
0603		was
0204		with a fever
2271		great
0296		and they begged
1388		him
1347		on account of her

VERSE 39 — And he stood over her and rebuked her fever and it left her. And immediately she rose up and served them.

2168		And he stood
1803		over
1388		her
1113		and rebuked
0204		her fever
2440		and it left her
0725		And immediately
2168		she rose up
2554		and served
0603		*
1261		them

VERSE 40 — And [at] the setting of the sun all those who had sick who were sick with various sicknesses brought them to him. And he placed his hand on each of them and healed them.

1884		[at] the setting of
2557		the sun
0518		And
1168		all
0066		those
0069		who had
0603		*
1261		*
1228		sick
1226		who were sick
1227		with sicknesses
0813		various
0208		brought
0592		them
1288		to him
0592		<he>
0518		And
1804		on
0721		each of them
0721		*
1388		*
0057		his hand
1625		he placed
0603		*
0136		and healed
0603		*
1261		them

VERSE 41 — And also demons were going out of many, crying out and saying, "You are the Messiah, the Son of God." And he rebuked them and did not allow them to say that they knew he was the Messiah.

1542		And going out
0603		were
0169		also
2469		demons
1388		of

LUKE — CHAPTER 4

#	Aramaic	Gloss
1596		many
1128		crying out
0683		*
0116		and saying
0133		You
0592		are
1446		the Messiah
0323		the Son
0093		of God
1113		And he rebuked
0603		*
0217		them
1262		and not
2440		did allow
0603		*
1261		them
0116		to say
1023		that they knew
0592		he was
1446		the Messiah

VERSE 42 — And on the morning of the day he went out [and] journeyed to a deserted place. And the crowds were seeking him and came up to him and were holding him captive so that he would not go away from them.

#	Aramaic	Gloss
2124		And on the morning
1036		of the day
1542		he went out
0042		[and] journeyed
1261		<to it>
0214		to a place
0892		deserted
1201		And the crowds
0296		seeking
0603		were
1261		him
0208		and came
1747		up to
1288		<toward> him
0047		were holding him captive
1262		so that not
0042		he would go away
1261		<to him>
1388		from
1288		them

VERSE 43 — But Jesus said to them, "It is necessary for me also to preach to other cities the kingdom of God, because for this I was sent."

#	Aramaic	Gloss
0592		<he>
0518		But
3257		Jesus
0116		said
1261		to them
0169		also
0499		to cities
0053		other
0626		It is necessary
1261		for me
1588		to preach
1385		the kingdom
0093		of God
1804		because for
0598		this
0592		<it>
2458		I was sent

VERSE 44 — And he was preaching in the synagogues of Galilee.

#	Aramaic	Gloss
0592		And <he>
1230		he was preaching
0603		*
1200		in the synagogues
3153		of Galilee

CHAPTER 5

VERSE 1 — And it happened [that] as the crowd gathered around him to hear the word of God and he was standing on the shore of the lake of Gennesaret,

#	Aramaic	Gloss
0603		it happened
0518		And
1128		[that] as

LUKE CHAPTER 5

1198		gathered		1093		[and] sat
1804		around him		0217		in it
1201		the crowd		0116		and told [them]
2547		to hear		0477		to take him
1364		the word		2203		a little way
0093		of God		1388		from
0592		and <he>		1019		dry land
2168		standing		1351		on the water
0603		he was		1093		And he sat
1804		on		0603		*
0057		the shore of		1053		and taught
1058		the lake		1388		from
3156		of Gennesaret		1692		the ship
				1201		the crowd

VERSE 2 — he saw two ships that were standing at the edge of the lake and the fishermen that had come down from them and they were washing their nets.

VERSE 4 — And after he stopped speaking, he said to Simon, "Row to deep [water] and cast your net for a catch."

0758		he saw		1128		And after
1692		ships		2623		he stopped
2709		two		1388		<from>
2168		that were standing		1365		speaking
1804		at		0116		he said
0439		the edge of		3521		to Simon
1058		the lake		0477		Row
2091		and the fishermen		1831		to deep [water]
1658		that had come down		2372		and cast
1388		from them		2090		your net
2466		and they were washing		2092		for a catch
2090		their nets				

VERSE 3 — And one of them belonged to Simon Peter. And Jesus boarded [and] sat in it and told [them] to take him a little way from dry land on the water. And he sat and taught the crowd from the ship.

VERSE 5 — Simon answered and said to him, "My Master, we have labored all night and have not caught anything. But at your word I will cast the net."

0721		And one		1838		answered
1388		of them		3521		Simon
3521		belonged to Simon		0116		and said
0603		*		1261		to him
3258		Peter		2275		My Master
1658		And boarded		1299		night
3257		Jesus		1168		all
				1265		we have labored
				1326		and anything

LUKE — CHAPTER 5

ID	Aramaic	English
1262		not
0047		have caught
1804		at
1364		your word
0518		But
2372		cast
0124		I will
2090		the net

VERSE 6 — And after they did this, they caught a great many fish and their net was tearing.

ID	Aramaic	English
1128		And after
0598		this
1724		they did
0716		they caught
1490		fish
1596		many
0938		a great
2129		and tearing
0603		was
2090		their net

VERSE 7 — And they made signs to their friends who were in the other ship to come to help them. And after they had come, they filled both ships, so that they were close to sinking.

ID	Aramaic	English
2374		And they made signs
0714		to their friends
1692		who were in the ship
0053		other
0208		to come
1751		to help
0592		them
1128		And after
0208		they had come
1366		they filled
0592		*
1692		ships
2709		both
0060		so that
2248		close
0603		they were
0945		to sinking

VERSE 8 — And when Simon Peter saw [this], he fell down before the feet of Jesus and said to him, "I beg you, my Lord, go away from me, for I am a sinful man."

ID	Aramaic	English
1128		when
0758		saw [this]
0518		And
3521		Simon
3258		Peter
1538		he fell down
2154		before
2293		the feet
3257		of Jesus
0116		and said
1261		to him
0296		beg
0124		I
1388		you
1426		my Lord
2042		go away
1261		<you>
1388		from me
0361		for a man
0124		I am
0772		sinful

VERSE 9 — For amazement had taken hold of him and all who were with him, because of that catch of fish that they had caught,

ID	Aramaic	English
2680		amazement
0403		For
0047		had taken hold of him
0603		*
1168		and all <of them>
1817		who were with him
1804		because of
2092		catch
0593		that
1490		of fish
2089		that they had caught

Vertical Interlinear

LUKE — CHAPTER 5

VERSE 10 — and so also James and John, the sons of Zebedee, who were partners of Simon. And Jesus said to Simon, "Do not be afraid. From now on, you will catch men to life."

Code	Aramaic	English
0595	ܗܟܘܬ	so
0518	ܕܝܢ	and
0169	ܐܦ	also
3255	ܠܝܥܩܘܒ	James
3233	ܘܠܝܘܚܢܢ	and John
0323	ܒܢܝ	the sons
3185	ܙܒܕܝ	of Zebedee
0069	ܐܝܬܝܗܘܢ	who were
0603	ܗܘܘ	*
2486	ܫܘܬܦܐ	partners
3521	ܕܫܡܥܘܢ	of Simon
0116	ܐܡܪ	said
0518	ܕܝܢ	And
3257	ܝܫܘܥ	Jesus
3521	ܠܫܡܥܘܢ	to Simon
1262	ܠܐ	not
0509	ܬܕܚܠ	Do not be afraid
1388	ܡܢ	From
0602	ܗܫܐ	now on
0323	ܒܢܝ	men
0131	ܐܢܫܐ	*
0603	ܬܗܘܐ	you will
2089	ܨܐܕ	catch
0781	ܠܚܝܐ	to life

VERSE 11 — And they brought those ships to land and left everything and followed him.

Code	Aramaic	English
2244	ܘܩܪܒܘ	And they brought
0592	ܐܢܝܢ	those
1692	ܣܦܝܢܐ	ships
0199	ܠܐܪܥܐ	to land
2440	ܘܫܒܩܘ	and left
1168	ܟܠ	everything
1326	ܡܕܡ	*
0208	ܘܐܬܘ	and followed him
0215	ܒܬܪܗ	*

VERSE 12 — And when Jesus was in one of the cities, a man who was completely covered with leprosy came. He saw Jesus and fell on his face and begged him and said to him, "My Lord, if you want to, you are able to cleanse me."

Code	Aramaic	English
1128	ܘܟܕ	And when
0603	ܗܘܐ	was
3257	ܝܫܘܥ	Jesus
0721	ܒܚܕܐ	in one
1388	ܡܢ	of
0499	ܡܕܝܢܬܐ	the cities
0208	ܐܬܐ	came
0361	ܓܒܪܐ	a man
1366	ܕܡܠܐ	who was completely covered
1168	ܟܠܗ	*
0457	ܓܪܒܐ	with leprosy
0758	ܚܙܐ	He saw
3257	ܠܝܫܘܥ	Jesus
1538	ܘܢܦܠ	and fell
1804	ܥܠ	on
0173	ܐܦܘܗܝ	his face
0296	ܘܒܥܐ	and begged
0603	ܗܘܐ	*
1388	ܡܢܗ	him
0116	ܘܐܡܪ	and said
1261	ܠܗ	to him
1426	ܡܪܝ	My Lord
0121	ܐܢ	if
2077	ܨܒܐ	want to
0133	ܐܢܬ	you
2510	ܡܫܟܚ	are able
0133	ܐܢܬ	you
0521	ܠܡܕܟܝܘܬܢܝ	to cleanse me

VERSE 13 — And Jesus stretched out his hand [and] touched him and said to him, "I want to. Be cleansed." And immediately his leprosy went away from him and he was cleansed.

Code	Aramaic	English
2054	ܘܦܫܛ	And stretched out
0057	ܐܝܕܗ	his hand
3257	ܝܫܘܥ	Jesus

LUKE   CHAPTER 5

#	Syriac	English		#	Syriac	English
2244		[and] touched		1198		and was gathered
1261		him		0603		*
0116		and said		1818		a crowd
1261		to him		1596		large
2077		I want to		2547		to hear
0124		*		1388		from him
0521		Be cleansed		0136		and to be healed
0323		And immediately		1388		from
2573		*		1227		their sicknesses

VERSE 16 And he went away to the desert land and was praying.

#	Syriac	English
0042		went away
1388		from him
0457		his leprosy
0521		and he was cleansed

#	Syriac	English
0592		\<he\>
0518		And
2561		he went away
0603		*
0478		to the desert land
2106		and was praying

VERSE 14 And he commanded him, "Do not tell anyone, but go [and] show yourself to the priests and offer for your purification, as Moses commanded for their witness."

#	Syriac	English
2007		And he commanded him
0131		anyone
1262		not
0116		Do tell
0090		but
0042		go
0739		[and] show
1547		yourself
1135		to the priests
2244		and offer
0812		for
0526		your purification
0061		as
2007		commanded
3305		Moses
1610		for their witness

VERSE 17 And it happened [that] on a certain day while Jesus was teaching, Pharisees and teachers of the law were sitting [there] who had come from all the villages of Galilee and of Judea and of Jerusalem, and there was the power of the LORD to heal them.

#	Syriac	English
0603		And it happened [that]
0721		on a certain
1388		\<of\>
1036		day
1128		while
1053		teaching
0603		was
3257		Jesus
1093		sitting [there]
0603		were
3439		Pharisees
1053		and teachers of
1524		the law
0208		who had come
0603		*
1388		from
1168		all

VERSE 15 And a report about him went out all the more and a large crowd was gathered to hear from him and to be healed from their sicknesses.

#	Syriac	English
1542		And went out
1804		about him
0944		a report
1101		all the more

403

Vertical Interlinear

LUKE   CHAPTER 5

2251		the villages
3153		of Galilee
3224		and of Judea
3022		and of Jerusalem
0786		and the power
1426		of the LORD
0069		there was
0603		*
0136		to heal them

VERSE 18 — And men brought on a pallet a certain paralyzed man and were seeking to bring [him] in to lay him before him.

0131		And men
0208		brought
1897		on a pallet
0361		a man
0721		certain
2598		paralyzed
0296		and seeking
0603		were
1796		to bring [him] in
1625		to lay him
2154		before him

VERSE 19 — And when they could not find how to bring him in because of the multitude of people, they went up to the roof and let him down on his pallet from the roof floor into the middle before Jesus.

1128		And when
1262		not
2510		they could find
0061		how
1796		to bring him in
1347		because of
1598		the multitude
1818		of people
1658		they went up
1261		*
0019		to the roof
2424		and let him down
1817		on

1897		his pallet
1388		from
0975		the roof floor
1416		into the middle
2154		before <him>
3257		Jesus

VERSE 20 — And when Jesus saw their faith, he said to that paralyzed man, "Your sins are forgiven."

1128		when
0758		saw
0518		And
3257		Jesus
0113		their faith
0116		he said
0593		to that
2598		paralyzed
0361		man
2440		are forgiven
1261		<you>
0771		Your sins

VERSE 21 — And the scribes and Pharisees began reasoning and saying, "Who is this [man] who speaks blasphemy? Who is able to forgive sins, except God alone?"

2597		And began
1699		the scribes
3439		and Pharisees
0914		reasoning
0116		and saying
1390		Who is
0598		this [man]
1362		who speaks
0371		blasphemy
1390		Who is
2510		able
2440		to forgive
0771		sins
0090		except
0121		*
0093		God

LUKE CHAPTER 5

1041	ܒܠܚܘܕ	alone

VERSE 22 — But Jesus knew their reasonings and answered and said to them, "Why are you reasoning in your heart?

3257	ܝܫܘܥ	Jesus
0518	ܕܝܢ	But
1023	ܝܕܥ	knew
0917	ܡܚܫܒܬܗܘܢ	their reasonings
1838	ܘܥܢܐ	and answered
0116	ܘܐܡܪ	and said
1261	ܠܗܘܢ	to them
1393	ܡܢܐ	Why
0914	ܡܬܚܫܒܝܢ	are reasoning
0133	ܐܢܬܘܢ	you
1268	ܒܠܒܟܘܢ	in your heart

VERSE 23 — Which [thing] is easier to say, 'Your sins are forgiven' or to say, 'Rise up, walk?'

0066	ܐܝܕܐ	Which [thing]
2061	ܦܫܝܩܐ	is easier
0116	ܠܡܐܡܪ	to say
2440	ܕܫܒܝܩܝܢ	are forgiven
1261	ܠܟ	<you>
0771	ܚܛܗܝܟ	Your sins
0024	ܐܘ	or
0116	ܠܡܐܡܪ	to say
2168	ܩܘܡ	Rise up
0608	ܘܗܠܟ	walk

VERSE 24 — But that you will know that it is lawful for the Son of Man to forgive sins on earth," he said to the paralytic, "I say to you, rise up, take up your pallet and go to your house."

1023	ܕܬܕܥܘܢ	that you will know
0518	ܕܝܢ	But
2528	ܕܫܠܝܛ	that it is lawful for
0592	ܗܘ	*
0323	ܠܒܪܗ	the Son
0131	ܕܐܢܫܐ	of Man
0199	ܒܐܪܥܐ	on earth
2440	ܕܢܫܒܘܩ	to forgive
0771	ܚܛܗܐ	sins
0116	ܐܡܪ	he said
2598	ܠܡܫܪܝܐ	to the paralytic
1261	ܠܟ	to you
0116	ܐܡܪ	say
0124	ܐܢܐ	I
2168	ܩܘܡ	Rise up
2587	ܫܩܘܠ	take up
1897	ܥܪܣܟ	your pallet
0042	ܘܙܠ	and go
0243	ܠܒܝܬܟ	to your house

VERSE 25 — And immediately he rose up before their eyes and took up his pallet and went to his house, praising God.

0725	ܘܡܚܕܐ	And immediately
2168	ܩܡ	he rose up
1794	ܠܥܢܝܗܘܢ	before their eyes
2587	ܘܫܩܠ	and took up
1897	ܥܪܣܗ	his pallet
0042	ܘܐܙܠ	and went
0243	ܠܒܝܬܗ	to his house
1128	ܟܕ	praising
2428	ܡܫܒܚ	*
0093	ܠܐܠܗܐ	God

VERSE 26 — And amazement took hold of everyone and they were praising God and were filled with fear and were saying, "We have seen wonders today."

2680	ܘܬܡܗܐ	And amazement
0047	ܐܚܕ	took hold of
1175	ܠܟܠܢܫ	everyone
2428	ܘܡܫܒܚܝܢ	and praising
0603	ܗܘܘ	they were
0093	ܠܐܠܗܐ	God
1366	ܘܐܬܡܠܝܘ	and were filled
0511	ܕܚܠܬܐ	with fear
0116	ܘܐܡܪܝܢ	and were saying
0758	ܚܙܝܢ	We have seen
1037	ܝܘܡܢܐ	today
0551	ܬܕܡܪܬܐ	wonders

LUKE CHAPTER 5

VERSE 27 — After these [things], Jesus went out and saw a tax collector, whose name was Levi, who was sitting at the customs-house, and he said to him, "Follow me."

Code	Syriac	English
0215		After
0598		these [things]
1542		went out
3257		Jesus
0758		and saw
1358		a tax collector
2539		whose name was
3280		Levi
1093		who was sitting at
0243		the customs-house
1358		*
0116		and he said
1261		to him
0208		Follow me
0215		*

VERSE 28 — And he left everything and stood up [and] followed him.

Code	Syriac	English
2440		And he left
1168		everything
1326		*
2168		and stood up [and]
0042		followed him
0215		*

VERSE 29 — And Levi made for him a great feast in his house, and there was a large crowd of tax collectors and of others who were eating with them.

Code	Syriac	English
1724		And made
1261		for him
3280		Levi
0243		in his house
2140		a feast
2271		great
0069		and there was
0603		*
1201		a crowd
1596		large
1358		of tax collectors
0053		and of others
1664		who eating
0603		were
1817		with them

VERSE 30 — And the scribes and Pharisees were murmuring and saying to his disciples, "Why are you eating and drinking with tax collectors and sinners?"

Code	Syriac	English
2360		And murmuring
0603		were
1699		the scribes
3439		and Pharisees
0116		and saying
1304		to his disciples
1394		Why
1817		with
1358		tax collectors
0772		and sinners
0075		are eating
0133		you
2620		and drinking

VERSE 31 — And Jesus answered and said to them, "The physician is not needed by the healthy, but by those who are very sick.

Code	Syriac	English
1838		And answered
3257		Jesus
0116		and said
1261		to them
1262		not
0296		is needed
0137		The physician
0808		by the healthy
0090		but
0066		by those
0220		who are very sick
0220		*
1724		*

VERSE 32 — I did not come to call the just, but sinners to repentance."

Code	Syriac	English
1262		not

LUKE   CHAPTER 5

Code	Aramaic	English
0208		I did come
2239		to call
0637		the just
0090		but
0772		sinners
2651		to repentance

VERSE 33 — And those were saying to him, "Why are the disciples of John, also of the Pharisees, fasting and praying continually, but yours are eating and drinking?"

Code	Aramaic	English
0592		those
0518		And
0116		were saying
1261		to him
1394		Why are
1304		the disciples
3233		of John
2093		fasting
0112		and continually
2106		praying
0169		also
3439		of the Pharisees
0517		yours
0518		but
0075		are eating
2620		and drinking

VERSE 34 — And he said to them, "You cannot make the wedding guests fast as long as the bridegroom [is] with them.

Code	Aramaic	English
0592		\<he\>
0518		And
0116		he said
1261		to them
1262		cannot
2510		*
0133		You
0323		the wedding guests
0431		*
1188		as long as
0933		the bridegroom [is]
1817		with them
1724		make
2093		fast

VERSE 35 — But the days will come when the bridegroom will be taken up from them. Then, in those days, they will fast."

Code	Aramaic	English
0208		will come
0518		But
1036		the days
1128		when
2331		will be taken up
0933		the bridegroom
1388		from them
0594		Then
2093		they will fast
0593		in those
1036		days

VERSE 36 — And he told them a parable: "No one cuts off a piece of cloth from a new garment and lays [it] on an old garment, lest he cuts off the new and the patch that is from the new does not repair the old.

Code	Aramaic	English
0116		And he told
1261		them
1454		a parable
1262		No
0131		one
2147		cuts off
2405		a piece of cloth
1388		from
1320		a garment
0735		new
2372		and lays [it]
1804		on
1320		an garment
0275		old
1262		lest
0735		the new
2147		he cuts off
0275		and the old

Vertical Interlinear

LUKE   CHAPTER 5

1262	ܠܐ	not
2530	ܡܚܠܡ	does repair
2405	ܪܘܩܥܬܐ	the patch
1388	ܗܘ	that is from
0735	ܚܕܬܐ	the new

VERSE 37 — And no one puts new wine into old wineskins, lest the new wine will burst the wineskins and the wine should be poured out and the wineskins ruined.

1262	ܘܠܐ	And no
0131	ܐܢܫ	one
2372	ܪܡܐ	puts
0831	ܚܡܪܐ	wine
0735	ܚܕܬܐ	new
0687	ܒܙܩܐ	in wineskins
0275	ܒܠܝܬܐ	old
0121	ܕܠܐ	lest
0518	ܕܝܢ	*
1262	ܠܐ	*
0249	ܡܒܙܥ	will burst
0831	ܚܡܪܐ	the wine
0735	ܚܕܬܐ	new
0687	ܠܙܩܐ	the wineskins
0592	ܘܗܘ	and <it>
0831	ܚܡܪܐ	the wine
0201	ܡܬܐܫܕ	should be poured out
0687	ܘܙܩܐ	and the wineskins
0005	ܐܒܕܢ	ruined

VERSE 38 — On the contrary, they put new wine into new wineskins and both of them are preserved.

0090	ܐܠܐ	On the contrary
0831	ܚܡܪܐ	wine
0735	ܚܕܬܐ	new
0687	ܒܙܩܐ	into wineskins
0735	ܚܕܬܬܐ	new
2372	ܪܡܝܢ	they put
2709	ܘܬܪܝܗܘܢ	and both of them
1502	ܡܬܢܛܪܝܢ	are preserved

VERSE 39 — And no one drinks old wine and immediately desires new, for he says, 'The old is delicious.'"

1262	ܘܠܐ	And no
0131	ܐܢܫ	one
2620	ܫܬܐ	drinks
0831	ܚܡܪܐ	wine
1917	ܥܬܝܩܐ	old
0725	ܘܡܚܕܐ	and immediately
0296	ܒܥܐ	desires
0735	ܚܕܬܐ	new
0116	ܐܡܪ	he says
0403	ܓܝܪ	for
1917	ܥܬܝܩܐ	The old
0288	ܒܣܝܡ	is delicious

CHAPTER 6

VERSE 1 — And it happened [that] on the Sabbath, while Jesus was walking [in] the sown fields, his disciples were picking the heads of grain and rubbing [them] in their hands and eating [them].

0603	ܗܘܐ	it happened [that]
0518	ܕܝܢ	And
2445	ܒܫܒܬܐ	on the Sabbath
1128	ܟܕ	while
0608	ܡܗܠܟ	was walking
3257	ܝܫܘܥ	Jesus
0243	ܒܝܬ	[in] the sown fields
0693	ܙܪܥܐ	*
1304	ܬܠܡܝܕܘܗܝ	his disciples
1376	ܡܠܓܝܢ	picking
0603	ܗܘܘ	were
2436	ܫܒܠܐ	the heads of grain
2028	ܘܦܪܟܝܢ	and rubbing [them]
0057	ܒܐܝܕܝܗܘܢ	in their hands
0075	ܘܐܟܠܝܢ	and eating [them]

VERSE 2 — And some of the Pharisees were saying to them, "Why are you doing that which is not lawful to do on the Sabbath?"

0131	ܐܢܫܝܢ	some
0518	ܕܝܢ	And
1388	ܡܢ	of

408

LUKE   CHAPTER 6

#		text		#		text
3439		the Pharisees		1532		took
0116		were saying		0075		[and] ate
1261		to them		1030		and gave
1393		Why		0066		to those
1724		are you doing		1817		who were with him
0133		*		0593		that
1326		that which		1262		which not
1262		not		2528		was lawful
2528		is lawful		0603		*
1724		to do		0075		for [anyone] to eat
2445		on the Sabbath		0090		but
				1135		the priests
				1041		alone

VERSE 3   Jesus answered and said to them, "And have you not read what David did when he was hungry, and those who were with him,

1838		answered
3257		Jesus
0116		and said
1261		to them
1262		And not
0598		<this>
2239		have you read
1326		what
1724		did
3159		David
1128		when
1212		he was hungry
0592		*
0066		and those
1817		who were with him

VERSE 4   how he entered the house of God and took the bread of the table of the LORD [and] ate and gave to those who were with him, that which was not lawful for [anyone] to eat, but only the priests alone?"

1796		how he entered
0243		the house
0093		of God
1293		and the bread
2069		of the table
1426		of the LORD

VERSE 5   And he said to them, "The Lord of the Sabbath is the Son of Man."

0116		And he said
1261		to them
1426		The Lord
0592		is
2445		of the Sabbath
0323		the Son
0131		of Man

VERSE 6   And it happened [that] on another Sabbath he entered the synagogue and was teaching. And there was there a man whose right hand was withered.

0603		it happened [that]
0518		And
2445		on Sabbath
0053		another
1796		he entered
1200		the synagogue
1053		and teaching
0603		was
0069		And there was
0603		*
2682		there
0361		a man
0057		whose hand
1061		right

409

LUKE CHAPTER 6

1018	ܝܒܝܫܐ	withered
0603	ܗܘܬ	was

VERSE 7 And the scribes and Pharisees were watching him, if he would heal on the Sabbath, so that they would be able to accuse him.

1699	ܘܣܦܪܐ	And the scribes
3439	ܘܦܪܝܫܐ	and Pharisees
1502	ܢܛܪܝܢ	watching
0603	ܗܘܘ	were
1261	ܠܗ	him
0121	ܐܢ	if
0592	ܗܘ	*
0136	ܡܐܣܐ	he would heal
2445	ܒܫܒܬܐ	on the Sabbath
2510	ܕܢܫܟܚܘܢ	so that they would be able
0075	ܠܡܐܟܠ ܩܪܨܘܗܝ	to accuse him
2257	ܩܪܨܘܗܝ	*

VERSE 8 And he knew their thoughts and said to that man whose hand was withered, "Stand up. Come to the middle of the synagogue." And when he came and stood,

0592	ܗܘ	<he>
0518	ܕܝܢ	And
1023	ܝܕܥ	he knew
0917	ܡܚܫܒܬܗܘܢ	their thoughts
0116	ܘܐܡܪ	and said
0593	ܠܗܘ	to that
0361	ܓܒܪܐ	man
1018	ܕܝܒܝܫܐ	was withered
0057	ܐܝܕܗ	whose hand
2168	ܩܘܡ	Stand up
0208	ܬܐ	Come
1261	ܠܟ	*
1416	ܠܡܨܥܬܐ	to the middle of
1200	ܟܢܘܫܬܐ	the synagogue
1128	ܘܟܕ	And when
0208	ܐܬܐ	he came
2168	ܩܡ	and stood

VERSE 9 Jesus said to them, "I will ask you, is it lawful on the Sabbath to do good or evil, to cause a soul to live or to destroy [it]?"

0116	ܐܡܪ	said
1261	ܠܗܘܢ	to them
3257	ܝܫܘܥ	Jesus
2420	ܐܫܐܠܟܘܢ	I will ask you
1393	ܡܢܐ	*
2528	ܫܠܝܛ	is it lawful
2445	ܒܫܒܬܐ	on the Sabbath
0938	ܕܛܒ	good
1724	ܠܡܥܒܕ	to do
0024	ܐܘ	or
0220	ܕܒܝܫ	evil
1547	ܢܦܫܐ	a soul
0780	ܠܡܚܝܘ	to cause to live
0024	ܐܘ	or
0005	ܠܡܘܒܕܘ	to destroy [it]

VERSE 10 And he gazed at all of them and said to him, "Stretch out your hand." And he stretched [it] out and his hand was restored like the other.

0756	ܘܚܪ	And he gazed
0217	ܒܗܘܢ	at them
1168	ܒܟܠܗܘܢ	all of
0116	ܘܐܡܪ	and said
1261	ܠܗ	to him
2054	ܦܫܘܛ	Stretch out
0057	ܐܝܕܟ	your hand
2054	ܘܦܫܛ	And he stretched [it] out
2699	ܘܬܩܢܬ	and was restored
0057	ܐܝܕܗ	his hand
0060	ܐܝܟ	like
0714	ܚܒܪܬܗ	the other

VERSE 11 And they were filled with envy and were speaking with each other about what they should do to Jesus.

0592	ܗܢܘܢ	<they>
0518	ܕܝܢ	And
1366	ܐܬܡܠܝܘ	they were filled with
0860	ܚܣܡܐ	envy

LUKE   CHAPTER 6

1362		and speaking
0603		were
0721		with each other
1817		*
0721		*
1393		about what
1724		they should do
1261		<to him>
3257		to Jesus

VERSE 12   And it happened [that] in those days Jesus went out to a mountain to pray. And there he spent the night in prayer to God.

0603		it happened [that]
0518		And
1036		in days
0593		those
1542		went out
3257		Jesus
0958		to a mountain
2106		to pray
2682		And there
1465		he spent the night
0603		*
2107		in prayer
0093		to God

VERSE 13   And when [day] dawned, he called his disciples and chose twelve of them, those whom he named apostles:

1128		And when
1465		[day] dawned
2239		he called
1304		his disciples
0351		and chose
1388		of them
2710		twelve
0593		those
2522		whom apostles
2540		he named
0592		<them>

VERSE 14   Simon, whom he called Peter, and Andrew, his brother, and James and John and Philip and Bartholomew

3521		Simon
0593		whom
2540		he called
3258		Peter
3061		and Andrew
0043		his brother
3255		and James
3233		and John
3420		and Philip
3133		and Bartholomew

VERSE 15   and Matthew and Thomas and James, the son of Alphaeus, and Simon, who was called the zealot,

3329		and Matthew
3528		and Thomas
3255		and James
0323		the son of
3196		Alphaeus
3521		and Simon
2239		who was called
0989		the zealot

VERSE 16   and Judas, the son of James, and Judas Iscariot, who was the betrayer.

3228		and Judas
0323		the son of
3255		James
3228		and Judas
3370		Iscariot
0593		who
0603		was
2531		the betrayer

VERSE 17   And Jesus came down with them and stood in the plain with a large crowd of his disciples and a multitude of a crowd of people from all Judea and from Jerusalem and from the sea coast of Tyre and of Sidon,

1499		And came down
1817		with them
3257		Jesus

LUKE CHAPTER 6

2168		and stood
2014		in the plain
1201		with a crowd
1596		large
1304		of his disciples
1598		and a multitude
1201		of a crowd
1818		of people
1388		from
1168		all
3224		Judea
1388		and from
3022		Jerusalem
1388		and from
1700		the coast
1057		sea
3450		of Tyre
3452		and of Sidon

VERSE 18 who had come to hear his message and to be healed of their sicknesses, and those who were tormented by unclean spirits, and they were healed.

0208		who had come
2547		to hear
1364		his message
0136		and to be healed
1388		of
1227		their sicknesses
0066		and those
0102		who were tormented
1388		by
2323		spirits
0991		unclean
0136		and they were healed
0603		*

VERSE 19 And the whole crowd was seeking to touch him, for power was going out of him, and he was healing all of them.

1168		And whole
1201		the crowd
0296		seeking
0603		was
2244		to touch
1261		him
0786		power
0403		for
1542		going out
0603		was
1388		of him
1168		and all of them
0136		healing
0603		he was

VERSE 20 And he lifted up his eyes to his disciples and said, "Blessed are you poor, because yours is the kingdom of God.

2331		And he lifted up
1794		his eyes
1804		to
1304		his disciples
0116		and said
0940		Blessed are you
1406		poor
0517		because yours
0592		is
1385		the kingdom
0093		of God

VERSE 21 Blessed are you who are hungry now, because you will be satisfied. Blessed are you who are weeping now, because you will laugh.

0940		Blessed are you
0066		<those>
1214		who are hungry
0602		now
1585		because you will be satisfied
0940		Blessed are you
0267		who are weeping
0602		now
0400		because you will laugh

LUKE — CHAPTER 6

VERSE 22 — Blessed are you when men hate you and discriminate against you and reproach you and cast out your name as evil for the sake of the Son of Man.

#	Syriac	English
0940		Blessed are you
1313		when
1673		hate
1261		you
0325		men
2046		and discriminate
1261		against you
0855		and reproach
1261		you
1542		and cast out
2539		your name
0060		as
0220		evil
0812		for the sake of
0323		the Son of
0131		of Man

VERSE 23 — Rejoice in that day and leap for joy, because your reward is great in heaven, for their fathers did the same to the prophets.

#	Syriac	English
0726		Rejoice
0593		in that
1036		day
0500		and leap for joy
0018		because your reward
1596		is great
2543		in heaven
0597		the same
0403		for
1724		did
0603		*
0002		their fathers
1457		to the prophets

VERSE 24 — But woe to you, rich [ones], because you have received your comfort!

#	Syriac	English
0342		But
0625		woe
1261		to you
1921		rich [ones]
2134		because you have received
0263		your comfort

VERSE 25 — Woe to you, satisfied [ones], because you will hunger! Woe to you who are laughing now, because you will cry and you will mourn!

#	Syriac	English
0625		Woe
1261		to you
1586		satisfied [ones]
1212		because you will hunger
0625		Woe
1261		to you
0400		who are laughing
0602		now
0267		because you will cry
0009		and you will mourn

VERSE 26 — Woe to you, when men will speak what is good about you, for their fathers did so to the false prophets!

#	Syriac	English
0625		Woe
1261		to you
1128		when
0603		will
0116		speak
1804		about you
0323		men
0131		*
2583		what is good
0597		so
0403		for
1724		did
0603		*
1457		to the prophets
0487		false
0002		their fathers

VERSE 27 — But to you who hear, I say, 'Love your enemies and do that which is good to those who hate you.

#	Syriac	English
1261		to you

LUKE   CHAPTER 6

0518	ܐܠܐ	But
0116	ܐܡܪ	say
0124	ܐܢܐ	I
2547	ܠܕܫܡܥܝܢ	who hear
0696	ܐܚܒܘ	Love
0307	ܠܒܥܠܕܒܒܝܟܘܢ	your enemies
1724	ܘܥܒܕܘ	and do
2583	ܕܫܦܝܪ	that which is good
0066	ܠܐܝܠܝܢ	to those
1673	ܕܣܢܝܢ	who hate
1261	ܠܟܘܢ	you

VERSE 28   And bless those who curse you and pray for those who take you by force.

0335	ܘܒܪܟܘ	And bless
0066	ܠܐܝܠܝܢ	those
1284	ܕܠܝܛܝܢ	who curse
1261	ܠܟܘܢ	you
2106	ܘܨܠܘ	and pray
1804	ܥܠ	for
0066	ܐܝܠܝܢ	those
0477	ܕܕܒܪܝܢ	who take
1261	ܠܟܘܢ	you
2188	ܒܩܛܝܪܐ	by force

VERSE 29   And to him, who strikes you on your cheek, offer to him the other, and from him who takes away your outer cloak, do not hold back your tunic also.

1341	ܘܠܡܢܕܡܚܐ	And to him who strikes
1261	ܠܟ	you
1804	ܥܠ	on
1961	ܦܟܟ	your cheek
2244	ܩܪܒ	offer
1261	ܠܗ	to him
0053	ܐܚܪܢܐ	the other
1388	ܘܡܢ	and from
1389	ܡܢ	him
2587	ܕܫܩܠ	who takes away
1439	ܡܪܛܘܛܟ	your outer cloak
1262	ܠܐ	not
1180	ܬܟܠܐ	do hold back
0169	ܐܦ	also
1256	ܟܘܬܝܢܟ	your tunic

VERSE 30   To everyone who asks you, give to him, and from him, who takes away your [things], do not demand [them] back.

1168	ܠܟܠ	To everyone
2420	ܕܫܐܠ	who asks
1261	ܠܟ	you
1030	ܗܒ	give
1261	ܠܗ	to him
1388	ܘܡܢ	and from
1389	ܡܢ	him
2587	ܕܫܩܠ	who takes away
0517	ܕܝܠܟ	your [things]
1262	ܠܐ	not
2631	ܬܬܒܥ	do demand [them] back

VERSE 31   And whatever you desire men to do to you, do the same to them also.

0061	ܘܐܝܟܢܐ	And whatever
2077	ܕܨܒܝܢ	desire
0133	ܐܢܬܘܢ	you
1724	ܕܢܥܒܕܘܢ	to do
1261	ܠܟܘܢ	to you
0323	ܒܢܝܢܫܐ	men
0131	ܐܢܫܐ	*
0595	ܗܟܘܬ	the same
1724	ܥܒܕܘ	do
1261	ܠܗܘܢ	to them
0169	ܐܦ	also
0133	ܐܢܬܘܢ	you

VERSE 32   For if you love those who love you, what is your goodness? For even sinners love those who love them.

0121	ܐܢ	if
0403	ܓܝܪ	For
0696	ܡܚܒܝܢ	love
0133	ܐܢܬܘܢ	you
0066	ܠܐܝܠܝܢ	those
0696	ܕܡܚܒܝܢ	who love
1261	ܠܟܘܢ	you
0066	ܐܝܕܐ	what

LUKE   CHAPTER 6

0592		is
0942		your goodness
0169		even
0403		For
0772		sinners
0066		those
0696		love
1261		them
2342		who love

VERSE 33 — And if you do that which is good to those who do good to you, what is your goodness? For even sinners do the same.

0121		And if
1724		do
0133		you
0938		that which is good
0066		to those
0937		who do good
1261		to you
0066		what
0592		is
0942		your goodness
0169		even
0772		sinners
0403		For
0597		the same
1724		do

VERSE 34 — And if you lend to [those] from whom you expect to be repaid, what is your goodness? For even sinners lend to sinners, that in the same way they might be repaid.

0121		And if
1039		lend
0133		you
1389		to whom
1588		expect
0133		you
2037		to be repaid
1388		[those] from

0066		what
0592		is
0942		your goodness
0169		even
0772		sinners
0403		For
0772		to sinners
1039		lend
0595		that in the same way
2037		they might be repaid

VERSE 35 — But love your enemies and do good to them and lend and do not cut off the hope of anyone, and your reward will be increased and you will be the sons of the Most High, because he is kind to the evil and to the unthankful.

0342		But
0696		love
0307		your enemies
0937		and do good
1261		to them
1039		and lend
1262		and not
1992		do cut off
1592		the hope
0131		of anyone
0603		and will be
1596		increased
0018		your reward
0603		and you will be
0323		sons
2336		of the Most High
0592		because <he>
0288		is kind
0592		he
1804		to
0220		the evil
1804		and to
1217		the unthankful

415

LUKE CHAPTER 6

VERSE 36 — Therefore be merciful, as your Father also is merciful.

Code	Syriac	Gloss
0603		be
0596		Therefore
2343		merciful
0061		as
0169		also
0002		your Father
2343		merciful
0592		is

VERSE 37 — Do not judge and you will not be judged. Do not condemn and you will not be condemned. Forgive and you will be forgiven.

Code	Syriac	Gloss
1262		not
0496		Do judge
1262		and not
0496		will be judged
0133		you
1262		not
0742		Do condemn
1262		and not
0742		you will be condemned
0133		*
2597		Forgive
2597		and you will be forgiven

VERSE 38 — Give and it will be given to you. With good and pressed down and abundant measure they will throw into your laps. For with the same measure that you measure, it will be measured to you."

Code	Syriac	Gloss
1030		Give
1030		and it will be given
1261		to you
1144		With measure
0938		good
2404		and pressed down
2578		and abundant
2372		they will throw
1760		into your laps
0593		with the same
0403		For
1144		measure
1142		that measure
0133		you
1142		it will be measured
1261		to you

VERSE 39 — And he told them a parable, "Are the blind able to lead the blind? Would not they both fall in a ditch?

Code	Syriac	Gloss
0116		And he told
0603		*
1261		them
1454		a parable
1316		<?>
2510		Are able
1662		the blind
1662		the blind
0477		to lead
1262		not
2709		both
0422		in a ditch
1538		Would they fall

VERSE 40 — There is no disciple who is greater than his master, for everyone who is mature should be as his master [is].

Code	Syriac	Gloss
1264		There is no
1304		disciple
1100		who is greater
1388		than
2271		his master
1175		everyone
0403		for
0426		who is mature
0603		should be
0060		as
2271		his master [is]

VERSE 41 — And why do you see the straw that is in the eye of your brother, but the plank that is in your [own] eye is not seen by you?

Code	Syriac	Gloss
1393		why
0518		And

LUKE CHAPTER 6

0758		do see
0133		you
0406		the straw
1794		that is in the eye
0043		of your brother
2252		the plank
0518		but
1794		that is your [own] eye
1262		not
0758		is seen
1261		by you

VERSE 42 Or how are you able to say to your brother, 'My brother, allow me to take out the straw from your eye,' when behold, the plank that is in your own eye is not seen by you? Hypocrite! First take out the plank from your [own] eye and then it will be clear for you to take out the straw from the eye of your brother.

0024		Or
0061		how
2510		are able
0133		you
0116		to say
0043		to your brother
0043		My brother
2440		allow me
1542		to take out
0406		the straw
1388		from
1794		your eye
0580		when behold
2252		the plank
1794		that is in eye
0517		your own
1262		not
0758		is seen
1261		by you
1532		Hypocrite
0173		*
1542		take out

2151		First
2252		the plank
1388		from
1794		your [own] eye
0594		and then
0758		it will be clear
1261		for you
1542		to take out
0406		the straw
1388		from
1794		the eye
0043		of your brother

VERSE 43 There is not a good tree that produces bad fruit or a bad tree that produces good fruit.

1262		not
0069		There is
0063		a tree
0938		good
1724		that produces
2016		fruit
0220		bad
0169		or
1262		<not>
0063		a tree
0220		bad
1724		that produces
2016		fruit
0938		good

VERSE 44 For every tree is known by its fruit. For they do not gather figs from thorn-bushes, nor do they gather grapes from a bramble-bush.

1168		every
0063		tree
0403		For
1388		by
2016		its fruit
0592		<it>
1023		is known
1262		not

LUKE CHAPTER 6

0403		For
1309		they do gather
1388		from
1139		thorn-bushes
2628		figs
0169		nor
1262		*
1388		from
1678		a bramble-bush
2186		do they gather
1840		grapes

VERSE 45 A good man, from the good treasures that are in his heart, produces good things, and an evil man, from the evil treasures that are in his heart, produces evil things. For from the abundant [things] of the heart the lips speak.

0361		A man
0938		good
1388		from
1627		the treasures
0938		good
1268		that are in his heart
1542		produces
0938		good things
0361		and man
0220		an evil
1388		from
1627		the treasures
0220		evil
1268		that are in his heart
1542		produces
0220		evil things
1388		from
1106		the abundant [things] of
1268		the heart
0403		For
1362		speak
1701		the lips

VERSE 46 Why do you call me, 'My Lord, my Lord,' and you do not do what I say?

1393		Why
2239		do call
0133		you
1261		me
1426		My Lord
1426		my Lord
1326		and what
0116		say
0124		I
1262		not
1724		do you do
0133		*

VERSE 47 I will show you what each one who comes to me and hears my words and does them is like.

1168		each
0131		one
0208		who comes
1288		to me
2547		and hears
1364		my words
1724		and does
1261		them
0739		I will show you
1394		what
0540		is like

VERSE 48 He is like the man who built a house and dug and went deep and laid the foundations on rock. And when there was a flood, the flood beat on that house and it was not able to shake it, for its foundation was placed on rock.

0540		He is like
0361		the man
0281		who built
0243		a house
0875		and dug
1830		and went deep
1625		and laid
0203		the foundations

LUKE CHAPTER 6

1804		on
2477		rock
1128		when
0603		there was
0518		And
1368		a flood
1004		beat
1368		the flood
0243		on house
0593		that
1262		and not
2510		it was able
0657		to shake it
1626		placed
0603		was
0403		for
0203		its foundation
1804		on
2477		rock

VERSE 49 And whoever hears [my words] and does not do [them] is like the man who built his house on ground without a foundation. And when the river beat on it, immediately it fell, and the fall of that house was great."

0593		And whoever
2547		hears [my words]
1262		and not
1724		does do [them]
0540		is like
0361		the man
0281		who built
0243		his house
1804		on
1859		ground
1262		without
0203		a foundation
1128		And when
1004		beat
0217		on it
1478		the river

0323		immediately
2573		*
1538		it fell
0603		and was
1539		the fall
2271		great
0243		of house
0593		that

CHAPTER 7

VERSE 1 And when he completed all the sayings for the hearing of the people, Jesus entered Capernaum.

1128		And when
2530		he completed
1364		sayings
1168		all the
2549		for the hearing
1818		of the people
1796		entered
3257		Jesus
3268		Capernaum

VERSE 2 And the servant of a certain centurion, who was dear to him, was very sick and was about to die.

1727		the servant
0518		And
2223		of a centurion
0721		certain
1724		was very sick
0603		*
0221		*
0066		who
1079		was dear
0603		*
1804		to him
2248		and was about
0603		*
1334		to die

419

Vertical Interlinear

LUKE CHAPTER 7

VERSE	3		And he heard about Jesus and sent to him elders of the Judeans and was begging him to come [and] give life to his servant.
2547		ܘܫܡܥ	And he heard
1804		ܥܠ	about
3257		ܝܫܘܥ	Jesus
2458		ܘܫܕܪ	and sent
1288		ܠܘܬܗ	to him
2263		ܩܫܝܫܐ	elders
3226		ܕܝܗܘܕܝܐ	of the Judeans
0296		ܘܒܥܐ	and begging
0603		ܗܘܐ	was
1388		ܡܢܗ	him
0060		ܐܝܟ	<so that>
0208		ܕܢܐܬܐ	to come
0780		ܢܚܐ	[and] give life
1727		ܠܥܒܕܗ	to his servant

VERSE	4		And when they came to Jesus, they were begging him earnestly and saying, "He is worthy that you do this for him,
0592		ܗܢܘܢ	<they>
0518		ܕܝܢ	And
1128		ܟܕ	when
0208		ܐܬܘ	they came
1288		ܠܘܬ	to
3257		ܝܫܘܥ	Jesus
0296		ܒܥܝܢ	begging
0603		ܗܘܘ	they were
1388		ܡܢܗ	him
0255		ܒܛܝܠܐܝܬ	earnestly
0116		ܘܐܡܪܝܢ	and saying
2461		ܫܘܐ	He is worthy
0592		ܗܘ	*
1724		ܕܬܥܒܕ	that you should do
1261		ܠܗ	for him
0598		ܗܕܐ	this

VERSE	5		for he loves our people and has even built a synagogue for us."
2342		ܪܚܡ	he loves
0403		ܓܝܪ	for

1818		ܠܥܡܢ	our people
0169		ܘܐܦ	and even
0243		ܒܝܬ	a synagogue
1200		ܟܢܘܫܬܐ	*
0592		ܗܘ	<he>
0281		ܒܢܐ	has built
1261		ܠܢ	for us

VERSE	6		And Jesus went with them. And when he was not very far from the house, the centurion sent his friends to him and said to him, "My Lord, do not trouble [yourself], for I am not worthy that you should come under my roof,
3257		ܝܫܘܥ	Jesus
0518		ܕܝܢ	And
0042		ܐܙܠ	went
0603		ܗܘܐ	*
1817		ܥܡܗܘܢ	with them
1128		ܟܕ	when
0518		ܕܝܢ	And
1262		ܠܐ	not
1596		ܣܓܝ	very
2355		ܪܚܝܩ	he was far
1388		ܡܢ	from
0243		ܒܝܬܐ	the house
2458		ܫܕܪ	sent
1288		ܠܘܬܗ	to him
2223		ܩܢܛܪܘܢܐ	the centurion
2345		ܪܚܡܘܗܝ	his friends
0116		ܘܐܡܪ	and said
1261		ܠܗ	to him
1426		ܡܪܝ	My Lord
1262		ܠܐ	not
1827		ܬܬܥܢܐ	do trouble [yourself]
1262		ܠܐ	not
0403		ܓܝܪ	for
2461		ܫܘܐ	am worthy
0124		ܐܢܐ	I
1796		ܕܬܥܘܠ	that you should come
2660		ܬܚܝܬ	under
0973		ܡܛܠܠܝ	my roof

LUKE — CHAPTER 7

VERSE 7 — [and] on account of that, I am not worthy to come to you. But speak with a word and my young man will be healed,

#	Syriac	Gloss
1347		[and] on account of
0593		that
0124		<I>
1262		not
2461		I am worthy
1288		to you
0208		to come
0090		But
0116		speak
1364		with a word
0136		and will be healed
0976		my young man

VERSE 8 — for I also am a man who is subject to authority and there are soldiers under my hand. And I say to this one, 'Go,' and he goes, and to another, 'Come,' and he comes, and to my servant, 'Do this,' and he does [it]."

#	Syriac	Gloss
0169		also
0124		I
0403		for
0361		a man
0124		am
1724		who is subject
0124		<I am>
2660		to
2527		authority
0069		and there are
2660		under
0057		my hand
0150		soldiers
0116		and say
0124		I
0598		to this one
0042		Go
0042		and he goes
0053		and to another
0208		Come
0208		and he comes
1727		and to my servant
1724		Do
0598		this
1724		and he does [it]

VERSE 9 — And when Jesus heard these [things], he marveled at him. And he turned and said to the crowd that was following him, "I say to you, not even [in] Israel have I found faith like this."

#	Syriac	Gloss
1128		when
2547		heard
0518		And
3257		Jesus
0598		these [things]
0549		he marveled
0217		at him
1984		And he turned
0116		and said
1201		to the crowd
0208		that was following him
0215		*
0116		say
0124		I
1261		to you
0169		not even
1262		*
0243		[in] Israel
3035		*
2510		have I found
0060		like
0598		this
0113		faith

VERSE 10 — And those who were sent returned to the house and found that servant who was sick made whole.

#	Syriac	Gloss
0616		And returned
0593		those
2458		who were sent
0243		to the house
2510		and found

LUKE   CHAPTER 7

1727		servant
0593		that
1226		who sick
0603		was
1128		made whole
0808		*

VERSE 11 — And it happened on the day that followed, [that] he went to a city by the name of Nain and his disciples and a large crowd [were] with him.

0603		And it happened [that]
1036		on the day
0215		that followed
0042		he went
0603		*
0499		to a city
2539		by the name of
3334		Nain
1304		and his disciples
1817		[were] with him
1201		and a crowd
1596		large

VERSE 12 — And when he approached the gate of the city, he saw a dead man being brought who was the only [son] of his mother, and his mother was a widow, and a large crowd of citizens [was] with her.

1128		And when
2244		he approached
2718		the gate
0499		of the city
0758		he saw
1128		being
1281		brought
1338		a dead man
1042		who the only [son]
0603		was
0106		of his mother
0592		and <she>
0106		his mother
0195		a widow

0603		was
1201		and a crowd
1596		large
0323		of citizens
0499		*
1817		[was] with her

VERSE 13 — And Jesus saw her and had compassion on her and said to her, "Do not cry."

0758		saw her
0518		And
3257		Jesus
2342		and had compassion
1804		on her
0116		and said
1261		to her
1262		not
0267		Do cry

VERSE 14 — And he went [and] touched the pallet. And those who were carrying it stood, and he said, "Young man, I say to you, rise up."

0042		And he went
2244		[and] touched
1897		the pallet
0593		And those
2587		who were carrying
0603		*
1261		it
2168		stood
0116		and he said
1811		Young man
1261		to you
0116		say
0124		I
2168		rise up

VERSE 15 — And that dead man sat up and began to speak and he gave him to his mother.

1093		And sat up
0593		that
1338		dead man
2597		and began

LUKE CHAPTER 7

#	Syriac	English
1362		to speak
1030		and he gave him
0106		to his mother

VERSE 16 — And fear took hold of all men and they were praising God and saying, "A great prophet has risen up among us and God has visited his people."

#	Syriac	English
0047		And took hold
0511		fear
0131		of men
1168		all
2428		and praising
0603		they were
0093		God
0116		and saying
1457		A prophet
2271		great
2168		has risen up
0217		among us
1684		and has visited
0093		God
1818		his people

VERSE 17 — And this saying went out about him into all Judea and into all the region around them,

#	Syriac	English
1542		And went out
1804		about him
1364		saying
0598		this
1168		into all
3224		Judea
1168		and into all
0214		the region
0732		around them

VERSE 18 — and his disciples reported all these [things] to John.

#	Syriac	English
2569		and reported
3233		to John
1304		his disciples
0598		these [things]
1168		all

VERSE 19 — And John called two of his disciples and sent them to Jesus and said, "Are you that one who is to come or should we wait for another?"

#	Syriac	English
2239		And called
3233		John
2709		two
1388		of
1304		his disciples
2458		and sent
0592		them
1288		to
3257		Jesus
0116		and said
0133		Are you
0592		one
0593		that
0208		who is to come
0024		or
0053		for another
0592		<one>
1646		should we wait
0124		*

VERSE 20 — And they came to Jesus and said to him, John the baptizer sent us to you and said, "Are you that one who is to come or should we wait for another?"

#	Syriac	English
0208		And they came
1288		to
3257		Jesus
0116		and said
1261		to him
3233		John
1820		the baptizer
2458		sent us
1288		to you
0116		and said
0133		Are you
0592		one
0593		that
0208		who is to come

LUKE CHAPTER 7

0024		or		2547		and heard
0053		for another		1662		that the blind
0592		<one>		0758		see
1646		should we wait		0719		and the lame
0124		*		0608		walk

VERSE 21 — And in that same hour he healed many of sicknesses and of plagues and of evil spirits and he gave sight to many blind.

				0456		and the lepers
				0521		are cleansed
0217		<in it>		0907		and the deaf
0518		And		2547		heard
0593		in that same		1338		and the dead
2573		hour		2168		rise up
1596		many		1406		and the poor
0136		he healed		1588		receive good news

VERSE 23 — And blessed is he who is not offended at me."

1388		of				
1227		sicknesses		0940		And blessed is he
1388		and of		1389		who
1342		plagues		1262		not
1388		and of		1242		is offended
2323		spirits		0217		at me
0220		evil				

VERSE 24 — And when the disciples of John went away, he began to speak to the crowds about John: "What did you go out to the desert to see, a reed that was shaken by the wind?

1596		and to many				
1662		blind				
1030		he gave				
0603		*		1128		when
0758		sight		0518		And

VERSE 22 — And Jesus answered and said to them, "Go [and] tell John everything that you have seen and heard, that the blind see and the lame walk and the lepers are cleansed and the deaf hear and the dead rise up and the poor receive good news.

				0042		went away
				1304		the disciples
				3233		of John
				2597		he began
				0116		to speak
1838		And answered		1201		to the crowds
3257		Jesus		1804		about
0116		and said		3233		John
1261		to them		1393		What
0042		Go		1542		did you go out
0116		[and] tell		0892		to the desert
3233		John		0758		to see
1173		everything		2224		a reed
0758		that you have seen		1388		that by

LUKE CHAPTER 7

2323	ܪܘܚܐ	the wind
0657	ܐܬܬܙܝܥ	was shaken

VERSE 25 — And if not, what did you go out to see, a man clothed with soft garments? Behold, those who are with fancy clothes and luxuries are [in] the house of kings.

0090	ܘܐܠܐ	And if not
1393	ܡܢܐ	what
1542	ܢܦܩܬܘܢ	did you go out
0758	ܠܡܚܙܐ	to see
0361	ܓܒܪܐ	a man
1501	ܠܒܘܫܐ	garments
2366	ܪܟܝܟܐ	soft
1272	ܠܒܝܫ	clothed with
0580	ܗܐ	Behold
0066	ܐܝܠܝܢ	those
1273	ܕܒܠܒܘܫܐ	who are with clothes
2429	ܡܫܒܚܐ	fancy
1987	ܘܒܦܘܢܩܐ	and luxuries
0069	ܐܝܬܝܗܘܢ	are
0243	ܒܝܬ	[in] the house of
1383	ܡܠܟܐ	kings
0592	ܐܢܘܢ	<they>

VERSE 26 — And if not, what did you go out to see, a prophet? Yes, I say to you, even greater than the prophets.

0090	ܘܐܠܐ	And if not
1393	ܡܢܐ	what
1542	ܢܦܩܬܘܢ	did you go out
0758	ܠܡܚܙܐ	to see
1457	ܢܒܝܐ	a prophet
0065	ܐܝܢ	Yes
0116	ܐܡܪ	say
0124	ܐܢܐ	I
1261	ܠܟܘܢ	to you
1100	ܘܝܬܝܪ	even greater
1388	ܡܢ	than
1457	ܢܒܝܐ	the prophets

VERSE 27 — This is he about whom it is written: BEHOLD, I WILL SEND MY MESSENGER BEFORE YOUR FACE TO PREPARE THE WAY BEFORE YOU.

0599	ܗܢܘ	This is he
1804	ܕܥܠܘܗܝ	about whom
1247	ܟܬܝܒ	it is written
0580	ܕܗܐ	BEHOLD
0124	ܐܢܐ	<I>
2458	ܡܫܕܪ	WILL SEND
0124	ܐܢܐ	I
1375	ܡܠܐܟܝ	MY MESSENGER
2154	ܩܕܡ	BEFORE
2041	ܦܪܨܘܦܟ	YOUR FACE
2699	ܕܢܬܩܢ	TO PREPARE
0038	ܐܘܪܚܐ	THE WAY
2154	ܩܕܡܝܟ	BEFORE YOU

VERSE 28 — I say to you, there is no prophet among those born of women who is greater than John the baptizer, but the least in the kingdom of God is greater than he."

0116	ܐܡܪ	say
0124	ܐܢܐ	I
1261	ܠܟܘܢ	to you
1264	ܕܠܝܬ	there is no
1457	ܢܒܝܐ	prophet
1046	ܒܝܠܝܕܝ	among those born
0135	ܢܫܐ	of women
2271	ܕܪܒ	who is greater
1388	ܡܢ	than
3233	ܝܘܚܢܢ	John
1820	ܡܥܡܕܢܐ	the baptizer
0686	ܙܥܘܪܐ	the least
0518	ܕܝܢ	but
1385	ܒܡܠܟܘܬܐ	in the kingdom
0093	ܕܐܠܗܐ	of God
2271	ܪܒ	greater
0592	ܗܘ	is
1388	ܡܢܗ	than he

LUKE CHAPTER 7

VERSE 29 — And all the people who heard, even the tax collectors, declared God [to be] just, because they had been baptized [with] the baptism of John.

1168	And all
1818	the people
2547	who heard
0169	even
1358	the tax collectors
0636	declared [to be] just
0093	God
1819	because they had been baptized [with]
1821	the baptism
3233	of John

VERSE 30 — And the Pharisees and the scribes rejected in themselves the will of God, because they were not baptized by him.

3439	the Pharisees
0518	And
1699	and the scribes
0979	rejected
1547	in themselves
2079	the will
0093	of God
1262	because not
1819	they were baptized
1388	by him

VERSE 31 — "To what therefore can I liken the men of this generation and to what are they like?

1389	To what
0596	therefore
0540	can I liken
0131	the men
2605	of generation
0598	this
1389	and to what
0540	are they like

VERSE 32 — They are like young boys who sit in the marketplace and call out to their friends and say, 'We have played music for you and you did not dance and we mourned for you and you did not weep.'

0540	They are like
0976	young boys
1093	who sit
2481	in the marketplace
2227	and call out
0714	to their friends
0116	and say
0672	We have played music
1261	for you
1262	and not
2403	you did dance
0091	and we mourned
1261	for you
1262	and not
0267	you did weep

VERSE 33 — For John the baptizer came neither eating bread nor drinking wine and you said, 'There is a demon in him.'

0208	came
0403	For
3233	John
1820	the baptizer
1262	neither
0075	eating
1293	bread
1262	nor
2620	drinking
0831	wine
0116	and said
0133	you
2469	a demon
0069	There is
0217	in him

LUKE CHAPTER 7

VERSE 34 — The Son of Man came eating and drinking and you say, 'Behold, a gluttonous man and [one] drinking wine and a friend of tax collectors and sinners.'

0208		came
0323		The Son
0131		of Man
0075		eating
2620		and drinking
0116		and say
0133		you
0580		Behold
0361		a man
0076		gluttonous
2620		and [one] drinking
0831		wine
2345		and a friend
1358		of tax collectors
0772		and sinners

VERSE 35 — Yet wisdom is declared just by all its children."

0636		Yet is declared just
0792		wisdom
1388		by
1168		all
0323		its children

VERSE 36 — Now one of the Pharisees came [and] begged him to eat with him. And he entered the house of that Pharisee and sat to eat.

0208		came
0518		Now
0296		[and] begged
1388		him
0721		one
1388		of
3439		the Pharisees
1308		to eat
1817		with him
1796		And he entered
0243		the house
3439		of Pharisee
0593		that
1664		and sat to eat

VERSE 37 — And there was a woman [who was] a sinner in that city. And when she learned that he was reclining in the house of that Pharisee, she took an alabaster box of ointment

0135		And a woman
0772		[who was] a sinner
0069		there was
0603		*
0499		in city
0593		that
1128		And when
1023		she learned
0243		that in the house
3439		of Pharisee
0593		that
1664		he was reclining
1532		she took
2502		an alabaster box
0291		of ointment

VERSE 38 — and stood behind him at his feet and she was crying. And she began washing his feet with her tears and wiping them with the hair of her head. And she was kissing his feet and anointed [them] with ointment.

2168		and stood
0295		behind him
1288		at
2293		his feet
0267		and she was crying
0603		*
2597		And she began
0548		with her tears
2080		washing
2293		his feet
1687		and with the hair
2362		of her head
2461		wiping

Vertical Interlinear

LUKE **CHAPTER 7**

1261		them
1573		And she was kissing
0603		*
2293		his feet
1443		and anointed [them] with
0291		ointment

VERSE 39 Now when that Pharisee who had invited him saw [this], he reasoned within himself and said, "This man, if he were a prophet, would have known who she is and what her reputation [is], because the woman who touched him is a sinner."

1128		when
0758		saw [this]
0518		Now
3439		Pharisee
0593		that
2239		who had invited him
0914		he reasoned
1547		within himself
0116		and said
0598		This [man]
0097		if
1457		a prophet
0603		he were
1023		would have known
0603		*
1389		who
0592		she is
1313		and what
0944		her reputation [is]
0772		because a sinner
0592		is
0135		the woman
0593		<she>
2244		who touched
1261		him

VERSE 40 But Jesus answered and said to him, "Simon, I have something to say to you." And he said to him, "Speak, my Master." Jesus said to him,

1838		answered
0518		But
3257		Jesus
0116		and said
1261		to him
3521		Simon
1326		something
0069		I have
1261		*
0116		to say
1261		to you
0592		<he>
0518		And
0116		he said
1261		to him
0116		Speak
2275		my Master
0116		said
1261		to him
3257		Jesus

VERSE 41 "There were two debtors to a certain lender. One owed five hundred denarii and the other fifty denarii.

2709		two
0745		debtors
0069		There were
0603		*
0721		to a certain
1426		lender
0743		*
0721		One
0745		owed
0603		*
0519		denarii
0835		five hundred
0053		and the other
0519		denarii

LUKE CHAPTER 7

0834	ܚܡܫܝܢ	fifty		0593	ܗܘ	that
VERSE	**42**	And because they had no way to repay, he forgave both of them. Now then, which of them will love him more?"		0135	ܐܢܬܬܐ	woman
				0116	ܘܐܡܪ	and said
				3521	ܠܫܡܥܘܢ	to Simon
1264	ܘܕܠܝܬ	And because they had no way		0758	ܚܙܐ	Do you see
				0133	ܐܢܬ	*
0603	ܗܘܐ	*		0135	ܐܢܬܬܐ	woman
1261	ܠܗܘܢ	*		0598	ܗܕܐ	this
2037	ܠܡܦܪܥ	to repay		0243	ܠܒܝܬܟ	your house
2709	ܠܬܪܝܗܘܢ	both of them		1796	ܥܠܬ	I entered
2440	ܫܒܩ	he forgave		1351	ܡܝܐ	[and] water
0066	ܐܝܢܐ	which		2293	ܠܪܓܠܝ	for my feet
0596	ܗܟܝܠ	Now then		1262	ܠܐ	not
1388	ܡܢܗܘܢ	of them		1030	ܝܗܒܬ	you did give [me]
1100	ܝܬܝܪ	more		0598	ܗܕܐ	this [woman]
0696	ܢܚܒܝܘܗܝ	will love him		0518	ܕܝܢ	but
VERSE	**43**	Simon answered and said, "I suppose that the one who was forgiven the most." Jesus said to him, "You have judged correctly."		0548	ܒܕܡܥܝܗ	with her tears
				2293	ܪܓܠܝ	my feet
				2080	ܨܒܥܬ	has washed
				1687	ܘܒܣܥܪܗ	and with her hair
1838	ܥܢܐ	answered		2461	ܫܘܝܬ	she has dried
3521	ܫܡܥܘܢ	Simon		0592	ܐܢܝܢ	them
0116	ܘܐܡܪ	and said		**VERSE**	**45**	You did not kiss me, but behold, this [woman], since I entered, has not ceased to kiss my feet.
1588	ܣܒܪ	suppose				
0124	ܐܢܐ	I				
0593	ܕܗܘ	that the one		0133	ܐܢܬ	<you>
2440	ܕܐܫܬܒܩ	who was forgiven		1262	ܠܐ	not
1261	ܠܗ	<to him>		1573	ܢܫܩܬܢܝ	You did kiss me
1596	ܣܓܝ	the most		0598	ܗܕܐ	this [woman]
0116	ܐܡܪ	said		0518	ܕܝܢ	but
1261	ܠܗ	to him		0580	ܗܐ	behold
3257	ܝܫܘܥ	Jesus		1388	ܡܢ	since
2722	ܬܪܝܨܐܝܬ	correctly		1796	ܕܥܠܬ	I entered
0496	ܕܢܬ	You have judged		1262	ܠܐ	not
VERSE	**44**	Then he turned to that woman and said to Simon, "Do you see this woman? I entered your house [and] you did not give [me] water for my feet, but this [woman] has washed my feet with her tears and she has dried them with her hair.		2516	ܫܠܝܬ	has ceased
				2293	ܪܓܠܝ	my feet
				1573	ܠܡܢܫܩܘ	to kiss
1984	ܘܐܬܦܢܝ	Then he turned				
1288	ܠܘܬ	to				

LUKE   CHAPTER 7

VERSE 46   You did not anoint my head [with] oil, but this [woman] has anointed my feet with perfumed ointment.

Code	Syriac	English
0133		<you>
1445		[with] oil
2362		my feet
1262		not
1443		You did anoint
0598		this [woman]
0518		but
1445		with ointment
0291		perfumed
2293		my feet
1443		has anointed

VERSE 47   Because of this I say to you, her many sins are forgiven, because she has loved much. But he to whom little is forgiven loves little."

Code	Syriac	English
0812		Because of
0598		this
0116		say
0124		I
1261		to you
2440		are forgiven
1261		<her>
0771		her sins
1596		many
1347		because
0696		she has loved
1596		much
0593		he
0518		But
2203		little
2440		is forgiven
1261		to whom
2203		little
0696		loves

VERSE 48   And he said to that woman, "Your sins are forgiven."

Code	Syriac	English
0116		And he said
0593		to that
0135		woman
2440		are forgiven
1261		<you>
0771		Your sins

VERSE 49   And those who were sitting to eat began saying among themselves, "Who is this who even forgives sins?"

Code	Syriac	English
2597		began
0518		And
0593		those
1664		who were sitting to eat
0116		saying
1547		among themselves
1390		Who is
0598		this
0169		who even
0771		sins
2440		forgives

VERSE 50   But Jesus said to that woman, "Your faith has given you life. Go in peace."

Code	Syriac	English
3257		Jesus
0518		But
0116		said
0593		to that
0135		woman
0113		Your faith
0780		has given you life
0042		Go
2535		in peace

CHAPTER 8

VERSE 1   And it happened [that] after these [things] Jesus was going around in the cities and in the villages and he was preaching and declaring the kingdom of God. And his twelve [were] with him

Code	Syriac	English
0603		And it happened [that]
1388		after
0215		*
0598		these [things]
1236		going around
0603		was

430

LUKE CHAPTER 8

#	Syriac	English
3257		Jesus
0499		in the cities
2251		and in the villages
1230		and he was preaching
0603		*
1588		and declaring
1385		the kingdom
0093		of God
2710		And his twelve [were]
1817		with him

VERSE 2 — and those women who had been healed of sicknesses and of evil spirits: Mary who was called Magdalene, from whom seven demons had gone out,

#	Syriac	English
0135		and women
0598		those
0136		who had been healed
1388		of
1227		sicknesses
1388		and of
2323		spirits
0220		evil
3325		Mary
2239		who was called
3297		Magdalene
0593		<who>
2437		seven
2469		demons
1542		had gone out
1388		from whom

VERSE 3 — and Joanna the wife of Chuza, the steward of Herod, and Susanna, and many others who were ministering to them from their properties.

#	Syriac	English
3232		and Joanna
0135		the wife of
3259		Chuza
2276		the steward
3179		of Herod
3508		and Susanna
0053		and others
1596		many
0066		<those>
2554		who were ministering
0603		*
1261		to them
1388		from
2217		their properties

VERSE 4 — And when a large crowd had gathered and they were coming to him from all the cities, he spoke in parables:

#	Syriac	English
1128		And when
1201		a crowd
1596		large
1198		had gathered
0603		*
1388		and from
1168		all
0499		the cities
0208		coming
0603		they were
1288		to him
0116		he spoke
1454		in parables

VERSE 5 — "A sower went to sow his seed, and as he sowed, some fell by the side of the road and was trampled and a bird ate it.

#	Syriac	English
1542		went
0692		A sower
0691		to sow
0693		his seed
1128		and as
0691		he sowed
0069		some
1538		fell
1804		by
0057		the side of
0038		the road
0507		and was trampled
0075		and ate it
2026		a bird

LUKE   CHAPTER 8

VERSE	**6**	And other [seed] fell on rock. And immediately it sprang up, but because it did not have moisture, it withered.
0053	ܘܐܚܪܢܐ	And other [seed]
1538	ܢܦܠ	fell
1804	ܥܠ	on
2477	ܫܘܥܐ	rock
0323	ܘܒܪ	And immediately
2573	ܫܥܬܗ	*
1065	ܝܥܐ	it sprang up
1264	ܘܕܠܝܬ	but because it did not have
0603	ܗܘܐ	*
1261	ܠܗ	*
2671	ܬܠܝܠܘܬܐ	moisture
1018	ܝܒܫ	it withered
VERSE	**7**	And other [seed] fell among thorns and the thorns sprang up with it and choked it.
0053	ܘܐܚܪܢܐ	And other [seed]
1538	ܢܦܠ	fell
0266	ܒܝܬ	among
1139	ܟܘܒܐ	thorns
1065	ܘܝܥܘ	and sprang up
1817	ܥܡܗ	with it
1139	ܟܘܒܐ	the thorns
0848	ܘܚܢܩܘܗܝ	and choked it
VERSE	**8**	And other [seed] fell on good and fertile earth and sprang up and produced fruit one hundred[fold]. When he had said these [things], he cried out, "He who has ears to hear should hear."
0053	ܘܐܚܪܢܐ	And other [seed]
1538	ܢܦܠ	fell
0199	ܒܐܪܥܐ	on earth
0938	ܛܒܬܐ	good
2583	ܘܫܦܝܪܬܐ	and fertile
1065	ܘܝܥܐ	and sprang up
1724	ܘܥܒܕ	and produced
2016	ܦܐܪܐ	fruit
0721	ܚܕ	one
1317	ܒܡܐܐ	hundred[fold]
0598	ܘܗܠܝܢ	these [things]
1128	ܟܕ	When
0116	ܐܡܪ	he had said
2227	ܩܥܐ	he cried out
0603	ܗܘܐ	*
1389	ܡܢ	He who
0069	ܕܐܝܬ	has
1261	ܠܗ	*
0021	ܐܕܢܐ	ears
2547	ܕܢܫܡܥ	to hear
2547	ܢܫܡܥ	should hear
VERSE	**9**	And his disciples asked him, "What is [the meaning of] this parable?"
2420	ܘܫܐܠܘܗܝ	And asked him
1304	ܬܠܡܝܕܘܗܝ	his disciples
1395	ܕܡܢܐ	What is
1454	ܡܬܠܐ	[the meaning of] parable
0598	ܗܢܐ	this
VERSE	**10**	And he said to them, "To you it is given to know the secret of the kingdom of God. But to the rest, it is spoken in comparisons: BECAUSE ALTHOUGH THEY SEE, THEY WILL NOT SEE AND ALTHOUGH THEY HEAR, THEY WILL NOT UNDERSTAND.
0592	ܗܘ	<he>
0518	ܕܝܢ	And
0116	ܐܡܪ	he said
1261	ܠܗܘܢ	to them
1261	ܠܟܘܢ	To you
0592	ܗܘ	it
1030	ܝܗܝܒ	is given
1023	ܠܡܕܥ	to know
0188	ܐܪܙܐ	the secret
1385	ܕܡܠܟܘܬܗ	of the kingdom
0093	ܕܐܠܗܐ	of God
0593	ܠܗܢܘܢ	to <them>
0518	ܕܝܢ	But
2611	ܫܪܟܐ	the rest
1967	ܒܦܠܐܬܐ	in comparisons
0116	ܐܬܐܡܪ	it is spoken
1128	ܕܟܕ	BECAUSE ALTHOUGH

Vertical Interlinear

LUKE — CHAPTER 8

Code	Syriac	English
0758		THEY SEE
1262		NOT
0758		THEY WILL SEE
1128		AND ALTHOUGH
2547		THEY HEAR
1262		NOT
1647		THEY WILL UNDERSTAND

VERSE 11 — Now, this is [the meaning of] the parable. The seed is the word of God.

Code	Syriac	English
0599		this is
0518		Now
1454		[the meaning of] the parable
0693		The seed
0069		is
1364		the word
0093		of God

VERSE 12 — And those [seeds] that [fell] by the side of the road are those who hear the word, yet the enemy comes [and] takes the word from their heart[s], so that they will not believe and live.

Code	Syriac	English
0593		those [seeds]
0518		And
1804		that [fell] by
0057		the side of
0038		the road
0069		are
0593		those
2547		who hear
1364		the word
0208		yet comes
0307		the enemy
2587		[and] takes
1364		the word
1388		from
1268		their heart[s]
1262		so that not
0109		they will believe
0780		and live

VERSE 13 — And those [seeds] that [fell] on rock are those that when they hear, receive the word with joy. But they have no root. On the contrary, their faith is for a while, yet in the time of temptation, they are offended.

Code	Syriac	English
0598		those [seeds]
0518		And
1804		that [fell] on
2477		rock
0598		those
0592		are
1313		that when
2547		they hear
0727		with joy
2134		receive
1261		<it>
1364		the word
1877		But root
1264		they have no
1261		*
0090		On the contrary
0633		for a while
0592		is
0113		their faith
0633		yet in the time of
1528		temptation
1242		they are offended

VERSE 14 — And that [seed] which fell among thorns are those who hear the word and are choked with the care and wealth and lusts of the world and they do not bear fruit.

Code	Syriac	English
0593		that [seed]
0518		And
1538		which fell
0266		among
1139		thorns
0598		<they>
0592		are
0066		those
2547		who hear

LUKE CHAPTER 8

1364		the word		1625		places
1072		and with the care		1261		it
1920		and wealth		2660		under
2288		and lusts		1897		a bed
1813		of the world		0090		On the contrary
0848		are choked		1625		he places
2016		and fruit		1261		it
1262		not		1803		on
1030		they do bear		1388		*

VERSE 15 And that [seed] which [fell] on good ground are those who with an honest and good heart hear the word and adhere [to it] and bear fruit with patience.

0593		that [seed]
0518		And
0199		which [fell] on ground
0938		good
0598		<they>
0592		are
0066		those
1268		who with heart
2574		an honest
0938		and good
2547		hear
1364		the word
0047		and adhere [to it]
1030		and bear
2016		fruit
1591		with patience

VERSE 16 No one lights a lamp and hides it in a vessel or places it under a bed. On the contrary, he places it on a lamp stand, so that all who enter will see its light.

1262		No
0131		one
1474		lights
2607		a lamp
0869		and hides
1261		it
1320		in a vessel
0024		or

1402		a lamp stand
1168		so that all
1796		who enter
0758		will see
1477		its light

VERSE 17 For there is not anything that is covered that will not be revealed or that is hidden that will not be known and come [out] openly.

1264		there is not
0403		For
1326		anything
1206		that is covered
1262		that not
0409		will be revealed
1262		or
1009		that is hidden
1262		that not
1023		will be known
0208		and come [out]
0411		openly

VERSE 18 Take heed how you hear, for whoever has, it will be given to him, and whoever does not have, even that which he thinks he has, will be taken from him."

0758		Take heed
0061		how
2547		you hear
1389		whoever
0069		has
1261		*
0403		for

LUKE CHAPTER 8

#	Aramaic	English
1030		it will be given
1261		to him
1389		and whoever
1264		does not have
1261		*
0169		even
0593		that
1588		which he thinks
0069		he has
1261		*
2587		will be taken
1388		from him

VERSE 19 Now his mother and his brothers came to him and were not able to speak with him because of the crowd.

#	Aramaic	English
0208		came
0518		Now
1288		to him
0106		his mother
0043		his brothers
1262		and not
2510		were able
0603		*
1362		to speak
1817		with him
1347		because of
1201		the crowd

VERSE 20 And they said to him, "Your mother and your brothers are standing outside and want to see you."

#	Aramaic	English
0116		And they said
1261		to him
0106		Your mother
0043		and your brothers
2168		are standing
0322		outside
2077		and want
0758		to see you

VERSE 21 But he answered and said to them, "My mother and my brothers are those who hear the word of God and do it."

#	Aramaic	English
0592		<he>
0518		But
1838		he answered
0116		and said
1261		to them
0598		<they>
0592		are
0106		My mother
0043		and my brothers
0066		those
2547		who hear
1364		the word
0093		of God
1724		and do
1261		it

VERSE 22 And it happened [that] on a certain day Jesus boarded [and] sat in a boat, he and his disciples, and he said to them, "Let us cross over to the other side of the lake."

#	Aramaic	English
0603		it happened [that]
0518		And
0721		on a certain
1388		<of>
1036		day
1658		boarded
3257		Jesus
1093		[and] sat
1692		in a boat
0592		he
1304		and his disciples
0116		and he said
1261		to them
1733		Let us cross over
0593		to <that>
1735		the other side
1058		of the lake

LUKE CHAPTER 8

VERSE 23 — And while they were journeying, Jesus was asleep. And there was a sudden wind storm on the lake and the boat was about to sink.

1128	ܘܟܕ	And while
2299	ܪܕܝܢ	they were journeying
0544	ܕܡܟ	was asleep
1261	ܠܗ	*
0592	ܗܘ	*
3257	ܝܫܘܥ	Jesus
0603	ܘܗܘܬ	And there was
1816	ܥܠܥܠܐ	a sudden storm
2323	ܕܪܘܚܐ	wind
1058	ܒܝܡܬܐ	on the lake
2248	ܘܩܪܝܒܐ	and was about
0603	ܗܘܬ	*
1692	ܣܦܝܢܬܐ	the boat
0945	ܠܡܛܒܥ	to sink

VERSE 24 — And they came near [and] woke him and said to him, "Our Master, our Master, we are being destroyed." And he stood up and rebuked the winds and the waves of the sea and they ceased and there was calm.

2244	ܘܩܪܒܘ	And they came near
1880	ܐܥܝܪܘܗܝ	[and] woke him
0116	ܘܐܡܪܝܢ	and said
1261	ܠܗ	to him
2271	ܪܒܢ	Our Master
2271	ܪܒܢ	our Master
0005	ܐܒܕܝܢܢ	we are being destroyed
0592	ܗܘ	<he>
0518	ܕܝܢ	And
2168	ܩܡ	he stood up
1113	ܘܟܐܐ	and rebuked
2323	ܒܪܘܚܐ	the winds
0926	ܘܒܡܚܫܘܠܐ	and the waves
1057	ܕܝܡܐ	of the sea
1483	ܘܢܚܘ	and they ceased
0603	ܘܗܘܐ	and there was
2519	ܫܠܝܐ	calm

VERSE 25 — And he said to them, "Where is your faith?" And, being afraid, they were amazed and said one to another, "Who indeed is this [man] who commands even the winds and the waves and the sea and they obey him?"

0116	ܘܐܡܪ	And he said
1261	ܠܗܘܢ	to them
1108	ܐܝܟܐ	Where
0592	ܗܝ	is
0113	ܗܝܡܢܘܬܟܘܢ	your faith
0592	ܗܢܘܢ	<they>
0518	ܕܝܢ	And
1128	ܟܕ	being
0509	ܕܚܝܠܝܢ	afraid
0549	ܡܬܕܡܪܝܢ	they were amazed
0603	ܗܘܘ	*
0116	ܘܐܡܪܝܢ	and said
0721	ܚܕ	one
0721	ܠܚܕ	to another
1390	ܡܢܘ	Who is
1163	ܟܝ	indeed
0598	ܗܢܐ	this [man]
0169	ܕܐܦ	who even
2323	ܠܪܘܚܐ	the winds
2007	ܦܩܕ	commands
0926	ܘܠܡܚܫܘܠܐ	and the waves
1057	ܘܠܝܡܐ	and the sea
2547	ܘܡܫܬܡܥܝܢ	and they obey
1261	ܠܗ	him

VERSE 26 — And they journeyed and came to the region of the Gadarenes that is on the shore opposite Galilee.

2299	ܘܪܕܘ	And they journeyed
0208	ܘܐܬܘ	and came
0214	ܠܐܬܪܐ	to the region
3147	ܕܓܕܪܝܐ	of the Gadarenes
0069	ܕܐܝܬܘܗܝ	that is
1735	ܥܠ ܥܒܪܐ	on the shore
2135	ܠܘܩܒܠ	opposite
3153	ܓܠܝܠܐ	Galilee

Vertical Interlinear

LUKE   **CHAPTER 8**

VERSE 27 — And when he had come onto the land, he met a certain man from the city who had had a devil for a long time. And he did not wear clothes and did not live in a house, but in the tombs.

1128		And when
1542		he had come
0199		onto the land
1928		he met
0217		*
0361		a man
0721		certain
1388		from
0499		the city
0069		who had had
0217		*
0514		a devil
1388		for
0633		a time
1596		long
1320		And clothes
1262		not
1272		he did wear
0603		*
0243		and in a house
1262		not
1833		did live
0603		*
0090		but
0243		in the tombs
2143		*

VERSE 28 — And when he saw Jesus, he cried out and fell down before him and spoke with a loud voice, "What do we have in common, Jesus, Son of the Most High God? I beg you, do not torment me."

1128		when
0758		he saw
0518		And
3257		Jesus
2227		he cried out
1538		and fell down
2154		before him
2204		and with a voice
2336		loud
0116		spoke
1313		What
1261		do we have in common
1261		*
3257		Jesus
0323		Son
0093		of God
2333		the Most High
0296		beg
0124		I
1388		you
1262		not
2565		do torment me

VERSE 29 — For Jesus was commanding the unclean spirit to go out of the man, for a long time had passed since he was [first] held captive by him. And he had been bound with chains and restrained with fetters, but he broke his bonds and was driven by the demon into the wilderness.

2007		commanding
0603		was
1261		<him>
0403		For
3257		Jesus
2323		the spirit
0991		unclean
1542		to go out
1388		of
0325		the man
1596		long
0603		had passed
0403		for
0633		a time
1388		since
2426		he was [first] held captive
0603		*
1261		by him

437

Vertical Interlinear

LUKE   CHAPTER 8

0160		And he had been bound
0603		*
2508		with chains
1123		and with fetters
1502		restrained
0603		*
1992		but he broke
0603		*
0161		his bonds
0477		and was driven
0603		*
1388		by
2469		the demon
0892		into the wilderness

VERSE 30 And Jesus asked him, "What is your name?" He said to him, "Legion," because many devils had entered into him.

2420		asked him
0518		And
3257		Jesus
1389		What is
2539		your name
0116		He said
1261		to him
1275		Legion
1347		because
0514		devils
1596		many
1796		had entered
0603		*
0217		into him

VERSE 31 And they were begging him that he would not command them to go to the abyss.

0296		And begging
0603		they were
1388		him
1262		that not
2007		he would command
1261		them
0042		to go
2643		to the abyss

VERSE 32 And there was there a herd of many pigs that was feeding on the mountain. And they were begging him to permit them to attack the pigs and he permitted them.

0069		there was
0603		*
0518		And
2682		there
0319		a herd
0766		of pigs
1596		many
2381		that was feeding
0958		on the mountain
0296		And begging
0603		they were
1388		him
1989		to permit
1261		them
0766		the pigs
1796		to attack
1989		and he permitted
1261		them

VERSE 33 And the demons went out from the man and attacked the pigs and that whole herd rushed to a steep place and fell into the lake and was drowned.

1542		And went out
2469		the demons
1388		from
0361		the man
1796		and attacked
0766		the pigs
2720		and rushed
0319		the herd
0593		<that>
1168		whole
2586		to a steep place
1538		and fell

LUKE   CHAPTER 8

1058		into the lake
0848		and was drowned

VERSE 34 — And when the herdsmen saw what had happened, they fled and reported [it] in the cities and villages.

1128		when
0758		saw
0518		And
2383		the herdsmen
1326		what
0603		had happened
1904		they fled
2569		and reported [it]
0499		in the cities
2251		and villages

VERSE 35 — And the men came out to see what had happened. And they came to Jesus and found the man, whose demons had gone out, clothed and sober and sitting at the feet of Jesus, and they were afraid.

1542		And came out
0131		the men
0758		to see
1326		what
0603		had happened
0208		And they came
1288		to
3257		Jesus
2510		and found
0361		the man
0593		<that>
1542		gone out
2469		whose demons
1128		clothed
1272		*
1517		and sober
1093		and sitting
1288		at
2293		the feet
3257		of Jesus
0509		and they were afraid

VERSE 36 — And those who had seen [it] reported to them how he healed the man possessed with a devil.

2569		And reported
1261		to them
0066		those
0758		who had seen [it]
0061		how
0136		he healed
0361		the man
0593		<who>
0515		possessed with a devil

VERSE 37 — And all the assembly of the Gadarenes begged him to go away from them, because great fear had taken hold of them. And Jesus boarded a ship and turned away from them.

0296		And begged
0603		*
1388		him
1168		all
1201		the assembly
3147		of the Gadarenes
0042		to go away
1261		*
1388		from
1288		them
1347		because
0511		fear
2271		great
0047		had taken hold of
0592		them
0592		<he>
0518		And
3257		Jesus
1658		boarded
1692		a ship
0616		and turned away
1388		from
1288		them

LUKE CHAPTER 8

VERSE 38 — And that man from whom the demons went out begged him that he might remain with him. But Jesus sent him away and said to him,

Code	Syriac	English
0593	ܗܘ	that
0518	ܕܝܢ	And
0361	ܓܒܪܐ	man
1542	ܐܦܩܘ	went out
1388	ܕܡܢܗ	from whom
2469	ܫܐܕܐ	the demons
0296	ܒܥܐ	begged
0603	ܗܘܐ	*
1388	ܡܢܗ	him
1288	ܕܠܘܬܗ	that with him
0603	ܢܗܘܐ	he might remain
2597	ܘܫܪܝܗܝ	But sent him away
3257	ܝܫܘܥ	Jesus
0116	ܘܐܡܪ	and said
1261	ܠܗ	to him

VERSE 39 — "Return to your house and report what God has done for you." And he went and was preaching in the whole city what Jesus had done for him.

Code	Syriac	English
0616	ܗܦܘܟ	Return
0243	ܠܒܝܬܟ	to your house
2569	ܘܐܫܬܥܐ	and report
1326	ܡܕܡ	what
1724	ܕܥܒܕ	has done
1261	ܠܟ	for you
0093	ܐܠܗܐ	God
0042	ܘܐܙܠ	And he went
1230	ܘܡܟܪܙ	and preaching
0603	ܗܘܐ	was
1168	ܒܟܠܗ	in the whole
0499	ܡܕܝܢܬܐ	city
1326	ܡܕܡ	what
1724	ܕܥܒܕ	had done
1261	ܠܗ	for him
3257	ܝܫܘܥ	Jesus

VERSE 40 — And when Jesus returned, a large crowd received him, for all were looking for him.

Code	Syriac	English
1128	ܟܕ	when
0616	ܗܦܟ	returned
0518	ܕܝܢ	And
3257	ܝܫܘܥ	Jesus
2134	ܩܒܠܗ	received him
1201	ܟܢܫܐ	a crowd
1596	ܣܓܝܐܐ	large
1168	ܟܠܗܘܢ	all
0403	ܓܝܪ	for
1261	ܠܗ	for him
0756	ܚܝܪܝܢ	looking
0603	ܗܘܘ	were

VERSE 41 — And a certain man whose name [was] Jairus, a chief of the synagogue, fell before the feet of Jesus and begged him to enter his house,

Code	Syriac	English
0361	ܘܓܒܪܐ	And a man
0721	ܚܕ	certain
2539	ܕܫܡܗ	whose name was
3231	ܝܘܐܪܫ	Jairus
2362	ܪܒ	a chief of
1200	ܟܢܘܫܬܐ	the synagogue
1538	ܢܦܠ	fell
2154	ܩܕܡ	before
2293	ܪܓܠܘܗܝ	the feet
3257	ܕܝܫܘܥ	of Jesus
0296	ܘܒܥܐ	and begged
0603	ܗܘܐ	*
1388	ܡܢܗ	him
1796	ܕܢܥܘܠ	to enter
0243	ܠܒܝܬܗ	his house

VERSE 42 — for he had an only daughter about twelve years old and she was about to die. And while Jesus went with him, a large crowd thronged him.

Code	Syriac	English
0327	ܒܪܬܐ	an daughter
0403	ܓܝܪ	for
1042	ܝܚܝܕܝܬܐ	only
0069	ܐܝܬ	he had

LUKE CHAPTER 8

#	Syriac	English
0603		*
1261		*
0060		about
0327		twelve years old
2559		*
2710		*
2248		and about
0603		she was
1334		to die
1128		And while
0042		went
1817		with him
0592		<he>
3257		Jesus
1201		a crowd
1596		large
0711		thronged
0603		*
1261		him

VERSE 43 — And a certain woman, whose blood had been flowing [for] twelve years, who had spent all her wealth among the doctors, but was not able to be healed by man,

#	Syriac	English
0135		a woman
0518		And
0721		certain
2717		had been flowing
0603		*
0539		whose blood
2559		[for] years
2710		twelve
0593		<she>
0266		who among
0137		the doctors
1168		all
2217		her wealth
1542		had spent
1262		but not
2510		was able
1388		by
0131		man
0136		to be healed

VERSE 44 — approached from behind him and touched the outer edge of his garment. And immediately the flow of her blood stopped.

#	Syriac	English
2244		approached
1388		from
0295		behind him
2244		and touched
1197		the outer edge
1320		of his garment
0725		And immediately
2168		stopped
2302		the flow
0539		of her blood

VERSE 45 — And Jesus said, "Who touched me?" And while all were denying [it], Simon Peter and those with him said to him, "Our Master, the crowds are pressing and thronging you, yet you say, 'Who touched me?'"

#	Syriac	English
0116		And said
3257		Jesus
1390		Who
2244		touched
1261		me
1128		And while
1168		all
1215		were denying [it]
0116		said
1261		to him
3521		Simon
3258		Peter
1817		and those with him
2271		Our master
1201		the crowds
0102		are pressing
1261		you
0711		and thronging
0116		yet say
0133		you

Vertical Interlinear

LUKE CHAPTER 8

1390	ܡܢܘ	Who
2244	ܩܪܒ	touched
1261	ܠܝ	me
VERSE 46		And he said, "Someone touched me, for I know that power went out of me."
0592	ܗܘ	\<he\>
0518	ܕܝܢ	And
0116	ܐܡܪ	he said
0131	ܐܢܫ	Someone
2244	ܩܪܒ	touched
1261	ܠܝ	me
0124	ܐܢܐ	\<I\>
0403	ܓܝܪ	for
1023	ܝܕܥܬ	I know
0786	ܕܚܝܠܐ	that power
1542	ܢܦܩ	went out
1388	ܡܢܝ	of me
VERSE 47		Now when that woman saw that she had not escaped his notice, she came trembling and fell down [and] worshipped him. And she declared before all the people for what reason she had touched [him] and how she was immediately healed.
0593	ܗܝ	that
0518	ܕܝܢ	Now
0135	ܐܢܬܬܐ	woman
1128	ܟܕ	when
0758	ܚܙܬ	saw
1262	ܕܠܐ	that not
0993	ܛܥܬܗ	she had escaped his notice
0208	ܐܬܬ	she came
1128	ܟܕ	trembling
2414	ܪܬܝܬܐ	*
1538	ܘܢܦܠܬ	and fell down
1599	ܣܓܕܬ	[and] worshipped
1261	ܠܗ	him
0116	ܘܐܡܪܬ	And she declared
1794	ܠܥܝܢ	before
1818	ܥܡܐ	the people
1168	ܟܠܗ	all

1347	ܡܛܠ	for
0066	ܐܝܕܐ	what
1801	ܥܠܬܐ	reason
2244	ܩܪܒܬ	she had touched [him]
0061	ܘܐܝܟܢܐ	and how
0725	ܡܚܕܐ	immediately
0136	ܐܬܐܣܝܬ	she was healed
VERSE 48		And Jesus said to her, "Be encouraged, my daughter. Your faith has given you life. Go in peace."
0592	ܗܘ	\<he\>
0518	ܕܝܢ	And
3257	ܝܫܘܥ	Jesus
0116	ܐܡܪ	said
1261	ܠܗ	to her
1267	ܐܬܠܒܒܝ	Be encouraged
0327	ܒܪܬܝ	my daughter
0113	ܗܝܡܢܘܬܟܝ	Your faith
0780	ܐܚܝܬܟܝ	has given you life
0042	ܙܠܝ	Go
2535	ܒܫܠܡܐ	in peace
VERSE 49		And while he was speaking, a man from the house of the chief of the synagogue came and said to him, "Your daughter has died. Do not trouble the teacher."
1744	ܘܥܕ	And while
0592	ܗܘ	\<he\>
1362	ܡܡܠܠ	he was speaking
0208	ܐܬܐ	came
0131	ܐܢܫ	a man
1388	ܡܢ	from
0243	ܕܒܝܬ	the house of
2271	ܪܒ	the chief of
1200	ܟܢܘܫܬܐ	the synagogue
0116	ܘܐܡܪ	and said
1261	ܠܗ	to him
1334	ܡܝܬܬ	has died
1261	ܠܗ	*
0327	ܒܪܬܟ	Your daughter
1262	ܠܐ	not
1827	ܬܥܡܠ	Do trouble

LUKE   CHAPTER 8

1055		the teacher
VERSE 50		But Jesus heard [it] and said to the father of the girl, "Do not fear, believe only and she will live."
3257		Jesus
0518		But
2547		heard [it]
0116		and said
0002		to the father
0978		of the girl
1262		not
0509		Do fear
1041		only
0109		believe
0780		and she will live
VERSE 51		And Jesus came to the house and did not allow anyone to enter with him, except Simon and James and John and the father of the girl and her mother.
0208		came
0518		And
3257		Jesus
0243		to the house
1262		and not
2440		did allow
0131		anyone
1796		to enter
1817		with him
0090		except
3521		Simon
3255		and James
3233		and John
0002		and the father
0978		of the girl
0106		and her mother
VERSE 52		And all were weeping and mourning over her. But Jesus said, "Do not weep, for she has not died, but sleeps."
1168		all
0518		And
0267		weeping

0603		were
2403		and mourning
1804		over her
3257		Jesus
0518		But
0116		said
1262		not
0267		Do weep
1262		not
0403		for
1334		she has died
0090		but
0544		sleeps
0592		*
VERSE 53		And they were laughing at him, because they knew that she had died.
0400		And laughing
0603		they were
1804		at him
1023		because they knew
1334		that she had died
1261		*
VERSE 54		And he put everyone outside and took her by her hand and called her and said, "Young girl, rise up."
0592		<he>
0518		And
1542		he put
1175		everyone
0322		outside
0047		and took her
0057		by her hand
2239		and called her
0116		and said
0978		Young girl
2168		rise up
VERSE 55		And her spirit returned and immediately she rose up. And he commanded them to give her [something] to eat.
0616		And returned
2323		her spirit

LUKE CHAPTER 8

#	Syriac	English
0725		and immediately
2168		she rose up
2007		And he commanded
1030		them to give
1261		her
0075		[something] to eat

VERSE 56 — And her parents were astonished. And he warned them not to tell anyone what had happened.

#	Syriac	English
2679		And were astonished
0002		her parents
0592		<he>
0518		And
0645		he warned
0592		them
0131		anyone
1262		not
0116		to tell
1313		what
0603		had happened

CHAPTER 9

VERSE 1 — And Jesus called his twelve and gave them power and authority over all demons and to heal sicknesses.

#	Syriac	English
2239		And called
3257		Jesus
2710		his twelve
1030		and gave
1261		them
0786		power
2527		and authority
1804		over
1168		all
2469		demons
1227		and sicknesses
0136		to heal

VERSE 2 — And he sent them to preach the kingdom of God and to heal the sick.

#	Syriac	English
2458		And he sent
0592		them
1230		to preach
1385		the kingdom
0093		of God
0136		and to heal
1228		the sick

VERSE 3 — And he said to them, "Do not take anything on the journey, neither staff nor bag nor bread nor money nor should you have two coats.

#	Syriac	English
0116		And he said
1261		to them
1326		anything
1262		not
2587		Do take
0038		on the journey
1262		neither
2433		staff
1262		nor
2712		bag
1262		nor
1293		bread
1262		nor
1209		money
1262		nor
2709		two
1256		coats
0603		should have
1261		you

VERSE 4 — And in whatever house you enter, remain there and leave from there.

#	Syriac	English
0066		And in whatever
0243		house
1796		you enter
0133		*
1261		<it>
2682		there
0603		remain
1388		and from
2682		there
1542		leave

LUKE — CHAPTER 9

VERSE 5 — And whoever does not receive you, when you leave that city, shake off even the dust from your feet for a witness against them."

#	Syriac	Gloss
1389		And whoever
1262		not
2134		does receive
1261		you
1313		when
1542		leave
0133		you
1388		<from>
0499		city
0593		that
0169		even
0795		the dust
1388		from
2293		your feet
1541		shake off
1804		against them
1610		for a witness

VERSE 6 — And the apostles left and were going around in the villages and cities and were preaching and healing in every place.

#	Syriac	Gloss
1542		And left
2522		the apostles
1236		and were going around
0603		*
2251		in the villages
0499		and cities
1588		and were preaching
0603		*
0136		and healing
1168		in every
0494		place

VERSE 7 — Now Herod the tetrarch heard of all [the things] that were done by his hand and he was wondering, because some were saying that John had risen from the dead.

#	Syriac	Gloss
2547		heard of
0518		Now
3179		Herod
0961		the tetrarch
1168		all [the things]
0603		that were done
0603		*
0057		by his hand
0549		and he was wondering
0603		*
1347		because
0116		saying
0603		were
0131		some
3233		that John
2168		had risen
1388		from
0243		the dead
1338		*

VERSE 8 — And others were saying that Elijah had appeared and others that a prophet from the first prophets had risen.

#	Syriac	Gloss
0053		others
0518		And
0116		saying
0603		were
3047		that Elijah
0758		had appeared
0053		and others
1457		that a prophet
1388		from
1457		the prophets
2157		first
2168		had risen

VERSE 9 — And Herod said, "I cut off the head of John, but who is this [man] about whom I hear these [things]?" And he wanted to see him.

#	Syriac	Gloss
0116		And said
3179		Herod
2362		the head
3233		of John
0124		<it>

LUKE CHAPTER 9

#	Aramaic	English
1992		I cut off
1390		who is
0518		but
0598		this [man]
0598		these [things]
2547		hear
0124		I
1804		about whom
2077		And he wanted
0603		*
0758		to see him

VERSE 10 And when the apostles returned, they reported to Jesus everything that they had done. And he took them privately to a desert place of Bethsaida.

#	Aramaic	English
1128		And when
0616		returned
2522		the apostles
2569		they reported
3257		to Jesus
1173		everything
1724		that they had done
0477		And he took
0592		them
1041		privately
0214		to a place
0892		desert
3118		of Bethsaida

VERSE 11 And when the crowds knew [it], they followed him. And he received them and spoke with them about the kingdom of God. And those who had a need for healing, he healed.

#	Aramaic	English
1201		the crowds
0518		And
1128		when
1023		knew [it]
0042		they followed him
0215		*
2134		And he received
0592		them
1362		and spoke
0603		*
1817		with them
1804		about
1385		the kingdom
0093		of God
0066		And those
1679		who had a need
0603		*
1804		for
0138		healing
0136		he healed
0603		*

VERSE 12 And when the day began to fade, his disciples came near and were saying to him, "Send away the crowds that they may go to the villages and to the towns around us to stay in them and to find food for themselves, because we are in a desert place.

#	Aramaic	English
1128		when
0518		And
2597		began
1036		the day
2106		to fade
2244		came near
1304		his disciples
0116		and were saying
1261		to him
2597		Send away
1201		the crowds
0042		that they may go
2251		to the villages
0732		around us
1219		and to the towns
2597		to stay
0217		in them
2510		and to find
1261		for themselves
1594		food
1347		because

LUKE CHAPTER 9

#	Syriac	English
0214		in a place
0892		desert
0069		we are

VERSE 13 — Jesus said to them, "You give them [something] to eat." But they were saying, "We do not have more than five [loaves of] bread and two fish, unless we go and buy food for all this people,"

#	Syriac	English
0116		said
1261		to them
3257		Jesus
1030		give
1261		them
0133		You
0075		[something] to eat
0592		<they>
0518		But
0116		they were saying
1264		We do not have
1261		*
1100		more
1388		than
0833		five
1293		[loaves of] bread
2709		and two
1490		fish
0090		unless
0121		*
0042		we go
0632		and buy
1594		food
0598		for this
1168		all
1818		people

VERSE 14 — for there were about five thousand men. Jesus said to them, "Cause them to sit to eat [in] groups, fifty men in a group."

#	Syriac	English
0603		there were
0603		*
0403		for
0060		about
0833		five
0099		thousand
0361		men
0116		said
1261		to them
3257		Jesus
1664		Cause to sit to eat
0592		them
1666		[in] groups
0834		fifty
0131		men
1666		in a group

VERSE 15 — And the disciples did so and caused them all to sit to eat.

#	Syriac	English
1724		And did
0595		so
1304		the disciples
1664		and caused to sit to eat
1168		them all

VERSE 16 — And Jesus took those five [loaves of] bread and two fish and gazed into heaven and blessed and broke [them] and gave [them] to his disciples to set before the crowds.

#	Syriac	English
1532		And took
3257		Jesus
0593		those
0833		five
1293		[loaves of] bread
2709		and two
1490		fish
0756		and gazed
2543		into heaven
0335		and blessed
2234		and broke [them]
1030		and gave [them]
1304		to his disciples
1625		to set
1201		before the crowds

LUKE CHAPTER 9

VERSE 17 — And all ate and were satisfied and they took up the fragments that were left over, twelve baskets.

0075	And ate
1168	all
1585	and were satisfied
2587	and they took up
2235	the fragments
1326	that
1098	were left over
2710	twelve
2176	baskets

VERSE 18 — And while he was praying alone and his disciples with him, he asked them and said, "What do the crowds say about me, who I am?"

1128	And while
2106	he was praying
1041	alone
1304	and his disciples
1817	with him
2420	he asked
0592	them
0116	and said
1390	What
0116	do say
1804	about me
1201	the crowds
0069	who I am

VERSE 19 — They answered and were saying to him, "John the baptizer, and others, Elijah, and others, that a certain prophet from the first prophets has risen."

1838	They answered
0116	and were saying
1261	to him
3233	John
1820	the baptizer
0053	and others
3047	Elijah
0053	others
0518	and
1457	that a prophet
0721	certain
1388	from
1457	the prophets
2157	first
2168	has risen

VERSE 20 — He said to them, "But who do you say that I am?" Simon answered and said, "The Messiah of God."

0116	He said
1261	to them
0133	<you>
0518	But
1390	who
0116	do say
0133	you
0069	that I am
1838	answered
3521	Simon
0116	and said
1446	The Messiah
0093	of God

VERSE 21 — And he reproved them and warned them not to say this to anyone.

0592	<he>
0518	and
1113	he reproved
0217	them
0645	and warned
0592	them
0598	this
0131	to anyone
1262	not
0116	to say

VERSE 22 — And he said to them that the Son of Man would suffer many things and he would be rejected by the elders and the chief priests and scribes and they would kill him and on the third day he would rise up.

| 0116 | And he said |
| 1261 | to them |

LUKE CHAPTER 9

#	Syriac	English
1914		that would
0592		<he>
0323		the Son
0131		of Man
1596		many [things]
0911		suffer
1655		and he would be rejected
1388		by
2263		the elders
2271		and chief priests
1135		*
1699		and scribes
2179		and they would kill him
1036		and on the day
2674		third
2168		he would rise up

VERSE 23 — And he said before everyone, "He who wants to follow me should deny himself and take up his cross every day and follow me.

#	Syriac	English
0116		And he said
0603		*
2154		before
1175		everyone
1389		He who
2077		wants
0208		to follow me
0215		*
1215		should deny
1547		himself
2587		and take up
0689		his cross
1172		every day
0208		and follow me
0215		*

VERSE 24 — For he who wants to save his soul will lose it, but he who will lose his soul because of me, this one will save it.

#	Syriac	English
1389		he who
0403		For
2077		wants
1547		his soul
0780		to save
0005		will lose
1261		it
1389		he who
0518		but
0005		will lose
1547		his soul
1347		because of me
0598		this one
0780		will save
1261		it

VERSE 25 — For what is a man helped who gains the whole world, but will lose or is deprived of his soul?

#	Syriac	English
1393		what
0403		For
1751		is helped
0323		a man
0131		*
1098		who gains
1813		the world
1168		whole
1547		his soul
0518		but
0005		will lose
0024		or
0865		is deprived

VERSE 26 — And whoever will be ashamed of me and of my words, the Son of Man will be ashamed of him when he comes in the glory of his Father with his holy angels.

#	Syriac	English
1389		<of>
0235		whoever will be ashamed
0217		of me
0518		And
1364		and of my words
0235		will be ashamed
0217		of him
0323		the Son
0131		of Man

LUKE CHAPTER 9

#	Aramaic	English
1313		when
0208		he comes
2431		in the glory
0002		of his Father
1817		with
1375		his angels
2162		holy

VERSE 27 I say the truth to you, there are men who stand here who will not taste death until they see the kingdom of God."

#	Aramaic	English
2596		the truth
0116		say
0124		I
1261		to you
0069		there are
0131		men
2168		who stand
0600		here
1262		who not
0998		will taste
1335		death
1747		until
0758		they see
1385		the kingdom
0093		of God

VERSE 28 And it happened [that] about eight days after these words, Jesus took Simon and James and John and climbed a mountain to pray.

#	Aramaic	English
0603		it happened [that]
0518		And
0215		after
1364		words
0598		these
0060		about
2683		eight
1036		days
0477		took
3257		Jesus
3521		Simon
3255		and James
3233		and John
1658		and climbed
0958		a mountain
2106		to pray

VERSE 29 And while he was praying, the appearance of his face was changed and his clothes were whitened and made to shine.

#	Aramaic	English
1128		And while
0592		he
2106		was praying
0811		was changed
0759		the appearance
0173		of his face
1501		and his clothes
0754		were whitened
0343		and made to shine
0603		*

VERSE 30 And behold, two men were talking with him, who were Moses and Elijah,

#	Aramaic	English
0580		And behold
2709		two
0361		men
1362		were talking
0603		*
1817		with him
0069		who were
3305		Moses
3047		and Elijah

VERSE 31 who appeared in glory. And they were talking about his departure that was about to be accomplished in Jerusalem.

#	Aramaic	English
0758		who appeared
2432		in glory
0116		talking
0603		they were
0518		And
1804		about
1544		his departure
1914		that about
0603		was

LUKE   CHAPTER 9

2530	ܕܢܬܡܠܐ	to be accomplished
3022	ܒܐܘܪܫܠܡ	in Jerusalem
VERSE 32		And Simon and those who were with him were heavy with sleep and scarcely awake and they saw his glory and those two men who were standing with him.
1076	ܘܝܩܪܘ	And were heavy
0603	ܗܘܘ	*
1261	ܠܗܘܢ	<to them>
2568	ܒܫܢܬܐ	with sleep
3521	ܫܡܥܘܢ	Simon
0593	ܘܗܢܘܢ	and those
1817	ܕܥܡܗ	who were with him
0864	ܘܠܡܚܣܢ	and scarcely
1880	ܐܬܬܥܝܪܘ	awake
0758	ܘܚܙܘ	and they saw
2431	ܫܘܒܚܗ	his glory
0593	ܘܠܗܢܘܢ	and those
2709	ܬܪܝܢ	two
0131	ܓܒܪܝܢ	men
2168	ܕܩܝܡܝܢ	who were standing
0603	ܗܘܘ	*
1288	ܠܘܬܗ	with him
VERSE 33		And when they began to go away from him, Simon said to Jesus, "My Master, it is good for us that we were here. Yet let us make three booths, one for you and one for Moses and one for Elijah," and he did not know what he said.
1128	ܘܟܕ	And when
2597	ܫܪܝܘ	they began
2046	ܠܡܦܪܩ	to go away
1388	ܡܢܗ	from him
0116	ܐܡܪ	said
3521	ܫܡܥܘܢ	Simon
3257	ܠܝܫܘܥ	to Jesus
2275	ܪܒܝ	My Master
2583	ܫܦܝܪ	is good
0592	ܗܘ	it
1261	ܠܢ	for us
0600	ܕܗܪܟܐ	that here
0603	ܢܗܘܐ	we were

1724	ܘܢܥܒܕ	Yet let us make
2674	ܬܠܬ	three
0974	ܡܛܠܠܝܢ	booths
1261	ܠܟ	for you
0721	ܚܕ	one
3305	ܘܠܡܘܫܐ	and for Moses
0721	ܚܕ	one
3047	ܘܠܐܠܝܐ	and for Elijah
0721	ܚܕ	one
1262	ܘܠܐ	and not
1023	ܝܕܥ	he did know
0603	ܗܘܐ	*
1393	ܡܢܐ	what
0116	ܐܡܪ	he said
VERSE 34		And when he said these [things], a cloud came and overshadowed them. And they were afraid when they saw that Moses and Elijah entered into the cloud.
1128	ܘܟܕ	And when
0116	ܐܡܪ	he said
0598	ܗܠܝܢ	these [things]
0603	ܗܘܬ	came
1844	ܥܢܢܐ	a cloud
0970	ܘܐܛܠܬ	and overshadowed
1804	ܥܠܝܗܘܢ	them
0509	ܘܕܚܠܘ	And they were afraid
1128	ܟܕ	when
0758	ܚܙܘ	they saw
3305	ܠܡܘܫܐ	that Moses
3047	ܘܠܐܠܝܐ	and Elijah
1796	ܕܥܠܘ	entered
1844	ܒܥܢܢܐ	into the cloud
VERSE 35		And a voice came from the cloud that said, "This is my beloved Son. Hear him."
2204	ܘܩܠܐ	And a voice
0603	ܗܘܐ	came
1388	ܡܢ	from
1844	ܥܢܢܐ	the could
0116	ܕܐܡܪ	that said
0599	ܗܢܘ	This is

LUKE CHAPTER 9

0323		my Son
0698		beloved
1261		him
2547		Hear

VERSE 36 And after the voice came, Jesus was found alone and they kept silent and did not tell anyone in those days anything that they had seen.

1128		And after
0603		came
2204		the voice
2510		was found
3257		Jesus
1041		alone
0592		and they
2623		kept silent
0131		and anyone
1262		not
0116		did tell
0593		in those
1036		days
1326		anything
0758		that they had seen

VERSE 37 And it happened [that] on the next day when they came down from the mountain, a large crowd met them.

0603		And it happened [that]
1036		on the day
0215		next
1128		when
1499		they came down
1388		from
0958		the mountain
1928		met
0217		them
1201		a crowd
1596		large

VERSE 38 And a certain man from that crowd cried out and said, "Teacher, I beg you, take notice of me. He is my only son

0361		And a man
0721		certain
1388		from
1201		crowd
0593		that
2227		cried out
0116		and said
1055		Teacher
0296		beg
0124		I
1388		you
1984		take notice
1804		of me
0323		my son
1042		only
0592		He is
1261		<to me>

VERSE 39 and a spirit quickly comes over him and suddenly he cries out and gnashes his teeth and foams and with difficulty does it go out of him when it has harassed him.

2323		and a spirit
1743		comes quickly
1804		over him
1388		and suddenly
2519		*
2227		he cries out
0904		and gnashes
2558		his teeth
2340		and foams
0864		and with difficulty
2042		does it go out
1388		of him
1313		when
2494		it has harassed him

VERSE 40 And I begged your disciples to cast it out and they were not able."

0296		And I begged
1388		<from>
1304		your disciples
1542		to cast it out

452

Vertical Interlinear

LUKE   CHAPTER 9

1262		and not
2510		they were able

VERSE 41 — And Jesus answered and said, "Oh faithless and perverted generation! How long should I be with you and endure you? Bring your son here."

1838		answered
0518		And
3257		Jesus
0116		and said
0033		Oh
2605		generation
1262		faithless
0114		*
1871		and perverted
1747		How long
0120		*
0603		should I be
1288		with you
1588		and endure you
2244		Bring
1111		here
0323		your son

VERSE 42 — And while he was bringing him, that devil cast him down and convulsed him. And Jesus rebuked that unclean spirit and he healed the young boy and gave him to his father.

1128		And while
2244		he was bringing
1261		him
2372		cast him down
0514		devil
0593		that
1412		and convulsed him
1113		And rebuked
3257		Jesus
2323		spirit
0593		that
0991		unclean
0136		and he healed
0976		the young boy
1030		and gave him
0002		to his father

VERSE 43 — And they were all amazed at the greatness of God. And while everyone was wondering about all that Jesus had done, he said to his disciples,

0549		And they were amazed
1168		all
2273		at the greatness
0093		of God
1128		And while
1175		everyone
0549		wondering
0603		was
1804		about
1168		all
1724		that had done
3257		Jesus
0116		he said
1304		to his disciples

VERSE 44 — Set these words in your ears, for the Son of Man is about to be delivered into the hands of men.

1625		Set
0133		*
1364		words
0598		these
0021		in your ears
0323		the Son
0403		for
0131		of Man
1914		is about to
2530		be delivered
0057		into the hands of
0323		men
0131		*

VERSE 45 — But they did not understand this saying, because it was hidden from them so that they did not know it, and they were afraid to ask him about this saying.

0592		<they>

453

LUKE   CHAPTER 9

0518		But
1262		not
1023		they did understand
1364		saying
0598		this
1347		because
1206		hidden
0603		it was
1388		from them
1262		so that not
1023		they did know it
0509		and afraid
0603		they were
2420		to ask him
1804		<about it>
1804		about
1364		saying
0598		this

VERSE 46 And the thought entered into them [as to] who was indeed great among them.

1796		And entered
0217		into them
0917		the thought
1390		[as to] who was
1163		indeed
2271		great
0217		among them

VERSE 47 And Jesus knew the thought of their heart[s] and he took a young child and set him by him.

3257		Jesus
0518		And
1023		knew
0917		the thought
1268		of their heart[s]
1532		and he took
0976		a young child
2168		and set him
1288		by him

VERSE 48 And he said to them, "He who receives a child like this in my name, receives me. And he who receives me, receives him who sent me. For whoever is least among all of you, this one will be great."

0116		And he said
1261		to them
1389		He who
2134		receives
0976		a child
0060		like
0598		this
2539		in my name
1261		me
0592		<he>
2134		receives
1389		And he who
1261		me
2134		receives
2134		receives
1389		him
2458		who sent me
0066		whoever
0403		For
0686		is least
1168		among all of you
0598		this one
0603		will be
2271		great

VERSE 49 And John answered and said, "Our Master, we saw a man who was casting out devils in your name and we prohibited him, because he did not follow you with us."

1838		And answered
3233		John
0116		and said
2271		Our Master
0758		we saw
0131		a man
1542		who was casting out
0514		devils

LUKE CHAPTER 9

#	Syriac	English
2539		in your name
1180		and we prohibited him
1804		*
1262		because not
0208		he did follow
1817		with us
0215		<after> you

VERSE 50 — Jesus said to them, "Do not prohibit [him], for he who is not against you is for you."

#	Syriac	English
0116		said
1261		to them
3257		Jesus
1262		not
1180		Do prohibit [him]
1389		he who
0403		for
1262		not
0603		is
2135		against you
0812		for you
0592		is

VERSE 51 — And it happened that when the days of his offering up were fulfilled, he directed his face to go to Jerusalem.

#	Syriac	English
0603		And it happened
1128		that when
1366		were fulfilled
1036		the days
1659		of his offering up
2699		he directed
2041		his face
0042		to go
3022		to Jerusalem

VERSE 52 — And he sent messengers before his face and they went [and] entered a village of the Samaritans in order to prepare for him.

#	Syriac	English
2458		And he sent
1375		messengers
2154		before
2041		his face
0042		and they went
1796		[and] entered
2251		a village
3524		of the Samaritans
0060		in order
2699		to prepare
1261		for him

VERSE 53 — And they did not receive him because his face was set to go to Jerusalem.

#	Syriac	English
1262		And not
2134		they did receive him
1347		because
2041		his face
3022		to Jerusalem
1625		was set
0603		*
0042		to go

VERSE 54 — And when James and John, his disciples, saw [it], they said to him, "Our Lord, do you want us to speak and have fire come down from heaven and consume them as also Elijah did?"

#	Syriac	English
1128		And when
0758		saw [it]
3255		James
3233		and John
1304		his disciples
0116		they said
1261		to him
1426		Our Lord
2077		do want
0133		you
0116		us to speak
1499		and have come down
1494		fire
1388		from
2543		heaven
1630		and consume
0592		them
0060		as

Vertical Interlinear

LUKE CHAPTER 9

0169		also
3047		Elijah
1724		did

VERSE 55 — And he turned and rebuked them and said, "You do not know of what spirit you are.

1984		And he turned
1113		and rebuked
0217		them
0116		and said
1262		not
1023		do know
0133		You
0066		of what
0133		you are
2323		spirit

VERSE 56 — For the Son of Man did not come to destroy souls, but to make [them] to live." And they went to another village.

0323		the Son
0403		For
0131		of Man
1262		not
0208		did come
0005		to destroy
1547		souls
0090		but
0780		to make [them] to live
0042		And they went
1261		*
2251		to village
0053		another

VERSE 57 — And while they were traveling on the road, a man said to him, "I will follow you wherever you go, my Lord."

1128		And while
0042		they were traveling
0038		on the road
0116		said
1261		to him
0131		a man
0208		I will follow you
0215		*
0214		wherever
0042		go
0133		you
1426		my Lord

VERSE 58 — Jesus said to him, "Foxes have holes and a bird of heaven a shelter, but the Son of Man has no where to lay his head."

0116		said
1261		to him
3257		Jesus
2695		Foxes
1564		holes
0069		have
1261		*
2026		and a bird
2543		of heaven
0973		a shelter
0323		the Son
0518		but
0131		of Man
1264		has no
1261		*
1108		where
1664		to lay
2362		his head

VERSE 59 — And he said to another, "Follow me." And he said to him, "My Lord, allow me first to go [and] bury my father."

0116		And he said
0053		to another
0208		Follow me
0215		*
0592		<he>
0518		And
0116		he said
1261		to him
1426		My Lord
1989		allow

Vertical Interlinear

LUKE   **CHAPTER 9**

1261	ܠܝ	me
2151	ܠܘܩܕܡ	first
0042	ܐܙܠ	to go
2142	ܐܩܒܘܪ	[and] bury
0002	ܐܒܝ	my father

VERSE 60   Jesus said to him, "Leave the dead burying their dead and go [and] preach the kingdom of God."

0116	ܐܡܪ	said
1261	ܠܗ	to him
3257	ܝܫܘܥ	Jesus
2440	ܫܒܘܩ	Leave
1338	ܡܝܬܐ	the dead
2142	ܩܒܪܝܢ	burying
1338	ܡܝܬܝܗܘܢ	their dead
0133	ܘܐܢܬ	and <you>
0042	ܙܠ	go
1588	ܣܒܪ	[and] preach
1385	ܡܠܟܘܬܗ	the kingdom
0093	ܕܐܠܗܐ	of God

VERSE 61   Another said to him, "I will follow you, my Lord, but first allow me to go [and] say goodbye to my household and [then] I will come."

0116	ܐܡܪ	said
1261	ܠܗ	to him
0053	ܐܚܪܢܐ	Another
0208	ܐܬܐ	I will follow you
0215	ܒܬܪܟ	*
1426	ܡܪܝ	my Lord
2151	ܠܘܩܕܡ	first
0518	ܕܝܢ	but
1989	ܐܦܣ	allow
1261	ܠܝ	me
0042	ܐܙܠ	to go
2530	ܐܫܠܡ	[and] say goodbye
0323	ܠܒܝܬ	to my household
0243	ܘܐܬܐ	*
0208	ܘܐܬܐ	and [then] I will come

VERSE 62   Jesus said to him, "No one places his hand on the handle of a plow and looks back and is useful for the kingdom of God."

0116	ܐܡܪ	said
1261	ܠܗ	to him
3257	ܝܫܘܥ	Jesus
1262	ܠܐ	No
0131	ܐܢܫ	one
2372	ܪܡܐ	places
0057	ܐܝܕܗ	his hand
1804	ܥܠ	on
0893	ܚܨܝܢܐ	the handle
1933	ܕܦܕܢܐ	of the plow
0756	ܘܚܐܪ	and looks
0295	ܠܒܣܬܪܗ	back
0918	ܘܚܫܚ	and is useful
1385	ܠܡܠܟܘܬܗ	for the kingdom
0093	ܕܐܠܗܐ	of God

CHAPTER 10

VERSE 1   After these [things], Jesus appointed from his disciples seventy others and sent them two by two before his face to every region and city that he was about to go.

0215	ܒܬܪ	After
0598	ܗܠܝܢ	these [things]
2046	ܦܪܫ	appointed
3257	ܝܫܘܥ	Jesus
1388	ܡܢ	from
1304	ܬܠܡܝܕܘܗܝ	his disciples
0053	ܐܚܪܢܐ	others
2439	ܫܒܥܝܢ	seventy
2458	ܘܫܕܪ	and sent
0592	ܐܢܘܢ	them
2709	ܬܪܝܢ	two by two
2709	ܬܪܝܢ	*
2154	ܩܕܡ	before
2041	ܦܪܨܘܦܗ	his face
1168	ܠܟܠ	to every
0214	ܐܬܪ	region

Vertical Interlinear

LUKE — CHAPTER 10

Code	Syriac	Gloss
0499		and city
1914		that about
0603		he was
0042		to go

VERSE 2 — And he said to them, "The harvest is great and the workers are few. Therefore, pray the Lord [of] the harvest to send out workers for his harvest.

Code	Syriac	Gloss
0116		And he said
1261		to them
0879		The harvest
1596		is great
1999		and the workers
0686		are few
0296		pray
0596		Therefore
1388		<from>
1426		the Lord [of]
0879		the harvest
1542		to send out
1999		workers
0879		for his harvest

VERSE 3 — Go! Behold, I send you as lambs among wolves.

Code	Syriac	Gloss
0042		Go
0580		Behold
0124		<I>
2458		I send
0124		*
1261		you
0060		as
0117		lambs
0266		among
0469		wolves

VERSE 4 — Do not carry bags or sacks or shoes and do not greet anyone on the way.

Code	Syriac	Gloss
1262		not
2587		Do carry
1261		<for you>
1165		bags
1262		or
2712		sacks
1262		or
1582		shoes
2535		and <with peace>
0131		anyone
0038		on the way
1262		not
2420		do greet

VERSE 5 — And in whatever house you enter, first say, 'Peace to this house.'

Code	Syriac	Gloss
0066		And in whatever
0243		house
1796		enter
0133		you
2151		first
0116		say
2535		Peace
0243		to house
0598		this

VERSE 6 — And if there is there a man of peace, your peace will rest on him, but if not, it will return on you.

Code	Syriac	Gloss
0121		And if
0069		there is
2682		there
0323		a man of
2535		peace
1483		will rest
1804		on him
2535		your peace
0121		if
0518		but
1262		not
1804		on you
0616		it will return

VERSE 7 — And remain in the same house, eating and drinking from their [food], for the worker is worthy of his wage and do not move from house to house.

Code	Syriac	Gloss
0217		in the same
0518		And

LUKE — CHAPTER 10

0243		house
0603		remain
1128		eating
1308		*
0133		<you>
2620		and drinking
1388		from
0517		their [food]
2461		worthy
0592		is
0403		for
1999		the worker of
0018		his wage
1262		and not
2561		do move
1388		from
0243		house
0243		to house

VERSE 8 And in whatever city you enter and they receive you, eat what is placed before you.

0066		And in whatever
0499		city
1796		enter
0133		you
2134		and they receive
1261		you
1308		eat
1326		what
1625		is placed
1261		before you

VERSE 9 And heal those who are sick in it and say to them, 'The kingdom of God has come near to you.'

0136		And heal
0066		those
1226		who are sick
0217		in it
0116		and say
1261		to them
2244		has come near
1804		to you
1385		The kingdom
0093		of God

VERSE 10 But in whatever city you enter and they do not receive you, go out in the marketplace and say,

0066		in whatever
0499		city
0518		But
1796		enter
0133		you
1262		and not
2134		they do receive you
1542		go out
1261		<to you>
2481		in the marketplace
0116		and say

VERSE 11 'Even the dust that sticks to us on our feet from your city, we shake off against you, but know this, that the kingdom of God has come near to you.'

0169		<and> Even
0795		the dust
0476		that sticks
1261		to us
2293		on our feet
1388		from
0499		your city
1541		shake off
0124		we
1261		against you
0342		but
0598		this
1023		know
2244		that has come near
1261		<to it>
1804		to you
1385		the kingdom
0093		of God

LUKE CHAPTER 10

VERSE 12 — I say to you, it will be [more] pleasant for Sodom in that day than for that city.

0116	ܐܡܪ	say
0124	ܐܢܐ	I
1261	ܠܟܘܢ	to you
3362	ܕܠܣܕܘܡ	for Sodom
0603	ܢܗܘܐ	it will be
1483	ܢܝܚ	[more] pleasant
1036	ܒܝܘܡܐ	in day
0593	ܗܘ	that
0024	ܐܘ	than
0499	ܠܡܕܝܢܬܐ	for city
0593	ܗܝ	that

VERSE 13 — Woe to you, Chorazin! Woe to you, Bethsaida! Because if the miracles that happened in you had happened in Tyre and Sidon, they would have long ago repented in sackclothes and in ash.

0625	ܘܝ	Woe
1261	ܠܟܝ	to you
3260	ܟܘܪܙܝܢ	Chorazin
0625	ܘܝ	Woe
1261	ܠܟܝ	to you
3118	ܒܝܬܨܝܕܐ	Bethsaida
0097	ܕܐܠܘ	Because if
3450	ܒܨܘܪ	in Tyre
3452	ܘܒܨܝܕܢ	and Sidon
0603	ܗܘܘ	had happened
0786	ܚܝܠܐ	the miracles
0603	ܕܗܘܘ	that happened
0217	ܒܟܝܢ	in you
1124	ܟܒܪ	long ago
0518	ܕܝܢ	<but>
1702	ܒܣܩܐ	in sackclothes
2182	ܘܒܩܛܡܐ	and in ash
2649	ܬܒܘ	they would have repented

VERSE 14 — But for Tyre and Sidon it will be [more] pleasant in the judgment than for you.

0342	ܒܪܡ	But
3450	ܠܨܘܪ	for Tyre
3452	ܘܠܨܝܕܢ	and Sidon
0603	ܢܗܘܐ	it will be
1483	ܢܝܚ	[more] pleasant
0497	ܒܕܝܢܐ	in the judgment
0024	ܐܘ	than
1261	ܠܟܝܢ	for you

VERSE 15 — And you, Capernaum, who are lifted up to heaven will be brought down low to Sheol.

0133	ܘܐܢܬܝ	And you
3268	ܟܦܪܢܚܘܡ	Capernaum
0593	ܗܝ	who
1747	ܕܥܕܡܐ	to
2543	ܠܫܡܝܐ	heaven
2331	ܐܬܬܪܝܡܬܝ	are lifted up
1747	ܥܕܡܐ	to
2422	ܠܫܝܘܠ	Sheol
2661	ܬܬܚܬܝܢ	will be brought down low

VERSE 16 — He who hears you hears me. And he who rejects you rejects me and he who rejects me rejects him who sent me."

1389	ܡܢ	He
1261	ܕܠܟܘܢ	who you
2547	ܫܡܥ	hears
1261	ܠܝ	me
2547	ܫܡܥ	hears
1389	ܘܡܢ	And he
1261	ܕܠܟܘܢ	who you
0979	ܛܠܡ	rejects
1261	ܠܝ	me
0592	ܗܘ	<is>
0979	ܛܠܡ	rejects
1389	ܘܡܢ	and he
1261	ܕܠܝ	who me
0979	ܛܠܡ	rejects
0979	ܛܠܡ	rejects
1389	ܠܡܢ	him
2521	ܕܫܠܚܢܝ	who sent me

LUKE CHAPTER 10

VERSE 17 — And those seventy whom he had sent returned with great joy and said to him, "Our Lord, even the demons were subject to us in your name."

Code	Syriac	English
0616		And returned
0593		those
2439		seventy
2458		whom he had sent
0727		with joy
2271		great
0116		and said
1261		to him
1426		Our Lord
0169		even
2469		the demons
1724		were subject
1261		to us
2539		in your name

VERSE 18 — And he said to them, "I was seeing Satan fall like lightning from heaven.

Code	Syriac	English
0592		<he>
0518		And
0116		he said
1261		to them
0758		seeing
0603		I was
1261		<him>
1642		Satan
1538		fall
0060		like
0344		lightning
1388		from
2543		heaven

VERSE 19 — Behold, I give to you authority to trample on serpents and scorpions and all the power of the enemy and nothing will hurt you.

Code	Syriac	English
0580		Behold
1030		give
0124		I
1261		you
2527		authority
0603		to trample on
0507		*
0740		serpents
1879		and scorpions
1168		and all
0786		the power
0307		of the enemy
1326		and nothing
1262		*
0621		will hurt you

VERSE 20 — But do not rejoice in this, that demons are subject to you, but rather rejoice that your names are written in heaven."

Code	Syriac	English
0342		But
0598		in this
1262		not
0726		do rejoice
2469		that demons
1724		are subject
1261		to you
0090		but rather
0726		rejoice
2539		that your names
1247		are written
2543		in heaven

VERSE 21 — Immediately, Jesus was joyful in the Holy Spirit and said, "I thank you, my Father, Lord of heaven and earth, that you have hidden these [things] from wise and intelligent [ones] and have revealed them to infants, yes, my Father, because so was the will before you."

Code	Syriac	English
0217		Immediately
2573		*
2320		was joyful
3257		Jesus
2323		in the Holy Spirit
2164		*
0116		and said
1020		thank

LUKE   CHAPTER 10

0124	ܐܢܐ	I
1261	ܠܟ	you
0002	ܐܒܝ	my Father
1426	ܡܪܐ	Lord
2543	ܕܫܡܝܐ	of heaven
0199	ܘܕܐܪܥܐ	and earth
1206	ܕܟܣܝܬ	that you have hidden
0598	ܗܠܝܢ	these [things]
1388	ܡܢ	from
0790	ܚܟܝܡܐ	the wise
1650	ܘܣܟܘܠܬܢܐ	and intelligent [ones]
0409	ܘܓܠܝܬ	and have revealed
0592	ܐܢܝܢ	them
1048	ܠܝܠܘܕܐ	to infants
0065	ܐܝܢ	yes
0002	ܐܒܝ	my Father
0597	ܕܗܟܢܐ	because so
0603	ܗܘܐ	was
2079	ܨܒܝܢܐ	the will
2154	ܩܕܡܝܟ	before you

VERSE 22   And he turned toward his disciples and said to them, "Everything is delivered to me from my Father and no man knows who is the Son, except the Father and who is the Father, except the Son and to whom the Son wants to reveal [him]?"

1984	ܘܐܬܦܢܝ	And he turned
1288	ܠܘܬ	toward
1304	ܬܠܡܝܕܘܗܝ	his disciples
0116	ܘܐܡܪ	and said
1261	ܠܗܘܢ	to them
1168	ܟܠ	Everything
1326	ܡܕܡ	*
2530	ܐܫܬܠܡ	is delivered
1261	ܠܝ	to me
1388	ܡܢ	from
0002	ܐܒܝ	my Father
1262	ܘܠܐ	and no
0131	ܐܢܫ	man
1023	ܝܕܥ	knows
1390	ܡܢܘ	who is
0323	ܒܪܐ	the Son
0090	ܐܠܐ	except
0121	ܐܢ	*
0002	ܐܒܐ	the Father
1390	ܘܡܢܘ	and who is
0002	ܐܒܐ	the Father
0090	ܐܠܐ	except
0121	ܐܢ	*
0323	ܒܪܐ	the Son
1389	ܘܠܡܢ	and to whom
0121	ܕܐܢ	<that if>
2077	ܨܒܐ	wants
0323	ܒܪܐ	the Son
0409	ܕܢܓܠܐ	to reveal [him]

VERSE 23   And he turned toward his disciples privately and said, "Blessed are the eyes that see what you see.

1984	ܘܐܬܦܢܝ	And he turned
1288	ܠܘܬ	toward
1304	ܬܠܡܝܕܘܗܝ	his disciples
1041	ܒܠܚܘܕܝܗܘܢ	privately
0116	ܘܐܡܪ	and said
0940	ܛܘܒܝܗܘܢ	Blessed are <they>
1794	ܠܥܝܢܐ	the eyes
0758	ܕܚܙܝܢ	that see
1326	ܡܕܡ	what
0133	ܕܐܢܬܘܢ	you
0758	ܚܙܝܢ	see

VERSE 24   For I say to you, many prophets and kings have wanted to see what you see and have not seen, and to hear what you hear and have not heard."

0116	ܐܡܪ	say
0124	ܐܢܐ	I
1261	ܠܟܘܢ	to you
0403	ܓܝܪ	For
1457	ܢܒܝܐ	prophets
1596	ܣܓܝܐܐ	many
1383	ܘܡܠܟܐ	and kings
2077	ܨܒܘ	have wanted
0758	ܕܢܚܙܘܢ	to see

LUKE — CHAPTER 10

Vertical Interlinear

#	Syriac	English
1326		what
0758		see
0133		you
1262		and not
0758		have seen
2547		and to hear
1326		what
0133		you
2547		hear
1262		and not
2547		have heard

VERSE 25 — And behold, a certain scribe stood up to tempt him and said, "Teacher, what must I do to inherit eternal life?"

#	Syriac	English
0580		And behold
1699		a scribe
0721		certain
2168		stood up
1527		to tempt him
0116		and said
1055		Teacher
1393		what
1724		must I do
1087		to inherit
0782		life
1813		eternal

VERSE 26 — And Jesus said to him, "How is it written in the law? How do you read?"

#	Syriac	English
0592		<he>
0518		And
3257		Jesus
0116		said
1261		to him
1524		in the law
0061		How
1247		is it written
0061		How
2239		do read
0133		you

VERSE 27 — He answered and said to him: YOU SHOULD LOVE THE LORD YOUR GOD WITH ALL YOUR HEART AND WITH ALL YOUR SOUL AND WITH ALL YOUR STRENGTH AND WITH ALL YOUR MIND, and YOUR NEIGHBOR AS YOURSELF.

#	Syriac	English
1838		He answered
0116		and said
1261		to him
2342		YOU SHOULD LOVE
1426		THE LORD
0093		YOUR GOD
1388		WITH
1168		ALL
1268		YOUR HEART
1388		AND WITH
1168		ALL
1547		YOUR SOUL
1388		AND WITH
1168		ALL
0786		YOUR STRENGTH
1388		AND WITH
1168		ALL
2385		YOUR MIND
2248		and YOUR NEIGHBOR
0060		AS
1547		YOURSELF

VERSE 28 — Jesus said to him, "You have spoken correctly; do this and you will live."

#	Syriac	English
0116		said
1261		to him
3257		Jesus
2722		correctly
0116		You have spoken
0598		this
1724		do
0780		and you will live

VERSE 29 — But wanting to justify himself, he said to him, "And who is my neighbor?"

#	Syriac	English
0592		<he>
0518		But

LUKE CHAPTER 10

#	Syriac	English		#	Syriac	English
1128		wanting		1499		to be going down
2077		*		0603		*
0636		to justify		0038		on road
1547		himself		0593		that
0116		he said		0758		and he saw him
1261		to him		1733		and passed by
1390		And who is		**VERSE 32**		And so also a Levite came [and] arrived at that place and saw him and passed by.
2248		my neighbor				
VERSE 30		Jesus said to him, "A certain man went down from Jerusalem to Jericho, and robbers fell on him and they stripped him and beat him and left him when little life remained in him and they went away.		0597		And so
				0169		also
				3281		a Levite
0116		said		0208		came
1261		Jesus		1346		[and] arrived
3257		to him		0593		at that
0361		A man		0494		place
0721		certain		0758		and saw him
1499		went down		1733		and passed by
0603		*		**VERSE 33**		Now a Samaritan man, while he was journeying, came where he was, and he saw him and had compassion on him.
1388		from				
3022		Jerusalem		0131		a man
3039		to Jericho		0518		Now
1538		and fell		3524		Samaritan
1804		on him		1128		while
1306		robbers		2299		he was journeying
2521		and they stripped him		0603		*
1341		and beat him		0208		came
2440		and left him		1108		where
1128		when		0069		he was
2203		little		0603		*
2174		remained		0758		and he saw him
0217		in him		2342		and had compassion
1547		life		1804		on him
0042		and they went away		**VERSE 34**		And he came near and bandaged his wounds and poured wine and oil on them and placed him on his donkey and brought him to an inn and took care of him.
VERSE 31		And a certain priest happened to be going down on that road and he saw him and passed by.				
				2244		And he came near
0373		And happened		1864		and bandaged
1135		a priest		1342		his wounds
0721		certain				

Vertical Interlinear

LUKE   CHAPTER 10

1558		and poured
1804		on them
0831		wine
1445		and oil
1625		and placed him
1804		on
0830		his donkey
0208		and brought him
1939		to an inn
0253		and took care
1261		*
1804		of him

VERSE 35 — And at the break of the day he went away, he gave two denarii to the innkeeper and said to him 'Care for him. And if you spend anything more, when I return I will give [it] to you.'

2124		And at the break
1036		of the day
1542		he went away
2709		two
0519		denarii
1030		he gave
1940		to the innkeeper
0116		and said
1261		to him
1069		Care for
0517		him
0121		And if
1326		anything
1100		more
1542		you spend
1313		when
0616		return
0124		I
1030		I will give [it]
0124		*
1261		to you

VERSE 36 — Therefore, which of these three seems to you to have been a neighbor to him who fell into the hands of robbers?"

1390		which
0596		Therefore
1388		of
0598		these
2674		three
0758		seems
1261		to you
0603		to have been
2248		a neighbor
0593		to him
1538		who fell
0057		into the hands of
0402		robbers

VERSE 37 — And he said, "The one who had compassion on him." Jesus said to him, "Go, you should also do the same."

0592		\<he\>
0518		And
0116		he said
0593		The one
2342		who had compassion
1804		on him
0116		said
1261		to him
3257		Jesus
0042		Go
0169		also
0133		\<you\>
0597		the same
0603		you should
1724		do

VERSE 38 — And it happened that while they were journeying on the road, he entered a certain village and a woman whose name [was] Martha received him into her house.

0603		And it happened
1128		that while
0592		they

465

LUKE CHAPTER 10

Vertical Interlinear

Code		English
2299		were journeying
0038		on the road
1796		he entered
2251		a village
0721		certain
0135		and a woman
2539		whose name [was]
3327		Martha
2134		received him
0243		into her house

VERSE 39 — And she had a sister whose name [was] Mary. And she came [and] seated herself at the feet of our Lord and was listening to his words.

Code		English
0069		And she had
0603		*
1261		<to her>
0046		a sister
2539		whose name [was]
3325		Mary
0208		And she came
1093		[and] seated
1261		herself
1288		at
2293		the feet
1426		of our Lord
2547		and listening to
0603		was
1364		his words

VERSE 40 — But Martha was occupied with much service and came [and] said to him, "My Lord, do you not care that my sister has left me alone to serve? Tell her to help me."

Code		English
3327		Martha
0518		But
1838		occupied
0603		was
2556		with service
1596		much
0208		and came
0116		[and] said
1261		to him
1426		My Lord
1262		not
0253		do you care
1261		*
0046		that my sister
2440		has left me
1041		alone
2554		to serve
0116		Tell
1261		her
1751		to help
1261		me

VERSE 41 — But Jesus answered and said to her, "Martha, Martha, you are anxious and troubled about many [things].

Code		English
1838		answered
0518		But
3257		Jesus
0116		and said
1261		to her
3327		Martha
3327		Martha
1069		You are anxious
2308		and troubled
1804		about
1596		many [things]

VERSE 42 — But there is one [thing] that is necessary and Mary has chosen that good part for herself that will not be taken from her."

Code		English
0721		one [thing]
0592		there is
0518		But
0296		that is necessary
3325		Mary
0518		and
1399		part
0938		good
0351		has chosen

Vertical Interlinear

LUKE   CHAPTER 10

1261		for herself		0133		you
0593		that		0597		so
1262		that not		0603		you should
1532		will be taken		0116		speak
1388		from her		0002		Our Father

CHAPTER 11

VERSE 1   And it happened that while he was praying in a certain place, when he had finished, one of his disciples said to him, "Our Lord, teach us to pray, as John also taught his disciples."

0603		And it happened
1128		that while
0592		he
2106		was praying
0494		in a place
0721		certain
1128		when
2530		he had finished
0116		said
1261		to him
0721		one
1388		of
1304		his disciples
1426		Our Lord
1053		teach us
2106		to pray
0061		as
0169		also
3233		John
1053		taught
1304		his disciples

VERSE 2   Jesus said to them, "When you pray, you should speak so: Our Father who is in heaven, your name will be made holy, your kingdom will come, your desire will occur, as in heaven, even also on earth.

0116		said
1261		to them
3257		Jesus
0120		When
2106		pray
0133		you
0597		so
0603		you should
0116		speak
0002		Our Father
2543		who is in heaven
2160		will be made holy
2539		your name
0208		will come
1385		your kingdom
0603		will occur
2079		your desire
0060		as
2543		in heaven
0169		even also
0199		on earth

VERSE 3   Give us the bread of our necessity every day,

1030		Give
1261		us
1293		the bread
1680		of our necessity
1172		every day

VERSE 4   and forgive us [of] our sins, for we also forgive all who have wronged us. And do not let us enter into temptation, but deliver us from the Evil [one]."

2440		and forgive
1261		us
0771		[of] our sins
0169		also
0124		we
0403		for
2440		forgive
1168		all
0745		who have wronged
1261		us
1262		And not
1796		do let us enter
1528		into temptation

Vertical Interlinear

LUKE   CHAPTER 11

0090	‏ܐܠܐ‏	but	
2042	‏ܦܨܢ‏	deliver us	
1388	‏ܡܢ‏	from	
0220	‏ܒܝܫܐ‏	the Evil [one]	

VERSE 5 — And he said to them, "Who is among you who has a friend and would go to him at midnight and say to him, 'My friend, lend me three loaves,

0116	‏ܘܐܡܪ‏	And he said
1261	‏ܠܗܘܢ‏	to them
1390	‏ܡܢܘ‏	Who is
1388	‏ܡܢܟܘܢ‏	among you
0069	‏ܐܝܬ‏	who has
1261	‏ܠܗ‏	*
2345	‏ܪܚܡܐ‏	a friend
0042	‏ܘܢܐܙܠ‏	and would go
1288	‏ܠܘܬܗ‏	to him
1973	‏ܒܦܠܓܗ‏	at midnight
1299	‏ܕܠܠܝܐ‏	*
0116	‏ܘܢܐܡܪ‏	and say
1261	‏ܠܗ‏	to him
2345	‏ܪܚܡܝ‏	My friend
2420	‏ܐܫܐܠܝܢܝ‏	lend me
2674	‏ܬܠܬ‏	three
0462	‏ܓܪܝܨܢ‏	loaves

VERSE 6 — because a friend has come to me from a journey and I have nothing to place before him;'

1347	‏ܡܛܠ‏	because
2345	‏ܕܪܚܡܐ‏	a friend
0208	‏ܐܬܐ‏	has come
1288	‏ܠܘܬܝ‏	to me
1388	‏ܡܢ‏	from
0038	‏ܐܘܪܚܐ‏	a journey
1264	‏ܘܠܝܬ‏	and I have nothing
1261	‏ܠܝ‏	*
1326	‏ܡܕܡ‏	*
1625	‏ܕܐܣܝܡ‏	to place
1261	‏ܠܗ‏	before him

VERSE 7 — and his friend would answer from within and say to him, 'Do not trouble me, for behold, the door is shut and my children are with me in bed. I am not able to rise and give to you.'

0593	‏ܘܗܘ‏	and <that>
2345	‏ܪܚܡܗ‏	his friend
1388	‏ܡܢ‏	from
0379	‏ܠܓܘ‏	within
1838	‏ܢܥܢܐ‏	would answer
0116	‏ܘܢܐܡܪ‏	and say
1261	‏ܠܗ‏	to him
1262	‏ܠܐ‏	not
0621	‏ܬܗܪܝܢܝ‏	Do trouble me
0580	‏ܕܗܐ‏	for behold
2718	‏ܬܪܥܐ‏	the door
0047	‏ܐܚܝܕ‏	is shut
0592	‏ܘܗܘ‏	*
0323	‏ܘܒܢܝ‏	and my children
1817	‏ܥܡܝ‏	are with me
1897	‏ܒܥܪܣܐ‏	in bed
1262	‏ܠܐ‏	not
2510	‏ܡܫܟܚ‏	am able
0124	‏ܐܢܐ‏	I
2168	‏ܕܐܩܘܡ‏	to rise
1030	‏ܘܐܬܠ‏	and give
1261	‏ܠܟ‏	to you

VERSE 8 — I say to you, if on account of friendship he will not give to him, because of his persistence, he will rise up and give to him as much as is needed by him.

0116	‏ܐܡܪ‏	say
0124	‏ܐܢܐ‏	I
1261	‏ܠܟܘܢ‏	to you
0121	‏ܐܢ‏	if
1347	‏ܡܛܠ‏	on account of
2347	‏ܪܚܡܘܬܐ‏	friendship
1262	‏ܠܐ‏	not
1030	‏ܢܬܠ‏	he will give
1261	‏ܠܗ‏	to him
1347	‏ܡܛܠ‏	because of

LUKE CHAPTER 11

#	Syriac	English
0882		his persistence
2168		he will rise up
1030		and give
1261		to him
1188		as much as
0296		is needed
1261		by him

VERSE 9 — I say to you also, 'Ask and it will be given to you, seek and you will find, knock and it will be opened to you,'

#	Syriac	English
0169		also
0124		<I>
0116		say
0124		I
1261		to you
2420		Ask
1030		and it will be given
1261		to you
0296		seek
2510		and you will find
1568		knock
2070		and it will be opened
1261		to you

VERSE 10 — for everyone who asks will receive and whoever seeks will find and who knocks, it will be opened to him.

#	Syriac	English
1168		everyone
0403		for
2420		who asks
1532		will receive
0296		and who seeks
2510		will find
1568		and who knocks
2070		it will be opened
1261		to him

VERSE 11 — For what father among you whose son asks him for bread will offer him a stone? And if he asks him for a fish, instead of a fish will he offer him a serpent?

#	Syriac	English
0066		what
0403		For
1388		among you
0002		father
2420		asks him for
0323		whose son
1293		bread
1316		?
1119		a stone
1091		will offer
1261		him
0121		And if
1490		a fish
2420		he asks him for
1316		<?>
0812		instead of
1490		a fish
0740		a serpent
1091		will he offer
1261		him

VERSE 12 — And if he asks him for an egg, will he offer him a scorpion?

#	Syriac	English
0121		And if
0327		an egg
2420		he asks him for
1316		<?>
0592		<he>
1879		a scorpion
1091		will he offer
1261		him

VERSE 13 — And if you who are evil know to give good gifts to your children, how much more will your Father from heaven give the Holy Spirit to those who ask him?"

#	Syriac	English
0121		And if
0133		<you>
0220		who evil
0069		are
1023		know
0133		you
1032		gifts
0938		good

LUKE   CHAPTER 11

1030		to give		2362		the prince
0323		to your children		0514		of devils
1188		how much		1542		casts out
1101		more		0598		This [man]
0002		your Father		0514		devils
1388		from		**VERSE 16**		And others, tempting him, were asking him for a sign from heaven.
2543		heaven				
1030		will give		0053		others
2323		the Holy Spirit		0518		And
2164		*		1128		tempting
0066		to those		1527		*
2420		who ask		1261		him
1261		him		0206		a sign
VERSE 14		And as he was casting out a demon because he was dumb, it occurred that after that demon went out that dumb [man] spoke and the crowds were amazed.		1388		from
				2543		heaven
				2420		asking for
				0603		were
				1261		him
1128		And as		**VERSE 17**		But Jesus, who knew their thoughts, said to them, "Every kingdom that is divided against itself will be ruined and a house that is separated from its essential [foundation] will fall.
1542		he was casting out				
2469		a demon				
0069		because he was				
0907		dumb				
0603		it occurred		3257		Jesus
1128		that after		0518		But
1542		went out		1023		who knew
0593		that		0603		*
2469		demon		0917		their thoughts
1362		spoke		0116		said
0593		that		1261		to them
0907		dumb [man]		1168		Every
0549		and were amazed		1385		kingdom
1201		the crowds		1968		that is divided
VERSE 15		And some of them said, "This [man] casts out devils by Beelzebub, the prince of devils."		1804		against
				1547		itself
				0891		will be ruined
0131		some		0243		and a house
0518		And		1804		that from
1388		of them		2219		its essential [foundation]
0116		said		1968		is separated
3127		by Beelzebub		1538		will fall

470

LUKE CHAPTER 11

VERSE 18 — And if Satan is divided against himself, how will his kingdom stand? For you say that I cast out devils by Beelzebub.

0121		And if
1642		Satan
1804		against
1547		himself
1968		is divided
0061		how
2168		will stand
1385		his kingdom
0116		For say
0133		you
3127		that by Beelzebub
1542		cast out
0124		I
0514		devils

VERSE 19 — And if I cast out devils by Beelzebub, by whom do your sons cast [them] out? Because of this, they will be judges to you.

0121		And if
0124		<I>
3127		by Beelzebub
1542		cast out
0124		I
0514		devils
0323		your sons
1393		by whom
1542		do cast [them] out
1347		Because of
0598		this
0592		they
0603		will be
1261		to you
0498		judges

VERSE 20 — But if I cast out devils by the finger of God, the kingdom of God has come near to you.

0121		if
0518		But
2081		by the finger
0093		of God
1542		cast out
0124		I
0514		devils
2244		has come near
1261		*
1804		to you
1385		the kingdom
0093		of God

VERSE 21 — When a strong man, being armed, guards his courtyard, his property is in quietness.

0120		When
0862		a strong man
1128		being
0655		armed
1502		guards
0505		his courtyard
2505		in quietness
0592		is
2217		his property

VERSE 22 — But if one who is stronger than him should come, he will conquer him [and] he will capture all of his armor on which he had relied and he will distribute his spoil.

0121		if
0518		But
0208		should come
1389		one
0862		who is stronger
1388		than him
0664		he will conquer him
1168		and all of
0656		his armor
2587		he will capture
0593		<that>
2665		he had relied
0603		*
1804		on which

LUKE CHAPTER 11

0245	ܘܒܙܬܗ	and his spoil
1968	ܢܦܠܓ	he will distribute

VERSE 23 He who is not with me is against me and he who does not gather with me actually scatters.

1389	ܡܢ	He who
1262	ܕܠܐ	not
0603	ܗܘܐ	is
1817	ܥܡܝ	with me
2135	ܠܘܩܒܠܝ	against me
0592	ܗܘ	is
1389	ܘܡܢ	and he who
1262	ܕܠܐ	not
1198	ܟܢܫ	does gather
1817	ܥܡܝ	with me
0229	ܡܒܕܪܘ	actually scatters
0229	ܡܒܕܪ	*

VERSE 24 When an unclean spirit leaves a man, it goes [and] wanders around in places in which there is no water to seek rest for itself. And when it does not find [rest], it says, "I will return to my house from where I left."

2323	ܪܘܚܐ	spirit
0991	ܛܢܦܬܐ	an unclean
1313	ܡܐ	When
1542	ܕܢܦܩܬ	leaves
1388	ܡܢ	<from>
0323	ܒܪ	a man
0131	ܐܢܫܐ	*
0042	ܐܙܠܐ	it goes
1236	ܡܬܟܪܟܐ	[and] wanders around
0214	ܒܐܬܪܘܬܐ	in places
1351	ܕܡܝܐ	where water
1264	ܠܝܬ	there is no
0217	ܒܗܘܢ	<in them>
0296	ܕܬܒܥܐ	to seek
1261	ܠܗ	for itself
1485	ܢܝܚܐ	rest
1313	ܘܡܐ	And when
1262	ܕܠܐ	not

2510	ܐܫܟܚܬ	it does find [rest]
0116	ܐܡܪܐ	it says
0616	ܐܗܦܘܟ	I will return
0243	ܠܒܝܬܝ	to my house
1110	ܐܝܡܟܐ	from where
1542	ܕܢܦܩܬ	I left

VERSE 25 And if it comes [and] finds that it is swept and furnished,

0121	ܘܐܢ	And if
0208	ܐܬܝܐ	it comes
2510	ܘܡܫܟܚܐ	[and] finds
0818	ܕܚܡܝܡ	that it is swept
2083	ܘܡܨܒܬ	and furnished

VERSE 26 then it goes [and] leads seven other spirits more evil that it and they enter and live there and the end [state] of that man becomes worse than his first [state]."

0594	ܗܝܕܝܢ	then
0042	ܐܙܠܐ	it goes
0477	ܕܒܪܐ	[and] leads
2437	ܫܒܥ	seven
2323	ܪܘܚܝܢ	spirits
0053	ܐܚܪܢܝܬܐ	other
0220	ܕܒܝܫܢ	more evil
1388	ܡܢܗ	than it
1796	ܘܥܐܠܢ	and they enter
1833	ܘܥܡܪܢ	and live
2682	ܬܡܢ	there
0603	ܘܗܘܝܐ	and becomes
0054	ܚܪܬܗ	the end [state]
0325	ܕܒܪܢܫܐ	of man
0593	ܗܘ	that
0220	ܒܝܫܐ	worse
1388	ܡܢ	than
2157	ܩܕܡܝܬܗ	his first [state]

VERSE 27 And while he was speaking these [things], a certain woman raised up her voice from the crowd and said to him, "Blessed is the womb that bore you and the breasts that nursed you."

1128	ܘܟܕ	And while

LUKE   CHAPTER 11

0598		these [things]
1362		speaking
0603		he was
2331		raised up
0135		a woman
0721		certain
2204		her voice
1388		from
1201		the crowd
0116		and said
1261		to him
0940		Blessed is
1241		the womb
0999		that bore you
2640		and the breasts
1063		that nursed you

VERSE 28 He said to her, "Blessed are those who have heard the word of God and keep it."

0116		He said
1261		to her
0592		\<he\>
0940		Blessed are
0066		those
2547		who have heard
1364		the word
0093		of God
1502		and keep
1261		it

VERSE 29 And when the crowds were gathered, he began to say, "This evil generation seeks a sign and a sign will not be given to it, except the sign of Jonah the prophet.

1128		And when
1198		were gathered
0603		*
1201		the crowds
2597		he began
0116		to say
2605		generation
0598		This
0220		evil
0206		a sign
0296		seeks
0206		and a sign
1262		not
1030		will be given
1261		to it
0090		except
0206		the sign
3242		of Jonah
1457		the prophet

VERSE 30 For as Jonah was a sign to the Ninevites, so also the Son of Man will be [a sign] to this generation.

0061		as
0403		For
0603		was
3242		Jonah
0206		a sign
3346		to the Ninevites
0597		so
0603		will be [a sign]
0169		also
0323		the Son
0131		of Man
2605		to generation
0598		this

VERSE 31 The queen of the south will stand in the judgment concerning the men of this generation and will condemn them, because she came from the far sides of the earth to hear the wisdom of Solomon, and behold, one who is greater than Solomon [is] here.

1386		The queen
1062		of the south
2168		will stand
0497		in the judgment
1817		concerning
0131		the men
2605		of generation
0598		this

473

LUKE CHAPTER 11

Vertical Interlinear

0742		and will condemn		1474		lights
0592		them		2607		a lamp
0208		because she came		1625		and places
1388		from		1261		it
1735		the far sides		1206		in a hidden place
0199		of the earth		0024		or
2547		to hear		2660		under
0792		the wisdom		1583		a basket
3518		of Solomon		0090		but rather
0580		and behold		1803		[he places it] on
1100		one who is greater		1388		*
1388		than		1402		a lamp stand
3518		Solomon		0066		so that those
0600		[is] here		1796		who enter
				0758		will see
				1477		its light

VERSE 32 The Ninevite men will stand in the judgment concerning this generation and will condemn it, because they repented at the preaching of Jonah, and behold, one who is greater than Jonah [is] here.

VERSE 34 The lamp of your body is the eye. So when your eye is simple, your whole body will also be lightened. But if it is evil, your [whole] body will also be darkened.

0361		the men
3346		Ninevite
2168		will stand
0497		in the judgment
1817		concerning
2605		generation
0598		this
0742		and will condemn it
2649		because they repented
1232		at the preaching
3242		of Jonah
0580		and behold
1100		one who is greater
1388		than
3242		Jonah
0600		[is] here

2607		The lamp
1929		of your body
0069		is
1794		your eye
0120		when
0596		So
1794		your eye
2055		is simple
0169		also
1168		whole
1929		your body
0603		will be
1474		lightened
0121		if
0518		But
0603		it is
0220		evil
0169		also
1929		your [whole] body

VERSE 33 No one lights a lamp and places it in a hidden place or under a basket, but rather [he places it] on a lamp stand, so that those who enter will see its light.

1262		No
0131		one

LUKE   CHAPTER 11

0603	ܢܗܘܐ	will be
0923	ܚܫܘܟ	darkened

VERSE 35 — Therefore, beware that the light that is in you is not darkness.

0645	ܐܙܕܗܪ	beware
0596	ܗܟܝܠ	Therefore
1314	ܕܠܡܐ	that not
1477	ܢܘܗܪܐ	the light
0217	ܕܒܟ	that is in you
0923	ܚܫܘܟܐ	darkness
0592	ܗܘ	is

VERSE 36 — Now if your whole body is lightened and does not have any dark portion, all of it will be giving light, as a lamp by its flame gives you light."

0121	ܐܢ	if
0518	ܕܝܢ	Now
1929	ܦܓܪܟ	your body
1168	ܟܠܗ	whole
1474	ܢܗܝܪ	is lightened
1264	ܘܠܝܬ	and does not have
0217	ܒܗ	*
1399	ܡܢܬܐ	portion
1326	ܡܕܡ	any
0923	ܚܫܘܟܬܐ	dark
0603	ܢܗܘܐ	will be
1474	ܢܗܝܪ	giving light
1168	ܟܠܗ	all of it
0060	ܐܝܟ	as
2607	ܫܪܓܐ	a lamp
0538	ܒܕܠܩܗ	by its flame
1474	ܢܗܪ	gives light
1261	ܠܟ	you

VERSE 37 — And while he was speaking, a certain Pharisee asked him to eat with him and he entered [and] sat to eat.

1128	ܟܕ	while
0518	ܕܝܢ	And
1362	ܡܡܠܠ	he was speaking
0296	ܒܥܐ	asked
1388	ܡܢܗ	him
3439	ܦܪܝܫܐ	a Pharisee
0721	ܚܕ	certain
2597	ܕܢܫܬܪܐ	to eat
1288	ܠܘܬܗ	with him
1796	ܘܥܠ	and he entered
1664	ܐܣܬܡܟ	[and] sat to eat

VERSE 38 — And that Pharisee, when he saw him, was amazed that he had not washed first before his meal.

0593	ܗܘ	that
0518	ܕܝܢ	And
3439	ܦܪܝܫܐ	Pharisee
1128	ܟܕ	when
0758	ܚܙܝܗܝ	he saw him
0549	ܐܬܕܡܪ	was amazed
1262	ܕܠܐ	that not
2151	ܠܘܩܕܡ	first
1819	ܥܡܕ	he had washed
1388	ܡܢ	<from>
2154	ܩܕܡ	before
2602	ܫܪܘܬܗ	his meal

VERSE 39 — And Jesus said to him, "Now you Pharisees cleanse the outside of the cup and of the dish, but your inside is full of rape and evil.

0116	ܐܡܪ	said
1261	ܠܗ	to him
0518	ܕܝܢ	And
3257	ܝܫܘܥ	Jesus
0602	ܗܫܐ	Now
0133	ܐܢܬܘܢ	<you>
3439	ܦܪܝܫܐ	Pharisees
0320	ܒܪܗ	the outside
1205	ܕܟܣܐ	of the cup
1954	ܘܕܙܒܘܪܐ	and of the dish
0521	ܡܕܟܝܢ	cleanse
0133	ܐܢܬܘܢ	you
0379	ܠܓܘ	inside
1388	ܡܢܟܘܢ	your
0518	ܕܝܢ	but
1366	ܡܠܐ	is full of

475

LUKE CHAPTER 11

0776	ܚܛܘܦܝܐ	rape		1086	ܥܣܒܐ	herb
0220	ܘܒܝܫܘܬܐ	and evil		1733	ܘܥܒܪܝܢ	yet pass
VERSE 40		Fools! Did not he who made the outside also make the inside?		0133	ܐܢܬܘܢ	you
				1804	ܥܠ	over
0867	ܣܟܠܐ	Fools		0497	ܕܝܢܐ	justice
2385	ܠܐ	*		1804	ܘܥܠ	and <over>
1262	ܠܐ	not		0699	ܚܘܒܐ	the love
0603	ܗܘܐ	Did		0093	ܕܐܠܗܐ	of God
1389	ܡܢ	he who		0598	ܗܠܝܢ	these [things]
1724	ܥܒܕ	made		0518	ܕܝܢ	Now
0322	ܕܠܒܪ	the outside		0626	ܘܠܐ	ought
0379	ܘܕܠܓܘ	also the inside		0603	ܗܘܐ	*
0592	ܗܘ	<he>		1724	ܠܡܥܒܕ	you to do
1724	ܥܒܕ	make		0598	ܘܗܠܝܢ	and these [things]
VERSE 41		But what you have, give in alms, and behold, everything will be clean to you.		1262	ܠܐ	not
				2440	ܠܡܫܒܩ	you should leave out
0342	ܒܪܡ	But		**VERSE 43**		Woe to you, Pharisees, because you love the chief seats in the synagogues and a greeting in the streets.
1326	ܡܕܡ	what				
0069	ܐܝܬ	you have		0625	ܘܝ	Woe
1030	ܗܒܘܗܝ	give		1261	ܠܟܘܢ	to you
0642	ܒܙܕܩܬܐ	in alms		3439	ܦܪܝܫܐ	Pharisees
0580	ܘܗܐ	and behold		2342	ܕܪܚܡܝܢ	because love
1173	ܟܠܡܕܡ	everything		0133	ܐܢܬܘܢ	you
0521	ܕܟܐ	will be clean		2362	ܪܝܫ	the chief
0592	ܗܘ	*		1094	ܡܘܬܒܐ	seats
1261	ܠܟܘܢ	to you		1200	ܒܟܢܘܫܬܐ	in the synagogues
VERSE 42		But woe to you, Pharisees, because you tithe of mint and rue and every herb, yet you pass over justice and the love of God. Now these [things] you ought to do and these [things] you should not leave out.		2535	ܘܫܠܡܐ	and a greeting
				2481	ܒܫܘܩܐ	in the streets
				VERSE 44		Woe to you, scribes and Pharisees, hypocrites, because you are like graves that are unknown and men walk over them and do not know [it]."
0090	ܐܠܐ	But				
0625	ܘܝ	woe				
1261	ܠܟܘܢ	to you		0625	ܘܝ	Woe
3439	ܦܪܝܫܐ	Pharisees		1261	ܠܟܘܢ	to you
1850	ܕܡܥܣܪܝܢ	because tithe of		1699	ܣܦܪܐ	scribes
0133	ܐܢܬܘܢ	you		3439	ܘܦܪܝܫܐ	and Pharisees
1526	ܢܢܥܐ	mint		1532	ܢܣܒܝ	hypocrites
1927	ܘܦܓܢܐ	and rue		0173	ܐܦܐ	*
1168	ܘܟܠ	and every		0069	ܕܐܝܬܝܟܘܢ	because you are
				0060	ܐܝܟ	like

LUKE CHAPTER 11

#	Aramaic	English
2146		graves
1262		that are unknown
1023		*
0323		and men
0131		*
0608		walk
1804		over them
1262		and not
1023		do know [it]

VERSE 45 And one of the scribes answered and said to him, "Teacher, when you say these [things], you reproach us also."

#	Aramaic	English
1838		And answered
0721		one
1388		of
1699		the scribes
0116		and said
1261		to him
1055		Teacher
1128		when
0598		these [things]
0116		say
0133		you
0169		also
1261		us
2119		reproach
0133		you

VERSE 46 And he said, "Woe also to you, scribes, because you make men carry heavy burdens, yet you do not touch the burdens with one of your fingers.

#	Aramaic	English
0592		<he>
0518		And
0116		he said
0169		also
1261		to you
1699		scribes
0625		Woe
0999		because make carry
0133		you
0323		men
0131		*
1017		burdens
1079		heavy
0133		yet <you>
0721		with one
1388		of
2081		your fingers
1262		not
2244		do touch
0133		you
1261		<them>
1017		the burdens

VERSE 47 Woe to you, because you build tombs for the prophets whom your fathers killed.

#	Aramaic	English
0625		Woe
1261		to you
0281		because build
0133		you
2146		tombs
1457		for the prophets
0002		your fathers
2179		killed
0592		whom

VERSE 48 Therefore, you bear witness to and approve of the works of your fathers, because they killed them and you build their graves.

#	Aramaic	English
1608		bear witness to
0133		you
0596		Therefore
2077		and approve
0133		<you>
1728		of the works
0002		of your fathers
0592		because <they>
2179		they killed
0592		them
0133		and <you>
0281		build
0133		you

LUKE CHAPTER 11

2146		their graves

VERSE 49 — Because of this, the wisdom of God also said, 'Behold, I will send them prophets and apostles, some of whom they will persecute and kill,'

1347		Because of
0598		this
0169		also
0792		the wisdom
0093		of God
0116		said
0580		Behold
0124		<I>
2458		I will send
1261		them
1457		prophets
2522		and apostles
1388		some of whom
2304		they will persecute
2179		and kill

VERSE 50 — so that the blood of all the prophets that was shed from when the world was established will be required from this generation,

2631		so that will be required
0539		the blood
1168		of all
1457		the prophets
0201		that was shed
1388		from
0328		when was established
1813		the world
1388		from
2605		generation
0598		this

VERSE 51 — from the blood of Abel up to the blood of Zacharias, who was killed between the temple [and] the altar, yes, I say to you, it will be required from this generation.

1388		from
0539		the blood
3171		of Abel
1747		up to
0539		the blood
3191		of Zachariah
0593		who
2179		was killed
0266		between
0607		the temple
0475		[and] the altar
0065		yes
0116		say
0124		I
1261		to you
2631		it will be required
1388		from
2605		generation
0598		this

VERSE 52 — Woe to you, scribes, because you have taken away the keys of knowledge. You have not entered and you have hindered those who were entering."

0625		Woe
1261		to you
1699		scribes
2587		because you have taken away
2205		the keys
1027		of knowledge
0133		<you>
1262		not
1796		You have entered
0066		and those
1796		who were entering
1180		you have hindered

VERSE 53 — And while he was speaking these [things] to them, the scribes and Pharisees began to be offended and they grew angry and were criticizing his words.

1128		And while
0598		these [things]
0116		he was speaking
0603		*

LUKE CHAPTER 11

Code	Syriac	English
1261		to them
2597		began
1699		the scribes
3439		and Pharisees
0219		to be offended
1261		*
0837		and they grew angry
2669		and were criticizing
1364		his words

VERSE 54 — And they were plotting against him in many [ways], seeking to catch something from his mouth in order to be able to accuse him.

Code	Syriac	English
1509		And they were plotting
1261		against him
1596		in many [ways]
1128		seeking
0296		*
0047		to catch
1326		something
1388		from
1936		his mouth
2510		in order to be able
0075		to accuse him
2257		*

CHAPTER 12

VERSE 1 — And when very large crowds were gathered, so that they were trampling one another, Jesus began to say to his disciples, "First, beware among yourselves of the leaven of the Pharisees, which is hypocrisy.

Code	Syriac	English
1128		And when
1198		were gathered
2274		very
1201		crowds
1596		large
0061		so that
0507		they were trampling
0721		one another
0721		*
2597		began
3257		Jesus
0116		to say
1304		to his disciples
2151		First
0645		beware
1547		among yourselves
1388		of
0832		the leaven
3439		of the Pharisees
0069		which is
1533		hypocrisy
0173		*

VERSE 2 — And there is not anything that is covered that will not be revealed or that is hidden that will not be known.

Code	Syriac	English
1264		there is not
0518		And
1326		anything
1206		that is covered
1262		that not
0409		will be revealed
1262		or
1009		that is hidden
1262		that not
1023		will be known

VERSE 3 — For everything that you speak in darkness will be heard in the light, and what you murmur in closets into ears will be proclaimed on the roofs.

Code	Syriac	English
1168		everything
0403		For
0923		in darkness
0116		that you speak
1475		in the light
2547		will be heard
1326		and what
0029		in closets
0021		into ears
1294		you murmur
1804		on
0019		the roofs

LUKE CHAPTER 12

1230	ܢܬܟܪܙ	will be proclaimed
VERSE	**4**	And I say to you, my friends, 'Do not fear those who kill the body and afterwards have nothing more to do.'
0116	ܐܡܪ	say
0124	ܐܢܐ	I
1261	ܠܟܘܢ	to you
0518	ܕܝܢ	And
2345	ܠܪܚܡܝ	my friends
1262	ܠܐ	not
0509	ܬܕܚܠܘܢ	Do fear
1388	ܡܢ	*
0066	ܐܝܠܝܢ	those
2179	ܕܩܛܠܝܢ	who kill
1929	ܦܓܪܐ	the body
1388	ܘܡܢ	and <from>
0216	ܒܬܪܟܢ	afterwards
1264	ܠܝܬ	have nothing
1261	ܠܗܘܢ	*
1326	ܝܬܝܪ	*
1100	ܡܕܡ	more
1724	ܠܡܥܒܕ	to do
VERSE	**5**	But I will show you whom you should fear, him who after he has killed, has authority to send into Gehenna, yes, I say to you, 'Fear this [one].'
0739	ܐܚܘܝܟܘܢ	I will show you
0518	ܕܝܢ	But
1388	ܡܢ	<of>
1389	ܡܢ	whom
0509	ܬܕܚܠܘܢ	you should fear
1388	ܡܢ	<of>
0593	ܗܘ	him
1388	ܕܡܢ	who after
0215	ܒܬܪ	*
2179	ܕܩܛܠ	he has killed
2528	ܫܠܝܛ	has authority
2372	ܠܡܫܕܐ	to send
3148	ܒܓܗܢܐ	into Gehenna
0065	ܐܝܢ	yes
0116	ܐܡܪ	say

0124	ܐܢܐ	I
1261	ܠܟܘܢ	to you
1388	ܕܡܢ	<of>
0598	ܗܢܐ	this [one]
0509	ܕܚܠܘ	Fear
VERSE	**6**	Are not five birds sold for two coins? And one of them is not forgotten before God.
1262	ܠܐ	not
0833	ܚܡܫ	five
2125	ܨܦܪܝܢ	birds
0632	ܡܙܕܒܢܢ	Are sold
2709	ܒܬܪܝܢ	for two
0166	ܐܣܪܝܢ	coins
0721	ܘܚܕܐ	And one
1388	ܡܢܗܝܢ	of them
1262	ܠܐ	not
0993	ܛܥܝܐ	is forgotten
2154	ܩܕܡ	before
0093	ܐܠܗܐ	God
VERSE	**7**	But even the separate hairs of your head are all numbered. Do not fear, therefore, because you are more valuable than a multitude of birds.
0517	ܕܝܠܟܘܢ	your
0518	ܕܝܢ	But
0169	ܐܦ	even
1403	ܡܢܐ	the separate hairs
1687	ܕܣܥܪܐ	*
2362	ܕܪܫܟܘܢ	of your head
1168	ܟܠܗܝܢ	all
1396	ܡܢܝܢ	are numbered
0592	ܐܢܝܢ	<them>
1262	ܠܐ	not
0596	ܗܟܝܠ	therefore
0509	ܬܕܚܠܘܢ	Do fear
1388	ܕܡܢ	because than
1598	ܣܘܓܐܐ	a multitude
2125	ܕܨܦܪܐ	of birds
1104	ܡܝܬܪܝܢ	are more valuable
0133	ܐܢܬܘܢ	you

480

Vertical Interlinear

LUKE   CHAPTER 12

VERSE 8 — And I say to you, whoever will confess me before men, the Son of Man also will confess him before the angels of God.

Code	Aramaic	English
0116		say
0124		I
1261		to you
0518		And
1168		whoever
1020		will confess
0217		me
2154		before
0325		men
0169		also
0323		the Son
0131		of Man
1020		will confess
0217		him
2154		before
1375		the angels
0093		of God

VERSE 9 — But he who denies me before men will be denied himself before the angels of God.

Code	Aramaic	English
0066		he who
0518		But
1215		denies
0217		me
2154		before
0325		men
1215		will be denied
0217		himself
2154		before
1375		the angels
0093		of God

VERSE 10 — And whoever speaks a word against the Son of Man will be forgiven, but he who blasphemes against the Holy Spirit will not be forgiven.

Code	Aramaic	English
1168		And whoever
0116		speaks
1364		a word
1804		against
0323		the Son
0131		of Man
2440		will be forgiven
1261		\<him\>
1389		he who
1804		against
2323		the Spirit
0518		but
2164		Holy
0370		blasphemes
1262		not
2440		will be forgiven
1261		\<him\>

VERSE 11 — And when they bring you to the synagogues before chiefs and rulers, do not be anxious how you should answer or what you should say,

Code	Aramaic	English
1313		when
2244		they bring
1261		you
0518		And
1200		to the synagogues
2154		before
2362		chiefs
2529		and rulers
1262		not
1069		do be anxious
0061		how
1542		you should answer
2323		*
0024		or
1393		what
0116		you should say

VERSE 12 — for the Holy Spirit will teach you at that moment what you ought to say."

Code	Aramaic	English
2323		the Spirit
0403		for
2164		Holy
1053		will teach you

LUKE CHAPTER 12

#	Aramaic	English
0593		at that
2573		moment
1326		what
0626		you ought
0116		to say

VERSE 13 And one of that crowd said to him, "Teacher, tell my brother to divide the inheritance with me."

#	Aramaic	English
0116		said
1261		to him
0518		And
0131		one
1388		of
0593		that
1201		crowd
1055		Teacher
0116		tell
0043		my brother
1968		to divide
1817		with me
1090		the inheritance

VERSE 14 And Jesus said to him, "Man, who set me [as] a judge and distributor over you?"

#	Aramaic	English
3257		Jesus
0518		And
0116		said
1261		to him
0361		Man
1390		who
2168		set me
1804		over you
0498		[as] a judge
1969		and distributor

VERSE 15 And he said to his disciples, "Beware of all greediness, because life is not in the abundance of possessions."

#	Aramaic	English
0116		And he said
1304		to his disciples
0645		Beware
1388		of
1168		all
1067		greediness
1347		because
1262		not
0603		<was>
1102		in the abundance
1515		of possessions
0069		is
0782		life

VERSE 16 And he spoke a parable to them, "A certain rich man's land brought to him many crops.

#	Aramaic	English
0116		And he spoke
1454		a parable
1288		to them
0361		A man's
0721		certain
1921		rich
1796		brought
1261		to him
0199		land
1800		crops
1596		many

VERSE 17 And he thought within himself and said, 'What shall I do, because I do not have anywhere I can gather in my crops?'

#	Aramaic	English
0914		And he thought
0603		*
1547		within himself
0116		and said
1393		What
1724		shall I do
1264		because I do not have
1261		*
1108		anywhere
0824		I can gather in
1800		my crops

482

Vertical Interlinear

LUKE   CHAPTER 12

VERSE 18 — And he said, 'I will do this. I will pull down my storehouses and I will build and enlarge them and I will gather in there all my harvest and my goods.'

0116		And he said
0598		this
1724		I will do
1719		I will pull down
0243		my storehouses
2232		*
0281		and I will build
1082		and enlarge
0592		them
0824		and I will gather in
2682		there
1168		all
1732		my harvest
0938		and my goods

VERSE 19 — And I will say to my soul, 'My soul, you have many goods that are laid up for many years. Take rest, eat, drink [and] be merry.'

0116		And I will say
1547		to my soul
1547		My soul
0069		you have
1261		*
0938		goods
1596		many
1626		that are laid up
2559		for years
1596		many
1483		Take rest
0075		eat
2620		drink
0286		[and] be merry

VERSE 20 — But God said to him, 'Fool! In this night they will require your soul from you, and those [things] that you have prepared, for whom will they be?'

0116		said
1261		to him
0518		But
0093		God
0867		Fool
2385		*
0598		In this
1299		night
1547		your soul
2631		they will require
1261		<it>
1388		from you
0598		and those [things]
0950		that you have prepared
1389		for whom
0603		will they be

VERSE 21 — So is he who lays up for himself treasures and does not abound in God."

0597		So
0592		is
1389		he who
1625		lays up
1261		for himself
1627		treasures
0093		and in God
1262		not
1921		does abound

VERSE 22 — And he said to his disciples, "Because of this, I say to you, do not be anxious for yourselves, what you will eat or for your body, what you will wear,

0116		And he said
1304		to his disciples
1347		Because of
0598		this
1261		to you
0116		say
0124		I
1262		not
1069		do be anxious
1547		for yourselves
1393		what

LUKE   CHAPTER 12

0075	ܬܐܟܠܘܢ	you will eat
1262	ܐܘ	or
1929	ܠܦܓܪܟܘܢ	for your body
1393	ܡܢܐ	what
1272	ܬܠܒܫܘܢ	you will wear

VERSE 23   for the soul is more than food, and the body than clothes.

1547	ܢܦܫܐ	the soul
0403	ܓܝܪ	for
1100	ܝܬܝܪܐ	is more
1388	ܡܢ	than
1594	ܣܝܒܪܬܐ	food
1929	ܘܦܓܪܐ	and the body
1388	ܡܢ	than
1273	ܠܒܘܫܐ	clothes

VERSE 24   Consider the ravens, for they neither sow nor reap and they do not have rooms and storehouses, yet God provides for them. Therefore, how much more important are you than birds?

0316	ܐܬܒܩܘ	Consider
1535	ܒܢܥܒܐ	the ravens
1262	ܕܠܐ	for neither
0691	ܙܪܥܝܢ	they sow
1262	ܘܠܐ	nor
0878	ܚܨܕܝܢ	reap
1264	ܘܠܝܬ	and they do not have
1261	ܠܗܘܢ	*
0029	ܬܘܢܐ	rooms
0243	ܘܒܝܬ	and storehouses
2232	ܩܦܣܐ	*
0093	ܘܐܠܗܐ	yet God
2715	ܡܬܪܣܐ	provides
1261	ܠܗܘܢ	for them
1188	ܟܡܐ	how much more
0596	ܗܟܝܠ	Therefore
0133	ܐܢܬܘܢ	are you
1100	ܝܬܝܪܝܢ	important
0133	ܐܢܬܘܢ	<you>
1388	ܡܢ	than
2026	ܦܪܚܬܐ	birds

VERSE 25   And which of you, being anxious, is able to add one cubit to his stature?

0066	ܐܝܢܐ	which
0518	ܕܝܢ	And
1388	ܡܢܟܘܢ	of you
1128	ܟܕ	being
1069	ܝܨܦ	anxious
2510	ܡܫܟܚ	is able
1064	ܠܡܘܣܦܘ	to add
1804	ܥܠ	to
2171	ܩܘܡܬܗ	his stature
0119	ܐܡܬܐ	cubit
0721	ܚܕܐ	one

VERSE 26   And if you are not even capable of a small [thing], why are you anxious about the rest?

0121	ܐܢ	if
0518	ܕܝܢ	And
0169	ܐܦܠܐ	even
1262	ܠܐ	not
0686	ܙܥܘܪܬܐ	a small [thing]
2510	ܡܫܟܚܝܢ	capable of
0133	ܐܢܬܘܢ	you are
1393	ܡܢܐ	why
1804	ܥܠ	about
2611	ܫܪܟܐ	the rest
1069	ܝܨܦܝܢ	are anxious
0133	ܐܢܬܘܢ	you

VERSE 27   Consider how the lilies grow, for they neither labor nor spin, but I say to you, not even Solomon in all his glory was covered as one of these.

0316	ܐܬܒܩܘ	Consider
2484	ܒܫܘܫܢܐ	the lilies
0061	ܐܝܟܢܐ	how
2280	ܪܒܝܢ	grow
1262	ܕܠܐ	for neither
1265	ܠܐܝܢ	they labor
1262	ܘܠܐ	nor
1782	ܥܙܠܢ	spin
0116	ܐܡܪ	say

LUKE — CHAPTER 12

0124		I
1261		to you
0518		but
0169		even
1262		not
3518		Solomon
1168		in all
2431		his glory
1206		was covered
0060		as
0721		one
1388		of
0598		these

VERSE 28 — And if God so clothes the grass that today is in the field and tomorrow falls into the oven, how much more you, [oh] little of faith?

0121		if
0518		And
1826		the grass
1037		that today
0069		is
0884		in the field
1345		and tomorrow
1538		falls
2692		into the oven
0093		God
0597		so
1272		clothes
1188		how much
1100		more
1261		you
0686		[oh] little of
0113		faith

VERSE 29 — And you should not seek what you will eat and what you will drink and your mind should not wander in these [things].

0133		And <you>
1262		not
0296		you should seek
1393		what
0075		you will eat
1393		and what
2620		you will drink
1262		and not
1934		should wander
2385		your mind
0598		in these [things]

VERSE 30 — For all these [things] the Gentiles of the world seek. Now your Father also knows that these [things] are necessary for you.

0598		these [things]
0403		For
1168		all
1818		the Gentiles
0592		<he>
1813		of the world
0296		seek
0169		also
1261		for you
0518		Now
0002		your Father
1023		knows
0296		that are necessary
1261		for you
0598		these [things]

VERSE 31 — But seek the kingdom of God and all these [things] will be added to you.

0342		But
0296		seek
1385		the kingdom
0093		of God
0598		and these [things]
1168		all
1064		will be added
1261		to you

VERSE 32 — Do not fear, little flock, because your Father wants to give you the kingdom.

1262		not
0509		Do fear
0398		flock

LUKE CHAPTER 12

#	Syriac	English
0686		little
2077		because wants
0002		you Father
1030		to give
1261		you
1385		the kingdom

VERSE 33 — Sell your possessions and give alms. Make for yourselves bags that do not grow old and a treasure that does not fail in heaven, where a thief does not approach and moth does not corrupt.

#	Syriac	English
0632		Sell
2217		your possessions
1030		and give
0642		alms
1724		Make
1261		for yourselves
1165		bags
1262		that not
0274		do grow old
1627		and a treasure
1262		that not
0380		does fail
2543		in heaven
1108		where
0437		a thief
1262		not
2244		does approach
1682		and moth
1262		not
0702		does corrupt

VERSE 34 — For wherever your treasure is, there will your heart be also.

#	Syriac	English
1108		wherever
0403		For
0069		is
1627		your treasure
2682		there
0603		will be
0169		also
1268		your heart

VERSE 35 — Your loins should be girded and your lamps lit.

#	Syriac	English
0603		should be
0160		girded
0876		Your loins
1474		and lit
2607		your lamps

VERSE 36 — And you should be like men who wait for their lord at that time when he returns from the wedding feast, so that when he comes and knocks, they may immediately open [the door] for him.

#	Syriac	English
0603		And you should be
0540		like
0131		men
1646		who wait
1426		for their lord
0120		at that time when
1984		he returns
1388		from
0243		the wedding feast
2621		*
1313		so that when
0208		he comes
1568		and knocks
0725		immediately
2070		they may open [the door]
1261		for him

VERSE 37 — Blessed are those servants whose lord comes and finds them awake. Truly I say to you, he will gird up his loins and cause them to sit to eat and will cross over [and] serve them.

#	Syriac	English
0940		Blessed are
1727		servants
0593		<those>
0066		those
0208		comes
1426		whose lord
2510		and finds
0592		them
1128		awake

LUKE CHAPTER 12

1880	ܐܡܝܢ	*		0208	ܐܬܐ	would come
0110	ܐܡܝܢ	Truly		0437	ܓܢܒܐ	the thief
0116	ܐܡܪ	say		1880	ܡܬܬܥܝܪ	he would have watched
0124	ܐܢܐ	I		0603	ܗܘܐ	*
1261	ܠܟܘܢ	to you		1262	ܘܠܐ	and not
0160	ܕܢܐܣܘܪ	he will gird up		2440	ܫܒܩ	would have allowed
0876	ܚܨܘܗܝ	his loins		0603	ܗܘܐ	*
1664	ܘܢܣܡܟ	and cause to sit to eat		1983	ܕܢܬܦܠܫ	to be broken into
0592	ܐܢܘܢ	them		0243	ܒܝܬܗ	his house
1733	ܘܢܥܒܪ	and will cross over		**VERSE 40**		Therefore, you should also be prepared, because the Son of Man will come at that moment that you do not expect."
2554	ܢܫܡܫ	[and] serve				
0592	ܐܢܘܢ	them		0169	ܐܦ	also
VERSE 38		And if he comes in the second or third watch and finds [them] so, blessed are those servants.		0133	ܐܢܬܘܢ	<you>
				0596	ܗܟܝܠ	Therefore
0121	ܘܐܢ	And if		0603	ܗܘܘ	you should be
1503	ܒܡܛܪܬܐ	in the watch		0950	ܡܛܝܒܝܢ	prepared
2709	ܕܬܪܬܝܢ	second		0593	ܕܒܗܝ	because at that
0024	ܐܘ	or		2573	ܫܥܬܐ	moment
2674	ܕܬܠܬ	third		1262	ܕܠܐ	that not
0208	ܐܬܐ	he comes		1588	ܣܒܪܝܢ	do expect
2510	ܘܢܫܟܚ	and finds [them]		0133	ܐܢܬܘܢ	you
0597	ܗܟܢܐ	so		0208	ܐܬܐ	will come
0940	ܛܘܒܝܗܘܢ	blessed are		0323	ܒܪܗ	the Son
1727	ܠܥܒܕܐ	servants		0131	ܕܐܢܫܐ	of Man
0593	ܗܢܘܢ	those		**VERSE 41**		Simon Peter said to him, "Our Lord, do you speak this parable to us or also to everyone?"
VERSE 39		Now know this, that if the lord of the house had known in what watch the thief would come, he would have watched and would not have allowed his house to be broken into.				
				0116	ܐܡܪ	said
				1261	ܠܗ	to him
0598	ܗܕܐ	this		3521	ܫܡܥܘܢ	Simon
0518	ܕܝܢ	Now		3258	ܟܐܦܐ	Peter
1023	ܕܥܘ	know		1426	ܡܪܢ	Our Lord
0097	ܕܐܠܘ	that if		1288	ܠܘܬܢ	to us
1023	ܝܕܥ	had known		0116	ܐܡܪ	do speak
0603	ܗܘܐ	*		0133	ܐܢܬ	you
1426	ܡܪܐ	the lord of		1261	ܠܗ	<to him>
0243	ܒܝܬܐ	the house		1454	ܡܬܠܐ	parable
0066	ܒܐܝܕܐ	in what		0598	ܗܢܐ	this
1503	ܡܛܪܬܐ	watch		0024	ܐܘ	or

LUKE   CHAPTER 12

0169		also		1804		over
1288		to		1168		all
1175		everyone		2217		his possessions

VERSE 42   Jesus said to him, "Who indeed is the faithful and wise steward, whose lord will place him over his service that he should give [him] a measured portion in its time?

VERSE 45   But if that servant says in his heart, 'My lord delays to come,' and begins to beat the servants and the handmaids of his lord and begins to eat and to drink and to be drunk,

0116		said		0121		if
1261		to him		0518		But
3257		Jesus		0116		says
1390		Who		1727		servant
1163		indeed		0593		that
0069		is		1268		in his heart
2276		the steward		1426		My lord
0114		faithful		0050		delays
0790		and wise		0208		to come
2168		will place him		2597		and begins
1426		whose lord		1341		to beat
1804		over		1727		the servants
2556		his service		0118		and the handmaids
1030		that he should give [him]		1426		of his lord
2035		a measured portion		2597		and begins
0633		it its time		1308		to eat
				2620		and to drink
				2315		and to be drunk

VERSE 43   Blessed is that servant whose lord comes [and] finds that he does so.

VERSE 46   the lord of that servant will come in a day that he does not expect and in an hour that he does not know and will separate him and place his lot with those who are not faithful.

0940		Blessed is				
0593		that				
1727		servant				
0208		comes		0208		will come
1426		whose lord		1426		the lord
2510		[and] finds <him>		1727		of servant
1724		that he does		0593		that
0597		so		1036		in a day
				1262		that not

VERSE 44   Truly I say to you, he will place him over all his possessions.

2594		Truly		1588		he does expect
0116		say		2573		and in an hour
0124		I		1262		that not
1261		to you		1023		he does know
2168		he will place him		1968		and will separate him

LUKE   CHAPTER 12

1625		and place
1399		his lot
1817		with
0593		those
1262		who not
0109		are faithful

VERSE 47 And the servant, who knows the will of his lord and does not prepare for him according to his will, will be beaten with many [stripes].

1727		the servant
0518		And
0066		who
1023		knows
2079		the will
1426		of his lord
1262		and not
0950		does prepare
1261		for him
0060		according to
2079		his will
0277		will be beaten with
1596		many [stripes]

VERSE 48 But he who did not know, yet did something that was worthy of stripes, will be beaten with a few stripes, for anyone who is given much, much is required, and to whom they have committed much, they will require more by his hand.

0593		<he>
0518		But
1262		who not
1023		he did know
1724		yet did
1326		something
2461		that was worthy of
1342		stripes
0277		will be beaten with
1342		stripes
0686		a few
1168		anyone

0403		for
1030		who is given
1261		<to him>
1596		much
1596		much
2631		is required
1388		<of him>
0593		and to whom
0448		they have committed
1261		<to him>
1596		much
1101		more
2631		they will require
0057		by his hand

VERSE 49 I have come to send fire on the earth and I want to. Oh that it was already kindled!

1494		fire
0208		I have come
2372		to send
0199		on the earth
2077		and want to
0124		I
0097		Oh that
1388		already
1129		*
0696		it was kindled

VERSE 50 And I have a baptism that I am baptized [with] and I am greatly pressured, until it is fulfilled.

1821		And a baptism
0069		I have
1261		*
1819		that I am baptized [with]
1596		and greatly
0102		pressured
0124		I am
1747		until
1366		it is fulfilled

LUKE   CHAPTER 12

VERSE 51 — Do you think that I have come to bring harmony on earth? I say to you, 'No, but rather division.'

Code	Syriac	Gloss
1588		Do think
0133		you
2505		that harmony
0208		I have come
2372		to bring
0199		on the earth
0116		say
0124		I
1261		to you
1262		No
0090		but rather
1972		division

VERSE 52 — For from now on, there will be five in one house who are divided, three against two and two against three.

Code	Syriac	Gloss
1388		from
0602		now on
0403		For
0603		there will be
0833		five
0243		in house
0721		one
1968		who are divided
2674		three
1804		against
2709		two
2709		and two
1804		against
2674		three

VERSE 53 — For father will be divided against his son and son against his father, mother against her daughter, and daughter against her mother, mother-in-law against her daughter-in-law, and daughter-in-law against her mother-in-law."

Code	Syriac	Gloss
1968		will be divided
0403		For
0002		father
1804		against
0323		his son
0323		and son
1804		against
0002		his father
0106		mother
1804		against
0327		her daughter
0327		and daughter
1804		against
0106		her mother
0823		mother-in-law
1804		against
1179		her daughter-in-law
1179		and daughter-in-law
1804		against
0823		her mother-in-law

VERSE 54 — And he said to the crowds, "When you see a cloud that rises from the west immediately you say, 'Rain will come,' and it happens so.

Code	Syriac	Gloss
0116		And he said
1201		to the crowds
1313		When
0758		you see
1844		a cloud
0555		that rises
1388		from
1884		the west
0725		immediately
0116		say
0133		you
1350		Rain
0208		will come
0603		and it happens
0597		so

VERSE 55 — And when the south [wind] blows, you say, 'There will be heat,' and it happens.

Code	Syriac	Gloss
1313		And when
1571		blows
1062		the south [wind]

LUKE — CHAPTER 12

0116	ܐܡܪܝܢ	say		0042	ܐܙܠ	go
0133	ܐܢܬܘܢ	you		0133	ܐܢܬ	you
0819	ܫܘܒܐ	heat		1817	ܥܡ	with
0603	ܗܘܐ	There will be		0309	ܒܥܠܕܝܢܟ	your adversary
0603	ܘܗܘܐ	and it happens		1288	ܠܘܬ	to

VERSE 56 — Hypocrites! You know [how] to distinguish the appearance of the earth and of heaven. So how do you not distinguish this time?

1532	ܢܣܒܝ	Hypocrites		0194	ܐܪܟܘܢܐ	the ruler
0173	ܐܦܐ	*		1744	ܥܕ	while
2041	ܦܪܨܘܦܐ	the appearance		0038	ܒܐܘܪܚܐ	on the road
0199	ܕܐܪܥܐ	of the earth		0133	ܐܢܬ	you are
2543	ܘܕܫܡܝܐ	and of heaven		1030	ܗܒ	make
1023	ܝܕܥܝܢ	know		2638	ܬܓܪܘܬܐ	terms [with him]
0133	ܐܢܬܘܢ	You		2042	ܘܐܬܦܪܩ	and be quit
2046	ܠܡܦܪܫ	[how] to distinguish		1388	ܡܢܗ	of him
0633	ܙܒܢܐ	time		1314	ܕܠܡܐ	so that not
0518	ܕܝܢ	So		1015	ܢܘܒܠܟ	he will conduct you
0598	ܗܢܐ	this		1288	ܠܘܬ	to
0061	ܐܝܟܢܐ	how		0498	ܕܝܢܐ	the judge
1262	ܠܐ	not		0498	ܘܕܝܢܐ	and the judge
2046	ܦܪܫܝܢ	do distinguish		2530	ܢܫܠܡܟ	deliver you
0133	ܐܢܬܘܢ	you		0352	ܠܓܒܝܐ	to the official

VERSE 57 — And why of yourselves do you not judge [with] truthfulness?

1394	ܠܡܢܐ	why		0352	ܘܓܒܝܐ	and the official
0518	ܕܝܢ	And		2372	ܢܪܡܝܟ	cast you in
1388	ܡܢ	of		0243	ܒܝܬ	prison
1547	ܢܦܫܟܘܢ	yourselves		0163	ܐܣܝܪܐ	*
1262	ܠܐ	not				
0496	ܕܝܢܝܢ	do judge				
0133	ܐܢܬܘܢ	you				
2269	ܩܘܫܬܐ	[with] truthfulness				

VERSE 58 — For when you go with your adversary to the ruler, while you are on the road, make terms [with him] and be quit of him, so that he will not conduct you to the judge and the judge deliver you to the official and the official cast you in prison.

1313	ܟܕ	when
0403	ܓܝܪ	For

VERSE 59 — And I say to you, you will not leave there until you give back the last coin."

0116	ܘܐܡܪ	And say
0124	ܐܢܐ	I
1261	ܠܟ	to you
1262	ܠܐ	not
1542	ܬܦܘܩ	you will leave
1388	ܡܢ	<from>
2682	ܬܡܢ	there
1747	ܥܕܡܐ	until
1030	ܬܬܠ	you give back
2541	ܫܡܘܢܐ	the coin
0051	ܐܚܪܝܐ	last

LUKE

CHAPTER 13

VERSE 1 — Now at that time, men came [and] told him about those Galileans, whose blood Pilate had mingled with their sacrifices.

Code	Syriac	English
0593		at that
0518		Now
0633		time
0208		came
0131		men
0116		[and] told
1261		him
1804		about
3154		Galileans
0593		those
3417		Pilate
0802		had mingled
0539		whose blood
1817		with
0474		their sacrifices

VERSE 2 — And Jesus answered and said to them, "Do you think that these Galileans were sinners more than all the Galileans because it happened to them so?

Code	Syriac	English
1838		And answered
3257		Jesus
0116		and said
1261		to them
1588		Do think
0133		you
0598		that these
3154		Galileans
0772		sinners
0603		were
1100		more
1388		than
1168		all
3154		the Galileans
0597		because so
0603		it happened
0592		to them

VERSE 3 — No! And I say to you, but all of you will also be destroyed likewise, [if] you do [not] repent.

Code	Syriac	English
1262		No
0116		say
0124		I
1261		to you
0518		And
0169		also
1168		all of you
0090		but
2649		[if] you do [not] repent
0597		likewise
0005		you will be destroyed

VERSE 4 — Or those eighteen, on whom the tower fell in Siloam and killed them, do you think that they were sinners more than all the men who lived in Jerusalem?

Code	Syriac	English
0024		Or
0593		those
2686		eighteen
1538		fell
1804		on whom
0369		the tower
3510		in Siloam
2179		and killed
0592		them
1588		do think
0133		you
0772		that sinners
0603		they were
1100		more
1388		than
1168		all
0325		the men
1833		who lived
3022		in Jerusalem

VERSE 5 — No! And I say to you, except all of you repent like them, you will be destroyed."

Code	Syriac	English
1262		No
0116		say

LUKE   CHAPTER 13

0124	ܐܢܐ	I	2016	ܦܐܪܐ	fruit
1261	ܠܟܘܢ	to you	2628	ܒܬܬܐ	on fig tree
0518	ܕܝܢ	And	0598	ܗܕܐ	this
0090	ܐܠܐ	except	1262	ܘܠܐ	and not
2649	ܬܬܘܒܘܢ	repent	2510	ܐܫܟܚܬ	have found [any]
1168	ܟܠܟܘܢ	all of you	0124	ܐܢܐ	I
0072	ܐܟܘܬܗܘܢ	like them	1992	ܦܣܘܩܝܗ	Cut it down
0005	ܬܐܒܕܘܢ	you will be destroyed	1394	ܠܡܢܐ	Why

VERSE 6   And he spoke this parable, "A man had a fig tree that was planted in his vineyard, and he came [and] looked on it for fruit and did not find [any].

0253		should be wasted
0199	ܐܪܥܐ	the ground

VERSE 8   The laborer said to him, 'My lord, leave it even this year, until I work with it and manure it

0116	ܘܐܡܪ	And he spoke	0116	ܐܡܪ	said
1454	ܡܬܠܐ	parable	1261	ܠܗ	to him
0598	ܗܢܐ	this	1977	ܦܠܚܐ	The laborer
2628	ܬܬܐ	a fig tree	1426	ܡܪܝ	My lord
0069	ܐܝܬ	had	2440	ܫܒܘܩܝܗ	leave it
0603	ܗܘܐ	*	0169	ܐܦ	even
0131	ܠܐܢܫ	A man	0598	ܗܕܐ	this
1554	ܕܢܨܝܒܐ	that was planted	2559	ܫܢܬܐ	year
1240	ܒܟܪܡܗ	in his vineyard	1744	ܥܕ	until
0208	ܘܐܬܐ	and he came	1974	ܐܦܠܘܚܝܗ	I work with it
0296	ܒܥܐ	[and] looked for	0630	ܘܐܙܒܠܝܗ	and manure it
0217	ܒܗ	on it			
2016	ܦܐܪܐ	fruit			
1262	ܘܠܐ	and not			
2510	ܐܫܟܚ	did find [any]			

VERSE 9   and perhaps it will produce fruit. Yet if not, next year you may cut it down.'"

VERSE 7   And he said to the laborer, 'Behold, [for] three years I have come [and] I looked for fruit on this fig tree and I have not found [any]. Cut it down. Why should the ground be wasted?'

0121	ܘܐܢ	and perhaps
1724	ܬܥܒܕ	it will produce
2016	ܦܐܪܐ	fruit
0090	ܘܐܠܐ	Yet if not
1391	ܠܫܢܐ	next year
1992	ܬܦܣܩܝܗ	you may cut it down

VERSE 10   And while Jesus was teaching on the Sabbath in one of the synagogues,

0116	ܘܐܡܪ	And he said	1128	ܟܕ	while
1977	ܠܦܠܚܐ	to the laborer	0518	ܕܝܢ	And
0580	ܗܐ	Behold	1053	ܡܠܦ	was teaching
2674	ܬܠܬ	[for] three	3257	ܝܫܘܥ	Jesus
2559	ܫܢܝܢ	years	2445	ܒܫܒܬܐ	on the Sabbath
0208	ܐܬܐ	have come	0721	ܒܚܕܐ	in one
0124	ܐܢܐ	I			
0296	ܒܥܐ	[and] looked for			
0124	ܐܢܐ	I			

LUKE CHAPTER 13

#	Syriac	English
1388		of
1200		the synagogues

VERSE 11 — there was a woman there who had had a spirit of infirmity [for] eighteen years and she was bent over and was not able to straighten at all.

#	Syriac	English
0069		there was
0603		*
2682		there
0135		a woman
0069		who had had
0603		*
1261		*
2323		a spirit
1227		of infirmity
2559		[for] years
2686		eighteen
1211		and bent over
0603		she was
1262		and not
2510		was able
0603		*
2054		to straighten
0429		at all

VERSE 12 — And Jesus saw her and called her and said to her, "Woman, you are free from your infirmity."

#	Syriac	English
0758		saw her
0518		And
3257		Jesus
2239		and called her
0116		and said
1261		to her
0135		Woman
2597		you are free
1388		from
1227		your infirmity

VERSE 13 — And he placed his hand on her and immediately she straightened and praised God.

#	Syriac	English
1625		And he placed
0057		his hand
1804		on her
0725		and immediately
2054		she straightened
2428		and praised
0093		God

VERSE 14 — And the ruler of the synagogue, being angered because Jesus had healed on the Sabbath, answered and said to the crowds, "There are six days in which you ought to work. You should come [and] be healed in them and not on the day of the Sabbath."

#	Syriac	English
1838		answered
0518		And
2271		the ruler of
1200		the synagogue
1128		being
0837		angered
1804		because
0136		had healed
2445		on the Sabbath
3257		Jesus
0116		and said
1201		to the crowds
2615		six
0592		There are
1036		days
0217		in which
0626		you ought
1974		to work
0217		in them
0603		You should
0208		come
0136		[and] be healed
1262		and not
1036		on the day
2445		of the Sabbath

Vertical Interlinear

LUKE   CHAPTER 13

VERSE 15 — And Jesus answered and said to him, "Hypocrite! What one of you on the Sabbath does not untie his ox or his donkey from the stall and go [and] water [it]?

Code	Aramaic	English
3257		Jesus
0518		And
1838		answered
0116		and said
1261		to him
1532		Hypocrite
0173		*
0721		What one
0721		*
1388		of you
2445		on the Sabbath
1262		not
2597		does untie
2657		his ox
0024		or
0830		his donkey
1388		from
0039		the stall
0042		and go
2585		[and] water [it]

VERSE 16 — And this [woman], because she is a daughter of Abraham, and the Accuser has bound her, behold, eighteen years, is it not right that she should be freed from this bondage on the day of the Sabbath?"

Code	Aramaic	English
0598		this [woman]
0518		And
0327		because a daughter
0592		she is
3005		of Abraham
0160		and has bound her
0078		the Accuser
0580		behold
2686		eighteen
2559		years
1262		not
0626		is it right
0603		*
2597		that she should be freed
1388		from
0598		this
0162		bondage
1036		on the day
2445		of the Sabbath

VERSE 17 — And when he said these [things], all those who were opposing were ashamed and all the people were rejoicing at all the wonders that occurred by his hand.

Code	Aramaic	English
1128		And when
0598		these [things]
0116		he said
0603		*
0235		ashamed
0603		were
1168		all
0066		those
2168		who were opposing
0603		*
2135		<against> him
1168		and all
1818		the people
0726		rejoicing
0603		were
1168		at all
2681		the wonders
0603		that occurred
0603		*
0057		by his hand

VERSE 18 — And Jesus said, "What is the kingdom of God like and to what can I compare it?

Code	Aramaic	English
0116		said
0603		*
0518		And
3257		Jesus
1394		What
0540		is like

Vertical Interlinear

LUKE   CHAPTER 13

1385		the kingdom
0093		of God
1394		and to what
0540		can I compare it

VERSE 19 It is like a grain of mustard seed, which a man took [and] threw into his garden. And it grew and became a large tree and a bird of heaven built a nest in its branches."

0540		It is like
2019		a grain
0895		of mustard seed
0593		which
1532		took
0361		a man
2372		[and] threw
0433		into his garden
2280		And it grew
0603		and became
0063		a tree
2271		large
2026		and a bird
2543		of heaven
2215		built a nest
1623		in its branches

VERSE 20 Jesus again said, "To what can I compare the kingdom of God?

2650		again
0116		said
3257		Jesus
1394		To what
0540		can I compare
1385		the kingdom
0093		of God

VERSE 21 It is like leaven that a woman took and hid in three measures [of] flour until all was leavened."

0540		It is like
0832		leaven
1532		that took
0135		a woman
0986		and hid
2210		in flour
2674		three
1583		measures [of]
1747		until
1168		all
0827		was leavened

VERSE 22 And he traveled into the villages and cities while teaching and going to Jerusalem.

2299		And he traveled
0603		*
2251		into the villages
0499		and cities
1128		while
1053		teaching
0042		and going
3022		to Jerusalem

VERSE 23 And a man asked him whether those who will live are few.

2420		asked him
0518		And
0131		a man
0121		whether
0686		are few
0592		<them>
0066		those
0780		who will live

VERSE 24 And Jesus said to them, "Strive to enter through the narrow door, for I say to you, many will seek to enter and not be able.

3257		Jesus
0518		And
0116		said
1261		to them
1259		Strive
1796		to enter
2718		through the door
0104		narrow
0116		say

Vertical Interlinear

LUKE — CHAPTER 13

Code	Aramaic	English
0124		I
1261		to you
0403		for
1596		many
0296		will seek
1796		to enter
1262		and not
2510		be able

VERSE 25 — From the time that the lord [of] the house will rise and shut the door, then you will stand outside and knock on the door and begin to say, 'Our lord, our lord, open to us,' and he will answer and say, 'I say to you, I do not know you. From where are you?'

Code	Aramaic	English
1388		From
2573		the time
2168		that will rise
1426		the lord
0243		[of] the house
0047		and shut
2718		the door
0603		then you will
2168		stand
0322		outside
1568		and knock
2718		on the door
2597		and begin
0116		to say
1426		Our lord
1426		Our lord
2070		open
1261		to us
1838		and he will answer
0592		*
0116		and say
0116		say
0124		I
1261		to you
1262		not
1023		do know
0124		I
1261		you
1110		From where
0133		are you

VERSE 26 — And you will begin to say, 'We have eaten and we drank before you and you have taught in our streets.'

Code	Aramaic	English
2597		And you will begin
0116		to say
2154		before you
0075		We have eaten
2620		and we drank
2481		and in our streets
1053		you have taught

VERSE 27 — And he will say to you, 'I do not know you. From where are you? DEPART FROM ME, WORKERS OF FALSEHOOD.'

Code	Aramaic	English
0116		And he will say
1261		to you
1262		not
1023		I do know
0124		*
1261		you
1110		From where
0133		are you
2042		DEPART
1261		*
1388		FROM ME
1976		WORKERS OF
2482		FALSEHOOD

VERSE 28 — There will be there weeping and gnashing of teeth when you see Abraham and Isaac and Jacob and all the prophets in the kingdom of God, but you will be thrown outside.

Code	Aramaic	English
2682		there
0603		There will be
0268		weeping
0905		and gnashing of
2558		teeth
1128		when

Vertical Interlinear

LUKE   CHAPTER 13

0758	ܬܚܙܘܢ	you see
3005	ܠܐܒܪܗܡ	Abraham
3033	ܘܠܐܝܣܚܩ	and Isaac
3255	ܘܠܝܥܩܘܒ	and Jacob
1168	ܘܠܟܠܗܘܢ	and all
1457	ܢܒܝܐ	the prophets
1385	ܒܡܠܟܘܬܐ	in the kingdom
0093	ܕܐܠܗܐ	of God
0133	ܐܢܬܘܢ	<you>
0518	ܕܝܢ	but
0603	ܬܗܘܘܢ	you will be
1542	ܡܦܩܝܢ	thrown
0322	ܠܒܪ	outside

VERSE 29 And they will come from the east and from the west and from the south and from the north and will sit to eat in the kingdom of God.

0208	ܘܢܐܬܘܢ	And they will come
1388	ܡܢ	from
0557	ܡܕܢܚܐ	the east
1388	ܘܡܢ	and from
1884	ܡܥܪܒܐ	the west
1388	ܘܡܢ	and from
1062	ܬܝܡܢܐ	the south
1388	ܘܡܢ	and from
0459	ܓܪܒܝܐ	the north
1664	ܘܢܣܬܡܟܘܢ	and will sit to eat
1385	ܒܡܠܟܘܬܐ	in the kingdom
0093	ܕܐܠܗܐ	of God

VERSE 30 And behold, there are last who will be first and there are first who will be last."

0580	ܘܗܐ	And behold
0069	ܐܝܬ	there are
0051	ܐܚܪܝܐ	last
0603	ܕܢܗܘܘܢ	who will be
2157	ܩܕܡܝܐ	first
0069	ܘܐܝܬ	and there are
2157	ܩܕܡܝܐ	first
0603	ܕܢܗܘܘܢ	who will be
0051	ܐܚܪܝܐ	last

VERSE 31 On the same day, some of the Pharisees approached and were saying to him, "Go away, leave here, because Herod wants to kill you."

0217	ܒܗ	On the same
0593	ܒܗܘ	*
1036	ܝܘܡܐ	day
2244	ܩܪܒܘ	approached
0131	ܐܢܫܐ	some
1388	ܡܢ	of
3439	ܦܪܝܫܐ	the Pharisees
0116	ܘܐܡܪܝܢ	and were saying
1261	ܠܗ	to him
1542	ܦܘܩ	Go away
0042	ܙܠ	leave
1261	ܠܟ	*
1112	ܡܟܐ	here
1347	ܡܛܠ	because
3179	ܕܗܪܘܕܣ	Herod
2077	ܨܒܐ	wants
2179	ܠܡܩܛܠܟ	to kill you

VERSE 32 Jesus said to them, "Go, tell this fox, 'Behold, I will cast out demons and do healings today and tomorrow and on the third day I will be finished.'

0116	ܐܡܪ	said
1261	ܠܗܘܢ	to them
3257	ܝܫܘܥ	Jesus
0042	ܙܠܘ	Go
0116	ܐܡܪܘ	tell
2695	ܠܬܥܠܐ	fox
0598	ܗܢܐ	this
0580	ܕܗܐ	Behold
1542	ܡܦܩ	I will cast out
0124	ܐܢܐ	*
2469	ܕܝܘܐ	demons
0138	ܘܐܣܘܬܐ	and healings
1724	ܥܒܕ	do
0124	ܐܢܐ	*
1037	ܝܘܡܢܐ	today
1345	ܘܡܚܪ	and tomorrow

Vertical Interlinear

LUKE   CHAPTER 13

1036		and on the day
2674		third
1366		I will be finished
0124		*

VERSE 33 — Nevertheless, it is right for me to heal today and tomorrow and I will go on another day, because it is not possible that the prophet should be hurt outside of Jerusalem.

0342		Nevertheless
0626		it is right
1261		for me
1037		today
1345		and tomorrow
1684		to heal
1036		and on day
0053		another
0042		I will go
1347		because
1262		not
2510		it is possible
1457		that the prophet
0005		should be hurt
0322		outside
1388		of
3022		Jerusalem

VERSE 34 — Jerusalem, Jerusalem, she has killed the prophets and stoned those who were sent to her. How many times did I want to gather your children as a hen who gathers her chicks under her wings and you did not want [it]?

3022		Jerusalem
3022		Jerusalem
2179		she has killed
1457		the prophets
2296		and stoned
0066		those
2521		who were sent
1288		to her
1188		How
0633		many times
2077		did I want
1198		to gather
0323		your children
0060		as
2714		a hen
1198		who gathers
2022		her chicks
2660		under
0451		her wings
1262		and not
2077		you did not want [it]

VERSE 35 — Behold, your house is left desolate, for I say to you, you will not see me until you say, 'Blessed is he who comes in the name of the LORD.'"

0580		Behold
2440		is left
1261		<to you>
0243		your house
0894		desolate
0116		say
0124		I
1261		to you
0403		for
1262		not
0758		you will see me
1747		until
0116		you say
0338		Blessed is
0592		he
0208		who comes
2539		in the name
1426		of the LORD

CHAPTER 14

VERSE 1 — And it happened that when he entered the house of one of the rulers of the Pharisees to eat bread on the day of the Sabbath, they were watching him.

0603		And it happened
1128		that when
1796		he entered

LUKE   CHAPTER 14

0243	ܒܝܬܐ	the house
0721	ܚܕ	of one
1388	ܡܢ	of
2362	ܪܫܐ	the rulers
3439	ܕܦܪܝܫܐ	of the Pharisees
0075	ܠܡܐܟܠ	to eat
1293	ܠܚܡܐ	bread
1036	ܒܝܘܡܐ	on the day
2445	ܕܫܒܬܐ	of the Sabbath
0592	ܘܗܢܘܢ	<and they>
1502	ܢܛܪܝܢ	watching
0603	ܗܘܘ	they were
1261	ܠܗ	him

VERSE 2   And behold, there was a certain man before him who was swollen with water.

0580	ܘܗܐ	And behold
0361	ܓܒܪܐ	a man
0721	ܚܕ	certain
1198	ܕܟܢܝܫ	who was swollen with
0603	ܗܘܐ	*
1351	ܡܝܐ	water
0069	ܐܝܬ	there was
0603	ܗܘܐ	*
2154	ܩܕܡܘܗܝ	before him

VERSE 3   And Jesus spoke out and said to the scribes and Pharisees, "Is it lawful to heal on the Sabbath?"

1838	ܘܥܢܐ	And spoke out
3257	ܝܫܘܥ	Jesus
0116	ܘܐܡܪ	and said
1699	ܠܣܦܪܐ	to the scribes
3439	ܘܠܦܪܝܫܐ	and Pharisees
0121	ܐܢ	<if>
2528	ܫܠܝܛ	Is it lawful
2445	ܒܫܒܬܐ	on the Sabbath
0136	ܠܡܐܣܝܘ	to heal

VERSE 4   And they were quiet and he took him and healed him and let him go.

0592	ܗܢܘܢ	<they>
0518	ܕܝܢ	And
2623	ܫܬܩܘ	they were quiet
0047	ܘܐܚܕܗ	and he took him
0592	ܗܘ	*
0136	ܘܐܣܝܗ	and healed him
2597	ܘܫܪܝܗܝ	and let him go

VERSE 5   And he said to them, "Which of you whose son or ox falls into a well on the day of the Sabbath does not immediately draw up [and] lift him out?"

0116	ܘܐܡܪ	And he said
1261	ܠܗܘܢ	to them
1390	ܡܢ	Which
1388	ܡܢܟܘܢ	of you
1538	ܢܦܠ	falls
0323	ܒܪܗ	whose son
0024	ܐܘ	or
2657	ܬܘܪܗ	ox
0218	ܒܒܪܐ	into a well
1036	ܒܝܘܡܐ	on the day
2445	ܕܫܒܬܐ	of the Sabbath
1262	ܘܠܐ	<and> not
0725	ܡܚܕܐ	immediately
0533	ܡܣܩ	does draw up
1658	ܡܣܩ	[and] lift out
1261	ܠܗ	him

VERSE 6   And they did not find an answer to give to him about this.

1262	ܘܠܐ	And not
2510	ܐܫܟܚܘ	they did find
1030	ܠܡܬܠ	to give
1261	ܠܗ	to him
2068	ܦܬܓܡܐ	an answer
1804	ܥܠ	about
0598	ܗܕܐ	this

VERSE 7   And he spoke a parable to those who were invited there because he saw those who were choosing the places that were the best seats.

0116	ܘܐܡܪ	And he spoke
0603	ܗܘܐ	*
1454	ܡܬܠܐ	a parable

LUKE — CHAPTER 14

#	Aramaic	English
1288		to
0593		those
0671		who were invited
2682		there
1804		because
0758		he saw
0603		*
1261		those
0351		who were choosing
0494		the places
2362		that were the best seats
1666		*

VERSE 8 — When you are invited by someone to a banquet, do not go [and] seat yourself in the best seat, lest someone who is more honorable than you should be invited there,

#	Aramaic	English
0120		When
0671		are invited
0133		you
1388		by
0131		someone
0243		to a banquet
2621		*
1262		not
0042		do go
1664		[and] seat
1261		yourself
2362		in the best seat
1666		*
1314		lest
0603		you should be
0671		invited
2682		there
0131		someone
1081		who is more honorable
1388		than you

VERSE 9 — And he who called you and him will come and say to you, 'Give place to this [man].' And you will be ashamed as you stand and take the last place.

#	Aramaic	English
0208		And will come
0593		he
1389		who
1261		you
1261		and him
2239		called
0116		and say
1261		to you
1030		Give
0494		place
0598		to this [man]
0235		And you will be ashamed
1128		as
2168		stand
0133		you
0047		and take
0133		<you>
0494		the place
0051		last

VERSE 10 — On the contrary, when you are invited, go [and] seat yourself at the end, so that when he who called you comes, he will say to you, 'My friend, move yourself up higher and be seated,' and you will have praise before all who sit to eat with you,

#	Aramaic	English
0090		On the contrary
1313		when
0671		you are invited
0042		go
1664		[and] seat
1261		yourself
0054		at the end
1313		so that when
0208		comes
0593		he
2239		who called you
0116		he will say
1261		to you

LUKE   CHAPTER 14

2345		My friend		0603		do
1802		move yourself		2239		call
1803		up higher		2345		your friends
1664		and be seated		0170		not even
0603		and you will have		0043		your brothers
1261		*		0024		or
2432		praise		0045		your kinsmen
2154		before		1262		and not
1168		all		2425		your neighbors
1664		who sit to eat		1921		rich
1817		with you		1314		lest

VERSE 11 because everyone who elevates himself will be humbled, and everyone who humbles himself will be raised up."

				0169		also
				0592		they
1347		because		2239		invite you
1168		everyone		0603		and you have
2331		who elevates		1261		*
1547		himself		2038		payment
1353		will be humbled		0598		this

VERSE 13 On the contrary, when you make a feast, call the poor, the hurt, the lame, [and] the blind.

1168		and everyone				
1353		who humbles		0090		On the contrary
1547		himself		1313		when
2331		will be raised up		1724		you make
				0133		*
				2140		a feast
				2239		call

VERSE 12 And he spoke also to him who invited him, "When you make a meal or a dinner, do not call your friends, not even your brothers or your kinsmen, and not your rich neighbors, lest they also invite you and you have this payment.

				1406		the poor
0116		he spoke		1603		the hurt
0518		And		0718		the lame
0169		also		1662		[and] the blind

VERSE 14 And you [will have] blessing, because they have nothing to repay you, for your payment will be in the resurrection of the just."

0593		to him				
2239		who invited him				
1313		When				
1724		you make				
0133		*		0940		and you [will have] blessing
2602		a meal		1264		because they have nothing
0024		or		1261		*
0928		a dinner		2037		to repay you
1262		not		0603		will be
				0403		for

LUKE — CHAPTER 14

2038		your payment
2173		in the resurrection
0637		of the just

VERSE 15 — And when one of those who were seated to eat heard these [things], he said to him, "Blessed is he who will eat bread in the kingdom of God."

1128		when
2547		heard
0518		And
0721		one
1388		of the just
0593		those
1664		who were seated to eat
0598		these [things]
0116		he said
1261		to him
0940		Blessed is he
1389		who
0075		will eat
1293		bread
1385		in the kingdom
0093		of God

VERSE 16 — Jesus said to him, "A certain man made a great supper and called many.

0116		said
1261		to him
3257		Jesus
0361		A man
0721		certain
1724		made
0928		a supper
2271		great
2239		and called
1596		many

VERSE 17 — And he sent his servant at the time of the supper to tell those who were called, 'Behold, everything is prepared for you. Come.'

2458		And he sent
1727		his servant
1750		at the time
0928		of the supper
0116		to tell
0066		those
2239		who were called
0580		Behold
1173		everything
0950		is prepared
1261		for you
0208		Come

VERSE 18 — And all began as one to excuse themselves. The first said to him, 'I have bought a field and I need to go out [and] see it. I beg you, allow me to be excused.'

2597		And began
1388		as
0721		one
1168		all
2420		to excuse themselves
0116		said
1261		to him
2157		The first
2251		a field
0632		I have bought
0104		and need
0124		I
1542		to go out
0758		[and] see it
0296		beg
0124		I
1388		you
2440		allow me
2420		to be excused
0124		*

VERSE 19 — Another said, 'I have bought five yoke [of] oxen and I am going to prove them. I beg you, allow me to be excused.'

0053		Another
0116		said
0833		five

503

LUKE   CHAPTER 14

0648		yoke [of]
2657		oxen
0632		I have bought
0042		and I am going
0124		*
0316		to prove
0592		them
0296		beg
0124		I
1388		you
2440		allow me
2420		to be excused
0124		*

VERSE 20 — And another said, 'I have taken a wife and because of this, I am not able to come.'

0053		And another
0116		said
0135		a wife
1532		I have taken
1347		and because of
0598		this
1262		not
2510		am able
0124		I
0208		to come

VERSE 21 — And that servant came and told his lord these [things]. Then the lord of the house was angry and said to his servant, 'Go out quickly into the marketplaces and streets of the city and bring here the poor and the afflicted and the lame and the blind.'

0208		And came
0593		that
1727		servant
0116		and told
1426		his lord
0598		these [things]
0594		Then
2290		was angry
1426		the lord of
0243		the house
0116		and said
1727		to his servant
1542		Go out
1738		quickly
2481		into the marketplaces
0341		and streets
0499		of the city
1796		and bring
1111		here
1406		the poor
1118		and the afflicted
0720		and the lame
1776		and the blind

VERSE 22 — And the servant said, 'My lord, it is as you commanded and yet there is room.'

0116		And said
1727		the servant
1426		My lord
0603		it is
0060		as
2007		you commanded
2650		and yet
0069		there is
0214		room

VERSE 23 — And the lord said to his servant, 'Go out into the roads and among the hedges and urge them to enter, so that my house may be full,

0116		And said
1426		the lord
1727		to his servant
1542		Go out
0038		into the roads
0266		and among
1617		the hedges
0102		and urge
1796		them to enter
1366		so that may be full
0243		my house

LUKE CHAPTER 14

VERSE 24 — for I say to you, not one of those men who were called will taste of my supper.'"

Code	Aramaic	English
0116		say
0124		I
1261		to you
0403		for
0721		one
1388		of
0593		those
0131		men
2239		who were called
0603		*
1262		not
0998		will taste
1388		of
0928		my supper

VERSE 25 — And while large crowds were going with him, he turned and said to them,

Code	Aramaic	English
1128		And while
0042		were going
0603		*
1817		with him
1201		crowds
1596		large
1984		he turned
0116		and said
1261		to them

VERSE 26 — "He who comes to me and does not hate his father and his mother and his brothers and his sisters and his wife and his children and also himself is not able to be a disciple of me.

Code	Aramaic	English
1389		He who
0208		comes
1288		to me
1262		and not
1673		does hate
0002		his father
0106		and his mother
0043		and his brothers
0046		and his sisters
0135		and his wife
0323		and his children
0169		and also
1547		himself
1304		a disciple
1262		not
2510		is able
0603		to be
1261		of me

VERSE 27 — And he who does not bear his cross and follow me is not able to be a disciple of me.

Code	Aramaic	English
1389		And he
1262		who not
2587		does bear
2109		his cross
0208		and follow me
0215		*
1304		a disciple
1262		not
2510		is able
0603		to be
1261		of me

VERSE 28 — For which of you who wants to build a tower does not first sit down [and] think about his expenses, whether he has [enough] to complete it,

Code	Aramaic	English
1390		which
0403		For
1388		of you
2077		who wants
0281		to build
0369		a tower
1262		<and> not
2151		first
1093		does sit down
0914		[and] think about
1546		his expenses
0121		whether
0069		he has
1261		*

LUKE CHAPTER 14

2530	ܠܡܫܠܡܘܬܗ	[enough] to complete it
VERSE 29		so that when he has not laid the foundation and is not able to finish [it], all who see will mock him
1262	ܕܠܐ	so that not
1128	ܟܕ	when
1625	ܢܣܝܡ	he has laid
0203	ܫܬܐܣܬܐ	the foundation
1262	ܘܠܐ	and not
2510	ܢܫܟܚ	is able
2530	ܠܡܫܠܡܘ	to finish [it]
1168	ܟܠ	all
0758	ܕܚܙܝܢ	who see
0603	ܢܗܘܘܢ	will
0246	ܡܡܝܩܝܢ	mock
0217	ܒܗ	him
VERSE 30		and say, 'This man began to build and was not able to finish [it]'?
0116	ܘܐܡܪܝܢ	and say
0598	ܕܗܢܐ	This
0361	ܒܪܢܫܐ	man
2597	ܫܪܝ	began
0281	ܠܡܒܢܐ	to build
1262	ܘܠܐ	and not
2510	ܐܫܟܚ	was able
2530	ܠܡܫܠܡܘ	to finish [it]
VERSE 31		Or what king who goes to war to fight with his neighboring king does not first think whether he is able to meet with ten thousand, him who comes against him with twenty thousand?
0024	ܐܘ	Or
1390	ܡܢܘ	what
1383	ܡܠܟܐ	king
0042	ܕܐܙܠ	who goes
2247	ܠܩܪܒܐ	to war
1259	ܠܡܬܟܬܫܘ	to fight
1817	ܥܡ	with
1383	ܡܠܟܐ	king
0714	ܚܒܪܗ	his neighboring
1262	ܘܠܐ	<and> not
2151	ܠܘܩܕܡ	first
2381	ܡܬܪܥܐ	does think
0121	ܐܢ	whether
2510	ܡܫܟܚ	he is able
1848	ܒܥܣܪܐ	with ten
0099	ܐܠܦܝܢ	thousand
0197	ܠܡܐܪܥ	to meet
0593	ܠܗܘ	him
0208	ܕܐܬܐ	who comes
1804	ܥܠܘܗܝ	against him
1851	ܒܥܣܪܝܢ	with twenty
0099	ܐܠܦܝܢ	thousand
VERSE 32		And if not, while he is far away from him, he will send an ambassador and ask for peace.
0121	ܘܐܢ	if
0518	ܠܐ	And
1262	ܠܐ	not
1744	ܥܕ	while
0592	ܗܘ	he
2355	ܪܚܝܩ	is far away
1388	ܡܢܗ	from him
2458	ܡܫܕܪ	he will send
0059	ܐܝܙܓܕܐ	an ambassador
0296	ܘܒܥܐ	and ask
1804	ܥܠ	for
2535	ܫܠܡܐ	peace
VERSE 33		So, every one of you who does not forsake all his wealth is not able to be a disciple of me.
0597	ܗܟܢܐ	So
1175	ܟܠܢܫ	every one
1388	ܡܢܟܘܢ	of you
1262	ܕܠܐ	who not
2440	ܫܒܩ	does forsake
1168	ܟܠ	all
2217	ܩܢܝܢܗ	his wealth
1262	ܠܐ	not
2510	ܡܫܟܚ	is able
0603	ܕܢܗܘܐ	to be

LUKE — CHAPTER 14

#	Syriac	Gloss
1261		of me
1304		a disciple

VERSE 34 — Salt is good, but if even the salt should lose its flavor, with what will it be salted?

#	Syriac	Gloss
2583		good
0592		is
1378		Salt
0121		if
0518		but
0169		even
1378		the salt
1962		should lose its flavor
1393		with what
1377		will it be salted

VERSE 35 — It is fit neither for the land nor for the dung-heap. They put it outside. He who has ears to hear should hear."

#	Syriac	Gloss
1262		neither
0199		for the land
1262		nor
0631		for the dung-heap
0042		It is fit
0322		outside
2455		They put
1261		it
1389		He who
0069		has
1261		*
0021		ears
2547		to hear
2547		should hear

CHAPTER 15

VERSE 1 — Now the tax collectors and sinners came near to him in order to hear him.

#	Syriac	Gloss
2244		came near
0603		*
0518		Now
1288		to him
1358		the tax collectors
0772		and sinners
2547		in order to hear him

VERSE 2 — And the scribes and Pharisees were murmuring and saying, "This [man] receives sinners and eats with them."

#	Syriac	Gloss
1699		And the scribes
3439		and Pharisees
2360		murmuring
0603		were
0116		and saying
0598		This [man]
0772		sinners
2134		receives
0075		and eats
1817		with them

VERSE 3 — And Jesus told them this parable.

#	Syriac	Gloss
0116		And told
1261		them
3257		Jesus
1454		parable
0598		this

VERSE 4 — "What man among you who has one hundred sheep and if one of them should be lost, does not leave the ninety-nine in the open country and go [and] seek that one which is lost until he finds it?

#	Syriac	Gloss
1390		What
1388		among you
0361		man
0069		who has
1261		*
1317		one hundred
1887		sheep
0121		and if
0005		should be lost
0721		one
1388		of them
1262		not
2440		does leave
2724		the ninety-nine
2723		*

LUKE — CHAPTER 15

#	Aramaic	English
0478		in the open country
0042		and go
0296		[and] seek
0593		that one
0005		which is lost
1747		until
2510		he finds it

VERSE 5 — And when he has found it, he will rejoice and take it on his shoulders

#	Aramaic	English
1313		And when
2510		he has found it
0726		he will rejoice
2587		and take
1261		it
1804		on
1257		his shoulders

VERSE 6 — and come to his house and call to his friends and his neighbors and say to them, 'Rejoice with me, because I have found my sheep that was lost.'

#	Aramaic	English
0208		and come
0243		to his house
2239		and call
2345		to his friends
2425		and his neighbors
0116		and say
1261		to them
0726		Rejoice
1817		with me
2510		because I have found
1887		my sheep
0007		that was lost
0603		*

VERSE 7 — I say to you, so there will be [more] joy in heaven for one sinner who repents than for ninety-nine just [ones] who do not need repentance.

#	Aramaic	English
0116		say
0124		I
1261		to you
0597		so
0603		there will be
0727		[more] joy
2543		in heaven
1804		for
0721		one
0772		sinner
2649		who repents
0024		than
1804		for
2724		ninety-nine
2723		*
0637		just [ones]
1262		who not
0296		do need
1261		<to them>
2651		repentance

VERSE 8 — Or what woman, who has ten coins and loses one of them, does not light a lamp and sweep the house and search for it carefully until she finds it?

#	Aramaic	English
0024		Or
0066		what
0592		<she>
0135		woman
0069		who has
1261		*
1848		ten
0651		coins
0005		and loses
0721		one
1388		of them
1262		<and> not
1474		does light
2607		a lamp
0818		and sweep
0243		the house
0296		and search
1261		for it
0255		carefully
1747		until

LUKE CHAPTER 15

2510		she finds it
VERSE 9		And when she has found it, she will call her friends and her neighbors and say to them, 'Rejoice with me, because I have found my coin that was lost.'
1313		And when
2510		she has found it
2239		she will call
2345		her friends
2425		and her neighbors
0116		and say
1261		to them
0726		Rejoice
1817		with me
2510		because I have found
0651		my coin
0007		that was lost
0603		*
VERSE 10		I say to you, so there will be joy before the angels of God over one sinner that repents."
0116		say
0124		I
1261		to you
0597		so
0603		there will be
0727		joy
2154		before
1375		the angels
0093		of God
1804		over
0721		one
0772		sinner
2649		that repents
VERSE 11		And Jesus spoke again to them,, "A certain man had two sons.
0116		And spoke
0603		*
1261		to them
2650		again
3257		Jesus
0361		A man
0721		certain
0069		had
0603		*
1261		*
0323		sons
2709		two
VERSE 12		And his younger son said to him, 'My father, give me the portion that is coming to me from your house, and he divided to them his wealth.'
0116		And said
1261		to him
0323		his son
0686		younger
0002		My father
1030		give
1261		me
1972		the portion
1346		that is coming
1261		to me
1388		from
0243		your house
1968		and he divided
1261		to them
2217		his wealth
VERSE 13		And after a few days, his younger son gathered up everything that came to him and went to a region far away and there spent his wealth living wastefully.
1388		And after
0215		*
1036		days
2203		a few
1198		gathered up
0593		<that>
0323		his son
0686		younger
1168		everything
1326		*
1346		that came to him

LUKE CHAPTER 15

#	Syriac	English		#	Syriac	English
0042		and went		2458		sent him
0214		to a region		2251		into the field
2355		far away		2381		to tend
2682		and there		0766		the pigs

VERSE 16 And he desired to fill his stomach from the carob husks that the pigs were eating, and no one gave to him.

#	Syriac	English
0229		spent
2217		his wealth
1128		living
0780		*
2025		wastefully

#	Syriac	English
2287		And he desired
0603		*
1366		to fill
1241		his stomach
1388		from

VERSE 14 And when he had used up everything that he had, a great famine occurred in that region and he began to have need.

#	Syriac	English
1128		And when
0423		he had used up
1168		everything
1326		*
0069		that he had
0603		*
1261		*
0603		occurred
1213		a famine
2271		great
0214		in region
0593		that
2597		and he began
0865		to have need
1261		*

#	Syriac	English
0896		the carob husks
0593		<those>
0075		that were eating
0603		*
0766		the pigs
1262		and no
0131		one
1030		gave
0603		*
1261		to him

VERSE 17 And when he came to himself, he said, 'How many hired servants are now [at] my father's house who have an abundance of bread and I am perishing here with my hunger?'

#	Syriac	English
1128		And when
0208		he came
1288		to
1547		himself
0116		he said
1188		How many
0602		now
0017		hired servants
0069		are
0243		[at] house
0002		my father's
1100		who an abundance of
1261		have
1293		bread

VERSE 15 And he went [and] joined himself to one of the citizens of that land and he sent him into the field to tend the pigs.

#	Syriac	English
0042		And he went
1565		[and] joined
1261		himself
0721		to one
1388		of
0323		the citizens
0499		*
0214		of land
0593		that
0592		and he

LUKE CHAPTER 15

0124		and <I>		0592		he
0600		here		2355		was far away
1213		with my hunger		0758		saw him
0005		I am perishing		0002		his father
0124		*		2342		and had compassion

VERSE 18 — I will rise up [and] go to my father and say to him, 'My father, I have sinned against heaven and before you,

				1804		on him
2168		I will rise up		2312		and ran
0042		[and] go		1538		[and] fell
1288		to		1804		on
0002		my father		2097		his neck
0116		and say		1573		and kissed him
1261		to him				
0002		My father				

VERSE 21 — And his son said to him, 'My father, I have sinned against heaven and before you and I am not worthy to be called your son.'

0770		I have sinned				
2543		against heaven		0116		And said
2154		and before you		1261		to him
				0323		his son
				0002		My father

VERSE 19 — and therefore I am not worthy to be called your son. Make me like one of your hired servants.'

				0770		I have sinned
1262		and not		2543		against heaven
1357		therefore		2154		and before you
2461		I am worthy		1262		and not
0124		*		2461		I am worthy
0323		your son		0124		*
2239		to be called		0323		your son
1724		Make me		2239		to be called
0060		like				
0721		one				
1388		of				
0017		your hired servants				

VERSE 22 — And his father said to his servants, 'Bring out the best robe, clothe him, and place a ring on his hand and put shoes on him

VERSE 20 — And he rose up [and] came to his father. And while he was far away, his father saw him and had compassion on him and ran [and] fell on his neck and kissed him.

				0116		said
				0518		And
2168		And he rose up		0002		his father
0208		[and] came		1727		to his servants
1288		to		1542		Bring out
0002		his father		0146		the robe
1744		And while		2365		best
				1272		clothe him
				1625		and place
				1783		a ring

511

LUKE CHAPTER 15

#	Aramaic	English
0057		on his hand
1581		and put on him
1582		shoes
VERSE 23		and bring [and] kill the ox that is fattened and let us eat and be merry,
0208		and bring
2179		[and] kill
2657		the ox
1949		that is fattened
0075		and let us eat
0286		and be merry
VERSE 24		because this, my son, was dead and [now] is alive, and he was lost and [now] is found,' and they began to be merry.
0598		because this
0323		my son
1338		dead
0603		was
0780		and [now] is alive
0007		and lost
0603		he was
2510		and [now] is found
2597		and they began
0286		to be merry
VERSE 25		Now his oldest son was in the field and when he arrived and came near to the house, he heard the sound of the singing of many.
0593		<that>
0518		Now
0323		his son
2263		oldest
2251		in the field
0603		was
1128		and when
0208		he arrived
2244		and came near
1288		to
0243		the house
2547		he heard
2204		the sound of
0674		the singing
1596		of many
VERSE 26		And he called to one of the boys and asked him, 'What is this?'
2239		And he called
0721		to one
1388		of
0976		the boys
2420		and asked him
1395		What is
0598		this
VERSE 27		He said to him, 'Your brother has come and your father has killed the ox that is fattened, because he has received him [back] healthy.'
0116		He said
1261		to him
0043		Your brother
0208		has come
2179		and has killed
0002		your father
2657		the ox
1949		that is fattened
1128		because healthy
0808		*
2134		he has received him [back]
VERSE 28		And he was angry and did not want to enter. So his father came out [and] begged him.
2290		And he was angry
1262		and not
2077		did want
0603		*
1796		to enter
1542		So came out
0002		his father
0296		[and] begged
1388		him

LUKE   CHAPTER 15

VERSE 29
And he said to his father, 'Behold, how many years have I worked for you [in] service and never transgressed your commandment, yet during all this time you did not give me a goat to make merry with my friends.

Code	Syriac	English
0592		\<he\>
0518		And
0116		he said
0002		to his father
0580		Behold
1188		how many
2559		years
1974		have I worked
0124		*
1261		for you
1729		[in] service
1262		and never
1451		*
1733		transgressed
2009		your commandment
1388		yet during all this time
1450		*
0366		a goat
1262		not
1030		you did give
1261		me
0286		to make merry
1817		with
2345		my friends

VERSE 30
But for this your son, after he has squandered your wealth with harlots and has come [home], you kill for him the ox that is fattened.'

Code	Syriac	English
0598		for this
0518		But
0323		your son
1128		after
2024		he has squandered
2217		your wealth
1817		with
0680		harlots
0208		and has come [home]
1514		you kill
1261		for him
2657		the ox
1949		that is fattened

VERSE 31
His father said to him, 'My son, you always are with me and everything of mine is yours,

Code	Syriac	English
0116		said
1261		to him
0002		His father
0323		My son
0133		\<you\>
1170		always
1817		with me
0133		you are
1173		and everything
0517		of mine
0517		yours
0592		is

VERSE 32
but it is right for us to make merry and to rejoice, because your brother was dead, yet [now] is alive and was lost, yet [now] is found."

Code	Syriac	English
0286		to make merry
0518		but
0626		it is right
0603		*
1261		for us
0726		and to rejoice
0598		because \<this\>
0043		your brother
1334		dead
0603		was
0780		yet [now] is alive
0007		and was lost
0603		*
2510		yet [now] is found

LUKE

CHAPTER	16	
VERSE	1	And he spoke a parable to his disciples, "There was a certain rich man, and he had a steward, and they had accused him of squandering his wealth.
0116		And he spoke
1454		a parable
1288		to
1304		his disciples
0361		a man
0721		certain
0069		There was
0603		*
1921		rich
0069		and he had
0603		*
1261		*
2276		a steward
0075		and they accused him
1261		*
2257		*
2217		of his wealth
2024		squandering
VERSE	2	And his lord called him and said to him, 'What is this that I hear about you? Give me an accounting of your stewardship, for you can no longer be a steward for me.'
2239		And called him
1426		his lord
0116		and said
1261		to him
1395		What is
0598		this
2547		that hear
0124		I
1804		about you
1030		Give
1261		me
0916		an accounting
2271		of your stewardship
2277		*
1262		<not>
0403		for
2510		can
0133		you
1357		no longer
2276		a steward
0603		be
1261		for me
VERSE	3	That steward said to himself, 'What should I do, for my lord has taken from me the stewardship? I am not able to dig, and I am ashamed to beg.
0116		said
0593		That
2276		steward
1547		to himself
1393		What
1724		should I do
1426		for my lord
2587		has taken
1261		<to him>
1388		from me
2271		the stewardship
2277		*
0875		to dig
1262		not
2510		able
0124		I am
0730		and to beg
0235		ashamed
0124		I am
VERSE	4	I know what I will do so that when I am dismissed from the stewardship, they will receive me into their houses.'
1023		I know
1393		what
1724		I will do
1313		so that when
1542		I am dismissed
1388		from

LUKE   CHAPTER 16

2271	ܪܒܬܐ	the stewardship
2277	ܕܒܝܬܐ	*
2134	ܢܩܒܠܘܢܢܝ	they will receive me
0243	ܒܒܬܝܗܘܢ	into their houses

VERSE 5 And he called each one of his lord's debtors and said to the first, 'How much do you owe my lord?'

2239	ܘܩܪܐ	And he called
0721	ܚܕ	each one
0721	ܚܕ	*
1388	ܡܢ	of
0745	ܚܝܒܐ	debtors
1426	ܕܡܪܗ	his lord's
0116	ܘܐܡܪ	and said
2157	ܠܩܕܡܝܐ	to the first
1188	ܟܡܐ	How much
0745	ܚܝܒ	do owe
0133	ܐܢܬ	you
1426	ܠܡܪܝ	my lord

VERSE 6 He said to him, 'One hundred measures [of] oil.' He said to him, 'Take your book and sit down quickly; write fifty measures.'

0116	ܐܡܪ	He said
1261	ܠܗ	to him
1317	ܡܐܐ	One hundred
1455	ܡܕܝܢ	measures [of]
1445	ܡܫܚܐ	oil
0116	ܐܡܪ	He said
1261	ܠܗ	to him
1532	ܣܒ	Take
1248	ܟܬܒܟ	your book
1093	ܘܬܒ	and sit down
1738	ܒܥܓܠ	quickly
1247	ܘܟܬܘܒ	[and] write
0834	ܚܡܫܝܢ	fifty
1455	ܡܕܝܢ	measures

VERSE 7 And he said to another, 'And what do you owe my lord?' He said to him, 'One hundred cors [of] wheat.' He said to him, 'Take your book and sit down; write eighty cors.'

0116	ܐܡܪ	And he said
0053	ܠܐܚܪܢܐ	to another
0133	ܘܐܢܬ	And <you>
1393	ܡܢܐ	what
0745	ܚܝܒ	do owe
0133	ܐܢܬ	you
1426	ܠܡܪܝ	my lord
0116	ܐܡܪ	He said
1261	ܠܗ	to him
1317	ܡܐܐ	One hundred
1158	ܟܘܪܝܢ	cors
0779	ܚܛܐ	[of] wheat
0116	ܐܡܪ	He said
1261	ܠܗ	to him
2134	ܩܒܠ	Take
1248	ܟܬܒܟ	your book
1093	ܘܬܒ	and sit down
1247	ܘܟܬܘܒ	[and] write
2685	ܬܡܢܝܢ	eighty
1158	ܟܘܪܝܢ	cors

VERSE 8 And our Lord praised the unjust steward because he had acted wisely, for the sons of this world are wiser than the sons of light, in this, their generation.

2428	ܘܫܒܚ	And praised
1426	ܡܪܢ	our Lord
2276	ܠܪܒܝܬܐ	the steward
1766	ܕܥܘܠܐ	unjust
0791	ܕܚܟܝܡܐܝܬ	because wisely
1724	ܥܒܕ	he had acted
0323	ܒܢܘܗܝ	the sons
0403	ܓܝܪ	for
1813	ܕܥܠܡܐ	of world
0598	ܗܢܐ	this
0790	ܚܟܝܡܝܢ	are wiser
0592	ܐܢܘܢ	<they>

515

LUKE   CHAPTER 16

1388	than
0323	the sons
1477	of light
2605	in their generation
0598	this

VERSE 9 — And also I say to you, 'Make friends for yourself from this wealth of evil that when it is fully spent, they may welcome you into their everlasting shelters.'

0169	And also
0124	<I>
0116	say
0124	I
1261	to you
1724	Make
1261	for yourself
2345	friends
1388	from
1387	mammon
0598	this
1766	of wickedness
1313	so that when
0423	it is fully spent
2134	they may welcome you
0973	into their shelters
1813	everlasting

VERSE 10 — He who is trustworthy in little also is trustworthy in much, and he who is unjust in little also is unjust in much.

1389	He who
2203	in little
0109	is trustworthy
0169	also
1596	in much
0109	trustworthy
0592	is
1389	and he who
2203	in little
1767	is unjust
0169	also
1596	in much

1767	unjust
0592	is

VERSE 11 — If therefore you are not trustworthy [ones] with the wealth of evil, who will entrust the truth to you?

0121	If
0596	therefore
1387	with the mammon
1766	of wickedness
0114	trustworthy [ones]
1262	not
0603	you are
2596	the truth
1261	to you
1390	who
0109	will entrust

VERSE 12 — And if you have not been found trustworthy [ones] in that which is not yours, who will give to you your own?"

0121	And if
0227	in that not
0517	which is yours
1262	not
2510	you have been found
0114	trustworthy [ones]
0517	your own
1390	who
1030	will give
1261	to you

VERSE 13 — There is no servant that is able to serve two masters, for either he will hate the one and love the other or honor the one and despise the other. You are not able to serve God and wealth.

1264	There is no
1727	servant
2510	that is able
2709	two
1426	masters
1974	to serve
0024	either
0403	for

516

Vertical Interlinear

LUKE CHAPTER 16

0721		the one	0592		those
1673		he will hate	0636		who justify
0053		and the other	1547		themselves
2342		love	2154		before
0024		or	0323		men
0721		the one	0131		*
1076		honor	0093		God
0053		and the other	0518		But
2474		despise	1023		knows
1262		not	1268		your hearts
2510		are able	1326		because what
0133		You	2331		is esteemed
1974		to serve	0266		among
0093		God	0325		men
1387		and mammon	2154		before
			0093		God
			1470		abominable
			0592		is

VERSE 14 — Now the Pharisees, when they heard all these [things], because they loved money, were mocking him.

3439		the Pharisees
0518		Now
1128		when
2547		they heard
0598		these [things]
1168		all
1347		because
2342		loved
0603		they
1209		money
1330		mocking
0603		were
0217		him

VERSE 15 — And Jesus said to them, "You are those who justify themselves before men. But God knows your hearts, because what is esteemed among men is abominable before God.

3257		Jesus
0518		And
0116		said
1261		to them
0133		You are

VERSE 16 — The law and the prophets [were] until John. Since then, the kingdom of God is preached and all crowd to enter it.

1524		The law
1457		and the prophets
1747		[were] until
3233		John
1388		Since
0594		then
1385		the kingdom
0093		of God
1588		is preached
1168		and all
1261		it
0711		crowd
1796		to enter

VERSE 17 — And it is easier for heaven and earth to pass away than [for] one letter of the law to pass away.

2061		easier
0592		it is
0518		And

517

LUKE   CHAPTER 16

2543		for heaven
0199		and earth
1733		to pass away
0024		than [for]
0207		letter
0721		one
1388		of
1524		the law
1733		to pass away

VERSE 18 Everyone who dismisses his wife and marries another commits adultery, and everyone who marries a forsaken woman commits adultery.

1168		Everyone
1389		*
2597		who dismisses
0135		his wife
1532		and marries
0053		another
0385		commits adultery
1168		and everyone
1389		*
1532		who marries
2440		a forsaken woman
0385		commits adultery

VERSE 19 Now there was a certain rich man and he wore linen and purple. And every day he lived in pleasure splendidly.

0361		a man
0518		Now
0721		certain
1921		rich
0069		there was
0603		*
1272		and he wore
0603		*
0238		linen
0186		and purple
1172		And every day
0286		he lived in pleasure
0603		*
0349		splendidly

VERSE 20 And there was a certain poor man whose name was Lazarus. And he lay at the gate of that rich man, stricken with boils.

1406		And a poor [man]
0721		certain
0069		there was
0603		*
2539		whose name was
3292		Lazarus
2372		And he lay
0603		*
1288		at
2718		the gate
0593		of that
1921		rich man
1128		stricken
1341		*
2493		with boils

VERSE 21 And he longed to fill his stomach from the crumbs that fell from the table of that rich man. But even the dogs came [and] licked his boils.

1014		And he longed
0603		*
1366		to fill
1241		his stomach
1388		from
2052		the crumbs
1538		that fell
1388		from
2069		the table
0593		of that
1921		rich man
0090		But
0169		even
1183		the dogs
0208		came
0603		*
1290		[and] licked

LUKE CHAPTER 16

2493	ܐܫܘܢܝܗܝ	his boils

VERSE 22 — Now it happened and that poor [man] died and the angels carried him to the bosom of Abraham. And also that rich man died and was buried.

0603	ܗܘܐ	it happened
0518	ܕܝܢ	Now
1334	ܘܡܝܬ	and died
0593	ܗܘ	that
1406	ܡܣܟܢܐ	poor [man]
1015	ܘܐܘܒܠܘܗܝ	and carried him
1375	ܡܠܐܟܐ	the angels
1760	ܠܥܘܒܗ	to the bosom
3005	ܕܐܒܪܗܡ	of Abraham
0169	ܐܦ	also
0593	ܗܘ	that
0518	ܕܝܢ	And
1921	ܥܬܝܪܐ	rich man
1334	ܡܝܬ	died
2142	ܘܐܬܩܒܪ	and was buried

VERSE 23 — And while he was tormented in Sheol, he lifted up his eyes from far away and saw Abraham and Lazarus in his bosom.

1128	ܘܟܕ	And while
2565	ܡܫܬܢܩ	he was tormented
2422	ܒܫܝܘܠ	in Sheol
2331	ܐܪܝܡ	he lifted up
1794	ܥܝܢܘܗܝ	his eyes
1388	ܡܢ	from
2354	ܪܘܚܩܐ	far away
0758	ܘܚܙܐ	and saw
3005	ܠܐܒܪܗܡ	Abraham
3292	ܘܠܠܥܙܪ	and Lazarus
1760	ܒܥܘܒܗ	in his bosom

VERSE 24 — And he cried with a loud voice and said, 'My father Abraham, have compassion on me and send Lazarus to dip the tip of his finger in water and to moisten my tongue for me, for, behold, I am tormented in this flame.'

2239	ܘܩܥܐ	And he cried out
2204	ܒܩܠܐ	with a voice
2336	ܪܡܐ	loud
0116	ܘܐܡܪ	and said
0002	ܐܒܝ	My father
3005	ܐܒܪܗܡ	Abraham
2342	ܐܬܪܚܡ	have compassion
1804	ܥܠܝ	on me
2458	ܘܫܕܪ	and send
3292	ܠܠܥܙܪ	Lazarus
2080	ܕܢܛܒܘܠ	to dip
2362	ܪܝܫ	the tip
2081	ܨܒܥܗ	of his finger
1351	ܒܡܝܐ	in water
2358	ܘܢܪܛܒ	and to moisten
1261	ܠܝ	for me
1312	ܠܫܢܝ	my tongue
0580	ܕܗܐ	for behold
2565	ܡܫܬܢܩ	tormented
0124	ܐܢܐ	I am
1278	ܒܫܠܗܒܝܬܐ	in flame
0598	ܗܕܐ	this

VERSE 25 — Abraham said to him, 'My son, remember that you received your good [things] during your life and Lazarus his bad [things] and now, behold, he is refreshed here and you are tormented.

0116	ܐܡܪ	said
1261	ܠܗ	to him
3005	ܐܒܪܗܡ	Abraham
0323	ܒܪܝ	My son
0527	ܐܬܕܟܪ	remember
2134	ܕܩܒܠܬ	that you received
0938	ܛܒܬܟ	your good [things]
0782	ܒܚܝܝܟ	during your life
3292	ܘܠܥܙܪ	and Lazarus
0220	ܒܝܫܬܗ	his bad [things]
0602	ܘܗܫܐ	and now
0580	ܗܐ	behold
1483	ܡܬܬܢܝܚ	he is refreshed
0600	ܗܪܟܐ	here
0133	ܘܐܢܬ	and you
2565	ܡܫܬܢܩ	are tormented

LUKE   CHAPTER 16

VERSE 26 — And with all these [things] a great chasm is placed between us and you, so that those who want to pass over from here to you are not able, nor from there to pass over to us.'

1817	ܗܕܐ	And with
0598	ܘܥܠ	these [things]
1168	ܟܠܗܝܢ	all
0606	ܦܚܬܐ	a chasm
2271	ܪܒܐ	great
1626	ܣܝܡ	is placed
0266	ܒܝܢܝܢ	between us
1261	ܘܠܟܘܢ	and you
0066	ܕܐܝܠܝܢ	so that those
2077	ܕܨܒܝܢ	who want
1112	ܡܟܐ	from here
1733	ܕܢܥܒܪܘܢ	to pass over
1288	ܠܘܬܟܘܢ	to you
1262	ܠܐ	not
2510	ܢܫܟܚܘܢ	are able
0170	ܘܐܦܠܐ	nor
1388	ܡܢ	from
2682	ܬܡܢ	there
1733	ܕܢܥܒܪܘܢ	to pass over
1288	ܠܘܬܢ	to us

VERSE 27 — Then he said to him, 'I beg of you, my father, to send him to the house of my father,

0116	ܐܡܪ	he said
1261	ܠܗ	to him
1324	ܗܟܝܠ	Then
0296	ܒܥܐ	beg
0124	ܐܢܐ	I
1388	ܡܢܟ	of you
0002	ܐܒܝ	my father
2458	ܕܬܫܕܪܝܘܗܝ	to send him
0243	ܠܒܝܬ	to the house
0002	ܐܒܝ	of my father

VERSE 28 — for I have five brothers. Let him go [and] witness to them so that they will not also come to this place of torment.'

0833	ܚܡܫܐ	five
0403	ܓܝܪ	for
0043	ܐܚܝܢ	brothers
0069	ܐܝܬ	I have
1261	ܠܝ	*
0042	ܢܐܙܠ	Let him go
1608	ܘܢܣܗܕ	[and] witness to
0592	ܐܢܘܢ	them
1262	ܕܠܐ	so that not
0169	ܐܦ	also
0592	ܗܢܘܢ	they
0208	ܢܐܬܘܢ	will come
0494	ܠܐܬܪܐ	to place
0598	ܗܢܐ	this
2567	ܕܬܫܢܝܩܐ	of torment

VERSE 29 — Abraham said to him, 'They have Moses and the prophets. They should hear them.'

0116	ܐܡܪ	said
1261	ܠܗ	to him
3005	ܐܒܪܗܡ	Abraham
0069	ܐܝܬ	They have
1261	ܠܗܘܢ	*
3305	ܡܘܫܐ	Moses
1457	ܘܢܒܝܐ	and the prophets
2547	ܢܫܡܥܘܢ	They should hear
0592	ܐܢܘܢ	them

VERSE 30 — And he said to him, 'No, my father Abraham, but if someone from the dead would go to them, they would repent.'

0592	ܗܘ	<he>
0518	ܕܝܢ	And
0116	ܐܡܪ	he said
1261	ܠܗ	to him
1262	ܠܐ	No
0002	ܐܒܝ	my father
3005	ܐܒܪܗܡ	Abraham
0090	ܐܠܐ	but
0121	ܐܢ	if
0131	ܐܢܫ	someone
1388	ܡܢ	from

LUKE — CHAPTER 16

#	Syriac	Gloss
1338		the dead
0042		would go
1288		to them
2649		they would repent

VERSE 31 — Abraham said to him, 'If they will not hear Moses and the prophets, even if someone would rise from the dead, they will not believe him.'"

#	Syriac	Gloss
0116		said
1261		to him
3005		Abraham
0121		If
3305		Moses
1457		and the prophets
1262		not
2547		they will hear
0169		even
1262		not
0121		if
0131		someone
1388		from
1338		the dead
2168		would rise
0109		they will believe
1261		him

CHAPTER 17

VERSE 1 — And Jesus said to his disciples, "It is not possible that offenses not come, but woe to him by whose hand they come!

#	Syriac	Gloss
0116		And said
0603		*
3257		Jesus
1304		to his disciples
1262		not
2510		It is possible
1262		that not
0208		come
1244		offenses
0625		woe
0518		but
0593		to him
0057		by whose hand
0208		they come

VERSE 2 — It would be better for him if a millstone of a donkey were hung on his neck and he were thrown into the sea, than to cause one of these little ones to stumble.

#	Syriac	Gloss
2010		It would be better
0603		*
1261		for him
0097		if
2341		a millstone
0830		of a donkey
2672		were hung
2097		on his neck
2455		and he were thrown
1057		into the sea
0024		than
1242		to cause to stumble
0721		one
1388		of
0598		these
0686		little ones

VERSE 3 — Take heed to yourselves. If your brother sins, reprove him. And if he repents, forgive him.

#	Syriac	Gloss
0645		Take heed
1547		to yourselves
0121		If
0770		sins
0043		your brother
1113		reprove
0217		him
0121		And if
2649		he repents
2440		forgive
1261		him

VERSE 4 — And if he offends you seven times in a day and in a day seven times he turns to you and says, 'I repent,' forgive him."

#	Syriac	Gloss
0121		And if
2437		seven

LUKE CHAPTER 17

0633		times		1876		Be uprooted
1036		in a day		1554		and be planted
1647		he offends		1057		in the sea
0217		you		2547		and it will obey
2437		and seven		0603		*
0633		times		1261		you
1036		in a day		**VERSE**	**7**	And which of you who has a servant who plows or tends a flock, and when he comes from the field says immediately to him, 'Pass through, sit down to eat?'
1984		he turns				
1288		to you				
0116		and says				
2649		I repent		1390		which
0124		*		0518		And
2440		forgive		1388		of you
1261		him		0069		who has
VERSE	**5**	And the apostles said to our Lord, "Increase faith to us."		1261		*
				1727		a servant
0116		And said		0477		who plows
2522		the apostles		1933		*
1426		to our Lord		0024		or
1064		Increase		2381		tends
1261		to us		1839		a flock
0113		faith		0121		and when
VERSE	**6**	He said to them, "If you have faith like a grain of mustard seed, you could say to this tree, 'Be uprooted and be planted in the sea,' and it will obey you.		0208		he comes
				1388		from
				0884		the field
0116		He said		0116		says
1261		to them		1261		to him
0121		If		0725		immediately
0069		you have		1733		Pass through
0603		*		1664		sit down to eat
1261		*		**VERSE**	**8**	On the contrary, he says to him, 'Prepare something to eat for me and gird up your loins [and] serve me until I have eaten and drunk, and afterwards you also may eat and drink.'
0113		faith				
0060		like				
2019		a grain				
0895		of mustard seed		0090		On the contrary
0116		say		0116		he says
0603		you could		1261		to him
2658		to tree		0950		Prepare
0598		this		1261		for me
				1326		something

Vertical Interlinear

LUKE CHAPTER 17

0927		to eat		1727		servant[s]
0160		and gird up		0124		We are
0876		your loins		0254		unprofitable
2554		[and] serve me		1326		because what
1747		until		0745		we ought
1308		I have eaten		0603		*
2620		and drunk		1724		to do
0216		and afterwards		1724		we have done
0169		also		**VERSE 11**		And it happened that when Jesus went to Jerusalem he passed through the Samaritans to Galilee.
0133		you				
1308		may eat		0603		And it happened
2620		and drink		1128		that when
VERSE 9		Does that servant receive his thanks because he did what was commanded him? I think not.		0042		went
				3257		Jesus
1316		<?>		3022		to Jerusalem
0942		his thanks		1733		he passed through
2134		Does receive		0603		*
0593		that		0266		<among>
1727		servant		3524		the Samaritans
1724		because he did		3153		to Galilee
1326		what		**VERSE 12**		And when he was about to enter a certain village, ten men, lepers, met him and stood at a distance.
2007		was commanded				
1261		him		1128		And when
1262		not		2248		he was about
1588		think		1796		to enter
0124		I		2251		a village
VERSE 10		So also, when you do all these [things] that are commanded to you, say, 'We are unprofitable servant[s],' because what we ought to do we have done."		0721		certain
				0197		met him
				1848		ten
0597		So		0131		men
0169		also		0456		lepers
0133		<you>		2168		and stood
1313		when		1388		at
1724		you do		2354		a distance
1168		all		**VERSE 13**		And they lifted their voice[s] and said, "Our Master, Jesus, have compassion on us."
0066		these [things]				
2007		that are commanded		2331		And they lifted
1261		to you		2204		their voice[s]
0116		say				

LUKE   CHAPTER 17

0116		and said		1804		on
2271		Our master		0173		his face
3257		Jesus		2154		before
2342		have compassion		2293		the feet
1804		on us		3257		of Jesus
VERSE 14		And when he saw them, he said to them, "Go [and] show yourselves to the priests." And as they went, they were cleansed.		1128		giving thanks
				1020		*
				1261		him
				0592		and <he>
1128		And when		0598		this [man]
0758		he saw		3524		a Samaritan
0592		them		0603		was
0116		he said		**VERSE 17**		And Jesus answered and said, "Were there not ten who were cleansed? Where are the nine?
1261		to them				
0042		Go				
0739		[and] show		1838		answered
1547		yourselves		0518		And
1135		to the priests		3257		Jesus
1128		And as		0116		and said
0042		they went		1262		not
0521		they were cleansed		0603		there
VERSE 15		And one of them, when he saw that he was cleansed, returned and with a loud voice was praising God.		1848		ten
				0603		Were
				0598		<those>
0721		one		0521		who were cleansed
0518		And		1108		Where
1388		of them		0592		are
1128		when		2723		the nine
0758		he saw		**VERSE 18**		Did [no one else] determine to come [and] give praise to God, except this [one] who is from a foreign nation?"
0521		that he was cleansed				
0616		returned				
1261		*		1316		<?>
2204		and with a voice		2046		Did determine [no one else]
2336		loud		0208		to come
2428		praising		1030		[and] give
0603		was		2432		praise
0093		God		0093		to God
VERSE 16		And he fell on his face before the feet of Jesus, giving him thanks, and this [man] was a Samaritan.		0090		except
				0598		this [one]
1538		And he fell		1388		who from

Vertical Interlinear

LUKE **CHAPTER 17**

1818		a nation
0592		is
1522		foreign

VERSE 19 And he said to him, "Stand up [and] go! Your faith has given you life."

0116		And he said
1261		to him
2168		Stand up
0042		[and] go
0113		Your faith
0780		has given you life

VERSE 20 And when some of the Pharisees asked Jesus when the kingdom of God would come, he answered and said to them, "The kingdom of God does not come with watching,"

1128		And when
2420		asked
3257		Jesus
1388		some of
3439		the Pharisees
0120		when
0208		would come
1385		The kingdom
0093		of God
1838		he answered
0116		and said
1261		to them
1262		not
0208		does come
1385		the kingdom
0093		of God
1505		with watching

VERSE 21 nor should they say, 'Behold, here it is,' and 'Behold, there it is,' for behold, the kingdom of God is in the middle of you."

1262		nor
0116		should they say
0580		Behold
0600		here
0592		it is
0580		and Behold
0601		there
0592		it is
0580		behold
0403		for
1385		the kingdom
0093		of God
0379		in the middle
1388		of you
0592		is

VERSE 22 And he said to his disciples, "The days will come when you will desire to see one of the days of the Son of Man and you will not see.

0116		And he said
1304		to his disciples
0208		will come
1036		The days
2287		when you will desire
0758		to see
0721		one
1388		of
1036		the days
0323		of the Son
0131		of Man
1262		and not
0758		you will see

VERSE 23 And if they say to you, 'Behold, here he is,' and 'Behold, there he is,' you should not go.

0121		And if
0116		they say
1261		to you
0580		Behold
0600		here
0592		he is
0580		and Behold
0601		there
0592		he is
1262		not
0042		you should go

LUKE CHAPTER 17

VERSE 24 — For as lightning shines from heaven and all under heaven is lightened, so the Son of Man will be in his day,

Code	Aramaic	Gloss
0061	ܐܝܟ	as
0403	ܓܝܪ	For
0344	ܒܪܩܐ	the lightning
0343	ܒܪܩ	shines
1388	ܡܢ	from
2543	ܫܡܝܐ	heaven
1168	ܘܟܠܗ	and all
2660	ܬܚܝܬ	under
2543	ܫܡܝܐ	heaven
1474	ܢܗܪ	is lightened
0597	ܗܟܢܐ	so
0603	ܢܗܘܐ	will be
0323	ܒܪܗ	the Son
0131	ܕܐܢܫܐ	of Man
1036	ܒܝܘܡܗ	in his day

VERSE 25 — but first he is going to suffer many [things] and be rejected by this generation.

Code	Aramaic	Gloss
2151	ܠܘܩܕܡ	first
0518	ܕܝܢ	but
1914	ܥܬܝܕ	he is going
0592	ܗܘ	*
0911	ܕܢܚܫ	to suffer
1596	ܣܓܝܐܬܐ	many [things]
1655	ܘܢܣܬܠܐ	and be rejected
1388	ܡܢ	by
2605	ܫܪܒܬܐ	generation
0598	ܗܕܐ	this

VERSE 26 — And as it was in the days of Noah, so will it be in the days of the Son of Man,

Code	Aramaic	Gloss
0061	ܘܐܝܟ	And as
0603	ܕܗܘܐ	it was
1036	ܒܝܘܡܬܗ	in the days
3339	ܕܢܘܚ	of Noah
0597	ܗܟܢܐ	so
0603	ܢܗܘܐ	will it be
1036	ܒܝܘܡܬܗ	in the days
0323	ܕܒܪܗ	of the Son
0131	ܕܐܢܫܐ	of Man

VERSE 27 — for they were eating and drinking and taking wives and being given to husbands, until the day that Noah entered the ark and the flood came and destroyed everyone.

Code	Aramaic	Gloss
0075	ܕܐܟܠܝܢ	for they were eating
0603	ܗܘܘ	*
2620	ܘܫܬܝܢ	and drinking
1532	ܘܢܣܒܝܢ	and taking
0135	ܢܫܐ	wives
1030	ܘܝܗܒܝܢ	and being given
0361	ܠܓܒܪܐ	to husbands
1747	ܥܕܡܐ	until
1036	ܠܝܘܡܐ	the day
1796	ܕܥܠ	that entered
3339	ܢܘܚ	Noah
1140	ܠܟܘܝܠܐ	the ark
0208	ܘܐܬܐ	and came
0954	ܛܘܦܢܐ	the flood
0005	ܘܐܘܒܕ	and destroyed
1168	ܠܟܠ	everyone
0131	ܐܢܫ	*

VERSE 28 — And [it will be] again as it was in the days of Lot, when they were eating and drinking and buying and selling and planting and building.

Code	Aramaic	Gloss
0061	ܘܐܝܟܢܐ	And [it will be]
2650	ܬܘܒ	again
0603	ܕܗܘܐ	as it was
1036	ܒܝܘܡܬܗ	in the days
3279	ܕܠܘܛ	of Lot
0075	ܕܐܟܠܝܢ	when they were eating
0603	ܗܘܘ	*
2620	ܘܫܬܝܢ	and drinking
0632	ܘܙܒܢܝܢ	and buying
0632	ܘܡܙܒܢܝܢ	and selling
1554	ܘܢܨܒܝܢ	and planting
0603	ܗܘܘ	*
0281	ܘܒܢܝܢ	and building

LUKE CHAPTER 17

VERSE 29 — And on the day that Lot went out from Sodom, the LORD rained fire and sulphur from heaven and destroyed all of them.

1036		on the day
0518		And
1542		that went out
3279		Lot
1388		from
3362		Sodom
1349		rained
1426		the LORD
1494		fire
1125		and sulfur
1388		from
2543		heaven
0005		and destroyed
1168		all of them

VERSE 30 — So it will be in the day that the Son of Man is revealed.

0597		So
0603		it will be
1036		in the day
0409		that is revealed
0323		the Son
0131		of Man

VERSE 31 — In that day, he who is on the roof and his goods are in the house should not come down to take them, and he who is in the field should not turn back.

0593		In that
1036		day
1389		he who
0019		on the roof
0592		is
1320		and his goods
0243		are in the house
1262		not
1499		should come down
2587		to take
0592		them
1389		and he who
0884		in the field
0592		is
1262		not
0616		should turn
0295		back

VERSE 32 — Remember the wife of Lot.

0527		Remember
0135		the wife
3279		of Lot

VERSE 33 — He who wants to save his soul will lose it, and he who loses his soul will save it.

1389		He who
2077		wants
0780		to save
1547		his soul
0005		will lose it
1389		and he who
0005		loses
1547		his soul
0780		will save it

VERSE 34 — I say to you, in that night, two will be in one bed. One will be taken and the other will be left.

0116		say
0124		I
1261		to you
0593		in that
1299		night
2709		two
0603		will be
0721		in one
1897		bed
0721		One
0477		will be taken
0053		and the other
2440		will be left

LUKE   CHAPTER 17

VERSE 35 — Two [women] will be grinding together. One will be taken and the other will be left.

2709		Two [women]
0603		will be
0960		grinding
0074		together
0721		One
0477		will be taken
0053		and the other
2440		will be left

VERSE 36 — Two [men] will be in the field. One will be taken and the other will be left."

2709		Two [men]
0603		will be
0884		in the field
0721		One
0477		will be taken
0053		and the other
2440		will be left

VERSE 37 — They answered and said to him, "To where, our Lord?" He said to them, "Where the body [is], there the eagles will be gathered."

1838		They answered
0116		and said
1261		to him
1108		To where
1426		our Lord
0116		He said
1261		to them
1108		Where
1929		the body [is]
2682		there
1198		will be gathered
1575		the eagles

CHAPTER 18

VERSE 1 — And he also spoke to them a parable that at all times they should pray and not be weary.

0116		he spoke
1261		to them
0518		And
0169		also
1454		a parable
1168		that at all
1750		times
2106		they should pray
1262		and not
1319		be weary
1261		*

VERSE 2 — "There was a certain judge in a certain city who did not fear God and did not reverence men.

0498		a judge
0721		certain
0069		There was
0603		*
0499		in a city
0721		certain
1388		who <from>
0093		God
1262		not
0509		did fear
0603		*
1388		and <from>
0325		men
1262		not
1161		did reverence
0603		*

VERSE 3 — And there was a certain widow in that city and she came to him and said, 'Avenge me of my adversary.'

0195		a widow
0518		And
0721		certain
0069		there was
0603		*
0499		in city
0593		that
0208		and she came
0603		*

528

LUKE   CHAPTER 18

1288		to him		1168		continually
0116		and said		1750		*
2631		Avenge me		0603		she is
1388		of		0208		coming
0306		my adversary		0621		[and] annoying
0497		*		1261		me

VERSE 4 — And he did not want to [for] a long time, but afterwards he said to himself, 'Although I do not fear God and I do not reverence men,

1262		And not
2077		he did want to
0603		*
0633		[for] a time
1596		long
0216		afterwards
0518		but
0116		he said
1547		to himself
0121		Although
1388		<from>
0093		God
1262		not
0509		do fear
0124		I
1388		and <from>
0325		men
1262		not
1161		do reverence
0124		I

VERSE 5 — yet, because this widow troubles me, I will avenge her, so that she is not coming continually [and] annoying me.'"

0172		yet
1347		because
1265		troubles
1261		me
0598		this
0195		widow
2631		I will avenge her
1262		so that not

VERSE 6 — And our Lord said, "Hear what the unjust judge said.

0116		And said
1426		our Lord
2547		Hear
1393		what
0116		said
0498		the judge
1766		unjust

VERSE 7 — And will not God perform vengeance even more for his chosen [ones], who call on him by day and by night, and be long-suffering with them?

0093		God
0518		And
1262		not
1101		even more
1724		will perform
2633		vengeance
0353		for his chosen [ones]
2239		who call
1261		on him
0064		by day
1299		and by night
1466		and be long-suffering
2323		*
1804		with them

VERSE 8 — I say to you, he will perform their vengeance quickly. Nevertheless, will the Son of Man come and will he indeed find faith on the earth?"

0116		say
0124		I
1261		to you
1724		he will perform

LUKE   CHAPTER 18

2633	ܬܒܥܬܗܘܢ	their vengeance
1738	ܒܥܓܠ	quickly
0342	ܒܪܡ	Nevertheless
0208	ܐܬܐ	will come
0323	ܒܪܗ	the Son
0131	ܕܐܢܫܐ	of Man
2510	ܘܢܫܟܚ	and will he find
1163	ܟܝ	indeed
0113	ܗܝܡܢܘܬܐ	faith
1804	ܥܠ	on
0199	ܐܪܥܐ	the earth

VERSE 9 And he spoke this parable against those men who were confident in themselves that they were just and were despising everyone.

0116	ܘܐܡܪ	And he spoke
0603	ܗܘܐ	*
1454	ܡܬܠܐ	parable
0598	ܗܢܐ	this
2135	ܠܘܩܒܠ	against
0131	ܐܢܫܐ	men
0066	ܐܝܠܝܢ	those
2665	ܕܬܟܝܠܝܢ	who were confident
1804	ܥܠ	in
1547	ܢܦܫܗܘܢ	themselves
0069	ܕܐܝܬܝܗܘܢ	that they were
0637	ܙܕܝܩܐ	just
0284	ܘܡܣܠܝܢ	and were despising
1804	ܥܠ	*
1175	ܠܟܠܢܫ	everyone

VERSE 10 "Two men went up to the temple to pray. One [was] a Pharisee and the other a tax collector.

2709	ܬܪܝܢ	Two
0361	ܓܒܪܝܢ	men
1658	ܣܠܩܘ	went up
0607	ܠܗܝܟܠܐ	to the temple
2106	ܠܡܨܠܝܘ	to pray
0721	ܚܕ	One [was]
3439	ܦܪܝܫܐ	a Pharisee
0053	ܘܐܚܪܢܐ	and the other
1358	ܡܟܣܐ	a tax collector

VERSE 11 And that Pharisee was standing by himself and so was praying, 'God, I thank you that I am not like the rest of men, extortioners and greedy [ones] and adulterers, nor like this tax collector.

0593	ܘܗܘ	And that
3439	ܦܪܝܫܐ	Pharisee
2168	ܩܐܡ	standing
0603	ܗܘܐ	was
0266	ܒܝܢܘܗܝ	by himself
1547	ܠܢܦܫܗ	*
0598	ܘܗܠܝܢ	and so
2106	ܡܨܠܐ	praying
0603	ܗܘܐ	was
0093	ܐܠܗܐ	God
1020	ܡܘܕܐ	thank
0124	ܐܢܐ	I
1261	ܠܟ	you
1262	ܕܠܐ	that not
0603	ܗܘܝܬ	I am
0060	ܐܝܟ	like
2611	ܫܪܟܐ	the rest
0131	ܕܐܢܫܐ	of men
0775	ܚܛܘܦܐ	extortioners
1808	ܘܥܠܘܒܐ	and greedy [ones]
0388	ܘܓܝܪܐ	and adulterers
1262	ܘܠܐ	and not
0060	ܐܝܟ	like
0598	ܗܢܐ	this
1358	ܡܟܣܐ	tax collector

VERSE 12 On the contrary, I fast twice in a week and I tithe everything that I gain.'

0090	ܐܠܐ	On the contrary
2093	ܨܐܡ	fast
0124	ܐܢܐ	I
2709	ܬܪܝܢ	twice
2445	ܒܫܒܬܐ	in a week
1850	ܘܡܥܣܪ	and tithe
0124	ܐܢܐ	I
1168	ܟܠ	everything

LUKE　　CHAPTER 18

1326	ܗܢܐ	*
2216	ܕܐܙܠ	that gain
0124	ܐܢܐ	I

VERSE 13 But that tax collector was standing far away and did not even want to raise his eyes to heaven, but was beating on his breast and saying, 'God, have mercy on me, a sinner.'

0593	ܗܘ	that
0518	ܕܝܢ	But
1358	ܡܟܣܐ	tax collector
2168	ܩܐܡ	standing
0603	ܗܘܐ	was
1388	ܡܢ	<from>
2354	ܪܘܚܩܐ	far away
1262	ܘܠܐ	and not
2077	ܨܒܐ	did want
0603	ܗܘܐ	*
0169	ܐܦ	even
1262	ܠܐ	not
1794	ܥܝܢܘܗܝ	his eyes
2331	ܢܪܝܡ	to raise
2543	ܠܫܡܝܐ	to heaven
0090	ܐܠܐ	but
1006	ܛܪܦ	beating
0603	ܗܘܐ	was
1804	ܥܠ	on
0729	ܚܕܝܗ	his breast
0116	ܘܐܡܪ	and saying
0093	ܐܠܗܐ	God
0840	ܚܘܢܝܢܝ	have mercy on me
0772	ܠܚܛܝܐ	a sinner

VERSE 14 I say to you, this [man] went down to his house more justified than that Pharisee, for everyone who raises himself up will be humbled, and everyone who humbles himself will be raised up."

0116	ܐܡܪ	say
0124	ܐܢܐ	I
1261	ܠܟܘܢ	to you
1499	ܢܚܬ	went down
0598	ܗܢܐ	this [man]
1326		
2216		that gain
0243	ܠܒܝܬܗ	to his house
1100	ܝܬܝܪ	more
1388	ܡܢ	than
0593	ܗܘ	that
3439	ܦܪܝܫܐ	Pharisee
1168	ܟܠ	everyone
0131	ܓܝܪ	*
0403	ܓܝܪ	for
2331	ܕܢܪܝܡ	who raises up
1547	ܢܦܫܗ	himself
1353	ܢܬܡܟܟ	will be humbled
1168	ܘܟܠ	and everyone
1353	ܕܢܡܟ	who humbles
1547	ܢܦܫܗ	himself
2331	ܢܬܬܪܝܡ	will be raised up

VERSE 15 And they also brought him infants that he would touch them, and his disciples saw them and rebuked them.

2244	ܩܪܒܘ	they brought
0603	ܗܘܘ	*
1261	ܠܗ	him
0518	ܕܝܢ	And
0169	ܐܦ	also
1048	ܛܠܝܐ	infants
2244	ܕܢܩܪܘܒ	that he would touch
1261	ܠܗܘܢ	them
0758	ܘܚܙܘ	and saw
0592	ܐܢܘܢ	them
1304	ܬܠܡܝܕܘܗܝ	his disciples
1113	ܘܟܐܘ	and rebuked
0217	ܒܗܘܢ	them

VERSE 16 And Jesus called them and said to them, "Let the children come to me, and do not hinder them, for the kingdom of heaven belongs to those who are like these.

0592	ܗܘ	<he>
0518	ܕܝܢ	And
3257	ܝܫܘܥ	Jesus
2239	ܩܪܐ	called

531

LUKE   CHAPTER 18

0592		them		0721		one
0116		and said		1388		of
1261		to them		2362		the rulers
2440		Let		0116		and said
0976		the children		1261		to him
0208		come		1055		teacher
1288		to me		0938		Good
1262		and not		1393		what
1180		do hinder		1724		must I do
0592		them		1087		to inherit
0066		to those		0782		life
0403		for		1813		eternal
0060		who are like				
0598		these				
0592		<they>				
0517		belongs				
0592		*				
1385		the kingdom				
2543		of heaven				

VERSE 19 — Jesus said to him, "Why do you call me good? There is none good, except one, God.

				0116		said
				1261		to him
				3257		Jesus
				1393		why
				2239		do call
				0133		you
				1261		me
				0938		good
				1264		There is none
				0938		good
				0090		except
				0121		*
				0721		one
				0093		God

VERSE 17 — Truly I say to you, whoever does not receive the kingdom of God as a child will not enter it."

0110		Truly
0116		say
0124		I
1261		to you
1389		whoever
1262		not
2134		does receive
1385		the kingdom
0093		of God
0060		as
0976		a child
1262		not
1796		will enter
1261		it

VERSE 18 — And one of the rulers asked him and said to him, "Good teacher, what must I do to inherit eternal life?"

| 2420 | | And asked him |

VERSE 20 — You know the commandments: DO NOT KILL, and DO NOT COMMIT ADULTERY, and DO NOT STEAL, and DO NOT BEAR WITNESS THAT IS FALSE. HONOR YOUR FATHER AND YOUR MOTHER."

2009		the commandments
1023		know
0133		You
1262		NOT
2179		DO KILL
1262		and NOT

LUKE CHAPTER 18

0385		DO COMMIT ADULTERY		1030		and give
1262		and NOT		1406		to the poor
0436		DO STEAL		0603		and you will have
1262		and NOT		1261		*
1608		DO BEAR		1627		a treasure
1610		WITNESS		2543		in heaven
2482		THAT IS FALSE		0208		and follow me
1076		HONOR		0215		*
0002		YOUR FATHER				
0106		AND YOUR MOTHER				

VERSE 23 But when he heard these [things], he was sad, for he was very rich.

VERSE 21 He said to him, "All these [things] I have kept from my youth."

0592		\<he\>
0518		But
1128		when
2547		he heard
0598		these [things]
1221		he was sad
1261		*
1921		rich
0603		he was
0403		for
0938		very

0116		He said
1261		to him
0598		these [things]
1168		All
1502		I have kept
0592		*
1388		from
0977		my youth

VERSE 22 And when Jesus heard these [things] he said to him, "You lack one [thing]. Go [and] sell everything that you have and give to the poor and you will have a treasure in heaven and follow me."

VERSE 24 And when Jesus saw that he was sad, he said, "How difficult [it is] for those who have possessions to enter the kingdom of God,

1128		And when
0758		saw
3257		Jesus
1221		that he was sad
1261		*
0116		he said
0061		How
1788		difficult [it is]
0066		for those
0069		who have
1261		*
1515		possessions
1796		to enter
1385		the kingdom
0093		of God

1128		when
2547		heard
0518		And
0598		these [things]
3257		Jesus
0116		he said
1261		to him
0721		one [thing]
0867		You lack
1261		*
0042		Go
0632		[and] sell
1168		everything
1326		*
0069		that you have
1261		*

LUKE CHAPTER 18

VERSE 25 — because it is easier for a camel to enter through the eye of a needle, than [for] a rich man [to enter] the kingdom of God."

0532	because it is easier
0592	*
0420	for a camel
0888	through the eye
0748	of a needle
1796	to enter
0024	than [for]
1921	a rich man [to enter]
1385	the kingdom
0093	of God

VERSE 26 — Those who heard were saying to him, "Then who is able to have life?"

0116	were saying
1261	to him
0066	Those
2547	who heard
1390	Then who
2510	is able
0780	to have life

VERSE 27 — And Jesus said, "Those [things] that with men are not possible, with God are possible."

3257	Jesus
0518	And
0116	said
0066	Those [things]
1288	that with
0323	men
0131	*
1262	not
2510	are possible
1288	with
0093	God
2510	possible
0603	are

VERSE 28 — Simon Peter said to him, "Behold, we have left everything and have followed you."

0116	said
1261	to him
3521	Simon
3258	Peter
0580	Behold
0124	we
2440	have left
1168	everything
1326	*
0208	and followed you
0215	*

VERSE 29 — Jesus said to him, "Truly I say to you, there is no man who has left houses or parents or brothers or wife or children because of the kingdom of God

0116	said
1261	to him
3257	Jesus
0110	Truly
0116	say
0124	I
1261	to you
1264	there is no
0131	man
2440	who has left
0243	houses
0024	or
0002	parents
0024	or
0043	brothers
0024	or
0135	wife
0024	or
0323	children
1347	because of
1385	the kingdom
0093	of God

VERSE 30 — and will not receive doubly many [things] in this time, and in the age to come, eternal life."

| 1262 | and not |
| 2134 | will receive |

LUKE   CHAPTER 18

1853		doubly
1596		many [things]
0598		in this
0633		time
1813		and in the age
0208		to come
0782		life
1813		eternal

VERSE 31 And Jesus took his twelve and said to them, "Behold, we go up to Jerusalem and all the things that are written in the prophets about the Son of Man will be fulfilled,

0477		And took
3257		Jesus
2710		his twelve
0116		and said
1261		to them
0580		Behold
1658		we go up
3022		to Jerusalem
2530		and will be fulfilled
1168		all the things
1247		that are written
1457		in the prophets
1804		about
0323		the Son
0131		of Man

VERSE 32 for he will be delivered to the Gentiles and they will mock him and they will spit in his face.

2530		he will be delivered
0403		for
1818		to the Gentiles
0246		and they will mock
0217		him
2400		and they will spit
0173		in his face

VERSE 33 And they will beat him and they will despise him and they will kill him, and on the third day he will rise up."

1461		And they will beat him
2119		and they will despise him
2179		and they will kill him
1036		and on the day
2674		third
2168		he will rise up

VERSE 34 And they did not understand any of these [things], but this saying was hidden from them and they did not know these [things] that were spoken to them.

0592		<they>
0518		And
0721		any
1388		of
0598		these [things]
1262		not
1647		they did understand
0090		but
1206		hidden
0603		was
1388		from them
1364		saying
0598		this
1262		and not
1023		they did know
0603		*
0598		these [things]
1362		that were spoken
1817		to them

VERSE 35 And when he was near to Jericho, a certain blind man was sitting by the side of the road, begging.

1128		And when
2248		he was near
3039		to Jericho
1662		a blind man
0721		certain
1093		was sitting
0603		*
1804		by
0057		the side of
0038		the road

LUKE   CHAPTER 18

0730			<and> begging
VERSE	**36**		And he heard the sound of the crowd that was passing by and he asked, "Who is this [man]?"
2547			And he heard
2204			the sound of
1201			the crowd
1733			that was passing by
2420			and he asked
0603			*
1390			Who is
0598			this [man]
VERSE	**37**		They said to him, "Jesus the Nazarene is passing by."
0116			They said
1261			to him
3257			Jesus
3355			the Nazarene
1733			is passing by
VERSE	**38**		And he cried out and said, "Jesus, Son of David, have compassion on me."
2227			And he cried out
0116			and said
3257			Jesus
0323			Son
3159			of David
2342			have compassion
1804			on me
VERSE	**39**		And those who were preceding Jesus rebuked him that he should be silent, but he cried out all the more, "Son of David, have compassion on me."
0066			And those
0042			who were preceding
0603			*
2154			*
3257			Jesus
1113			rebuked
0603			*
0217			him
2623			that he should be silent
0592			<he>
0518			but
1101			all the more
2227			he cried out
0603			*
0323			Son
3159			of David
2342			have compassion
1804			on me
VERSE	**40**		And Jesus stopped and commanded that they bring him to him. And when he was near to him, he asked him
2168			And stopped
3257			Jesus
2007			and commanded
0208			that they bring him
1288			to him
1128			And when
2244			he was near
1288			to him
2420			he asked him
VERSE	**41**		and said to him, "What do you want me to do for you?" And he said, "My Lord, that I may see."
0116			and said
1261			to him
1393			What
2077			do want
0133			you
1724			me to do
1261			for you
0592			<he>
0518			And
0116			he said
1426			My Lord
0758			that I may see
VERSE	**42**		And Jesus said to him, "See! Your faith has given you life."
3257			And Jesus
0116			said
1261			to him
0758			See

536

Vertical Interlinear

LUKE CHAPTER 18

0113		Your faith
0780		has given you life

VERSE 43 — And immediately, he saw and followed him and praised God. And all the people who saw [it] were giving glory to God.

0323		And immediately
2573		*
0758		he saw
0208		and followed him
0603		*
0215		*
2428		and praised
0093		God
1168		And all
1818		the people
0758		who saw [it]
1030		were giving
0603		*
2431		glory
0093		to God

CHAPTER 19

VERSE 1 — And when Jesus entered and passed through into Jericho,

1128		And when
1796		entered
3257		Jesus
1733		and passed through
3039		into Jericho

VERSE 2 — there was a certain man whose name was Zacchaeus, a rich man and the chief of the tax collectors.

0361		a man
0721		certain
2539		whose name was
3190		Zacchaeus
1921		a rich man
0603		there was
2271		and the chief of
1358		the tax collectors

VERSE 3 — And he wanted to see who Jesus was, and was not able to from the crowd, because Zacchaeus was small in his stature.

2077		And he wanted
0603		*
0758		to see
3257		Jesus
1390		who was
1262		and not
2510		was able to
0603		*
1388		from
1201		the crowd
1347		because
2171		in his stature
0686		small
0603		was
3190		Zacchaeus

VERSE 4 — And he ran before Jesus and climbed up a barren fig tree to see him, because he was going to pass by that way.

2312		And he ran
2150		before
3257		Jesus
1658		and climbed up
1261		*
2628		a fig tree
1963		barren
0758		to see him
1347		because
0595		that way
1914		going
0603		was
1733		to pass by

VERSE 5 — And when Jesus came to that place, he saw him and said to him, "Hurry, come down, Zacchaeus, for today I must be in your house."

1128		And when
0208		came
0593		to that

537

LUKE CHAPTER 19

0494	ܐܬܪܐ	place		0518	ܕܝܢ	and
3257	ܝܫܘܥ	Jesus		3190	ܙܟܝ	Zacchaeus
0758	ܚܙܝܗܝ	he saw him		0116	ܘܐܡܪ	and said
0116	ܘܐܡܪ	and said		3257	ܠܝܫܘܥ	to Jesus
1261	ܠܗ	to him		0580	ܗܐ	Behold
2308	ܐܣܬܪܗܒ	Hurry		1426	ܡܪܝ	my Lord
1499	ܚܘܬ	come down		1973	ܦܠܓܗ	half of
3190	ܙܟܝ	Zacchaeus		1515	ܕܢܟܣܝ	my possessions
1037	ܝܘܡܢܐ	today		1030	ܝܗܒ	I give
0403	ܓܝܪ	for		0124	ܐܢܐ	*
0626	ܘܠܐ	I must		1406	ܠܡܣܟܢܐ	to the poor
0243	ܒܒܝܬܟ	in your house		1175	ܘܠܟܠܢܫ	and to everyone
0603	ܐܗܘܐ	be		1326	ܡܕܡ	anything
				0417	ܕܛܠܡܬ	I have defrauded

VERSE 6 — And he hurried [and] came down and received him, rejoicing.

				0721	ܚܕ ܒܐܪܒܥܐ	fourfold
2308	ܘܐܣܬܪܗܒ	And he hurried		0179	ܐܢܐ	*
1499	ܘܢܚܬ	[and] came down		2037	ܦܪܥ	I repay
2134	ܘܩܒܠܗ	and received him		0124	ܐܢܐ	*
1128	ܟܕ	rejoicing				
0726	ܚܕܐ	*				

VERSE 9 — Jesus said to him, "Today life has come to this house, because this [man] also is a son of Abraham,

VERSE 7 — And when all of them saw, they were murmuring and saying that he had entered [and] lodged with a sinful man.

				0116	ܐܡܪ	said
1128	ܟܕ	when		1261	ܠܗ	to him
0758	ܚܙܘ	saw		3257	ܝܫܘܥ	Jesus
0518	ܕܝܢ	And		1037	ܝܘܡܢܐ	Today
1168	ܟܠܗܘܢ	all of them		0603	ܗܘܘ	has come
2360	ܪܛܢܝܢ	they were murmuring		0782	ܚܝܐ	life
0603	ܗܘܘ	*		0243	ܠܒܝܬܐ	to house
0116	ܘܐܡܪܝܢ	and saying		0598	ܗܢܐ	this
1288	ܕܠܘܬ	with		1347	ܡܛܠ	because
0361	ܐܢܫܐ	a man		0169	ܐܦ	also
0772	ܚܛܝܐ	sinful		0598	ܗܢܐ	this [man]
1796	ܥܠ	he had entered		0323	ܒܪܗ	a son
2597	ܫܪܐ	[and] lodged with		0592	ܗܘ	is
				3005	ܕܐܒܪܗܡ	of Abraham

VERSE 8 — And Zacchaeus stood up and said to Jesus, "Behold, my Lord, half of my possessions I give to the poor and to everyone I have defrauded anything I repay fourfold."

VERSE 10 — for the Son of Man is come to seek and to give life to him who was perishing."

				0208	ܐܬܐ	is come
2168	ܩܡ	stood up		0403	ܓܝܪ	for
				0323	ܒܪܗ	the Son

LUKE CHAPTER 19

Vertical Interlinear

0131		of Man
0296		to seek
0780		and to give life
0593		to him
1326		who
0007		was perishing
0603		*

VERSE 11 — And when they heard these [things], he went on to speak a parable because he was near to Jerusalem and they thought that the kingdom of God was going to be revealed at that time.

1128		And when
2547		they heard
0603		*
0598		these [things]
1064		he went on
0116		to speak
1454		a parable
1347		because
2248		near
0603		he was
3022		to Jerusalem
1588		and they thought
0603		*
0593		that at that time
2573		*
1914		was going
0409		to be revealed
1385		the kingdom
0093		of God

VERSE 12 — And he said, "A certain man, a great nobleman, went to a far country to receive a kingdom for himself and [then] to return.

0116		And he said
0361		A man
0721		certain
0323		a nobleman
0952		*
2271		great

0042		went
0214		to a country
2355		far
1532		to receive
1261		for himself
1385		a kingdom
0616		and [then] to return

VERSE 13 — And he called his ten servants and gave them ten coins, and said to them, 'Do business until I come.'

2239		And he called
1848		ten
1727		his servants
1030		and gave
1261		them
1848		ten
1397		coins
0116		and said
1261		to them
2637		Do business
1744		until
0208		come
0124		I

VERSE 14 — But his citizens hated him, and sent ambassadors after him and were saying, 'We do not want this [man] to rule over us.'

0323		his citizens
0499		*
0518		But
1673		hated
0603		*
1261		him
2458		and sent
0059		ambassadors
0215		after him
0116		and were saying
1262		not
2077		do want
0124		We
1381		to rule

LUKE CHAPTER 19

1804	ܥܠܢ	over us
0598	ܠܗܢܐ	this [man]
VERSE 15		And when he received the kingdom and was returning, he said that they should call to him those [of] his servants to whom he had given money, to know what each and every one of them had gained.
1128	ܘܟܕ	And when
1532	ܢܣܒ	he received
1385	ܡܠܟܘܬܐ	the kingdom
0616	ܘܗܦܟ	and was returning
0116	ܐܡܪ	he said
2239	ܕܢܩܪܘܢ	that they should call
1261	ܠܗ	to him
0593	ܗܢܘܢ	those [of]
1727	ܥܒܕܘܗܝ	his servants
1030	ܕܝܗܒ	he had given
1261	ܠܗܘܢ	to whom
1209	ܟܣܦܐ	money
1023	ܕܢܕܥ	to know
1393	ܡܢܐ	what
1168	ܟܠ	each and every one
0721	ܚܕ	*
0721	ܚܕ	*
1388	ܡܢܗܘܢ	of them
2637	ܐܬܬܓܪ	had gained
VERSE 16		And the first came said, 'My lord, your coin has gained ten coins.'
0208	ܘܐܬܐ	And came
2157	ܩܕܡܝܐ	the first
0116	ܘܐܡܪ	and said
1426	ܡܪܝ	My lord
1397	ܡܢܝܟ	your coin
1848	ܥܣܪܐ	ten
1397	ܡܢܝܢ	coins
1098	ܐܘܬܪ	has gained
VERSE 17		He said to him, 'Well done, good servant. Because you have been found faithful with little, you will be a ruler over ten walled cities.'
0116	ܐܡܪ	He said

1261	ܠܗ	to him
0058	ܐܝܘ	Well done
1727	ܥܒܕܐ	servant
0938	ܛܒܐ	good
2203	ܕܒܩܠܝܠ	Because with little
2510	ܐܫܬܟܚܬ	you have been found
0109	ܡܗܝܡܢ	faithful
0603	ܬܗܘܐ	you will be
2528	ܫܠܝܛ	a ruler
1804	ܥܠ	over
1848	ܥܣܪܐ	ten
1237	ܟܪܟܝܢ	walled cities
VERSE 18		And the second came and said, 'My lord, your coin has made five coins.'
0208	ܘܐܬܐ	And came
2709	ܕܬܪܝܢ	the second
0116	ܘܐܡܪ	and said
1426	ܡܪܝ	My lord
1397	ܡܢܝܟ	your coin
0833	ܚܡܫܐ	five
1397	ܡܢܝܢ	coins
1724	ܥܒܕ	has made
VERSE 19		He also said to this [man], 'You also will be a ruler over five walled cities.'
0116	ܐܡܪ	He said
0169	ܐܦ	also
0598	ܠܗܢܐ	to this [man]
0169	ܐܦ	also
0133	ܐܢܬ	You
0603	ܬܗܘܐ	will be
2528	ܫܠܝܛ	a ruler
1804	ܥܠ	over
0833	ܚܡܫܐ	five
1237	ܟܪܟܝܢ	walled cities
VERSE 20		And another came and said, 'My lord, behold, your coin has been with me since it was placed in a linen cloth,
0208	ܘܐܬܐ	And came
0053	ܐܚܪܢܐ	another
0116	ܘܐܡܪ	and said

LUKE   CHAPTER 19

#	Syriac	English		#	Syriac	English
1426		My lord		0220		evil
0580		behold		1023		You knew
1397		your coin		0603		*
0593		<that>		1261		me
0069		has been		0361		that a man
0603		*		0124		I am
1288		with me		2265		harsh
1128		since		2587		and [that] I take up
1625		it was placed		0124		*
1605		in a linen cloth		1326		what
				1262		not

VERSE 21   for I feared you because you are a harsh man and you take up what you have not laid down and you reap what you have not sown.'

#	Syriac	English
1625		I have laid down
0878		and [that] I reap
0124		*
1326		what
1262		not
0691		I have sown

VERSE 23   Why did you not give my money to the exchange and I could come [and] demand it with its interest?'

#	Syriac	English
0509		I feared
0403		for
1388		you
0361		because a man
0133		you are
2265		harsh
2587		and take up
0133		you
1326		what
1262		not
1625		you have laid down
0878		and reap
0133		you
1326		what
1262		not
0691		you have sown

#	Syriac	English
1394		Why
1262		not
1030		did you give
1209		my money
1804		to
2069		the exchange
0124		and <I>
0208		come
0603		I could
2631		[and] demand
1261		it
1817		with
2282		its interest

VERSE 22   He said to him, 'From your mouth I will judge you, evil servant. You knew me, that I am a harsh man and [that] I take up what I have not laid down and [that] I reap what I have not sown.

#	Syriac	English
0116		He said
1261		to him
1388		From
1936		your mouth
0496		I will judge you
1727		servant

VERSE 24   And to those who were standing before him, he said, 'Take from him the coin and give [it] to the one who has ten coins.'

#	Syriac	English
0593		And to those
2168		who were standing
2154		before him
0116		he said

LUKE CHAPTER 19

1532	ܣܒܘ	Take
1388	ܡܢܗ	from him
1397	ܡܢܝܐ	the coin
1030	ܘܗܒܘ	and give [it]
0593	ܠܗܘ	to the one
0069	ܐܝܬ	who had
1288	ܠܘܬܗ	*
1848	ܥܣܪܐ	ten
1397	ܡܢܝܢ	coins

VERSE 25 They were saying to him, 'Our lord, he has ten coins.'

0116	ܐܡܪܝܢ	They were saying
1261	ܠܗ	to him
1426	ܡܪܢ	Our lord
0069	ܐܝܬ	he has
1288	ܠܘܬܗ	*
1848	ܥܣܪܐ	ten
1397	ܡܢܝܢ	coins

VERSE 26 He said to them, 'I say to you, to whomever has, it will be given, and whoever does not have, even that which he has will be taken from him.

0116	ܐܡܪ	He said
1261	ܠܗܘܢ	to them
0116	ܐܡܪ	say
0124	ܐܢܐ	I
1261	ܠܟܘܢ	to you
1168	ܕܠܟܠ	to whomever
1389	ܡܢ	*
0069	ܐܝܬ	has
1261	ܠܗ	*
1030	ܬܬܝܗܒ	it will be given
1261	ܠܗ	<to him>
1388	ܘܡܢ	and whoever
0593	ܗܘ	*
1264	ܠܝܬ	does not have
1261	ܠܗ	*
0169	ܐܦ	even
0593	ܗܘ	that
0069	ܐܝܬ	which he has
1261	ܠܗ	*
1532	ܢܫܬܩܠ	will be taken
1388	ܡܢܗ	from him

VERSE 27 But my enemies, those who did not want me to rule over them, bring them and kill them before me.'"

0342	ܒܪܡ	But
0593	ܗܢܘܢ	<those>
0307	ܒܥܠܕܒܒܝ	my enemies
0066	ܐܝܠܝܢ	those
1262	ܕܠܐ	who not
2077	ܨܒܘ	did want
1381	ܕܐܡܠܟ	me to rule
1804	ܥܠܝܗܘܢ	over them
0208	ܐܝܬܘ	bring
0592	ܐܢܘܢ	them
2179	ܘܩܛܠܘ	and kill
0592	ܐܢܘܢ	them
2154	ܩܕܡܝ	before me

VERSE 28 And when he had said these [things], Jesus left to travel on to Jerusalem.

1128	ܘܟܕ	And when
0116	ܐܡܪ	he had said
0598	ܗܠܝܢ	these [things]
3257	ܝܫܘܥ	Jesus
1542	ܢܦܩ	left
2154	ܠܩܕܡܘܗܝ	on
0042	ܕܢܐܙܠ	to travel
3022	ܠܐܘܪܫܠܡ	to Jerusalem

VERSE 29 And when he arrived at Bethphage and Bethany on the side of the mountain that is called the Mount of Olives, he sent two of his disciples.

1128	ܘܟܕ	And when
1346	ܡܛܝ	he arrived
3117	ܠܒܝܬܦܓܐ	at Bethphage
3116	ܘܠܒܝܬܥܢܝܐ	and Bethany
1804	ܥܠ	on
0439	ܓܢܒ	the side of
0958	ܛܘܪܐ	the mountain
2239	ܕܡܬܩܪܐ	that is called

LUKE CHAPTER 19

0243	ܛܘܪܐ	the Mount of
0663	ܕܙܝܬܐ	Olives
2458	ܫܕܪ	he sent
2709	ܬܪܝܢ	two
1388	ܡܢ	of
1304	ܬܠܡܝܕܘܗܝ	his disciples

VERSE 30 And he said to them, "Go to the village that is opposite us, and when you enter it, behold, you will find a colt that is tied, on which a man has never ridden. Untie [and] bring it.

0116	ܘܐܡܪ	And he said
1261	ܠܗܘܢ	to them
0042	ܙܠܘ	Go
2251	ܠܩܪܝܬܐ	to the village
0593	ܗܝ	that
2135	ܕܠܩܘܒܠܢ	is opposite us
1128	ܘܡܐ	and when
1796	ܥܐܠܝܢ	enter
0133	ܐܢܬܘܢ	you
1261	ܠܗ	it
0580	ܗܐ	behold
2510	ܡܫܟܚܝܢ	will find
0133	ܐܢܬܘܢ	you
1793	ܥܝܠܐ	a colt
0160	ܕܐܣܝܪ	that is tied
0131	ܐܢܫ	a man
1451	ܡܡܬܘܡ	never
1262	ܠܐ	*
2367	ܪܟܒ	has ridden
1804	ܥܠܘܗܝ	on which
2597	ܫܪܘ	Untie
0208	ܐܝܬܐܘܗܝ	[and] bring it

VERSE 31 And if anyone asks you, 'Why are you untying it,' say thus to him, 'Our Lord needs [it].'"

0121	ܘܐܢ	And if
0131	ܐܢܫ	anyone
2420	ܡܫܐܠ	asks
1261	ܠܟܘܢ	you
1394	ܠܡܢܐ	Why
2597	ܫܪܝܢ	are untying
0133	ܐܢܬܘܢ	you
1261	ܠܗ	it
0597	ܗܟܢܐ	thus
0116	ܐܡܪܘ	say
1261	ܠܗ	to him
1426	ܕܠܡܪܢ	Our lord
0296	ܡܬܒܥܐ	needs [it]

VERSE 32 And those, who were sent, went and found [it] as he had told them.

0042	ܘܐܙܠܘ	And went
0593	ܗܢܘܢ	those
2458	ܕܐܫܬܕܪܘ	who were sent
2510	ܘܐܫܟܚܘ	and found [it]
0061	ܐܝܟܢܐ	as
0116	ܕܐܡܪ	he had told
1261	ܠܗܘܢ	them

VERSE 33 And while they were untying the colt, its owners said to them, "Why are you untying that colt?"

1128	ܘܟܕ	And while
2597	ܫܪܝܢ	they were untying
1261	ܠܗ	<it>
1793	ܠܥܝܠܐ	the colt
0116	ܐܡܪܝܢ	said
1261	ܠܗܘܢ	to them
1426	ܡܪܘܗܝ	its owners
1393	ܡܢܐ	Why
2597	ܫܪܝܢ	are untying
0133	ܐܢܬܘܢ	you
1793	ܥܝܠܐ	colt
0593	ܗܘ	that

VERSE 34 And they said to them, "Our Lord needs [it]."

0116	ܘܐܡܪܘ	And they said
1261	ܠܗܘܢ	to them
1426	ܕܠܡܪܢ	Our lord
0296	ܡܬܒܥܐ	needs [it]

LUKE CHAPTER 19

VERSE 35 — And they brought it to Jesus and they threw their garments on the colt and mounted Jesus on it.

0208		And they brought it
1288		to
3257		Jesus
2372		and they threw
1804		on
1793		the colt
1320		their garments
2367		and mounted
3257		Jesus
1804		on it

VERSE 36 — And as he went along, they were spreading their garments on the road.

1128		as
0518		And
0042		he went along
2031		spreading
0603		they were
1320		their garments
0038		on the road

VERSE 37 — And when he came near to the descent of the Mount of Olives, the whole crowd of disciples began rejoicing and praising God with a loud voice for all the miracles that they had seen.

1128		And when
2244		he had come near
1500		to the descent
0958		of the Mount
0243		of Olives
0663		*
2597		began
1168		whole
1201		the crowd
1304		of disciples
0726		rejoicing
2428		and praising
0093		God
2204		with a voice
2336		loud
1804		for
1168		all
0786		the miracles
0758		that they had seen

VERSE 38 — And they were saying: BLESSED IS THE KING WHO HAS COME IN THE NAME OF THE LORD. PEACE IN HEAVEN AND GLORY IN THE HIGHEST.

0116		And saying
0603		they were
0338		BLESSED
0592		IS
1383		THE KING
0208		WHO HAS COME
2539		IN THE NAME
1426		OF THE LORD
2535		PEACE
2543		IN HEAVEN
2431		AND GLORY
2332		IN THE HIGHEST

VERSE 39 — And some of the Pharisees from among the crowds were saying to him, "My Master, rebuke your disciples."

0131		some
0518		And
1388		of
3439		the Pharisees
1388		from
0266		among
1201		the crowds
0116		were saying
1261		to him
2275		Rabbi
1113		rebuke
1304		your disciples

VERSE 40 — He said to them, "I say to you, if these would be quiet, the stones would cry out."

0116		He said
1261		to them

LUKE CHAPTER 19

#	Syriac	English
0116		say
0124		I
1261		to you
0121		if
0598		these
2623		would be quiet
1119		the stones
2227		would cry out

VERSE 41 — And when he came near and saw the city, he wept over it.

#	Syriac	English
1128		And when
2244		he came near
0758		and saw
0499		the city
0267		he wept
1804		over it

VERSE 42 — And he said, "Would that you had known those [things] that were for your peace, even in this your day, but now they are hidden from your eyes.

#	Syriac	English
0116		And he said
0097		Would that
1163		*
1023		you had known
0066		those [things]
0069		that were
2535		for your peace
0172		even
0598		in this
1036		your day
0602		now
0518		but
1206		they are hidden
1261		<to them>
1388		from
1794		your eyes

VERSE 43 — But the days will come to you when your enemies will surround you and will pressure you on every side.

#	Syriac	English
0208		will come
1261		to you
0518		But
1036		the days
0730		when will surround you
0307		your enemies
0102		and will pressure you
1388		on
1168		every
0494		side

VERSE 44 — And they will overthrow you and your children within you and they will not leave a stone on a stone in you, for you did not know the time of your visitation."

#	Syriac	English
1636		And they will overthrow you
0323		and your children
0376		within you
1262		and not
2440		they will leave
0217		in you
1119		a stone
1804		on
1119		a stone
0812		for
1262		not
1023		you did know
0633		the time
1685		of your visitation

VERSE 45 — And when he entered the temple, he began to throw out those who were selling and buying in it.

#	Syriac	English
1128		And when
1796		he entered
0607		the temple
2597		he began
1542		to throw out
0066		those
0632		who were selling
0217		in it
0632		and buying

LUKE CHAPTER 19

VERSE 46 — And he said to them, "It is written: MY HOUSE IS A HOUSE OF PRAYER, but you have made it a den of robbers."

0116		And he said
1261		to them
1247		It is written
0243		MY HOUSE
0243		IS A HOUSE OF
2107		PRAYER
0069		<are>
0133		you
0518		but
1724		have made it
1775		a den
1306		of robbers

VERSE 47 — And he taught everyday in the temple and the chief priests and scribes and elders of the people were seeking to destroy him.

0592		And <he>
1053		he taught
0603		*
1168		everyday
1036		*
0607		in the temple
2271		the chief priests
1135		*
0518		and
1699		and scribes
2263		and elders
1818		of the people
0296		seeking
0603		were
0005		to destroy him

VERSE 48 — And they were not able to find to do to him, for all the people were intent to hear him.

1262		and not
2510		able to find
0603		they were
1393		what
1724		to do
1261		to him
1168		all
0403		for
1818		the people
2672		intent
0603		were
0217		him
2547		to hear

CHAPTER 20

VERSE 1 — And it happened [that] on one of the days when he was teaching to the people in the temple and preaching, the chief priests and scribes with the elders rose up against him.

0603		And it happened [that]
0721		on one
1388		of
1036		the days
1128		when
1053		he was teaching
0607		in the temple
1818		to the people
1588		and preaching
2168		rose up
1804		against him
2271		the chief priests
1135		*
1699		and scribes
1817		with
2263		the elders

VERSE 2 — And they were saying to him, "Tell us with what authority you do these [things] and who is it who gave you this authority?"

0116		And they were saying
1261		to him
0116		Tell
1261		us
0066		with what
2527		authority

LUKE — CHAPTER 20

Vertical Interlinear

ID	Syriac	English
0598		these [things]
1724		do
0133		you
1390		and who is it
0593		who
1030		gave
1261		you
2527		authority
0598		this

VERSE 3 — Jesus answered and said to them, "I will also ask you a question and [you] tell me,

ID	Syriac	English
1838		answered
3257		Jesus
0116		and said
1261		to them
2420		I will ask you
0169		also
0124		<I>
1364		a question
0116		and [you] tell
1261		me

VERSE 4 — the baptism of John, was it from heaven or from men?"

ID	Syriac	English
1821		the baptism
3233		of John
1388		from
2543		heaven
0603		was it
0024		or
1388		from
0323		men
0131		*

VERSE 5 — And they were reasoning among themselves and were saying, "If we say from heaven, he will say to us, 'Then why do you not believe him?'

ID	Syriac	English
0592		<they>
0518		And
0914		reasoning
0603		they were
1547		among themselves
0116		and were saying
0121		If
0116		we say
1388		from
2543		heaven
0116		he will say
1261		to us
1347		Then why
1393		*
1262		not
0109		do you believe him

VERSE 6 — And if we say from men, the people will stone us, for they all are convinced that John was a prophet."

ID	Syriac	English
0121		if
0518		And
0116		we say
1388		from
0323		men
0131		*
2296		will stone
1261		us
1818		the people
1168		all
1955		are convinced
0403		for
3233		that John
1457		a prophet
0592		was

VERSE 7 — And they said to him, "We do not know from where it is."

ID	Syriac	English
0116		And they said
1261		to him
1262		not
1023		We do know
1388		from
1110		where
0592		it is

LUKE CHAPTER 20

VERSE 8 — Jesus said to them, "Neither will I tell you with what authority I do these [things]."

#	Aramaic	Gloss
0116		said
1261		to them
3257		Jesus
1262		Neither
0124		<I>
0116		will I tell
0124		*
1261		you
0066		with what
2527		authority
0598		these [things]
1724		do
0124		I

VERSE 9 — And he began to speak this parable to the people. "A certain man planted a vineyard and handed it over to workers and stayed away [for] a long time.

#	Aramaic	Gloss
2597		And he began
0116		to speak
1818		to the people
1454		parable
0598		this
0361		A man
0721		certain
1554		planted
1240		a vineyard
0047		and handed it over
1977		to workers
0299		and stayed away
0633		[for] a time
1596		long

VERSE 10 — And in time, he sent his servant to the workers that they should give him of the fruit of the vineyard. But the workers beat him and sent him away empty-handed.

#	Aramaic	Gloss
0633		And in time
2458		he sent
1727		his servant
1288		to
1977		the workers
1030		that they should give
1261		him
1388		of
2016		the fruit
1240		of the vineyard
1977		the workers
0518		But
1341		beat him
2458		and sent him away
1128		empty-handed
1714		*

VERSE 11 — And in addition he sent another servant. And they also beat that one and shamefully treated him and sent him away empty-handed.

#	Aramaic	Gloss
1064		And in addition
2458		<and> he sent
1727		servant
0053		another
0592		<they>
0518		And
0169		also
0593		that one
1341		they beat <him>
2119		and shamefully treated him
2458		and sent him away
1128		empty-handed
1714		*

VERSE 12 — And in addition he sent a third. And also they wounded that one and threw him out.

#	Aramaic	Gloss
1064		And in addition
2458		<and> he sent
2674		a third
0592		<they>
0518		And
0169		also
0593		that one
2113		they wounded <him>

Vertical Interlinear

LUKE   CHAPTER 20

1542		and threw him out
VERSE 13		The lord of the vineyard said, 'What should I do? I will send my beloved son. Perhaps they will see him and respect [him].'
0116		said
1426		The lord of
1240		the vineyard
1393		What
1724		should I do
2458		I will send
0323		my son
0698		beloved
1124		Perhaps
0758		they will see him
1161		and respect [him]
VERSE 14		But when the workers saw him they were reasoning among themselves and were saying, 'This is the heir. Come, let us kill him and the inheritance will be ours.'
1128		when
0758		saw him
0518		But
1977		the workers
0914		reasoning
0603		they were
1547		among themselves
0116		and were saying
0599		This is
1089		the heir
0208		Come
2179		let us kill him
0603		and will be
1090		the inheritance
0517		ours
VERSE 15		And they threw him outside of the vineyard and killed him. Therefore what should the lord of the vineyard do to them?
1542		And they threw him
0322		outside
1388		of
1240		the vineyard
2179		and killed him
1393		what
0596		Therefore
1724		should do
1261		to them
1426		the lord of
1240		the vineyard
VERSE 16		He will come and destroy those workers and will give the vineyard to others." And when they heard [it] they said, "This should not be."
0208		He will come
0005		and destroy
1977		workers
0593		those
1030		will give
1240		the vineyard
0053		to others
1128		when
2547		they heard [it]
0518		And
0116		they said
1262		not
0603		should be
0598		This
VERSE 17		And he gazed at them and said, "And what is that which is written: THE STONE THAT THE BUILDERS REJECTED HAS BECOME THE HEAD OF THE CORNER OF THE CORNERSTONE?
0592		\<he\>
0518		And
0756		he gazed
0217		at them
0116		and said
1393		And what
0592		is
0593		that
1247		which is written
1119		THE STONE

LUKE CHAPTER 20

1655		THAT REJECTED		1023		they knew
0282		THE BUILDERS		0403		for
0592		HAS BECOME		1804		that against them
0603		*		0116		he had spoken
2362		THE HEAD OF		1454		parable
2255		THE CORNER		0598		this
0654		OF THE CORNERSTONE				

VERSE 20 And they sent to him spies who were acting like just [men] to catch him in speech and to deliver him to the judge and to the authority of the governor.

VERSE 18 And whoever will fall on that stone will be bruised, and whomever it falls on, it will blow him away [as chaff]."

1168		And whoever		2458		And they sent
1538		will fall		1288		to him
1804		on		0468		spies
0593		that		0540		who were acting like
1119		stone		0637		just [men]
2380		will be bruised		0047		to catch him
1168		and whomever		1364		in speech
1389		*		2530		and to deliver him
0592		it		0497		to the judge
1538		falls		2527		and to the authority
1804		on <him>		0586		of the governor
0569		it will blow him away [as chaff]				

VERSE 21 And they asked him and said to him, "Teacher, we know that you speak and teach rightly and do not respect persons, but rather you teach the way of God with truthfulness.

VERSE 19 And the chief priests and scribes were wanting to lay hands on him at that time, yet they were afraid of the people, for they knew that he had spoken this parable against them.

0296		were wanting		2420		And they asked him
0603		*		0116		and said
0518		And		1261		to him
2271		the chief priests		1055		Teacher
1135		*		1023		we know
1699		and scribes		2722		that rightly
2372		to lay		1362		speak
1804		on him		0133		you
0057		hands		1053		and teach
0593		at that time		1262		and not
2573		*		1532		do respect persons
0509		yet they were afraid		0133		*
1388		of		0173		*
1818		the people		0090		but
				2269		with truthfulness

Vertical Interlinear

LUKE   CHAPTER 20

ID	Syriac	English
0038		the way
0093		of God
1053		teach
0133		you

VERSE 22 — Is it lawful for us to give the poll tax to Caesar or not?"

ID	Syriac	English
2528		Is it lawful
1261		for us
1030		to give
1209		the poll tax
2362		*
3483		to Caesar
0024		or
1262		not

VERSE 23 — But he perceived their craftiness and said, "Why do you tempt me?

ID	Syriac	English
0592		<he>
0518		But
1647		he perceived
0900		their craftiness
0116		and said
1393		Why
1527		do tempt
0133		you
1261		me

VERSE 24 — Show me a denarius. Whose image and inscriptions are on it?" And they said, "That of Caesar."

ID	Syriac	English
0739		Show me
0519		a denarius
1389		Whose
0069		are
0217		on it
2112		image
1251		and inscriptions
0592		<they>
0518		And
0116		they said
3483		That of Caesar

VERSE 25 — Jesus said to them, "Give therefore that which is of Caesar to Caesar and that which is of God to God."

ID	Syriac	English
0116		said
1261		to them
3257		Jesus
1030		Give
0596		therefore
3483		that which is of Caesar
3483		to Caesar
0093		and that which is of God
0093		to God

VERSE 26 — And they were not able to capture a word from him before the people, and they marveled at his answer and were silent.

ID	Syriac	English
1262		And not
2510		they were able
0047		to capture
1388		from him
1364		a word
2154		before
1818		the people
0549		and they marveled
1804		at
2068		his answer
2623		and were silent

VERSE 27 — And some of the Sadducees came near, those who were saying that there is no resurrection, and they asked him

ID	Syriac	English
2244		came near
0518		And
0131		some
1388		of
3188		the Sadducees
0593		those
0116		who were saying
2173		that resurrection
1264		there is no
2420		and they asked him

LUKE   CHAPTER 20

VERSE 28 — and said to him, "Teacher, Moses wrote to us, 'If a brother of a man, who has a wife, should die without children, he should take the wife of his brother and raise up seed for his brother.'

0116	and said
1261	to him
1055	Teacher
3305	Moses
1247	wrote
1261	to us
0121	If
0131	a man
1334	should die
0043	a brother of
0069	who has
1261	*
0135	a wife
1262	without
0323	children
1532	he should take
0043	his brother
0135	the wife of
2168	and raise up
0693	seed
0043	for his brother

VERSE 29 — Now there were seven brothers. The first took a wife and died without children.

2437	seven
0518	Now
0043	brothers
0069	there were
0603	*
2157	The first
1532	took
0135	a wife
1334	and died
1262	without
0323	children

VERSE 30 — And the second took her for his wife, and this [one] died without children.

1532	And took her
2709	the second
0135	for his wife
0598	and this [one]
1334	died
1262	without
0323	children

VERSE 31 — And the third took her again, and so also the seven of them. And they died and did not leave children.

2674	And the third
2650	again
1532	took her
0595	and so
0169	also
2437	the seven of them
1334	And they died
1262	and not
2440	did leave
0323	children

VERSE 32 — And finally the woman also died.

1334	and died
0054	finally
0169	also
0135	the woman

VERSE 33 — Therefore, in the resurrection, whose wife will she be, for seven of them married her?"

2173	in the resurrection
0596	Therefore
0066	whose
1388	*
0603	will she be
0135	wife
2437	seven of them
0403	for
1532	married her

LUKE CHAPTER 20

VERSE 34
Jesus said to them, "The children of this world take women and women are [given] to men,

0116		said
1261		to them
3257		Jesus
0323		The children
1813		of world
0598		this
1532		take
0135		women
0135		and women
0603		are [given]
0361		to men

VERSE 35
but those who are worthy of that world and of the resurrection that is from the dead neither take women nor are women [given] to men.

0593		those
0518		but
0593		who of that
1813		world
2461		are worthy
2173		and of the resurrection
1388		that is from
0243		the dead
1338		*
1262		neither
1532		take
0135		women
0169		nor
1262		*
0135		women
0603		are
0361		[given] to men

VERSE 36
For neither are they able to die again, for they are like the angels and are sons of God, because they are sons of the resurrection.

0170		neither
0403		For
2650		again
1334		to die
2510		are they able
0060		like
1375		the angels
0592		they are
0403		for
0323		and sons
0069		are
0093		of God
1347		because
0603		they are
0323		sons
2173		of the resurrection

VERSE 37
Now that the dead will rise even Moses showed, for he mentioned [it] at the bush when he said: THE LORD, THE GOD OF ABRAHAM AND THE GOD OF ISAAC AND THE GOD OF JACOB.

2168		that will rise
0518		Now
1338		the dead
0169		even
3305		Moses
0228		showed
0527		he mentioned [it]
0403		for
1678		at the bush
1128		when
0116		he said
1426		THE LORD
0093		THE GOD
3005		OF ABRAHAM
0093		AND THE GOD
3033		OF ISAAC
0093		AND THE GOD
3255		OF JACOB

VERSE 38
And he is not the God of the dead, but of the living, for all are alive to him."

0093		the God
0518		And
1262		not

LUKE CHAPTER 20

Strong's	Aramaic	English
0603		he is
1338		of the dead
0090		but
0781		of the living
1168		all
0403		for
0781		alive
0592		are
1261		to him

VERSE 39 And some of the scribes answered and said to him, "Teacher, you have spoken well."

Strong's	Aramaic	English
1838		And answered
0131		some
1388		of
1699		the scribes
0116		and said
1261		to him
1055		Teacher
2583		well
0116		have spoken
0133		you

VERSE 40 And they did not dare to ask him about anything again.

Strong's	Aramaic	English
1262		And not
2650		again
1435		they did dare
2420		to ask him
1804		about
1326		anything

VERSE 41 And he said to them, "In what way do the scribes say concerning the Messiah that he is the Son of David?

Strong's	Aramaic	English
0116		And he said
0603		*
1261		to them
0061		In what way
0116		do say
1699		the scribes
1804		concerning
1446		the Messiah
0323		that the Son
0592		he is
3159		of David

VERSE 42 Even David said in the book of Psalms: THE LORD SAID TO MY LORD, SIT AT MY RIGHT [HAND]

Strong's	Aramaic	English
0592		Even <he>
3159		David
0116		said
1248		in the book
0676		of the Psalms
0116		SAID
1426		THE LORD
1426		TO MY LORD
1093		SIT
1261		*
1388		AT
1061		MY RIGHT [HAND]

VERSE 43 UNTIL I PLACE YOUR ENEMIES UNDER YOUR FEET.

Strong's	Aramaic	English
1747		UNTIL
1625		I PLACE
0307		YOUR ENEMIES
2660		UNDER
2293		YOUR FEET

VERSE 44 If therefore David called him, 'My Lord,' how is he his son?"

Strong's	Aramaic	English
0121		If
0596		therefore
3159		David
1426		My Lord
2239		called
1261		him
0061		how
0323		his son
0592		is he

VERSE 45 And while all the people were listening, he said to his disciples,

Strong's	Aramaic	English
1128		And while
1168		all
1818		the people

LUKE CHAPTER 20

2547	ܫܡܥ	were listening
0603	ܗܘܐ	*
0116	ܐܡܪ	he said
1304	ܠܬܠܡܝܕܘܗܝ	to his disciples

VERSE 46 "Beware of the scribes who want to walk in robes and love a greeting in the streets and the chief places in the synagogues and the best seats at meals.

0645	ܐܙܕܗܪܘ	Beware
1388	ܡܢ	of
1699	ܣܦܪܐ	the scribes
2077	ܕܨܒܝܢ	who want
0608	ܠܡܗܠܟܘ	to walk
0146	ܒܐܣܛܠܐ	in robes
2342	ܘܪܚܡܝܢ	and love
2535	ܫܠܡܐ	a greeting
2481	ܒܫܘܩܐ	in the streets
2362	ܘܪܝܫ	and the chief
1094	ܡܘܬܒܐ	places
1200	ܒܟܢܘܫܬܐ	in the synagogues
2362	ܘܪܝܫ	and the best seats
1666	ܣܡܟܐ	*
0928	ܒܚܫܡܝܬܐ	at meals

VERSE 47 Those who devour the houses of widows with the pretext of lengthening their prayers, the same will receive a greater judgment."

0593	ܗܢܘܢ	Those
0075	ܕܐܟܠܝܢ	who devour
0243	ܒܬܐ	the houses
0195	ܕܐܪܡܠܬܐ	of widows
1801	ܒܥܠܬܐ	with the pretext
0192	ܕܡܘܪܟܝܢ	of lengthening
2107	ܨܠܘܬܗܘܢ	their prayers
0592	ܗܢܘܢ	the same
2134	ܢܩܒܠܘܢ	will receive
0497	ܕܝܢܐ	a judgment
1100	ܝܬܝܪܐ	greater

CHAPTER 21

VERSE 1 And Jesus looked at the rich [men] who were putting their gifts in the treasury.

0756	ܚܪ	looked
0518	ܕܝܢ	And
3257	ܝܫܘܥ	Jesus
1921	ܒܥܬܝܪܐ	at the rich [men]
0066	ܐܝܠܝܢ	<those>
2372	ܕܪܡܝܢ	who were putting in
0603	ܗܘܘ	*
0243	ܒܝܬ	the treasury
0393	ܓܙܐ	*
2246	ܩܘܪܒܢܝܗܘܢ	their gifts

VERSE 2 And he also saw a certain poor widow who put in two small coins.

0758	ܘܚܙܐ	And he saw
0169	ܐܦ	also
0195	ܐܪܡܠܬܐ	a widow
0721	ܚܕܐ	certain
1406	ܡܣܟܢܬܐ	poor
2372	ܕܐܪܡܝܬ	who put in
2541	ܫܡܘܢܐ	small coins
2709	ܬܪܝܢ	two

VERSE 3 And he said, "I speak the truth to you that this poor widow has put in more than everyone.

0116	ܘܐܡܪ	And he said
2596	ܫܪܪܐ	the truth
0116	ܐܡܪ	I speak
0124	ܐܢܐ	*
1261	ܠܟܘܢ	to you
0598	ܕܗܕܐ	that this
0195	ܐܪܡܠܬܐ	widow
1406	ܡܣܟܢܬܐ	poor
2372	ܐܪܡܝܬ	has put in
1100	ܝܬܝܪ	more
1388	ܡܢ	than
1175	ܟܠܢܫ	everyone

LUKE   CHAPTER 21

VERSE	4	For all of these have put into the place of the offerings of God from what was left over to them, but this [widow] from her need has put in all that she owned."
1168		all of
0403		For
0598		these
1388		from
1313		what
1100		was left over
0603		*
1261		to them
2372		have put into
0243		the place of the offerings
2246		*
0093		of God
0598		this [widow]
0518		but
1388		from
0868		her need
1168		all
2216		that she owned
0603		*
2372		has put in

VERSE	5	And while some were speaking about the temple, how it was adorned with beautiful stones and with gifts, Jesus said to them,
1128		And while
0116		were speaking
0603		*
0131		some
1804		about
0607		the temple
1119		how with stones
2583		beautiful
2246		and with gifts
2083		it was adorned
0116		said
1261		to them
3257		Jesus

VERSE	6	These [things] that you see, the days will come in which [one] stone will not be left on [another] stone that is not pulled down.
0598		These [things]
0758		that see
0133		you
0208		will come
1036		the days
0217		in which
1262		not
2440		will be left
1119		[one] stone
1804		on
1119		[another] stone
1262		that not
1719		is pulled down

VERSE	7	And they asked him and said, "Teacher, when will these [things] be and what is the sign when these [things] are about to happen?"
2420		And they asked
0603		*
1261		him
0116		and said
1055		Teacher
0120		when
0598		these [things]
0603		will be
1393		and what
0592		is
0206		the sign
1313		when
2248		about
0598		these [things]
0603		are

VERSE	8	And he said to them, "See [that] you are not deceived, for many will come in my name and will say, 'I am the Messiah, and the time draws near,' but you should not follow them.
0592		<he>
0518		And

556

LUKE   CHAPTER 21

0116		he said
1261		to them
0758		See
1316		[that] not
0993		you are deceived
1596		many
0403		for
0208		will come
2539		in my name
0116		and will say
0124		I am
0124		*
1446		the Messiah
0633		and the time
2244		draws near
1262		not
0518		but
0042		you should follow them
0215		*

VERSE 9 — And when you hear of wars and riots, do not fear, for these [things] are going to happen first, but the end will not yet have arrived,

1313		And when
2547		hear of
0133		you
2247		wars
2454		and riots
1262		not
0509		do fear
1914		going
0592		are
0403		for
0598		These [things]
2151		first
0603		to happen
0090		but
1262		not
1745		yet
1346		will have arrived

0054		the end

VERSE 10 — for nation will rise against nation and kingdom against kingdom

2168		will rise
0403		for
1818		nation
1804		against
1818		nation
1385		and kingdom
1804		against
1385		kingdom

VERSE 11 — and great earthquakes will occur in various places, and famines and plagues, and there will be fears and panic, and great signs from heaven will be seen and there will be much foul weather.

0658		and earthquakes
2271		great
0603		will occur
0494		in various places
0494		*
1213		and famines
1336		and plagues
0603		and there will be
0511		fears
1707		and panic
0206		and signs
2271		great
1388		from
2543		heaven
0758		will be seen
1718		and foul weather
2271		much
0603		there will be

VERSE 12 — But before all these [things], they will lay hands on you and persecute you and deliver you to the synagogues and to prison, and they will bring you before kings and governors on account of my name.

2154		before
0518		But

LUKE   CHAPTER 21

0598	ܗܠܝܢ	these [things]
1168	ܟܠܗܝܢ	all
2372	ܢܪܡܘܢ	they will lay
1804	ܥܠܝܟܘܢ	on you
0057	ܐܝܕܝܐ	hands
2304	ܘܢܪܕܦܘܢܟܘܢ	and persecute you
2530	ܘܢܫܠܡܘܢܟܘܢ	and deliver you
1200	ܠܟܢܘܫܬܐ	to the synagogues
0243	ܘܠܒܝܬ	and to prison
0163	ܐܣܝܪܐ	*
2244	ܘܢܩܪܒܘܢܟܘܢ	and they will bring you
2154	ܩܕܡ	before
1383	ܡܠܟܐ	kings
0586	ܘܗܓܡܘܢܐ	and governors
1347	ܡܛܠ	on account of
2539	ܫܡܝ	my name

VERSE 13 But it will happen to you for a testimony.

0603	ܘܗܘܐ	it will happen
1261	ܠܟܘܢ	to you
0518	ܕܝܢ	But
1610	ܠܣܗܕܘܬܐ	for a testimony

VERSE 14 And put [it] in your heart[s] that you should not be learning to make a defense,

1625	ܣܝܡܘ	put [it]
0518	ܕܝܢ	And
1268	ܒܠܒܟܘܢ	in your heart[s]
1262	ܕܠܐ	that not
0603	ܬܗܘܘܢ	you should be
1053	ܝܠܦܝܢ	learning
1543	ܠܡܦܩ	to make a defense
2323	ܪܘܚܐ	*

VERSE 15 for I will give to you a mouth and wisdom, so that all your enemies will not be able to stand against it.

0124	ܐܢܐ	<I>
0403	ܓܝܪ	for
1030	ܐܬܠ	I will give
1261	ܠܟܘܢ	to you
1936	ܦܘܡܐ	a mouth
0792	ܘܚܟܡܬܐ	and wisdom
0066	ܐܝܕܐ	<which>
1262	ܕܠܐ	so that not
2510	ܢܫܟܚܘܢ	will be able
2168	ܠܡܩܡ	to stand
2135	ܠܘܩܒܠܗ	against it
1168	ܟܠܗܘܢ	all
0307	ܒܥܠܕܒܒܝܟܘܢ	your enemies

VERSE 16 And your fathers and your brothers and your kinsmen and your friends will betray you and they will kill some of you.

2530	ܢܫܠܡܘܢܟܘܢ	will betray you
0518	ܕܝܢ	And
0002	ܐܒܗܝܟܘܢ	your fathers
0043	ܘܐܚܝܟܘܢ	and your brothers
0045	ܘܐܚܝܢܝܟܘܢ	and your kinsmen
2345	ܘܪܚܡܝܟܘܢ	and your friends
1334	ܘܢܡܝܬܘܢ	and they will kill
1388	ܡܢܟܘܢ	some of you

VERSE 17 And you will be hated by everyone on account of my name,

0603	ܘܬܗܘܘܢ	And you will be
1675	ܣܢܝܐܝܢ	hated
1388	ܡܢ	by
1168	ܟܠ	everyone
0131	ܐܢܫ	*
1347	ܡܛܠ	on account of
2539	ܫܡܝ	my name

VERSE 18 yet not a hair from your head will be hurt.

1403	ܘܡܢܬܐ	yet a hair
1388	ܡܢ	from
2362	ܪܫܟܘܢ	your head
1262	ܠܐ	not
0005	ܬܐܒܕ	will be hurt

VERSE 19 And by your patience you will gain your life.

1591	ܒܡܣܝܒܪܢܘܬܟܘܢ	by your patience
0518	ܕܝܢ	And
2216	ܬܩܢܘܢ	you will gain
1547	ܢܦܫܟܘܢ	your life

LUKE — CHAPTER 21

Vertical Interlinear

VERSE 20 — And when you see Jerusalem [with] an army surrounding it, then know that its destruction draws near.

#	Syriac	Gloss
1313	ܕ	when
0518	ܕܝܢ	And
0758	ܬܚܙܘܢ	you see
3022	ܠܐܘܪܫܠܡ	Jerusalem
0730	ܚܕܝܪܐ	surrounding
1261	ܠܗ	it
0786	ܚܝܠܐ	[with] an army
0594	ܗܝܕܝܢ	then
1023	ܕܥܘ	know
2244	ܕܩܪܒ	that draws near
1261	ܠܗ	*
0892	ܚܘܪܒܗ	its destruction

VERSE 21 — Then those who are in Judea should flee to the mountain and those who are within it should flee and [those] in the villages should not enter it,

#	Syriac	Gloss
0594	ܗܝܕܝܢ	Then
0066	ܐܝܠܝܢ	those
3224	ܕܒܝܗܘܕ	who in Judea
0592	ܐܢܘܢ	are
1904	ܢܥܪܩܘܢ	should flee
0958	ܠܛܘܪܐ	to the mountain
0066	ܘܐܝܠܝܢ	and those
0376	ܕܒܓܘܗ	who within
0592	ܐܢܘܢ	are
1904	ܢܥܪܩܘܢ	should flee
2251	ܘܕܒܩܘܪܝܐ	and [those] in the villages
1262	ܠܐ	not
1796	ܢܥܠܘܢ	should enter
1261	ܠܗ	it

VERSE 22 — because these are the days of vengeance that everything that is written will be fulfilled.

#	Syriac	Gloss
1036	ܕܝܘܡܬܐ	because the days
0592	ܐܢܘܢ	are
0598	ܗܠܝܢ	these
2633	ܕܬܒܥܬܐ	of vengeance
2530	ܕܢܫܠܡ	that will be fulfilled
1168	ܟܠ	everything
1313	ܕ	*
1247	ܕܟܬܝܒ	that is written

VERSE 23 — And woe to those who are pregnant and to those who are nursing in those days, for there will be a great torment in the land and wrath on this people.

#	Syriac	Gloss
0625	ܘܝ	woe
0518	ܕܝܢ	And
0066	ܠܐܝܠܝܢ	to those
0260	ܕܒܛܢܢ	who are pregnant
0066	ܘܠܐܝܠܝܢ	and to those
1063	ܕܡܝܢܩܢ	who are nursing
0593	ܒܗܢܘܢ	in those
1036	ܝܘܡܬܐ	days
0603	ܢܗܘܐ	there will be
0403	ܓܝܪ	for
0103	ܐܘܠܨܢܐ	a torment
2271	ܪܒܐ	great
0199	ܒܐܪܥܐ	in the land
2291	ܘܪܘܓܙܐ	and wrath
1804	ܥܠ	on
1818	ܥܡܐ	people
0598	ܗܢܐ	this

VERSE 24 — And they will fall by the edge of the sword and be led away captive to every land. And Jerusalem will be trampled by the Gentiles until the times of the Gentiles will be fulfilled.

#	Syriac	Gloss
1538	ܘܢܦܠܘܢ	And they will fall
1936	ܒܦܘܡܐ	by the edge
0893	ܕܚܪܒܐ	of the sword
2426	ܘܢܫܬܒܘܢ	and be led away captive
1168	ܠܟܠ	to every
0214	ܐܬܪ	land
3022	ܘܐܘܪܫܠܡ	And Jerusalem
0603	ܬܗܘܐ	will be
0507	ܡܬܕܝܫܐ	trampled
1388	ܡܢ	by
1818	ܥܡܡܐ	the Gentiles
1747	ܥܕܡܐ	until

LUKE CHAPTER 21

Code	Aramaic	English
2530		will be fulfilled
0633		the times
1818		of the Gentiles

VERSE 25 — And there will be signs in the sun and in the moon and in the stars, and on the earth the torment of the nations and anxiety from the roaring of the sea,

Code	Aramaic	English
0603		And there will be
0206		signs
2557		in the sun
1611		and in the moon
1141		and in the stars
0199		and on the earth
0103		the torment
1818		of the nations
2060		and anxiety
0057		*
1388		from
2654		the roaring
2204		<of the voice>
1057		of the sea

VERSE 26 — and a shaking that draws out the lives of men from the fear of what is about to come on the earth, and the powers of heaven will be shaken.

Code	Aramaic	English
0658		and a shaking
1542		that draws out
1547		the lives
0325		of men
1388		from
0511		the fear
1326		of what
1914		is about
0208		to come
1804		on
0199		the earth
0657		and will be shaken
0786		the powers
2543		of heaven

VERSE 27 — And then they will see THE SON OF MAN WHO WILL COME IN THE CLOUDS with much power and great glory.

Code	Aramaic	English
0594		And then
0758		they will see
0323		THE SON
0131		OF MAN
0208		WHO WILL COME
1844		IN THE CLOUDS
1817		with
0786		power
1596		much
2431		and glory
2271		great

VERSE 28 — And when these [things] begin to happen, take heart and lift up your heads, because your deliverance is near."

Code	Aramaic	English
1313		when
0518		And
2597		begin
0598		these [things]
0603		to happen
1267		take heart
2331		and lift up
2362		your heads
1347		because
2244		is near
1261		*
2043		your deliverance

VERSE 29 — And he told them a parable: "Look at the fig tree and all the trees,

Code	Aramaic	English
0116		And he told
0603		*
1261		them
1454		a parable
0758		Look at
2628		the fig tree
1168		and all
0063		the trees

LUKE — CHAPTER 21

Vertical Interlinear

VERSE 30 — because when they bud, you understand immediately from them that summer is near.

Code	Aramaic	English
1313		because when
2037		they bud
0725		immediately
1388		from them
1647		understand
0133		you
2244		that is near
1261		*
2194		summer

VERSE 31 — Likewise also, when you see these [things] that are happening, know that the kingdom of God is near.

Code	Aramaic	English
0597		Likewise
0169		also
0133		<you>
1313		when
0758		you see
0598		these [things]
0603		that are happening
1023		know
2248		that near
0592		is
1385		the kingdom
0093		of God

VERSE 32 — Truly I say to you, this generation will not pass away until all these [things] happen.

Code	Aramaic	English
0110		Truly
0116		say
0124		I
1261		to you
1262		not
1733		will pass away
2605		generation
0598		this
1747		until
0598		these [things]
1168		all
0603		happen

VERSE 33 — Heaven and earth will pass away, yet my words will not pass away.

Code	Aramaic	English
2543		Heaven
0199		and earth
1733		will pass away
1364		yet my words
1262		not
1733		will pass away

VERSE 34 — And take heed to yourselves that your hearts should never become heavy in excess and in drunkenness and in the anxiety of the world, and that day should come suddenly on you.

Code	Aramaic	English
0645		take heed
0518		And
1547		to yourselves
1262		that never
1450		*
1076		should become heavy
1268		your hearts
0140		in excess
2317		and in drunkenness
1072		and in the anxiety
1813		of the world
1388		and suddenly
2519		*
0208		should come
1804		on you
1036		day
0593		that

VERSE 35 — For as a snare it will ensnare all those who live on the face of all the earth.

Code	Aramaic	English
0060		as
2123		a snare
0403		For
2122		it will ensnare
1804		*
1168		all
0066		those
1093		who live

LUKE   CHAPTER 21

Code	Syriac	English
1804		on
0173		the face
1168		of all
0199		the earth

VERSE 36 — Therefore, watch always and pray that you will be worthy to escape these [things] that are going to happen and [that] you will stand before the Son of Man."

Code	Syriac	English
0603		<be>
0596		Therefore
2459		watch
1170		always
2106		and pray
2461		that you will be worthy
1904		to escape
1388		<from>
0598		these [things]
1914		that are going
0603		to happen
2168		and [that] you will stand
2154		before
0323		the Son
0131		of Man

VERSE 37 — And in the daytime, he was teaching in the temple and at night he went out [and] was staying in the mountain that was called the Mount of Olives.

Code	Syriac	English
0064		in the daytime
0518		And
1053		he was teaching
0603		*
0607		in the temple
1299		and at night
1542		he went out
0603		*
0242		[and] was staying
0958		in the mountain
2239		that was called
0243		the Mount of Olives
0663		*

VERSE 38 — And all the people were preceding him to the temple to hear his word.

Code	Syriac	English
1168		And all
1818		the people
2150		preceding
0603		were
1288		him
0607		to the temple
2547		to hear
1364		his word

CHAPTER 22

VERSE 1 — Now the Feast of Unleavened Bread, that is called the Passover, was near

Code	Syriac	English
2248		was near
0603		*
0518		Now
1721		the Feast
1951		of Unleavened Bread
2239		that is called
3433		the Passover

VERSE 2 — and the chief priests and scribes were seeking how to kill him, for they were afraid of the people.

Code	Syriac	English
0296		and seeking
0603		were
2271		the chief priests
1135		*
1699		and scribes
0061		how
2179		to kill him
0509		afraid
0603		they were
0403		for
1388		of
1818		the people

VERSE 3 — And Satan entered into Judas, who was called Iscariot, who was from the number of the twelve.

Code	Syriac	English
1796		entered
0603		*
0518		And

LUKE — CHAPTER 22

Code	Syriac	Gloss
1642		Satan
3228		into Judas
2239		who was called
3370		Iscariot
0069		who was
0603		*
1388		from
1398		the number
2710		of the twelve

VERSE 4 — And he went [and] talked with the chief priests and scribes and captains of the temple about how he might deliver him to them.

Code	Syriac	Gloss
0042		And he went
1362		[and] talked
1817		with
2271		the chief priests
1135		*
1699		and scribes
2271		and captains
0786		*
0607		of the temple
0060		about how
2530		he might deliver him
1261		to them

VERSE 5 — And they rejoiced and pledged to give him money.

Code	Syriac	Gloss
0726		And they rejoiced
2168		and pledged
1030		to give
1261		him
1209		money

VERSE 6 — And he promised them and sought an opportunity to deliver him to them apart from the crowd.

Code	Syriac	Gloss
1020		And he promised
1261		them
0296		and sought
0603		*
1982		an opportunity
2530		to deliver him
1261		to them
0279		apart
1388		from
1201		the crowd

VERSE 7 — And the day of the Feast of Unleavened Bread arrived, during which was the custom that the Passover be killed.

Code	Syriac	Gloss
1346		And arrived
1036		the day
1951		of the Feast of Unleavened Bread
0217		during which
0069		was
0603		*
1762		the custom
1514		that be killed
3433		the Passover

VERSE 8 — And Jesus sent Peter and John and said to them, "Go [and] prepare for us the Passover that we may eat."

Code	Syriac	Gloss
2458		And sent
3257		Jesus
3258		Peter
3233		and John
0116		and said
1261		to them
0042		Go
0950		[and] prepare
1261		for us
3433		the Passover
1308		that we may eat

VERSE 9 — And they said to him, "Where do you want us to prepare [it]?"

Code	Syriac	Gloss
0592		<they>
0518		And
0116		they said
1261		to him
1108		Where
2077		do want
0133		you
0950		us to prepare [it]

Vertical Interlinear

LUKE — CHAPTER 22

VERSE 10 — He said to them, "Behold, when you enter the city, a man will meet you who is bearing a jar of water. Follow him.

Code	Syriac	Gloss
0116		He said
1261		to them
0580		Behold
1313		when
1796		you enter
0133		*
0499		the city
1928		will meet
0217		you
0361		a man
2587		who is bearing
0458		a jar
1351		of water
0042		Follow him
0215		*

VERSE 11 — And where he enters, say to the lord of the house, 'Our Master says, Where is a place of lodging where I may eat the Passover with my disciples?'

Code	Syriac	Gloss
1108		And where
1796		he enters
0116		say
1426		to the lord
0243		of the house
2271		Our Master
0116		says
0067		Where is
0243		a place of lodging
2599		*
1108		where
0075		I may eat
3433		the Passover
1817		with
1304		my disciples

VERSE 12 — And behold, he will show you a certain large upper room that is furnished. There make ready."

Code	Syriac	Gloss
0580		And behold
0592		he
0739		will show
1261		you
1805		upper room
0721		certain
2271		large
2461		that is furnished
2682		There
0950		make ready

VERSE 13 — And they went [and] found [the man] as he had told them and they prepared the Passover.

Code	Syriac	Gloss
0042		And they went
2510		[and] found [the man]
0060		as
0116		he had told
1261		them
0950		and they prepared
3433		the Passover

VERSE 14 — And when the time was come, Jesus and the twelve apostles with him came [and] sat to eat.

Code	Syriac	Gloss
1128		And when
0603		was come
1750		the time
0208		came
3257		Jesus
1664		[and] sat to eat
2710		and twelve
2522		the apostles
1817		with him

VERSE 15 — And he said to them, "I have greatly desired to eat this Passover with you before I suffer.

Code	Syriac	Gloss
0116		And he said
1261		to them
2289		I have greatly desired
2287		*
0598		this
3433		Passover
0075		to eat

LUKE   CHAPTER 22

1817	ܥܡܟܘܢ	with you		0169	ܐܦ	also
2154	ܩܕܡ	before		1804	ܥܠ	concerning
0911	ܕܐܚܫ	I suffer		1205	ܟܣܐ	the cup
VERSE	16	For I say to you, from now on I will not eat until it is fulfilled in the kingdom of God."		1388	ܡܢ	after
				0215	ܒܬܪ	*
0116	ܐܡܪ	say		0927	ܕܐܚܫܡܘ	they had eaten the supper
0124	ܐܢܐ	I		0116	ܐܡܪ	he said
1261	ܠܟܘܢ	to you		0598	ܗܢܐ	This
0403	ܓܝܪ	For		1205	ܟܣܐ	cup
1357	ܕܡܟܝܠ	from now on		0520	ܕܝܬܩܐ	[is] the covenant
1262	ܠܐ	not		0735	ܚܕܬܐ	new
0075	ܐܟܘܠ	I will eat		0539	ܒܕܡܝ	in my blood
1747	ܥܕܡܐ	until		0812	ܕܚܠܦܝܟܘܢ	that on behalf of you
2530	ܕܢܬܡܠܐ	it is fulfilled		0201	ܡܬܐܫܕ	is shed
1385	ܒܡܠܟܘܬܗ	in the kingdom		VERSE	21	But, behold, the hand of my betrayer [is] on the table
0093	ܕܐܠܗܐ	of God				
VERSE	19	And he took bread and gave thanks and broke [it] and gave [it] to them and said, "This is my body that is given for your sakes. This do for my remembrance."		0342	ܒܪܡ	But
				0580	ܗܐ	behold
				0057	ܐܝܕܗ	the hand
1532	ܘܢܣܒ	And he took		2531	ܕܡܫܠܡܢܝ	of my betrayer
1293	ܠܚܡܐ	bread		1804	ܥܠ	[is] on
1020	ܘܐܘܕܝ	and gave thanks		2069	ܦܬܘܪܐ	the table
2234	ܘܩܨܐ	and broke [it]		VERSE	22	and the Son of Man dies as it was determined. But woe to that man by whose hand he is betrayed!"
1030	ܘܝܗܒ	and gave [it]				
1261	ܠܗܘܢ	to them		0323	ܘܒܪܗ	and the Son
0116	ܘܐܡܪ	and said		0131	ܕܐܢܫܐ	of Man
0599	ܗܢܘ	This is		0042	ܐܙܠ	dies
1929	ܦܓܪܝ	my body		0061	ܐܝܟܢܐ	as
1804	ܕܥܠ	that for		2046	ܕܐܬܦܪܫ	it was determined
0173	ܐܦܝܟܘܢ	your sakes		0342	ܒܪܡ	But
1030	ܡܬܝܗܒ	is given		0625	ܘܝ	woe
0598	ܗܢܐ	This		0593	ܠܗܘ	to that
0603	ܗܘܝܬܘܢ	do		0361	ܓܒܪܐ	man
1724	ܥܒܕܝܢ	*		0057	ܕܒܐܝܕܗ	by whose hand
0528	ܠܕܘܟܪܢܝ	for my remembrance		2530	ܡܫܬܠܡ	he is betrayed
VERSE	20	And likewise also, concerning the cup, after they had eaten supper he said, "This cup [is] the new covenant in my blood that is shed on behalf of you.		VERSE	23	And they began to examine among themselves which one of them indeed it was who was going to do this.
				2597	ܘܫܪܝܘ	And they began
0595	ܘܗܟܢܐ	And likewise		1867	ܠܡܒܚܢ	to examine

565

LUKE CHAPTER 22

0266	ܒܝܢܬܗܘܢ	among themselves
1390	ܕܐܝܢܐ	which
1163	ܟܝ	indeed
1388	ܡܢܗܘܢ	one of them
0593	ܗܘ	who
0598	ܗܢܐ	this
1914	ܥܬܝܕ	was going
1684	ܠܡܥܒܕ	to do

VERSE 24 — And there was also a conflict among them about which of them was the greatest.

0603	ܗܘܐ	there was
0518	ܕܝܢ	And
0169	ܐܦ	also
0890	ܚܪܝܢܐ	a conflict
0266	ܒܝܢܬܗܘܢ	among them
1389	ܕܐܝܢܐ	about which
0069	ܐܝܬ	was
0217	ܒܗܘܢ	of them
2271	ܪܒ	the greatest

VERSE 25 — And Jesus said to them, "The kings of the Gentiles are their lords and those who are authorities over them are called workers of good.

0592	ܗܘ	\<he\>
0518	ܕܝܢ	And
3257	ܝܫܘܥ	Jesus
0116	ܐܡܪ	said
1261	ܠܗܘܢ	to them
1383	ܡܠܟܝܗܘܢ	The kings
1818	ܕܥܡܡܐ	of the Gentiles
1426	ܡܪܝܗܘܢ	their lords
0592	ܐܢܘܢ	are
2528	ܘܫܠܝܛܝܗܘܢ	and those who are authorities
1804	ܥܠܝܗܘܢ	over them
1724	ܥܒܕܝ	workers of
0938	ܛܒܬܐ	good
2239	ܡܬܩܪܝܢ	are called

VERSE 26 — But you are not so, but he who is the greatest among you must be as the least and he who is chief as a servant.

0133	ܐܢܬܘܢ	you are
0518	ܕܝܢ	But
1262	ܠܐ	not
0597	ܗܟܢܐ	so
0090	ܐܠܐ	but
0066	ܐܝܢܐ	he who
2271	ܕܪܒ	is the greatest
0217	ܒܟܘܢ	among you
0603	ܢܗܘܐ	must be
0060	ܐܝܟ	as
0686	ܙܥܘܪܐ	the least
0066	ܘܐܝܢܐ	and he who
2362	ܪܫܐ	chief
0592	ܗܘ	is
0060	ܐܝܟ	as
2555	ܡܫܡܫܢܐ	a servant

VERSE 27 — For who is greater, he who sits to eat or he who serves? Is it not he who sits to eat? But I am among you as one who serves.

1390	ܐܝܢܐ	who is
0403	ܓܝܪ	For
2271	ܪܒ	greater
0593	ܗܘ	he
1664	ܕܣܡܝܟ	who sits to eat
0024	ܐܘ	or
0593	ܗܘ	he
2554	ܕܡܫܡܫ	who serves
1262	ܠܐ	not
0603	ܗܘܐ	Is it
0593	ܗܘ	he
1664	ܕܣܡܝܟ	who sits to eat
0124	ܐܢܐ	I
0518	ܕܝܢ	But
0069	ܐܝܬܝ	am
0266	ܒܝܢܬܟܘܢ	among you
0060	ܐܝܟ	as
0593	ܗܘ	one

Vertical Interlinear

LUKE   **CHAPTER 22**

2554	ܕܡܫܡܫ	who serves

VERSE 28   But you are those who have continued with me in my trials.

0133	ܐܢܬܘܢ	you are
0592	ܐܢܘܢ	those
0518	ܕܝܢ	But
1258	ܕܟܬܪܬܘܢ	who have continued
1288	ܠܘܬܝ	with me
1528	ܒܢܣܝܘܢܝ	in my trials

VERSE 29   And I promise to you, as my Father has promised a kingdom to me,

0124	ܘܐܢܐ	And \<I\>
1020	ܡܫܬܘܕܐ	promise
0124	ܐܢܐ	I
1261	ܠܟܘܢ	to you
0060	ܐܝܟ	as
1020	ܐܫܬܘܕܝ	has promised
1261	ܠܝ	to me
0002	ܐܒܝ	my Father
1385	ܡܠܟܘܬܐ	a kingdom

VERSE 30   that you will eat and drink at the table of my kingdom and you will sit on thrones and you will judge the twelve tribes of Israel."

0075	ܕܬܐܟܠܘܢ	that you will eat
2620	ܘܬܫܬܘܢ	and drink
1804	ܥܠ	at
2069	ܦܬܘܪܐ	the table
1385	ܕܡܠܟܘܬܝ	of kingdom
0517	ܕܝܠܝ	my
1093	ܘܬܬܒܘܢ	and you will sit
1804	ܥܠ	on
1159	ܟܘܪܣܘܬܐ	thrones
0496	ܘܬܕܘܢܘܢ	and you will judge
2710	ܬܪܥܣܪ	twelve
2433	ܫܒܛܐ	the tribes
3035	ܕܐܝܣܪܝܠ	of Israel

VERSE 31   And Jesus said to Simon, "Simon, behold, Satan is resigned to sift you like wheat."

0116	ܘܐܡܪ	and said
3257	ܝܫܘܥ	Jesus
3521	ܠܫܡܥܘܢ	to Simon
3521	ܫܡܥܘܢ	Simon
0580	ܗܐ	behold
1642	ܣܛܢܐ	Satan
2420	ܫܐܠ	is resigned
1883	ܕܢܥܪܘܒܟܘܢ	to sift you
0060	ܐܝܟ	as
0779	ܚܛܐ	wheat

VERSE 32   And I have prayed for you that your faith would not be lacking. You also in time will turn and strengthen your brothers."

0124	ܘܐܢܐ	And \<I\>
0296	ܒܥܝܬ	I have prayed
1804	ܥܠܝܟ	for you
1262	ܕܠܐ	that not
0865	ܬܚܣܪ	would be lacking
0113	ܗܝܡܢܘܬܟ	your faith
0169	ܐܦ	also
0133	ܐܢܬ	You
0633	ܒܙܒܢ	in time
1984	ܐܬܦܢܝ	will turn
2591	ܘܐܫܪ	and strengthen
0043	ܐܚܝܟ	your brothers

VERSE 33   And Simon said to him, "My Lord, I am ready [to go] with you even to prison and to death."

3521	ܫܡܥܘܢ	Simon
0518	ܕܝܢ	And
0116	ܐܡܪ	said
1261	ܠܗ	to him
1426	ܡܪܝ	My Lord
1817	ܥܡܟ	with you
0950	ܡܛܝܒ	I am ready [to go]
0124	ܐܢܐ	*
0243	ܘܠܒܝܬ	even to prison
0163	ܐܣܝܪܐ	*
1335	ܘܠܡܘܬܐ	and to death

LUKE   CHAPTER 22

VERSE 34 — Jesus said to him, "I say to you, Simon, that the rooster will not crow today before you insist three times that you do not know me."

Code	Syriac	Gloss
0116		said
1261		to him
3257		Jesus
0116		say
0124		I
1261		to you
3521		Simon
1262		that not
2239		will crow
2713		the rooster
1037		today
1747		before
2674		three
0633		times
1215		you insist
1262		that not
1023		do know
0133		you
1261		me

VERSE 35 — And he said to them, "When I sent you out without purses and without bags and shoes, what did you lack?" They said to him, "Nothing."

Code	Syriac	Gloss
0116		And he said
1261		to them
1128		When
2458		I sent you out
1262		without
1165		bags
1262		and without
2712		wallets
1582		and shoes
1316		<?>
0865		did you lack
1261		*
1326		what
0116		They said
1261		to him
1262		Nothing
1326		*

VERSE 36 — He said to them, "From now on, he who has a purse should take [it] and likewise also a bag. And he who does not have a sword should sell his garment and buy a sword for himself.

Code	Syriac	Gloss
0116		He said
1261		to them
1388		From
0602		now on
1389		he who
0069		has
1261		*
1165		a bag
1532		should take [it]
0597		and likewise
0169		also
2712		a wallet
1389		And he who
1264		does not have
1261		*
1645		a sword
0632		should sell
1501		his garment
0632		and buy
1261		for himself
1645		a sword

VERSE 37 — For I say to you, this also that was written must be fulfilled in me: I WILL BE NUMBERED WITH THE UNJUST, for all [things] that concern me will be fulfilled."

Code	Syriac	Gloss
0116		say
0124		I
1261		to you
0403		For
0169		also
0598		this
1247		that was written
0626		must

LUKE CHAPTER 22

ID	Aramaic	English
1366		be fulfilled
0217		in me
1817		WITH
1767		THE UNJUST
1396		I WILL BE NUMBERED
1168		all [things]
0403		for
1804		that concern me
2530		will be fulfilled

VERSE 38 And they said to him, "Our Lord, behold, here are two swords." He said to them, "They are sufficient."

ID	Aramaic	English
0592		And they
0116		said
1261		to him
1426		Our Lord
0580		behold
0600		here
0069		are
2709		two
1645		swords
0116		He said
1261		to them
1694		They are sufficient

VERSE 39 And he left and traveled (as he was accustomed) to the Mount of Olives and his disciples also followed him.

ID	Aramaic	English
1542		And he left
0042		and traveled
0060		as
1761		accustomed
0603		he was
0958		to the Mount of Olives
0243		*
0663		*
0042		and followed him
0215		*
0169		also
1304		his disciples

VERSE 40 And when he arrived at the place, he said to them, "Pray, so that you should not enter into temptation."

ID	Aramaic	English
1128		And when
1346		he arrived
0494		at the place
0116		he said
1261		to them
2106		Pray
1262		so that not
1796		you should enter
1528		into temptation

VERSE 41 And he went away from them about [the distance] one throws a stone and he knelt and was praying.

ID	Aramaic	English
0592		And he
2042		went away
1388		from them
0060		about [the distance]
2455		one throws
1119		a stone
1625		and he knelt
0336		*
2106		and was praying
0603		*

VERSE 42 And he said, "Father, if you want, let this cup pass by me. Nevertheless, not my will, but yours be done."

ID	Aramaic	English
0116		And he said
0002		Father
0121		if
2077		want
0133		you
1733		let pass by me
1205		cup
0598		this
0342		Nevertheless
1262		not
2079		my will
0090		but
0517		yours

LUKE CHAPTER 22

0603	ܗܘܐ	be done

VERSE 43 And an angel from heaven appeared to him to strengthen him.

0758	ܘܐܬܚܙܝ	And appeared
1261	ܠܗ	to him
1375	ܡܠܐܟܐ	an angel
1388	ܡܢ	from
2543	ܫܡܝܐ	heaven
0787	ܕܢܚܝܠ	to strengthen
1261	ܠܗ	him

VERSE 44 And being in fear, he prayed earnestly and his sweat was as drops of blood and he fell down on the ground.

1128	ܘܟܕ	And being
0603	ܗܘܐ	*
0511	ܒܕܚܠܬܐ	in fear
2664	ܬܟܝܒܐܝܬ	earnestly
2106	ܡܨܠܐ	he prayed
0603	ܗܘܐ	*
0603	ܘܗܘܬ	and was
0562	ܕܘܥܬܗ	his sweat
0060	ܐܝܟ	as
2538	ܫܠܬܐ	drops
0539	ܕܕܡܐ	of blood
1538	ܘܢܦܠ	and he fell down
1804	ܥܠ	on
0199	ܐܪܥܐ	the ground

VERSE 45 And he rose up from his prayer and came to his disciples and found them asleep from sorrow.

2168	ܘܩܡ	And he rose up
1388	ܡܢ	from
2107	ܨܠܘܬܗ	his prayer
0208	ܘܐܬܐ	and came
1288	ܠܘܬ	to
1304	ܬܠܡܝܕܘܗܝ	his disciples
2510	ܘܐܫܟܚ	and found
0592	ܐܢܘܢ	them
1128	ܟܕ	asleep
0544	ܕܡܟܝܢ	*
1388	ܡܢ	from
1773	ܥܩܬܐ	sorrow

VERSE 46 And he said to them, "Why are you sleeping? Rise up [and] pray, so that you should not enter into temptation."

0116	ܘܐܡܪ	And he said
1261	ܠܗܘܢ	to them
1393	ܡܢܐ	Why
0544	ܕܡܟܝܢ	sleeping
0133	ܐܢܬܘܢ	are you
2168	ܩܘܡܘ	Rise up
2106	ܨܠܘ	[and] pray
1262	ܕܠܐ	so that not
1796	ܬܥܠܘܢ	you should enter
1528	ܠܢܣܝܘܢܐ	into temptation

VERSE 47 And while he was speaking, behold, a crowd with him who was called Judas, one of the twelve, came before them. And he came near to Jesus and kissed him, for he had given this sign to them, "Whomever I kiss is him."

1744	ܘܥܕ	And while
0592	ܗܘ	he
1362	ܡܡܠܠ	was speaking
0580	ܗܐ	behold
1201	ܟܢܫܐ	a crowd
0593	ܘܥܡܗ	and him
2239	ܕܡܬܩܪܐ	who was called
3228	ܝܗܘܕܐ	Judas
0721	ܚܕ	one
1388	ܡܢ	of
2710	ܬܪܥܣܪ	the twelve
0208	ܐܬܐ	came
2154	ܩܕܡܝܗܘܢ	before them
2244	ܘܩܪܒ	And he came near
1288	ܠܘܬ	to
3257	ܝܫܘܥ	Jesus
1573	ܘܢܫܩܗ	and kissed him
0598	ܗܕܐ	this
0403	ܓܝܪ	for
0206	ܐܬܐ	sign
1030	ܝܗܒ	he had given

LUKE — CHAPTER 22

#	Aramaic	English
0603		*
1261		to them
0066		Whomever
1573		I kiss
0124		*
0592		is him

VERSE 48 — Jesus said to him, "Judas, do you betray the Son of Man with a kiss?"

#	Aramaic	English
0116		said
1261		to him
3257		Jesus
3228		Judas
1574		with a kiss
2530		do you betray
0133		*
1261		<him>
0323		the Son
0131		of Man

VERSE 49 — And when those who were with him saw what happened, they said to him, "Our Lord, should we strike them with swords?"

#	Aramaic	English
1128		when
0758		saw
0518		And
0066		those
1817		who were with him
1326		what
0603		happened
0116		they said
1261		to him
1426		Our Lord
1341		should we strike
0592		them
1645		with swords

VERSE 50 — And one of them struck the servant of the chief priests and took off his right ear.

#	Aramaic	English
1341		And struck
0721		one
1388		of them
1727		the servant
2271		of the chief priests
1135		*
1532		and took off
0021		his ear
1061		right

VERSE 51 — And Jesus answered and said, "This is enough." And he touched the ear of the one who was wounded and healed him.

#	Aramaic	English
1838		answered
0518		And
3257		Jesus
0116		and said
1129		is enough
1747		*
0598		This
2244		And he touched
0021		the ear
0593		of the one
0277		who was wounded
0136		and healed him

VERSE 52 — And Jesus said to those who had come against him, the chief priests and the elders and the captains of the temple, "Do you come out against me as against a robber with swords and with clubs to arrest me?

#	Aramaic	English
0116		And said
3257		Jesus
0593		to those
0208		who had come
1804		against him
2271		the chief priests
1135		*
2263		and the elders
2271		and the captains
0786		*
0607		of the temple
0060		as
1804		against
1306		a robber

LUKE CHAPTER 22

1542		Do you come out		0518		And
1804		against me		1494		a fire
1645		with swords		1416		in the middle
0778		and with clubs		0505		of the enclosure
0047		to arrest me		1093		and sitting
				0603		they were
				0732		around it
				1093		and was sitting
				0603		*

VERSE 53 Every day I was with you in the temple and you did not lay hands on me. But this is your hour and the power of darkness."

1172		Every day		0169		also
1817		with you		0592		\<he\>
0603		I was		3521		Simon
0607		in the temple		0266		among them
1262		and not				
1091		you did lay				
1804		on me				
0057		hands				
0090		But				
0598		this				
0592		is				
2573		your hour				
2527		and the power				
0923		of darkness				

VERSE 56 And a certain young woman saw him while he was sitting by the fire and she looked at him and said, "This [man] was also with him."

0758		And saw him
1812		a young woman
0721		certain
1093		while he was sitting
1288		by
1494		the fire
0756		and she looked
0217		at him
0116		and said
0169		also
0598		This [man]
1817		with him
0603		was

VERSE 54 And they arrested [him and] brought him to the house of the high priest and Simon followed him from a distance.

0047		And they arrested [him and]
0208		brought him
0243		to the house
2271		of the high priest
1135		*
3521		and Simon
0208		followed him
0603		*
0215		*
1388		from
2354		a distance

VERSE 57 And he denied [it] and said, "Woman, I do not know him."

0592		\<he\>
0518		And
1215		he denied [it]
0116		and said
0135		Woman
1262		not
1023		do know
0124		I

VERSE 55 And they kindled a fire in the middle of the enclosure and they were sitting around it and Simon also was sitting among them.

0047		they kindled

Vertical Interlinear

LUKE CHAPTER 22

1261		him

VERSE 58 — And after a little while another saw him and said to him, "You also are of them," but Peter said, "I am not."

0215		And after
2203		a little while
0758		saw him
0053		another
0116		and said
1261		to him
0169		also
0133		<you>
1388		of them
0133		You are
3258		Peter
0518		but
0116		said
1262		not
0603		I am

VERSE 59 — And after one hour another argued and said, "Truly this [man] also was with him, for he is also a Galilean."

0215		And after
2573		hour
0721		one
0053		another
0889		argued
0603		*
0116		and said
2594		Truly
0169		also
0598		this [man]
1817		with him
0603		was
0169		also
3154		a Galilean
0592		he is
0403		for

VERSE 60 — Peter said, "Man, I do not know what you are talking about." And immediately while he was speaking the rooster crowed.

0116		said
3258		Peter
0361		Man
1262		not
1023		do know
0124		I
1393		what
0116		talking about
0133		you are
0725		And immediately
1128		while
0592		he
1362		was speaking
2239		crowed
2713		the rooster

VERSE 61 — And Jesus turned and looked at Peter, and Simon remembered the word of our Lord that he had spoken to him, "Before the rooster will crow, you will deny me three times."

1984		And turned
3257		Jesus
0756		and looked
3258		at Peter
0527		and remembered
3521		Simon
1364		the word
1426		of our Lord
0116		that he had spoken
0603		*
1261		to him
2154		Before
2239		will crow
2713		the rooster
1215		you will deny
0217		me
2674		three

LUKE CHAPTER 22

0633		times

VERSE 62 — And Simon went outside [and] cried bitterly.

1542		And went
0322		outside
3521		Simon
0267		[and] cried
1421		bitterly

VERSE 63 — And the men who held Jesus captive were mocking him and were covering him

0361		And the men
0047		who held captive
0603		*
3257		Jesus
0246		mocking
0603		were
0217		him
0869		and covering
0603		were
1261		him

VERSE 64 — and were striking him on his face and saying, "Prophesy who struck you."

1341		and striking
0603		were
1261		him
1804		on
0173		his face
0116		and saying
1456		Prophesy
1390		who
1341		struck you

VERSE 65 — And many other [things] they were reviling and saying against him.

0053		And other [things]
1596		many
0370		they were reviling
0603		*
0116		and saying
1804		against him

VERSE 66 — And when [day] dawned, the elders and chief priests and scribes were gathered together and they took him to their council.

1128		And when
1465		[day] dawned
1198		were gathered together
2263		the elders
2271		and chief priests
1135		*
1699		and scribes
1658		and they took him
0243		to their council
1200		*

VERSE 67 — And they said to him, "If you are the Messiah, tell us." He said to them, "If I tell you, you will not believe me.

0116		And they said
1261		to him
0121		If
0133		you
0592		are
1446		the Messiah
0116		tell
1261		us
0116		He said
1261		to them
0121		If
0116		I tell
1261		you
1262		not
0109		you will believe me

VERSE 68 — And if I ask you, you will not restore or will you release me.

0121		And if
2420		I ask you
1262		not
1984		you will restore
0133		*
1261		me
2068		<an answer>

LUKE   CHAPTER 22

0024		or
2597		will release
0133		you
1261		me

VERSE 69 — From now on, the Son of Man will be seated at the right [hand] of the power of God."

1388		From
0602		now on
0603		will be
0323		the Son
0131		of Man
1093		seated
1388		at
1061		the right [hand]
0786		of the power
0093		of God

VERSE 70 — And all of them were saying, "Are you therefore the Son of God?" Jesus said to them, "You say that I am."

0116		were saying
0518		And
1168		all of them
0133		you
0592		Are
0596		therefore
0323		the Son
0093		of God
0116		said
1261		to them
3257		Jesus
0133		<you>
0116		say
0133		You
0124		that I am
0124		*

VERSE 71 — They said, "Why do we need more witnesses? For we have heard [it] from his mouth."

0116		They said
1393		Why
2650		more
0296		do we need
1261		*
1609		witnesses
0124		<we>
0403		for
2547		we have heard [it]
1388		from
1936		his mouth

CHAPTER 23

VERSE 1 — And the whole company of them rose up and brought him to Pilate.

2168		And rose up
1168		the whole
1201		company of them
0208		and brought him
1288		to
3417		Pilate

VERSE 2 — And they began to accuse him and say, "We have found that this [man] is deceiving our nation and he denies that the poll tax should be given to Caesar. And he says about himself that he is a king, the Messiah."

2597		And they began
0075		to accuse him
2257		*
0116		and say
0598		this [man]
2510		We have found
0993		that is deceiving
1818		our nation
1180		and he denies
1209		that the poll tax
2362		*
3483		to Caesar
1262		<not>
1030		should be given
0116		And he says
1804		about
1547		himself

LUKE CHAPTER 23

Num	Aramaic	English
1383		that a king
0592		he is
1446		the Messiah

VERSE 3 — And Pilate asked him and said to him, "Are you the king of the Judeans?" He said to him, "You have said [it]."

Num	Aramaic	English
3417		Pilate
0518		And
2420		asked him
0116		and said
1261		to him
0133		you
0592		Are
1383		the king
3226		of the Judeans
0116		He said
1261		to him
0133		<you>
0116		You have said [it]

VERSE 4 — And Pilate said to the chief priests and to the crowd, "I do not find any cause against this man."

Num	Aramaic	English
0116		And said
3417		Pilate
2271		to the chief priests
1135		*
1201		and to the crowd
0124		<I>
1326		any
1801		cause
1262		not
2510		I do find
0124		*
1804		against
0361		man
0598		this

VERSE 5 — And they were shouting and saying, "He incites our nation, teaching in all of Judea. And he began from Galilee up to here."

Num	Aramaic	English
0592		<they>
0518		And
0683		shouting
0603		they were
0116		and saying
2452		He incites
1818		our nation
1128		teaching
1053		*
1168		in all of
3224		Judea
2597		And he began
1388		from
3153		Galilee
1747		up to
0600		here

VERSE 6 — And Pilate, when he heard the name of Galilee, asked if the man was a Galilean.

Num	Aramaic	English
3417		Pilate
0518		And
1128		when
2547		he heard
2539		the name
3153		of Galilee
2420		asked
0121		if
0361		the man
0592		was
3154		a Galilean

VERSE 7 — And when he knew that he was under the authority of Herod, he sent him to Herod, because he was in Jerusalem in those days.

Num	Aramaic	English
1128		And when
1023		he knew
1388		that <from>
2660		under
2527		the authority
0592		he was
3179		of Herod
2458		he sent him

LUKE CHAPTER 23

#	Syriac	Translation
1288		to <him>
3179		<of> Herod
1347		because
3022		in Jerusalem
0603		he was
0593		in those
1036		days

VERSE 8 — And Herod, when he saw Jesus, was very glad, for he had wanted to see him for a long time because he had heard many [things] about him, and he thought that he might see some sign from him.

#	Syriac	Translation
3179		Herod
0518		And
1128		when
0758		he saw
3257		Jesus
0726		was glad
0938		very
2077		he had wanted
0603		*
0403		for
0758		to see him
1388		for
0633		a time
1596		long
1347		because
2547		he had heard
0603		*
1804		about him
1596		many [things]
1588		and he thought
0603		*
1326		that some
0206		sign
0758		he might see
1388		from him

VERSE 9 — And he asked him many questions, but Jesus did not give him any answer.

#	Syriac	Translation
1364		And questions
1596		many
2420		he asked
0603		*
1261		him
3257		Jesus
0518		but
1326		any
2068		answer
1262		not
2649		did give him

VERSE 10 — And the chief priests and scribes rose up and were vehemently accusing him.

#	Syriac	Translation
2168		rose up
0603		*
0518		And
2271		the chief priests
1135		*
1699		and scribes
1780		and vehemently
0075		were accusing him
0603		*
2257		*

VERSE 11 — And Herod and his soldiers treated him with contempt and when he had mocked [him], he clothed him with garments of purple and sent him to Pilate.

#	Syriac	Translation
3179		Herod
0518		And
2474		treated him with contempt
0592		*
1976		and his soldiers
1128		and when
0246		he had mocked [him]
1272		he clothed him with
1501		garments
0660		of purple
2458		and sent him
1288		to
3417		Pilate

Vertical Interlinear

LUKE   CHAPTER 23

VERSE 12 — And in that day Pilate and Herod became friends with one another, for there had been a conflict between them from the start.

Code	Syriac	English
0593		And in that
1036		day
0603		became
2345		friends
3417		Pilate
3179		and Herod
1817		with
0723		one another
0308		a conflict
0603		there had been
0403		for
1388		from
2153		the start
0266		between them

VERSE 13 — And Pilate called the chief priests and the rulers and the people

Code	Syriac	English
2239		called
0518		And
3417		Pilate
2271		the chief priests
1135		*
0194		and the rulers
1818		and the people

VERSE 14 — and he said to them, "You have brought me this man as a rebel against of your nation and behold, I have examined him before your eyes and I have not found any fault in this man of all you have accused him.

Code	Syriac	English
0116		and he said
1261		to them
2244		You have brought
1261		me
0361		man
0598		this
0060		as
0616		a rebel against
1818		your nation
0580		and behold
0124		I
1867		have examined him
1794		before your eyes
1801		and fault
1326		any
1262		not
2510		I have found
0361		in man
0598		this
1388		of
1168		all
2406		that you have accused
0133		*
0217		him

VERSE 15 — Not even Herod [found anything], for I sent him to him and behold, nothing that is worthy of death has been done by him.

Code	Syriac	English
0090		Not even
0170		*
3179		Herod [found anything]
2458		I sent him
0403		for
1288		to him
0580		and behold
1262		nothing
1326		*
2461		that is worthy
1335		of death
1684		has been done
1261		by him

VERSE 16 — I will therefore punish him and let him go."

Code	Syriac	English
2299		I will punish him
0596		therefore
2440		and let him go

VERSE 17 — For it was a custom that he would release one [prisoner] to them at the feast.

Code	Syriac	English
1762		a custom
0403		For

LUKE CHAPTER 23

#	Syriac	English
0069		it was
0603		*
2597		that he would release
1261		to them
0721		one [prisoner]
1721		at the feast

VERSE 18 — And the whole crowd cried out and said, "Take this [man] away and release Barabbas to us,"

#	Syriac	English
2227		cried out
0518		And
1168		the whole
1201		crowd
0116		and said
2587		Take
0598		this [man]
2597		and release
1261		to us
3128		Barabbas

VERSE 19 — him who was thrown into prison because of insurrection and murder that had happened in the city.

#	Syriac	English
0593		him
0066		who
1347		because of
0147		insurrection
0603		that had happened
0499		in the city
2181		and murder
2372		was thrown into
0603		*
0243		prison
0163		*

VERSE 20 — And again Pilate spoke to them, wanting to release Jesus.

#	Syriac	English
2650		again
0518		And
1362		spoke
1817		to them
3417		Pilate
1128		wanting
2077		*
2597		to release
3257		Jesus

VERSE 21 — But they cried out and said, "Crucify him, crucify him."

#	Syriac	English
0592		<they>
0518		But
2227		they cried out
0603		*
0116		and said
0688		Crucify him
0688		crucify him

VERSE 22 — And the third time he said to them, "For what evil has this [man] done? I have not found any cause that is worthy of death in him. Therefore, I will punish him and let him go."

#	Syriac	English
0592		<he>
0518		And
2674		third
0633		the time
0116		he said
1261		to them
1393		what
0403		For
0220		evil
1724		has done
0598		this [man]
1326		any
1801		cause
2461		that is worthy
1335		of death
1262		not
2510		I have found
0217		in him
2299		I will punish him
0596		Therefore
2440		and let him go

LUKE CHAPTER 23

VERSE 23 — But they were insisting with a loud voice and asking him to crucify him. And their voice and [that] of the chief priests prevailed.

Code	Syriac	Gloss
0592		<they>
0518		But
2663		insisting
0603		they were
2204		with a voice
2336		loud
2420		and asking
0603		*
1261		him
0688		to crucify him
1907		And prevailed
0603		*
2204		their voice
0517		<their own>
2271		and [that] of the chief priests
1135		*

VERSE 24 — And Pilate commanded that their request be done.

Code	Syriac	Gloss
3417		Pilate
0518		And
2007		commanded
0603		that be done
2421		their request

VERSE 25 — And he released to them him who because of insurrection and murder was thrown into prison, whom they had requested, but he delivered Jesus to their will.

Code	Syriac	Gloss
2597		And he released
1261		to them
0593		him
1347		who because of
0147		insurrection
2181		and murder
2372		was thrown into
0603		*
0243		prison
0163		*
0593		whom
2420		they had requested
3257		Jesus
0518		but
2530		he delivered
2079		to their will

VERSE 26 — And as they were leading him, they took hold of Simon, a Cyrenian, who was coming from the country, and set the cross on him to carry [it] after Jesus.

Code	Syriac	Gloss
1128		And as
1015		they were leading
1261		him
0047		they took hold
3521		of Simon
3465		a Cyrenian
0208		who was coming
1388		from
2251		the country
1625		and set
1804		on him
0689		the cross
0999		to carry [it]
0215		after
3257		Jesus

VERSE 27 — And a large group of people were following him and women who were lamenting and mourning for him.

Code	Syriac	Gloss
0208		And were following him
0603		*
0215		*
1598		a large group
1818		of people
0135		and women
0066		<those>
2403		who were lamenting
0603		*
0091		and mourning
1804		for him

LUKE CHAPTER 23

VERSE 28
And Jesus turned to them and said, "Daughters of Jerusalem, do not weep for me, but weep for yourselves and for your sons.

1984	ܘܐܬܦܢܝ	And turned
3257	ܝܫܘܥ	Jesus
1288	ܠܘܬܗܝܢ	to them
0116	ܘܐܡܪ	and said
0327	ܒܢܬ	Daughters of
3022	ܐܘܪܫܠܡ	Jerusalem
1262	ܠܐ	not
0267	ܬܒܟܝܢ	do weep
1804	ܥܠܝ	for me
0342	ܒܪܡ	but
1804	ܥܠ	for
1547	ܢܦܫܟܝܢ	yourselves
0267	ܒܟܝܢ	weep
1804	ܘܥܠ	and for
0323	ܒܢܝܟܝܢ	your sons

VERSE 29
For behold, the days are coming in which they will say, 'Blessed are the barren and the wombs that have not given birth and the breasts that have not nursed.'

0580	ܕܗܐ	For behold
0208	ܐܬܝܢ	are coming
1036	ܝܘܡܬܐ	the days
0217	ܕܒܗܘܢ	in which
0116	ܢܐܡܪܘܢ	they will say
0940	ܛܘܒܝܗܝܢ	Blessed are
1878	ܠܥܩܪܬܐ	the barren
1241	ܘܠܟܪܣܬܐ	and the wombs
1262	ܕܠܐ	that not
1046	ܝܠܕ	have given birth
2640	ܘܠܬܕܝܐ	and the breasts
1262	ܕܠܐ	that not
1063	ܐܝܢܩܘ	have nursed

VERSE 30
THEN YOU WILL BEGIN TO SAY TO THE MOUNTAINS, 'FALL ON US,' AND TO THE HILLS, 'COVER US.'

0594	ܗܝܕܝܢ	THEN
2597	ܬܫܪܘܢ	YOU WILL BEGIN
0116	ܠܡܐܡܪ	TO SAY
0958	ܠܛܘܪܐ	TO THE MOUNTAINS
1538	ܦܠܘ	FALL
1804	ܥܠܝܢ	ON US
2337	ܘܠܪܡܬܐ	AND TO THE HILLS
1206	ܕܟܣܝܢ	COVER US

VERSE 31
For if they do these [things] in a green tree, what will happen in the dry?"

0121	ܕܐܢ	For if
2199	ܒܩܝܣܐ	in a tree
2359	ܪܛܝܒܐ	green
0598	ܗܠܝܢ	these [things]
1724	ܥܒܕܝܢ	they do
1018	ܒܝܒܝܫܐ	in the dry
1393	ܡܢܐ	what
0603	ܢܗܘܐ	will happen

VERSE 32
And two others, evildoers were coming with him to be killed.

0208	ܘܐܬܝܢ	And were coming
0603	ܗܘܘ	*
1817	ܥܡܗ	with him
2709	ܬܪܝܢ	two
0053	ܐܚܪܢܐ	others
1724	ܥܒܕܝ	evildoers
0220	ܒܝܫܬܐ	*
2179	ܕܢܬܩܛܠܘܢ	to be killed

VERSE 33
And when they had come to a certain place that was called 'The Skull,' they crucified him there, and those evildoers, one on his right and one on his left.

1128	ܘܟܕ	And when
0208	ܐܬܘ	they had come
0494	ܠܕܘܟܬܐ	to a place
0721	ܚܕܐ	certain
2239	ܕܡܬܩܪܝܐ	that was called
2259	ܩܪܩܦܬܐ	The Skull
0688	ܨܠܒܘܗܝ	they crucified him
2682	ܬܡܢ	there
0593	ܘܠܗܢܘܢ	and those
1724	ܥܒܕܝ	evildoers
0220	ܒܝܫܬܐ	*

LUKE   CHAPTER 23

0721	ܚܕ	one
1388	ܡܢ	on
1061	ܝܡܝܢܗ	his right
0721	ܘܚܕ	and one
1388	ܡܢ	on
1668	ܣܡܠܗ	his left

VERSE 34 And Jesus said, "Father, forgive them, for they do not know what they are doing." And they divided his garments and cast a lot for them.

0592	ܗܘ	\<he\>
0518	ܕܝܢ	And
3257	ܝܫܘܥ	Jesus
0116	ܐܡܪ	said
0603	ܗܘܐ	*
0002	ܐܒܐ	Father
2440	ܫܒܘܩ	forgive
1261	ܠܗܘܢ	them
1262	ܠܐ	not
0403	ܓܝܪ	for
1023	ܝܕܥܝܢ	they know
1393	ܡܢܐ	what
1724	ܥܒܕܝܢ	they are doing
1968	ܘܦܠܓܘ	And they divided
1501	ܢܚܬܘܗܝ	his garments
2372	ܘܐܪܡܝܘ	and cast
1804	ܥܠܝܗܘܢ	for them
1991	ܦܣܐ	a lot

VERSE 35 And the people were standing and observing and the rulers also were mocking him and saying, "He saved others. Let him save himself if he is the Messiah, the chosen of God."

2168	ܩܐܡ	were standing
0603	ܗܘܐ	*
0518	ܕܝܢ	And
1818	ܥܡܐ	the people
0758	ܘܚܙܐ	and observing
1330	ܘܡܡܝܩܝܢ	and mocking
0603	ܗܘܘ	were
0217	ܒܗ	him
0169	ܐܦ	also
0194	ܐܪܟܘܢܐ	the rulers
0116	ܘܐܡܪܝܢ	and saying
0053	ܠܐܚܪܢܐ	others
0780	ܐܚܝ	He saved
0780	ܢܚܐ	Let him save
1547	ܢܦܫܗ	himself
0121	ܐܢ	if
0592	ܗܘܝܘ	he is
1446	ܡܫܝܚܐ	the Messiah
0353	ܓܒܝܗ	the chosen
0093	ܕܐܠܗܐ	of God

VERSE 36 And the soldiers were also mocking him, while drawing near to him and offering him vinegar.

0246	ܘܡܒܙܚܝܢ	And mocking
0603	ܗܘܘ	were
0217	ܒܗ	him
0169	ܐܦ	also
0150	ܐܣܛܪܛܝܘܛܐ	the soldiers
1128	ܟܕ	while
2244	ܩܪܒܝܢ	drawing near
1288	ܠܘܬܗ	to him
2244	ܘܡܩܪܒܝܢ	and offering
1261	ܠܗ	him
0794	ܚܠܐ	vinegar

VERSE 37 And they were saying to him, "If you are the king of the Judeans, save yourself."

0116	ܘܐܡܪܝܢ	And they were saying
1261	ܠܗ	to him
0121	ܐܢ	If
0133	ܐܢܬ	you
0592	ܗܘ	are
1383	ܡܠܟܐ	the king
3226	ܕܝܗܘܕܝܐ	of the Judeans
0780	ܐܚܐ	save
1547	ܢܦܫܟ	yourself

Vertical Interlinear

LUKE — CHAPTER 23

VERSE 38 — And there was also an inscription that was written over him in Greek and Latin and Hebrew: "This is the king of the Judeans."

Code	Aramaic	English
0069		there was
0603		*
0518		And
0169		also
1248		an inscription
1247		that was written
1803		over
1388		him
3238		in Greek
3492		and Latin
3388		and Hebrew
0599		This is
1383		the king
3226		of the Judeans

VERSE 39 — And one of those evildoers who was crucified with him was blaspheming against him and said, "If you are the Messiah, rescue yourself and rescue us also."

Code	Aramaic	English
0721		one
0518		And
1388		of
0593		those
1724		evildoers
0220		*
2108		who was crucified
0603		*
1817		with him
0370		blaspheming
0603		was
1804		against him
0116		and said
0121		If
0133		you
0592		are
1446		the Messiah
2002		rescue
1547		yourself
2002		and rescue
0169		also
1261		us

VERSE 40 — And his companion rebuked him and said to him, "Are you not afraid even of God, because indeed you are in the same judgment?

Code	Aramaic	English
1113		And rebuked
0217		him
0714		his companion
0116		and said
1261		to him
0169		even
1262		not
1388		of
0093		God
0509		Are you afraid
0133		*
0169		because indeed
0133		you
0217		in the same
0133		are
0497		judgment

VERSE 41 — And we justly, for as we deserve and as we have done we have been repaid, but nothing that is hateful has been done by this [man]."

Code	Aramaic	English
0124		And we
1151		justly
0060		as
2461		we deserve
0603		*
0403		for
0060		and as
1724		we have done
2037		we have been repaid
0598		this [man]
0518		but
1326		nothing
1673		that is hateful

LUKE   CHAPTER 23

#	Syriac	English
1262		<not>
1724		has been done
1261		by <him>

VERSE 42 — And he said to Jesus, "Remember me, my Lord, when you come in your kingdom."

#	Syriac	English
0116		And he said
3257		to Jesus
0527		Remember me
1426		my Lord
1313		when
0208		you come
0133		*
1385		in your kingdom

VERSE 43 — Jesus said to him, "Truly I say to you, today you will be with me in paradise."

#	Syriac	English
0116		said
1261		to him
3257		Jesus
0110		Truly
0116		say
0124		I
1261		to you
1037		today
1817		with me
0603		you will be
2020		in paradise

VERSE 44 — Now it was about the sixth hour and darkness was on all the land until the ninth hour.

#	Syriac	English
0069		it was
0603		*
0518		Now
0060		about
2573		the hour
2615		sixth
0603		and was
0923		darkness
1804		on
1168		all
0199		the land

#	Syriac	English
1747		until
2723		the ninth
2573		hour

VERSE 45 — And the sun was dark and the veil of the temple was torn from the middle of it.

#	Syriac	English
2557		And the sun
0922		was dark
2129		and was torn
0173		the veil
2718		*
0607		of the temple
1388		from
1416		the middle of it

VERSE 46 — And Jesus cried out with a loud voice and said, "MY FATHER, INTO YOUR HANDS I PLACE MY SPIRIT." He said this and died.

#	Syriac	English
2227		And cried out
3257		Jesus
2204		with a voice
2336		loud
0116		and said
0002		MY FATHER
0057		INTO YOUR HANDS
1625		PLACE
0124		I
2323		MY SPIRIT
0598		this
0116		He said
2530		and died

VERSE 47 — And when the centurion saw what had happened, he praised God and said, "Truly this man was just."

#	Syriac	English
1128		when
0758		saw
0518		And
2223		the centurion
1326		what
0603		had happened
2428		he praised
0093		God

LUKE   CHAPTER 23

0116		and said
2594		Truly
0598		this
0361		man
0637		just
0603		was

VERSE 48 And all the crowds, who were gathered for this sight, when they saw what had happened, returned, beating their breast[s].

1168		And all
1201		the crowds
0066		<those>
1198		who were gathered
0603		*
0763		for spectacle
0598		this
1128		when
0758		they saw
1326		what
0603		had happened
0616		returned
1128		beating
1006		*
1804		<on>
0729		their breast[s]

VERSE 49 And all the acquaintances of Jesus were standing at a distance, and the women, who had come with him from Galilee, and they saw these [things].

2168		And were standing
0603		*
1388		at
2354		a distance
1168		all
1024		the acquaintances
3257		of Jesus
0135		and the women
0066		<those>
0208		who had come
0603		*

1817		with him
1388		from
3153		Galilee
0758		and they saw
0603		*
0598		these [things]

VERSE 50 And a certain man, whose name [was] Joseph, a counselor from Arimathaea, a city of Judea, was a good and just man.

0361		a man
0518		And
0721		certain
2539		whose name [was]
3246		Joseph
0237		a counselor
1388		from
3502		Arimathaea
0499		a city
3224		of Judea
0361		a man
0603		was
0938		good
0637		and just

VERSE 51 This [man] did not agree with their will and with their deed and was waiting for the kingdom of God.

0598		This [man]
1262		not
2530		did agree
0603		*
2079		with their will
1685		and with their deed
1646		and waiting
0603		was
1385		for the kingdom
0093		of God

VERSE 52 This [man] came near to Pilate and asked for the body of Jesus.

0598		This [man]
2244		came near
1288		to

LUKE CHAPTER 23

#	Aramaic	English
3417		Pilate
2420		and asked for
1929		the body
3257		of Jesus

VERSE 53 — And he took it down and wrapped it in a sheet of linen and placed it in a hewn tomb in which no man yet had been placed.

#	Aramaic	English
1499		And he took it down
1236		and wrapped it
0752		in a sheet
1255		of linen
1625		and placed it
0243		in a tomb
2143		*
1567		hewn
0593		which
1262		no
0131		man
1745		yet
1625		had been placed in
0603		*
0217		*

VERSE 54 — And it was the preparation day and the Sabbath was dawning.

#	Aramaic	English
1036		And the day
1886		preparation
0603		it was
2445		and the Sabbath
1465		was dawning
0603		*

VERSE 55 — And the women who had come with him from Galilee were near and they saw the grave and how his body had been placed.

#	Aramaic	English
2248		near
0603		were
0518		And
0135		the women
0598		<those>
0208		who had come
1817		with him
1388		from
3153		Galilee
0758		and they saw
2146		the grave
0061		and how
1625		had been placed
1929		his body

VERSE 56 — And they returned [and] prepared spices and ointments and rested on the Sabbath as was commanded.

#	Aramaic	English
0616		And they returned
0950		[and] prepared
0622		spices
0291		and ointments
2445		and on the Sabbath
2516		rested
0060		as
2007		was commanded

CHAPTER 24

VERSE 1 — Now on the first [day] of the week, at dawn while [it was] dark, they came to the tomb and brought the spices they had prepared, and there were with them other women.

#	Aramaic	English
0721		on the first [day]
2445		of the week
0518		Now
2582		at dawn
1744		while
0923		[it was] dark
0208		they came
0243		to the tomb
2143		*
0208		and brought
0622		the spices
0598		<those>
0950		that they had prepared
0603		*
0069		and there were
0603		*

LUKE CHAPTER 24

1817	ܥܡܗܝܢ	with them
0135	ܢܫܐ	women
0053	ܐܚܪܢܝܬܐ	other

VERSE 2 — And they found the stone that was rolled from the tomb.

2510	ܘܐܫܟܚ	And they found
1119	ܟܐܦܐ	the stone
1737	ܕܡܥܓܠܐ	that was rolled
1388	ܡܢ	from
0243	ܒܝܬ	the tomb
2143	ܩܒܘܪܐ	*

VERSE 3 — And they entered, yet did not find the body of Jesus.

1796	ܘܥܠܝܢ	And they entered
1262	ܘܠܐ	yet not
2510	ܐܫܟܚܘܗܝ	did find
1929	ܠܦܓܪܐ	the body
3257	ܕܝܫܘܥ	of Jesus

VERSE 4 — And it happened that while they were astonished about this, behold, two men stood above them and their clothing was shining.

0603	ܘܗܘܐ	And it happened
1128	ܟܕ	that while
0592	ܗܢܝܢ	they
2679	ܬܡܝܗܢ	were astonished
1804	ܥܠ	about
0598	ܗܕܐ	this
0580	ܗܐ	behold
2709	ܬܪܝܢ	two
0361	ܓܒܪܝܢ	men
2168	ܩܡܘ	stood
1803	ܠܥܠ	above
1388	ܡܢܗܝܢ	them
0343	ܘܡܒܪܩ	and was shining
0603	ܗܘܐ	*
1273	ܠܒܘܫܗܝܢ	their clothing

VERSE 5 — And they were in fear and bowed their faces to the ground. And they said to them, "Why do you seek the living with the dead?

0603	ܘܗܘܝ	And they were
0511	ܒܕܚܠܬܐ	in fear
1210	ܘܟܦܝ	and bowed
0173	ܐܦܝܗܝܢ	their faces
0199	ܒܐܪܥܐ	to the ground
0116	ܘܐܡܪܝܢ	And they said
1261	ܠܗܝܢ	to them
1393	ܡܢܐ	Why
0296	ܒܥܝܢ	do seek
0133	ܐܢܬܝܢ	you
0781	ܠܚܝܐ	the living
1817	ܥܡ	with
1338	ܡܝܬܐ	the dead

VERSE 6 — He is not here. He has risen! Remember what he spoke to you while he was in Galilee

1264	ܠܝܬܘܗܝ	He is not
2694	ܬܢܢ	here
2168	ܩܡ	He has risen
1261	ܠܗ	*
1756	ܐܬܕܟܪܝܢ	Remember
1362	ܕܡܠܠ	what he spoke
1817	ܥܡܟܝܢ	to you
1128	ܟܕ	while
0592	ܗܘ	he was
3153	ܒܓܠܝܠܐ	in Galilee

VERSE 7 — and he said that the Son of Man will be delivered into the hands of men [who are] sinners and would be crucified, and after three days would rise?"

0116	ܘܐܡܪ	and he said
0603	ܗܘܐ	*
1914	ܕܥܬܝܕ	that will
0592	ܗܘ	be
0323	ܒܪܗ	the Son
0131	ܕܐܢܫܐ	of Man
2530	ܕܢܫܬܠܡ	delivered
0057	ܒܐܝܕܝ	into the hands
0131	ܐܢܫܐ	of men
0772	ܚܛܝܐ	[who are] sinners
2108	ܘܢܙܕܩܦ	and would be crucified
2674	ܘܠܬܠܬܐ	and after three

LUKE CHAPTER 24

#	Aramaic	English
1036		days
2168		would rise
VERSE 8		**And they remembered his words.**
0592		And they
0527		remembered
1364		his words
VERSE 9		**And they returned from the grave and told all these [things] to the eleven and to the rest.**
0616		And they returned
1388		from
2146		the grave
0116		and told
0598		these [things]
1168		all
0724		to the eleven
2611		and to the rest
VERSE 10		**Now there was Mary Magdalene and Joanna and Mary the mother of James and the rest who were with them, who had told the apostles.**
0069		there was
0603		*
0518		Now
3325		Mary
3297		Magdalene
3232		and Joanna
3325		and Mary
0106		the mother
3255		of James
2611		and the rest
1817		who were with them
0598		<those>
0116		who had told
0603		*
2522		the apostles
VERSE 11		**And these words seemed crazy in their eyes and they did not believe them.**
0758		And seemed
1794		in their eyes
1364		words
0598		these
0060		<as>
2561		crazy
1262		and not
0109		they did believe
0592		them
VERSE 12		**And Simon stood up and ran to the grave and looked in [and] saw the linen clothes placed alone, and went away wondering in himself about what had happened.**
3521		Simon
0518		And
2168		stood up
2312		and ran
2146		to the grave
0501		and looked in
0758		[and] saw
1255		the linen clothes
1625		placed
1041		alone
0042		and went away
1128		wondering
0549		*
1547		in himself
1804		about
1326		what
0603		had happened
VERSE 13		**And behold, two of them on the same day went to a village by the name of Emmaus, and it was sixty furlongs distant from Jerusalem.**
0580		And behold
2709		two
1388		of them
0217		on the same
1036		day
0042		went
0603		*
2251		to a village
2539		by the name of

LUKE CHAPTER 24

Vertical Interlinear

Number	Syriac	English
3396		Emmaus
2042		And it was distant
1388		from
3022		Jerusalem
0141		furlongs
2616		sixty

VERSE 14 And they were speaking with each other about all those [things] that had happened.

Number	Syriac	English
0592		And <they>
1362		speaking
0603		they were
0721		with each other
1817		*
0721		*
1804		about
0598		those [things]
1168		all
0373		that had happened

VERSE 15 And while they were speaking and questioning one another, Jesus came and approached them and was walking with them.

Number	Syriac	English
1128		And while
0592		they
1362		were speaking
0296		and questioning
0721		one another
1817		*
0721		*
0208		came
0592		<he>
3257		Jesus
1346		and approached
0592		them
0608		and was walking
0603		*
1817		with them

VERSE 16 And their eyes were closed so that they did not recognize him.

Number	Syriac	English
1794		And their eyes
0047		closed
0603		were
1262		so that not
1647		they did recognize him

VERSE 17 And he said to them, "What are these words that you are speaking with each other while you walk and are sad?"

Number	Syriac	English
0116		And he said
1261		to them
1393		What
0592		are
1364		words
0598		these
1362		that you are speaking
0133		*
0721		with each other
1817		*
0721		*
1128		while
0608		walk
0133		you
1193		and are sad
0133		*

VERSE 18 One of them whose name was Cleopas answered and said to him, "Are you indeed only a stranger from Jerusalem that you do not know what has happened in it in these days?"

Number	Syriac	English
1838		answered
0721		One
1388		of them
2539		whose name was
3477		Cleopas
0116		and said
1261		to him
0133		you
0592		Are
1163		indeed
1041		only
1522		a stranger
1388		from

LUKE   CHAPTER 24

Code	Syriac	English
3022	ܐܘܪܫܠܡ	Jerusalem
1262	ܠܐ	that not
1023	ܝܕܥ	you do know
0133	ܐܢܬ	*
1326	ܡܢܐ	what
0603	ܗܘܐ	has happened
0217	ܒܗ	in it
0593	ܒܗܠܝܢ	in these
1036	ܝܘܡܬܐ	days

VERSE 19   He said to them, "What [things]?" They said to him, "About Jesus who was from Nazareth, a man who was a prophet and was mighty in word and in deeds before God and before all the people.

Code	Syriac	English
0116	ܐܡܪ	He said
1261	ܠܗܘܢ	to them
1393	ܡܢܐ	What [things]
0116	ܐܡܪܝܢ	They said
1261	ܠܗ	to him
1804	ܥܠ	About
3257	ܝܫܘܥ	Jesus
0593	ܗܘ	who
1388	ܕܡܢ	was from
3354	ܢܨܪܬ	Nazareth
0361	ܓܒܪܐ	a man
0603	ܕܗܘܐ	who was
1457	ܢܒܝܐ	a prophet
0788	ܘܚܝܠܬܢ	and was mighty
0603	ܗܘܐ	*
1364	ܒܡܠܬܐ	in word
1728	ܘܒܥܒܕܐ	and in deeds
2154	ܩܕܡ	before
0093	ܐܠܗܐ	God
2154	ܘܩܕܡ	and before
1168	ܟܠܗ	all
1818	ܥܡܐ	the people

VERSE 20   And the chief priests and elders delivered him to the judgment of death and they crucified him.

Code	Syriac	English
2530	ܘܐܫܠܡܘܗܝ	And delivered him
2271	ܪܒܝ	the chief priests
1135	ܟܗܢܐ	*
2263	ܘܩܫܝܫܐ	and elders
0497	ܠܕܝܢܐ	to the judgment
1335	ܕܡܘܬܐ	of death
0688	ܘܙܩܦܘܗܝ	and crucified him

VERSE 21   But we had hoped that he was going to deliver Israel and behold, three days [have passed] since all these [things] happened.

Code	Syriac	English
0124	ܚܢܢ	<we>
0518	ܕܝܢ	But
1588	ܣܒܪܝܢ	we had hoped
0603	ܗܘܝܢ	*
0592	ܕܗܘܝܘ	that he was
1914	ܥܬܝܕ	going
0603	ܗܘܐ	*
2042	ܠܡܦܪܩܘܬܗ	to deliver
3035	ܠܐܝܣܪܝܠ	Israel
0580	ܘܗܐ	and behold
2674	ܬܠܬܐ	three
1036	ܝܘܡܝܢ	days
0580	ܗܐ	<behold>
1388	ܡܢ	since
0598	ܕܗܠܝܢ	these [things]
1168	ܟܠܗܝܢ	all
0603	ܗܘܝ	happened

VERSE 22   But also [some of] our women astonished us, for they went early to the tomb

Code	Syriac	English
0090	ܐܠܐ	But
0169	ܐܦ	also
0135	ܢܫܐ	[some of] women
1388	ܡܢܢ	our
2679	ܐܬܗܪܢ	astonished us
2150	ܩܕܡ	early
0603	ܗܘܝ	they went
0403	ܓܝܪ	for
0243	ܠܒܝܬ	to the tomb
2143	ܩܒܘܪܐ	*

Vertical Interlinear

LUKE   CHAPTER 24

VERSE 23 — and when they did not find his body, they came [and] told us, 'We saw angels there and they said about him that he is alive.'

1128		and when
1262		not
2510		they did find
1929		his body
0208		they came
0116		[and] told
1261		us
1375		angels
0758		We saw
2682		there
0116		and they said
1804		about him
0781		that alive
0592		he is

VERSE 24 — And also, [some of] our men went to the tomb and found the same as what the women had said, but they did not see him."

0169		And also
0131		[some of] men
1388		our
0042		went
0243		to the tomb
2143		*
2510		and found
0597		the same
0060		as
1313		what
0116		had said
0135		the women
1261		him
0518		but
1262		not
0758		they did see

VERSE 25 — Then Jesus said to them, "Oh fools and dull of heart to believe in all those [things] that the prophets spoke!

0594		Then
0116		said
1261		to them
3257		Jesus
0025		Oh
0867		fools
2385		*
1079		and dull of
1268		heart
0109		to believe
1168		in all
0066		those [things]
1362		that spoke
1457		the prophets

VERSE 26 — Were not for these [things] Messiah intended to endure and to enter into his glory?"

1262		not
0603		Were
0598		these [things]
1914		intended
0603		*
1588		for to endure
1446		the Messiah
1796		and to enter
2432		into his glory

VERSE 27 — And he began from Moses and from all the prophets and expounded to them about himself from all the scriptures.

2597		And he began
0603		*
1388		from
3305		Moses
1388		and from
1168		all
1457		the prophets
2061		and expounded
0603		*
1261		to them
1804		about
1547		himself

LUKE CHAPTER 24

#	Syriac	English
1388		from
1168		all
1248		the scriptures

VERSE 28 — And they came near the village to which they were going and he caused them to think that he was going to a more distant place.

#	Syriac	English
2244		And they came near
0603		*
2251		to the village
0593		which
0042		they were going
0603		*
1261		<to it>
0592		and <he>
1588		he caused to think
0603		*
1261		them
0060		that <as>
0494		to a place
2355		more distant
0042		he was going
0603		*

VERSE 29 — And they constrained him and said to him, "Remain with us because the day now is at an end [and it is starting] to become dark." And he entered to continue with them.

#	Syriac	English
0102		And they constrained him
0116		and said
1261		to him
1938		Remain
1288		with us
1347		because
1036		the day
0602		is now
2370		at an end
1261		*
0922		[and it is starting] to become dark
1796		And he entered
2165		to continue

#	Syriac	English
1288		with them

VERSE 30 — And it happened that while he sat to eat with them, he took bread and blessed [it] and broke [it] and gave [it] to them.

#	Syriac	English
0603		And it happened
1128		that while
1664		he sat to eat
1817		with them
1532		he took
1293		bread
0335		and blessed [it]
2234		and broke [it]
1030		and gave [it]
1261		to them

VERSE 31 — And immediately their eyes were opened and they knew him. And he was taken from them.

#	Syriac	English
0725		And immediately
2070		were opened
1794		their eyes
1023		and they knew him
0592		And he
2587		was taken
1261		*
1388		from them

VERSE 32 — And they said one to another, "Were not our heart[s] heavy within us while he talked with us along the road and expounded to us the scriptures?"

#	Syriac	English
0116		And they said
0603		*
0721		one
0721		to another
1262		not
0603		Were
1268		our heart[s]
1079		heavy
0603		*
0376		within us
1128		while
1362		he talked

LUKE — CHAPTER 24

Vertical Interlinear

1817	ܠܢ	with us
0038	ܒܐܘܪܚܐ	along the road
2061	ܘܦܫܩ	and expounded
1261	ܠܢ	to us
1248	ܟܬܒܐ	the scriptures

VERSE 33 — And they rose up immediately and returned to Jerusalem. And they found the eleven, who were gathered together and those who were with them,

2168	ܘܩܡܘ	And they rose up
0217	ܒܗ	immediately
2573	ܒܫܥܬܐ	*
0616	ܘܗܦܟܘ	and returned
3022	ܠܐܘܪܫܠܡ	to Jerusalem
2510	ܘܐܫܟܚܘ	And they found
0724	ܠܚܕܥܣܪ	the eleven
1198	ܕܟܢܝܫܝܢ	who were gathered together
0066	ܘܠܐܝܠܝܢ	and those
1817	ܕܥܡܗܘܢ	who were with them

VERSE 34 — saying, "Truly our Lord has risen and appeared to Simon."

1128	ܟܕ	saying
0116	ܐܡܪܝܢ	*
2594	ܫܪܝܪܐܝܬ	Truly
2168	ܩܡ	has risen
1426	ܡܪܢ	our Lord
0758	ܘܐܬܚܙܝ	and appeared
3521	ܠܫܡܥܘܢ	to Simon

VERSE 35 — And those also related these [things] that had happened on the road and how he was made known to them while breaking bread.

0169	ܘܐܦ	And also
0592	ܗܢܘܢ	those
2569	ܐܫܬܥܝܘ	related
0066	ܐܝܠܝܢ	these [things]
0603	ܕܗܘܝ	that had happened
0038	ܒܐܘܪܚܐ	on the road
0061	ܘܐܝܟܢܐ	and how
1023	ܐܬܝܕܥ	he was made known
1261	ܠܗܘܢ	to them
1128	ܟܕ	while
2234	ܩܨܐ	breaking
1293	ܠܚܡܐ	bread

VERSE 36 — And while they were saying these [things], Jesus stood among them and said to them, "Peace [be] with you. It is I. Do not be afraid."

1128	ܘܟܕ	And while
0598	ܗܠܝܢ	these [things]
1362	ܡܡܠܠܝܢ	saying
0603	ܗܘܘ	they were
3257	ܝܫܘܥ	Jesus
2168	ܩܡ	stood
0266	ܒܝܢܬܗܘܢ	among them
0116	ܘܐܡܪ	and said
1261	ܠܗܘܢ	to them
2535	ܫܠܡܐ	Peace [be]
1817	ܥܡܟܘܢ	with you
0124	ܐܢܐ	It is
0124	ܐܢܐ	I
1262	ܠܐ	not
0509	ܬܕܚܠܘܢ	Do be afraid

VERSE 37 — And they were astonished and were in fear, for they supposed that they had seen a spirit.

0592	ܘܗܢܘܢ	And they
2308	ܐܬܪܗܒܘ	were astonished
0603	ܘܗܘܘ	and were
0511	ܒܕܚܠܬܐ	in fear
1588	ܣܒܪܝܢ	they supposed
0603	ܗܘܘ	*
0403	ܓܝܪ	for
2323	ܕܪܘܚܐ	that a spirit
0758	ܚܙܝܢ	they had seen

VERSE 38 — And Jesus said to them, "Why are you troubled and why do thoughts well up in your hearts?

0116	ܘܐܡܪ	And said
1261	ܠܗܘܢ	to them
3257	ܝܫܘܥ	Jesus
1393	ܡܢܐ	Why

LUKE CHAPTER 24

0657	ܡܬܕܘܕܝܢ	are you troubled
0133	ܐܢܬܘܢ	*
1393	ܘܡܢܐ	and why
1658	ܣܠܩܢ	do well up
0917	ܡܚܫܒܬܐ	thoughts
1804	ܥܠ	in
1268	ܠܒܘܬܟܘܢ	your hearts

VERSE 39 Look at my hands and my feet, for it is I. Touch me and know that a spirit has no flesh and bones as you see that I have."

0758	ܚܙܘ	Look at
0057	ܐܝܕܝ	my hands
2293	ܘܪܓܠܝ	and my feet
0124	ܕܐܢܐ	for it is
0124	ܐܢܐ	I
0467	ܓܘܫܘܢܢܝ	Touch me
1023	ܘܕܥܘ	and know
2323	ܕܠܪܘܚܐ	that a spirit
0294	ܒܣܪܐ	flesh
0464	ܘܓܪܡܐ	and bones
1264	ܠܝܬ	has no
1261	ܠܗ	*
0060	ܐܝܟ	as
0758	ܕܚܙܝܢ	you see
0133	ܐܢܬܘܢ	*
0069	ܐܝܬ	that I have
1261	ܠܝ	*

VERSE 40 And while he said these [things], he showed them his hands and his feet.

1128	ܘܟܕ	And while
0598	ܗܠܝܢ	these [things]
0116	ܐܡܪ	he said
0739	ܚܘܝ	he showed
0592	ܐܢܘܢ	them
0057	ܐܝܕܘܗܝ	his hands
2293	ܘܪܓܠܘܗܝ	and his feet

VERSE 41 And while they did still not believe from their joy and were astonished, he said to them, "Do you have anything here to eat?"

1128	ܘܟܕ	And while
1747	ܥܕܟܝܠ	still
0602	ܠܐ	*
1262	ܠܐ	not
0109	ܡܗܝܡܢܝܢ ܗܘܘ	they did believe
0603	ܗܘܘ	*
1388	ܡܢ	from
0727	ܚܕܘܬܗܘܢ	their joy
2679	ܘܡܬܬܡܗܝܢ	and were astonished
0603	ܗܘܘ	*
0116	ܐܡܪ	he said
1261	ܠܗܘܢ	to them
0069	ܐܝܬ	Do you have
1261	ܠܟܘܢ	*
2694	ܬܢܢ	here
1326	ܡܕܡ	anything
0075	ܠܡܐܟܠ	to eat

VERSE 42 And they gave him a portion of fish that was broiled and of a comb of honey.

0592	ܗܢܘܢ	<they>
0518	ܕܝܢ	And
1030	ܝܗܒܘ	they gave
1261	ܠܗ	him
1399	ܡܢܬܐ	a portion
1388	ܡܢ	of
1490	ܢܘܢܐ	fish
0949	ܕܛܘܝܐ	that was broiled
1388	ܘܡܢ	and of
1167	ܟܟܪܝܬܐ	a comb
0484	ܕܕܒܫܐ	of honey

VERSE 43 And he took [and] ate [it] before them.

1532	ܘܢܣܒ	And he took
0075	ܐܟܠ	[and] ate [it]
1794	ܠܥܢܝܗܘܢ	before them

VERSE 44 And he said to them, "These are the words that I spoke to you while I was with you, that it was necessary that everything be fulfilled that was written in the law of Moses and in the prophets and in the Psalms about me."

0116	ܘܐܡܪ	And he said
1261	ܠܗܘܢ	to them

LUKE CHAPTER 24

Vertical Interlinear

0598		These
0592		are
1364		the words
1362		that I spoke
1817		to you
1128		while
1288		with you
0603		I was
0626		that necessary
0592		it was
2530		that be fulfilled
1168		everything
1326		*
1247		that was written
1524		in the law
3305		of Moses
1457		and in the prophets
0676		and in the Psalms
1804		about me

VERSE 45 Then he opened their minds to understand the scriptures.

0594		Then
2070		he opened
2385		their minds
1647		to understand
1248		the scriptures

VERSE 46 And he said to them, "So it is written and so it was right that the Messiah should suffer and rise from the dead after three days

0116		And he said
1261		to them
0597		So
1247		it is written
0597		and so
0641		it was right
0603		*
0911		that should suffer
1446		the Messiah
2168		and rise
1388		from
0243		the dead
1338		*
2674		after three
1036		days

VERSE 47 and that repentance will be preached through his name for the forgiveness of sins in all the nations and [that] the beginning will be from Jerusalem.

1230		and that will be preached
2539		through his name
2651		repentance
2441		for the forgiveness
0771		of sins
1168		in all
1818		the nations
2601		and [that] the beginning
0603		will be
1388		from
3022		Jerusalem

VERSE 48 And you are a witness of these [things]

0133		And you
0592		are
1609		a witness
0598		of these [things]

VERSE 49 and I will send to you the promise of my Father. But remain in the city, Jerusalem, until you be clothed with power from on high."

0124		and I
2458		will send
1804		you
1382		the promise
0002		of my Father
0133		<you>
0518		But
2165		remain
3022		in Jerusalem
0499		the city
1747		until
1272		you be clothed with

595

LUKE CHAPTER 24

0786	ܚܝܠܐ	power
1388	ܡܢ	from
2334	ܪܘܡܐ	on high

2428	ܕܡܫܒܚܝܢ	*
0335	ܘܡܒܪܟܝܢ	and blessing
0093	ܠܐܠܗܐ	God
0110	ܐܡܝܢ	Amen

VERSE 50 And he took them out up to Bethany and raised his hands and blessed them.

1542	ܘܐܦܩ	And he took out
0592	ܐܢܘܢ	them
1747	ܠܒܪ	up
3116	ܠܒܝܬ ܥܢܝܐ	to Bethany
2331	ܘܐܪܝܡ	and raised
0057	ܐܝܕܘܗܝ	his hands
0335	ܘܒܪܟ	and blessed
0592	ܐܢܘܢ	them

VERSE 51 And it happened that while he blessed them, he was separated from them and taken up to heaven.

0603	ܘܗܘܐ	And it happened
1128	ܕܟܕ	that while
0335	ܡܒܪܟ	he blessed
1261	ܠܗܘܢ	them
2046	ܐܬܦܪܫ	he was separated
1388	ܡܢܗܘܢ	from them
1658	ܘܣܠܩ	and taken up
2543	ܠܫܡܝܐ	to heaven

VERSE 52 And they worshipped him and returned to Jerusalem with great joy.

0592	ܗܢܘܢ	<they>
0518	ܕܝܢ	And
1599	ܣܓܕܘ	they worshipped
1261	ܠܗ	him
0616	ܘܗܦܟܘ	and returned
3022	ܠܐܘܪܫܠܡ	to Jerusalem
0727	ܒܚܕܘܬܐ	with joy
2271	ܪܒܬܐ	great

VERSE 53 And they were always in the temple praising and blessing God. Amen.

1170	ܘܒܟܠܙܒܢ	And always
0069	ܐܝܬܝܗܘܢ	they were
0603	ܗܘܘ	*
0607	ܒܗܝܟܠܐ	in the temple
1128	ܟܕ	praising

Vertical Interlinear

Vertical Interlinear

CPSIA information can be obtained at www.ICGtesting.com
Printed in the USA
BVOW09*2340030116

431631BV00009B/241/P